Fodor's

SOUTHERN
CALIFORNIA

Welcome to Southern California

Balmy weather, blissful beaches, Hollywood glamour—Southern California delivers fun and relaxation year-round. Outdoor enthusiasts revel in the natural beauty and excellent outdoor activities in the dramatic Mojave Desert and iconic Big Sur coastline, and at relaxing Palm Springs resorts. Beachgoers are drawn to the seemingly endless strands that line the stunning coast. For urban culture-vultures, trendy Los Angeles and sunny San Diego hold a wealth of treasures, including movie studio tours, America's preeminent zoo, and superb restaurants.

TOP REASONS TO GO

★ **Cool Cities:** San Diego's bay, Los Angeles's movie lore, Palm Springs' spa resorts.

★ **Beaches:** For swimming, surfing, or tanning, the beaches can't be beat.

★ **Feasts:** Cutting-edge cuisine, food trucks, fusion flavors, farmers' markets.

★ **Theme Parks:** From Disneyland to LEGOLAND, SoCal has some of the biggest and best.

★ **Outdoor Adventures:** Hiking, golfing, and national park excursions are all excellent.

★ **Road Trips:** The Pacific Coast Highway offers spectacular views and thrills aplenty.

Contents

MAPS

Fodor's Features

San Diego Zoo 81

Chapter 1

EXPERIENCE SOUTHERN CALIFORNIA

20 ULTIMATE EXPERIENCES

Southern California offers terrific experiences that should be on every traveler's list. Here are Fodor's top picks for a memorable trip.

1 Hike the Hollywood Sign

The iconic Hollywood sign was originally erected in 1923 and read "Hollywoodland." The easiest path starts from the Griffith Park Observatory. *(Ch. 7)*

2 Find the Weird at Venice Beach

California counterculture can be found at Venice Beach:
bodybuilders at Muscle Beach and head shops on the
boardwalk, and multimillion-dollar homes along the
Venice Canals. *(Ch. 7)*

3 Surf the Waves in Malibu

Surfrider Beach is a stretch of Malibu that includes the
Malibu Pier and is a popular point for surfing buffs and
beach bums alike. On Zuma Beach surfers share the water
with sealions. *(Ch. 7)*

4 Suspend Disbelief at Universal Studios

Universal is more a theme park with lots of roller coasters and thrill rides than a backstage pass, though its tour provides a good firsthand look at familiar TV and movie sets. *(Ch. 6)*

5 Take the Ferry to Coronado

The 15-minute ferry ride between downtown San Diego and Coronado provides great views of Downtown and Naval Air Station North Island. *(Ch. 4)*

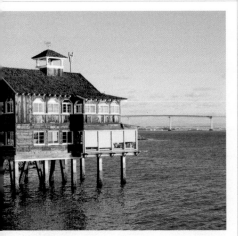

6 Shop and Dine in Seaport Village

Situated along the water, Seaport Village is a 14-acre, open-air shopping and dining complex that's home to shops and eateries, special events, and winding walking paths. *(Ch. 4)*

7 Explore Old Town San Diego

San Diego's oldest and most storied neighborhood is also California's earliest settlement. Today, it's a hub for Mexican restaurants, souvenir shops, and cultural and historical attractions and celebrations. *(Ch. 4)*

8 Spend the Day Exploring Balboa Park

This 1,200-acre urban park houses 17 museums, performing arts venues, gardens, sculptures, and other attractions like the San Diego Zoo. *(Ch. 4)*

9 Explore the Gaslamp Quarter

Covering more than 16 city blocks, this bustling neighborhood is great for shopping, dining, and nightlife. Guided walking tours of the historic district are available. *(Ch. 4)*

10 Explore Your Wild Side at San Diego Safari Park

A great way to learn about wildlife without the typical claustrophobic animal cages. *(Ch. 4)*

11 Camp in Joshua Tree

Just east of Palm Springs is this National Park, named for the Yucca trees, which Mormons named after the biblical Joshua, who raised his hands into the sky. *(Ch. 8)*

12 Traverse Death Valley

One of the hottest places on Earth, Death Valley sits on the eastern edge of California along the border with Nevada. *(Ch. 12)*

13 Spend the Night at Madonna Inn

San Luis Obispo is home to one of the most eccentric hotels in the country. No two rooms are the same, making each stay unique. *(Ch. 11)*

14 Seals at La Jolla

Seals and sea lions love the Children's Pool Beach, but keep your distance. For good views from Coast Avenue, walk along the sea cliffs toward the seawall. *(Ch. 4)*

15 Find Your Inner Child at Disneyland

"The Happiest Place on Earth" continues to delight children and all but the most cynical adults. *(Ch. 6)*

16 Go to a Show Taping in L.A.

Dozens of sitcoms, talk shows, and game shows film every day in Los Angeles, and you can get tickets to be an audience member. *(Ch. 7)*

17 See a Concert at the Hollywood Bowl

A live music amphitheater built into the side of the Hollywood Hills, the venue is known for its incredible acoustics. *(Ch. 7)*

18 See Stars on the Hollywood Walk of Fame

When this theater opened in 1927, the tradition of stars imprinting their hands or feet into the cement began, with an "accidental" footprint by Norma Talmadge. Today, the Walk of Fame runs a mile along Hollywood Boulevard. *(Ch. 7)*

19 Experience Opulence at the Hearst Castle

Once a celebrity hotspot hosting Roaring '20s parties, you can tour the palace's zoo, gold-leaf Roman pool, and priceless art collection. *(Ch. 11)*

20 Get a Bird's-Eye View of Palm Springs

Ride the Palm Springs Aerial Tramway—the largest rotating tramway in the world. At the top (8,516 feet) are restaurants and hiking trails. *(Ch. 5)*

WHAT'S WHERE

1 San Diego. San Diego's Gaslamp Quarter and early California–themed Old Town have a human scale—but big-ticket animal attractions like the San Diego Zoo pull in visitors.

2 Orange County. A diverse destination with premium resorts and restaurants, strollable waterfront communities, and kid-friendly attractions.

3 Los Angeles. Go for the glitz of the entertainment industry, but stay for the rich cultural attributes and communities.

4 The Central Coast. Three of the state's top stops—swanky Santa Barbara, Hearst Castle, and Big Sur—sit along the scenic 200-mile route. A quick boat trip away lies scenic Channel Islands National Park.

5 Palm Springs and the Desert Resorts. Golf on some of the West's most challenging courses, lounge at fabulous resorts, check out mid-20th-century-modern architectural gems, and trek through primitive desert parks.

6 Joshua Tree National Park. Proximity to major urban areas—as well as world-class rock climbing and nighttime celestial displays—help make this one of the most visited national parks.

7 Mojave Desert. Material pleasures are in short supply here, but Mother Nature's stark beauty more than compensates.

8 Death Valley National Park. America's second-largest national park is vast, beautiful, and often the hottest place in the nation.

9 Sequoia and Kings Canyon National Parks. The sight of ancient redwoods towering above jagged mountains is breathtaking.

Southern California Today

THE PEOPLE

California is as much a state of mind as a state in the union—a kind of perpetual promised land that has represented many things to many people. In the 18th century, Spanish missionaries came seeking converts and gold. In the 19th, miners rushed here to search for gold. And, in the years since, a long line of Dust Bowl farmers, land speculators, Haight-Ashbury hippies, migrant workers, dot-commers, real estate speculators, and would-be actors have come chasing their own dreams.

The result is a population that leans toward idealism—without necessarily always being as liberal as you might think. (Remember, this is Ronald Reagan's old stomping ground.) And despite the stereotype of the blue-eyed, blond surfer, California's population is not homogeneous either. Ten million people who live here (more than 27% of Californians) are foreign born. Almost half hail from Latin American countries; another third emigrated from Asia, following the waves of Chinese workers who arrived in the 1860s to build the railroads and subsequent waves of Indochinese refugees from the Vietnam War.

THE POLITICS

What's blue and red and green all over? California: a predominantly Democratic state with an aggressive "go green" agenda and policies that make California the greenest state in the nation, supporting more green construction, wind farms, and solar panels.

THE ECONOMY

Leading all other states in terms of the income generated by agriculture, tourism, entertainment, and industrial activity, California has the country's most diverse state economy. Moreover, with a gross state product of more than $2.7 trillion, California would be one of the top 10 economies *in the world* if it were an independent nation.

Despite its wealth ($71,805 median household income) and productivity, California took a large hit in the 2007 recession, but the Golden State's economic history is filled with boom and bust cycles—beginning with the mid-19th-century gold rush that started it all. Optimists already have their eyes on the next potential boom: high-tech and bioresearch, "green companies" focused on alternative energy, renewables, electric cars, and the like.

THE CULTURE

Art and culture thrive in San Diego. Balboa Park alone holds 17 museums, opulent gardens, and three performance venues, in addition to the San Diego Zoo. The Old Globe Theater and La Jolla Playhouse routinely originate plays that capture coveted Tony Awards in New York.

But California's *real* forte is pop culture, and L.A. and its environs are the chief arbiters. Movie, TV, and video production have been centered here since the early 20th century. Capitol Records set up shop in L.A. in the 1940s, and this area has been instrumental in the music industry ever since. And while these industries continue to influence national trends, today they are only part of the pop culture equation. Websites are also a growing part of that creativity—Facebook, YouTube, and Google are (northern) California companies.

THE PARKS AND PRESERVES

Cloud-spearing redwood groves, snow-tipped mountains, canyon-slashed deserts, primordial lava beds, and a seemingly endless coast: California's natural diversity is staggering—and efforts to protect it started early. Yosemite, the first national park, was established here in 1890, and the National Park Service now oversees 32 sites in California (more than in any other state). When you factor in 280 state parks—which encompass underwater preserves, historic sites, wildlife reserves, dune systems, and other sensitive habitats—the number of acres involved is almost as impressive as the topography itself.

Due to encroaching development and pollution, keeping these natural treasures in pristine condition is an ongoing challenge. For instance, Sequoia and Kings Canyon (which is plagued by pesticides and other agricultural pollutants blown in from the San Joaquin Valley) has been named America's "smoggiest park" by the National Parks Conservation Association, and the Environmental Protection Agency has designated it as an "ozone nonattainment area with levels of ozone pollution that threaten human health."

There is no question that Californians love their 280 state parks. Nearly every park has its grass-roots supporters, who volunteer to raise money, volunteer as rangers, and work other jobs to keep the parks open.

THE CUISINE

California gave us McDonald's, Denny's, Carl's Jr., Taco Bell, and, of course, In-N-Out Burger. Fortunately for those of us with fast-clogging arteries, the state also kick-started the health-food movement. Back in the 1970s, California-based chefs put American cuisine on the culinary map by focusing on freshly prepared seasonal ingredients.

Today, this focus has spawned the "locavore" or sustainable food movement—followers try to consume only food produced within a 100-mile radius of where they live, since processing and refining food and transporting goods over long distances is bad for both the body and the environment. This isn't much of a restriction in California, where a huge variety of crops grow year-round. Some 350 cities and towns have certified farmers' markets—and their stalls are bursting with a variety of goods. California has been America's top agricultural producer for the last 50 years, growing more fruits and vegetables than any other state. Dairies and ranches also thrive here, and fishing fleets harvest fish and shellfish from the rich waters offshore.

What to Eat and Drink in Southern California

Avocado toast

CRAFT BEER
Dubbed the "Capital of Craft," San Diego has more than 150 craft breweries, a movement that began with Karl Strauss Brewing Company in 1989. Since then, the San Diego Brewers Guild established an annual San Diego Beer Week every November, and a few neighborhoods have become craft brewery destinations in their own right.

L.A. HOTDOGS
While every major city in the country has their own take on street hot dogs, L.A.'s Mexican-inspired version is arguably the best. Wrapped in bacon and topped with grilled onions, bell peppers, ketchup, mustard, mayo, and jalapenos, it's practically a ritual for anyone stumbling home drunk to grab one. Look for street carts in areas with a lot of bars.

KOREAN BBQ TACOS
If you like Korean BBQ and you enjoy street tacos, then you might be ready for Korean BBQ tacos, one of the few culinary creations that originated in La La Land. They're exactly what it sounds like—tacos but with Korean BBQ meats, and the best place to get them is from one of Roy Choi's legendary Kogi food trucks. To find a location, go to kogibbq.com.

In-N-Out

FISH TACOS
There's a great debate about who makes the best fish tacos in San Diego. Rubio's Coastal Grill is credited with popularizing fish tacos in the U.S.; the original location is still in Pacific Beach. The original tacos have fried pollock, white sauce, salsa, cabbage, and a corn tortilla.

MEZCAL
Mezcal is made from the agave plant, typically in Oaxaca, Mexico, so naturally the best Oaxacan restaurant in L.A. (Guelaguetza) would have a top-shelf selection. Other great spots include Petty Cash, and Madre! in Torrance.

IN-N-OUT
No California food list is complete without the legendary In-N-Out. "Where's the closest In-N-Out" is asked by just about every tourist the moment they arrive. In-N-Out burgers and fries are made fresh and made to order, which is why they're so good in the first place.

FRENCH DIP
Not only was the French Dip invented in Los Angeles, two different restaurants claim its origin. Philippe the Original in Downtown opened in 1908 and is a counter-style diner; Cole's also opened in 1908, is (slightly) more upscale, and features a hidden speakeasy in the back of the restaurant.

SEAFOOD FRESH FROM THE OCEAN
You don't have to go far to find a bounty of fresh seafood in San Diego, most likely sourced from the waters off Southern California. Always check out the day's catch—usually served as a sandwich, salad, or plate—and what's been shucked on ice.

VEGETARIAN FOOD
Californians are generally known to be health conscious, eating lots of fresh local produce (including adding avocado to everything). There are plentiful vegetarian and vegan options throughout almost all of Southern California.

TIKI COCKTAILS
Tiki culture has obvious parallels to San Diego's tropical, laid-back vacation vibe, so it's no surprise that the concept took root here with rum as the star spirit. Sure bets include The Grass Skirt, False Idol, and Fairweather Bar. If you're heading to Palm Springs, check out Bootlegger Tiki. And L.A.'s got Tiki Ti.

Best Beaches in San Diego

CORONADO

Often praised for its sparkling sand, the island is home to Hotel del Coronado, a 130-year-old luxury hotel perfect for post-beach snacks; Del Beach, which is open to the public; and Dog Beach where pooches can run free sans leash.

MISSION BEACH

Located near SeaWorld San Diego, Mission Beach is home to a bustling boardwalk that's frequented by walkers, cyclists, and people-watchers. The bay is popular for water sports such as stand-up paddle boarding and Jet Skiing, but the beach is best known for Belmont Park, its oceanfront amusement park.

WINDANSEA BEACH

Seasoned surfers should head to La Jolla's Windansea Beach for powerful waves. Tucked away in a residential area, Windansea's entrance is marked by large rocks that make for a great place to watch or dry out, but recreational swimming is not advised here due to the strong surf.

TORREY PINES STATE BEACH

Situated at the base of a 1,500-acre natural reserve, La Jolla's Torrey Pines State Beach offers a long, narrow stretch of pristine beach framed by picturesque sea cliffs. Beachgoers can add a hike to their itinerary that starts or finishes on the sand, with plenty of lookout areas for great photo ops. Beyond the bluffs, a salt marsh provides seclusion from businesses and their associated street noise.

LA JOLLA SHORES

Pack up the whole family for a beach day in La Jolla Shores, which is known for its calm waves, two parks, and playground. Sea caves and underwater canyons that are part of La Jolla Underwater Park and Ecological Reserve—a marine protected area—attract kayakers and scuba divers.

DEL MAR CITY BEACH

In the upscale coastal neighborhood of Del Mar lie two beach parks that are popular for special events because of their stunning views of the Pacific. Seagrove Park is perched on the hill at the end of 15th Street, with benches for ocean gazing and winding paths along the bluffs. Farther north across the railroad tracks, Powerhouse Park offers easy beach access, a playground area, and a volleyball court.

SWAMI'S STATE BEACH

West of the magnificent Self-Realization Fellowship Temple and Meditation Gardens in Encinitas, this beach draws surfers and yogis in with its Zen vibes, while others treat the steep staircase leading down to the beach as a workout, with a rewarding view of sea cliffs waiting at the bottom. At low tide, shells and other sea creatures are left behind for beachcombers to easily discover.

FLETCHER COVE BEACH PARK
Nestled in the heart of Solana Beach, Fletcher Cove Beach Park doubles as a recreational park and beach access area. Here you'll find a basketball court, playground, lawn area, and picnic tables. A paved ramp leads down to the crescent-shaped beach that's flanked by cliffs on both sides.

For sweeping views of the ocean, position yourself at one of the lookouts outfitted with seating and/or binoculars—yup, binoculars are waiting for you.

BEACON'S BEACH
Follow the windy dirty path laden with switchbacks down to find Beacon's Beach in Encinitas, a well-known beach spot and favorite locals' hangout; on maps it may be labeled Leucadia State Beach. Since its entrance is hidden below sea cliffs on a one-way residential street, Beacon's Beach has an air of exclusivity. With plenty of space to spread out here, you won't have to infringe on sun-worshipping neighbors.

MOONLIGHT STATE BEACH
Fans of active beach days should head to this Encinitas beach. Volleyball courts, picnic tables, and playgrounds line the beach, with a concession stand, equipment rentals, and free Sunday concerts in high season.

10 Best Celebrity Hangouts in L.A.

CAFÉ GRATITUDE LARCHMONT

Round out your L.A. vacation with a plant-based meal at local chain, Café Gratitude. For a celeb sighting, head to their Larchmont Blvd. location where Jake Gyllenhaal and Beyoncé, obligingly declare what they're grateful for before digging in.

THE HOLLYWOOD ROOSEVELT

The Hollywood Roosevelt is one of L.A.'s oldest hotels, and has hosted numerous celebrities and dignitaries in its Spanish Colonial Revival rooms. Set in the heart of Hollywood, it offers a convenient location as well as a number of watering holes, including Tropicana Pool & Café and The Spare Room. Incidentally, it's also one of the city's most haunted places, so if you don't spot a celeb, you may bump into a ghost.

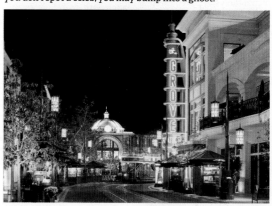

THE GROVE

L.A. may be strewn with outdoor malls, but it's The Grove that gets the highest billing, not just for its collection of mid- to high-end shops and restaurants, but also for its next-door neighbor, the Farmers Market. It's also one of the best places to see stars like Lena Headey, Zendaya, and Mario Lopez.

PINZ BOWLING CENTER

For a bit of family-friendly fun, head to Pinz in Studio City, where bowling is more than just a game, it's also a neon- and black-light party. Every lane comes with an automated ordering system so you can overload on wings and fries without ever leaving your spot. Celebrities often pop in here for bowling night, from A-listers like Vin Diesel and Jessica Alba to performers like Bruno Mars and Missy Elliott.

1

Experience Southern California 10 BEST CELEBRITY HANGOUTS IN L.A.

NOBU MALIBU
Nobu is a known A-list hotspot that's hosted everyone from Keanu Reeves to Kendall Jenner. Even if you don't spot a star, it's still worth the trip for its impeccable sushi and sashimi. Be warned, though: mingling with A-listers doesn't come cheap.

TOSCANA
Upscale Brentwood is home to many celebrities, and rustic trattoria Toscana is one of their neighborhood haunts. It may not be L.A.'s best Italian restaurant—for that, check out Jon & Vinny's —but for star sightings, it's your best bet. Jennifer Garner, Reese Witherspoon, and Heidi Klum have dined here.

CHATEAU MARMONT
The Chateau Marmont is possibly L.A.'s best-known celebrity haunt. Come for brunch in the garden terrace or drop in at night for the Hollywood-inspired cocktails. Photos not allowed.

Catch

CATCH
Secure a table at the flora-cluttered Catch in West Hollywood and rub elbows with the likes of David Beckham and the Jenner-Kardashian clan. This eatery is as L.A. as you can get, with its alfresco setting, vegan and gluten-free offerings, and locally and sustainably grown ingredients.

CRAIG'S
A West Hollywood dining staple, Craig's plain facade provides a safe haven for the movie industry's most important names and well-known faces like John Legend and Chrissy Teigen. We're not going to lie: this joint is always busy, so you might not even get a table. It's a good thing the food is worth the effort.

RUNYON CANYON
Out of L.A.'s numerous beautiful hiking spots, Runyon Canyon gets the biggest share of celebrity regulars, probably because it's strategically tucked between the Hollywood Hills, where many stars live, and the Hollywood strip. It's also a great venue for getting some fresh air, not to mention an ideal spot to take panoramic sunset photos.

Southern California Books and Movies

MOVIE: *ANCHORMAN*

In this raunchy comedy, Will Ferrell plays Ron Burgundy, a beloved San Diego news anchor who faces challenges to his job and sexist way of thinking when a female news anchor (Christina Applegate) comes on the scene. While the loud comedy boasts San Diego as its setting, much was filmed in L.A., with great pains taken to make everything look like San Diego.

MOVIE: *FAST TIMES AT RIDGEMONT HIGH*

This humorous coming-of-age film has become somewhat of a cult classic, but many people don't know it's based on the book and journalistic efforts of Cameron Crowe (the young *Rolling Stone* prodigy reporter). Cameron spent a year undercover in Clairemont High School in San Diego, and the book and movie tell the account of this wild, adolescent year and the characters he meets.

MOVIE: *SUNSET BOULEVARD*

This 1950s Billy Wilder classic is a wild ride and entertaining glimpse into the film business and its eccentric characters. A has-been star and a young screenwriter hope to use each other in some way, while things get more complicated—proving that what happens behind the scenes in Hollywood isn't the same as what appears on the big screen.

MOVIE: *TANGERINE*

Shot entirely with an iPhone camera, this indie film explores the streets of Hollywood with a close lens on a few characters. Recently out of prison, a transgender prostitute tries to track down her pimp and his new girlfriend with the help of a friend. It's hard to explain just how much light, humor, and beauty fills this film—you just have to see it for yourself.

MOVIE: *CHINATOWN*

In this classic crime noir, a young private eye (Jack Nicholson) in Depression-era Los Angeles gets in over his head with a client's case involving her husband's death and the city's sketchy water rights dealings. Incorporating fictionalized details of L.A.'s historic water wars, it's a tale of corruption and mystery.

BOOK: *THE GANGSTER WE ARE ALL LOOKING FOR* **BY LE THI DIEM THUY**

The characters of Thuy's novel are Vietnamese refugees in the late '70s, adjusting to life in crowded bungalows and apartments of Normal Heights, Linda Vista, and East San Diego. The protagonist, a young girl, flees Vietnam with her father and is sponsored by a churchgoing family in San Diego after their long journey. The novel is based on the author's own childhood.

BOOK: *THE HOUSE OF BROKEN ANGELS* **BY LUIS ALBERTO AURREA**

Centered on three generations of a Mexican-American family, with a history in the California Territories since World War I, this is a full, happy novel about family love and heartbreak, teeming with big personalities and vivid characters.

BOOK: *THE REVOLT OF THE COCKROACH PEOPLE* **BY OSCAR ZETA ACOSTA**

This story about Chicano radicalization in East Los Angeles is based on real events. The protagonist lawyer is based on Oscar Zeta Acosta himself, an author, activist, and lawyer/politician with his own fascinating life (and mysterious disappearance), and a key player in the movement.

BOOK: *ASK THE DUST* BY JOHN FANTE

Set in Los Angeles during the Great Depression, an Italian American writer lives in a seedy hotel in Bunker Hill and struggles with poverty, love, and creativity. Downtown L.A. is rendered well, and the character's relationship with Los Angeles—his love and hopes for the city—remains complicated.

BOOK: *HAM ON RYE* BY CHARLES BUKOWSKI

America's favorite degenerate poet writes an off-the-cuff novel about growing up in L.A. during the mid-20th century as the child of German immigrants. As told through Henry Chinaski, the author's alter ego and antihero, the book starts with family violence, alcoholism, Model Ts, and orange trees, and segues into schoolyard bullying and some realist, gritty views on the America (and Southern California) of the times.

What's New in Southern California

FOODIE'S PARADISE

Great dining is a staple of the California lifestyle, and a new young generation of chefs is challenging old ideas about preparing and presenting great food. The food-truck frenzy continues to fuel movable feasts up and down the state. Esteemed chefs and urban foodies follow the trucks on Twitter as they move around cities 24/7 purveying delicious, cheap, fresh meals. You can find food-laden trucks at sports and entertainment venues, near parks and attractions, and on busy roads and boulevards.

Diners are also embracing the pop-up concept, where guest chefs offer innovative menus in unconventional settings for a limited time. These pop-up engagements are hosted anywhere from inside a warehouse to outside in a field. Often there is an air of secrecy and anticipation to them, with key details being revealed at the last moment. Visitors can look for local pop-ups listed on foodie websites such as Eater (⊕ *www.eater.com*).

FAMILY FUN

California's theme parks work overtime to keep current and attract patrons of all ages. LEGOLAND California Resort keeps expanding with additional attractions such as the LEGOLAND Water Park and its 250-room LEGO-theme hotel.

Disneyland also continues to grow. Return visitors will notice huge changes with the unveiling of the much-anticipated Star Wars Land. Visitors will also enjoy the addition of new shows, parades, and attractions, such as the transformation of the Tower of Terror into the Marvel Guardians of the Galaxy ride.

WINE DISCOVERIES

In the hillsides of San Diego County, the Ramona Valley AVA is seeing an increasing number of visitors, and Escondido-based Orfila keeps snagging awards.

North of Los Angeles, the boutique wineries in the hillsides of Malibu are garnering increased attention.

ALL ABOARD

Riding the rails can be a satisfying experience, particularly in California where the distances between destinations sometimes run into the hundreds of miles. You can save money on gas and parking, avoid freeway traffic, and see some of the best the state has to offer. California broke ground on a high-speed rail project linking San Francisco to Los Angeles, but the controversial project looks to be dead after huge cost overruns

But, there's still the long scenic-route. Hop on the luxuriously appointed *Coast Starlight,* a long-distance train with sleeping cars that runs between Seattle and Los Angeles, passing some of California's most beautiful coastline as it hugs the beach. For the best surf-side viewing, get a seat or a room on the left side of the train and ride south to north.

Amtrak also has frequent Pacific Surfliner service between San Diego and Los Angeles, and San Diego and Santa Barbara. These are coach cars, but many of the trains have been upgraded and are comfortable and convenient, especially if you want to get off and on the train at several destinations—Anaheim near Disneyland, Downtown Los Angeles, coastal Ventura, Santa Barbara, and San Luis Obispo.

STATE OF THE ARTS

The Los Angeles County Museum of Art (LACMA) keeps expanding its Wilshire Boulevard campus following the 2010 opening of the Renzo Piano–designed Resnick Pavilion. It is now gearing up for a major expansion under the direction of architect Peter Zumthor, estimated to be complete in 2023.

Chapter 2

TRAVEL SMART SOUTHERN CALIFORNIA

Updated by
Paul Feinstein and
Marlise Kast-Myers

★ **CAPITAL:**
Sacramento

👫 **POPULATION:**
40.1 million

💬 **LANGUAGE:**
English

$ **CURRENCY:**
U.S. dollar

📞 **COUNTRY CODE:**
1

⚠ **EMERGENCIES:**
911

🚗 **DRIVING:**
On the right

⚡ **ELECTRICITY:**
120–240 v/60 cycles; plugs have two or three rectangular prongs

�途 **TIME:**
Three hours behind New York

🌐 **WEB RESOURCES:**
www.visitcalifornia.com,
www.parks.ca.gov,
www.dot.ca.gov/cttravel,
travel.state.gov

Things to Know Before You Go

IT AIN'T SMALL

California is the third largest state behind Alaska and Texas and in square miles is similar in size to France, Spain, Sweden, and Thailand. And even if you're only visiting half the state—it's still plenty big. Even the cities are massive. Often, tourists arrive in Los Angeles expecting to do Malibu and Disneyland on the same day. Here's some perspective—that drive is 77 miles and, depending on traffic, can take more than three hours from end to end.

SPEAKING OF TRAFFIC

One of the downsides to exploring the Golden State is the lack of high-speed rail. If you want to see all this part of the state has to offer, you'll probably want to rent a car. But that means sitting in a lot of traffic. Get used to it. Traveling between Los Angeles and San Diego can take anywhere from two to four hours; between Los Angeles and Santa Barbara between one and three. And, of course, Los Angeles is infamously awful at rush hour, but there are some rules to live by: First, only get in a car before 7 am, after 10 am, before 3 pm, or after 7 pm. If you MUST drive at any other times, find routes that don't involve L.A.'s maze of freeways. Side streets are your friends and give you lots of alternatives. If you get stuck on the 405 at 5:30, you will miss your dinner reservation.

YOUR WEATHER FORECAST

Despite the perception of Southern California, the weather can occasionally be tricky. Both San Diego and Los Angeles are typically sunny with temperatures in the 70s. But tourists who have never visited are often surprised to find out how cool it gets at night. Many businesses and residences—particularly older buildings—do not have central heating or air conditioning, so it's advised to bring a light jacket or sweater for summer evenings, and heavier knits during winter. Coastal neighborhoods can turn particularly chilly from ocean breezes. The deserts, however, tend to stay warm year-around, though will occasionally dip down in the winter months.

IF YOU DECIDE TO GO TO MEXICO, BRING YOUR PASSPORT

San Diego's an international border city, located only 17 miles from Tijuana, making it easy to plan a trip to both cities in a single visit. But gone are the days when Americans could cross the border into Mexico and return by simply showing their driver's license. For the last decade, U.S. Customs and Border Protection has required Americans to show a valid passport to return home after a day of tacos and margaritas in Mexico. From San Diego, the easiest way to travel to the border is by taking the trolley ($5 round-trip) to San Ysidro on the blue line, and then walk across—retracing your steps on the way back. Check the CBP Border Wait Times mobile app for estimated wait times around the clock.

ENTERTAINMENT!

You'd have to be living in a cave to not know that California, specifically Hollywood, is the entertainment capital of the world. But seeing stars isn't the only fun to be had. California packs a big punch on the entertainment front. There's Universal Studios, Disneyland, Disney's California Adventure, Knott's Berry Farm, Six Flags Magic Mountain, LEGOLAND, and Sea World. If you're not having fun here, you're doing it wrong.

CELEBRITIES LIVE HERE, TOO

If you want to see celebs in L.A., you need to know where to find them. But this isn't a safari—they're not animals—so be cool. If you want some guarantees, go to lunch at the Chateau Marmont or Polo Lounge. Hit up dinner at Craig's or Catch LA. If you're more into movie stuff than movie people, head over to the Warner Bros. and Universal Studios lots, where you can tour sound stages and movie sets and maybe, just maybe, see an A-lister eating lunch at the commissary—again, be cool.

MARIJUANA IS LEGAL

OK, stoners, this is what you've been waiting for. California has legalized marijuana and you want to know where to get high. First off, think of the marijuana rules like the alcohol rules. You need to be 21. You can't consume in public. You can't smoke and drive (and really, you shouldn't). Fines can be as high (not a pun) as $250 just for driving with an open container. So, if you need a pick-me-up or take-me-down, look for the green crosses on storefronts.

GOOD LUCK FINDING A HOTEL DURING THESE TIMES

In San Diego during Comic Con? In Palm Springs during Coachella? In Los Angeles during the Oscars? Don't already have a hotel? You're outta luck. Rooms are at an all-time premium during these events. In San Diego and Palm Springs, Airbnb rentals will be completely booked. If you plan to travel anytime near these events, plan on booking at least six months in advance.

TACO TUESDAYS ARE A WEEKLY TRADITION

If you like happy hour, then you'll love Taco Tuesdays throughout Southern California. Many local restaurants, especially in beach communities, offer discounts on Tuesdays that may also include drink specials. And it's not just Mexican restaurants that join in the tradition—eateries of all types and every price point have tempting deals. Browse Instagram for drool-worthy #TacoTuesday posts to begin plotting out your next tortilla-filled meal.

STAY AWAY FROM THE SEALS

They might look cute and cuddly, but keep away from the seals and sea lions that congregate at La Jolla's Children's Pool Beach. Do not feed them, and go with the knowledge that these playful creatures often leave a strong odor of feces in their wake.

Getting Here and Around

From Los Angeles To:	By Air	By Car
San Diego	55 mins	2 hrs
Death Valley	No flights	5 hrs
San Francisco	1 hr 30 mins	5 hrs 40 mins
Monterey	1 hr 10 mins	5 hrs
Santa Barbara	50 mins	1 hr 40 mins
Big Sur	No flights	5 hrs 40 mins
Sacramento	1 hr 30 mins	6 hrs 15 mins

From Los Angeles To:	Route	Distance
San Diego	I–5 or I–405	127 miles
Las Vegas	I–10 to I–15	270 miles
Death Valley	I–10 to I–15 to Hwy. 127 to Hwy. 190	290 miles
San Francisco	I–5 to I–580 to I–80	382 miles
Monterey	U.S. 101 to Salinas, Hwy. 68 to Hwy. 1	320 miles
Santa Barbara	U.S. 101	95 miles
Big Sur	U.S. 101 to Hwy. 1	349 miles
Sacramento	I–5	391 miles

 ## Air

Flying time to California is about 6½ hours from New York and 4¾ hours from Chicago. Travel from London to either Los Angeles or San Francisco is 11 hours and from Sydney approximately 15. Flying between San Francisco and Los Angeles takes about 90 minutes.

 ## Bus

Greyhound is the major bus carrier in California. Regional bus service is available in metropolitan areas.

 ## Car

Two main north–south routes run through California: Interstate 5 through the middle of the state, and U.S. 101, a parallel route closer to the coast. Slower but more scenic is Highway 1, which winds along much of the coast.

From north to south, the state's main east–west routes are Interstate 80, Interstate 15, Interstate 10, and Interstate 8. Much of California is mountainous, and you may encounter winding roads and steep mountain grades.

GASOLINE

Gas stations are plentiful throughout the state. Many stay open late, except in rural areas, where Sunday hours are limited and where you may drive long stretches without a chance to refuel.

ROAD CONDITIONS

Rainy weather can make driving along the coast or in the mountains treacherous. Some smaller routes over mountain ranges and in the deserts are prone to flash flooding. When the weather is particularly bad, Highway 1 may be closed due to mud and rock slides.

WEATHER CONDITIONS
National Weather Service
☎ *707/443–6484 northernmost California, 831/656–1725 San Francisco Bay area and central California, 775/673–8100 Reno, Lake Tahoe, and northern Sierra, 805/988–6610 Los Angeles, 858/675–8700 San Diego, 916/979–3051 Sacramento.*

ROADSIDE EMERGENCIES

Dial 911 to report accidents and to reach the police, the California Highway Patrol (CHP), or the fire department. On some rural highways and on most interstates, look for emergency phones on the side of the road.

In Los Angeles, the Metro Freeway Service Patrol provides assistance to stranded motorists under nonemergency conditions. Dial 511 from a cell phone and choose the "motorist aid" option to reach them 24 hours a day.

RULES OF THE ROAD

All passengers must wear a seat belt at all times. A child must be secured in a federally approved child passenger restraint system and ride in the back seat until at least eight years of age or until the child is at least 4 feet 9 inches tall. Children who are eight but don't meet the height requirement must ride in a booster seat or a car seat. It is illegal to leave a child six years of age or younger unattended in a motor vehicle. Unless indicated, right turns are allowed at red lights after you've come to a full stop. Left turns between two one-way streets are allowed at red lights after you've come to a full stop. Drivers with a blood-alcohol level higher than 0.08 who are stopped by police are subject to arrest.

The speed limit on some interstate highways is 70 mph; unlimited-access roads are usually 55 mph. In cities, freeway speed limits are between 55 mph and 65 mph. Many city routes have commuter lanes during rush hour.

You must turn on your headlights whenever weather conditions require the use of windshield wipers. Texting on a wireless device is illegal for all drivers. If using a mobile phone while driving it must be hands-free and mounted (i.e.,

it's not legal having it loose on the seat or your lap). For more driving rules, refer to the Department of Motor Vehicles driver's handbook at ⊕ *www.dmv.ca.gov.*

CAR RENTAL

When you reserve a car, ask about cancellation penalties, taxes, drop-off charges (if you're planning to pick up the car in one city and leave it in another), and surcharges (for being under or over a certain age, for additional drivers, or for driving across state or country borders or beyond a specific distance from your point of rental). All these things can add substantially to your costs. Request car seats and extras such as GPS when you book.

Rates are sometimes—but not always—better if you book in advance or reserve through a rental agency's website. There are other reasons to book ahead, though: for popular destinations, during busy times of the year, or to ensure that you get certain types of cars (vans, SUVs, exotic sports cars).

■ TIP→ **Make sure that a confirmed reservation guarantees you a car. Agencies sometimes overbook, particularly for busy weekends and holiday periods.**

A car is essential in most parts of California. In sprawling cities such as Los Angeles and San Diego, you'll have to take the freeways to get just about anywhere.

Rates statewide for the least expensive vehicle begin as low as $30 a day, usually on weekends, and less than $200 a week. This does not include additional fees or the tax on car rentals (8%–10%). Be sure to shop around—you can get a decent deal by shopping the major car-rental companies' websites. A few companies rent specialty cars such as convertibles or sport-utility vehicles.

Getting Here and Around

In California you must have a valid driver's license and be 21 to rent a car; rates may be higher if you're under 25. Some agencies will not rent to those under 25; check when you book. Non-U.S. residents must have a license, valid for the entire rental period, with text in the Roman alphabet that clearly identifies it as a driver's license. In addition, most companies also require an international license; check in advance.

Train

Amtrak provides rail service within California. On some trips—to Yosemite National Park, for example—passengers board motor coaches part of the way. The rail service's scenic *Coast Starlight* trip begins in Los Angeles and hugs the Pacific Coast to San Luis Obispo before it turns inland for the rest of its journey to Portland and Seattle.

Essentials

Lodging

The lodgings we review are the top choices in each price category. *For an expanded review of each property, please see www.fodors.com.* We don't specify whether the facilities cost extra; when pricing accommodations, ask what's included and what costs extra. *For price information, see the planner in each chapter.*

Be sure you understand the hotel's cancellation policy. Some places allow you to cancel without any kind of penalty—even if you prepaid to secure a discounted rate—if you cancel at least 24 hours in advance. Others require you to cancel a week in advance or penalize you the cost of one night. Small inns and B&Bs are most likely to require you to cancel far in advance. Most hotels allow children under a certain age to stay in their parents' room at no extra charge, but others charge for them as extra adults; find out the cutoff age for discounts.

BED-AND-BREAKFASTS

California has more than 1,000 bed-and-breakfasts. You'll find everything from simple homestays to lavish luxury lodgings, many in historic hotels and homes. The California Association of Boutique and Breakfast Inns has about 300 member properties that you can locate and book through its website.

Communications

INTERNET

Internet access is widely available in urban areas, but it can be difficult to get online in rural communities. Most hotels offer some kind of connection—usually broadband or Wi-Fi. Many hotels charge a daily fee ($10–$15) for Internet access.

Cafés with free Wi-Fi are common throughout California.

Dining

California has led the pack in bringing natural and organic foods to the forefront of American dining. Though rooted in European cuisine, California cooking has strong Asian and Latin influences. Wherever you go, you're likely to find that dishes are made with fresh produce and other local ingredients.

The restaurants we list are the cream of the crop in each price category. *For price information, see the planner in each chapter.*

CUTTING COSTS

The better grocery and specialty-food stores have grab-and-go sections, with prepared foods on a par with restaurant cooking, perfect for picnicking (remember, it infrequently rains between May and October). At resort areas in the off-season you can often find two-for-one dinner specials at upper-end restaurants; check coupon apps or local papers or with visitor bureaus.

RESERVATIONS AND DRESS

Regardless of where you are, it's a good idea to make a reservation if you can. For popular restaurants, book as far ahead as you can (often 30 days), and reconfirm as soon as you arrive in California. (Large parties should always call ahead to check the reservations policy.)

Online reservation services make it easy to book a table. OpenTable covers many California cities.

Essentials

➕ Health

Smoking is illegal in all California bars and restaurants, including on outdoor dining patios in some cities. If you have an existing medical condition that may require emergency treatment, be aware that many rural and mountain communities have only daytime clinics, not hospitals with 24-hour emergency rooms.

Outdoor sports are a huge draw in California's moderate climate, but caution, especially in unfamiliar areas, is key. Drownings occur each year because beach lovers don't heed warnings about high surfs with their deadly rogue waves. Do not fly within 24 hours of scuba diving.

If you're spending time in the national parks or forests, be sure to follow posted instructions that outline how to avoid encounters with bears (e.g., store your food in bear lockers) and how to prevent exposure to hantavirus, carried in deer mouse droppings in remote areas.

📅 Hours of Operation

Banks in California are typically open weekdays 9–6; most are open on Saturday but close on Sunday and most holidays. Smaller shops usually operate 10 or 11–6, with larger stores remaining open until 8 or later. Hours vary for museums, historical sites, and state parks, and many are closed one or more days a week, or for extended periods during off-season months.

💲 Money

Los Angeles and San Diego are expensive cities to visit, and rates at coastal and desert resorts are also high. A day's admission to a major theme park is more than $100 per person, though you may be able to get discounts by purchasing tickets in advance online. Hotel rates average $150 to $250 a night (though you can find cheaper places), and dinners at even moderately priced restaurants often cost $20 to $40 per person. Costs in Death Valley/Mojave Desert region are considerably less—some motels in the Mojave charge less than $100.

CREDIT CARDS

It's a good idea to inform your credit-card company before you travel. Otherwise, unusual activity might prompt the company to put a hold on your card. Record all your credit-card numbers—as well as the phone numbers to call if your cards are lost or stolen—so you're prepared should something go wrong.

➕ Safety

California is a safe place to visit, as long as you take the usual precautions. In large cities ask the concierge or desk clerk to point out areas on your map that you should avoid. Lock valuables in a hotel safe when you're not using them. Keep an eye on your handbag when you're out in public. Security is high (but mostly invisible) at theme parks and resorts.

When hiking, stay on trails—rangers say that the majority of hikers needing to be rescued have gone off trail—and heed signs at trailheads about dangerous situations such as cliffs with loose rocks and how to react if you encounter predatory animals that live in the area. Bring plenty of water, hike with a companion if possible, and learn to identify and avoid contact with poison oak, a ubiquitous plant in California that causes a severe rash.

⑤ Taxes

Sales tax in the state of California is 7.25%, but local taxes vary and may be as much as an additional 2.5%. Sales tax applies to all purchases except for food bought in a grocery store; food consumed in a restaurant is taxed, but takeout food is not. Hotel taxes vary widely by region, from about 8% to 16.5%.

⑨ Time

California is in the Pacific time zone. Pacific daylight time (PDT) is in effect from mid-March through early November; the rest of the year the clock is set to Pacific standard time (PST).

⑨ Tours

Guided tours are a good option when you don't want to do it all yourself. You travel along with a group (sometimes large, sometimes small), stay in prebooked hotels, eat with your fellow travelers (the cost of meals is sometimes included in the price of your tour, sometimes not), and follow a schedule.

But not all guided tours are an if-it's-Tuesday-this-must-be-Yosemite experience. A knowledgeable guide can take you places that you might never discover on your own, and you may be pushed to see

Tipping Guidelines for California	
Bartender	$1–$3 per drink, or 15%–20% per round
Bellhop	$2–$3 per bag, depending on the level of the hotel
Hotel Concierge	$5–$10 for advice and reservations, more for difficult tasks
Hotel Doorman	$2–$3 for hailing a cab
Valet Parking Attendant	$3–$5 when you get your car
Hotel Maid	$3–$5 per day; more in high-end hotels
Waiter	18%–22% (20%–25% is standard in upscale restaurants); nothing additional if a service charge is added to the bill
Skycap at Airport	$1–$2 per bag
Hotel Room-Service Waiter	15%–20% per delivery, even if a service charge was added since that fee goes to the hotel, not the waiter
Taxi Driver	15%–20%, but round up the fare to the next dollar amount
Tour Guide	15% of the cost of the tour, more depending on quality

more than you would have otherwise. Tours aren't for everyone, but they can be just the thing for trips to places where making travel arrangements is difficult or time-consuming.

Essentials

Whenever you book a guided tour, find out what's included and what isn't. A "land-only" tour includes all your travel (by bus, in most cases) in the destination, but not necessarily your flights to and from or even within it. Also, in most cases prices in tour brochures don't include fees and taxes. And remember that you'll be expected to tip your guide (in cash) at the end of the tour.

◉ Visitor Information

The California Travel and Tourism Commission's website takes you to each region of California, with digital visitor guides in multiple languages, driving tours, maps, welcome center locations, information on local tours, links to bed-and-breakfasts, and a complete booking center. It also links you—via the Destinations menu—to the websites of city and regional tourism offices and attractions. *For the numbers and websites of regional and city visitor bureaus and chambers of commerce, see the Planning section in each chapter.*

Contacts

Air

AIRLINE SECURITY ISSUES

Transportation Security Administration (*TSA*). ☎ 866/289–9673 ⊕ www.tsa.gov.

AIRPORTS

SOUTHERN CALIFORNIA Hollywood Burbank Airport (*Bob Hope Airport*). ☎ 818/840–8840 ⊕ www.hollywoodburbankairport.com. **John Wayne Airport.** ☎ 949/252–5200 ⊕ www.ocair.com. **Long Beach Airport.** ☎ 562/570–2600 ⊕ www.lgb.org. **Los Angeles International Airport.** ☎ 855/463–5252 ⊕ www.flylax.com. **Ontario International Airport.** ☎ 909/937–2700 ⊕ www.flyontario.com. **San Diego International Airport.** ☎ 619/400–2400 ⊕ www.san.org.

AIRLINES

Air Canada. ☎ 888/247–2262 ⊕ www.aircanada.com. **Alaska Airlines/Horizon Air.** ☎ 800/252–7522 ⊕ www.alaskaair.com. **American Airlines.** ☎ 800/433–7300 ⊕ www.aa.com. **Delta Airlines.** ☎ 800/221–1212 for U.S. reservations, 800/241–4141 for international reservations ⊕ www.delta.com. **Frontier Airlines.** ☎ 801/401–9000 ⊕ www.flyfrontier.com. **JetBlue.** ☎ 800/538–2583 ⊕ www.jetblue.com. **Southwest Airlines.** ☎ 800/435–9792 ⊕ www.southwest.com. **United Airlines.** ☎ 800/864–8331 ⊕ www.united.com.

🚌 Bus

BUS INFORMATION Greyhound. ☎ 800/231–2222 ⊕ www.greyhound.com.

🚗 Car

SPECIALTY CAR AGENCIES

Beverly Hills Rent a Car. ☎ 310/448–2018 ⊕ www.bhrentacar.com. **Enterprise Exotic Car Rentals.** ☎ 866/458–9227 ⊕ exoticcars.enterprise.com. **MCar** (*Midway Car Rental*). ☎ 866/717–6802 ⊕ www.midwaycarrental.com.

MAJOR RENTAL AGENCIES

Alamo. ☎ 800/462–5266 ⊕ www.alamo.com. **Avis.** ☎ 800/633–3469 ⊕ www.avis.com. **Budget.** ☎ 800/218–7992 ⊕ www.budget.com. **Hertz.** ☎ 800/654–3131 ⊕ www.hertz.com. **National Car Rental.** ☎ 877/222–9058 ⊕ www.nationalcar.com.

ROAD CONDITIONS

Caltrans Current Highway Conditions. ☎ 800/427–7623 ⊕ www.dot.ca.gov.

🚆 Train

INFORMATION Amtrak. ☎ 800/872–7245 ⊕ www.amtrak.com.

➕ Health/Safety

Ambulance, fire, police ☎ 911 emergency.

🛏 Lodging

RESERVATION SERVICES

California Association of Boutique and Breakfast Inns (*CABBI*). ☎ 800/373–9251 ⊕ www.cabbi.com.

Chapter 3

SOUTHERN CALIFORNIA'S BEST ROAD TRIPS

Updated by
Daniel Mangin

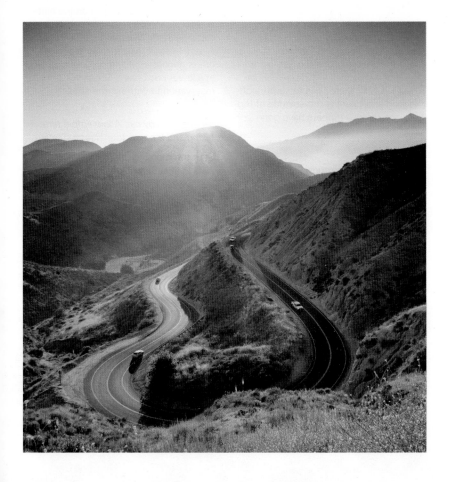

Great Itineraries

No trip to California would be complete without a drive through the state's spectacular scenery. However, adding a road trip to your itinerary is not just a romantic idea: it's often a practical one, too. A road trip is a great way to link together more than one urban area or to venture into some more remote areas of this massive state. Whether you have just a few days or longer to spare, these itineraries will help you hit the road.

Big Sur, 2 Days

In a nutshell, this drive is all about the jaw-dropping scenery of the Pacific Coast. Visitors pressed for time often make the drive through Big Sur in one day. However, those who linger will be rewarded with more time to venture off the road and to enjoy the solitude of Big Sur once the day-trippers have gone.

DAY 1: BIG SUR
(30 mins by car.)

The coastal drive through **Big Sur** is justifiably one of the most famous stretches of road in the world. The winding curves, endless views, and scenic waypoints are the stuff of road-trip legend. Keep your camera handy, fill up the tank, and prepare to be wowed. Traffic can easily back up along the route and drivers should take caution navigating the road's twists and turns. While you will only drive about 30 miles today, allow several hours for hikes and stops.

Heading into Big Sur you will first come upon the extremely photogenic **Bixby Creek Bridge.** Pull over in the turnout on the north side of the bridge to get that perfect shot. About 10 miles down the road look for a small cluster of services known as Big Sur Village just before the entrance to **Pfeiffer Big Sur State Park,** the perfect place to stop for a hike.

One mile south of the park, watch carefully for the sharp turnout and unmarked road leading to **Pfeiffer Beach.** Following the unpaved road 2 miles toward the sea you may question whether you are lost, but your perseverance will be rewarded when you reach the secluded beach with its signature rocky arch just offshore. Don't miss it!

There are several lodging options around this portion of Big Sur, ranging from rustic to luxurious. If room rates at the legendary **Post Ranch Inn** are not in your budget, consider splurging on the nine-course tasting menu at its spectacular cliff-side **Sierra Mar** restaurant instead. Alternatively, the terrace at **Nepenthe** offers decent food and gorgeous views at a lower price point. Time your dinner reservation to witness the sunset.

DAY 2: BIG SUR TO CAMBRIA
(About 2 hrs by car. Allow ample time for hiking and 2 hrs to tour Hearst Castle.)

Start the morning off with a hike in **Julia Pfeiffer Burns State Park,** popular for its waterfall tumbling dramatically into the sea. Back on the road, several scenic overlooks will beckon as you head through the southern stretch of Big Sur. A pullout north of the entrance near mile marker 36.2 affords views of McWay Falls. If the trail to the falls is open (check the park's website), you can hike in a short way for an up-close view.

As you enter **San Simeon,** don't miss the **Piedras Blancas Elephant Seal Rookery.** Depending on your timing, you might catch a late afternoon tour at **Hearst Castle.** If not, you can make a reservation for a tour early the following morning. End the day with a walk at **Moonstone Beach** in the town of **Cambria,** 10 miles south of the castle, and overnight in one of the reasonably priced lodgings here.

From here, you can continue your travels south through the central coast to **Santa Barbara.** Or head inland to visit the **Paso Robles** wine region.

Santa Barbara Wine Country, 3 Days

It has been well over a decade since the popular movie *Sideways* brought the Santa Barbara Wine Country to the world's attention, and interest in this wine-growing area continues to grow. On this trip you will explore one of the most beautiful cities in the West, enjoy time along the gorgeous coast, and then head inland for a delightful wine-tasting adventure. This itinerary makes a perfect add-on to a trip to Los Angeles, or for those driving the coastal route between Los Angeles and San Francisco.

DAY 1: SANTA BARBARA
(2 hrs by car from LAX to Santa Barbara without traffic.)

Santa Barbara is a gem, combining elegance with a laid-back coastal vibe. It provides a tranquil escape from the congestion of Los Angeles and a dose of sophistication to the largely rural central coast.

Start your day at the beautiful **Old Mission Santa Barbara,** known as the "Queen" of the 21 missions that comprise the California Mission Trail. Plan to spend some time here; if your visit doesn't coincide with one of the 60-minute docent-led tours, self-guided tours are also available. From here, head to the waterfront and spend some time enjoying the wide stretch of sand at **East Beach** and a seafood lunch at one of the restaurants on **Stearns Wharf.** After lunch, consider kicking off your wine tour early by checking out some of the Funk Zone tasting rooms just north of the wharf.

Next stop is a tour of the **Santa Barbara County Courthouse.** Don't miss the murals in the ceremonial chambers or the incredible views from the top of the courthouse tower, the incredible views of downtown's beautiful red-tile-roofed buildings and beyond them the Pacific Ocean.

Back on the ground, enjoy superb shopping along **State Street.** Enjoy the lively dining and nightlife scene downtown, or head toward tony **Montecito** for an elegant dinner. Splurge on an overnight stay at the posh **Four Seasons Resort The Biltmore Santa Barbara,** or check into the Funk Zone's **Hotel Indigo.**

DAY 2: SANTA RITA HILLS, LOMPOC, AND LOS OLIVOS

(Without stops, this route takes about 2 hrs by car. Plan to linger and to detour down side roads to reach the wineries.)

Take the scenic drive along the coast on Highway 101 before heading inland towards Buellton. Exit onto Santa Rosa Road to begin your loop through the Santa Rita Hills. This area's cooler climate produces top-notch Chardonnay and Pinot Noir. Vineyards line the loop as you head out on Santa Rosa Road and return on Highway 246 toward Buellton. A good stop midway along the route is the so-called **Lompoc Wine Ghetto**. Don't let the industrial-park setting deter you—the tasting rooms here include well-regarded producers such as **Longoria**. In Buellton, drop by **Lafond Winery and Vineyards** and **Alma Rosa Winery,** the latter part of the **Industrial Way** food-and-drink complex.

Back on Highway 101, head north about 6 miles before exiting towards **Los Olivos,** where you can park the car and spend the rest of the day exploring on foot. Tasting rooms, galleries, boutiques, and restaurants have made this former stage-coach town quite wine-country chic. **Blair Fox Cellars** and **Coquelicot Estate Vineyard** are just two of the producers with tasting

rooms in town. Los Olivos is a good base to dine—**Bear and Star** at **Fess Parker's Wine Country Inn and Spa** is the star here. Stay at Fess Parker's or just outside town at the lovely Ballard Inn, or slip over to nearby **Solvang,** checking into the **Hotel Corque** and dining in its chic locavore **Root 246** restaurant.

DAY 3: SOLVANG, FOXEN CANYON, AND THE SANTA YNEZ VALLEY

(The drive from Santa Ynez to Santa Barbara is about 45 mins by car via Hwy. 154.)

Start the next morning with pastries at the Danish town of **Solvang,** 10 minutes south of Los Olivos. The windmills and distinct half-timber architecture of this village are charming, if a bit touristy. Spend some time exploring the town before hitting the road.

The towns of Los Olivos, **Santa Ynez,** and Solvang are located just a few minutes apart, with wineries spread between them in an area known as the Santa Ynez Valley. Heading north from Los Olivos, the Foxen Canyon wine trail extends all the way to Santa Maria and is home to excellent producers. Expect some backtracking along your route today as you wind between the towns and venture into Foxen Canyon. Allow 30 to 45 minutes for the well-conceived walking tour at **Firestone Vineyard,** a must if you're interested in the wine-making process. Don't blink or you might miss the tiny town of **Santa Ynez,** worth a wander or a stop for lunch. A mile east of the tiny town's commercial drag you'll find **Gainey Vineyard,** whose wines impress major wine critics.

When you've had your fill of the wine region, take scenic Highway 154 over the San Marcos Pass and back to Santa Barbara. Wind down the day with a stroll along the beach, and perhaps one last glass of wine at sunset.

Route 66 and the Mojave Desert, 4 Days

Route 66 was the original road trip "from Chicago to L.A.," with California the ultimate destination. The Mother Road travels west from the Arizona border, skirting the Mojave Desert before passing through Los Angeles and ending at the Pacific Ocean. What makes this journey so compelling is actually what it lacks. Desolate stretches of road through windswept towns are reminders of the harsh conditions 1930s pioneers fleeing the central United States dust storms faced, while faded neon signs and abandoned motels offer nostalgic glimpses of Route 66's mid-century heyday. Nearby, the solitary beauty of the Mojave National Preserve beckons with its volcanic rock formations, Joshua trees, and seemingly endless dunes.

DAY 1: SANTA MONICA
By reversing the typical Route 66 journey and traveling from west to east you can hit the road upon arrival at LAX, or spend a few days exploring Los Angeles first. Starting your voyage in **Santa Monica** may feel a bit like eating your dessert first.

For road-trippers on Route 66, reaching the Pacific Ocean after a long dusty drive through the desert was certainly a treat. The official end of Route 66 is marked with a plaque in **Palisades Park,** on a bluff overlooking **Santa Monica State Beach.** Soak in the quintessential SoCal beach scene on the wide expanse of sand below before heading to the famous **Santa Monica Pier.** From here, you can rent a bike and cruise south to **Venice Beach** for the ultimate people-watching experience.

In the evening, stroll the pedestrian-only **Third Street Promenade** and neighboring **Santa Monica Place** mall for a good selection of shopping, dining, and entertainment. Relax in luxury at the legendary **Shutters on the Beach.** Or, in keeping with the true Route 66 spirit, opt for the more modest motor-lodge vibe of the **Sea Shore Motel.**

DAY 2: HOLLYWOOD AND PASADENA
(1½ hrs by car from Santa Monica to Pasadena and another 1½–2 hrs by car to Victorville.)

Heading inland through **Beverly Hills** and **Hollywood,** the remnants of Route 66 are easily overshadowed by the surrounding glitz and glamour. A stop at the **Hollywood Museum** or the **Hollywood Walk of Fame** will help transport you back in time to Tinseltown's golden age.

The route continues through **Pasadena,** with its stately homes and spacious gardens. Fans of Craftsman architecture won't want to miss a tour of the **Gamble House,** while a stroll around **Old Town Pasadena** is a great way to stretch your legs and grab a bite to eat.

Depending on your interests and how much sightseeing you've done, you might choose to stay in Pasadena for the night to enjoy a wider choice of dining and lodging options. Or, head to **Victorville** to maximize time on Route 66 tomorrow.

DAY 3: ROUTE 66

(The drive from Pasadena to Victorville takes about 1¼ hrs, not counting traffic. Driving from Victorville to Barstow takes less than an hr. From there, you can follow as much of Route 66 as time permits.)

Hit the road early if you didn't spend the night in Victorville. First stop is the **California Route 66 Museum** in **Victorville,** where you'll learn all about the history of the Mother Road. Pick up a copy of the museum's self-guided tour book and consult one of the many Route 66–related websites, among them ⊕ *www. historic66.com*, to help you navigate the old road as it crosses back and forth alongside Interstate 40 between Barstow and Needles. Abandoned service stations, shuttered motels, and faded signs dot the desert landscape in various states of alluring decay. Grab a meal at the famous **Baghdad Café** in Barstow. For a diversion unrelated to Route 66, spend a few hours exploring **Calico Ghost Town,** a restored old mining town just north of Barstow. In the evening, turn back the hands of time and catch a flick at the **Skyline Drive-In Theatre.**

Accommodations in this area are mostly of the chain-motel variety. Victorville and Barstow are your best bets for lodging unless you follow Route 66 into Arizona, where **Lake Havasu City,** 43 miles south of Needles on Highway 95, offers several options. Staying overnight in nondescript Needles is not recommended.

DAY 4: MOJAVE NATIONAL PRESERVE

(There are several access points to the park along I–15 and I–40. Kelso Dunes Visitor Center is about 1½ hrs by car from Barstow. Within the park stick to paved or gravel roads—others require four-wheel drive.)

In the morning, head north from Route 66 into the beautiful and remote landscape of the **Mojave National Preserve.** Reaching the top of the stunning golden **Kelso Dunes** requires some athleticism, but your efforts will be rewarded with incredible scenery and the eerie sounds of "singing" sand caused by the wind. If you spent the night in Lake Havasu City, explore the volcanic gas formations of **Hole-in-the-Wall** first. Farther north in the park, the Cima Road will bring you to the Teutonia Peak Trailhead and the largest concentration of Joshua trees in the world. Visitor centers at **Kelso Depot** and **Hole-in-the-Wall** provide information on additional sights, hiking trails, and campgrounds in the park.

There are several options for the next leg of your journey. You can drive back to Los Angeles in about three hours or drive onward to **Las Vegas** even faster. If you have more time, you can continue north and spend a few days in **Death Valley National Park,** or head south to **Joshua Tree** and **Palm Springs** before making your way back to **Los Angeles.**

Palm Springs and the Desert, 5 Days

Many visitors consider the Palm Springs area pure paradise, and not just for the opportunity to get a good tan or play golf on championship courses. Expect fabulous and funky spas, a dog-friendly atmosphere, and sparkling stars at night.

DAY 1: PALM SPRINGS
(Just over 2 hrs by car from LAX, without traffic.)

Somehow in harmony with the harsh environment, mid-century-modern homes and businesses with clean, low-slung lines define the **Palm Springs** style. Although the desert cities—Cathedral City, Rancho Mirage, Palm Desert, Indian Wells, Indio, and La Quinta—comprise a trendy destination with beautiful hotels, fabulous multicultural food, abundant nightlife, and plenty of culture, a quiet atmosphere prevails. Fans of Palm Springs' legendary architecture won't want to miss the home tours, lectures, and other events at the annual Modernism Week held each February, or the smaller fall preview event in October. If your visit doesn't coincide with these happenings, swing by the Palm Springs Visitor's Center for information on self-guided architecture tours. The city seems far away when you hike in hushed **Tahquitz** or **Indian Canyon**; cliffs and palm trees shelter rock art, irrigation works, and other remnants of Agua Caliente culture. If your boots aren't made for walking, you can always practice your golf game or indulge in spa treatments at an area resort instead. Embrace the Palm Springs vibe and park yourself at the modern-chic **Kimpton Rowan Palm Springs Hotel** or the legendary **Parker Palm Springs.** Alternatively, base yourself at the desert oasis, **La Quinta Resort,** about 40 minutes from downtown Palm Springs.

DAY 2: EXPLORE PALM SPRINGS
(The Aerial Tram is 15 mins by car from central Palm Springs. Plan at least a half day for the excursion.)

If riding a tram up an 8,516-foot mountain for a stroll or even a snowball fight above the desert sounds like fun to you, then show up at the **Palm Springs Aerial Tramway** before the first morning tram leaves (later, the line can get discouragingly long). Dress in layers and wear decent footwear as it can be significantly colder when you reach the top. Afterward stroll through the **Palm Springs Art Museum** where you can see a shimmering display of contemporary studio glass, an array of enormous Native American baskets, and significant 20th-century sculptures by Henry Moore and others. After all that walking you may be ready for an early dinner. Nearly every restaurant in Palm Springs offers a happy hour, when you can sip a cocktail and nosh on a light entrée, usually for half price. Using your hotel as a base, take a few day trips to discover the natural beauty of the desert.

DAY 3: JOSHUA TREE NATIONAL PARK
(1 hr by car from Palm Springs.)

Due to its proximity to Los Angeles and the highway between Las Vegas and coastal cities, **Joshua Tree** is among the most accessible of the national parks. You can see most of it in a day, entering the park at the town of Joshua Tree, exploring sites along **Park Boulevard,** and exiting at **Twentynine Palms.** With the signature trees, piles of rocks, glorious spring wildflowers, starlit skies, and colorful pioneer history, the experience is a bit more like the Wild West than Sahara dunes. Whether planning to take a day hike or a scenic drive, load up on drinking water before entering the park.

DAY 4: ANZA-BORREGO DESERT STATE PARK AND THE SALTON SEA
(About 2 hrs by car from Palm Springs.)

The **Salton Sea,** about 60 miles south of Palm Springs via Interstate 10 and Highway 86S, is one of the largest inland seas on earth. Formed by the flooding of the Colorado River in 1905, it attracts thousands of migrating birds and bird-watchers every fall. **Anza-Borrego Desert State**

Park to the west, California's largest state park, contains 600,000 acres of mostly untouched wilderness. The springtime wildflower displays here rank among the state's best. Just east of the park lies **Borrego Springs,** a tiny hamlet most notable for its 130 life-size bronze sculptures of animals that roamed this space millions of years ago. The desert is home to an archaeological site, where scientists continue to uncover remnants of prehistoric animals ranging from mastodons to horses. If you have four-wheel drive, a detour down the sandy track to **Font's Point** rewards the intrepid with spectacular views of the Borrego badlands. However, do not take the challenging road conditions lightly—inquire with park rangers before setting out.

DAY 5: RETURN TO L.A.
(LAX is just over 2 hrs by car from Palm Springs without traffic, but the drive often takes significantly more time.)

If you intend to depart from LAX, plan for a full day of driving from the desert to the airport. Be prepared for heavy traffic at any time of day or night. If possible, fly out of Palm Springs International Airport or Ontario International Airport instead.

Southern California with Kids, 7 Days

SoCal offers many opportunities to entertain the kids beyond the Magic Kingdom. LEGOLAND is a blast for kids 12 and under, and families can't beat the San Diego Zoo and San Diego's historic Old Town.

DAYS 1–2: DISNEYLAND

(45 mins by car from LAX to Disneyland.)

Get out of Los Angeles International Airport as fast as you can. Pick up your rental car and head south on the Interstate 405 freeway, which can be congested day or night, toward Orange County (aka the O.C.) and **Disneyland.** Skirt the lines at the box office with advance-purchased tickets in hand and storm the gates of the Magic Kingdom. You can cram the highlights into a single day, but if you get a two-day ticket and stay the night you can see the end-of-day parade and visit **Downtown Disney** before heading south. The **Grand Californian Hotel** is a top choice for lodging within the Disney Resort. If tackling Disneyland after a long flight is too much, head south from LAX to the surfer's haven at **Huntington Beach,** where you can relax at the beach and spend the night in one of several beachfront hotels before heading inland to Anaheim the next morning.

DAY 3: LEGOLAND

(1 to 1½ hrs by car from Huntington Beach or Anaheim, depending on traffic.)

Get an early start for your next roller-coaster ride at **LEGOLAND,** about an hour's drive south of Huntington Beach via the Pacific Coast Highway. Check into the **LEGOLAND Hotel** or the **Sheraton Carlsbad Resort & Spa**; both offer direct access to the park. LEGOLAND has a water park and aquarium in addition to

Tips

No matter how carefully you plan your movements to avoid busy routes at peak hours, you will inevitably encounter heavy traffic in L.A., Orange County, and San Diego. If your plans include a trip from L.A. to San Diego or Orange County, you can save time (and maybe money) by booking your flight to L.A. and returning from the airport nearest to your last destination.

Allow yourself twice as much time as you think you'll need to negotiate LAX.

the LEGO-based rides, shows, and roller coasters. The little ones can live out their fairy-tale fantasies and bigger ones can spend all day on waterslides, shooting water pistols, driving boats, or water fighting with pirates.

DAY 4: LA JOLLA AND SAN DIEGO

(La Jolla is just over an hr's drive from Carlsbad along scenic S21, or 40 mins on the I-5 freeway; Downtown San Diego is a 20-min drive from La Jolla.)

Take a leisurely drive south to San Diego by using the "old road," the original Pacific Coast Highway that hugs the shore all the way. It's a slow drive through Leucadia, Encinitas, Solana Beach, and Del Mar, all with popular surfing beaches. When you get to **La Jolla,** swing around the cove to see one of the area's most beautiful beaches. Look, but don't go in the water at the Children's Pool, as it's likely to be filled with barking seals. The **Birch Aquarium at Scripps** here offers a look at how scientists study the oceans.

Hop onto Interstate 5 and head for Downtown **San Diego.** Go straight for the city's nautical heart by exploring the

DAY 6: SEAWORLD AND OLD TOWN

(From Downtown San Diego, both Sea-World and Old Town are 10 mins by car.)

Two commercial and touristy sights are on the agenda today. **SeaWorld,** with its walk-through shark tanks, can be a lot of fun if you surrender to the experience. Also touristy, but with genuine historical significance, **Old Town** drips with Mexican and early Californian heritage. Soak it up in the plaza at **Old Town San Diego State Historic Park,** then browse the stalls and shops at **Fiesta de Reyes** and along San Diego Avenue. Unwind after a long day with dinner and margaritas at one of Old Town's many Mexican restaurants.

DAY 7: DEPARTURE FROM SAN DIEGO OR LOS ANGELES

(San Diego Airport is 10 mins by car from Downtown. Depending on traffic, allow 2½–4 hrs to drive from Downtown San Diego to LAX.)

Pack up your Mouseketeer gear and give yourself ample time to reach the airport. San Diego International Airport lies within a 10-minute drive from Old Town. Although you'll be driving on freeways the entire way to LAX, traffic is always heavy and you should allot at least a half day to get there.

The Southern Pacific Coast Highway: Sand, Surf, and Sun, 3 Days

This tour along the southern section of the Pacific Coast Highway (PCH) is a beach vacation on wheels, taking in the highlights of the Southern California coast and its world-famous surfer-chic vibe. If at any point the drive feels like something out of a movie, that's

restored ships of the **Maritime Museum** at the waterfront in Downtown. Victorian buildings—and plenty of other tourists—surround you on a stroll through the **Gaslamp Quarter.** Plant yourself at a Downtown hotel and graze your way through the neighborhood's many restaurants.

DAY 5: SAN DIEGO ZOO

(10 mins by car from Downtown San Diego.)

Malayan tapirs in a faux-Asian rain forest, polar bears in an imitation Arctic, and pandas frolicking in the trees—the **San Diego Zoo** maintains a vast and varied collection of creatures in a world-renowned facility comprised of meticulously designed habitats. Come early, and wear comfy shoes. Have dinner in the nearby **Hillcrest** neighborhood or Downtown.

because it likely is—this is the California of Hollywood legend. The itinerary is easily combined with the Big Sur and Northern Coast itineraries to do a full run of the legendary coastal route. Roll the top down on the convertible and let the adventure begin.

DAY 1: SANTA BARBARA TO SANTA MONICA

(About 2 hrs by car via the 101 and Hwy. 1. Allow plenty of time for beach stops and be aware of rush-hour traffic as you approach Santa Monica.)

Don't leave **Santa Barbara** without exploring the highlights of this Mediterranean-inspired city. Take a stroll along State Street, through the red-tile-roofed buildings of downtown to the gorgeous **Santa Barbara County Courthouse** and take in the views from its tower. Before leaving town, make a stop at the **Mission Santa Barbara,** widely considered the finest of the 21 California missions.

Heading south out of town the 101 runs along the coast past the low-key beach communities of Carpinteria and Mussel Shoals. Approaching **Ventura** on a clear day, the Channel Islands are visible in the distance. Stretch your legs on the **Ventura Oceanfront** with a walk on San Buenaventura State Beach, or around the picturesque Ventura Harbor. There are several spots to grab lunch at the harbor, too, including an outpost of Santa Barbara's famous **Brophy Bros.** seafood restaurant.

Leaving Ventura, trade the 101 for Highway 1 and continue south through miles of protected, largely unpopulated coastline. Hike the trails at **Point Mugu State Park,** scout for offshore whales at **Point Dume State Beach,** or ride a wave at **Zuma Beach.** The PCH follows the curve of Santa Monica Bay from Point Mugu through Malibu and on to Santa Monica. Chances are you'll experience déjà vu

driving this stretch of road: mountains on one side, ocean on the other, opulent homes perched on hillsides; you've seen this piece of coast countless times on TV and film. As you approach Malibu proper, affectionately known as "the 'bu," be sure to walk out on the **Malibu Pier** for a great photo op, then check out **Surfrider Beach,** with three famous points where perfect waves ignited a worldwide surfing rage in the 1960s.

If you plan to visit the **Getty Villa Malibu,** with its impressive antiquities collection and jaw-dropping setting overlooking the Pacific, you will need to obtain free timed-entry tickets online prior to your arrival. Otherwise, continue the drive to Santa Monica where you can overnight near the **Santa Monica Pier** and grab dinner along the **Third Street Promenade** or at Santa Monica Place.

DAY 2: SANTA MONICA TO NEWPORT BEACH

(About 2 hrs by car without traffic, but plan for traffic.)

Start the day with a morning walk along **Santa Monica State Beach** and, if you didn't visit it the night before, the **Santa Monica Pier.** Rent some beach cruisers and pedal your way south along the bike path to **Venice Beach** (about 3 miles each way) to take in the action along the boardwalk. Once you tire of the skateboarders, bodybuilders, and street performers, head inland a few blocks to Abbott Kinney Boulevard for lunch at **Gjelina** and a browse in the local boutiques.

Pedal back to Santa Monica and trade two wheels for four to continue the drive toward Newport Beach. If time permits, you can follow Highway 1 through Marina del Ray and the trio of beach towns well known among beach-volleyball enthusiasts: Manhattan, Hermosa, and Redondo Beach. From here Highway 1 skirts through Long Beach and continues into Orange County. If time is short, skip this section of the PCH in favor of the 405 freeway. However, as is always advisable near L.A., check current traffic reports before choosing your route.

The affluent coastal cities of Orange County (aka the O.C.) are familiar to many thanks to *Arrested Development*, *The Real Wives of Orange County*, and other TV shows set here. However, the dazzling yachts and multimillion-dollar mansions of Newport Beach still may take you by surprise after the more laid-back brand of luxe found elsewhere on the coast.

Choose from among the many excellent restaurants and overnight at **The Island Hotel.**

DAY 3: NEWPORT BEACH TO DANA POINT
(1 hr by car.)

The next morning, head to Balboa Island in the middle of Newport Harbor. This far quainter (but equally expensive) commu-nity is a getaway for locals and tourists alike. Browse the boutiques along Marine Avenue before hopping in a Duffy (elec-tric boat) for a harbor tour. Back on land, don't leave without enjoying a Balboa

Bar—the ice-cream treat is virtually mandatory for all Balboa Island visitors. Leaving Newport Beach on the PCH, your next stop is Crystal Cove State Park, 6 miles southeast. If the tide is low, this is a great spot for tide pooling. Otherwise, don't miss the historic beach cottages dating as far back as 1935.

Back on the road, **Laguna Beach** is this journey's final stop. In an area not often noted for its cultural offerings, Laguna Beach is the exception. Browse the art galleries and enjoy a meal in the charming downtown before taking one last walk along the Pacific. The PCH ter-minates 10 miles south of Laguna Beach near Dana Point, a town famous for its harbor and whale-watching excursions. From here, you can continue to San Diego or return north to Anaheim or Los Angeles via Interstate 5.

Hooray for Hollywood, 4 Days

If you are a movie fan, there's no better place to see it all than L.A. Always keep your eyes out for a familiar face: you nev-er know when you might spot a celebrity.

DAY 1: LOS ANGELES

As soon as you land at LAX, make like a local and hit the freeway. Even if L.A.'s top-notch art, history, and science museums don't tempt you, the hodgepodge of art deco, Beaux Arts, and futuristic architecture begs at least a drive-by. Heading east from Santa Monica, Wilshire Boulevard cuts through a historical and cultural cross section of the city. Two stellar sights on its Miracle Mile are the encyclopedic **Los Angeles County Museum of Art** and the fossil-filled **La Brea Tar Pits.** Come evening, the open-air **Farmers Market** and its many eateries hum. Hotels in Beverly Hills or West Hollywood beckon, just a few minutes away.

DAY 2: HOLLYWOOD AND THE MOVIE STUDIOS

(Avoid driving to the studios during rush hour. Studio tours vary in length—plan at least a half day for the excursion.)

Every L.A. tourist should devote at least one day to the movies and take at least one studio tour in the San Fernando Valley. For fun, choose the special-effects theme park at **Universal Studios Hollywood**; for the nitty-gritty, choose **Warner Bros. Studios.** Nostalgic musts in Hollywood include the **Hollywood Walk of Fame** along **Hollywood Boulevard** and the celebrity footprints cast in concrete outside **Grauman's Chinese Theatre** (now known as the TCL Chinese Theater). When evening arrives, the Hollywood scene boasts a bevy of trendy restaurants and nightclubs.

DAYS 3 AND 4: BEVERLY HILLS AND SANTA MONICA

(15–20 mins by car between destinations, but considerably longer in traffic.)

The **Getty Center**'s pavilion architecture, hilltop gardens, and frame-worthy L.A. views make it a dazzling destination— and that's before you experience the extensive art collection. From the museum, descend to the sea via Santa Monica Boulevard for lunch along **Third Street Promenade,** followed by a ride on the historic carousel on the pier. The buff and the bizarre meet at Venice Beach's **Ocean Front Walk**—strap on some Rollerblades if you want to join them! Over in Beverly Hills, **Rodeo Drive** specializes in exhibitionism with a heftier price tag, but voyeurs are still welcome.

Splurge on breakfast or brunch at a posh café in the **Farmers Market,** then stroll through aisles and aisles of gorgeous produce and specialty food before you take a last look at the Pacific Ocean through the camera obscura at **Palisades Park** in Santa Monica.

Chapter 4

SAN DIEGO

Updated by
Claire Deeks Van
Der Lee, Marlise
Kast-Myers,
Jeff Terich, and
Kai Oliver-Kurtin

4

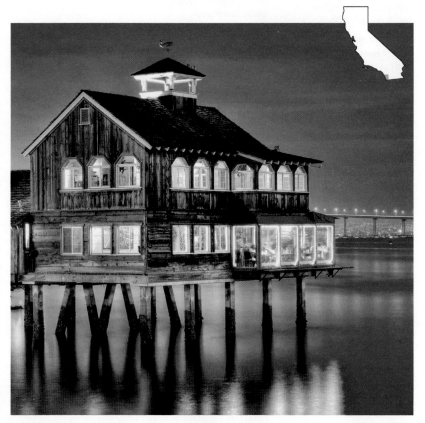

⊙ Sights	🍴 Restaurants	🛏 Hotels	🛍 Shopping	🍸 Nightlife
★★★★★	★★★★★	★★★★★	★★★★☆	★★★☆☆

WELCOME TO SAN DIEGO

TOP REASONS TO GO

★ **Sun and Surf:** Legendary beaches and surfing in La Jolla, Coronado, and Point Loma.

★ **Good Eats:** Brewpubs, a wide mix of ethnic cuisines, fresh seafood and produce, and modern cafés delight diners.

★ **Great Golf:** A concentration of beautiful courses with sweeping ocean views and light breezes.

★ **Stellar Shopping:** From hip boutiques and fine Mexican crafts to the upscale Fashion Valley Mall.

★ **Family Time:** Fun for all ages at LEGOLAND, Balboa Park, the San Diego Zoo, and more.

★ **Outdoor Sports:** A perfect climate for biking, hiking, sailing—anything—outdoors.

1 Downtown. San Diego's Downtown area is delightfully urban and accessible, filled with walkable A-list attractions like the Gaslamp Quarter and the waterfront.

2 Balboa Park, Bankers Hill, and San Diego Zoo. San Diego's cultural heart is where you'll find most of the city's museums and its world-famous zoo.

3 Old Town and Uptown. California's first permanent European settlement is now preserved as a state historic park in Old Town. Uptown is composed of several smaller neighborhoods that showcase a unique blend of historical charm and modern urban community.

4 Mission Bay and the Beaches. Home to 27 miles of shoreline, this 4,600-acre aquatic park is San Diego's monument to sports and fitness.

5 La Jolla. This luxe, bluff-top enclave fittingly means "the jewel" in Spanish. Come here for fantastic upscale shopping and unspoiled stretches of the coast.

6 Point Loma Peninsula. Visit the site of the first European landfall on Point Loma.

7 Coronado. Home to the Hotel Del, Coronado's island-like isthmus is a favorite celebrity haunt.

PACIFIC OCEAN

0   2 mi

0   2 km

S21

Miramar Rd.

MIRAMAR

Escondido Fwy.

Kearney Villa Rd.

805

MARINE CORPS
AIR STATION,
MIRAMAR

15

La Jolla
Shores

La Jolla Cove

Children's Pool/
Shell Beach

Gilman Dr.

San Diego Fwy.

Genesee Av.

Jacob Dekema Freeway

52

Torrey Pines Rd.

Marine
St. Beach

LA JOLLA

5

La Jolla
Pkwy.

Clairemont

Mesa

Blvd.

163

La Jolla Blvd.

Windansea
Beach

Balboa

Ave.

Murphy Canyon Rd.

Tourmaline
Surfing Park

5

Genesee Av.

Aero Dr.

PACIFIC BEACH

Grand Ave.

Clairemont Dr.

Mission Blvd.

Mission
Bay

Rd.

Cabrillo Fwy.

805

MISSION
BAY

4

Ingraham St.

Linda

Vista

MISSION
VALLEY

San Diego River

15

SeaWorld

Friars

Rd.

8

Adams Ave.

MISSION
BEACH

Mission Bay Dr.

MISSION
HILLS

163

UPTOWN

University Ave.

Ocean Beach

Sunset Cliffs Blvd.

Nimitz Blvd.

209

OLD
TOWN

3

HILLCREST

San Diego
Zoo

NORTH
PARK

BUS
8

Rosecrans St.

Pacific

Hwy.

N. Harbor Dr.

BANKERS
HILL

2

BALBOA
PARK

SOUTH
PARK

Catalina Blvd.

POINT
LOMA

6

Shelter
Island

Harbor Island

North
Island

DOWNTOWN

1

Imperial Ave.

94

Harbor Dr.

National Ave.

Cabrillo Memorial Dr.

NAVAL
AIR STATION

7

CORONADO

75

5

Sunset
Cliffs

Coronado Beach

Hotel Del
Coronado

San Diego Bay

Cabrillo
National
Monument

San Diego is a vacationer's paradise, complete with idyllic year-round temperatures and 70 miles of pristine coastline. Recognized as one of the nation's leading family destinations, with LEGOLAND and the San Diego Zoo, San Diego is equally attractive to those in search of art, history, world-class shopping, and culinary exploration. San Diego's beaches are legendary, offering family-friendly sands, killer surf breaks, and spectacular scenery. San Diego's cultural sophistication often surprises visitors, as the city is better known for its laid-back vibe. Tourists come for some fun in the sun, only to discover a city with much greater depth.

San Diego is a big California city—second only to Los Angeles in population—with a small-town feel. San Diego's many neighborhoods offer diverse adventures: from the tony boutiques in La Jolla to the yoga and surf shops of Encinitas; from the subtle sophistication of Little Italy to the flashy nightlife of the Downtown Gaslamp Quarter, each community adds flavor and flair to San Diego's personality.

San Diego County also covers a lot of territory, roughly 400 square miles of land and sea. To the north and south of the city are its famed beaches. Inland, a succession of chaparral-covered mesas is punctuated with deep-cut canyons that step up to forested mountains.

Known as the birthplace of California, San Diego was claimed for Spain by explorer Juan Rodríguez Cabrillo in 1542 and eventually came under Mexican rule. You'll find reminders of San Diego's Spanish and Mexican heritage throughout the region—in architecture and place-names, in distinctive Mexican cuisine, and in the historic buildings of Old Town.

In 1867 developer Alonzo Horton, who called the town's bay front "the prettiest place for a city I ever saw," began building a hotel, a plaza, and prefab homes on 960 Downtown acres. A remarkable number of these buildings are preserved in San Diego's historic Gaslamp Quarter today. The city's fate was sealed in the 1920s when the U.S. Navy, impressed by the city's excellent harbor and temperate climate, decided to build a destroyer base on San Diego Bay. Today, the military operates many bases and installations throughout the county (which, added together, form the largest military base in the world) and continues to be a major contributor to the local economy.

Planning

Getting Here and Around

AIR TRAVEL

The major airport is San Diego International Airport (SAN), formerly called Lindbergh Field. Most airlines depart and arrive at Terminal 2. Southwest, Frontier, and Alaska Airlines are reserved for Terminal 1. Free, color-coded shuttles loop the airport and match the parking lot they serve.

AIRPORT San Diego International Airport.
⊠ 3225 N. Harbor Dr., off I–5 ☎ 619/400–2400 ⊕ www.san.org.

AIRPORT TRANSFERS SuperShuttle.
⊠ 123 Caminio de la Riena ☎ 800/258–3826 ⊕ www.supershuttle.com. **San Diego Transit.** ☎ 619/233–3004 ⊕ www.511sd.com.

BUS AND TROLLEY TRAVEL

Under the umbrella of the Metropolitan Transit System, there are two major transit agencies in the area: San Diego Transit and North County Transit District (NCTD). The bright-red trolleys of the San Diego Trolley light-rail system operate on three lines that serve Downtown San Diego,

Mission Valley, Old Town, South Bay, the U.S. border, and East County. The trolley system connects with San Diego Transit bus routes—connections are posted at each trolley station.

San Diego Transit bus fares range from $2.25 to $5; North County Transit District bus fares are $4. You must have exact change in coins and/or bills. Pay upon boarding. Transfers are not included; the $5 day pass is the best option for most bus travel and can be purchased on board.

San Diego Trolley tickets cost $2.50 and are good for two hours, but for one-way travel only. For a round-trip journey or longer, day passes are available for $5.

BUS AND TROLLEY INFORMATION North County Transit District. ☎ 760/966–6500 ⊕ www.gonctd.com. **San Diego Transit.** ☎ 619/233–3004 ⊕ www.511sd.com. **Transit Store.** ⊠ 102 Broadway ☎ 619/234–1060 ⊕ www.sdmts.com.

CAR TRAVEL

A car is necessary for getting around greater San Diego on the sprawling freeway system and for visiting the North County beaches, mountains, and desert. Driving around San Diego County is pretty simple: most major attractions are within a few miles of the Pacific Ocean. Interstate 5, which stretches north–south from Oregon to the Mexican border, bisects San Diego. Interstate 8 provides access from Yuma, Arizona, and points east. Drivers coming from the Los Angeles area, Nevada, and the mountain regions beyond can reach San Diego on Interstate 15. During rush hours there are jams on Interstate 5 and on Interstate 15 between Interstate 805 and Escondido.

There are a few border inspection stations along major highways in San Diego County, the largest just north of Oceanside on Interstate 5 near San Clemente. Travel with your driver's license, and passport if you're an international traveler.

TAXI TRAVEL

Fares vary among companies. If you're heading to the airport from a hotel, ask about the flat rate, which varies according to destination; otherwise you'll be charged by the mile (which works out to $20 or so from any Downtown location). Taxi stands are at shopping centers and hotels; otherwise you must call and reserve a cab. For on-demand private transportation, Uber is readily available throughout San Diego County with competitive rates up to 40% less than that of a taxi. The companies listed *below* don't serve all areas of San Diego County. If you're going somewhere other than Downtown, ask if the company serves that area.

TAXI COMPANIES Orange Cab. ☎ *619/223–5555* ⊕ *www.orange-cabsandiego.net.* **Silver Cabs.** ☎ *619/280–5555* ⊕ *www.sandiegosilvercab.com.* **Yellow Cab.** ☎ *619/444–4444* ⊕ *www.driveu.com.*

TRAIN TRAVEL

Amtrak serves Downtown San Diego's Santa Fe Depot with daily trains to and from Los Angeles, Santa Barbara, and San Luis Obispo. Amtrak trains stop in San Diego North County at Solana Beach and Oceanside. Coaster commuter trains, which run between Oceanside and San Diego Monday through Saturday, stop at the same stations as Amtrak as well as others. The frequency is about every half hour during the weekday rush hour, with four trains on Saturday. One-way fares are $4 to $5.50, depending on the distance traveled. The *Sprinter* runs between Oceanside and Escondido, with many stops along the way.

Metrolink operates high-speed rail service ($17) between the Oceanside Transit Center and Union Station in Los Angeles.

INFORMATION Coaster. ☎ *760/966–6500* ⊕ *www.gonctd.com/coaster.* **Metrolink.** ☎ *800/371–5465* ⊕ *www.metrolinktrains.com.*

Activities

San Diego offers bountiful opportunities for bikers, from casual boardwalk cruises to strenuous rides into the hills. The mild climate makes biking in San Diego a year-round delight. Bike culture is respected here, and visitors are often impressed with the miles of designated bike lanes running alongside city streets and coastal roads throughout the county.

If you're a beginner surfer, consider paddling in the waves off Mission Beach, Pacific Beach, Tourmaline Surfing Park, La Jolla Shores, Del Mar, or Oceanside. More experienced surfers usually head for Sunset Cliffs, La Jolla reef breaks, Black's Beach, or Swami's in Encinitas. All necessary equipment is included in the cost of all surfing schools. Beach-area Y's offer surf lessons and surf camp in the summer months and during spring break.

Beaches

San Diego's beaches have a different vibe from their northern counterparts in neighboring Orange County and glitzy Los Angeles farther up the coast. San Diego is more laid-back and less of a scene. Cyclists on cruiser bikes whiz by as surfers saunter toward the waves and sunbathers bronze under the sun, be it July or November.

Even at summer's hottest peak, San Diego's beaches are cool and breezy. Ocean waves are large, and the water will be colder than what you experience at tropical beaches—temperatures range from 55°F to 65°F from October through June, and 65°F to 73°F from July through September.

Finding a parking spot near the ocean can be hard in summer. Del Mar has a pay lot and metered street parking around the 15th Street Beach. La Jolla Shores has free street parking up to two hours. Mission Beach and other large beaches have unmetered parking lots, but space can be limited. Your best bet is to arrive early.

Pay attention to signs listing illegal activities; undercover police often patrol the beaches. Smoking and alcoholic beverages are completely banned on city beaches. Drinking in beach parking lots, on boardwalks, and in landscaped areas is also illegal. Glass containers are not permitted on beaches, cliffs, and walkways, or in park areas and adjacent parking lots. Littering is not tolerated, and skateboarding is prohibited at some beaches. Fires are allowed only in fire rings or elevated barbecue grills. Although it may be tempting to take a sea creature from a tide pool as a souvenir, it may upset the delicate ecological balance, and it's illegal, too.

Year-round, lifeguards are stationed at nine permanent stations from Sunset Cliffs to Black's Beach. All other beaches are covered by roving patrols in the winter, and seasonal towers in the summer. When swimming in the ocean be aware of rip currents, which are common in California shores. For a surf and weather report, call San Diego's Lifeguard Services at ☎ *619/221–8899*. Visit ⊕ *www.surfline. com* for live webcams on surf conditions and water temperature forecasts.

Restaurants

San Diego is an up-and-coming culinary destination, thanks to its stunning Pacific Ocean setting, proximity to Mexico, diverse population, and the area's extraordinary farming community. Increasingly the city's veteran top chefs are being joined by a new generation of talented chefs and restaurateurs who are adding stylish restaurants with innovative food and drink programs to the dining scene at a record pace. Yes, visitors still are drawn to the San Diego Zoo and miles of beaches, but now they come for memorable dining experiences as well.

The city's culinary scene got a significant boost when San Diego emerged as one of the world's top craft beer destinations, with artisan breweries and gastropubs now in almost every neighborhood. These neighborhoods are also ethnically diverse with modest eateries offering affordable authentic international cuisines that add spice to the dining mix.

The trendy Gaslamp Quarter delights visitors looking for a broad range of innovative and international dining and nightlife, while bustling Little Italy offers a mix of affordable Italian fare and posh new eateries. Modern restaurants and cafés thrive in East Village, amid the luxury condos near PETCO Park. The Uptown neighborhoods centered on Hillcrest—an urbane district with San Francisco flavor—are a mix of bars and independent restaurants, many of which specialize in ethnic cuisine. North Park, in particular, has a happening restaurant and craft beer scene, with just about every kind of cuisine you can think of, and laid-back prices to boot. And scenic La Jolla offers some of the best fine dining in the city with dramatic water views as an added bonus.

PRICES

Meals in San Diego popular dining spots can be pricey, especially in areas like La Jolla, the Gaslamp Quarter, and Coronado. Many other restaurants are very affordable or offer extra value with fixed-price menus, early-dining specials and early and late happy hours.

Restaurant reviews have been shortened. For full information, visit Fodors.com.

What It Costs			
$	**$$**	**$$$**	**$$$$**
RESTAURANTS			
under $18	$18–$27	$28–$35	over $35

Hotels

Sharing the city's postcard-perfect sunny skies are neighborhoods and coastal communities that offer great diversity; San Diego is no longer the sleepy beach town it once was. In action-packed Downtown, luxury hotels cater to solo business travelers and young couples with trendy restaurants and cabana-encircled pools. Budget-friendly options can be found in smaller neighborhoods just outside the Gaslamp Quarter such as Little Italy and Uptown.

You'll need a car if you stay outside Downtown, but the beach communities are rich with lodging options. Across the bridge, Coronado's hotels and resorts offer access to a stretch of glistening white sand that's often recognized as one of the best beaches in the country. La Jolla offers many romantic, upscale ocean-view hotels and some of the area's best restaurants and specialty shopping. But it's easy to find a water view in any price range: surfers make themselves at home at the casual inns and budget stays of Pacific Beach and Mission Bay. If you're planning to fish, check out hotels located near the marinas in Shelter Island, Point Loma, or Coronado.

For families, Uptown, Mission Valley, and Old Town are close to the San Diego Zoo, offering good-value accommodations with extras like sleeper sofas and video games. Mission Valley is ideal for business travelers; there are plenty of well-known chain hotels with conference space, modern business centers, and kitchenettes for extended stays.

When you make reservations, book well in advance and ask about specials. Several properties in the Hotel Circle area of Mission Valley offer reduced rates and even free tickets to the San Diego Zoo and other attractions. You can save on hotels and attractions by visiting the San Diego Tourism Authority website (⊕ www.sandiego.org) for special seasonal offers.

PRICES

Note that even in the most expensive areas, you can find affordable rooms. High season is summer, and rates are lowest in fall. If an ocean view is important, request it when booking, but it will cost you.

Hotel reviews have been shortened. For full information, visit Fodors.com.

What It Costs			
$	$$	$$$	$$$$
HOTELS			
under $150	$150– $225	$226– $300	over $300

Nightlife

A couple of decades ago, San Diego scraped by on its superb daytime offerings. Those sleepy-after-dark days are over; San Diego now sizzles when the sun goes down. Of particular interest to beer lovers, the city has become internationally acclaimed for dozens of breweries, beer pubs, and festivals.

The Gaslamp Quarter is still one of the most popular areas to go for a night on the town. Named for actual gaslights that once provided illumination along its once-seedy streets (it housed a number of gambling halls and brothels), the neighborhood bears only a trace of its debauched roots. Between the Gaslamp and nearby East Village, Downtown San Diego mostly comprises chic nightclubs, tourist-heavy pubs, and a handful of live music venues. Even most of the hotels Downtown have a street-level or rooftop bar—so plan on making it a late night if that's where you intend to bunk. On weekends, parking can be tricky; most lots run about $20, and though there is metered parking (free after 6 pm and all day Sunday), motorists don't give up those coveted spots so easily. Some restaurants and clubs offer valet, though that can get pricey.

Hillcrest is a popular area for LGBTQ nightlife and culture, whereas just a little bit east of Hillcrest, ever-expanding North Park features a diverse range of bars and lounges that cater to a twenty- and thirtysomething crowd, bolstering its reputation as the city's hipster capital. Nearby Normal Heights is a slightly less pretentious alternative, though whichever of these neighborhoods strikes your fancy, a cab from Downtown will run about the same price: $15.

Nightlife along the beaches is more of a mixed bag. Where the scene in Pacific Beach might feel like every week is Spring Break, La Jolla veers toward being more cost-prohibitive. And although Point Loma is often seen as a sleeper neighborhood in terms of nightlife, it's coming into its own with some select destinations.

If your drink involves caffeine and not alcohol, there's no shortage of coffeehouses in San Diego, and some of the better ones in Hillcrest and North Park stay open past midnight.

Shopping

San Diego's retail landscape has changed radically in recent years with the opening of several new shopping centers—some in historic buildings—that are focused more on locally owned boutiques than national retailers. Where once the Gaslamp was the place to go for urban apparel and unique home decor, many independently owned boutiques have decided to set up shop in the charming neighborhoods east of Balboa Park known as North Park and South Park. Although Downtown is still thriving, any shopping trip to San Diego should include venturing out to the city's diverse

and vibrant neighborhoods. Not far from Downtown, Little Italy is the place to find contemporary art, modern furniture, and home accessories.

Old Town is a must for pottery, ceramics, jewelry, and handcrafted baskets. Uptown is known for its mélange of funky bookstores, offbeat gift shops, and nostalgic collectibles and vintage stores. The beach towns offer the best swimwear and sandals. La Jolla's chic boutiques offer a more intimate shopping experience, along with some of the classiest clothes, jewelry, and shoes in the county. The new La Plaza La Jolla is an open-air shopping center with boutiques and galleries in a Spanish-style building overlooking the cove. Point Loma's Liberty Station shopping area in the former Naval Training Center has art galleries, restaurants, and home stores. Trendsetters will have no trouble finding must-have handbags and designer apparel at the world-class Fashion Valley mall in Mission Valley, a haven for luxury brands such as Hermès, Gucci, and Jimmy Choo.

Enjoy near-perfect weather year-round as you explore shops along the scenic waterfront. The Headquarters at Seaport is a new open-air shopping and dining center in the city's former Police Headquarters building. Here there are some big names, but mostly locally owned boutiques selling everything from gourmet cheese to coastal-inspired home accessories. Just next door, Seaport Village is still the place to go for trinkets and souvenirs. If you don't discover what you're looking for in the boutiques, head to Westfield Horton Plaza, the Downtown mall with more than 120 stores. The sprawling mall completed a major restoration project in 2016 to include a new public plaza, amphitheater, and fountains.

Most malls have free parking in a lot or garage, and parking is not usually a problem. Some of the shops in the Gaslamp Quarter offer validated parking or valet parking.

Tours

BOAT TOURS

Visitors to San Diego can get a great overview of the city from the water. Tour companies offer a range of harbor cruises, from one-hour jaunts to dinner and dancing cruises. In season, whale-watching voyages are another popular option.

Flagship Cruises and Events

BOAT TOURS | One- and two-hour tours of the San Diego Harbor loop north or south from the Broadway Pier throughout the day. Other offerings include dinner and dance cruises, brunch cruises, and winter whale-watching tours December–mid-April. ⊠ *990 N. Harbor Dr., Embarcadero* ☎ *619/234–4111* ⊕ *www.flagshipsd.com* ⊠ *From $27.*

H&M Landing

BOAT TOURS | From mid-December to March, this outfitter offers three-hour tours to spot migrating gray whales just off the San Diego coast. ⊠ *2803 Emerson St.* ☎ *619/222–1144* ⊕ *www.hmlanding.com* ⊠ *From $50.*

Hornblower Cruises & Events

BOAT TOURS | One- and two-hour cruises around San Diego Harbor depart from the Embarcadero several times a day and alternate between the northern and southern portion of the bay. If you're hoping to spot some sea lions, take the North Bay route. Dinner and brunch cruises are also offered, as well as whale-watching tours in winter. ⊠ *970 N. Harbor Dr.* ☎ *619/686–8700, 888/467–6256* ⊕ *www.hornblower.com* ⊠ *From $27.*

San Diego SEAL Tours

BOAT TOURS | This amphibious tour drives along the Embarcadero before splashing into the San Diego Harbor for a cruise. The 90-minute tours depart daily from 10 am to 5 pm from Seaport Village and the Embarcadero. Call for daily departure times and locations. ⊠ *500 Kettner Blvd.,* *Embarcadero* ☎ *619/298–8687* ⊕ *www.sealtours.com* ⊠ *$42.*

Seaforth Boat Rentals

BOAT TOURS | For those seeking a private tour on the water, this company can provide a skipper along with your boat rental. Options include harbor cruises, whale-watching, and sunset sails. Seaforth has four locations and a diverse fleet of sail and motorboats to choose from. ⊠ *1641 Quivira Rd., Mission Bay* ☎ *888/834–2628* ⊕ *www.seaforthboatrental.com* ⊠ *From $160.*

BUS AND TROLLEY TOURS

For those looking to cover a lot of ground in a limited time, narrated trolley tours include everything from Balboa Park to Coronado. To venture farther afield, consider a coach tour to the desert, Los Angeles, or even Baja, Mexico.

DayTripper Tours

BUS TOURS | **FAMILY** | Single- and multiday trips throughout Southern California, the Southwest, and Baja depart from San Diego year-round. Popular day trips include the Getty Museum, and theater performances in Los Angeles. Call or check the website for pickup locations. ☎ *619/334–3394, 800/679–8747* ⊕ *www.daytripper.com* ⊠ *From $89.*

Five Star Tours

BUS TOURS | Private and group sightseeing bus tour options around San Diego and beyond include everything from the San Diego Zoo and brewery tours to city tours and trips to Baja, Mexico. ⊠ *1050 Kettner Blvd.* ☎ *619/232–5040* ⊕ *www.fivestartours.com* ⊠ *From $50.*

Old Town Trolley Tours

GUIDED TOURS | **FAMILY** | Combining points of interest with local history, trivia, and fun anecdotes, this hop-on, hop-off trolley tour provides an entertaining overview of the city and offers easy access to all the highlights. The tour is narrated, and you can get on and off as you please. Stops include Old Town, Seaport Village, the Gaslamp Quarter, Coronado, Little

Italy, and Balboa Park. The trolley leaves every 30 minutes, operates daily, and takes two hours to make a full loop. ✉ *San Diego* ☎ *866/754–0966* ⊕ *www.trolleytours.com/san-diego* 💲 *From $40.*

San Diego Scenic Tours

BUS TOURS | Half- and full-day bus tours of San Diego and Tijuana depart daily, and some include a harbor cruise. Tours depart from several hotels around town. ✉ *San Diego* ☎ *858/273–8687* ⊕ *www.sandiegoscenictours.com* 💲 *From $38.*

WALKING TOURS

Several fine walking tours are available on weekdays or weekends; upcoming walks are usually listed in the *San Diego Reader.*

Balboa Park Offshoot Tours

GUIDED TOURS | On Saturday at 10 am, free, hour-long walks start from the Balboa Park Visitor Center. The tour's focus rotates weekly, covering topics such as the park's history, palm trees, and desert vegetation. Reservations are not required, but no tours are scheduled between Thanksgiving and the New Year. ✉ *Balboa Park Visitor Center, 1549 El Prado, Balboa Park* ☎ *619/239–0512* ⊕ *www.balboapark.org* 💲 *Free.*

Coronado Walking Tours

WALKING TOURS | Departing from the Glorietta Bay Inn at 11 am Tuesday, Thursday, and Saturday, this 90-minute stroll through Coronado's historic district takes in the island's mansions, old Tent City, the Hotel del Coronado, and the castles and cottages that line the beautiful beach. Reservations are recommended. ✉ *1630 Glorietta Blvd.* ☎ *619/435–5993* ⊕ *www.coronadowalkingtour.com* 💲 *$15* ☞ *Cash only.*

Gaslamp Quarter Historical Foundation

WALKING TOURS | Two-hour walking tours of the Downtown historic district depart from the William Heath Davis House at 11 am on Saturday. ✉ *410 Island Ave.* ☎ *619/233–4692* ⊕ *gaslampfoundation.org* 💲 *$20.*

Urban Safaris

GUIDED TOURS | Led by longtime San Diego resident Patty Fares, these two-hour Saturday walks through diverse neighborhoods like Hillcrest, Ocean Beach, and Point Loma are popular with tourists and locals alike. The tours, which always depart from a neighborhood coffeehouse, focus on art, history, and ethnic eateries, among other topics. Reservations are required, and private walks can be arranged during the week. ☎ *619/944–9255* ⊕ *www.walkingtoursofsandiego.com* 💲 *$15.*

Visitor Information

For general information and brochures before you go, contact the San Diego Tourism Authority, which publishes the helpful *San Diego Visitors Planning Guide.* When you arrive, stop by one of the local visitor centers for general information.

When to Go

San Diego's weather is so ideal that most locals shrug off the high cost of living and relatively lower wages as a "sunshine tax." Along the coast, average temperatures range from the mid-60s to the high 70s, with clear skies and low humidity. Annual rainfall is minimal, less than 10 inches per year.

The peak season for sun seekers is July through October. In July and August, the mercury spikes and everyone spills outside. From mid-December to mid-March, whale-watchers can glimpse migrating gray whales frolicking in the Pacific. In spring and early summer, a marine layer hugs the coastline for much or all of the day (locals call it "June Gloom"), which can be dreary and disappointing for those who were expecting to bask in Southern California sunshine.

Downtown

Nearly written off in the 1970s, today Downtown San Diego is a testament to conservation and urban renewal. Once derelict Victorian storefronts now house the hottest restaurants, and the *Star of India,* the world's oldest active sailing ship, almost lost to scrap, floats regally along the Embarcadero. Like many modern U.S. cities, Downtown San Diego's story is as much about its rebirth as its history. Although many consider Downtown to be the 16½-block Gaslamp Quarter, it's actually comprised of eight neighborhoods, including East Village, Little Italy, and Embarcadero.

Gaslamp Quarter

Considered the liveliest of the Downtown neighborhoods, the Gaslamp Quarter's 4th and 5th avenues are peppered with trendy nightclubs, swanky lounge bars, chic restaurants, and boisterous sports pubs. The Gaslamp has the largest collection of commercial Victorian-style buildings in the country. Despite this, when the move for Downtown redevelopment gained momentum in the 1970s, there was talk of bulldozing them and starting from scratch. In response, concerned history buffs, developers, architects, and artists formed the Gaslamp Quarter Council to clean up and preserve the quarter. The majority of the quarter's landmark buildings are on 4th and 5th avenues, between Island Avenue and Broadway.

 Sights

Gaslamp Museum at the Davis-Horton House

HISTORIC SITE | The oldest wooden house in San Diego houses the Gaslamp Quarter Historical Foundation, the district's curator. Before developer Alonzo Horton came to town, Davis, a prominent San

Franciscan, had made an unsuccessful attempt to develop the waterfront area. In 1850 he had this prefab saltbox-style house, built in Maine, shipped around Cape Horn, and assembled in San Diego (it originally stood at State and Market streets). Ninety-minute walking tours ($20) of the historic district leave from the house on Thursday at 1 pm (summer only) and Saturday at 11 am (year-round). If you can't time your visit with the tour, a self-guided tour map ($2) is available. ⊠ *410 Island Ave., at 4th Ave., Gaslamp Quarter* ☎ *619/233–4692* ⊕ *www. gaslampfoundation.org* ✉ *$5 self-guided, $10 with audio tour* ⊗ *Closed Mon.*

 Restaurants

Searsucker

$$$ | AMERICAN | Since opened by celebrity chef Brian Malarkey a few years ago, this high-energy flagship restaurant has become the Gaslamp's best for food and energetic atmosphere. Foodies from near and far savor the upscale down-home fare like small plates of biscuits with spicy honey, duck fat fries, and shrimp and grits. **Known for:** detailed, home-inspired decor; crispy duck fat fries; late-night menu on Friday and Saturday 11 pm–1 am. ⑤ *Average main: $30* ⊠ *611 5th Ave., Gaslamp Quarter* ☎ *619/233–7327* ⊕ *www.searsucker.com.*

Taka

$$ | JAPANESE | Pristine fish imported from around the world and presented creatively attracts crowds nightly to this intimate Gaslamp restaurant. Table service is available inside and outside where an *omakase* (tasting menu) or eight-piece rolls can be shared and savored; take a seat at the bar to watch one of the sushi chefs preparing appetizers. **Known for:** uni sushi topped with wasabi; omakase tasting menu; upscale sake offerings. ⑤ *Average main: $18* ⊠ *555 5th Ave., Gaslamp Quarter* ☎ *619/338–0555* ⊕ *www.takasushi.com* ⊗ *No lunch.*

Hotels

★ Andaz San Diego

$$$$ | **HOTEL** | The lobby of the luxury, Hyatt-managed Andaz—with its dark, sexy vibe, tall columns wrapped in braided leather, buckets of chilled wine awaiting guests, and welcoming service—pretty much sums up the experience here: high-style stay without the attitude. **Pros:** luxurious rooms; romantic vibe; friendly service. **Cons:** noisy on weekends; not a good choice for families; small pool. ⓢ *Rooms from: $319* ✉ *600 F St., Gaslamp Quarter* ☎ *619/849–1234* ⊕ *www.sandiego.andaz.hyatt.com* ⤳ *159 rooms* ❏ *No meals.*

★ Kimpton Hotel Solamar

$$$ | **HOTEL** | **FAMILY** | Best known for Upper East Bar, its poolside rooftop bar, and stylish lobby decor, Solamar's guest rooms reflect this urban escape's mixture of luxury and fun, with prints galore and subtle nods to San Diego's happy beach culture. **Pros:** great restaurant; attentive service; upscale rooms. **Cons:** busy valet parking; daily facility fee; no coffeemaker or teakettle in rooms. ⓢ *Rooms from: $279* ✉ *435 6th Ave., Gaslamp Quarter* ☎ *619/819–9500, 877/230–0300* ⊕ *www.hotelsolamar. com* ⤳ *235 rooms* ❏ *No meals.*

★ Pendry San Diego

$$$$ | **HOTEL** | Opened in early 2017, the Pendry San Diego is the Gaslamp's newest stunner. **Pros:** well situated in Gaslamp Quarter; excellent dining options; complimentary coffee in the mornings. **Cons:** pricey room rates; meals are expensive; not very family-friendly. ⓢ *Rooms from: $480* ✉ *550 J St., Gaslamp Quarter* ☎ *619/738–7000* ⊕ *www.pendryhotels. com* ⤳ *317 rooms* ❏ *No meals.*

★ The Sofia Hotel

$$$ | **HOTEL** | This stylish and centrally located boutique hotel may have small rooms, but it more than compensates with pampering extras like motion-sensor temperature controls, a Zen-like 24-hour yoga studio, an updated lobby, and a brand-new spa suite. **Pros:** upscale amenities; historic building; near shops and restaurants. **Cons:** busy area; small rooms; spotty Wi-Fi. ⓢ *Rooms from: $259* ✉ *150 W. Broadway, Gaslamp Quarter* ☎ *619/234–9200, 800/826–0009* ⊕ *www.thesofiahotel.com* ⤳ *211 rooms* ❏ *No meals.*

 # Nightlife

BARS

★ The Grant Grill

BARS/PUBS | Though the Grant Grill—located on the ground floor of the historic U.S. Grant Hotel—is a full-service restaurant, it's built up a reputation in recent years for stepping up San Diego's craft cocktail game. The cocktail menu is updated seasonally with fresh ingredients and themes (one recently featured a mini "Voodoo" doll frozen inside of a large ice cube), all of which are both innovative and palate pleasant. The atmosphere is comfortable and elegant, even on its busiest nights. ✉ *U.S. Grant Hotel, 326 Broadway, Gaslamp Quarter* ☎ *619/744–2077* ⊕ *www.grantgrill.com.*

★ The Rooftop by STK

DANCE CLUBS | At this rooftop bar and lounge atop the Andaz hotel, a fashionable crowd sips cocktails poolside while gazing at gorgeous views of the city. Thursday through Saturday, the scene heats up with a DJ spinning dance music, while velvet ropes and VIP bottle service please the A-listers (like Prince Harry) in the crowd. ✉ *Andaz San Diego, 600 F St., Gaslamp Quarter* ☎ *619/814–2060* ⊕ *www.hyatt.com/en-US/hotel/california/andaz-san-diego/sanas/dining.*

PIANO BARS

★ Vin de Syrah

WINE BARS—NIGHTLIFE | This "spirit and wine cellar" sends you down a rabbit hole (or at least down some stairs) to a whimsical spot straight out of Alice in Wonderland. Behind a hidden door (look for a handle in the grass wall), you'll find visual delights (grapevines suspended from the ceiling, vintage jars with flittering "fireflies," cozy chairs nestled around a faux fireplace and pastoral vista) that rival the culinary ones—the wine list is approachable and the charcuterie boards are exquisitely curated. ■ **TIP**➔ **More than just a wine bar, the cocktails are also worth a try.** ⊠ *901 5th Ave., Gaslamp Quarter* ☎ *619/234–4166* ⊕ *www.syrahwineparlor.com.*

★ Westgate Hotel Plaza Bar

PIANO BARS/LOUNGES | The old-money surroundings, including leather-upholstered seats, marble tabletops, and a grand piano, supply one of the most elegant and romantic settings for a drink in San Diego. ⊠ *1055 2nd Ave., Gaslamp Quarter* ☎ *619/238–1818* ⊕ *www.westgatehotel.com.*

 Performing Arts

DANCE
California Ballet Company
DANCE | The company performs high-quality contemporary and classical works September–May at the **Civic Theatre.** The *Nutcracker* is staged annually around the holiday season. ⊠ *San Diego Civic Theatre, 1100 3rd Ave., Gaslamp Quarter* ☎ *858/560–5676* ⊕ *www.californiaballet.org.*

MUSIC
★ Copley Symphony Hall
MUSIC | The great acoustics here are surpassed only by the incredible Spanish baroque interior. Not just the home of the San Diego Symphony Orchestra, the renovated 2,200-seat 1920s-era theater has also hosted major stars like Elvis Costello, Leonard Cohen, and Sting. ⊠ *750 B St., Gaslamp Quarter* ☎ *619/235–0804* ⊕ *www.sandiegosymphony.org.*

San Diego Symphony Orchestra
MUSIC | The orchestra's events include classical concerts and summer and winter pops, nearly all of them at Copley Symphony Hall. The outdoor Summer

Pops series is held on the Embarcadero, on North Harbor Drive beyond the convention center. ⊠ *Box office, 750 B St., Gaslamp Quarter* ☎ *619/235–0804* ⊕ *www.sandiegosymphony.org.*

Embarcadero

The Embarcadero cuts a scenic swath along the harbor front and connects today's Downtown San Diego to its maritime routes. The bustle of Embarcadero comes less these days from the activities of fishing folk than from the throngs of tourists, but this waterfront walkway, stretching from the convention center to the Maritime Museum, remains the nautical soul of the city. There are several seafood restaurants here, as well as sea vessels of every variety—cruise ships, ferries, tour boats, and navy destroyers.

A huge revitalization project is under way along the northern Embarcadero. The overhaul seeks to transform the area with large mixed-use development projects, inviting parks, walkways, and public art installations. The redevelopment will eventually head south along the waterfront, with plans under way for a major overhaul of the entire Central Embarcadero and Seaport Village.

◉ Sights
★ Maritime Museum
MARINA | **FAMILY** | From sailing ships to submarines, the Maritime Museum is a must for anyone with an interest in nautical history. This collection of restored and replica ships affords a fascinating glimpse of San Diego during its heyday as a commercial seaport. The jewel of the collection, the *Star of India,* was built in 1863 and made 21 trips around the world in the late 1800s. Saved from the scrap yard and painstakingly restored, the windjammer is the oldest active iron sailing ship in the world. The newly constructed *San Salvador* is a detailed historic replica

of the original ship first sailed into San Diego Bay by explorer Juan Rodriguez Cabrillo back in 1542. And, the popular HMS *Surprise* is a replica of an 18th-century British Royal Navy frigate. The museum's headquarters are on the *Berkeley*, an 1898 steam-driven ferryboat, which served the Southern Pacific Railroad in San Francisco until 1958.

Numerous cruises of San Diego Bay are offered, including a daily 45-minute narrated tour aboard a 1914 pilot boat and three-hour weekend sails aboard the topsail schooner the *Californian*, the state's official tall ship, and 75-minute tours aboard a historic swift boat, which highlights the city's military connection. Partnering with the museum, the renowned yacht *America* also offers sails on the bay, and whale-watching excursions are available in winter. ✉ *1492 N. Harbor Dr., Embarcadero* ☎ *619/234–9153* ⊕ *www. sdmaritime.org* 🎟 *$18.*

★ Museum of Contemporary Art San Diego (MCASD)

MUSEUM | At the Downtown branch of the city's contemporary art museum, explore the works of international and regional artists in a modern, urban space. The Jacobs Building—formerly the baggage building at the historic Santa Fe Depot—features large gallery spaces, high ceilings, and natural lighting, giving artists the flexibility to create large-scale installations. MCASD's collection includes many pop art, minimalist, and conceptual works from the 1950s to the present. The museum showcases both established and emerging artists in temporary exhibitions, and has permanent, site-specific commissions by Jenny Holzer and Richard Serra. ✉ *1100 and 1001 Kettner Blvd., Downtown* ☎ *858/454–3541* ⊕ *www. mcasd.org* 🎟 *$10; free 3rd Thurs. of the month 5–7* ⊗ *Closed Wed.*

★ The New Children's Museum (NCM)

MUSEUM | FAMILY | The NCM blends contemporary art with unstructured play to create an environment that appeals to children as well as adults. The 50,000-square-foot structure was constructed from recycled building materials, operates on solar energy, and is convection-cooled by an elevator shaft. It also features a nutritious and eco-conscious café. Interactive exhibits include designated areas for toddlers and teens, as well as plenty of activities for the entire family. Several art workshops are offered each day, as well as hands-on studios where visitors are encouraged to create their own art. The studio projects change frequently and the entire museum changes exhibits every 18 to 24 months, so there is always something new to explore. The adjoining 1-acre park and playground is across from the convention center trolley stop. ✉ *200 W. Island Ave., Embarcadero* ☎ *619/233–8792* ⊕ *www. thinkplaycreate.org* 🎟 *$14* ⊗ *Closed Tues.*

Seaport Village

PEDESTRIAN MALL | FAMILY | You'll find some of the best views of the harbor at Seaport Village, three bustling shopping plazas designed to reflect the New England clapboard, and Spanish Mission architectural styles of early California. On a prime stretch of waterfront the dining, shopping, and entertainment complex connects the harbor with hotel towers and the convention center. Specialty shops offer everything from a kite store and swing emporium to a shop devoted to hot sauces. You can dine at snack bars and restaurants, many with harbor views.

Live music can be heard daily from noon to 4 at the main food court. Additional free concerts take place every Sunday from 1 to 4 at the East Plaza Gazebo. The **Seaport Village Carousel** (rides $3) has 54 animals, hand-carved and hand-painted by Charles Looff in 1895. Across the street, the **Headquarters at Seaport Village** converted the historic police headquarters into several trendsetting shops and restaurants. ✉ *849 W. Harbor Dr., Downtown* ☎ *619/235–4014 office and events hotline* ⊕ *www.seaportvillage.com.*

★ **USS *Midway* Museum**

MILITARY SITE | FAMILY | After 47 years of worldwide service, the retired USS *Midway* began a new tour of duty on the south side of the Navy pier in 2004. Launched in 1945, the 1,001-foot-long ship was the largest in the world for the first 10 years of its existence. The most visible landmark on the north Embarcadero, it now serves as a floating interactive museum—an appropriate addition to the town that is home to one-third of the Pacific fleet and the birthplace of naval aviation. A free audio tour guides you through the massive ship while offering insight from former sailors. As you clamber through passageways and up and down ladder wells, you'll get a feel for how the *Midway's* 4,500 crew members lived and worked on this "city at sea."

Though the entire tour is impressive, you'll really be wowed when you step out onto the 4-acre flight deck—not only the best place to get an idea of the ship's scale, but also one of the most interesting vantage points for bay and city skyline views. An F-14 Tomcat jet fighter is just one of many vintage aircraft on display. Free guided tours of the bridge and primary flight control, known as "the Island," depart every 10 minutes from the flight deck. Many of the docents stationed throughout the ship served in the Navy, some even on the *Midway*, and they are eager to answer questions or share stories. The museum also offers multiple flight simulators for an additional fee, climb-aboard cockpits, and interactive exhibits focusing on naval aviation. There is a gift shop and a café with pleasant outdoor seating. This is a wildly popular stop, with most visits lasting several hours. ⚠ **Despite efforts to provide accessibility throughout the ship, some areas can only be reached via fairly steep steps; a video tour of these areas is available on the hangar deck.** ✉ *910 N. Harbor Dr., Embarcadero* ☎ *619/544–9600* ⊕ *www.midway.org* 🎫 *$21.*

🍴 Restaurants

★ **Eddie V's Prime Seafood**

$$$ | SEAFOOD | Don't be put off by the name, or that it is part of a small chain. This fine-dining restaurant at the Headquarters at Seaport in Downtown has won a devoted following for classic seafood, casual but sophisticated settings, and nightly live jazz. **Known for:** wallet-friendly happy hour deals; indulgent truffled mac and cheese. ⑤ *Average main: $34* ✉ *789 W. Harbor Dr., Embarcadero* ☎ *619/615–0281* ⊕ *www.eddiev. com* ⊙ *No lunch.*

★ **Puesto**

$ | MEXICAN | Bold graffiti graphics, chandeliers with tangled telephone wires, and beat-heavy music energize this Downtown eatery that celebrates Mexican street food with a modern twist. Settle into one of the interior rooms or the sunny patio under orange umbrellas to sip margaritas and other specialty cocktails, Baja wines, or fruity aguas frescas made daily. **Known for:** taco trio plates; unique Parmesan guacamole; fruit-infused margaritas made in-house. ⑤ *Average main: $16* ✉ *789 W. Harbor Dr., Downtown* ☎ *619/233–8880* ⊕ *www. eatpuesto.com.*

🏨 Hotels

Manchester Grand Hyatt San Diego

$$$ | HOTEL | FAMILY | Primarily a draw for business travelers, this hotel between Seaport Village and the convention center also works well for leisure and family travelers. **Pros:** great views; conference facilities; good location; spacious rooms. **Cons:** lots of convention-goers; some trolley noise; not as stylish as many other Downtown hotels. ⑤ *Rooms from: $259* ✉ *1 Market Pl., Embarcadero* ☎ *619/232–1234, 800/233–1234* ⊕ *www.manchester. grand.hyatt.com* 🛏 *1628 rooms* ⏐⊙⏐ *No meals.*

Shopping

★ The Headquarters at Seaport

OUTDOOR/FLEA/GREEN MARKETS | This new upscale shopping and dining center is in the city's former police headquarters, a beautiful and historic Mission-style building featuring an open courtyard with fountains. Restaurants and shops, many locally owned, occupy former jail facilities and offices. Pop into **Urban Beach House** for coastal-inspired fashion from popular surf brands for men and women, including accessories and home decor. Swing by **Madison San Diego** for a great selection of leather goods and accessories, from apparel and handbags to belts and travel accessories. **Dallmann Fine Chocolates** sells truffles in flavors like bananas Foster and coconut curry. **Venissimo Cheese** dishes up the best cheese from around the world, from goat milk chevre filled with Italian truffle salt to French triple crème Brie topped with tangy cranberries. **Geppetto's** has been a San Diego staple for more than 40 years, offering classic toys and games that inspire creativity for the entire family. ⊠ *789 W. Harbor Dr., Downtown* ☎ *619/235–4013* ⊕ *theheadquarters.com.*

East Village

The most ambitious of the Downtown projects is East Village, not far from the Gaslamp Quarter, and encompassing 130 blocks between the railroad tracks up to J Street, and from 6th Avenue east to around 10th Street. Sparking the rebirth of this former warehouse district was the 2004 construction of the San Diego Padres' baseball stadium, PETCO Park. The Urban Art Trail has added pizzazz to drab city thoroughfares by transforming such things as trash cans and traffic controller boxes into works of art. As the city's largest Downtown neighborhood, East Village is continually broadening its boundaries with its urban design of redbrick cafés, spacious galleries, rooftop bars, sleek hotels, and warehouse restaurants.

Sights

PETCO Park

SPORTS VENUE | **FAMILY** | PETCO Park is home to the city's major league baseball team, the San Diego Padres. The ballpark is strategically designed to give fans a view of San Diego Bay, the skyline, and Balboa Park. Reflecting San Diego's beauty, the stadium is clad in sandstone from India to evoke the area's cliffs and beaches; the 42,000 seats are dark blue, reminiscent of the ocean, and the exposed steel is painted white to reflect the sails of harbor boats on the bay. The family-friendly lawnlike berm, "Park at the Park," is a popular and affordable place for fans to view the game. The ballpark underwent a huge effort to improve dining in the park, and local food vendors and craft breweries now dominate the dining options. Behind-the-scenes guided tours of PETCO, including the press box and the dugout, are offered throughout the year. ⊠ *100 Park Blvd., East Village* ☎ *619/795–5011 tour hotline* ⊕ *sandiego.padres.mlb.com* ⊠ *$20 tour.*

🍴 Restaurants

The Blind Burro

$$ | **MODERN MEXICAN** | **FAMILY** | East Village families, baseball fans heading to or from PETCO Park, and happy-hour bound singles flock to this airy restaurant with Baja-inspired food and drink. Traditional margaritas get a fresh kick from fruit juices or jalapeño peppers; other libations include sangria and Mexican beers, all perfect pairings for house-made guacamole, ceviche, or salsas with chips. **Known for:** house margarita with fruit infusions; surf-and-turf Baja-style tacos; gluten-free menu. ⑤ *Average main: $18* ⊠ *639 J St., East Village* ☎ *619/795–7880* ⊕ *www.theblindburro.com.*

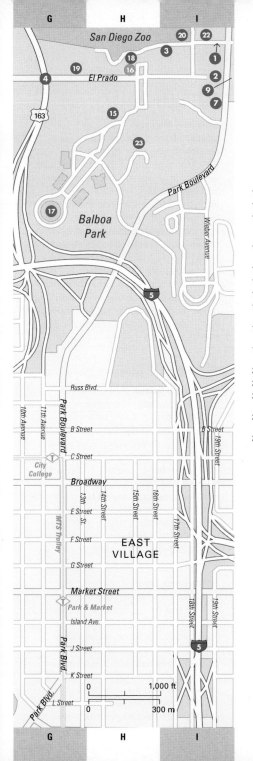

Sights ▼

1 Balboa Park Carousel....**I1**
2 Bea Evenson Fountain...**I1**
3 Botanical Building.......**I1**
4 Cabrillo Bridge.........**G1**
5 Chicano Park............**F9**
6 Coronado Ferry
   Landing **C9**
7 Fleet Science Center.....**I1**
8 Gaslamp Museum at the
   Davis-Horton House.....**E8**
9 Inez Grant Parker
   Memorial Rose Garden
   and Desert Garden.......**I1**
10 Little Italy Mercato......**C4**
11 Maritime Museum......**A5**
12 Museum of Contemporary
   Art San Diego
   (MCASD)................**B6**
13 The New Children's
   Museum (NCM).........**D8**
14 Orange Avenue **C9**
15 Palm Canyon **H2**
16 Petco Park...............**F9**
17 San Diego Air & Space
   Museum **G3**
18 The San Diego Museum
   of Art **H1**
19 San Diego Museum of
   Man **G1**
20 San Diego Zoo **I1**
21 Seaport Village..........**B9**
22 Spanish Village Art
   Center **I1**
23 Spreckels Organ
   Pavilion **H2**
24 USS Midway
   Museum **A7**

Restaurants ▼

1 Azuki Sushi **E2**
2 Bankers Hill Bar and
   Restaurant...............**E2**
3 The Blind Burro **F9**
4 Born and Raised **C3**
5 Cucina Urbana **E1**
6 Cafe 1134 ....**C9**
7 Chez Loma **C9**
8 Coronado Brewing
   Company.................**C9**
9 The Crack Shack........**B2**
10 Eddie V's Prime
   Seafood.................**B8**
11 Extraordinary
   Desserts **D5**
12 Herb & Wood............**B3**
13 Juniper and Ivy **B2**
14 Las Cuatro Milpas **F9**
15 Little Italy Food Hall......**C4**
16 Panama 66................**H1**
17 Prep Kitchen Little
   Italy......................**C4**
18 Puesto....................**B8**
19 ¡SALUD! **F9**
20 Searsucker **E8**
21 Taka **E8**
22 Tartine....................**C9**

Hotels ▼

1 Andaz San Diego **F7**
2 Coronado Island Marriott
   Resort & Spa.............**C9**
3 Found Hotel...............**C3**
4 Hotel del Coronado......**C9**
5 Kimpton Hotel
   Solamar..................**F8**
6 Loews Coronado Bay
   Resort...................**C9**
7 Manchester Grand Hyatt
   San Diego................**C8**
8 1906 Lodge at
   Coronado Beach........**C9**
9 Pendry San Diego **E8**
10 The Sofia Hotel.........**D6**

Nightlife

★ Fairweather

BARS/PUBS | Hidden in plain sight next to PETCO Park, Fairweather is an urban tiki oasis with a top-notch cocktail menu that boasts classics like daiquiris and their signature frozen piña colada alongside modern interpretations of old-school tiki drinks like Corpse Revivers and mai tais. ■TIP→ **Come by during Comic-Con in July to view the parade of costumed characters while sipping rum refreshments on the balcony.** ⊠ *793 J St., 2nd fl., East Village* ☎ *619/578–2392* ⊕ *www.fairweatherbar.com.*

★ Noble Experiment

PIANO BARS/LOUNGES | There are a handful of speakeasy-style bars in San Diego, though none deliver so far above and beyond the novelty quite like this cozy-yet-swank cocktail lounge hidden in the back of a burger restaurant. Seek out the hidden door (hint: look for the stack of kegs), tuck into a plush leather booth next to the wall of golden skulls, and sip on the best craft cocktails in the city. ■TIP→ **Reservations are almost always a must, so be sure to call ahead.** ⊠ *777 G St., East Village* ☎ *619/888–4713* ⊕ *nobleexperimentsd.com.*

Little Italy

Home to many in San Diego's design community, Little Italy exudes a sense of urban cool while remaining authentic to its roots and marked by old-country charms: church bells ring on the half hour, and Italians gather daily to play bocce in Amici Park. The main thoroughfare, India Street, is filled with lively cafés, chic shops, and many of the city's trendiest restaurants. Little Italy is one of San Diego's most walkable neighborhoods, and a great spot to wander. Art lovers can browse gallery showrooms, while shoppers adore the Fir Street cottages. The neighborhood bustles each Saturday during the wildly popular Mercato farmers' market.

◉ Sights

Little Italy Mercato

MARKET | Each Saturday tourists and residents alike flock to the Little Italy Mercato, one of the most popular farmers' markets in San Diego. Over 150 vendors line Date Street selling everything from paintings and pottery to flowers and farm-fresh eggs. Come hungry, as several booths and food trucks serve prepared foods. Alternatively, the neighborhood's many cafés and restaurants are just steps away. The Mercato is a great opportunity to experience one of San Diego's most exciting urban neighborhoods. ⊠ *Date and India Sts., Little Italy* ⊕ *www.littleitalysd.com/events/mercato.*

🍴 Restaurants

★ Born and Raised

$$$$ | STEAKHOUSE | The name is cheeky if a little morbid; the title refers to the restaurant's speciality—steak. It's a twist on a classic steak house, with a menu full of aged, prime cuts of beef served with a number of sauces, or perhaps try the table-side-prepared steak Diane with flambéed jus. **Known for:** table-side Caesar salad; aged New York steak; cheeky, glamorous decor. Ⓢ *Average main: $45* ⊠ *1909 India St., Little Italy* ☎ *619/202–4577* ⊕ *www.bornandraisedsteak.com.*

★ The Crack Shack

$ | AMERICAN | FAMILY | Next to his successful fine dining restaurant, Juniper and Ivy, celebrity chef Richard Blais has opened this more casual eatery complete with a walk-up counter, picnic-style tables, a boccie court, and a giant rooster—a nod to the egg- and chicken-themed menu. Ingredients are sourced from high-quality vendors and used for sandwiches, of which the fried chicken varieties shine, as well as salads and sides like fluffy minibiscuits with a miso-maple butter and a Mexican spin on poutine. **Known for:** Señor Croque fried chicken sandwich with smoked pork belly; biscuits with miso-maple butter; all-outdoor seating with boccie court. $ *Average main: $12* ✉ *2266 Kettner Blvd., Little Italy* ☎ *619/795–3299* ⊕ *www.crackshack.com.*

★ Extraordinary Desserts

$ | **CAFÉ** | For Paris-perfect cakes and tarts embellished California-style with fresh flowers, head to this sleek, serene branch of Karen Krasne's pastry shop and café. The space with soaring ceilings hosts breakfasts, lunches, and light dinners, accompanied by a wide selection of teas, coffee, organic wines, and craft beers. **Known for:** blueberry coffee cake for breakfast; chocolate dulce de leche cake; house-made dips including onion dip and Parmesan pesto. $ *Average main: $14* ✉ *1430 Union St., Little Italy* ☎ *619/294–7001* ⊕ *www.extraordinarydesserts.com.*

★ Herb & Wood

$$ | **AMERICAN** | Design lovers will fall for celebrity chef Brian Malarkey's sprawling restaurant, a former art store that has been refashioned into four luxe spaces in one—an entryway lounge, outdoor lounge, fireplace-dotted patio, and the main dining room, which is flanked by beaded chandeliers, lush banquettes, and paintings in rich jewel tones. The menu is heavy on wood-roasted dishes, many of which are apt for sharing like the roasted baby carrots or hiramasa with crispy quinoa. **Known for:** roasted baby carrots with cashew sesame dukkah; pillow-soft oxtail gnocchi; the secret menu Parker House rolls topped with Maldon sea salt. $ *Average main: $20* ✉ *2210 Kettner Blvd., Little Italy* ☎ *619/955–8495* ⊕ *www.herbandwood.com* ◷ *No lunch.*

Juniper and Ivy

$$$ | **MODERN AMERICAN** | Celebrity chef Richard Blais's addition to San Diego's restaurant scene fills an open-beamed space with seating for 250 and an open stainless-steel dream kitchen where diners can watch the chef and team in action. Blais sources local farm-fresh ingredients for his "left coast cookery" with a molecular gastronomy twist. **Known for:** California-Baja-inspired carne crudo asada topped with quail eggs; off-menu "In & Haute" burger; very shareable Yodel chocolate dessert. $ *Average main: $35* ✉ *2228 Kettner Blvd., Little Italy* ☎ *619/269–9036* ⊕ *www.juniperandivy.com* ◷ *No lunch.*

Little Italy Food Hall

$ | **FUSION** | **FAMILY** | A recently opened, chic update on the food court, Food Hall brings together a half dozen different innovative food counters to offer quick bites vastly more interesting than mall fare. Among its offerings are the seafood-centric Single Fin Kitchen and Wicked Maine Lobster, and an update on a local delicacy, Not Not Tacos. **Known for:** fusion tacos; bustling crowds of Mercato shoppers; beer/wine cart dispensing refreshments in the outdoor seating area. $ *Average main: $10* ✉ *550 W. Date St., Suite B, Little Italy* ☎ *619/269–7187* ⊕ *www.littleitalyfoodhall.com.*

★ Prep Kitchen Little Italy

$$ | **MODERN AMERICAN** | Urbanites craving a hip casual setting and gourmet menu pack architectural salvage–styled Prep Kitchen Little Italy, tucked upstairs above a busy corner in this thriving neighborhood. With first-date cocktails, after-work brews, or birthday champagne, diners relish familiar choices like meatball sandwiches, chops, and pork belly with kimchi Brussels. **Known for:** weekend brunch featuring popular chilaquiles dish; bacon-wrapped dates; $6 tapas during the daily happy hour. $ *Average main: $23* ✉ *1660 India St., Little Italy* ☎ *619/398–8383* ⊕ *www.prepkitchenlittleitaly.com.*

Hotels

Found Hotel

$ | **B&B/INN** | You'll find more amenities at other Downtown hotels but it's hard to beat this property's value and charm. **Pros:** good location; historic property; welcoming staff. **Cons:** some shared baths; no parking; not great for couples or families. $ *Rooms from: $139* ✉ *505 W. Grape St., Little Italy* ☎ *619/230–1600, 800/518–9930* ⊕ *sandiego.foundhotels. com* 🗫 *23 rooms* ❍❘ *Free Breakfast.*

Nightlife

BARS

★ False Idol

BARS/PUBS | A walk-in refrigerator harbors the secret entrance to this tiki-themed speakeasy, which is attached to Craft & Commerce. Beneath fishing nets full of puffer-fish lights and elaborate tiki-head wall carvings, the knowledgeable staff serves up creative takes on tropical classics with the best selection of rums in town. ■TIP→ **The bar fills up quickly, especially on weekends. Make a reservation online a week or more in advance.** ✉ *675 W. Beech St., Little Italy* ⊕ *falseidoltiki.com.*

The Waterfront Bar & Grill

BARS/PUBS | It isn't really *on* the waterfront, but San Diego's oldest bar was once the hangout of Italian fishermen. Most of the collars are now white, and patrons enjoy an excellent selection of beers, along with chili, burgers, fish-and-chips, and other great-tasting grub, including fish tacos. Get here early, as there's almost always a crowd. ✉ *2044 Kettner Blvd., Little Italy* ☎ *619/232–9656* ⊕ *www.waterfrontbarandgrill.com.*

BREWPUBS

★ Ballast Point Brewing Co.

BREWPUBS/BEER GARDENS | Until recently, you had to head to the Miramar/Scripps Ranch area for a tasting at Ballast Point, but now there's a local taproom in Little

Italy. The Sculpin IPA is outstanding. ✉ *2215 India St., Little Italy* ☎ *619/255–7213* ⊕ *www.ballastpoint.com.*

Karl Strauss' Brewing Company

BARS/PUBS | San Diego's first microbrewery now has multiple locations, but the original one remains a staple. This locale draws an after-work crowd for pints of Red Trolley Ale and later fills with beer connoisseurs from all walks of life to try Karl's latest concoctions. The German-inspired pub food is above average. ✉ *1157 Columbia St., Little Italy* ☎ *619/234–2739* ⊕ *www.karlstrauss.com.*

MUSIC CLUB

★ The Casbah

MUSIC CLUBS | This small club near the airport, the unofficial headquarters of the city's indie music scene, has a national reputation for showcasing up-and-coming acts of all genres. Nirvana, Smashing Pumpkins, and the White Stripes all played here on the way to stardom. ✉ *2501 Kettner Blvd., Middletown* ☎ *619/232–4355* ⊕ *www.casbahmusic.com.*

Barrio Logan

San Diego's Mexican-American community is centered in Barrio Logan, under the San Diego–Coronado Bay Bridge on the Downtown side. Chicano Park, spread along National Avenue from Dewey to Crosby streets, is the barrio's recreational hub. It's worth taking a short detour to see the huge murals of Mexican history painted on the bridge supports at National Avenue and Dewey Street; they're among the best examples of folk art in the city. Art enthusiasts will also enjoy the burgeoning gallery scene in the Barrio Logan neighborhood, rapidly becoming a hub for artists in San Diego.

GETTING HERE AND AROUND

Barrio Logan is located right off Interstate 5, at the Cesar E. Chavez Parkway exit. Driving is the easiest way to get there, especially coming from Downtown—in fact, it's only a mile from PETCO Park, and easily accessible via Imperial and Logan avenues. However, the Blue Line trolley also stops in Barrio Logan, and several bus lines also cross through the neighborhood, including the 9, 6, 20, 705, and 923.

When staying Downtown, Barrio Logan is also just a 15-minute walk, but with its somewhat isolated location under a bridge, visitors should exercise caution visiting the Chicano Park murals after dark.

◉ Sights

★ Chicano Park

PUBLIC ART | FAMILY | The cultural center of the Barrio Logan neighborhood, Chicano Park—designated a National Historic Landmark in 2017—was born in 1970 from the activism of local residents who occupied the space after the state rescinded its promise to designate the land a park. Signed into law a year later, the park is now a protected area that brings together families and locals for both public and private events, a welcoming gathering space as well as an outdoor gallery featuring large murals documenting Mexican-American history and Chicano activism. Every year Chicano Park Day is held on April 21, filling the park with the sights and sounds of music, dancers, vintage cars, and food and clothing vendors. ⊠ *Logan Ave. and Cesar Chavez Pkwy., Barrio Logan* ⊕ *chicano-park.com; www.chicanoparksandiego.com.*

Restaurants

Las Cuatros Milpas

$ | MEXICAN | One of the oldest restaurants in San Diego, having opened in 1933, Las Cuatros Milpas feels like a closely held secret in Barrio Logan. Open daily until 3 pm, it almost inevitably attracts a big lunchtime rush, though the wait is worth it for the homemade tortillas, beans with chorizo, and rolled tacos.

Known for: homemade tortillas; checkered picnic tables; chorizo con huevos. ⑤ *Average main: $5* ⊠ *1857 Logan Ave., Barrio Logan* ☎ *619/234–4460* ⊘ *Closed Sun.* ▭ *No credit cards.*

★ ¡Salud!

$ | MEXICAN | The line that inevitably wraps around the building is indicative of the quality of the tacos and the large selection of local craft beers on tap. Indeed, these are some of the best tacos in all of San Diego, ranging from the classic carne asada and Baja fish tacos to fried-shell beef tacos and Califas, which features french fries inside the tortilla. Just remember—alcohol isn't allowed at the outdoor tables. **Known for:** Baja-style street tacos; Pruno de Piña (beer and fermented pineapple); churros and ice cream. ⑤ *Average main: $3* ⊠ *2196 Logan Ave., Barrio Logan* ☎ *619/255–3856* ⊕ *www.saludsd.com.*

Balboa Park, Bankers Hill, and San Diego Zoo

Overlooking Downtown and the Pacific Ocean, 1,200-acre Balboa Park is the cultural heart of San Diego. Ranked as one of the world's best parks by the Project for Public Spaces, it's also where you can find most of the city's museums, art galleries, the Tony Award–winning Old Globe Theatre, and the world-famous San Diego Zoo. Often referred to as the "Smithsonian of the West" for its concentration of museums, Balboa Park is also a series of botanical gardens, performance spaces, and outdoor playrooms endeared to the hearts of residents and visitors alike.

In addition, the captivating architecture of Balboa's buildings, fountains, and courtyards gives the park an enchanted feel. Historic buildings dating from San Diego's 1915 Panama–California International Exposition are strung along the park's main east–west thoroughfare,

El Prado, which leads from 6th Avenue eastward over the Cabrillo Bridge (formerly the Laurel Street Bridge), the park's official gateway. If you're a cinema fan, many of the buildings may be familiar—Orson Welles used exteriors of several Balboa Park buildings to represent the Xanadu estate of Charles Foster Kane in his 1941 classic, *Citizen Kane*. Prominent among them was the California Building, whose 200-foot tower, housing a 100-bell carillon that tolls the hour, is El Prado's tallest structure. Missing from the black-and-white film, however, was the magnificent blue of its tiled dome shining in the sun.

Bankers Hill is a small neighborhood west of Balboa Park, with gorgeous views ranging from Balboa Park's greenery in the east to the San Diego Bay in the west. It's become one of San Diego's hottest restaurant destinations.

Sights

★ Balboa Park Carousel
CAROUSEL | FAMILY | Suspended an arm's length away on this antique merry-go-round is the brass ring that could earn you an extra free ride (it's one of the few carousels in the world that continue this bonus tradition). Hand-carved in 1910, the carousel features colorful murals, big-band music, and bobbing animals including zebras, giraffes, and dragons; real horsehair was used for the tails. ⊠ *1889 Zoo Pl., behind zoo parking lot, Balboa Park* ☎ *619/239–0512* ⊕ *www.balboapark.org* ⊠ *$3* ⊗ *Closed weekdays Labor Day–mid-June.*

Bea Evenson Fountain
FOUNTAIN | A favorite of barefoot children, this fountain shoots cool jets of water upwards of 50 feet. Built in 1972 between the Fleet Center and Natural History Museum, the fountain offers plenty of room to sit and watch the crowds go by. ⊠ *Balboa Park* ✥ *East end of El Prado* ⊕ *www.balboapark.org.*

★ Botanical Building
GARDEN | The graceful redwood-lath structure, built for the 1915 Panama–California International Exposition, now houses more than 2,000 types of tropical and subtropical plants plus changing seasonal flower displays. Ceiling-high tree ferns shade fragile orchids and feathery bamboo. There are benches beside miniature waterfalls for resting in the shade. The rectangular pond outside, filled with lotuses and water lilies that bloom in spring and fall, is popular with photographers. ⊠ *1549 El Prado, Balboa Park* ☎ *619/239–0512* ⊕ *www.balboapark.org* ⊠ *Free* ⊗ *Closed Thurs.*

Cabrillo Bridge
BRIDGE/TUNNEL | The official gateway into Balboa Park soars 120 feet above a canyon floor. Pedestrian-friendly, the 1,500-foot bridge provides inspiring views of the California Tower and El Prado beyond. ■ TIP→ **This is a great spot for photo-capturing a classic image of the park.** ⊠ *Balboa Park* ✥ *On El Prado, at 6th Ave. park entrance* ⊕ *www.balboapark.org.*

Fleet Science Center
MUSEUM | FAMILY | Interactive exhibits here are artfully educational and for all ages: older kids can get hands-on with inventive projects in Studio X, while the five-and-under set can be easily entertained with interactive play stations like the Ball Wall and Fire Truck in the center's Kid City. The IMAX Dome Theater, which screens exhilarating nature and science films, was the world's first, as was the Fleet's "NanoSeam" (seamless) dome ceiling that doubles as a planetarium. ⊠ *1875 El Prado, Balboa Park* ☎ *619/238–1233* ⊕ *www.rhfleet.org* ⊠ *The Fleet experience includes gallery exhibits and 1 IMAX film $21.95; additional cost for special exhibits or add-on 2nd IMAX film or planetarium show.*

★ Inez Grant Parker Memorial Rose Garden and Desert Garden
GARDEN | These neighboring gardens sit just across the Park Boulevard pedestrian

bridge and offer gorgeous views over Florida Canyon. The formal rose garden contains 1,600 roses representing nearly 130 varieties; peak bloom is usually in April and May. The adjacent Desert Garden provides a striking contrast, with 2.5 acres of succulents and desert plants seeming to blend into the landscape of the canyon below. ⊠ *2525 Park Blvd., Balboa Park* ⊕ *www.balboapark.org.*

Palm Canyon

CANYON | Enjoy an instant escape from the buildings and concrete of urban life in this Balboa Park oasis. Lush and tropical, with hundreds of palm trees, the 2-acre canyon has a shaded path perfect for those who love walking through nature. ⊠ *1549 El Prado, south of House of Charm, Balboa Park.*

★ San Diego Air & Space Museum

MUSEUM | FAMILY | By day, the streamlined edifice looks like any other structure in the park; at night, outlined in blue neon, the round building appears—appropriately enough—to be a landed UFO. Every available inch of space in the rotunda is filled with exhibits about aviation and aerospace pioneers, including examples of enemy planes from the world wars. In all, there are more than 60 full-size aircraft on the floor and hanging from the rafters. In addition to exhibits from the dawn of flight to the jet age, the museum displays a growing number of space-age exhibits, including the actual *Apollo 9* command module. To test your own skills, you can ride in a two-seat Max Flight simulator or try out the Talon Racing simulator. Movies in the 3-D/4-D theater are included with admission. ⊠ *2001 Pan American Pl., Balboa Park* ☎ *619/234–8291* ⊕ *www. sandiegoairandspace.org* ⊡ *Museum $19.95 (more for special exhibitions); Flight Simulators $5–$8 extra; restoration tour $5 extra and subject to availability.*

★ San Diego Museum of Art

MUSEUM | Known for its Spanish baroque and Renaissance paintings, including works by El Greco, Goya, Rubens, and van Ruisdael, San Diego's most comprehensive art museum also has strong holdings of South Asian art, Indian miniatures, and contemporary California paintings. The museum's exhibits tend to have broad appeal, and if traveling shows from other cities come to town, you can expect to see them here. Free docent tours are offered throughout the day. An outdoor Sculpture Court and Garden exhibits both traditional and modern pieces. Enjoy the view over a craft beer and some locally sourced food in the adjacent Panama 66 courtyard restaurant. ◾TIP→ **The museum hosts "Art After Hours" most Friday nights, with discounted admission 5–8 pm.** ⊠ *1450 El Prado, Balboa Park* ☎ *619/232–7931* ⊕ *www.sdmart.org* ⊡ *$15; $5 Fri. 5–8 pm; sculpture garden free* ⊘ *Closed Wed.*

★ San Diego Museum of Man

MUSEUM | FAMILY | If the facade of this building—the landmark California Building—looks familiar, it's because filmmaker Orson Welles used it and its dramatic tower as the principal features of the Xanadu estate in his 1941 classic, *Citizen Kane.* Closed for 80 years, the tower was recently reopened for public tours. An additional timed ticket and a climb up 125 steps is required, but the effort will be rewarded with spectacular 360-degree views of the coast, Downtown, and the inland mountains. Back inside, exhibits at this highly respected anthropological museum focus on Southwestern, Mexican, and South American cultures. Carved monuments from the Mayan city of Quirigua in Guatemala, cast from the originals in 1914, are particularly impressive. Exhibits might include examples of intricate beadwork from across the Americas, the history of Egyptian mummies, or the lifestyles of the Kumeyaay peoples, Native Americans who live in the San Diego area. ⊠ *California Bldg., 1350 El Prado, Balboa Park* ☎ *619/239–2001* ⊕ *www.museumofman. org* ⊡ *$13; special exhibits extra; Tower tickets (including museum admission)*

$23 ☞ *Tower tours are timed-entry and can be booked in advance through website or on arrival at museum.*

★ San Diego Zoo

ZOO | FAMILY | Balboa Park's—and perhaps the city's—most famous attraction is its 100-acre zoo. Nearly 4,000 animals of some 800 diverse species roam in hospitable, expertly crafted habitats that replicate natural environments as closely as possible. The flora in the zoo, including many rare species, is even more dear than the fauna. Walkways wind over bridges and past waterfalls ringed with tropical ferns; elephants in a sandy plateau roam so close you're tempted to pet them.

Exploring the zoo fully requires the stamina of a healthy hiker, but open-air double-decker buses that run throughout the day let you zip through three-quarters of the exhibits on a guided 35- to 40-minute, 3-mile tour. There are also express buses, used for quick transportation, that make five stops around the grounds and include some narration. The Skyfari Aerial Tram, which soars 170 feet above the ground, gives a good overview of the zoo's layout and, on clear days, a panorama of the park, Downtown San Diego, the bay, and the ocean, far beyond the San Diego–Coronado Bridge. ■ **TIP →** **Unless you come early, expect to wait for the regular bus, and especially for the top tier— the line can take more than 45 minutes; if you come at midday on a weekend or school holiday, you'll be doing the in-line shuffle for a while.**

Don't forget the San Diego Safari Park, the zoo's 1,800-acre extension to the north at Escondido. ✉ *2920 Zoo Dr., Balboa Park* ☎ *619/234–3153,* ⊕ *www.sandiegozoo. org* 🎟 *$54 adult, $44 children ages 3–11 (includes Skyfari and bus tour).*

★ Spanish Village Art Center

MUSEUM | More than 200 local artists, including glassblowers, enamel workers, wood-carvers, sculptors, painters, jewelers, and photographers work and give demonstrations of their craft on a rotating basis in these red tile–roof studio-galleries that were set up for the 1935–36 exposition in the style of an old Spanish village. The center is a great source for memorable gifts. ✉ *1770 Village Pl., Balboa Park* ☎ *619/233–9050* ⊕ *www.spanishvillageart.com* 🎟 *Free.*

★ Spreckels Organ Pavilion

ARTS VENUE | The 2,400-bench-seat pavilion, dedicated in 1915 by sugar magnates John D. and Adolph B. Spreckels, holds the 4,518-pipe Spreckels Organ, the largest outdoor pipe organ in the world. You can hear this impressive instrument at one of the year-round, free, 2 pm Sunday concerts, regularly performed by the city's civic organist Raúl Prieto Ramírez and guest artists—a highlight of a visit to Balboa Park. On Monday evenings from late June to mid-August, internationally renowned organists play evening concerts. At Christmastime the park's Christmas tree and life-size Nativity display turn the pavilion into a seasonal wonderland. ✉ *2211 Pan American Rd., Balboa Park* ☎ *619/702–8138* ⊕ *spreckelsorgan.org.*

🍴 Restaurants

★ Azuki Sushi

$$ | SUSHI | Sushi should be a no-brainer when visiting San Diego, especially for tourists from landlocked states who don't often get fresh fish. This menu is based on the seasons, and you'll find innovative sushi, sashimi, and a raw bar, all utilizing the freshest local fish (some is flown in daily from Japan) and produce; there are options for non-sushi fans. **Known for:** reservations recommended; specialty rolls like the R U Kidding Me? (snow crab, diver scallops, tempura asparagus, seared tuna, white truffle oil, and mixed greens, topped with garlic ponzu and flash-fried leeks); surprising pairings with wine and sake. ⑤ *Average main: $21* ✉ *2321 5th Ave., Bankers Hill* ☎ *619/238–4760* ⊕ *azukisushi.com* ⊙ *No lunch weekends.*

Continued on page 86

Polar bear, San Diego Zoo

LIONS AND TIGERS AND BEARS:
The World-Famous San Diego Zoo

From diving polar bears and 6-ton elephants to swinging great apes, San Diego's most famous attraction has it all. Nearly 4,000 animals representing 800 species roam the 100-acre zoo in expertly crafted habitats that replicate the animals' natural environments. The pandas may have gone home (in 2019), but there are plenty of other cool creatures to see here, from teeny-tiny mantella frogs to two-story-tall giraffes. But it's not all just fun and games. Known for its exemplary conservation programs, the zoo educates visitors on how to go green and explains its efforts to protect endangered species.

SAN DIEGO ZOO TOP ATTRACTIONS

Underwater viewing area at the Hippo Trail

❶ Children's Zoo (Discovery Outpost). Goats and sheep beg to be petted, and there is a viewer-friendly nursery where you may see baby animals bottle-feed and sleep peacefully in large cribs.

❷ Monkey Trails and Forest Tales (Lost Forest). Follow an elevated trail at treetop level and trek through the forest floor observing African mandrill monkeys, Asia's clouded leopard, the rare pygmy hippopotamus, and Visayan warty pigs.

❸ Orangutan and Siamang Exhibit (Lost Forest). Orangutans and siamangs climb and swing in this lush, tropical environment lined with 110-foot-long and 12-foot-high viewing windows.

Express Bus Stop

PARK WAY

Polar Bear Plunge **❿**

Skyfari West

PARK WAY

POLAR RIM

Arctic Trader

Ituri Hut

Ituri Forest Outpost

Express Bus Stop

Elephant Odyssey Entrance

PANDA CANYON

LOST FOREST

Albert's Restaurant

Giant Panda Research Station

❻

Treehouse Trader

Panda Shop

Treehouse Cafe

Treetops Room

PARK WAY

Hua Mei Cafe

❼ Gorilla Exhibit

❷

Monkey Trail

Scripps Aviary

Parker Aviary

Owens Aviary

❹ Greenzoo Coffee Co.

Hippo Trail

Tiger Trail

Monkey Trail

❺

Monkey Trail

CENTER STREET

Fern Canyon Trail

Tiger Trail

EASY STREET

Orangutan Trail

❸ Orangutan and Siamang Exhibit

CENTENNIAL PLAZA

Wegeforth Bowl

First Aid & Nursing Station

Jungle Java

Fern Canyon Trail

Bus Tour Loading

Birthday Bake Shop

DISCOVERY OUTPOST

Reptile House

Safari Kitchen

Front St. Photos

FRONTSTREET

Cinnamon Tree

Lagoon Terrace

Clark Theater

Poppy's Patio

Zoofari Photos

Kidsfore

Nestle Tollhouse Cafe by Chip

Flamingo Sandwich Co.

Rondavel Room

Insect House

Front St. Cafe

San Diego Zoo Store

Rondavel Room

Warner Administration Center

Petting Zoo

Children's Zoo

Skyfari East

Zoofari Party Area

ENTRANCE

Fisher Price Discovery Playground

Otto Center

❶

Balboa Park Railroad (MiniatureTrain)

P

④ Scripps, Parker, and Owens Aviaries (Lost Forest). Wandering paths climb through the enclosed aviaries where brightly colored tropical birds swoop between branches inches from your face.

⑤ Tiger Trail (Lost Forest). The mist-shrouded trails of this simulated rainforest wind down a canyon. Tigers, Malayan tapirs, and Argus pheasants wander among the exotic trees and plants.

⑥ Hippo Trail (Lost Forest). Glimpse huge but surprisingly graceful hippos frolicking in the water through an underwater viewing window and buffalo cavorting with monkeys on dry land.

⑦ Gorilla Exhibit (Lost Forest). The gorillas live in one of the zoo's bioclimatic zone exhibits modeled on their native habitat with waterfalls, climbing areas, and an open meadow. The sounds of the tropical rain forest emerge from a 144-speaker sound system that plays CDs recorded in Africa.

⑧ Africa Rocks. This massive exhibit consists of six different rocky habitats designed to showcase the diversity of topography and species on the African continent. Penguins, meerkats, and a band of baboons are just a few of the animals that call this ambitious exhibit home.

Lories at Owen's Aviary

⑨ Sun Bear Forest (Asian Passage). Playful beasts claw apart the trees and shrubs that serve as a natural playground for climbing, jump¬ing, and general merrymaking.

⑩ Polar Bear Plunge (Polar Rim). Watch polar bears take a chilly dive from the underwater viewing room. There are also Siberian reindeer, white foxes, and other Arctic creatures here. Kids can learn about the Arctic and climate change through interactive exhibits.

⑪ Elephant Odyssey. Get a glimpse of the animals that roamed Southern California 12,000 years ago and meet their living counterparts. The 7.5-acre, multispecies habitat features elephants, California condors, jaguars, and more.

⑫ Koala Exhibit (Outback). The San Diego Zoo houses the largest number of koalas outside Australia. Walk through the exhibit for photo ops of these marsupials from Down-Under curled up on their perches or dining on eucalyptus branches.

MUST-SEE ANIMALS

❶ GORILLA

This troop of primates engages visitors with their human-like expressions and behavior. The youngsters are sure to delight, especially when hitching a ride on mom's back. Up-close encounters might involve the gorillas using the glass partition as a backrest while peeling cabbage. By dusk the gorillas head inside to their sleeping quarters, so don't save this for your last stop.

❷ ELEPHANT

Asian and African elephants coexist at the San Diego Zoo. The larger African elephant is distinguished by its big flapping ears—shaped like the continent of Africa—which it uses to keep cool. An elephant's trunk has over 40,000 muscles in it—that's more than humans have in their whole body.

❸ ORANGUTAN

Bornean and Sumatran orangutans have been entertaining San Diego visitors since 1928. The exhibit has rope climbing structures, a man-made "termite mound" that's often filled with treats, rocky caves, and tall "sway poles" that allow the orangutans to swing like they would in trees. Don't be surprised if the orangutans come right up to the glass to observe the humans observing them!

❹ KOALA

While this collection of critters is one of the cutest in the zoo, don't expect a lot of activity from the koala habitat. These guys spend most of their day curled up asleep in the branches of the eucalyptus tree—they can sleep up to 20 hours a day. Although eucalyptus leaves are poisonous to most animals, bacteria in koalas' stomachs allow them to break down the toxins.

❺ POLAR BEAR

The trio of polar bears is one of the San Diego Zoo's star attractions, and their brand-new exhibit gets you up close and personal. Visitors sometimes worry about polar bears living in the warm San Diego climate, but there is no cause for concern. The San Diego-based bears eat a lean diet, thus reducing their layer of blubber and helping them keep cool.

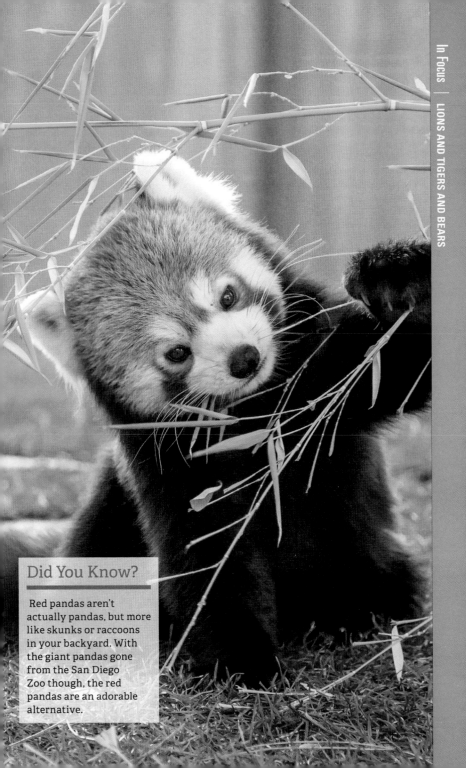

Did You Know?

Red pandas aren't actually pandas, but more like skunks or raccoons in your backyard. With the giant pandas gone from the San Diego Zoo though, the red pandas are an adorable alternative.

★ Bankers Hill Bar and Restaurant

$$ | **MODERN AMERICAN** | The living wall of succulents, hip warehouse interior, and wine bottle chandeliers suit this vibrant restaurant where good times and great eats meet. An after-work crowd joins residents of this quiet stretch of Bankers Hill for happy hour served from the zinc bar while diners enjoy sophisticated comfort food often with Southwest flair. **Known for:** popular burger with truffle fries; butterscotch pudding topped with shortbread cookies and crème fraîche; living plant wall on the sun-drenched patio. ⑤ *Average main: $23* ✉ *2202 4th Ave., Bankers Hill* ☎ *619/231–0222* ⊕ *www. bankershillsd.com* ⊗ *No lunch.*

★ Cucina Urbana

$$ | **ITALIAN** | Twentysomethings mingle with boomers in this convivial Bankers Hill dining room and bar, one of the most popular restaurants in town. The open kitchen turns out innovative Italian food with a California sensibility including a selection of small plates and family-style pasta dishes alongside traditional entrées. **Known for:** in-house wineshop with reasonably priced bottles and $9 corkage fee; seasonal polenta with ragu; ricotta-stuffed zucchini blossoms. ⑤ *Average main: $21* ✉ *505 Laurel St., Bankers Hill* ☎ *619/239–2222* ⊕ *www.cucinaurbana.com* ⊗ *No lunch Sat.–Mon.*

Panama 66

$ | **AMERICAN** | Adding a dose of hip to Balboa Park, this gastropub, located adjacent to the San Diego Museum of Art's sculpture garden, offers a stylish pit stop pretheater or between museum-hopping. The menu features upscale pub fare with several vegan options as well as a weekend brunch. **Known for:** rotating cocktails pegged to museum exhibits; live music most nights; local San Diego and Tijuana brews. ⑤ *Average main: $12* ✉ *1450 El Prado, Balboa Park* ☎ *619/696–1966* ⊕ *www.panama66.com* ⊗ *No dinner Mon. and Tues. Labor Day–Memorial Day.*

🎭 Performing Arts

THEATER

★ The Old Globe

THEATER | This complex, comprising the Sheryl and Harvey White Theatre, the Lowell Davies Festival Theatre, and the Old Globe Theatre, offers some of the finest theatrical productions in Southern California. Theater classics such as *The Full Monty* and *Dirty Rotten Scoundrels,* both of which went on to Broadway, premiered on these famed stages. The Old Globe presents the family-friendly *How the Grinch Stole Christmas* around the holidays, as well as a renowned summer Shakespeare Festival with three to four plays in repertory. ✉ *1363 Old Globe Way, Balboa Park* ☎ *619/234–5623* ⊕ *www. oldglobe.org.*

Old Town and Uptown

San Diego's Spanish and Mexican roots are most evident in Old Town and the surrounding hillside of Presidio Park. Visitors can experience settlement life in San Diego from Spanish and Mexican rule to the early days of U.S. statehood. Nearby Uptown is composed of several smaller neighborhoods near Downtown and around Balboa Park: the vibrant neighborhoods of Hillcrest, Mission Hills, North Park, and South Park showcase their unique blend of historical charm and modern urban community.

As the first European settlement in Southern California, Old Town began to develop in the 1820s. But its true beginnings took place on a nearby hillside in 1769 with the establishment of a Spanish military outpost and the first of California's missions, San Diego de Alcalá. In 1774 the hilltop was declared a *presidio reál*, a fortress built by the Spanish Empire, and the mission was relocated along the San Diego River. Over time, settlers moved down from the presidio to establish Old Town. A central plaza was laid out, surrounded by adobe and, later, wooden structures. San Diego became an incorporated U.S. city in 1850, with Old Town as its center. In the 1860s, however, the advent of Alonzo Horton's New Town to the southeast caused Old Town to wither. Efforts to preserve the area began early in the 20th century, and Old Town became a state historic park in 1968.

Today Old Town is a lively celebration of history and culture. The Old Town San Diego State Historic Park re-creates life during the early settlement, while San Diego Avenue buzzes with art galleries, gift shops, festive restaurants, and open-air stands selling inexpensive Mexican handicrafts.

 ## Sights

★ Fiesta de Reyes

HISTORIC SITE | FAMILY | North of San Diego's Old Town Plaza lies the area's unofficial center, built to represent a colonial Mexican plaza. The collection of more than a dozen shops and restaurants around a central courtyard in blossom with magenta bougainvillea, scarlet hibiscus, and other flowers in season reflects what early California might have looked like from 1821 to 1872. Mariachi bands and folklorico dance groups frequently perform on the plaza stage—check the website for times and upcoming special events. ■TIP→ Casa de Reyes is a great stop for a margarita and some chips and guacamole. ⊠ 4016 Wallace St., Old Town ☎ 619/297–3100 ⊕ www.fiestadereyes.com.

★ Old Town San Diego State Historic Park

HISTORIC SITE | FAMILY | The six square blocks on the site of San Diego's original pueblo are the heart of Old Town. Most of the 20 historic buildings preserved or re-created by the park cluster around **Old Town Plaza,** bounded by Wallace Street on the west, Calhoun Street on the north, Mason Street on the east, and San Diego Avenue on the south. The plaza is

a pleasant place to rest, plan your tour of the park, and watch passersby. San Diego Avenue is closed to vehicle traffic here.

Some of Old Town's buildings were destroyed in a fire in 1872, but after the site became a state historic park in 1968, reconstruction and restoration of the remaining structures began. Five of the original adobes are still intact.

Facing Old Town Plaza, the **Robinson-Rose House** was the original commercial center of Old San Diego, housing railroad offices, law offices, and the first newspaper press. The largest and most elaborate of the original adobe homes, the **Casa de Estudillo** was occupied by members of the Estudillo family until 1887 and later gained popularity for its billing as "Ramona's Marriage Place" based on a popular novel of the time. Albert Seeley, a stagecoach entrepreneur, opened the **Cosmopolitan Hotel** in 1869 as a way station for travelers on the daylong trip south from Los Angeles. Next door to the Cosmopolitan Hotel, the **Seeley Stable** served as San Diego's stagecoach stop in 1867 and was the transportation hub of Old Town until 1887, when trains became the favored mode of travel.

Several reconstructed buildings serve as restaurants or as shops purveying wares reminiscent of those that might have been available in the original Old Town. **Racine & Laramie**, a painstakingly reproduced version of San Diego's first cigar store in 1868, is especially interesting.

Pamphlets available at the Robinson-Rose House give details about all the historic houses on the plaza and in its vicinity. Free tours of the historic park are offered daily at 11:30 and 2; they depart from the Robinson-Rose House. ■TIP→ The covered wagon located near the intersection of Mason and Calhoun streets provides a great photo op. ⊠ Visitor center (Robinson-Rose House), 4002 Wallace St., Old Town ☎ 619/220–5422 ⊕ www.parks.ca.gov ➔ Free.

Old Town and Uptown

The Whaley House Museum

HISTORIC SITE | A New York entrepreneur, Thomas Whaley came to California during the gold rush. He wanted to provide his East Coast wife with all the comforts of home, so in 1857 he had Southern California's first two-story brick structure built, making it the oldest double-story brick building on the West Coast. The house, which served as the county courthouse and government seat during the 1870s, stands in strong contrast to the Spanish-style adobe residences that surround the nearby historic plaza and marks an early stage of San Diego's "Americanization." A garden out back includes many varieties of prehybrid roses from before 1867. The place is perhaps most famed, however, for the ghosts that are said to inhabit it. You can tour on your own during the day, but must visit by guided tour after 4:30 pm. The evening tours are geared toward the supernatural aspects of the house. Tours start at 6 pm (5 pm on Saturday) and are offered every half hour, with the last tour departing at 9:30 pm. ✉ *2476 San Diego Ave., Old Town* ☎ *619/297–7511* ⊕ *www.whaleyhouse. org* 🔖 *$10 before 5 pm; $13 after 5 pm* ⊘ *Closed Sept.–May and Wed.*

🍴 Restaurants

El Agave

$$$ | MEXICAN | Not a typical San Diego taco shop, this Mexican eatery is upstairs in a shopping complex in the middle of a tequila museum with some 2,000 bottles dating from the 1930s. The owners are equally serious about food, calling their cuisine Hispanic-Mexican Gastronomy, which means meat and fish dishes with lots of unusual spicy chilies, herbs, spices, and moles. **Known for:** impressive tequila selection and tequila flights; variety of mole dishes; upscale option in generally casual Old Town. 🔖 *Average main: $32* ✉ *2304 San Diego Ave., Old Town* ☎ *619/220–0692* ⊕ *www.elagave.com.*

🛏 Hotels

Best Western Plus Hacienda Hotel Old Town

$$ | HOTEL | FAMILY | Perched on a hill in the heart of Old Town, this hotel is known for its expansive courtyards, outdoor fountains, and maze of stairs that connects eight buildings of guest rooms. **Pros:** airport shuttle; well-maintained outdoor areas; excellent location for exploring Old Town. **Cons:** some rooms need renovating; complicated layout; can be noisy in some areas. 🔖 *Rooms from: $219* ✉ *4041 Harney St., Old Town* ☎ *800/888–1991* ⊕ *www.haciendahotel-oldtown.com* 🛏 *200 rooms* 🍽 *No meals.*

🛍 Shopping

★ Bazaar del Mundo Shops

SHOPPING CENTERS/MALLS | With a Mexican villa theme, the Bazaar hosts riotously colorful gift shops such as **Ariana,** for ethnic and artsy women's fashions; **Artes de Mexico,** which sells handmade Latin American crafts and Guatemalan weavings; and **The Gallery,** which carries handmade jewelry, Native American crafts, collectible glass, and original silk-screen prints. The **Laurel Burch Gallerita** carries the complete collection of its namesake artist's signature jewelry, accessories, and totes. ✉ *4133 Taylor St., at Juan St., Old Town* ☎ *619/296–3161* ⊕ *www. bazaardelmundo.com.*

Mission Valley

Although Mission Valley's charms may not be immediately apparent, it offers many conveniences to visitors and residents alike. One of the area's main attractions is the Fashion Valley mall, with its mix of high-end and mid-range retail stores and dining options, and movie theater. The Mission Basilica San Diego de Alcalá provides a tranquil refuge from the surrounding suburban sprawl.

Sights

★ Mission Basilica San Diego de Alcalá

HISTORIC SITE | It's hard to imagine how remote California's earliest mission must have once been; these days, however, it's accessible by major freeways (I–15 and I–8) and via the San Diego Trolley. The first of a chain of 21 missions stretching northward along the coast, Mission San Diego de Alcalá was established by Father Junípero Serra on Presidio Hill in 1769 and moved to this location in 1774. In 1775, it proved vulnerable to enemy attack, and Padre Luís Jayme, a young friar from Spain, was clubbed to death by the Kumeyaay Indians he had been trying to convert. He was the first of more than a dozen Christians martyred in California. The present church, reconstructed in 1931 following the outline of the 1813 church, is the fifth built on the site. It measures 150 feet long but only 35 feet wide because, without easy means of joining beams, the mission buildings were only as wide as the trees that served as their ceiling supports were tall. Father Jayme is buried in the sanctuary; a small museum named for him documents mission history and exhibits tools and artifacts from the early days; there is also a gift shop. From the peaceful, palm-bedecked gardens out back you can gaze at the 46-foot-high *campanario* (bell tower), the mission's most distinctive feature, with five bells. Mass is celebrated on the weekends. ⊠ *10818 San Diego Mission Rd., Mission Valley* ⊹ *From I–8 east, exit and turn left on Mission Gorge Rd., then left on Twain Rd.; mission is on right* ☎ *619/281–8449* ⊕ *www.mission-sandiego.com* ▱ *$5.*

Nightlife

★ Blanco Tacos + Tequila

BARS/PUBS | Get your margarita skinny, spicy, or standard, with house-made sours and fresh-squeezed juices, at this prime new spot within Fashion Valley Mall. Don't miss Margarita Monday ($5 classic margaritas until 6 pm) or Taco Tuesday ($4 happy hour tacos until 6 pm). ⊠ *Fashion Valley Mall, 7007 Friars Rd., Mission Valley* ☎ *619/810–2931* ⊕ *www.blancotacostequila.com.*

🛍 Shopping

★ Fashion Valley

SHOPPING CENTERS/MALLS | San Diego's most upscale mall has a contemporary Mission theme, lush landscaping, and more than 200 shops and restaurants. Acclaimed retailers like Nordstrom, Neiman Marcus, Bloomingdale's, and Tiffany & Co. are here, along with boutiques from fashion darlings like Michael Kors, Tory Burch, and Ted Baker. H&M is a favorite of fashionistas in search of edgy and affordable styles. Free wireless Internet service is available throughout the mall. Select "Simon WiFi" from any Wi-Fi–enabled device to log onto the network. ■**TIP**→ **If you're visiting from out of state, are a member of the military, or have a AAA membership, you can pick up a complimentary Style Pass at Simon Guest Services (located on the lower level beneath AMC Theaters near Banana Republic), which can get you savings at more than 70 of Fashion Valley's stores and restaurants.** ⊠ *7007 Friars Rd., Mission Valley* ☎ *619/688–9113* ⊕ *www.simon.com/mall/fashion-valley.*

Mission Bay and the Beaches

Mission Bay and the surrounding beaches are the aquatic playground of San Diego. The choice of activities available is astonishing, and the perfect weather makes you want to get out there and play. If you're craving downtime after all the activity, there are plenty of peaceful spots to relax and simply soak up the sunshine.

Mission Bay welcomes visitors with its protected waters and countless opportunities for fun. The 4,600-acre **Mission Bay Park** is the place for water sports like sailing, stand-up paddleboarding, and waterskiing. With 19 miles of beaches and grassy areas, it's also a great place for a picnic.

Mission Beach is a famous and lively fun zone for families and young people; if it isn't party time at the moment, it will be five minutes from now. The pathways in this area are lined with vacation homes, many for rent by the week or month.

North of Mission Beach is the college-packed party town of Pacific Beach, or "PB" as locals call it. The laid-back vibe of this surfer's mecca draws in free-spirited locals who roam the streets on skateboards and beach cruisers. The energy level peaks during happy hour, when PB's cluster of nightclubs, bars, and 150 restaurants open their doors to those ready to party.

Sights

★ Belmont Park

AMUSEMENT PARK/WATER PARK | **FAMILY** | The once-abandoned amusement park between the bay and Mission Beach Boardwalk is now a shopping, dining, and recreation complex. Twinkling lights outline the **Giant Dipper,** an antique wooden roller coaster on which screaming thrill seekers ride more than 2,600 feet of track and 13 hills (riders must be at least 4 feet, 2 inches tall). Created in 1925 and listed on the National Register of Historic Places, this is one of the few old-time roller coasters left in the United States.

Other Belmont Park attractions include miniature golf, a laser maze, video arcade, bumper cars, a tilt-a-whirl, and an antique carousel. The zip line thrills as it soars over the crowds below, while the rock wall challenges both junior climbers and their elders. ⊠ *3146 Mission Blvd., Mission Bay* ☎ *858/488–1549 for rides*

⊕ *www.belmontpark.com* ⊠ *Unlimited ride day package $32 for 48 inches and taller, $22 for under 48 inches, some attractions not included in price; individual ride tickets and other ride/attraction combo packages are also available.*

★ Crystal Pier

BEACH—SIGHT | Stretching out into the ocean from the end of Garnet Avenue, Crystal Pier is Pacific Beach's landmark. A stroll to the end of the pier will likely reveal fishermen hoping for a good catch. Surfers make catches of their own in the waves below. ⊠ *Pacific Beach* ⊕ *At end of Garnet Ave.*

★ Mission Bay Park

BEACH—SIGHT | San Diego's monument to sports and fitness, this 4,600-acre aquatic park has 27 miles of shoreline including 19 miles of sandy beaches. Playgrounds and picnic areas abound on the beaches and low, grassy hills. On weekday evenings, joggers, bikers, and skaters take over. In the daytime, swimmers, water-skiers, paddleboarders, anglers, and boaters—some in single-person kayaks, others in crowded powerboats—vie for space in the water. ⊠ *2688 E. Mission Bay Dr., Mission Bay* ⊕ *Off I–5 at Exit 22, E. Mission Bay Dr.* ☎ *858/581–7602 park ranger's office* ⊕ *www.sandiego.gov/park-and-recreation* ⊠ *Free.*

★ Mission Beach Boardwalk

BEACH—SIGHT | The cement pathway lining the sand from the southern end of Mission Beach north to Pacific Beach is always bustling with activity. Cyclists ping the bells on their beach cruisers to pass walkers out for a stroll alongside the oceanfront homes. Vacationers kick back on their patios, while friends play volleyball in the sand. The activity picks up alongside Belmont Park, where people stop to check out the action at the amusement park and beach bars. ⊠ *Mission Beach* ⊕ *Alongside sand from Mission Beach Park to Pacific Beach.*

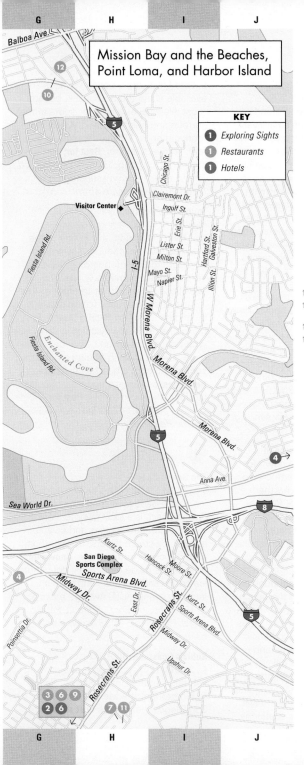

Mission Bay and the Beaches, Point Loma, and Harbor Island

KEY

- **1** *Exploring Sights*
- **1** *Restaurants*
- **1** *Hotels*

Sights ▼

1	Belmont Park	**C6**
2	Cabrillo National Monument	**C9**
3	Crystal Pier	**B2**
4	Mission Basilica San Diego de Alcalá	**J6**
5	Mission Bay Park	**F5**
6	Mission Beach Boardwalk	**C6**
7	Ocean Beach Pier	**C8**

Restaurants ▼

1	Azucar	**D9**
2	The Baked Bear	**C2**
3	Bali Hai	**G9**
4	The Cravory	**G8**
5	Hodad's	**C9**
6	Island Prime and C Level	**G9**
7	Liberty Public Market	**H9**
8	The Little Lion	**C9**
9	Point Loma Seafoods	**G9**
10	Rubio's Coastal Grill	**G1**
11	Stone Brewing World Bistro & Gardens	**H9**
12	Sushi Ota	**G1**
13	Waterbar	**C2**

Hotels ▼

1	The Dana on Mission Bay	**E6**
2	Homewood Suites San Diego Airport Liberty Station	**G9**
3	Hyatt Regency Mission Bay Spa And Marina	**E6**
4	Pacific Terrace Hotel	**B2**
5	Paradise Point Resort & Spa	**E5**
6	The Pearl Hotel	**G9**

Beaches

Mission Beach

BEACH—SIGHT | FAMILY | With a roller coaster, arcade, and hot dog stands, this 2-mile-long beach has a carnival vibe and is the closest thing you'll find to Coney Island on the West Coast. It's lively year-round but draws a huge crowd on hot summer days. A wide boardwalk paralleling the beach is popular with walkers, joggers, skateboarders, and bicyclists. To escape the crowds, head to South Mission Beach. It attracts surfers, swimmers, and volleyball players, who often play competitive pickup games on the courts near the north jetty. The water near the Belmont Park roller coaster can be a bit rough but makes for good bodyboarding and bodysurfing. For free parking, you can try for a spot on the street, but your best bets are the two big lots at Belmont Park. **Amenities:** lifeguards; parking (no fee); showers; toilets. **Best for:** swimming; surfing; walking. ⊠ *3000 Mission Blvd., Mission Bay* ✛ *Parking near roller coaster at West Mission Bay Dr.* ⊕ *www.sandiego. gov/lifeguards/beaches/mb.shtml.*

Pacific Beach/North Pacific Beach

BEACH—SIGHT | This beach, known for attracting a young college-age crowd and surfers, runs from the northern end of Mission Beach to Crystal Pier. The scene here is lively on weekends, with nearby restaurants, beach bars, and nightclubs providing a party atmosphere. In PB (as the locals call it) Sundays are known as "Sunday Funday," and pub crawls can last all day. So although drinking is no longer allowed on the beach, it's still likely you'll see people who have had one too many. The mood changes just north of the pier at North Pacific Beach, which attracts families and surfers. Although not quite pillowy, the sand at both beaches is nice and soft, which makes for great sunbathing and sand-castle building. ■ TIP→ **Kelp and flies can be a problem on this stretch, so**

choose your spot wisely. Parking at Pacific Beach can also be a challenge. A few coveted free angle parking spaces are available along the boardwalk, but you'll most likely have to look for spots in the surrounding neighborhood. **Amenities:** food and drink; lifeguards; parking (no fee); showers, toilets. **Best for:** partiers; swimming; surfing. ⊠ *4500 Ocean Blvd., Pacific Beach* ⊕ *www.sandiego.gov/ lifeguards/beaches/pb.shtml.*

Tourmaline Surfing Park

BEACH—SIGHT | Offering slow waves and frequent winds, this is one of the most popular beaches for surfers. For windsurfing and kiteboarding, it's only sailable with northwest winds. The 175-space parking lot at the foot of Tourmaline Street normally fills to capacity by midday. Just like Pacific Beach, Tourmaline has soft, tawny-colored sand, but when the tide is in the beach becomes quite narrow, making finding a good sunbathing spot a bit of a challenge. **Amenities:** seasonal lifeguards; parking (no fee); showers; toilets. **Best for:** windsurfing; surfing. ⊠ *600 Tourmaline St., Pacific Beach.*

Restaurants

The Baked Bear

$ | BAKERY | FAMILY | This build-your-own ice cream–sandwich shop a block from Pacific Beach is a local favorite thanks to its homemade cookies and diverse array of ice-cream flavors, from birthday cake to peanut butter fudge. **Known for:** Bear Bowls made of cookies; doughnut ice cream sandwiches; long lines on summer evenings. $ *Average main: $5* ⊠ *4516 Mission Blvd., Suite C, Pacific Beach* ☎ *858/886–7433* ⊕ *www.the-bakedbear.com.*

Rubio's Coastal Grill

$ | SEAFOOD | Credited with popularizing fish tacos in the United States, Ralph Rubio brought the Mexican staple to San Diego, opening his first restaurant in Pacific Beach where it still stands today. The original beer-battered fish tacos have fried pollock topped with white sauce, salsa, and cabbage atop a corn tortilla. **Known for:** the original fish taco; Taco Tuesday deal—fish taco and a beer for $5; $7 lunch specials. $ *Average main: $10* ✉ *4504 Mission Bay Dr., Pacific Beach* ☎ *858/272–2801* ⊕ *www.rubios.com.*

★ Sushi Ota

$$ | SUSHI | One fan called it "a notch above amazing"—an accolade not expected for a Japanese eatery wedged in a strip mall in Pacific Beach. But it's a destination for lovers of high-quality, superfresh raw fish from around San Diego and abroad; reservations strongly encouraged. **Known for:** velvety hamachi belly; sea urchin specials; chef's omakase tasting menu. $ *Average main: $25* ✉ *4529 Mission Bay Dr., Pacific Beach* ☎ *858/270–5670* ⊕ *www.sushiota.com* ⊙ *No lunch Sat.–Mon.*

★ Waterbar

$$ | SEAFOOD | Occupying a prime oceanfront lot just south of Crystal Pier, the views from the raised dining room are impressive. Throw in an excellent raw bar, a wide selection of shared plates, and a buzzy bar scene and you get Waterbar's "social seafood" concept. **Known for:** late-night "Boardwalk hour" oyster specials; boozy weekend brunch; ocean views. $ *Average main: $24* ✉ *4325 Ocean Blvd., Pacific Beach* ☎ *858/888–4343* ⊕ *www.waterbarsd.com.*

🛏 Hotels

The Dana on Mission Bay

$$$ | RESORT | FAMILY | This waterfront resort, just down the road from SeaWorld, has an ideal location for active leisure travelers. **Pros:** water views; many outdoor activities; shuttle to SeaWorld. **Cons:** expensive resort fee; popular wedding venue; rooms vary in quality and view. $ *Rooms from: $289*

✉ *1710 W. Mission Bay Dr., Mission Bay* ☎ *619/222–6440, 800/445–3339* ⊕ *www.thedana.com* ⇄ *271 rooms* ⦿ *No meals.*

Hyatt Regency Mission Bay Spa and Marina

$$$ | RESORT | FAMILY | This modern property has many desirable amenities, including balconies with excellent views of the garden, bay, ocean, or swimming pool courtyard. **Pros:** proximity to water sports; 120-foot waterslides in pools, plus kiddie slide; several suite configurations good for families. **Cons:** daily resort fee; not centrally located; some areas in need of updates. $ *Rooms from: $299* ✉ *1441 Quivira Rd., Mission Bay* ☎ *619/224–1234, 800/233–1234* ⊕ *www.missionbay.regency.hyatt.com* ⇄ *429 rooms* ⦿ *No meals.*

Pacific Terrace Hotel

$$$$ | RESORT | Travelers love this terrific beachfront hotel and the ocean views from most rooms; it's a perfect place for watching sunsets over the Pacific. **Pros:** beach views; large rooms; friendly service. **Cons:** busy and sometimes noisy area; expensive in peak season; resort fee. $ *Rooms from: $569* ✉ *610 Diamond St., Pacific Beach* ☎ *858/581–3500, 800/344–3370* ⊕ *www.pacificterrace.com* ⇄ *73 rooms* ⦿ *No meals.*

Paradise Point Resort & Spa

$$$ | RESORT | FAMILY | Minutes from SeaWorld but hidden in a quiet part of Mission Bay, the beautiful landscape of this 44-acre resort offers plenty of space for families to play and relax. **Pros:** water views; five pools; good service. **Cons:** not centrally located; motel-thin walls; parking and resort fees. $ *Rooms from: $296* ✉ *1404 Vacation Rd., Mission Bay* ☎ *858/274–4630, 800/344–2626* ⊕ *www.paradisepoint.com* ⇄ *462 rooms* ⦿ *No meals.*

Nightlife

BARS

★ The Grass Skirt

BARS/PUBS | Accessed through a false freezer door inside Good Time Poke, this speakeasy-styled tiki bar serves a wide selection of rum-based tropical cocktails in delightfully kitsch surroundings. The Polynesian-inspired menu features shareable poke and pupus, but call ahead to reserve a table—this hidden gem is no secret! ✉ *910 Grand Ave., Pacific Beach* ☎ *858/412–5237* ⊕ *www.thegrassskirt.com.*

JRDN

BARS/PUBS | This contemporary lounge (pronounced "Jordan") occupies the ground floor of Pacific Beach's chicest boutique hotel, Tower23, and offers a more sophisticated vibe in what is a very party-happy neighborhood. Sleek walls of windows and an expansive patio overlook the boardwalk. ✉ *723 Felspar St., Pacific Beach* ☎ *858/270–2323* ⊕ *www.t23hotel.com.*

Activities

DIVING

Scuba San Diego

SCUBA DIVING | This center is well regarded for its top-notch instruction and certification programs, as well as for guided dive tours. Scuba Adventure classes for non-certified divers are held daily in Mission Bay, meeting near Mission Point. Trips for certified divers depart from La Jolla and include dives to kelp reefs in La Jolla Cove, and night diving at La Jolla Canyon. They also have snorkeling tours to La Jolla's Sea Caves. ✉ *San Diego Hilton Hotel, 1775 E. Mission Bay Dr., Mission Bay* ☎ *619/260–1880* ⊕ *www.scubasandiego.com* ✉ *From $70* ☞ *Scuba Adventure meeting point is 2615 Bayside La. in South Mission Bay, near Mission Point.*

SURFING

Cheap Rentals

SURFING | One block from the boardwalk, this place has good daily and weekly prices for surfboards, paddleboards, kayaks, snorkel gear, skateboards, coolers, umbrellas, chairs, and bike rentals, including beach cruisers, tandems, hybrids, and two-wheeled baby carriers. Kids bikes are also available. Demand is high during the busy season (May through September) so call to reserve equipment ahead of time. ✉ *3689 Mission Blvd., Mission Beach* ☎ *858/488–9070, 800/941–7761* ⊕ *www.cheap-rentals.com* ✉ *From $7/hr.*

WATER SPORTS

Mission Bay Aquatic Center

BOATING | **FAMILY** | The world's largest instructional waterfront facility offers lessons in wakeboarding, sailing, surfing, waterskiing, rowing, kayaking, and windsurfing. Equipment rental is also available, but the emphasis is on instruction, and most rentals require a minimum two-hour orientation lesson before you can set out on your own. Reservations are recommended, particularly during the summer. Skippered keelboats and boats for waterskiing or wakeboarding can be hired with reservations. Free parking is available. ✉ *1001 Santa Clara Pl., Mission Beach* ☎ *858/488–1000* ⊕ *www.mbaquaticcenter.com.*

★ Seaforth Boat Rentals

BOATING | The Mission Bay outpost of this popular rental company offers a wide variety of motorized and nonmotorized craft. Jet Skis, SUPs, kayaks, and fishing skiffs are available alongside sailboats and powerboats of all sizes. For added relaxation, charter a skippered pontoon party boat, some with waterslides for added fun. ✉ *1641 Quivira Rd., Mission Bay* ☎ *888/834–2628* ⊕ *www.seaforthboatrental.com.*

La Jolla

La Jolla (pronounced La Hoya) means "the jewel" in Spanish and appropriately describes this small, affluent village and its beaches. Some beautiful coastline can be found here, as well as an elegant upscale atmosphere.

Sights

Birch Aquarium at Scripps

ZOO | FAMILY | Affiliated with the world-renowned Scripps Institution of Oceanography, this excellent aquarium sits at the end of a signposted drive leading off North Torrey Pines Road and has sweeping views of La Jolla coast below. More than 60 tanks are filled with colorful saltwater fish, and a 70,000-gallon tank simulates a La Jolla kelp forest. A special exhibit on sea horses features several examples of the species, plus mesmerizing sea dragons and a sea horse nursery. Besides the fish themselves, attractions include interactive educational exhibits based on the institution's ocean-related research and a variety of environmental issues. ✉ *2300 Expedition Way, La Jolla* ☎ *858/534–3474* ⊕ *www.aquarium.ucsd. edu* 🖃 *$19.50.*

San Diego-La Jolla Underwater Park Ecological Reserve

BODY OF WATER | Four habitats across 6,000 acres make up this underwater park and ecological reserve. When the water is clear, this is a diver's paradise with reefs, kelp beds, sand flats, and a submarine canyon. Plunge deeper to see guitarfish rays, perch, sea bass, anchovies, squid, and hammerhead sharks. Snorkelers, kayakers, and stand-up paddleboarders are likely to spot sea lions, seals, and leopard sharks. The Seven La Jolla Sea Caves, 75-million-year-old sandstone caves, are at the park's edge. ■ **TIP→ While the park can be explored on your own, the best way to view it is with a professional guide.** ✉ *La Jolla* ⊹ *La Jolla Cove.*

★ Torrey Pines State Natural Reserve

NATIONAL/STATE PARK | *Pinus torreyana,* the rarest native pine tree in the United States, enjoys a 1,500-acre sanctuary at the northern edge of La Jolla. About 6,000 of these unusual trees, some as tall as 60 feet, grow on the cliffs here. The park is one of only two places in the world (the other is Santa Rosa Island, off Santa Barbara) where the Torrey pine grows naturally. The reserve has several hiking trails leading to the cliffs, 300 feet above the ocean; trail maps are available at the park station. Wildflowers grow profusely in spring, and the ocean panoramas are always spectacular. From December to March, whales can be spotted from the bluffs. When in this upper part of the park, respect the restrictions. Not permitted: picnicking, smoking, leaving the trails, dogs, alcohol, or collecting plant specimens.

You can unwrap your sandwiches, however, at Torrey Pines State Beach, just below the reserve. When the tide is out, it's possible to walk south all the way past the lifeguard towers to Black's Beach over rocky promontories carved by the waves (avoid the bluffs, however; they're unstable). **Los Peñasquitos Lagoon** at the north end of the reserve is one of the many natural estuaries that flow inland between Del Mar and Oceanside. It's a good place to watch shorebirds. Volunteers lead guided nature walks at 10 and 2 on most weekends and holidays. ✉ *12600 N. Torrey Pines Rd., La Jolla* ⊹ *N. Torrey Pines Rd. exit off I–5 onto Carmel Valley Rd. going west, then turn left (south) on Coast Hwy. 101* ☎ *858/755–2063* ⊕ *www.torreypine. org* 🖃 *Parking $15–$20, varies by day of week and by season.*

Beaches

Black's Beach

BEACH—SIGHT | The powerful waves at this beach attract world-class surfers, and the strand's relative isolation appeals

La Jolla

KEY
- Exploring Sights
- Restaurants
- Hotels

Pacific Ocean

Torrey Pines State Beach

Black's Beach

0 ___ 1 mi
0 ___ 1 km

La Jolla Cove

Children's Pool

La Jolla Shores Park

La Jolla Shores Beach

Torrey Pines Rd.

Fay Ave.

Prospect St.

Pearl St.

La Jolla Blvd.

Marine Street Beach

Windansea Beach

Hermosa Terrace Park

La Jolla Natural Park

LA JOLLA

La Jolla Country Culb

Nautilus St.

La Mesa Dr.

THE MUIRLANDS

Genesee Ave.

UCSD Park

University of California San Diego (UCSD)

N Torrey Pines Rd.

Torrey Pines Rd.

La Jolla Scenic Dr. N.

Gilman Dr.

La Jolla Pkwy.

Via Capri

Soledad Natural Park

Soledad Fwy. 52

ROSE CANYON

Rose Creek

805

805

5

5

5

5

Sights ▼
1 Birch Aquarium at Scripps................... **D4**
2 Black's Beach............**C2**
3 La Jolla Cove............. **B5**
4 La Jolla Shores **C5**
5 San Diego - La Jolla Underwater Park Ecological Reserve......**C5**
6 Torrey Pines State Natural Reserve **C1**
7 Windansea Beach...... **B7**

Restaurants ▼
1 A.R. Valentien **D1**
2 El Pescador Fish Market **B6**
3 George's at the Cove ... **B5**
4 Piatti La Jolla.............**C5**

Hotels ▼
1 Grande Colonial......... **B6**
2 La Valencia Hotel **B5**
3 The Lodge at Torrey Pines **D1**

to nudist nature lovers (although by law nudity is prohibited) as well as gays and lesbians. Backed by 300-foot-tall cliffs whose colors change with the sun's angle, Black's can be accessed from Torrey Pines State Beach to the north, or by a narrow path descending the cliffs from Torrey Pines Glider Port. Beware the city has posted a "do not use" sign there because the cliff trails are unmaintained and highly dangerous so use at your own risk. If you plan to access Black's from the beaches to the north or south, do so at low tide. High tide and waves can restrict access. Strong rip currents are common—only experienced swimmers should take the plunge. Lifeguards patrol the area only between spring break and mid-October. Also keep your eyes peeled for the hang gliders and paragliders who ascend from atop the cliffs. Parking is available at the Glider Port and Torrey Pines State Beach. **Amenities:** none. **Best for:** solitude; nudists; surfing. ⊠ *Between Torrey Pines State Beach and La Jolla Shores, La Jolla ⊹ 2 miles south of Torrey Pines State Beach parking lot* ⊕ *www.sandiego.gov/lifeguards/beaches/blacks.shtml.*

★ La Jolla Cove

BEACH—SIGHT | FAMILY | This shimmering blue-green inlet surrounded by cliffs is what first attracted everyone to La Jolla, from Native Americans to the glitterati. "The Cove," as locals refer to it, beyond where Girard Avenue dead-ends into Coast Boulevard, is marked by towering palms that line a promenade where people strolling in designer clothes are as common as Frisbee throwers. Ellen Browning Scripps Park sits atop cliffs formed by the incessant pounding of the waves and offers a great spot for picnics with a view. The Cove has beautiful white sand that is a bit course near the water's edge, but the beach is still a great place for sunbathing and lounging. At low tide, the pools and cliff caves are a destination for explorers. With visibility at 30-plus feet, this is the best place in San Diego for snorkeling, where bright-orange Garibaldi

fish and other marine life populate the waters of the **San Diego–La Jolla Underwater Park Ecological Reserve.** From above water, it's not uncommon to spot sea lions and birds basking on the rocks, or dolphin fins just offshore. The cove is also a favorite of rough-water swimmers, while the area just north is best for kayakers wanting to explore the Seven La Jolla Sea Caves. **Amenities:** lifeguards; showers; toilets. **Best for:** snorkeling; swimming; walking. ⊠ *1100 Coast Blvd., east of Ellen Browning Scripps Park, La Jolla* ⊕ *www.sandiego.gov/lifeguards/beaches/cove.*

La Jolla Shores

BEACH—SIGHT | FAMILY | This is one of San Diego's most popular beaches due to its wide sandy shore, gentle waves, and incredible views of La Jolla Peninsula. There's also a large grassy park, and adjacent to La Jolla Shores lies the **San Diego-La Jolla Underwater Park Ecological Reserve**, 6,000 acres of protected ocean bottom and tide lands, bordered by the Seven La Jolla Sea Caves. The white powdery sand at La Jolla Sands is some of San Diego's best, and several surf and scuba schools teach here. Kayaks can also be rented nearby. A concrete boardwalk parallels the beach, and a boat launch for small vessels lies 300 yards south of the lifeguard station at Avenida de Playa. Arrive early to get a parking spot in the lot near Kellogg Park at the foot of Calle Frescota. Street parking is limited to one or two hours. **Amenities:** lifeguards; parking (no fee); showers; toilets. **Best for:** surfing; swimming; walking. ⊠ *8200 Camino del Oro, in front of Kellogg Park, La Jolla ⊹ 2 miles north of downtown La Jolla* ⊕ *www.sandiego.gov/lifeguards/beaches/shores.shtml.*

★ Windansea Beach

BEACH—SIGHT | With its rocky shoreline and strong shore break, Windansea stands out among San Diego beaches for its dramatic natural beauty. It's one of the best surf spots in San Diego County. Professional surfers love the unusual

A surfer prepares to head out before sunset at La Jolla's Torrey Pines State Beach and Reserve.

A-frame waves the reef break here creates. Although the large sandstone rocks that dot the beach might sound like a hindrance, they actually serve as protective barriers from the wind, making this one of the best beaches in San Diego for sunbathing. The beach's palm-covered surf shack is a protected historical landmark, and a seat here at sunset may just be one of the most romantic spots on the West Coast. The name Windansea comes from a hotel that burned down in the late 1940s. You can usually find nearby street parking. **Amenities:** seasonal lifeguards; toilets. **Best for:** sunset; surfing; solitude. ✉ *Neptune Pl. at Nautilus St., La Jolla* ⊕ *www.sandiego.gov/lifeguards/beaches/windan.shtml.*

🍴 Restaurants

★ A.R. Valentien

$$$$ | **AMERICAN** | Champions of in-season, fresh-today produce, the chefs at this cozy room in the luxurious, Craftsman-style Lodge at Torrey Pines have made A.R. Valentin one of San Diego's

top fine dining destinations. **Known for:** red-wine braised short rib; creamy chicken liver pâté; smooth dirty martinis. $ *Average main: $45* ✉ *The Lodge at Torrey Pines, 11480 N. Torrey Pines Rd., La Jolla* ☎ *858/777–6635* ⊕ *www.arvalentien.com.*

El Pescador Fish Market

$ | **SEAFOOD** | This bustling fish market and café in the heart of La Jolla Village has been popular with locals for its super-fresh fish for more than 30 years. Order the char-grilled, locally caught halibut, swordfish, or yellowtail on a toasted torta roll to enjoy in-house or to go for an oceanfront picnic at nearby La Jolla Cove. **Known for:** clam chowder; bustling on-site fish market; daily-caught cuts to go. $ *Average main: $15* ✉ *634 Pearl St., La Jolla* ☎ *858/456–2526* ⊕ *www.elpescadorfishmarket.com.*

★ George's at the Cove

$$$$ | **AMERICAN** | La Jolla's ocean-view destination restaurant includes three distinct levels: California Modern on the bottom floor, the Level2 bar in the

middle, and Ocean Terrace on the roof. At the sleek main dining room, open only for dinner, give special consideration to the legendary "fish tacos" and the six-course chef's tasting menu; for a more casual and inexpensive lunch or dinner option, head to the outdoor-only Ocean Terrace for spectacular views; for unique craft cocktails, like the "La Jolla" chilled with seaweed-laced ice cubes, and a seasonal happy hour with small bites, cocktails, beer, and wine, it's the Level2 lounge. **Known for:** beef tartare with 67-degree egg; excellent ocean views; attention to detail for special occasion dinners. ⑤ *Average main: $37 ⊠ 1250 Prospect St., La Jolla ☎ 858/454–4244 ⊕ www. georgesatthecove.com.*

★ Piatti La Jolla

$$ | MODERN ITALIAN | FAMILY | Blocks from the beach in La Jolla Shores, this comfortably modern dining room and shaded patio hits all the right notes—affordable, polished, and family-friendly. From lunch through close, it bustles with regulars from the neighborhood and visitors from around the world who are guided through the extensive Italian menu by the professional staff, some of whom have worked here for decades. **Known for:** stone-hearth oven pizza; tree-covered patio; house-made ravioli. ⑤ *Average main: $18 ⊠ 2182 Av. de la Playa, La Jolla ☎ 858/454–1589 ⊕ www.piatti.com.*

Hotels

★ Grande Colonial

$$$$ | HOTEL | This white wedding cake–style hotel in the heart of La Jolla Village has ocean views and charming European details that include chandeliers, mahogany railings, a wooden elevator, crystal doorknobs, and French doors. **Pros:** great location; superb restaurant; no resort fees. **Cons:** somewhat busy street; no fitness center; valet parking only. ⑤ *Rooms from: $369 ⊠ 910 Prospect St., La Jolla ☎ 888/828–5498 ⊕ www.thegrandecolonial.com ⤵ 93 rooms ⑩ No meals.*

La Valencia Hotel

$$$$ | HOTEL | This pink Spanish-Mediterranean confection drew Hollywood film stars in the 1930s and '40s with its setting and views of La Jolla Cove; now it draws the Kardashians. **Pros:** upscale rooms; views; near beach. **Cons:** standard rooms are tiny; lots of traffic outside; strange layout. ⑤ *Rooms from: $449 ⊠ 1132 Prospect St., La Jolla ☎ 858/454–0771 ⊕ www.lavalencia.com ⤵ 114 rooms ⑩ No meals.*

★ The Lodge at Torrey Pines

$$$$ | RESORT | Best known for its two 18-hole championship golf courses, this beautiful Craftsman-style lodge sits on a bluff between La Jolla and Del Mar with commanding coastal views, excellent service, a blissful spa, and the upscale A.R. Valentien restaurant (named after a San Diego plein air artist of the early 1900s), which serves farm-to-table California cuisine. **Pros:** spacious upscale rooms; remarkable service; adjacent the famed Torrey Pines Golf Course; warm decor with Craftsman accents and hardwoods. **Cons:** not centrally located; expensive; $30 daily parking fee. ⑤ *Rooms from: $379 ⊠ 11480 N. Torrey Pines Rd., La Jolla ☎ 858/453–4420, 888/826–0224 ⊕ www.lodgetorreypines. com ⅄ Two 18-hole championship golf courses ⤵ 170 rooms ⑩ No meals.*

🎭 Performing Arts

★ La Jolla Playhouse

THEATER | Under the artistic direction of Christopher Ashley, the playhouse presents exciting and innovative plays and musicals on three stages. Many Broadway shows—among them *Memphis, Come From Away, Tommy,* and *Jersey Boys*—have previewed here before their East Coast premieres. Its Without Walls program also ensures that the productions aren't limited to the playhouse, having put on site-specific shows in places like outdoor art spaces, cars, and even the ocean. ⊠ *University* of California at San Diego, 2910 La Jolla Village Dr., La Jolla ☎ 858/550–1010 ⊕ www.lajollaplayhouse.org.

Activities

BIKING

Route S21 (*Coast Highway 101*)

BICYCLING | On many summer days, Route S21, more commonly known as "the 101," from La Jolla to Oceanside looks like a freeway for cyclists. About 24 miles long, it's easily the most popular and scenic bike route around, never straying far from the beach. Although the terrain is fairly easy, the long, steep Torrey Pines grade is famous for weeding out the weak. Another Darwinian challenge is dodging slow-moving pedestrians and cars pulling over to park in towns like Encinitas and Del Mar. ☒ La Jolla.

GOLF

★ Torrey Pines Golf Course

GOLF | Due to its cliff-top location overlooking the Pacific and its classic championship holes, Torrey Pines is one of the best public golf courses in the United States. The course was the site of the 2008 U.S. Open and has been the home of the Farmers Insurance Open since 1968. The par-72 South Course, redesigned by Rees Jones in 2001, receives rave reviews from touring pros; it is longer, more challenging, and more expensive than the North Course. Tee times may be booked from 8 to 90 days in advance (*858/552–1662*) and are subject to an advance booking fee ($45). ☒ 11480 N. Torrey Pines Rd., La Jolla ☎ 858/452–3226, 800/985–4653 ⊕ www.torreypinesgolfcourse.com 🎫 South: $202 weekdays, $252 weekends. North: $110 weekdays, $138 weekends; $40 for golf cart 🏌 South: 18 holes, 7227 yards, par 72. North: 18 holes, 7258 yards, par 72.

HIKING AND NATURE TRAILS

Los Peñasquitos Canyon Preserve

HIKING/WALKING | Trails at this inland park north of Mira Mesa accommodate equestrians, runners, walkers, and cyclists as well as leashed dogs. Look at maps for trails specific to bikes and horses. A 7-mile loop passes a small waterfall among large volcanic rock boulders—it's an unexpected oasis amid the arid valley landscape. ☒ 12020 Black Mountain Rd., Rancho Peñasquitos ✛ From I–15, exit Mercy Rd., and head west to Black Mountain Rd.; turn right then left at first light; follow road to Ranch House parking lot ☎ 858/484–7504 ⊕ www.sdparks.org.

Torrey Pines State Reserve

HIKING/WALKING | Hikers and runners will appreciate this park's many winning features: switchback trails that descend to the sea, an unparalleled view of the Pacific, and a chance to see the Torrey pine tree, one of the rarest pine breeds in the United States. The reserve hosts guided nature walks as well. Dogs and food are prohibited at the reserve. Parking is $15–$20, depending on day and season. ☒ 12600 N. Torrey Pines Rd., La Jolla ✛ Exit I–5 at Carmel Valley Rd. and head west toward Coast Hwy. 101 until you reach N. Torrey Pines Rd.; turn left. ☎ 858/755–2063 ⊕ www.torreypine.org 🎫 Parking $15–$20.

KAYAKING

Hike Bike Kayak Adventures

KAYAKING | This shop offers several kayak tours, from easy excursions in La Jolla Cove that are well suited to families and beginners to more advanced jaunts. Tours include kayaking the caves off La Jolla coast, and whale-watching (from a safe distance) December through March. Tours last two to three hours and require a minimum of four people. ☒ 2222 Av. de la Playa, La Jolla ☎ 858/551–9510 ⊕ www.hikebikekayak.com 🎫 From $50.

SURFING
★ Surf Diva Surf School

SURFING | Check out clinics, surf camps, and private lessons especially formulated for girls and women. Most clinics and trips are for women only, but there are some coed options. Guys can also book group or private lessons from the nationally recognized staff. Surf Diva is also home to a boutique that sells surf and stand-up paddleboard equipment. They also offer surf retreats in Costa Rica. ✉ *2160 Ave. de la Playa, La Jolla* ☎ *858/454–8273* ⊕ *www.surfdiva.com* ✉ *Group lessons $65; private lessons $90.*

Point Loma

The hilly peninsula of Point Loma curves west and south into the Pacific and provides protection for San Diego Bay. Its high elevations and sandy cliffs provide incredible views, and make Point Loma a visible local landmark. Its maritime roots are evident, from its longtime ties to the U.S. Navy to its bustling sportfishing and sailing marinas. The funky community of Ocean Beach coexists alongside the stately homes of Sunset Cliffs and the honored graves at Fort Rosecrans National Cemetery.

At the northern end of Point Loma lies the chilled-out, hippyesque town of Ocean Beach, commonly referred to as "OB." The main thoroughfare of this funky neighborhood is dotted with dive bars, coffeehouses, surf shops, and 1960s diners. OB is a magnet for everyone from surfers to musicians and artists. Fans of OB applaud its resistance to "selling out" to upscale development, whereas detractors lament its somewhat scruffy edges.

 Sights

★ Cabrillo National Monument
LIGHTHOUSE | **FAMILY** | This 166-acre preserve marks the site of the first European

visit to San Diego, made by 16th-century Spanish explorer Juan Rodríguez Cabrillo when he landed at this spot on September 15, 1542. Today the site, with its rugged cliffs and shores and outstanding overlooks, is one of the most frequently visited of all the national monuments. There's a good visitor center and useful interpretive stations along the cliff-side walkways. Highlights include the moderately difficult Bayside Trail, the Old Point Loma Lighthouse, and the tide pools. There's also a sheltered viewing station where you can watch the gray whales' yearly migration from Baja California to Alaska (including high-powered telescopes). ✉ *1800 Cabrillo Memorial Dr., Point Loma* ☎ *619/557–5450* ⊕ *www.nps. gov/cabr* ✉ *$15 per car, $5 per person on foot/bicycle, entry good for 7 days.*

Ocean Beach Pier
MARINA | This T-shaped pier is a popular fishing spot and home to the Ocean Beach Pier Café and a small tackle shop. Constructed in 1966, it is the longest concrete pier on the West Coast and a perfect place to take in views of the harbor, ocean, and Point Loma Peninsula. Surfers flock to the waves that break just below. ✉ *1950 Abbott St., Ocean Beach.*

 Beaches

Sunset Cliffs
BEACH—SIGHT | As the name would suggest, this natural park near Point Loma Nazerene University is one of the best places in San Diego to watch the sunset thanks to its cliff-top location and expansive ocean views. Some limited beach access is accessible via an extremely steep stairway at the foot of Ladera Street. Beware of the treacherous cliff trails and pay attention to warning signs. The cliffs are very unstable and several fatalities have occurred over the last few years. If you're going to make your way to the narrow beach below, it's best to go at low tide when the southern end, near Cabrillo Point, reveals tide pools teeming

with small sea creatures. Farther north the waves lure surfers, and Osprey Point offers good fishing off the rocks. Keep your eyes peeled for migrating California gray whales during the winter months. Check WaveCast (⊕ *www.wavecast. com/tides*) for tide schedules. **Amenities:** parking (no fee). **Best for:** solitude; sunset; surfing. ⊠ *Sunset Cliffs Blvd., between Ladera St. and Adair St., Point Loma* ⊕ *www.sunsetcliffs.info.*

🍴 Restaurants

★ Azucar

$ | CUBAN | For a taste of Cuba in San Diego, head to this colorful Ocean Beach bakery where owner Vivian Hernandez Jackson combines her Cuban heritage, Miami childhood, and London culinary training in breakfast and lunch offerings. Morning specialties like raspberry scones with passion fruit icing, a traditional guava-and-cheese puff pastry, and ham-and-spinach quiche can be savored with café con leche, a sweet Cuban espresso with hot milk. **Known for:** tangy, citrus-centric desserts; traditional Cuban pastries; a quick bite before shopping or hitting the beach. ⑤ *Average main: $7* ⊠ *4820 Newport Ave., Ocean Beach* ☎ *619/523–2020* ⊕ *www.iloveazucar.com* ⊗ *No dinner.*

★ The Cravory

$ | BAKERY | San Diego's best cookies come in crowd-pleasing flavors such as birthday cake, red velvet, and pancakes and bacon. There's also craft sodas, Cravory flavored milks, edible cookie dough, ice cream, and cold brew to round out your snack. **Known for:** amazing cookies; cookie-of-the-month club; ships anywhere. ⑤ *Average main: $5* ⊠ *3960 W. Point Loma Blvd., Suite G, Point Loma* ✛ *next to Souplantation* ☎ *619/795–9077* ⊕ *thecravory.com.*

★ Hodad's

$ | BURGER | FAMILY | Surfers with big appetites chow down on huge, messy burgers, fries, onion rings, and shakes at this funky, hippie-beach joint adorned with beat-up surfboards and license plates from almost every state. Don't be put off by lines out the door, they move quickly and the wait is worth it. **Known for:** legendary bacon-cheeseburgers and thick-cut onion rings; surf-shack vibe; a little sass with your burger. ⑤ *Average main: $9* ⊠ *5010 Newport Ave., Ocean Beach* ☎ *619/224–4623* ⊕ *www.hodadies.com.*

★ Liberty Public Market

$ | INTERNATIONAL | FAMILY | The city's former Naval Training Center is now home to more than 30 vendors so even the pickiest of diners will be pleased. Options include tacos and quesadillas at Cecilia's Taqueria; fried rice, pad Thai, and curries at Mama Made Thai; artisan cheeses and charcuteries at Venissimo; lavender lattes from Westbean Coffee Roasters; more than a dozen Argentinian empanadas at Parana Empanadas; and croissants, eclairs, and macarons at Le Parfait Paris. **Known for:** cuisines from around the world; lively kid- and dog-friendly patio; the best regional foods under one roof. ⑤ *Average main: $10* ⊠ *2820 Historic Decatur Rd., Liberty Station* ☎ *619/487–9346* ⊕ *www.libertypublicmarket.com.*

★ The Little Lion

$$ | MODERN AMERICAN | Amid surf shacks and hippie beach bars, this restaurant perched on stunning Sunset Cliffs feels like a hidden European bistro. The sisters who run the show come from a long line of successful local restaurateurs and have brought their passed-down expertise to the simple, healthy menu and thoughtful service. **Known for:** light, healthy breakfast fare; cozy bistro setting; flash-fried cauliflower. ⑤ *Average main: $20* ⊠ *1424 Sunset Cliffs Blvd., Ocean Beach* ☎ *619/756–6921* ⊕ *www.thelittlelioncafe.com* ⊗ *Closed Mon.; no dinner Tues., Wed., and Sun.*

★ Point Loma Seafoods

$ | SEAFOOD | FAMILY | When fishing boats unload their catch on-site, a seafood restaurant and market earns the right to boast that they offer "The Freshest Thing in Town." At first, mostly sport fishermen came here, but word got out about the just-caught fried fish on San Francisco–style sourdough bread and now locals and visitors come to enjoy bay views, sunshine, and a greatly expanded menu of seafood dishes. A friendly efficient crew takes orders for food and drinks at the counter, keeping the wait down even on the busiest days. **Known for:** San Francisco–style seafood on sourdough; dockside bay views; seafood so fresh it's right from the boat. ⓢ *Average main: $15* ✉ *2805 Emerson St., Point Loma* ☎ *619/223–1109* ⊕ *www.pointlomaseafoods.com.*

★ Stone Brewing World Bistro and Gardens

$$ | ECLECTIC | FAMILY | This 50,000 square-foot monument to beer and good food is a crowd-pleaser, especially for fans of San Diego's nationally known craft beer scene. The global menu features dishes like the Bavarian pretzel and Korean-style BBQ ribs that pair perfectly with on-tap and bottled beers from around the world and Stone's famous IPAs. **Known for:** massive outdoor patio; brew-friendly eats; Meatless Mondays. ⓢ *Average main: $22* ✉ *2816 Historic Decatur Rd., Liberty Station* ☎ *619/269–2100* ⊕ *www.stonelibertystation.com.*

Hotels

★ Homewood Suites San Diego Airport Liberty Station

$$$ | HOTEL | FAMILY | Families and business travelers will benefit from the space and amenities at this all-suites hotel. **Pros:** outstanding central location near attractions; close to paths for joggers and bikers; complimentary airport shuttle. **Cons:** breakfast area can get crowded; far from nightlife. ⓢ *Rooms from: $249* ✉ *2576 Laning Rd., Point Loma* ☎ *619/222–0500* ⊕ *www.homewoodsuites.com* ⤳ *150 suites* ❙◯❙ *Free Breakfast.*

★ The Pearl Hotel

$$$ | HOTEL | This 1960s Sportsman's Lodge received a mid-century modern makeover, turning it into a retro-chic hangout decorated with kitschy lamps and original, in-room art by local children. **Pros:** near marina; hip bar/restaurant on-site (dinner only, except for seasonal specials); "Oysters and Bubbles" Mondays with $1 oysters and $7 bubbly. **Cons:** not centrally located; one bed in rooms; noise on movie night. ⓢ *Rooms from: $233* ✉ *1410 Rosecrans St., Point Loma* ☎ *619/226–6100* ⊕ *www.thepearlsd.com* ⤳ *23 rooms* ❙◯❙ *No meals.*

🏃 Activities

★ Bayside Trail at Cabrillo National Monument

HIKING/WALKING | Driving here is a treat in itself, as a vast view of the Pacific unfolds before you. The view is equally enjoyable on Bayside Trail (2 miles round-trip), which is home to the same coastal sagebrush that Juan Rodriguez Cabrillo saw when he first discovered the California coast in the 16th century. After the hike, you can explore nearby tide pools, the monument statue, and the Old Point Loma Lighthouse. Don't worry if you don't see everything on your first visit; your entrance receipt ($15 per car) is good for seven days. ✉ *1800 Cabrillo Memorial Dr., Point Loma* ⊕ *From I–5, take Rosecrans exit and turn right on Canon St. then left on Catalina Blvd. (also known as Cabrillo Memorial Dr.); follow until end* ☎ *619/557–5450* ⊕ *www.nps.gov/cabr* 🅿 *Parking $15.*

Shelter Island

In 1950 San Diego's port director decided to raise the shoal that lay off the eastern shore of Point Loma above sea level with the sand and mud dredged up during the course of deepening a ship channel in the 1930s and '40s. The resulting peninsula, **Shelter Island,** became home to several marinas and resorts, many with Polynesian details that still exist today, giving them a retro flair. This reclaimed peninsula now supports towering palms and resorts, restaurants, and side-by-side marinas. A long sidewalk runs past boat brokerages to the hotels and marinas that line the inner shore, facing Point Loma. On the bay side, fishermen launch their boats and families relax at picnic tables along the grass, where there are fire rings and permanent barbeque grills.

 Restaurants

Bali Hai

$$ | HAWAIIAN | For more than 50 years, generations of San Diegans and visitors have enjoyed this Polynesian-themed icon with its stunning bay and city skyline views. The menu is a fusion of Hawaiian and Asian cuisines with standouts like the Hawaiian tuna poke, Mongolian lamb with pad Thai, and wok-fried bass. **Known for:** potent Bali Hai mai tais; Sunday brunch buffet with a DIY sundae bar; Hawaiian and Asian-themed menu. ⑤ *Average main: $25* ⊠ *2230 Shelter Island Dr., Shelter Island* ☎ *619/222–1181* ⊕ *www.balihairestaurant.com* ⊙ *No lunch Sun.*

 Nightlife

Humphrey's Concerts by the Bay

MUSIC CLUBS | From June through September this dining and drinking oasis surrounded by water hosts the city's best outdoor jazz, folk, and light-rock concert series and is the stomping ground of such musicians as the Cowboy Junkies, Kenny G, and Chris Isaak. The rest of the year the music moves indoors for first-rate jazz, blues, and more. ⊠ *2241 Shelter Island Dr., Shelter Island* ☎ *619/224–3577* ⊕ *www.humphreysconcerts.com.*

Harbor Island

Following the successful creation of Shelter Island, in 1961 the U.S. Navy used the residue from digging berths deep enough to accommodate aircraft carriers to build **Harbor Island**. Restaurants and high-rise hotels dot the inner shore of this 1½-mile-long peninsula adjacent to the airport. Restaurants and high-rise hotels dot the inner shore while the bay's shore is lined with pathways, gardens, and scenic picnic spots. On the west point, the restaurant Tom Ham's Lighthouse has a U.S. Coast Guard–approved beacon shining from its tower and a sweeping view of San Diego's bay front.

 Restaurants

Island Prime and C Level

$$$$ | MODERN AMERICAN | Two restaurants in one share this enviable spot on the shore of Harbor Island: the splurge-worthy Island Prime steak house and the relaxed C Level with a choice terrace. Both venues tempt with unrivaled views of Downtown San Diego's skyline. **Known for:** sunset views; popovers served with jalapeño jelly butter; waterfront dining. ⑤ *Average main: $39* ⊠ *880 Harbor Island Dr., Harbor Island* ☎ *619/298–6802* ⊕ *www.cohnrestaurants.com/island-prime* ⊙ *No lunch at Island Prime.*

Tom Ham's Lighthouse

$$$ | SEAFOOD | It's hard to top this longtime Harbor Island restaurant's incredible views across San Diego Bay to the Downtown skyline and Coronado Bridge. Now a new alfresco dining deck and a contemporary seafood-focused menu ensure the dining experience at this working lighthouse doesn't take a back seat to the scenery. **Known for:** bottom-less mimosa Sunday brunch; alfresco dining deck with skyline and Corona-do bridge views; fresh seafood and beer-battered cod. ⑤ *Average main: $30* ✉ *2150 Harbor Island Dr., Harbor Island* ☎ *619/291–9110* ⊕ *www.tomhamslight-house.com* ☾ *No lunch Sun.*

Nightlife

Humphrey's Concerts by the Bay

MUSIC CLUBS | From June through September this dining and drinking oasis surrounded by water hosts the city's best outdoor jazz, folk, and light-rock concert series and is the stomping ground of such musicians as the Cowboy Junkies, Kenny G, and Chris Isaak. The rest of the year the music moves indoors for first-rate jazz, blues, and more. ✉ *2241 Shelter Island Dr., Shelter Island* ☎ *619/224–3577* ⊕ *www. humphreysconcerts.com.*

Coronado

As if freeze-framed in the 1950s, Coronado's quaint appeal is captured in its old-fashioned storefronts, well-manicured gardens, and charming **Ferry Landing Marketplace.** The streets of Coronado are wide, quiet, and friendly, and many of today's residents live in grand Victorian homes handed down for generations. Naval Air Station North Island was established in 1911 on Coronado's north end, across from Point Loma, and was the site of Charles Lindbergh's departure on the transcontinental flight that preceded his famous solo flight across the Atlantic. Coronado's long relationship with the U.S. Navy and its desirable real estate have made it an enclave for military personnel; it's said to have more retired admirals per capita than anywhere else in the United States.

Coronado is accessible via the arching blue 2.2-mile-long San Diego–Coronado Bay Bridge, which offers breathtaking views of the harbor and Downtown. Alternatively, pedestrians and bikes can reach Coronado via the popular ferry service. Bus 904 meets the ferry and travels as far as Silver Strand State Beach. Bus 901 runs daily between the Gaslamp Quarter and Coronado.

Sights

Coronado Ferry Landing

STORE/MALL | FAMILY | This collection of shops at Ferry Landing is on a smaller scale than the Embarcadero's Seaport Village, but you do get a great view of the Downtown San Diego skyline. The little bay-side shops and restaurants resemble the gingerbread domes of the Hotel Del Coronado. ✉ *1201 1st St., at B Ave., Coronado* ⊕ *www.coronadoferrylanding.com.*

★ Orange Avenue

NEIGHBORHOOD | Comprising Coronado's business district and its village-like heart, this avenue is surely one of the most charming spots in Southern California. Slow-paced and very "local" (the city fights against chain stores), it's a blast from the past, although entirely up to date in other respects. The military presence—Coronado is home to the U.S. Navy Sea, Air, and Land (SEAL) forces—is reflected in shops selling military gear and places like **McP's Irish Pub,** at No. 1107. A family-friendly stop for a good, all-American meal, it's the unofficial SEALs headquarters. Many clothing boutiques, home-furnishings stores, and upscale restaurants cater to visitors with deep pockets, but you can buy plumbing supplies, too, or get a genuine military haircut at **Crown Barber Shop,** at No. 947. If you need a break, stop for a latte at the sidewalk café of **Bay Books,** San Diego's largest independent bookstore, at No. 1029. ✉ *Orange Ave., near 9th St., Coronado.*

⚐ Beaches

★ Coronado Beach

BEACH—SIGHT | FAMILY | This wide beach is one of San Diego's most picturesque thanks to its soft white sand and sparkly blue water. The historic Hotel Del Coronado serves as a backdrop, and it's perfect for sunbathing, people-watching, and Frisbee tossing. The beach has limited surf, but it's great for bodyboarding and swimming. Exercisers might include Navy SEAL teams or other military units that conduct training runs on beaches in and around Coronado. There are picnic tables, grills, and popular fire rings, but don't bring lacquered wood or pallets. Only natural wood is allowed for burning. There's also a dog beach on the north end. There's free parking along Ocean Boulevard, though it's often hard to snag a space. **Amenities:** food and drink; lifeguards; showers; toilets. **Best for:** walking; swimming. ⊠ *Ocean Blvd., between S. O St. and Orange Ave., Coronado* ✛ *From the San Diego–Coronado bridge, turn left on Orange Ave. and follow signs.*

Silver Strand State Beach

BEACH—SIGHT | FAMILY | This quiet beach on a narrow sand-spit allows visitors a unique opportunity to experience both the Pacific Ocean and the San Diego Bay. The 2½ miles of ocean side is great for surfing and other water sports while the bay side, accessible via foot tunnel under Highway 75, has calmer, warmer water and great views of the San Diego skyline. Lifeguards and rangers are on duty year-round, and there are places for biking, volleyball, and fishing. Picnic tables, grills, and firepits are available in summer, and the Silver Strand Beach Cafe is open Memorial Day through Labor Day. The beach is close to Loews Coronado Bay Resort and the Coronado Cays, an exclusive community popular with yacht owners. You can reserve RV sites ($65 beach; $50 inland) online (⊕ *www.reserveamerica.com*). Three day-use parking lots provide room for 800 cars. **Amenities:** food and drink; lifeguards; parking (fee); showers; toilets. **Best for:** walking; swimming; surfing. ⊠ *5000 Hwy. 75, Coronado* ✛ *4½ miles south of city of Coronado* ☏ *619/435–5184* ⊕ *www.parks.ca.gov/silverstrand* 🅿 *Parking $10, motor home $30.*

Restaurants

Cafe 1134

$ | CAFÉ | Locals flock to this hip mini-bistro to start the day with flavorful omelets or fresh pastries and coffee. Lunch and dinner patrons enjoy a variety of classic deli sandwiches and salads in a relaxed and friendly atmosphere. **Known for:** hearty breakfast; fresh sandwiches and salads for lunch; friendly service. ⑤ *Average main: $5* ⊠ *1134 Orange Ave., Coronado* ☏ *619/437–1134* ⊕ *www.cafe1134.net* ⊟ *No credit cards.*

Chez Loma

$$ | FRENCH | French meets Southern Californian cuisine at this charming historic Victorian home in the heart of Coronado. A favorite of locals and guests at nearby Hotel Del Coronado, the romantic bistro offers French favorites like boeuf bourguignonne and moules marinière as well as California standbys like rockfish ceviche in tomatillo sauce. **Known for:** eclectic Sunday brunch; solid dessert selection; romantic atmosphere. ⑤ *Average main: $25* ⊠ *1132 Loma Ave., Coronado* ☏ *619/435–0661* ⊘ *No lunch.*

Coronado Brewing Company

$ | AMERICAN | FAMILY | Perfect for beer lovers with kids, this popular, laid-back Coronado brewpub offers a menu that features large portions of basic bar food like burgers, sandwiches, pizza, and salads. Enjoy a brew at a pair of sidewalk terraces or belly up to the bar and a new batch being made such as the Islander Pale Ale (IPA) or Mermaid's Red Ale. **Known for:** a good selection of house-crafted beers; kids' menu; more strollers than bar stools. $ *Average main: $12* ⊠ *170 Orange Ave., Coronado* ☎ *619/437–4452* ⊕ *www.coronado-brewing.com.*

Tartine

$ | FRENCH | FAMILY | Dine any time of day at this French-inspired café a block from San Diego Bay, as breakfast commences at 6 am with house-made granola, quiche, and just-baked coffee cakes and croissants. Sandwiches, salads, and soups round out the daytime menu, while dinner highlights include the catch of the day; just be sure be sure to save room for the Paris-pretty desserts. **Known for:** Coronado's best bet for casual but satisfying fare; in-house pastries and desserts; quiche any time of the day. $ *Average main: $15* ⊠ *1106 1st St., Coronado* ☎ *619/435–4323* ⊕ *www.tartinecoronado.com.*

Hotels

★ Coronado Island Marriott Resort & Spa

$$$$ | RESORT | FAMILY | Near San Diego Bay, this snazzy hotel has rooms with great Downtown skyline views. **Pros:** spectacular views; on-site spa; close to water taxis. **Cons:** not in downtown Coronado; resort fee; expensive self-parking. $ *Rooms from: $329* ⊠ *2000 2nd St., Coronado* ☎ *619/435–3000* ⊕ *www.marriott.com/hotels/travel/sanci-coronado-island-marriott-resort-and-spa* ⊃ *300 rooms* ⦿ *No meals.*

★ Hotel Del Coronado

$$$$ | RESORT | FAMILY | As much of a draw today as it was when it opened in 1888, the Victorian-style "Hotel Del" is always alive with activity, as guests—including U.S. presidents and celebrities—and tourists marvel at the fanciful architecture and ocean views. **Pros:** 17 on-site shops; on the beach; well-rounded spa. **Cons:** some rooms are small; expensive dining; hectic public areas. $ *Rooms from: $425* ⊠ *1500 Orange Ave., Coronado* ☎ *800/468–3533, 619/435–6611* ⊕ *www.hoteldel.com* ⊃ *757 rooms* ⦿ *No meals.*

Loews Coronado Bay Resort

$$$$ | RESORT | FAMILY | You can park your boat at the 80-slip marina of this romantic retreat set on a secluded 15-acre peninsula on the Silver Strand. **Pros:** great restaurants; lots of activities; all rooms have furnished balconies with water views. **Cons:** far from anything; confusing layout; not ideal for couples. $ *Rooms from: $349* ⊠ *4000 Coronado Bay Rd., Coronado* ☎ *619/424–4000, 800/815–6397* ⊕ *www.loewshotels.com/coronado-bay-resort* ⊃ *439 rooms* ⦿ *No meals.*

★ 1906 Lodge at Coronado Beach

$$$$ | B&B/INN | Smaller but no less luxurious than the sprawling beach resorts of Coronado, this lodge—whose name alludes to the main building's former life as a boardinghouse built in 1906—welcomes couples for romantic retreats two blocks from the ocean. **Pros:** most suites feature Jacuzzi tubs, fireplaces, and porches; historic property; free underground parking. **Cons:** too quiet for families; no pool; limited on-site dining options. $ *Rooms from: $329* ⊠ *1060 Adella Ave., Coronado* ☎ *619/437–1900, 866/435–1906* ⊕ *www.1906lodge.com* ⊃ *17 rooms* ⦿ *Free Breakfast.*

⬤ Shopping

SHOPPING CENTER

★ Hotel Del Coronado

SHOPPING CENTERS/MALLS | At the gift shops within the peninsula's main historic attraction, you can purchase sportswear, designer handbags, jewelry, and antiques. **Babcock & Story Emporium** carries an amazing selection of home decor items, garden accessories, and classy gifts. **Blue Octopus** is a children's store featuring creative toys, gifts, and apparel. **Spreckels Sweets & Treats** offers old-time candies, freshly made fudge, and decadent truffles. **Kate's** has designer fashions and accessories, while **Brady's for Men,** with its shirts and sport coats, caters to well-dressed men. **Crown Jewels Coronado** features fine jewelry, some inspired by the sea. ⊠ *1500 Orange Ave., Coronado* ☎ *619/435–6611* ⊕ *www.hoteldel.com/ coronado-shopping.*

Activities

BIKING
Holland's Bicycles

BICYCLING | This is a great bike rental source on Coronado Island, so you can ride the Silver Strand Bike Path on an electric bike, beach cruiser, road bike, or tandem. ⊠ *977 Orange Ave., Coronado* ☎ *619/435–3153* ⊕ *www.hollandsbicy-cles.com* ⊠ *From $25.*

PALM SPRINGS

Updated by
Cheryl Crabtree

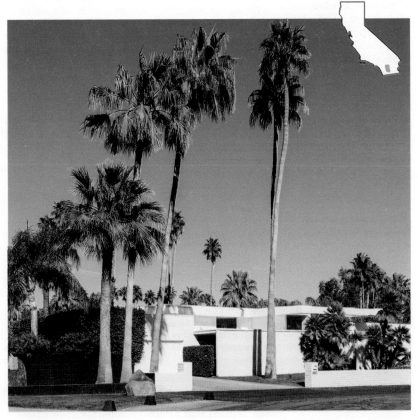

⊙ **Sights**
★★★★★

🍴 **Restaurants**
★★★★☆

🛏 **Hotels**
★★★★★

🛍 **Shopping**
★☆☆☆☆

🍸 **Nightlife**
★☆☆☆☆

WELCOME TO PALM SPRINGS

TOP REASONS TO GO

★ **Year-round sunshine:** The Palm Springs area has 350 days of sun each year, and the weather is usually ideal for playing one of the area's more than 100 golf courses.

★ **Spa under the stars:** Many resorts and small hotels now offer after-dark spa services, including outdoor soaks and treatments you can savor while sipping wine under the clear, starry sky.

★ **Personal pampering:** The resorts here have it all, beautifully appointed rooms packed with amenities, professional staffs, sublime spas, and delicious dining options.

★ **Divine desert scenery:** You'll probably spend a lot of time taking in the gorgeous 360-degree natural panorama, a flat desert floor surrounded by 10,000-foot mountains rising into a brilliant blue sky.

★ **The Hollywood connection:** The Palm Springs area has more celebrity ties than any other resort community. So keep your eyes open for your favorite star.

The Palm Springs resort area is within the Colorado Desert, on the western edge of the Coachella Valley. The area holds seven cities strung out along Highway 111, with Palm Springs at the northwestern end of the strip and Indio at the southeastern end. North of Palm Springs is Desert Hot Springs. Northeast the towns of the Morongo Valley stand along Twentynine Palms Highway, which leads to Joshua Tree National Park. Head south on Highway 86 from Indio to reach Anza-Borrego Desert State Park and the Salton Sea.

1 Palm Springs. A mid-century modern vibe and many restaurants, bars, and galleries line the avenues of Palm Springs. Hiking trails and an aerial tramway lead from the desert floor up to the San Jacinto mountain peaks.

2 Rancho Mirage. An elegant, upscale residential community, Rancho Mirage has resorts, golf courses and gated estates. A main draw here is Annenberg Retreat at Sunnylands, a grand garden estate open to the public for tours.

3 Palm Desert. The mile-long El Paseo shopping and restaurant district is the heart of Palm Desert, a peaceful community also known for its challenging golf

courses and the Living Desert Zoo and Gardens.

4 Indian Wells. Exclusive Indian Wells hosts major golf and tennis tournaments at posh resorts, where spas and upscale restaurants pamper players and spectators alike.

5 La Quinta. Coachella Valley's first golf course opened at La Quinta in 1920 and morphed into a quaint town alongside a sprawling resort and club with multiple courses.

6 Indio. The date capital of the nation, Indio lures visitors with date shakes and date palm fields.

7 Desert Hot Springs. A concentrated network of hot mineral springs flows through Desert Hot Springs, where visitors come to soak in the soothing waters and rejuvenate mind and body.

8 Yucca Valley. A laidback roadside city, Yucca Valley is a convenient stop on the way to Joshua Tree National Park. In nearby Pioneertown, Pappy and Harriet's Pioneertown Palace serves classic Western food and big-name musical entertainment.

9 Borrego Springs. Superb wildflower viewing and numerous nature trails are among the draws at Borrego Springs within Anza-Borrego Desert State Park.

10 Salton Sea. Nature lovers retreat to the shores of the Salton Sea, a haven for birdwatching and lakefront activities.

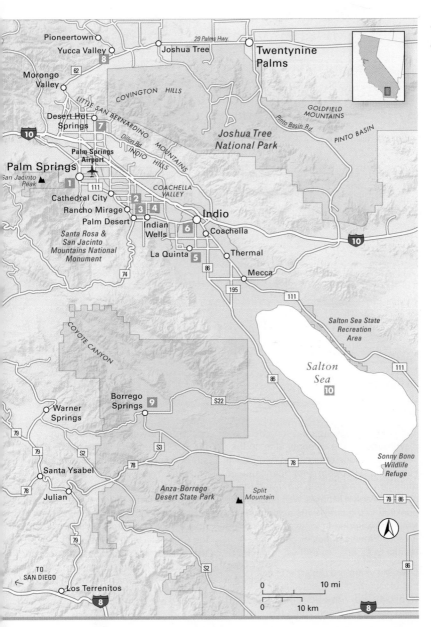

With the Palm Springs area's year-round sunshine, luxurious spas, chef-driven restaurants, and see-and-be-seen pool parties, it's no wonder that Hollywood A-listers and weekend warriors make the desert a getaway. Stretching south and east of the city along Highway 111, the desert resort towns—Cathedral City, Rancho Mirage, Palm Desert, Indian Wells, La Quinta, and Indio, along with Desert Hot Springs to the north—teem with resorts, golf courses, and shopping centers. Yucca Valley, Joshua Tree, and other artistic communities lie farther north and northeast. To the south, the wildflowers of Anza-Borrego Desert State Park herald the arrival of spring.

The Palm Springs area has long been a playground for the celebrity elite. In the 1920s Al Capone opened the Two Bunch Palms Hotel in Desert Hot Springs (with multiple tunnels to help him avoid the police); Marilyn Monroe was discovered poolside in the late 1940s at a downtown Palm Springs tennis club; Elvis and Priscilla Presley honeymooned here—the list goes on.

Over the years the desert arts scene has blossomed as spectacularly as the wildflowers of Anza-Borrego. Downtown Palm Springs is laden with urban-chic contemporary artwork (check out the Backstreet Arts District), but the surrounding rural areas are also artist enclaves: Yucca Valley, Joshua Tree, Pioneertown, and Twentynine Palms all have noteworthy galleries, art installations, and natural scenic views. Each April attention centers on Indio, where the Coachella Valley Music and Arts Festival, California's largest outdoor concert, culls droves of Angelenos, and music lovers from all over the world.

Planning

When to Go

Desert weather is best between January and April, the height of the visitor season. The fall months are nearly as lovely, but less crowded and less expensive (although autumn draws many conventions and business travelers). In summer, a popular time with European visitors, daytime temperatures may rise above 110°F (though evenings cool to the mid-70s); some attractions and restaurants close or reduce their hours during this time.

Getting Here and Around

AIR TRAVEL

Palm Springs International Airport serves California's desert communities. Air Canada, Alaska, Allegiant, American, Delta, Flair, Frontier, JetBlue, Sun Country, United, and WestJet all fly to Palm Springs, some only seasonally. Yellow Cab of the Desert and Desert City Cab serve the airport, which is about 3 miles from downtown. The fare is $3 to enter the cab and about $3.12 per mile.

AIRPORT INFORMATION Palm Springs International Airport. ⌧ *3200 E. Tahquitz Canyon Way, Palm Springs* ☎ *760/320–3882 info line, 760/318–3800* ⊕ *www.palmspringsairport.com.*

AIRPORT TRANSFERS Desert City Cab. ⌧ *3465 E. La Campana Way, Palm Springs* ☎ *760/328–3000* ⊕ *www.desertcitycab.com.* **Yellow Cab of the Desert.** ⌧ *75150 St. Charles Pl., Palm Desert* ☎ *760/340–8294* ⊕ *www.yellowcabofthedesert.com.*

BUS TRAVEL

Greyhound provides service to Palm Springs from many cities. SunBus, operated by the SunLine Transit Agency, serves the entire Coachella Valley, from Desert Hot Springs to Mecca.

BUS CONTACTS Greyhound. ☎ *800/231–2222 toll-free in U.S., 214/849–8100 from outside U.S.* ⊕ *www.greyhound.com.* **SunLine Transit Agency.** ☎ *760/343–3451* ⊕ *www.sunline.org.*

CAR TRAVEL

The desert resort communities occupy a 20-mile stretch between Interstate 10 to the east, and Palm Canyon Drive (Highway 111), to the west. The region is about a two-hour drive east of the Los Angeles area and a three-hour drive northeast of San Diego. It can take twice as long to make the trip from Los Angeles to the desert on winter and spring weekends because of heavy traffic. From Los Angeles take the San Bernardino Freeway (Interstate 10) east to Highway 111. From San Diego, Interstate 15 heading north connects with the Pomona Freeway (Highway 60), leading to the San Bernardino Freeway east.

To reach Borrego Springs from Los Angeles, take Interstate 10 east past the desert resorts area to Highway 86 south to the Borrego Salton Seaway (Highway S22) west. You can reach the Borrego area from San Diego via Interstate 8 to Highway 79 through Cuyamaca State Park. This will take you to Highway 78 in Julian, which you follow east to Yaqui Pass Road (S3) into Borrego Springs.

TAXI TRAVEL

Yellow Cab of the Desert and Desert City Cab serve the entire Coachella Valley. The fare is $3 to enter a cab and about $3.12 per mile.

TRAIN TRAVEL

The Amtrak *Sunset Limited*, which runs between Florida and Los Angeles, stops in Palm Springs.

TRAIN CONTACT Amtrak. ☎ *800/872–7245* ⊕ *www.amtrak.com.*

Health and Safety

Never travel alone in the desert. Let someone know your trip route, destination, and estimated time and date of return. Before setting out, make sure your vehicle is in good condition. Stay on main roads, and watch out for horses and range cattle.

Drink at least a gallon of water a day (three gallons if you're hiking or otherwise exerting yourself). Dress in layered clothing and wear comfortable, sturdy shoes and a hat. Keep snacks, sunscreen, and a first-aid kit on hand. If you suddenly have a headache or feel dizzy or nauseous, you could be suffering from dehydration. Get out of the sun immediately and drink plenty of water. Dampen your clothing to lower your body temperature.

Do not enter mine tunnels or shafts. Avoid canyons during rainstorms. Never place your hands or feet where you can't see them: rattlesnakes, scorpions, and black widow spiders may be hiding there.

Restaurants

An influx of talented chefs has expanded the dining possibilities of a formerly staid scene. The meat-and-potatoes crowd still has plenty of options, but you'll also find fresh seafood superbly prepared and contemporary Californian, Asian, Indian, and vegetarian cuisine, and Mexican food abounds. Most restaurants have early-evening happy hours, with discounted drinks and small-plate menus. Restaurants that remain open in July and August frequently discount deeply; others close in July and August or offer limited service. *Restaurant reviews have been shortened. For full information, visit Fodors.com.*

Hotels

In general you can find the widest choice of lodgings in Palm Springs, from tiny bed-and-breakfasts and chain motels to business and resort hotels. Massive resort properties predominate in down-valley communities, such as Palm Desert and Rancho Mirage. You can stay in the desert for as little as $100, or splurge for luxury digs at more than $1,000 a night. Rates vary widely by season and expected occupancy—a $200 room midweek can jump in price to $450 on Saturday.

Hotel and resort prices are frequently 50% cheaper in summer and fall than in winter and early spring. From January through May prices soar, and lodgings book up far in advance. You should book well ahead for stays during events such as Modernism Week or the Coachella and Stagecoach music festivals.

Most resort hotels charge a daily fee of up to $40 that is not included in the room rate; be sure to ask about extra fees when you book. Many hotels are pet-friendly and offer special services, though these also come with additional fees. Small boutique hotels and bed-and-breakfasts have plenty of character and are popular with hipsters and artsy types; discounts are sometimes given for extended stays. Casino hotels often offer good deals on lodging. Take care, though, when considering budget lodgings; other than reliable chains, they may not be up to par. *Hotel reviews have been shortened. For full information, visit Fodors.com.*

WHAT IT COSTS			
$	**$$**	**$$$**	**$$$$**
RESTAURANTS			
under $16	$16–$22	$23–$30	over $30
HOTELS			
under $120	$120–$175	$176–$250	over $250

Nightlife

Desert nightlife is concentrated and abundant in Palm Springs, with plenty of bars and clubs, but the action centers on hotel bars and lively pool parties. Arts festivals occur on a regular basis, especially in winter and spring. *Palm Springs Life* magazine (⊕ *www.palmspringslife. com*), available at hotels and visitor centers, has nightlife listings, as does the *Desert Sun* newspaper (⊕ *www. desertsun.com*).

Tours

Best of the Best Tours
GUIDED TOURS | One of the valley's largest outfits leads tours into Andreas Canyon, along the celebrity circuit, or to view windmills up close. ☎ *760/320–1365* ⊕ *www.thebestofthebesttours.com* ⊠ *From $40.*

Big Wheel Bike Tours
BICYCLING | This outfit delivers rental mountain, three-speed, and tandem bikes to area hotels. The company also conducts full- and half-day escorted on- and off-road bike tours, and also offers hiking and jeep tours to Joshua Tree National Park and the San Andreas Fault. Guides are first-rate. ⊠ *Palm Springs* ☎ *760/779–1837* ⊕ *www.bwbtours.com* ⊠ *$105 per person.*

Desert Adventures
SPECIAL-INTEREST | This outfit's three- to six-hour jeep, SUV, or van tours explore Joshua Tree National Park, Indian Canyon, Mecca Hills Painted Canyons, and the San Andreas Fault. The groups are small and the guides are knowledgeable. Departures are from Palm Desert and/or Palm Springs; hotel pickups are available. ☎ *760/324–5337* ⊕ *www.red-jeep.com* ⊠ *From $140.*

Trail Discovery Hiking Guides
GUIDED TOURS | For more than two decades, this outfit has been guiding

hikers of all abilities through the desert canyons of the Palm Springs area. Tours include Joshua Tree National Park, Indian Canyons, San Jacinto State Park, and sections of the Pacific Crest Trail. ☎ *760/413–1575* ⊕ *www.palmspringshiking.com* ⊠ *From $75.*

Palm Springs

A tourist destination since the late 19th century, Palm Springs evolved into an ideal hideaway for early Hollywood celebrities who slipped into town to play tennis, lounge poolside, attend a party or two, and unless things got out of hand, steer clear of gossip columnists. But the area blossomed in the 1930s after actors Charlie Farrell and Ralph Bellamy bought 200 acres of land for $30 an acre and opened the Palm Springs Racquet Club, which soon listed Ginger Rogers, Humphrey Bogart, and Clark Gable among its members.

Today, Palm Springs is embracing its glory days. Owners of resorts, bed-and-breakfasts, and galleries have renovated mid-century modern buildings, luring a new crop of celebs and high-powered executives. LGBTQ travelers, twenty-somethings, and families also sojourn here. Pleasantly touristy Palm Canyon Drive is packed with alfresco restaurants, many with views of the bustling sidewalk, along with indoor cafés and semi-chic shops. Farther west is the Uptown Design District, the area's shopping and dining destination. Continuing east on Palm Canyon Drive just outside downtown lie resorts and boutique hotels that host lively pool parties and house exclusive dining establishments and trendy bars.

GETTING HERE AND AROUND
Palm Springs is 90 miles southeast of Los Angeles on Interstate 10. Most visitors arrive in the Palm Springs area by car from the Los Angeles or San

Diego area via this freeway, which intersects with Highway 111 north of Palm Springs. Tahquitz Canyon Way marks the division between north and south on major streets (e.g., North and South Palm Canyon Drive). Once in Palm Springs, take advantage of the free Palm Springs Buzz, an air-conditioned pet-friendly trolley that loops around town Thursday through Sunday every 20 minutes from Via Escuela to Smoketree (⊕ *sunline.org*).

ESSENTIALS

VISITOR INFORMATION Greater Palm Springs Convention & Visitors Bureau.
⊠ *Visitor Center, 70–100 Hwy. 111, at Via Florencia, Rancho Mirage* ☎ *760/770–9000, 800/967–3767* ⊕ *www.visitgreaterpalmsprings.com.* **Palm Springs Visitors Center Downtown.** ⊠ *100 S. Palm Canyon Dr.* ⊹ *In Welwood Murray Memorial Library* ☎ *760/323–8296* ⊕ *www.visitpalmsprings.com.* **Palm Springs Visitors Center North.** ⊠ *2901 N. Palm Canyon Dr.* ☎ *760/778–8418, 800/347–7746* ⊕ *www.visitpalmsprings.com.*

 Sights

Backstreet Art District

MUSEUM | Galleries and live-work studios just off East Canyon Drive showcase the works of a number of highly acclaimed artists. Painter and ceramicist Linda Maxson, innovative digital photographer Taylor Mickle, and new and emerging artists at Galleria Marconi are among the stars here. ■TIP→ **On the first Wednesday evening of the month, the galleries are open from 5 to 8.** ⊠ *2600 S. Cherokee Way* ⊕ *www.backstreetartdistrict.com* ⊠ *Free* ⊘ *Most galleries closed Mon. and Tues.*

Elvis's Honeymoon Hideaway

HOUSE | The hideaway of the King of rock 'n' roll and his young bride, Priscilla, during their first year of marriage, this house perches on a hilltop abutting the San Jacinto Mountains. A stunning example of local mid-century modern architecture, it is rich in Elvis lore, photos, and furnishings. Docents describe the fabulous parties that took place here, attended by celebrities and local legends. Built in 1962 by Robert Alexander, one of Palm Spring's largest developers, the house consists of four perfect circles, each set on a different level. At the time, *Look* magazine described the structure as the "house of tomorrow," and indeed many of its features are standard in the homes of today. ⊠ *1350 Ladera Circle* ☎ *760/322–1192* ⊕ *www.elvishoneymoon.com* ⊠ *$35.*

★ Indian Canyons

CANYON | **FAMILY** | The Indian Canyons are the ancestral home of the Agua Caliente, part of the Cahuilla people. You can see remnants of their ancient life, including rock art, house pits and foundations, irrigation ditches, bedrock mortars, pictographs, and stone houses and shelters atop cliff walls. Short easy walks through the canyons reveal palm oases, waterfalls, and, in spring, wildflowers. Tree-shaded picnic areas are abundant. The attraction includes three canyons open for touring: Palm Canyon, noted for its stand of Washingtonia palms; Murray Canyon, home of Peninsula bighorn sheep; and Andreas Canyon, where a stand of fan palms contrasts with sharp rock formations. Ranger-led hikes to Palm and Andreas canyons are offered Friday–Sunday for an additional charge (no dogs allowed). The trading post at the entrance to Palm Canyon has hiking maps and refreshments, as well as Native American art, jewelry, and weaving. ⊠ *38520 S. Palm Canyon Dr., south of Acanto Dr.* ☎ *760/323–6018* ⊕ *www.indian-canyons. com* ⊠ *$9, ranger hikes $3* ⊘ *Closed Mon.–Thurs. July–Sept.*

Moorten Botanical Garden

GARDEN | In 1938, Chester "Cactus Slim" Moorten and his wife Patricia opened this showpiece for desert

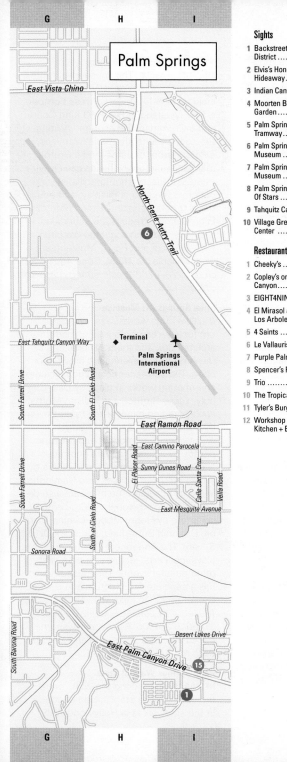

Palm Springs

East Vista Chino

North Gene Autry Trail

Terminal
Palm Springs International Airport

East Tahquitz Canyon Way

South Farrell Drive
South El Cielo Road

East Ramon Road

East Camino Parocela
El Placer Road
Sunny Dunes Road
Calle Santa Cruz
Vella Road

East Mesquite Avenue

South Farrell Drive
South El Cielo Road

Sonora Road

South Barona Road

Desert Lakes Drive
East Palm Canyon Drive

Sights ▼

1 Backstreet Art District **I9**
2 Elvis's Honeymoon Hideaway **A2**
3 Indian Canyons **D9**
4 Moorten Botanical Garden **C8**
5 Palm Springs Aerial Tramway **C1**
6 Palm Springs Air Museum **H3**
7 Palm Springs Art Museum **B4**
8 Palm Springs Walk Of Stars **C5**
9 Tahquitz Canyon **A7**
10 Village Green Heritage Center **C5**

Restaurants ▼

1 Cheeky's **C3**
2 Copley's on Palm Canyon.................... **C3**
3 EIGHT4NINE.............. **C3**
4 El Mirasol at Los Arboles **C3**
5 4 Saints **C5**
6 Le Vallauris **B5**
7 Purple Palm **C3**
8 Spencer's Restaurant... **B5**
9 Trio **C3**
10 The Tropicale............. **C4**
11 Tyler's Burgers **C5**
12 Workshop Kitchen + Bar............. **C3**

Hotels ▼

1 Ace Hotel and Swim Club **D8**
2 Alcazar Palm Springs **C3**
3 ARRIVE.................... **C1**
4 Avalon Hotel Palm Springs **C5**
5 Casa Cody **C5**
6 Colony Palms Hotel...... **C3**
7 East Canyon Hotel & Spa.............. **C2**
8 Hilton Palm Springs **C4**
9 Hotel California **C8**
10 The Hyatt Palm Springs **C4**
11 Kimpton Rowan Palm Springs Hotel **C5**
12 Korakia Pensione **B5**
13 La Maison **E8**
14 Orbit In Hotel **B5**
15 The Parker Palm Springs **I9**
16 Riviera Resort & Spa **C1**
17 The Saguaro.............. **E8**
18 Smoke Tree Ranch **F8**
19 Sparrows Lodge **E8**
20 Willows Historic Palm Springs Inn........ **B5**

plants—now numbering in the thousands—that include an ocotillo, a massive elephant tree, a boojum tree, and vine cacti. Their son Clark now operates the garden. ■TIP→ **Take a stroll through the Cactarium to spot rare finds such as the welwitschia, which originated in the Namib Desert in southwestern Africa.** ⊠ *1701 S. Palm Canyon Dr.* ☎ *760/327–6555* ⊕ *www.moortengarden.com* ⊠ *$5* ⊗ *Closed Wed.*

★ Palm Springs Aerial Tramway

VIEWPOINT | FAMILY | A trip on the tramway provides a 360-degree view of the desert through the picture windows of rotating cars. The 2½-mile ascent through Chino Canyon, the steepest vertical cable ride in the United States, brings you to an elevation of 8,516 feet in less than 20 minutes. On clear days, which are common, the view stretches 75 miles—from the peak of Mt. San Gorgonio in the north to the Salton Sea in the southeast. Stepping out into the snow at the summit is a winter treat. At the top, a bit below the summit of Mt. San Jacinto, are several diversions. Mountain Station has an observation deck, two restaurants, a cocktail lounge, apparel and gift shops, picnic facilities, a small wildlife exhibit, and a theater that screens movies on the history of the tramway and the adjacent Mount San Jacinto State Park and Wilderness. Take advantage of free guided and self-guided nature walks through the state park, or if there's snow on the ground, rent skis, snowshoes, or snow tubes. The tramway generally closes for maintenance in mid-September. ■TIP→ **Ride-and-dine packages are available in late afternoon. The tram is a popular attraction; to avoid a two-hour or longer wait, arrive before the first car leaves in the morning.** ⊠ *1 Tramway Rd., off N. Palm Canyon Dr. (Hwy. 111)* ☎ *888/515–8726* ⊕ *www.pstramway.com* ⊠ *From $26* ⊗ *Closed 2 wks in Sept. for maintenance.*

★ Palm Springs Air Museum

MUSEUM | FAMILY | This museum's impressive collection of World War II aircraft includes a B-17 Flying Fortress bomber, a P-51 Mustang, a Bell P-63 King Cobra, and a Grumman TBF Avenger. Among the cool exhibits are model warships, a Pearl Harbor diorama, and a Grumman Goose into which kids can crawl. Photos, artifacts, memorabilia, and uniforms are also on display, and educational programs take place on Saturday. Flight demonstrations are scheduled regularly. Rides in a vintage Warbird C-47 Skytrain and P-51D Mustang are also available. ⊠ *745 N. Gene Autry Trail* ☎ *760/778–6262* ⊕ *palmspringsairmuseum.org* ⊠ *$18.*

Palm Springs Art Museum

MUSEUM | This world-class art museum focuses on photography, modern architecture, and the traditional arts of the Americas. Galleries are bright and open. The permanent collection includes shimmering works in glass by Dale Chihuly, Ginny Ruffner, and William Morris. You'll also find handcrafted furniture by the late actor George Montgomery, mid-century modern architectural photos by Julius Shulman, enormous Native American baskets, and works by artists like Allen Houser, Arlo Namingha, and Fritz Scholder. The museum also displays significant works of 20th-century sculpture by Henry Moore, Marino Marina, Deborah Butterfield, and Mark Di Suvero. The Annenberg Theater presents plays, concerts, lectures, operas, and other cultural events. The museum also has a separate Architecture and Design Center at 300 S. Palm Canyon Dr. ⊠ *101 Museum Dr., off W. Tahquitz Canyon Dr.* ☎ *760/322–4800* ⊕ *www.psmuseum.org* ⊠ *$14, free Thurs. 4–8 and 2nd Sun. each month* ⊗ *Closed Wed.*

Palm Springs Walk of Stars

NEIGHBORHOOD | Along the walk, more than 300 bronze stars are embedded in the sidewalk (à la Hollywood Walk of Fame) to honor celebrities with a Palm Springs connection. Frank, Elvis, Marilyn, Dinah, Lucy, Ginger, Liz, and Liberace have all received their due. Those still around to walk the Walk and see their stars include Nancy Sinatra and Kathy Griffin. ✉ *Palm Canyon Dr., around Tahquitz Canyon Way, and Tahquitz Canyon Way, between Palm Canyon and Indian Canyon Drs.* ☎ *760/325–1577* ⊕ *www.palmsprings. com/walk-of-stars.*

Tahquitz Canyon

CANYON | On ranger-led tours of this secluded canyon on the Agua Caliente Reservation you can view a spectacular 60-foot waterfall, rock art, ancient irrigation systems, and native wildlife and plants. Tours are conducted several times daily; participants must be able to navigate 100 steep rock steps. (You can also take a self-guided tour of the 1.8-mile trail.) At the visitor center at the canyon entrance, watch a short video, look at artifacts, and pick up a map. ✉ *500 W. Mesquite Ave., west of S. Palm Canyon Dr.* ☎ *760/416–7044* ⊕ *www.tahquitzcanyon.com* 🗺 *$13* ⊘ *Closed Mon.–Thurs. July–Sept.*

Village Green Heritage Center

MUSEUM | Three small museums at the Village Green Heritage Center illustrate early life in Palm Springs. The centerpiece, the Agua Caliente Cultural Museum, traces the culture and history of the Cahuilla tribe with several exhibits. The **McCallum Adobe** and the **Cornelia White House** hold the collection of the Palm Springs Historical Society. **Ruddy's General Store Museum** is a re-creation of a 1930s general store. ✉ *219–221 S. Palm Canyon Dr.* ☎ *760/323–8297* ⊕ *www.pshistoricalsociety.org* 🗺 *Agua Caliente free, McCallum $2, Ruddy's $1* ⊘ *Closed Tues.*

🍴 Restaurants

★ Cheeky's

$ | AMERICAN | The artisanal bacon bar and hangover-halting mimosas attract legions to this breakfast and lunch joint, but brioche French toast and other favorites also contribute to the epic wait on weekends (no reservations accepted). Huevos rancheros, a gem salad with green goddess dressing, and other farm-centric dishes entice the foodie crowd. **Known for:** homemade pastries and sausages; local organic ingredients; grass-fed burger topped with house bacon. ⑤ *Average main: $13* ✉ *622 N. Palm Canyon Dr., at E. Granvia Valmonte* ☎ *760/327–7595* ⊕ *www.cheekysps. com* ⊘ *Closed Tues. No dinner.*

Copley's on Palm Canyon

$$$$ | MODERN AMERICAN | Chef Manion Copley prepares innovative cuisine in a setting that's straight out of Hollywood—a hacienda once owned by Cary Grant. Dine in the clubby house or under the stars in the garden. **Known for:** romantic patio dining; fresh seafood and meats with innovative flavors; sweet and savory herb ice creams. ⑤ *Average main: $32* ✉ *621 N. Palm Canyon Dr., at E. Granvia Valmonte* ☎ *760/327–9555* ⊕ *www.copleyspalmsprings.com* ⊘ *Closed July and Aug. No lunch.*

★ EIGHT4NINE

$$$ | AMERICAN | The dazzling interior design and eclectic Pacific Coast dishes made from scratch lure locals and visitors alike to this swank yet casual restaurant and lounge in the Uptown Design District. Sink into white patent leather chairs or comfy sofas in the lounge where you can gaze at historic celebrity photos, or choose a table in a grand corridor with a collection of private rooms, or in the outdoor patio with mountain views. **Known for:** nearly everything made from scratch; four-course chef's menu; all-day happy hour in lounge. ⑤ *Average*

main: $28 ✉ *849 N. Palm Canyon Dr.*
☎ *760/325–8490* ⊕ *eight4nine.com.*

El Mirasol at Los Arboles

$$ | MODERN MEXICAN | Chef Felipe
Castañeda owns two Mexican restaurants in Palm Springs—this one, part
of Los Arboles Hotel, is outside on a
charming patio set amid flower gardens
and shaded by red umbrellas. Castañeda prepares classic combinations of
tacos, tamales, and enchiladas, along
with specialties such as double-cooked
pork and *pollo en pipián* (chicken
with a pre-Columbian sauce made of
ground roasted pumpkin seeds and
dry chilies). **Known for:** classic Mexican
dishes; great vegetarian options; garden
setting. ⑤ *Average main: $22* ✉ *266
Via Altamira, off N. Indian Canyon Dr.*
☎ *760/459–3136* ⊕ *www.elmirasolres-
taurants.com.*

★ 4 Saints

$$$$ | CONTEMPORARY | Perched on the
seventh-floor rooftop of the Kimpton
Rowan Palm Springs, where stunning
views unfold from nearly every table,
4 Saints serves inventive farm-to-table
dishes in a slick, hipster dining room
and outdoor patio. The eclectic, globally
inspired menu focuses on small plates
and main dishes made with locally
sourced ingredients (e.g., seafood,
duck, and short ribs), intended for
sharing. **Known for:** creative and classic
cocktails; lively social vibe; stellar
seafood. ⑤ *Average main: $43* ✉ *100
W. Tahquitz Cyn. Way* ☎ *760/392–2020*
⊕ *www.4saintspalmsprings.com.*

Le Vallauris

$$$$ | FRENCH | A longtime favorite that
occupies the historic Roberson House,
Le Vallauris is popular with ladies who
lunch, all of whom get a hug from the
maître d'. The Belgian-French-inspired
menu changes daily, and each day it's
handwritten on a white board. **Known
for:** prix-fixe menus for lunch and dinner;
lovely tree-shaded garden; romantic
setting. ⑤ *Average main: $36* ✉ *385

W. Tahquitz Canyon Way, west of Palm
Canyon Dr.* ☎ *760/325–5059* ⊕ *www.
levallauris.com* ⊗ *Closed July and Aug.*

Purple Palm

$$$$ | MODERN AMERICAN | The hottest
tables in Palm Springs are those that
surround the pool at the Colony Palms
Hotel, where the hip and elite pay
homage to Purple Gang mobster Al
Wertheimer, who reportedly built the
hotel in the mid-1930s. Now it's a
casual, convivial place where you can
dine alfresco surrounded by a tropical
garden near the pool. **Known for:** craft
cocktails; happy hour and weekend
brunch; extensive international wine list.
⑤ *Average main: $32* ✉ *572 N. Indian
Canyon Dr., at E. Granvia Valmonte*
☎ *800/557–2187* ⊕ *www.colonypalms-
hotel.com.*

Spencer's Restaurant

$$$$ | MODERN AMERICAN | The swank
dining space inside the Palm Springs
Tennis Club Resort occupies a historic
mid-century modern structure. Crab
cakes, kung pao calamari, and crispy
flash-fried oysters are favorite starters.
Known for: French–Pacific Rim influences; romantic patio; elegant dining room.
⑤ *Average main: $35* ✉ *701 W. Baristo
Rd.* ☎ *760/327–3446* ⊕ *www.spencers-
restaurant.com.*

Trio

$$ | MODERN AMERICAN | The owners of
this high-energy Uptown Design District
restaurant claim that it's "where Palm
Springs eats," and it certainly seems
so on nights when the lines to get in
run deep. The menu includes home-
style staples such as Yankee pot roast,
crawfish pie, and other dishes, along
with veggie burgers and other vegetarian and gluten-free items. **Known for:**
local artwork; inventive desserts; ample
vegetarian and gluten-free options.
⑤ *Average main: $22* ✉ *707 N. Palm
Canyon Dr.* ☎ *760/864–8746* ⊕ *www.
triopalmsprings.com.*

The Tropicale

$$$ | INTERNATIONAL | Tucked onto a side-street corner, the Tropicale is a mid-century-style watering hole with a contemporary vibe. The bar and main dining room hold cozy leather booths; flowers and water features brighten the outdoor area. **Known for:** globe-trotting menu; happy hour (all night on Wednesday); weekly specials. ⑤ *Average main: $30* ⊠ *330 E. Amado Rd., at N. Calle Encilia* ☎ *760/866–1952* ⊕ *www.thetropicale. com* ⊗ *No lunch.*

★ Tyler's Burgers

$ | AMERICAN | FAMILY | Families, singles, and couples head to Tyler's for simple lunch fare that appeals to carnivores and vegetarians alike. Expect mid-20th-century America's greatest hits: heaping burgers, stacks of fries, root beer floats, milk shakes; on weekends, be prepared to wait with the masses. **Known for:** house-made cole slaw and potato salad; excellent burgers and fries; delicious shakes. ⑤ *Average main: $11* ⊠ *149 S. Indian Canyon Dr., at La Plaza* ☎ *760/325–2990* ⊕ *www.tylersburgers. com* ⊗ *Closed Sun. late May–mid-Feb. Closed mid-July–early Sept.*

Workshop Kitchen + Bar

$$$$ | AMERICAN | Chef Michael Beckman's Uptown Design District hot spot pairs high-quality California cuisine with creative cocktails in a sleek, almost utilitarian setting. The outdoor patio lures the oversize sunglasses Sunday brunch crowd, who slurp cava mimosas and artisanal cocktails; inside, the sleek concrete booths are topped with black leather cushions. **Known for:** most ingredients sourced from within a 100-mile radius; artisanal cocktails; communal seating options. ⑤ *Average main: $32* ⊠ *800 N. Palm Canyon Dr., at E. Tamarisk Rd.* ☎ *760/459–3451* ⊕ *www. workshoppalmsprings.com* ⊗ *No lunch Mon.–Sat.*

Hotels

Ace Hotel and Swim Club

$$$ | RESORT | With the hotel's vintage feel and hippie-chic decor, it would be no surprise to find guests gathered around cozy communal fire pits enjoying feel-good '60s music. **Pros:** Amigo Room has late-night dining; poolside stargazing deck; weekend DJ scene at the pool. **Cons:** party atmosphere not for everyone; limited amenities; casual staff and service. ⑤ *Rooms from: $189* ⊠ *701 E. Palm Canyon Dr.* ☎ *760/325–9900* ⊕ *www.acehotel.com/palmsprings* ⤴ *188 rooms* ⦿ *No meals.*

Alcazar Palm Springs

$$ | HOTEL | Tucked at the border of the Uptown Design District and an area known as the Movie Colony, the hip, modern, and affordable Alcazar features ample, blazing-white guest rooms that wrap around a sparkling pool; some rooms have Jacuzzis, and many have private patios or fireplaces. **Pros:** walking distance of downtown; parking on-site; bikes available. **Cons:** limited service; wall air-conditioners; resort fee. ⑤ *Rooms from: $159* ⊠ *622 N. Indian Canyon Dr.* ☎ *760/318–9850* ⊕ *www. alcazarpalmsprings.com* ⤴ *34 rooms* ⦿ *No meals.*

★ ARRIVE

$$$$ | HOTEL | During the day, sip cocktails from the indoor outdoor bar (which doubles as the reception desk), and lounge in the pool on an inflatable seahorse, or dance to a live DJ; at night, relax outside in the hot tub and socialize around the communal fire pits (half of the rooms also come with a private patio and fireplace), or cozy up in your king-size bed among tasteful modern furnishings, and wake to sunny mountain views. **Pros:** private cabanas with misting systems; great restaurant, artisanal ice-cream shop, and local coffee shop on-site; easy access to Uptown Design District shops, restaurants, galleries. **Cons:** only

king rooms available; shower offers little privacy; party scene may not suit everyone. ⑤ *Rooms from: $329* ✉ *1551 N. Palm Canyon Dr.* ☎ *760/507–1650* ⊕ *www.arrivehotels.com* ⤵ *32 rooms* ⑩ *No meals.*

Avalon Hotel Palm Springs

$$$$ | RESORT | With three pools and a spa spread over 4 acres of gardens, the upscale Avalon Hotel Palm Springs calls back to 1960s swanky, with private bungalows, lush gardens, and an emphasis on style. **Pros:** poolside cabanas; complimentary fitness classes; luxurious on-site Estrella Spa and stylish restaurant Chi Chi. **Cons:** popular wedding site. ⑤ *Rooms from: $400* ✉ *415 S. Belardo Rd.* ☎ *844/328–2566* ⊕ *www. avalonpalmsprings.com* ⤵ *79 rooms* ⑩ *No meals.*

Casa Cody

$$$$ | B&B/INN | An historic 1920s bed-and-breakfast near the Palm Springs Art Museum, Casa Cody has a retro coolness that embodies an old west feel (the founder, Harriet Cody, was Buffalo Bill's cousin). **Pros:** easy walk to restaurants, hikes, museums; relatively affordable rates for location; some rooms come with fireplaces, patios, and/or kitchens. **Cons:** old buildings; limited amenities; office closes in the early evening. ⑤ *Rooms from: $209* ✉ *175 S. Cahuilla Rd.* ☎ *760/320–9346* ⊕ *www.casacody.com* ⤵ *29 rooms* ⑩ *Breakfast.*

Colony Palms Hotel

$$$$ | HOTEL | This hotel has been a hip place to stay since the 1930s, when gangster Al Wertheimer built it to front his casino, bar, and brothel; it later became the Howard Hotel, owned by local luminaries Robert Stewart Howard (his dad owned the fabled racehorse Seabiscuit) and actress Andrea Leeds (the couple hosted a young Frank Sinatra, Elizabeth Taylor, and Liberace), and today it still attracts a younger crowd. **Pros:** rooms open to pool and gardens

in the central courtyard; attentive staff; fireplaces and whirlpool tubs in many rooms. **Cons:** high noise level outside; some rooms need updating; service sometimes inconsistent. ⑤ *Rooms from: $299* ✉ *572 N. Indian Canyon Dr.* ☎ *760/969–1800, 800/577–2187* ⊕ *www.colonypalmshotel.com* ⤵ *57 rooms* ⑩ *No meals.*

East Canyon Hotel & Spa

$$$ | B&B/INN | The vibe is social and the rooms are spacious at this classy resort whose gracious hosts welcome LGBTQ and all couples looking for romantic and relaxing getaways. **Pros:** elegant but laid-back feel; attentive service; complimentary poolside cocktails. **Cons:** long walk to downtown; grounds need sprucing up; tiny hot tub. ⑤ *Rooms from: $189* ✉ *288 E. Camino Monte Vista* ☎ *760/320–1928, 877/324–6835* ⊕ *www.eastcanyonps. com* ⤵ *15 rooms* ⑩ *Breakfast.*

Hilton Palm Springs

$$$ | HOTEL | This venerable hotel across the street from the Spa Casino and a few blocks from the main Palm Canyon dining and shopping scene has spacious rooms decorated in soft desert colors. **Pros:** a short walk to downtown strip; three dining venues; classy full-service spa. **Cons:** not right on Palm Canyon Drive; average service; many business meetings. ⑤ *Rooms from: $189* ✉ *400 E. Tahquitz Canyon Way* ☎ *760/320–6868, 855/271–3617* ⊕ *www.hiltonpalmsprings. com* ⤵ *260 rooms* ⑩ *No meals.*

★ Hotel California

$$$ | HOTEL | Expect homey accommodations for all budgets at this delightful hotel that's decked out in rustic Mexican furniture. **Pros:** comfortable design; friendly hosts; free off-street parking. **Cons:** far from downtown; property needs updating; fronts a busy road. ⑤ *Rooms from: $185* ✉ *424 E. Palm Canyon Dr.* ☎ *760/322–8855* ⊕ *www. palmspringshotelcalifornia.com* ⤵ *14 rooms* ⑩ *No meals.*

The Hyatt Palm Springs

$$$ | HOTEL | The best-situated downtown hotel in Palm Springs, the Hyatt has spacious suites where you can watch the sun rise over the city, or set behind the mountains from your bedroom's balcony. **Pros:** underground parking; restaurant plus two outdoor bar-lounges; daily sunset hour with free wine, beer, and appetizers. **Cons:** lots of business travelers; some street noise; valet parking only. $ *Rooms from: $179* ✉ *285 N. Palm Canyon Dr.* ☎ *760/322–9000* ⊕ *palmsprings. hyatt.com* ⌂ *197 suites* ⦿ *No meals.*

★ Kimpton Rowan Palm Springs Hotel

$$$$ | HOTEL | One of the newest arrivals on the downtown Palm Springs scene, the Rowan Palm Springs dazzles locals and guests (especially the under-40 set) with stunning views from myriad picture windows and a rooftop deck, and an unpretentious vibe that puts guests of all ages at ease. **Pros:** friendly, attentive service; stunning mountain and valley views; in the heart of downtown. **Cons:** rooftop pool area can get crowded; valet parking only; $35 resort fee. $ *Rooms from: $259* ✉ *100 W. Tahquitz Canyon Way* ☎ *760/904–5015, 800/532–7320* ⊕ *www.rowanpalmsprings.com* ⌂ *153 rooms* ⦿ *No meals.*

★ Korakia Pensione

$$$ | B&B/INN | The painter Gordon Coutts, best known for desert landscapes, constructed this Moroccan villa in 1924 as an artist's studio, and these days creative types gather in the main house and nearby Mediterranean-style villas, spread across 1.5 acres on both sides of the street, to soak up the spirit of that era. **Pros:** two pools; lunch and dinner available on request (fee); yoga on weekends. **Cons:** might not appeal to those who prefer standard resorts; no TVs or phones in rooms; no children under 13. $ *Rooms from: $249* ✉ *257 S. Patencio Rd.* ☎ *760/864–6411* ⊕ *www.korakia.com* ⌂ *28 rooms* ⦿ *Free Breakfast.*

La Maison

$$$ | B&B/INN | Offering all the comforts of home, this small bed-and-breakfast contains large rooms that surround the terra-cotta–tiled and very comfortable pool area, where you can spend quiet time soaking up the sun or taking a dip. **Pros:** restaurants nearby; quiet; genial hosts. **Cons:** on busy Highway 111; rooms open directly onto pool deck; some rooms on the small side. $ *Rooms from: $239* ✉ *1600 E. Palm Canyon Dr.* ☎ *760/325–1600* ⊕ *www.lamaisonpalmsprings.com* ⌂ *13 rooms* ⦿ *Breakfast.*

★ Orbit In Hotel

$$$ | B&B/INN | The architectural style of this hip inn on a quiet backstreet dates back to its 1955 opening—and nearly flat roofs, wide overhangs, glass everywhere—and the period feel continues inside. **Pros:** saltwater pool; Orbitini cocktail hour; free breakfast served poolside. **Cons:** best for couples; style not to everyone's taste; staff not available 24 hours. $ *Rooms from: $169* ✉ *562 W. Arenas Rd.* ☎ *760/323–3585, 877/996–7248* ⊕ *www.orbitin.com* ⌂ *9 rooms* ⦿ *Breakfast.*

★ The Parker Palm Springs

$$$$ | RESORT | A cacophony of color and over-the-top contemporary art assembled by New York City–based designer Jonathan Adler mixes well with the brilliant desert garden, three pools (two outdoor), fire pits, and expansive spa of this hip hotel that attracts a stylish, worldly clientele. **Pros:** celebrity clientele; on-site restaurants, bars, and spa; design-centric. **Cons:** pricey drinks and wine; a bit of a drive from downtown; resort fee ($35). $ *Rooms from: $399* ✉ *4200 E. Palm Canyon Dr.* ☎ *760/770–5000, 800/543–4300* ⊕ *www.theparkerpalmsprings.com* ⌂ *144 rooms* ⦿ *No meals.*

Riviera Resort & Spa

$$$$ | RESORT | A party place built in 1958 and renovated in 2016, the Riviera attracts young, well-heeled, bikini-clad guests who hang out around the pool by day, and

at the Bikini Bar by night. **Pros:** personal fire pits throughout the property; hip vibe; excellent spa. **Cons:** high noise level outdoors; party atmosphere; location at north end of Palm Springs. $ *Rooms from: $300* ✉ *1600 N. Indian Canyon Dr.* ☎ *760/327–8311* ⊕ *rivierapalmsprings.com* ⇨ *449 rooms* ⦿ *No meals.*

★ The Saguaro

$$ | **HOTEL** | A startling, rainbow-hued oasis—the brainchild of Manhattan-based architects Peter Stamberg and Paul Aferiat—the Saguaro caters to young, hip, pet-toting partygoers who appreciate its lively pool party scene. **Pros:** lively pool scene with weekend DJ parties; daily yoga, on-site spa, 24-hour fitness center, beach cruisers; shuttle service to downtown. **Cons:** a few miles from downtown; pool area can be noisy and crowded; $33 resort fee. $ *Rooms from: $169* ✉ *1800 E. Palm Canyon Dr.* ☎ *760/323–1711* ⊕ *thesaguaro.com* ⇨ *244 rooms* ⦿ *No meals.*

Smoke Tree Ranch

$$$$ | **RESORT** | **FAMILY** | A laid-back genteel retreat since the mid-1930s for some of the world's foremost families, including Walt Disney's, the area's most under-the-radar resort complex occupies 385 pristine desert acres surrounded by mountains and unspoiled vistas, and still provides an experience reminiscent of the Old West. **Pros:** priceless privacy; simple luxury; recreational activities like horseback riding and more. **Cons:** no glitz; limited entertainment options; family atmosphere not for everyone. $ *Rooms from: $400* ✉ *1850 Smoke Tree La.* ☎ *760/327–1221, 800/787–3922* ⊕ *www.smoketreeranch.com* ⊙ *Closed Apr.–late Oct.* ⇨ *49 cottages, includes 18 suites* ⦿ *All-inclusive.*

Sparrows Lodge

$$$ | **B&B/INN** | Rustic earthiness meets haute design at the adult-centered Sparrows, just off Palm Springs's main drag. **Pros:** unique design; intimate property; private patios. **Cons:** not family-oriented, minimum age 21; daily resort fee;

no TVs or phones in rooms. $ *Rooms from: $249* ✉ *1330 E. Palm Canyon Dr.* ☎ *760/327–2300* ⊕ *www.sparrowshotel.com* ⇨ *20 rooms* ⦿ *Breakfast.*

★ Willows Historic Palm Springs Inn

$$$$ | **B&B/INN** | A set of two adjacent opulent Mediterranean-style mansions built in the 1920s to host the rich and famous, this luxurious hillside bed-and-breakfast has gleaming hardwood and slate floors, stone fireplaces, frescoed ceilings, hand-painted tiles, iron balconies, antiques throughout, and a 50-foot waterfall that splashes into a pool outside the dining room. **Pros:** short walk to art museum, restaurants, shops; pool; expansive breakfast and afternoon wine hour. **Cons:** closed from June to September; pricey; some rooms on the small side. $ *Rooms from: $425* ✉ *412 W. Tahquitz Canyon Way* ☎ *760/320–0771* ⊕ *www.thewillowspalmsprings.com* ⇨ *17 rooms* ⦿ *Breakfast.*

Nightlife

BARS AND PUBS

Bootlegger Tiki

BARS/PUBS | Palm Springs tiki-drink traditions, especially during the two daily happy hours (4 to 6 pm and midnight to 2 am), draw loyal patrons to Bootlegger, which occupies the same space as Don the Beachcomber in the 1950s. ✉ *1101 N. Palm Canyon Dr.* ☎ *760/318–4154* ⊕ *www.bootleggertiki.com.*

★ Draughtsman

BARS/PUBS | In the Uptown Design District and part of the ARRIVE hotel, this upscale pub focuses on Palm Springs and SoCal craft beers, classic cocktails, and modern comfort food, as well as classics like chicken potpie and short rib poutine. Hang out in the contemporary indoor space with soaring ceilings and watch sports, or chill on the patio where you can play cornhole or foosball. ✉ *1501 N. Palm Canyon Dr.* ☎ *760/507–1644* ⊕ *draughtsmanpalmsprings.com.*

Palm Springs Modernism

Some of the world's most forward-looking architects designed and constructed buildings around Palm Springs between 1940 and 1970; and modernism, also popular elsewhere in California in the years after World War II, became an ideal fit for desert living, because it minimizes the separation between indoors and outdoors. See-through houses with glass exterior walls are common. Oversize flat roofs provide shade from the sun, and many buildings' sculptural forms reflect nearby landforms. The style is notable for elegant informality, clean lines, and simple landscaping.

Most obvious to visitors are three buildings that are part of the Palm Springs Aerial Tramway complex, built in the 1960s. Albert Frey, a Swiss-born architect, designed the soaring A-frame Tramway Gas Station, visually echoing the pointed peaks behind it. Frey also created the glass-walled Valley Station, from which you get your initial view of the Coachella Valley before you board the tram to the Mountain Station, designed by E. Stewart Williams.

Frey, a Palm Springs resident for more than 60 years, also designed the indoor-outdoor City Hall, Fire Station No. 1, and numerous houses. His second home, perched atop stilts on the hillside above the Palm Springs Art Museum, affords a sweeping view of the Coachella Valley through glass walls. The classy Movie Colony Hotel, one of the first buildings Frey designed in the desert, may seem like a typical 1950s motel with rooms surrounding a swimming pool now, but when it was built in 1935, it was years ahead of its time.

Donald Wexler, who honed his vision with Los Angeles architect Richard Neutra, brought new ideas about the use of materials to the desert, where he teamed up with William Cody on a number of projects, including the terminal at the Palm Springs Airport. Many of Wexler's buildings have soaring overhanging roofs, designed to provide shade from the blazing desert sun. Wexler also experimented with steel framing back in 1961, but the metal proved too expensive. Seven of his steel-frame houses can be seen in a neighborhood off Indian Canyon and Frances drives.

The Palm Springs Modern Committee sponsors Modernism Week in mid-February, when you can visit some of the most remarkable buildings in the area. Visit ⊕ www.psmodcom.org for an app that guides you to the most interesting buildings.

Purple Room Supper Club
BARS/PUBS | In an elegant venue within the Club Trinidad Hotel, this swinging '60s-era supper club offers live entertainment six nights a week. Come for drinks, dinner, and dancing Tuesday through Thursday night (no cover charge, but reservations are recommended). On Friday and Saturday night, dine at 6 pm and watch a scheduled show at 8 pm (reserve tickets in advance). Try to time your visit to catch *The Judy Show*, actor/owner Michael Holmes's Sunday evening comical tribute to Judy Garland, Bette Davis, Katharine Hepburn, and other stars (tickets required). ✉ *1900 E. Palm Canyon Dr.* ☎ *760/322–4422* ⊕ *www.purpleroompalmsprings.com.*

Tonga Hut

BARS/PUBS | The younger sibling of L.A.'s oldest tiki hut (opened in 1958 in North Hollywood), Tonga Hut Palm Springs transports guests to Polynesia with an authentic tiki vibe, pupu platters, and tropical drinks. It's on the second floor of a building in the heart of the downtown strip—try to nab a table on the lanai where you can experience the action from above. The bar and dining area are also fun and lively spaces; ask about the telephone booth that leads to a secret room, available for private parties. ⊠ *254 N. Palm Canyon Dr.* ☎ *760/322–4449* ⊕ *www.tongahut.com.*

★ **Village Pub**

BARS/PUBS | With live entertainment, DJs, and friendly service, this popular bar caters to a young crowd. Happy hour is fantastic. On weekend days there is live music as well. ⊠ *266 S. Palm Canyon Dr., at Baristo Rd.* ☎ *760/323–3265* ⊕ *www.palmspringsvillagepub.com.*

CASINOS

Casino Morongo

CASINOS | A 20-minute drive west of Palm Springs, this casino has 2,600 slot machines, video games, the Vibe nightclub, plus Vegas-style shows. ⊠ *49500 Seminole Dr., off I–10, Cabazon* ☎ *800/252–4499, 951/849–3080* ⊕ *www.morongocasinoresort.com.*

Spa Resort Casino

CASINOS | This resort holds 1,000 slot machines, blackjack tables, a high-limit room, four restaurants, two bars, and the Cascade Lounge for entertainment. ⊠ *401 E. Amado Rd., at N. Calle Encilia* ☎ *888/999–1995* ⊕ *www.sparesortcasino.com.*

DANCE CLUBS

Zelda's Nightclub

DANCE CLUBS | At this Palm Springs institution, the high-energy DJs, dancing, and drinking are still going strong and the dance floor is still thumping with Latin, hip-hop, and sounds from the '60s, '70s, and '80s. Zelda's offers bottle service in the VIP Sky Box. ⊠ *611 S. Palm Canyon Dr., at E. Camino Parocela* ☎ *760/325–2375* ⊕ *www.zeldasnightclub.com* ☾ *Closed Mon.*

GAY AND LESBIAN

The Dinah

FESTIVALS | In late March, when the world's finest female golfers hit the links for the Annual LPGA ANA Inspiration Championship in Rancho Mirage, thousands of lesbians converge on Palm Springs for a four-day party popularly known as The Dinah. ☎ *888/923–4624* ⊕ *thedinah.com.*

Hunter's Video Bar

DANCE CLUBS | Drawing a young gay and straight crowd, Hunter's is a club-scene mainstay. ⊠ *302 E. Arenas Rd., at Calle Encilia* ☎ *760/323–0700* ⊕ *huntersnightclubs.com.*

★ **Toucans Tiki Lounge**

BARS/PUBS | A friendly place with a tropical–rain forest setting, Toucans serves festive drinks and hosts live entertainment and theme nights. On Sunday it seems as though all of Palm Springs has turned out for drag night. ⊠ *2100 N. Palm Canyon Dr., at W. Via Escuela* ☎ *760/416–7584* ⊕ *www.toucanstikilounge.com* ☾ *Closed Wed.*

White Party Palm Springs

FESTIVALS | Held during spring break, the White Party draws tens of thousands of gay men from around the world for four days of parties and events. ⊠ *Palm Springs* ☎ *323/782–9924* ⊕ *jeffreysanker.com.*

THEMED ENTERTAINMENT

★ **Ace Hotel and Swim Club**

THEMED ENTERTAINMENT | Events are held here nearly every night, including film screenings, full moon parties, live concerts, DJs, and dancing. Many are free, and some are family friendly. The poolside venue makes most events fun and casual. ⊠ *701 E. Palm Canyon Dr., at Calle Palo Fierro* ☎ *760/325–9900* ⊕ *www.acehotel.com.*

Performing Arts

ARTS CENTERS

Annenberg Theater

CONCERTS | Broadway shows, operas, lectures, Sunday-afternoon chamber concerts, and other events take place at the Palm Springs Art Museum's handsome theater. ⊠ *101 N. Museum Dr., at W. Tahquitz Canyon Way* ☎ *760/325–4490* ⊕ *www.psmuseum.org.*

FESTIVALS

Modernism Week

FESTIVALS | Each February the desert communities celebrate the work of the architects and designers who created the Palm Springs "look" in the '40s, '50s, and '60s. Described these days as mid-century modern—you'll also see the term "desert modernism" used—these structures were created by Albert Frey, Richard Neutra, William F. Cody, John Lautner, and other notables. The 11-day event features lectures, a modernism show, films, vintage car and trailer shows, galas, and home and garden tours. A shorter preview week happens in October. ⊠ *Palm Springs* ⊕ *www. modernismweek.com.*

FILM

Palm Springs International Film Festival

FILM | In mid-January this 12-day festival brings stars and nearly 200 feature films from several dozen countries, plus panel discussions, short films, and documentaries, to various venues. The weeklong "Shortfest," celebrating more than 300 short films, takes place in June. ⊠ *Palm Springs* ☎ *760/322–2930, 800/898–7256* ⊕ *www.psfilmfest.org.*

Shopping

BOUTIQUES

★ Just Fabulous

LOCAL SPECIALTIES | Find everything from original photography and art, coffee table books, greeting cards, designer home decor, candles, and many other eclectic items at this fun gift shop that celebrates the area's retro-modern lifestyle and desert dolce vita. ⊠ *515 N. Palm Canyon Dr.* ☎ *760/864–1300* ⊕ *bjustfabulous.com.*

★ Trina Turk Boutique

CLOTHING | Celebrity designer Trina Turk's empire takes up a city block in the Uptown Design District. Turk, famous for men's and women's outdoor wear, reached out to another celebrity, interior designer Kelly Wearstler, to create adjoining clothing and residential boutiques. Lively fabrics brighten up the many chairs and couches for sale at the residential store, which also carries bowls, paintings, and other fun pieces to spiff up your home. ⊠ *891 N. Palm Canyon Dr.* ☎ *760/416–2856* ⊕ *www.trinaturk.com.*

OUTLET MALLS

★ Desert Hills Premium Outlets

OUTLET/DISCOUNT STORES | About 20 miles west of Palm Springs lies one of California's largest outlet centers. The 180 brand-name discount fashion shops include Jimmy Choo, Neiman Marcus, Versace, Saint Laurent Paris, J. Crew, Armani, Gucci, and Prada. ⊠ *48400 Seminole Rd., off I–10, Cabazon* ☎ *951/849–5018* ⊕ *www.premiumoutlets.com.*

SHOPPING DISTRICTS

★ Uptown Design District

SHOPPING NEIGHBORHOODS | A loose-knit collection of consignment and second-hand shops, galleries, and lively restaurants extends north of Palm Springs's downtown. The theme here is decidedly retro. Many businesses sell mid-century modern furniture and decorator items, and others carry clothing and estate jewelry. One spot definitely worth a peek is **The Shag Store,** the gallery of fine art painter Josh Agle. For antique costume jewelry check out **Dazzles.** If you dig the mid-mod aesthetic, breeze through the furnishings at **Towne Palm Springs.** ⊠ *N. Palm Canyon Dr., between Amado Rd. and Vista Chino.*

SPAS

★ Estrella Spa at the Avalon Hotel Palm Springs

SPA/BEAUTY | This spa earns top honors each year for the indoor/outdoor experience it offers with a touch of Old Hollywood ambience. You can enjoy your massage in one of four outdoor treatment cabanas in a garden, experience a sugar or salt scrub, get a facial or pedicure fireside, or receive a full-body treatment with a honey-sugar blend. Whatever the treatment, you can use the spa's private pool, take a break for lunch, and order a drink from the hotel's bar. ⊠ *Avalon Hotel Palm Springs, 415 S. Belardo Rd.* ☎ *760/318–3000* ⊕ *www. avalonpalmsprings.com* ⌂ *Salon. Services: facials, specialty massages, prenatal massages, outdoor treatments, wellness classes. $155, 60-min massage, $260, spa package.*

Feel Good Spa at the Ace Hotel

SPA/BEAUTY | The Feel Good Spa within its own dedicated facility at the Ace Hotel has five treatment rooms. The estheticians use local clay, mud, sea algae, and other natural ingredients, which you can purchase at the on-site shop. ⊠ *701 E. Palm Canyon Dr.* ☎ *760/866–6188* ⊕ *www.acehotel.com/palmsprings* ⌂ *Fully equipped gym. Services: wraps and scrubs, massage, facials, in-room treatments, salon, wellness classes, yoga. $115, 60-min massage.*

Palm Springs Yacht Club

SPA/BEAUTY | It's all about fun at this nautical-theme spa with 15 treatment rooms on the grounds of the Parker estate. Guests receive a complimentary cucumber-infused cocktail while lounging in a poolside tent. Before spa treatments, you can choose music from a playlist and the staff will stream it to your room. Treatments might feature local clay or stones, or a Thai massage. ⊠ *4200 E. Palm Canyon Dr.* ☎ *760/321–4606* ⊕ *www.theparkerpalmsprings.com/ spa* ⌂ *Sauna, steam room, indoor pool.*

Services: scrubs and wraps, massage, facials, manicures, pedicures, waxing, salon, fitness center with TechnoGym equipment, dining and cocktails. $195, 60-min massage.

Rancho Mirage

4 miles southeast of Cathedral City.

The rich and famous of Rancho Mirage live in beautiful estates and patronize elegant resorts and expensive restaurants. Although many mansions here are concealed behind the walls of gated communities and country clubs, the grandest of them all, Sunnylands, the Annenberg residence, is open to the public as a museum and public garden.

The city's golf courses host many high-profile tournaments. You'll find some of the desert's fanciest resorts in Rancho Mirage, and plenty of peace and quiet.

GETTING HERE AND AROUND

Due east of Cathedral City, Rancho Mirage stretches from Ramon Road on the north to the hills south of Highway 111. The western border is Da Vall Drive, the eastern one Monterey Avenue. Major east–west cross streets are Frank Sinatra Drive and Country Club Drive. Most shopping and dining spots are on Highway 111.

◉ Sights

★ The Annenberg Retreat at Sunnylands

HOUSE | The stunning 25,000-square-foot winter home and retreat of the late Ambassador Walter H. and Leonore Annenberg opened to the public in 2012. You can spend a whole day enjoying the 15 glorious acres of gardens (see website schedule of free guided walks, classes, and other programs), or take a guided 90-minute tour of the residence (reservations essential), a striking mid-century modern edifice designed by A. Quincy Jones. Floor-to-ceiling

The Desert Resorts

windows frame views of the gardens and Mt. San Jacinto, and the expansive rooms hold furnishings from the 1960s and later, along with impressionist art (some original, some replicas). The history made here is as captivating as the surroundings. Eight U.S. presidents—from Dwight Eisenhower to Barack Obama—and their First Ladies have visited Sunnylands; Ronald and Nancy Reagan were frequent guests. Britain's Queen Elizabeth and Prince Philip also relaxed here, as did Princess Grace of Monaco and Japanese Prime Minister Toshiki Kaifu. Photos, art, letters, journals, and mementos provide insight into some of the history that unfolded here. ⊠ *37–977 Bob Hope Dr., south of Gerald Ford Dr.* ☎ *760/202–2222* ⊕ *www.sunnylands.org* 🎟 *House tours $48, tickets available online 2 wks in advance; guided bird tour $35; open-air*

shuttle tour of grounds, $21; visitor center and gardens free ⊘ Closed Mon. and Tues. Closed June–mid-Sept. and during retreats.

Children's Discovery Museum of the Desert

MUSEUM | FAMILY | This museum features more than 80 hands-on exhibits, including a miniature rock-climbing area, a magnetic sculpture wall, make-it-and-take-it-apart projects, a rope maze, and an area for toddlers. Kids can make music on oversize drums, chimes, and a metallophone, work as chefs in the museum's pizza parlor, assemble their own cars on a racetrack, and build pies out of arts and crafts supplies. ⊠ *71–701 Gerald Ford Dr., at Bob Hope Dr.* ☎ *760/321–0602* ⊕ *www.cdmod.org* 🎟 *$10* ⊘ *Closed Mon. Sept.–mid-Nov.*

Palm Springs is a golfer's paradise: the area is home to more than 125 courses.

Koffi

RESTAURANT—SIGHT | Locals often hit this chain to get their caffeine fix, and it's a fine pit stop for pastries, premade sandwiches, and bagels. This outpost is the roasting facility, so the beans here are as fresh as they come. ⊠ *71–380 Hwy. 111* ☎ *760/340-2444* ⊕ *www.kofficoffee.com*.

Restaurants

Catalan

$$$ | **MEDITERRANEAN** | At this restaurant known for its beautifully prepared Mediterranean cuisine you can dine inside or under the stars in the atrium. The service here is attentive, and the menu roams Spain, Italy, California and beyond. **Known for:** two-course prix-fixe menu; delicious paella with clams; happy hour with inventive cocktails. ⑤ *Average main: $28* ⊠ *70026 Hwy. 111* ☎ *760/770-9508* ⊕ *www.catalanrestaurant.com* ⊙ *Closed Mon.*

Las Casuelas Nuevas

$$ | **MEXICAN** | **FAMILY** | Hundreds of artifacts from Guadalajara, Mexico, lend festive charm to this casual restaurant, which has an expansive garden patio. Tamales and shellfish dishes are among the specialties—expect more traditional Mexican fare, rather than California-influenced creations. **Known for:** vast tequila menu; weekend live entertainment; lively happy hour. ⑤ *Average main: $16* ⊠ *70–050 Hwy. 111* ☎ *760/328-8844* ⊕ *www.lascasuelasnuevas.com*.

🛏 Hotels

Agua Caliente Casino, Resort, Spa

$$$ | **RESORT** | As in Las Vegas, the Agua Caliente casino is in the lobby, but once you get into the spacious, beautifully appointed rooms of the resort, all of the cacophony at the entrance is forgotten. **Pros:** poolside cabanas outfitted with TV and Wi-Fi; package deals include access to Indian Canyons Golf Course; on-site Sunstone Spa. **Cons:** casino ambience; not appropriate for kids;

some live performances draw huge crowds. ⑤ *Rooms from: $250* ✉ *32–250 Bob Hope Dr.* ☎ *888/999–1995* ⊕ *www. hotwatercasino.com* ⤳ *366 rooms* ⦿ *No meals.*

Omni Rancho Las Palmas Resort & Spa

$$$$ | **RESORT** | **FAMILY** | The desert's most family-friendly resort, this large venue holds Splashtopia, a huge water-play zone. **Pros:** rooms come with private balconies or patios; trails for hiking and jogging; nightly entertainment. **Cons:** second-floor rooms accessed by very steep stairs; golf course surrounds rooms; resort hosts conventions. ⑤ *Rooms from: $299* ✉ *41-000 Bob Hope Dr.* ☎ *760/568–2727, 888/444–6664* ⊕ *www.rancholaspalmas.com* ⤳ *444 rooms* ⦿ *No meals.*

★ The Ritz Carlton, Rancho Mirage

$$$$ | **RESORT** | **FAMILY** | On a hilltop perch overlooking the Coachella Valley, this luxury resort spoils guests with exemplary service and comforts that include a trio of pools, access to the desert's finest spa, and private outdoor sitting areas for each room. **Pros:** fire pit overlooking Coachella Valley; access to Mission Hills golf courses and tennis; spa that's a destination in itself. **Cons:** hefty rates; some airport noise; resort and parking fees ($40 each). ⑤ *Rooms from: $289* ✉ *68900 Frank Sinatra Dr.* ☎ *760/321–8282* ⊕ *www.ritz-carlton.com* ⤳ *244 rooms* ⦿ *No meals.*

The Westin Mission Hills Golf Resort & Spa

$$$$ | **RESORT** | **FAMILY** | A sprawling resort on 360 acres, the Westin offers a slew of activities for all ages and is surrounded by fairways and putting greens, two family-friendly pools (one lagoon-style with a 75-foot waterslide) and an adults-only pool. **Pros:** gorgeous grounds; first-class golf facilities; daily activity programs for kids and adults. **Cons:** rooms are spread out; some buildings seem dated; far from town. ⑤ *Rooms from: $369* ✉ *71333 Dinah Shore Dr.* ☎ *760/328–5955, 877/253–0041* ⊕ *www.westinmission-hills.com* ⤳ *552 rooms* ⦿ *No meals.*

Nightlife

Agua Caliente Casino

CASINOS | This elegant and surprisingly quiet casino contains 1,300 slot machines, 36 table games, an 18-table poker room, a high-limit room, a no-smoking area, and six restaurants. The Show, the resort's concert theater, presents acts such as The Moody Blues, Joe Bonamassa, Toni Braxton, and Sophia Loren, as well as live sporting events. ✉ *32–250 Bob Hope Dr., at E. Ramon Rd.* ☎ *760/321–2000* ⊕ *www. hotwatercasino.com.*

Activities

GOLF

ANA Inspiration Championship

GOLF | The best female golfers in the world compete in this championship held in late March or early April. ✉ *Mission Hills Country Club* ☎ *760/834–8872* ⊕ *www.anainspiration.com.*

★ Westin Mission Hills Resort Golf Club

GOLF | Golfers at the Westin Mission Hills have two courses to choose from, the Pete Dye and the Gary Player Signature. They're both great, with amazing mountain views and wide fairways, but if you've only got time to play one, choose the Dye. The club is a member of the Troon Golf Institute, and has several teaching facilities, including the Westin Mission Hills Resort Golf Academy and the *Golf Digest* Golf School. ■ **TIP→ The resort's Best Available Rate program guarantees golfers (with a few conditions) the best Internet rate possible.** ✉ *71333 Dinah Shore Dr.* ☎ *760/328–3198* ⊕ *www.play-missionhills.com* 🏌 *Gary Player, from $74; Pete Dye, from $114* 🏌 *Pete Dye Resort: 18 holes, 5525 yards, par 72; Gary Player Signature: 18 holes, 5327 yards, par 70.*

🛍 Shopping

MALL

The River at Rancho Mirage

SHOPPING CENTERS/MALLS | This shopping-dining-entertainment complex holds 20 high-end shops, including the SoCal darling Diane's Beachwear, all fronting a faux river with cascading waterfalls. Also here are a 12-screen cinema, an outdoor amphitheater, and many restaurants including Fleming's Prime Steakhouse & Wine Bar and Babe's Bar-B-Que and Brewery. ⊠ 71–800 Hwy. 111, at Bob Hope Dr. ☎ 760/341–2711 ⊕ www.theriveratranchomirage.com.

SPAS

★ The Ritz Carlton Spa, Rancho Mirage

SPA/BEAUTY | Two hundred–plus suspended quartz crystals guard the entrance of the desert's premier spa. With private men's and women's areas, a co-ed outdoor soaking tub, food service, and some of the kindest spa technicians around, guests can expect pampering par excellence. The signature Spirit of the Mountains treatment, which starts with a full-body exfoliation, includes a massage, and ends with a body wrap and a scalp massage with lavender oil, is a blissful experience. The gym, equipped with state-of-the-art machines, is open 24/7. Private trainers are available to guide your workout; wellness classes are also available. ⊠ 68900 Frank Sinatra Dr. ☎ 760/202–6170 ⊕ www.ritzcarlton.com ⌂ Fully equipped gym. Salon. Services: body wraps, body scrubs, facials, mineral baths, specialty massages, outdoor treatments, waxing, wellness classes. $170, 50-min massage; $340, signature package.

The Spa at Mission Hills

SPA/BEAUTY | The emphasis at this spa in a quiet corner of the Westin Mission Hills Resort is on comfort rather than glitz and glamour. Attentive therapists incorporate coconut lemon balm, thyme, lavender, hydrating honey, and other botanicals into their treatments. Yoga and other wellness classes are also available. ⊠ 71333 Dinah Shore Dr. ☎ 760/770–2180 ⊕ www.spaatmissionhills.com ⌂ Steam room. Gym with: machines, cardio, pool. Services: rubs and scrubs, massages, facials, nail services. $160, 50-min massage.

Palm Desert

2 miles southeast of Rancho Mirage.

Palm Desert is a thriving retail and business community with popular restaurants, private and public golf courses, and premium shopping along the main commercial drag, El Paseo. Each October, the Palm Desert Golf Cart Parade launches "the season" with a procession of 80 golf carts decked out as floats buzzing up and down El Paseo. The town's stellar sight to see is the Living Desert complex.

GETTING HERE AND AROUND

Palm Desert stretches from north of Interstate 10 to the hills south of Highway 111. West–east cross streets north to south are Frank Sinatra Drive, Country Club Drive (lined on both sides with gated golfing communities), and Fred Waring Drive. Monterey Avenue marks the western boundary, and Washington Street forms the eastern edge.

TOURS

Art in Public Places

SELF-GUIDED | Several self-guided tours cover the works in Palm Desert's 150-piece Art in Public Places collection. Each tour is walkable or drivable. Maps and information about guided tours (one Saturday each month) are available at the city's visitor center and online. ⊠ Palm Desert Visitor Center, 73510 Fred Waring Dr. ☎ 760/568–1441 ⊕ www.palm-desert.org/arts-entertainment/public-art ☑ Free.

Sights

★ El Paseo

PEDESTRIAN MALL | West of and parallel to Highway 111, this mile-long Mediterranean-style shopper's paradise is lined with fountains, courtyards, and upscale boutiques. You'll find shoe salons, jewelry stores, children's shops, two dozen restaurants, and nearly as many art galleries. The strip is a pleasant place to stroll, window-shop, people-watch, and exercise your credit cards. ■TIP→ **In winter and spring a free bright-yellow shuttle ferries shoppers from store to store and back to their cars.** ⊠ Between Monterey and Portola Aves. ☎ 877/735-7273 ⊕ www.elpaseo.com.

★ The Living Desert Zoo and Gardens

GARDEN | FAMILY | Come eye-to-eye with wolves, coyotes, mountain lions, cheetahs, bighorn sheep, golden eagles, warthogs, and owls at the Living Desert, which showcases the flora and fauna of the world's deserts. Easy to challenging scenic trails traverse desert terrain populated with plants of the Mojave, Colorado, and Sonoran deserts. In recent years the park has expanded its vision to include Australia and Africa. At the 3-acre African WaTuTu village you'll find a traditional marketplace as well as camels, leopards, hyenas, and other African animals. Children can pet African domesticated animals, including Nigerian dwarf goats, in a "petting kraal." Gecko Gulch is a children's playground with crawl-through underground tunnels, climb-on snake sculptures, a carousel, and a Discovery Center that holds ancient Pleistocene animal bones. Elsewhere, a small aviary hosts seasonal bird exhibits, and a cool model train travels through miniatures of historic California towns. ■TIP→ **Time your visit to begin in the early morning to beat the heat and feed the giraffes.** ⊠ 47900 Portola Ave., south from Hwy. 111 ☎ 760/346-5694 ⊕ www.livingdesert.org ⊠ $20.

Palm Springs Art Museum in Palm Desert

MUSEUM | A satellite branch of the Palm Springs Art Museum, this gallery space tucked into a desert garden at the west entrance to El Paseo exhibits cutting-edge works by contemporary sculptors and painters. The on-site restaurant **Cuistot** (☎ 760/340-1000, ⊕ www.cuistotrestaurant.com) is a splendid, if pricey, place to enjoy French cuisine. ⊠ 72-567 Hwy. 111 ✛ At western entrance to El Paseo ☎ 760/346-5600 ⊕ www.psmuseum.org/palm-desert ⊠ Free ☉ Closed Mon.

Santa Rosa and San Jacinto Mountains National Monument

NATURE PRESERVE | Administered by the U.S. Bureau of Land Management, this monument protects Peninsula bighorn sheep and other wildlife on 280,000 acres of desert habitat. Stop by the visitor center for an introduction to the site and information about the natural history of the desert. A landscaped garden displays native plants and frames an impressive view. The well-informed staff can recommend hiking trails that show off the beauties of the desert. ■TIP→ **Free guided hikes are offered on Thursday and Saturday.** ⊠ 51-500 Hwy. 74 ☎ 760/862-9984 ⊕ www.blm.gov ⊠ Free.

🍴 Restaurants

★ Bouchee Café & Deli

$ | AMERICAN | Devotees of this La Quinta favorite come here for farm-to-table Euro-style meals and deli items. Order the salads or gorgeous sandwiches—the salmon salad is to die for—at the counter, then retire to the French-inspired dining area, or the shaded outdoor terrace. **Known for:** premade dinner to go; gourmet wine and cheese shop; locally sourced ingredients. ⑤ Average main: $12 ⊠ 72-785 Hwy. 111 ✛ Off Plaza Way near El Paseo ☎ 442/666-3296 ⊕ www.boucheecafeanddeli.com ☉ No dinner.

Pacifica Seafood

$$$$ | SEAFOOD | Choice seafood and rooftop dining draw locals and visitors to this busy restaurant on the second floor of the Gardens of El Paseo. Seafood that shines in dishes such as twin lobster tails, grilled Pacific swordfish, and barbecued sugar-spiced salmon arrives daily from San Diego; the menu also includes chicken, steaks, and meal-size salads. **Known for:** inventive sauces and glazes; craft cocktails and bourbon; lower-price sunset menu from 3 to 5:30. ⑤ *Average main: $38* ⊠ *73505 El Paseo* ☎ *760/674–8666* ⊕ *www.pacificaseafoodrestaurant.com* ⊙ *No lunch June–Aug.*

 ## Hotels

Desert Springs J. W. Marriott Resort and Spa

$$$ | RESORT | FAMILY | With a dramatic U-shape design, this sprawling hotel, which attract business travelers, couples, and families alike, is set on 450 landscaped acres and wraps around the desert's largest private lake. **Pros:** gondola rides on the lake to restaurants; popular lobby bar; wonderful spa. **Cons:** crowded in-season; high resort fee; long walk from lobby to rooms. ⑤ *Rooms from: $249* ⊠ *74–855 Country Club Dr.* ☎ *760/341–2211, 888/538–9459* ⊕ *www.desertspringsresort.com* ⊃ *884 rooms* ⦿ *No meals.*

Hotel Paseo

$$$$ | HOTEL | FAMILY | A half block from El Paseo's main drag, this hip luxury hotel, which opened in 2018 as a new member of Marriott's Autograph Collection, reflects the mid-century modern history and upscale, yet casual lifestyle of the desert. **Pros:** on-site restaurant owned by famed Palm Springs restaurateurs; full-service spa ; walk to El Paseo restaurants, shops, attractions. **Cons:** some rooms on the small side; pool area can seem small and crowded; street parking unless you pay for valet. ⑤ *Rooms from:*

$289 ⊠ *45400 Larkspur La.* ☎ *760/340–9001* ⊕ *www.hotelpaseo.com* ⊃ *149 rooms* ⦿ *No meals.*

 ## Performing Arts

McCallum Theatre

THEATER | The principal cultural venue in the desert, this theater hosts productions from fall through spring. *The Phantom of the Opera* has played here; Lily Tomlin and Willie Nelson have performed; and Shen Yun dancers have twirled across the stage. ⊠ *73–000 Fred Waring Dr.* ☎ *760/340–2787* ⊕ *www.mccallumtheatre.com.*

 ## Activities

BALLOONING

Fantasy Balloon Flights

BALLOONING | Sunrise excursions over the southern end of the Coachella Valley lift off at 6 am and take from 60 to 90 minutes; a traditional champagne toast follows the landing. Afternoon excursions are timed to touch down at sunset. ⊠ *Palm Desert* ☎ *760/568–0997* ⊕ *www.fantasyballoonflight.com* ⊠ *$195.*

GOLF

Desert Willow Golf Resort

GOLF | Praised for its environmentally smart design, this public golf resort planted water-thrifty turf grasses and doesn't use pesticides. The Mountain View course has four configurations; Firecliff is tournament quality with five configurations. A public facility, Desert Willow is one of the country's top-rated golf courses. ⊠ *38–995 Desert Willow Dr., off Country Club Dr.* ☎ *760/346–0015* ⊕ *www.desertwillow.com* ⊠ *Mountain View from $120, Firecliff from $120* ⚘ *Mountain View: 18 holes, 7079 yards, par 72; Firecliff: 18 holes, 7056 yards, par 72.*

Indian Wells

5 miles east of Palm Desert.

For the most part a quiet and exclusive residential enclave, Indian Wells hosts major golf and tennis tournaments throughout the year, including the BNP Paribus Open tennis tournament. Three hotels share access to championship golf and tennis facilities, and there are several noteworthy resort spas and restaurants.

GETTING HERE AND AROUND

Indian Wells lies between Palm Desert and La Quinta, with most resorts, restaurants, and shopping set back from Highway 111.

 Restaurants

Vue Grille and Bar at the Indian Wells Golf Resort

$$$$ | AMERICAN | This not-so-private restaurant at the Indian Wells Golf Resort offers a glimpse of how the country-club set lives. The service is impeccable, and the outdoor tables provide views of mountain peaks that seem close enough to touch. **Known for:** farm-to-table cuisine; grilled steaks and seafood; flatbreads and burgers. $ *Average main: $36* ⊠ *44–500 Indian Wells La.* ☎ *760/834–3800* ⊕ *www.vuegrilleand-bar.com.*

 Hotels

★ Hyatt Grand Regency Indian Wells Resort & Spa

$$$$ | RESORT | FAMILY | This stark-white resort adjacent to the Golf Resort at Indian Wells is one of the grandest in the desert, with seven pools (one with a waterslide and one adults-only), an outdoor game area and a kids club, and a spa. **Pros:** excellent business services; butler service in some rooms; very pet friendly. **Cons:** big and impersonal; spread out over 45 acres; noisy public areas. $ *Rooms from: $370* ⊠ *44–600 Indian Wells La.* ☎ *760/776–1234* ⊕ *indianwells.regency.hyatt.com* ⇨ *520 rooms* ⦿ *No meals.*

Miramonte Resort & Spa

$$$$ | RESORT | Guest rooms at the most intimate of the Indian Wells hotels are in red-roof villas on 11 acres of bougainvillea-filled gardens against a backdrop of the Santa Rosa Mountains. **Pros:** three swimming pools (one adults only); on-site farm-to-fork restaurant and lounge; one of the desert's best spas. **Cons:** extra resort fee; limited resort facilities on-site; long walk to lobby from some rooms. $ *Rooms from: $279* ⊠ *45000 Indian Wells La.* ☎ *760/341–2200* ⊕ *www.miramonteresort.com* ⇨ *215 rooms* ⦿ *No meals.*

Renaissance Indian Wells Resort and Spa

$$$$ | RESORT | FAMILY | The centerpiece of this luxurious resort, adjacent to the Golf Resort at Indian Wells, is an eight-story atrium lobby, onto which most rooms open. **Pros:** adjacent to golf-tennis complex; kids club; bicycles available. **Cons:** higher noise level in rooms surrounding pool; somewhat impersonal ambience. $ *Rooms from: $289* ⊠ *44–400 Indian Wells La.* ☎ *760/773–4444* ⊕ *www.renaissancehotels.com* ⇨ *560 rooms* ⦿ *No meals.*

 Activities

GOLF

★ Indian Wells Golf Resort

GOLF | Adjacent to the Hyatt Regency Indian Wells, this complex includes the Celebrity Course, designed by Clive Clark and twice a host to the PGA's Skins game (lots of water here, including streams, lakes, and waterfalls), and the Players Course, designed by John Fought to incorporate views of the surrounding mountain ranges. Both courses consistently rank among the best public courses in California. ■TIP→ **It's a good idea to book tee times well in advance,**

up to 60 days. ✉ 44–500 Indian Wells La. ☎ 760/346–4653 ⊕ www.indianwells-golfresort.com ⊘ Both courses from $69 ⛳ Celebrity Course: 18 holes, 7050 yards, par 72; Players Course: 18 holes, 7376 yards, par 72.

TENNIS

BNP Paribas Open

TENNIS | Drawing 200 of the world's top players, this tennis tournament takes place at Indian Wells Tennis Garden for two weeks in March. Various ticket plans are available, with some packages including stays at the adjoining Hyatt Regency Indian Wells or Renaissance resorts. ✉ 78200 Miles Ave. ☎ 800/999–1585 ⊕ www.bnpparibasopen.com.

Shopping

★ The Well Spa

SPA/BEAUTY | A luxurious 12,000-square-foot facility, The Well draws on international treatments and ingredients to indulge the senses and relax the body. Treatments such as hot stone, Himalayan salt, and full-body massages and table yoga are well worth the splurge. Sugar or salt exfoliating scrubs may well restore the soul in addition to the skin. ✉ Miramonte Resort, 45–000 Indian Wells La. ☎ 866/843–9355 ⊕ www.miramonteresort.com ☞ Services: facials, nail care, solo and couple's massages, scrubs, and other body therapies. $165, 60-min massage.

La Quinta

4 miles south of Indian Wells.

The desert became a Hollywood hideout in the 1920s, when La Quinta Hotel (now La Quinta Resort and Club) opened, introducing the Coachella Valley's first golf course. Old Town La Quinta is a popular attraction; the area holds dining spots, shops, and galleries.

GETTING HERE AND AROUND

Most of La Quinta lies south of Highway 111. The main drag through town is Washington Street.

Restaurants

Arnold Palmer's

$$$$ | AMERICAN | From the photos on the walls to the trophy-filled display cases, Arnie's essence infuses this restaurant. Families gather in the spacious restaurant for birthdays and Sunday dinners, and the service is always attentive. **Known for:** homemade meat loaf, double-cut pork chops, mac and cheese; top-notch wine list; entertainment most nights. $ Average main: $34 ✉ 78164 Ave. 52, near Desert Club Dr. ☎ 760/771–4653 ⊕ www.arnoldpalmers-restaurant.com.

★ Lavender Bistro

$$$$ | BISTRO | This romantic bistro with a spacious outdoor atrium decked out with flowers, fountains, and twinkling lights makes diners feel like they've been transported to southern France. Choices on the large menu include steamed mussels, a honey-brine pork chop, and lobster ravioli; for dessert you can't go wrong with the baked apple tart or the banana walnut brioche bread pudding. **Known for:** live music on the patio and in the fireside lounge; organic ingredients; extensive locavore menu. $ Average main: $34 ✉ 78073 Calle Barcelona ☎ 760/564–5353 ⊕ www.lavenderbistro.com ☉ Closed June–Sept.

Hotels

La Quinta Resort and Club

$$$$ | RESORT | FAMILY | Opened in 1926 and now a member of the Waldorf-Astoria Collection, the desert's oldest resort is a lush green oasis with 23 tennis courts and 41 pools set on 45 acres. **Pros:** individual swimming pools in some rooms; gorgeous gardens; pet and family friendly. **Cons:** a party atmosphere

sometimes prevails; spotty house-keeping/maintenance; swimming pools can be crowded. $ *Rooms from: $329* ✉ *49499 Eisenhower Dr.* ☎ *760/564–4111* ⊕ *www.laquintaresort.com* ⇌ *586 rooms, 210 villas* ⊙ *No meals.*

Performing Arts

La Quinta Arts Festival

FESTIVALS | More than 200 artists participate each March in a four-day juried show that's considered one of the best in the West. The event, held at La Quinta Civic Center, includes sculptures, paintings, watercolors, fiber art, and ceramics. ✉ *78495 Calle Tampico* ☎ *760/564–1244* ⊕ *www.lqaf.com* ✉ *From $17.*

Shopping

SPAS

Spa La Quinta

SPA/BEAUTY | The gorgeous Spa La Quinta may be the grandest spa in the entire desert. At this huge stand-alone facility you'll find everything from massages to facials to salon services and classes, plus a beautiful garden setting with a large fountain, flowers galore, plenty of nooks where you can hide out and enjoy the sanctuary, and a Jacuzzi with a waterfall. ✉ *49499 Eisenhower Dr.* ☎ *760/777–4800* ⊕ *www.laquintaresort. com* ☞ *Fitness center with cardio. Services: aromatherapy, body wraps and scrubs, massage, skin care, salon services, water therapies. $170, 50-min massage; $195, 30-min HydraFacial.*

Activities

GOLF

★ PGA West

GOLF | A world-class golf destination where Phil Mickelson and Jack Nicklaus play, this facility includes five resort courses and four private ones. Courses meander through indigenous desert landscapes, water features, and bunkers. The Norman, Nick Tournament, and TPC Stadium courses are "shot-makers" courses made for pros. TPC highlights include its two lakes, "San Andreas Fault" bunker, and island green called "Alcatraz." The Norman course has tight fairways and small greens. ✉ *49–499 Eisenhower Dr.* ☎ *760/564–5729 for tee times* ⊕ *www. pgawest.com* ✉ *Mountain Course, from $159; Dunes, from $119; Greg Norman, from $159; TPC Stadium, from $189; Jack Nicklaus Tournament, from $159* ⅄. *Mountain Course: 18 holes, 6732 yards, par 72; Dunes: 18 holes, 6712 yards, par 72; Greg Norman: 18 holes, 7156 yards, par 72; TPC Stadium: 18 holes, 7300 yards, par 72; Jack Nicklaus Tournament: 18 holes, 7204 yards, par 72.*

Indio

5 miles east of Indian Wells.

Indio is the home of the renowned date shake: an extremely thick and sweet milk shake made with dates. The city and surrounding countryside generate 95% of the dates grown and harvested in the United States. If you take a hot-air balloon ride, you will likely drift over the tops of date palm trees.

GETTING HERE AND AROUND

Indio is east of Indian Wells and north of La Quinta. Highway 111 runs right through Indio, and Interstate 10 skirts it to the north.

◉ Sights

National Date Festival and Riverside County Fair

FESTIVAL | FAMILY | Indio celebrates its raison d'être each February at its date festival and county fair. The mid-month festivities include an Arabian Nights pageant, camel and ostrich races, and exhibits of local dates, plus monster truck shows, a demolition derby, a nightly musical pageant, and a rodeo. ⊠ *Riverside County Fairgrounds, 82–503 Hwy. 111* ☎ *800/811–3247, 760/863–8247* ⊕ *www.datefest.org* ⊠ *$11, parking $10.*

Shields Date Garden and Café

STORE/MALL | Sample, select, and take home some of Shields's locally grown dates. Ten varieties are available, including the giant supersweet royal medjools, along with specialty date products such as date crystals, stuffed dates, confections, and local honey. At the Shields Date Garden Café you can try an iconic date shake, dig into date pancakes, or go exotic with a date tamale. Breakfast and lunch are served daily. ⊠ *80–225 Hwy. 111* ☎ *760/347–0996* ⊕ *www.shieldsdategarden.com* ☉ *No dinner.*

 Restaurants

Ciro's Ristorante and Pizzeria

$$ | **SICILIAN** | Serving pizza and pasta since the 1960s, this popular casual restaurant has a few unusual pies on the menu, including cashew with three cheeses. The decor is classic pizza joint, with checkered tablecloths and bentwood chairs. **Known for:** daily pasta specials; classic Italian dishes; house-made, hand-tossed pizza dough. ⑤ *Average main: $16* ⊠ *81–963 Hwy. 111* ☎ *760/347–6503* ⊕ *www.cirosofindio.com* ☉ *No lunch weekends.*

Jackalope Ranch

$$$ | **AMERICAN** | It's worth the drive to Indio to sample flavors of the Old West, 21st-century style. Inside a rambling 21,000-foot building, holding a clutch of indoor/outdoor dining spaces, you may be seated near an open kitchen, a bar, fountains, fireplaces, or waterworks. **Known for:** Western-style barbecue, spicy and savory sauces, and sumptuous desserts; casual, down-home locals hangout; lively vibe. ⑤ *Average main: $30* ⊠ *80–400 Hwy. 111* ☎ *760/342–1999* ⊕ *www.thejackaloperanch.com.*

 Performing Arts

MUSIC FESTIVALS

★ **Coachella Valley Music and Arts Festival**

FESTIVALS | Among Southern California's biggest parties, the festival draws hundreds of thousands of rock music fans to Indio each April for two weekends of live concerts. Headliners include acts such as Lady Gaga, Childish Gambino, Ariana Grande, Tame Impala, Kendrick Lamar, Jack Johnson, and Radiohead. Many attendees camp on-site, but to give your ears a rest post-concert you might want to stay at a nearby hotel. ■**TIP**→ **The festival sells out before the lineup is announced, so expect to pay big bucks if you haven't purchased tickets by late fall.** ⊠ *Empire Polo Club, 81–800 Ave. 51* ⊕ *www.coachella.com.*

Coachella Valley Preserve

NATURE PRESERVE | **FAMILY** | For a glimpse of how the desert appeared before development, head northeast from Palm Springs to this preserve. It has a system of sand dunes and several palm oases that were formed because the San Andreas Fault lines here allow water flowing underground to rise to the surface. A mile-long walk along Thousand Palms Oasis reveals pools supporting the tiny endangered desert pupfish and more than 183 bird species. Families like the relatively flat trail that is mostly shaded. The preserve has a visitor center, nature and equestrian trails, restrooms, and picnic facilities. Guided hikes are offered October–March. ■**TIP**→ **Be aware that it's exceptionally hot in summer here.** ⊠ *29200 Thousand Palms Canyon Rd., Thousand Palms* ☎ *760/343–2733* ⊕ *www.coachellavalleypreserve.org* ⊠ *Free* ☉ *Visitor center closed May–Sept. Parking lot and hiking closed Aug.*

Desert Hot Springs

9 miles north of Palm Springs.

Desert Hot Springs's famous hot mineral waters, thought by some to have curative powers, bubble up at temperatures of 90°F to 148°F and flow into the wells of more than 40 hotel spas.

GETTING HERE AND AROUND

Desert Hot Springs lies due north of Palm Springs. Take Gene Autry Trail north to Interstate 10, where the street name changes to Palm. Continue north to Pierson Boulevard, the town's center.

Sights

Cabot's Pueblo Museum

MUSEUM | Cabot Yerxa, the man who found the spring that made Desert Hot Springs famous, built a quirky four-story, 35-room pueblo between 1939 and his death in 1965. Now a museum run by the city of Desert Hot Springs, the Hopi-inspired adobe structure is filled with memorabilia of his time as a homesteader; his encounters with Hollywood celebrities at the nearby Bar-H Ranch; his expedition to the Alaskan gold rush; and many other events. The home, much of it crafted out of materials Yerxa recycled from the desert, can only be seen on hour-long tours. Outside, walk the grounds to a lookout with amazing desert views. ⊠ *67–616 E. Desert View Ave., at Eliseo Rd.* ☎ *760/329–7610* ⊕ *www.cabotsmuseum.org* 🎟 *$13* 🕙 *Closed Mon. Oct.–May, closed Mon. and Tues. June–Sept.* ☞ *Tours 9:30, 10:30, 11:30, 1:30, 2:30 Oct.–May, and 9:30, 10:30, 11:30 June–Sept. Tours limited to 12 people.*

Hotels

The Spring

$$$ | HOTEL | Designed for those who want to detox, lose weight, or chill out in the mineral pools, The Spring delivers quiet and personal service atop a Desert Hot Springs hill. **Pros:** access to mineral pools 24 hours a day; complimentary continental breakfast; spa and lodging packages available. **Cons:** rooms lack character; no TVs or phones; not much poolside privacy. $ *Rooms from: $239* ⊠ *12699 Reposo Way* ☎ *760/251–6700* ⊕ *www.the-spring.com* 🛏 *12 rooms* 🍽 *Breakfast.*

Two Bunch Palms

$$$ | RESORT | This adults-only hotel on a gorgeous 72-acre property with stunning views of Mt. San Jacinto provides a luxurious and relaxing experience with full-service access to natural hot springs. **Pros:** on-site restaurant serves breakfast, lunch, and dinner; fresh juice bar open all day; full-service spa, popular since the 1940s. **Cons:** some rooms have no TV; no pets allowed; minimum age 18. $ *Rooms from: $245* ⊠ *67425 Two Bunch Palms Trail* ☎ *760/676–5000* ⊕ *twobunchpalms. com* 🛏 *68 rooms* 🍽 *No meals.*

Yucca Valley

30 miles northeast of Palm Springs.

One of the high desert's fastest-growing cities, Yucca Valley is emerging as a bedroom community for people who work as far away as Ontario, 85 miles to the west. In this suburb you can shop for necessities, get your car serviced, grab coffee or purchase vintage furnishings, and chow down at fast-food outlets. Just up Pioneertown Road you'll find the most-talked-about dining establishment in the desert, Pappy & Harriet's, the famed performance venue that hosts big-name talent.

GETTING HERE AND AROUND

The drive to Yucca Valley on Highway 62/Twentynine Palms Highway passes through the Painted Hills and drops down into a valley. Take Pioneertown Road north to the Old West outpost.

Sights

Hi-Desert Nature Museum

MUSEUM | FAMILY | Natural and cultural history of the Morongo Basis and High Desert are the focus here. A small live-animal display includes scorpions, snakes, lizards, and small mammals. You'll also find gems and minerals, fossils from the Paleozoic era, taxidermy, and Native American artifacts. There's also a children's area and art exhibits. ⌧ Yucca Valley Community Center, 57090 Twentynine Palms Hwy. ☎ 760/369–7212 ⊕ hidesertnaturemuseum.org ⌧ Free ⊙ Closed Sun.–Tues.

Pioneertown

TOWN | In 1946 Roy Rogers, Gene Autry, the Sons of the Pioneers (the music group for whom the town is named), and Russ Hayden built Pioneertown, an 1880s-style Wild West movie set complete with hitching posts, saloon, and an OK Corral. You can stroll past wooden and adobe storefronts and feel like you're back in the Old West. Pappy & Harriet's Pioneertown Palace, now the town's top draw, has evolved into a hip venue for indie and mainstream performers such as Dengue Fever, Neko Case, and Robert Plant. ⌧ 53688 Pioneertown Rd., Pioneertown ✛ 4 miles north of Yucca Valley ⊕ pappyandharriets.com.

 Restaurants

★ Pappy & Harriet's Pioneertown Palace

$$$ | AMERICAN | FAMILY | Smack in the middle of what looks like the set of a Western is this cozy saloon where you can have dinner, relax over a drink at the bar, and catch some great indie bands or legendary artists—Leon Russell, Lorde, Paul McCartney, and Robert Plant have all played here. Pappy & Harriet's may be in the middle of nowhere, but you'll need reservations for dinner on weekends. **Known for:** live music several days/nights a week; Tex-Mex, Santa Maria–style barbecue; fun and lively atmosphere. ⑤ Average main: $25 ⌧ 53688 Pioneertown Rd., Pioneertown ☎ 760/365–5956 ⊕ www.pappyandharriets.com ⊙ Closed Tues. and Wed.

 Hotels

Best Western Joshua Tree Hotel & Suites

$$ | HOTEL | FAMILY | This hotel has spacious, nicely appointed rooms decorated in soft desert colors. **Pros:** convenient to Joshua Tree National Park; pleasant lounge; pool and hot tub. **Cons:** on a busy highway; limited service; some rooms need updating. ⑤ Rooms from: $130 ⌧ 56525 Twentynine Palms Hwy. ☎ 760/365–3555 ⊕ www.bestwestern.com ⌁ 95 rooms ⑩ Breakfast.

Rimrock Ranch Cabins

$$ | RENTAL | The quiet beauty of the surrounding desert attracts Hollywood writers, artists, and musicians to circa-1940s housekeeping cabins, an Airstream trailer, the Hatch House duplex, and lodge rooms. **Pros:** quiet desert hideaway; outdoor fireplaces and fully equipped kitchens; rich music heritage on site. **Cons:** rustic cabins will not appeal to resort seekers; far from most services; some rooms are sparsely furnished. ⑤ Rooms from: $120 ⌧ 53688 Pioneertown Rd., Pioneertown ☎ 760/228–0130 ⊕ www.rimrockranchpioneertown.com ⌁ 7 rental units ⑩ No meals.

Borrego Springs

59 miles south of Indio.

The permanent population of Borrego Springs, set squarely in the middle of Anza-Borrego Desert State Park, hovers around 2,500. From September through June, when temperatures stay in the '80s and '90s, you can engage in outdoor activities such as hiking, nature study, golfing, tennis, horseback riding, and mountain biking. If winter rains cooperate, Borrego Springs puts on some of the best wildflower displays in the low desert. In some years the desert floor is carpeted with color: yellow dandelions and sunflowers, pink primrose, purple sand verbena, and blue wild heliotrope. The bloom generally lasts from late February through April. For current information on wildflowers around Borrego Springs, call Anza-Borrego Desert State Park's wildflower hotline (☎ 760/767–4684).

GETTING HERE AND AROUND

You can access Anza Borrego by taking the Highway 86 exit from Interstate 10, south of Indio. Highway 86 passes through Coachella and along the western shore of the Salton Sea. Turn west on Highway S22 at Salton City and follow it to Peg Leg Road, where you turn south until you reach Palm Canyon Drive. Turn west and the road leads to the center of Borrego Springs, Christmas Circle, where most major roads come together. Well-marked roads radiating from the circle will take you to the most popular sites in the state park. If coming from the San Diego area, drive east on Interstate 8 to the Cuyamaca Mountains, exit at Highway 79, and enjoy the lovely 23-mile drive through the mountains until you reach Julian; head east on Highway 78 and follow signs to Borrego Springs.

ESSENTIALS

VISITOR INFORMATION Borrego Springs Chamber of Commerce & Visitors Bureau. ☒ 786 Palm Canyon Dr. ☎ 760/767–5555, 800/559–5524 ⊕ www.borregosprings-chamber.com.

Sights

★ Anza-Borrego Desert State Park

NATIONAL/STATE PARK | One of the richest living natural-history museums in the nation, this state park is a vast, nearly uninhabited wilderness where you can step through a field of wildflowers, cool off in a palm-shaded oasis, count zillions of stars in the black night sky, and listen to coyotes howl at dusk. The landscape, largely undisturbed by humans, reveals a rich natural history. There's evidence of a vast inland sea in the piles of oyster beds near Split Mountain and of the power of natural forces such as earthquakes and flash floods. In addition, recent scientific work has confirmed that the Borrego Badlands, with more than 6,000 meters of exposed fossil-bearing sediments, is likely the richest such deposit in North America, telling the story of 7 million years of climate change, upheaval, and prehistoric animals. Evidence has been unearthed of saber-toothed cats, flamingos, zebras, and the largest flying bird in the northern hemisphere beneath the now-parched sand. Today the desert's most treasured inhabitants are the herds of elusive and endangered native bighorn sheep, or borrego, for which the park is named. Among the strange desert plants you may observe are the gnarly elephant trees. As these are endangered, rangers don't encourage visitors to seek out the secluded grove at Fish Creek, but there are a few examples at the visitor center garden. After a wet winter you can see a short-lived but stunning display of cacti, succulents, and desert wildflowers in bloom.

The park is unusually accessible to visitors. Admission to the park is free, and few areas are off-limits. There are two developed campgrounds, but you can camp anywhere; just follow the trails and pitch a tent wherever you like. There are more than 500 miles of dirt roads, two huge wilderness areas, and 110 miles of riding and hiking trails. Many sites can be seen from paved roads, but some require driving on dirt roads, for which rangers recommend you use a four-wheel-drive vehicle. When you do leave the pavement, carry the appropriate supplies: a cell phone (which may be unreliable in some areas), a shovel and other tools, flares, blankets, and plenty of water. The canyons are susceptible to flash flooding, so inquire about weather conditions (even on sunny days) before entering. ■TIP→ **Borrego resorts, restaurants, and the state park have Wi-Fi, but the service is spotty at best. If you need to talk to someone in the area, it's best to find a phone with a landline.**

The sites and hikes listed below are arranged by region of the park and distance from the visitor center: in the valley and hills surrounding Borrego Springs, near Tamarisk Campground, along Highway S2, south of Scissors Crossing, and south of Ocotillo Wells.

Stop by the **visitor center** to get oriented, to pick up a park map, and to learn about weather, road, and wildlife conditions. Designed to keep cool during the desert's blazing-hot summers, the center is built underground, beneath a demonstration desert garden containing examples of most of the native flora and a little pupfish pond. Displays inside the center illustrate the natural history of the area. Picnic tables are scattered throughout, making this a good place to linger and enjoy the view.

A 1½-mile trail leads to **Borrego Palm Canyon,** one of the few native palm groves in North America. The canyon, about 1 mile west of the visitor center, holds a grove of more than 1,000 native fan palms, a stream, and a waterfall. Wildlife is abundant along this route. This moderate hike is the most popular in the park.

With a year-round stream and lush plant life, **Coyote Canyon,** approximately 4½ miles north of Borrego Springs, is one of the best places to see and photograph spring wildflowers. Portions of the canyon road follow a section of the old Anza Trail. This area is closed between June 15 and September 15 to allow native bighorn sheep undisturbed use of the water. The dirt road that gives access to the canyon may be sandy enough to require a four-wheel-drive vehicle.

The late-afternoon vista of the Borrego badlands from **Font's Point,** 13 miles east of Borrego Springs, is one of the most breathtaking views in the desert, especially when the setting sun casts a golden glow in high relief on the eroded mountain slopes. The road from the Font's Point turnoff can be rough enough to make using a four-wheel-drive vehicle advisable; inquire about road conditions at the visitor center before starting out. Even if you can't make it out on the paved road, you can see some of the view from the highway.

East of Tamarisk Grove campground (13 miles south of Borrego Springs), the **Narrows Earth Trail** is a short walk off the road. Along the way you can see evidence of the many geologic processes involved in forming the canyons of the desert, such as a contact zone between two earthquake faults, and sedimentary layers of metamorphic and igneous rock.

The 1.6-mile round-trip **Yaqui Well Nature Trail** takes you along a path to a desert water hole where birds and wildlife are abundant. It's also a good place to look for wildflowers in spring. At the trailhead across from Tamarisk Campground you can pick up a brochure describing what can be seen along the trail.

Traversing a boulder-strewn trail is the easy, mostly flat **Pictograph/Smuggler's Canyon Trail.** At the end is a collection of rocks covered with muted red and yellow pictographs painted within the last hundred years or so by Native Americans. Walk about ½ mile beyond the pictures to reach Smuggler's Canyon, where an overlook provides views of the Vallecito Valley. The hike, from 2 to 3 miles round-trip, begins in Blair Valley, 6 miles southeast of Highway 78, off Highway S2, at the Scissors Crossing intersection.

Just a few steps off the paved road, **Carrizo Badlands Overlook** offers a view of eroded and twisted sedimentary rock that obscures the fossils of the mastodons, saber-tooths, zebras, and camels that roamed this region a million years ago. The route to the overlook through Earthquake Valley and Blair Valley parallels the Southern Emigrant Trail. It's off Highway S2, 40 miles south of Scissors Crossing.

Geology students from all over the world visit the Fish Creek area of Anza-Borrego to explore the canyon through Split Mountain. The narrow gorge with 600-foot walls was formed by an ancient stream. Fossils in this area indicate that a sea once covered the desert floor. From Highway 78 at Ocotillo Wells, take Split Mountain Road south 9 miles. ⌧ *Visitor Center, 200 Palm Canyon Dr., Hwy. S22* ☎ *760/767–4205, 760/767–4684 wildflower hotline* ⊕ *www.parks.ca.gov* ☒ *Free; day-use parking in campground areas $10* ☞ *Make a campground reservation at: reservecalifornia.com.*

★ Galleta Meadows

PUBLIC ART | FAMILY | At Galleta Meadows, camels, llamas, saber-toothed tigers, tortoises, and monumental gomphotherium (a sort of ancient elephant) appear to roam the earth again. These life-size bronze figures are of prehistoric animals whose fossils can be found in the Borrego Badlands. The collection of more than 130 sculptures created by Ricardo Breceda was commissioned by the late Dennis Avery, who installed the works of art on property he owned for the entertainment of locals and visitors. Maps are available from Borrego Springs Chamber of Commerce. ⌧ *Borrego Springs Rd., from Christmas Circle to Henderson Canyon* ☎ *760/767–5555* ☒ *Free.*

🍴 Restaurants

The Arches

$$$ | MODERN AMERICAN | On the edge of the Borrego Springs Resort, Golf Club & Spa's golf course, set beneath a canopy of grapefruit trees, The Arches is a pleasant place to eat. For breakfast you'll find burritos alongside French toast, omelets, and eggs Benedict; or for lunch (best enjoyed on the patio) or dinner, the options include sandwiches, salads, and hearty pasta, seafood, grilled meats, and fish entrées. **Known for:** light fare; nightly specials; popular happy hour. ⑤ *Average main: $24* ⌧ *1112 Tilting T Dr.* ☎ *760/767–5700* ⊕ *www.borregospringsresort.com/dining.asp* ⊙ *Summer hrs vary; call ahead.*

Carlee's Place

$$$ | AMERICAN | Sooner or later most visitors to Borrego Springs wind up at Carlee's Place for a drink and a bite to eat, drawn by the extra-large menu with everything from burgers, salads, seafood, sandwiches, and prime rib. It's an all-American type of establishment, where your server might call you "honey" while setting a huge steak in front of you, and diners play pool and dance to jukebox music. **Known for:** all-American down-home setting; martinis and classic cocktails; everything made from scratch. ⑤ *Average main: $25* ⌧ *660 Palm Canyon Dr.* ☎ *760/767–3262* ⊕ *www.carleesplace.com.*

Carmelita's Mexican Grill and Cantina

$ | MEXICAN | A friendly, family-run eatery tucked into a back corner of what is called "The Mall," Carmelita's draws locals and visitors all day, whether it's for a hearty breakfast, a cooked-to-order enchilada or burrito, or to tip back a brew or margarita at the bar. The menu lists typical combination plates (enchiladas, burritos, tamales, and tacos). **Known for:** dog-friendly outdoor patio; house-made masa dough and salsas;

full bar with sports TVs. $ *Average main: $15* ✉ *575 Palm Canyon Dr.* ☎ *760/767–5666.*

Coyote Steakhouse

$$$ | **MODERN AMERICAN** | The upscale Coyote Steakhouse at the Palms at Indian Head hotel caters to those who want a fancy dinner, particularly hunks of filet mignon or rack of lamb served at candlelit tables with white tablecloths overlooking the pool. Pet owners will appreciate the canine menu, whose treats include house-made peanut-butter dog cookies. **Known for:** romantic candlelit dining room; pork tenderloin and prime rib; classic mid-century setting. $ *Average main: $30* ✉ *2220 Hoberg Rd.* ☎ *760/767–7788* ⊕ *www.thepalmsatindianhead.com* ☾ *No breakfast or lunch.*

Los Jilberto's Taco Shop

$ | **MEXICAN** | A casual local favorite for affordable Mexican dishes, Jilberto's serves up big burritos and meaty enchiladas. **Known for:** authentic Mexican dishes cooked to order; all-day breakfast menu; reasonable prices. $ *Average main: $10* ✉ *655 Palm Canyon Dr.* ☎ *760/767–1008* ⊕ *www.losjilbertostacoshop.com* ▭ *No credit cards.*

Hotels

Borrego Springs Resort, Golf Club & Spa

$$$ | **RESORT** | The large rooms at this quiet resort set around a swimming pool and with golf, tennis, and golf options come with either a shaded balcony or a patio with desert views. **Pros:** golf, tennis, and bikes available; good desert views from most rooms; close to sculpture gardens. **Cons:** rooms slightly dated; average service; breakfast not included. $ *Rooms from: $182* ✉ *1112 Tilting T Dr.* ☎ *760/767–5700, 888/826–7734* ⊕ *www.borregospringsresort.com* ⇥ *100 rooms* ☉ *No meals.*

★ Borrego Valley Inn

$$$$ | **B&B/INN** | Those looking for desert landscapes and some stargazing—guests must be 21 or older—may enjoy the adobe Southwestern-style buildings here that house spacious rooms, which boasts plenty of natural light, original art, pine beds, and corner fireplaces. **Pros:** swim under the stars in the clothing-optional pool; exquisite desert gardens; breakfast included. **Cons:** no kids and no pets; rooms could use sprucing up; service inconsistent. $ *Rooms from: $285* ✉ *405 Palm Canyon Dr.* ☎ *760/767–0311, 800/333–5810* ⊕ *www.borregovalleyinn.com* ⇥ *15 rooms* ☉ *Free Breakfast.*

★ La Casa Del Zorro

$$$ | **RESORT** | **FAMILY** | The draws at this desert hideaway a short drive from Anza Borrego State Park include three guest-only pools, a hot tub, five night-lit tennis courts and two pickle ball courts, a yoga studio, a spa, a restaurant, and the lively Fox Den Bar. The 42-acre property pays tribute to its surroundings with a cactus garden, a fire pit, and two tall, welded-metal animal sculptures by local artist Ricardo Breceda. **Pros:** private pool or hot tub in many casitas; 26 pools and 14 water features; on-site spa, bar, and restaurant. **Cons:** service can be spotty; casitas need updating; occasional strong desert winds sweep sand across the property. $ *Rooms from: $189* ✉ *3845 Yaqui Pass Rd.* ☎ *760/767–0100* ⊕ *www.lacasadelzorro.com* ⇥ *44 rooms, 19 casitas* ☉ *No meals.*

Activities

GOLF

Borrego Springs Resort, Golf Club & Spa

GOLF | The two 9-hole courses here, Mesquite and Desert Willow, are generally played as an 18-hole round by most golfers, starting with Mesquite. Both courses have natural desert landscaping and mature date palms. ✉ *1112 Tilting T Dr.* ☎ *760/767–3330* ⊕ *www.*

borregospringsresort.com *From $45* 🏌 *18 holes, 6760 yards, par 71* ☞ *Closed June–Sept.*

Roadrunner Golf and Country Club

GOLF | Adjacent to the Springs at Borrego course and with some shared facilities, this club has an 18-hole par-3 golf course. Though the course has views of the Santa Rosa, San Ysidro, and Vallecito mountains and Indian Head Mountain, the terrain is relatively flat. Another bonus: there's rarely a wait for a tee time. ✉ *1010 Palm Canyon Dr.* ☎ *760/767–5374* ⊕ *www. roadrunnerclub.com* *$40* 🏌 *18 holes, 2445 yards, par 3.*

🛍 Shopping

Anza-Borrego State Park Store

SPECIALTY STORES | The Anza-Borrego Foundation, a land conservation group, runs this store that sells guidebooks, maps, clothing, desert art, and gifts for kids. Its enthusiastic staffers also assist with trip planning. Foundation guides organize hikes, naturalist talks, classes, research programs, and nature walks. ✉ *587 Palm Canyon Dr., No. 110* ☎ *760/767–0446* ⊕ *www.theabf.org* ⊘ *Closed weekends June–Sept., and Wed. and Thurs. Oct.–May.*

Borrego Outfitters

CONVENIENCE/GENERAL STORES | This contemporary general store stocks high-end outdoor gear, hiking essentials, personal care items from Burt's Bees, footwear from Teva and Thymes, swimsuits, and tabletop items. You can browse through racks of clothing and piles of hats, all suited to the desert climate. ✉ *579 Palm Canyon Dr.* ☎ *760/767–3502* ⊕ *www.borregooutfitters.com.*

Salton Sea

30 miles southeast of Indio, 29 miles east of Borrego Springs.

The Salton Sea, one of the largest inland seas on Earth, is the product of both natural and artificial forces. The sea occupies the Salton Basin, a remnant of prehistoric Lake Cahuilla. Over the centuries the Colorado River flooded the basin and the water drained into the Gulf of California. In 1905 a flood once again filled the Salton Basin, but the exit to the gulf was blocked by sediment. The floodwaters remained in the basin, creating a saline lake 228 feet below sea level, about 35 miles long and 15 miles wide, with a surface area of nearly 380 square miles. The sea, which lies along the Pacific Flyway, supports 400 species of birds. Fishing for tilapia, boating, camping, and bird-watching are popular activities year-round.

GETTING HERE AND AROUND

Salton Sea State Recreation Area includes about 14 miles of coastline on the northeastern shore of the sea, about 30 miles south of Indio via Highway 111. The Sonny Bono Salton Sea National Wildlife Refuge fills the southernmost tip of the sea's shore. To reach it from the recreation area, continue south about 60 miles to Niland; continue south to Sinclair Road, and turn west following the road to the Refuge Headquarters.

👁 Sights

Salton Sea State Recreation Area

NATIONAL/STATE PARK | FAMILY | This huge recreation area on the sea's north shore draws thousands each year to its playgrounds, hiking trails, fishing spots, and boat launches. Ranger-guided bird walks take place on Saturday; you'll see migrating and native birds including Canada geese, pelicans, and shorebirds. ✉ *100–225 State Park Rd., North Shore* ☎ *760/393–3059, 760/393–3810 visitor center* ⊕ *www.parks.ca.gov* *$7.*

Sonny Bono Salton Sea National Wildlife Refuge

NATURE PRESERVE | The 2,200-acre wildlife refuge here, on the Pacific Flyway, is a wonderful spot for viewing migratory birds. There's an observation deck where you can watch Canada geese, and along the trails you might view eared grebes, burrowing owls, great blue herons, ospreys, and yellow-footed gulls. ⚠ **Though the scenery is beautiful, the waters here give off an unpleasant odor, and the New River, which empties into the sea, is quite toxic.** ✉ *906 W. Sinclair Rd., Calipatria* ☎ *760/348–5278* ⊕ *www.fws.gov/refuge/sonny_bono_salton_sea/* ✉ *Free* ⊙ *Closed weekends Mar.–Oct.*

Chapter 6

ORANGE COUNTY AND CATALINA ISLAND

Updated by
Kathy A. McDonald

6

Sights	Restaurants	Hotels	Shopping	Nightlife
★★★★★	★★★★☆	★★★★★	★☆☆☆☆	★☆☆☆☆

WELCOME TO ORANGE COUNTY AND CATALINA ISLAND

TOP REASONS TO GO

★ **Disney Magic:** Walking down Main Street, U.S.A., with Sleeping Beauty Castle straight ahead, you really will feel like you're in one of the happiest places on Earth.

★ **Beautiful Beaches:** Surf, swim, paddleboard, or just relax on one of the state's most breathtaking stretches of coastline. Keep in mind the water may be colder and rougher than you expect.

★ **Island Getaway:** Just a short high-speed catamaran ride from the shore, Catalina Island feels 1,000 miles away from the mainland. Wander around charming Avalon, dive or snorkel through the state's first underwater park, or explore the unspoiled beauty of the island's wild interior.

★ **The Fine Life:** Some of the state's wealthiest communities are in coastal Orange County, so spend at least part of your stay here experiencing how the other half lives.

★ **Family Fun:** Ride roller coasters, eat ice cream, bike on oceanfront paths, fish off ocean piers, or try bodysurfing.

1 Disneyland Resort. Once a humble vision of Walt Disney's, Southern California's top family and tourist destination has grown to become a megaresort, with more attractions spilling over into Disney's California Adventure. There's plenty here to entertain kids and adults alike.

2 Knott's Berry Farm. Amusement park lovers should check out this Buena Park attraction, with thrill rides, the *Peanuts* gang, and lots of fried chicken and boysenberry pie.

3 The Coast. The O.C.'s beach communities may not be quite as glamorous as they appear on TV, but coastal spots like Newport Harbor and Laguna Beach are perfect for chilling out in an oceanfront hotel.

4 Catalina Island. This unspoiled island paradise—with its pocket-size town, Avalon, and large nature preserve—is just off the Orange County coast.

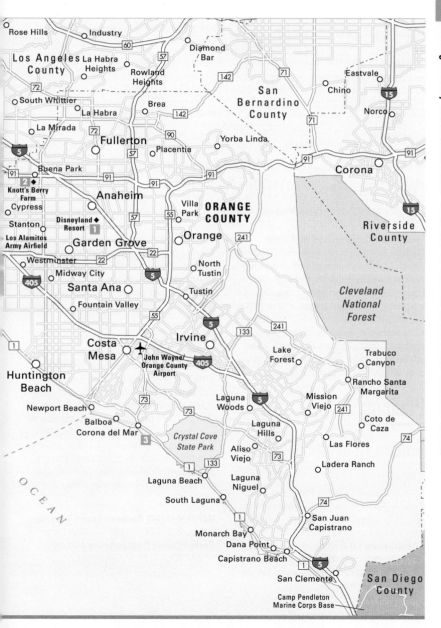

With its tropical flowers and palm trees, the stretch of coast between Seal Beach and San Clemente is often called the California Riviera. Exclusive Newport Beach and artsy Laguna are the stars, but lesser-known gems on the glistening coast—such as Corona del Mar—are also worth visiting. Offshore, meanwhile, lies gorgeous Catalina Island, a terrific spot for boating, diving, snorkeling, and hiking.

Few of the citrus groves that gave Orange County its name remain. This region south and east of Los Angeles is now ruled by tourism and high-tech business rather than agriculture. Despite a building boom that began in the 1990s, the area is still a place to find wilderness trails, canyons, greenbelts, and natural environs. Just offshore is a deep-water wilderness that's possible to explore via daily whale-watching excursions.

Planning

Getting Here and Around

AIR TRAVEL
Orange County's main facility is John Wayne Airport Orange County (SNA), which is served by six major domestic airlines and one commuter line. Long Beach Airport (LGB) is served by four airlines, including its major player, Jet-Blue. It's roughly 20 to 30 minutes by car from Anaheim.

Super Shuttle and Prime Time Airport Shuttle provide transportation from John Wayne and LAX to the Disneyland area of Anaheim. Round-trip fares average about $28 per person from John Wayne and $34 to $80 from LAX.

BUS TRAVEL
The Orange County Transportation Authority will take you virtually anywhere in the county, but it will take time; OCTA buses go from Knott's Berry Farm and Disneyland to Newport Beach. Bus 1 travels along the coast; Buses 701 and 721 provide express service to Los Angeles. Anaheim offers Anaheim Resort Transportation (ART) service that connects hotels to Disneyland Resort, downtown Anaheim, Buena Park, and the Metrolink train center. Rides are $3 each way.

INFORMATION Anaheim Resort Transportation. ☎ 714/563–5287 ⊕ rideart.org. **Orange County Transportation Authority.** ☎ 714/636–7433 ⊕ www.octa.net.

CAR TRAVEL

The San Diego Freeway (Interstate 405), the coastal route, and the Santa Ana Freeway (Interstate 5), the inland route, run north–south through Orange County. South of Laguna, Interstate 405 merges into Interstate 5 (called the San Diego Freeway south from this point). A toll road, Highway 73, runs 15 miles from Newport Beach to San Juan Capistrano; it costs $6.22–$8.48 (lower rates are for weekends and off-peak hours) and is usually less jammed than the regular freeways. Do your best to avoid all Orange County freeways during rush hours (6–9 am and 3:30–6:30 pm). Highway 55 leads to Newport Beach. The Pacific Coast Highway (Highway 1) allows easy access to beach communities and is the most scenic route but expect it to be crowded, especially on summer weekends and holidays.

FERRY TRAVEL

There are two ferries that service Catalina Island; Catalina Express runs from Long Beach (about 90 minutes) and from Newport Beach (about 75 minutes). Reservations are strongly advised for summers and weekends. During the winter months, ferry crossings are not as frequent as in the summer high season.

TRAIN TRAVEL

Amtrak makes daily stops in Orange County at all major towns. Metrolink is a weekday commuter train that runs to and from Los Angeles and Orange County.

INFORMATION Amtrak. ☎ 800/872–7245 ⊕ www.amtrak.com. **Metrolink.** ☎ 800/371–5465 ⊕ www.metrolink-trains.com.

Restaurants

Much like in L.A., restaurants in Orange County are generally casual, and you'll rarely see suits and ties. However, at top resort hotel dining rooms, many guests choose to dress up.

Of course, there's also a swath of casual places along the beachfronts—seafood takeout, taquerias, burger joints—that won't mind if you wear flip-flops. Reservations are recommended for the nicest restaurants.

Many places don't serve past 11 pm, and locals tend to eat early. Remember that according to California law, smoking is prohibited in all enclosed areas.

Hotels

Along the coast there are remarkable luxury resorts; if you can't afford a stay, pop in for the view at Laguna Beach's Montage or the always welcoming Ritz-Carlton at Dana Point. For a taste of the O.C. glam life, have lunch overlooking the yachts of Newport Bay at the Balboa Bay Resort.

As a rule, lodging prices tend to rise the closer the hotels are to the beach. If you're looking for value, consider a hotel that's inland along the Interstate 405 freeway corridor.

In most cases, you can take advantage of some of the facilities of the high-end resorts, such as restaurants and spas, even if you aren't an overnight guest.

Restaurant and hotel reviews have been shortened. For full information, visit Fodors.com.

WHAT IT COSTS			
$	$$	$$$	$$$$
RESTAURANTS			
under $20	$20–$30	$30–$40	over $40
HOTELS			
under $200	$200–$300	$301–$400	over $400

Visitor Information

Visit Anaheim is an excellent resource for both leisure and business travelers and can provide materials on many area attractions. Kiosks at the Anaheim Convention Center act as a digital concierge and allow visitors to plan itineraries and buy tickets to area attractions.

The Orange County Visitors Association's website is also a useful source of information.

INFORMATION Orange County Visitors Association. ⊕ *www.visittheoc.com.* **Visit Anaheim.** ✉ *Anaheim Convention Center, 800 W. Katella Ave., Anaheim* ☎ *714/765–2800* ⊕ *www.visitanaheim.org.*

Disneyland Resort

26 miles southeast of Los Angeles, via I–5.

The snowcapped Matterhorn, the centerpiece of Disneyland, punctuates the skyline of Anaheim. Since 1955, when Walt Disney chose this once-quiet farming community for the site of his first amusement park, Disneyland has attracted more than 650 million visitors and tens of thousands of workers, and Anaheim has been their host.

The resort is a sprawling complex that includes Disney's two amusement parks; three hotels; and Downtown Disney, a shopping, dining, and entertainment promenade. Anaheim's tourist center includes Angel Stadium of Anaheim, home of baseball's 2002 World Series Champion, Los Angeles Angels of Anaheim; the Honda Center (formerly the Arrowhead Pond), which hosts concerts and the Anaheim Ducks hockey team; and the enormous Anaheim Convention Center.

GETTING THERE

Disney is about a 30-mile drive from either LAX or Downtown. From LAX, follow Sepulveda Boulevard south to the Interstate 105 freeway and drive east 16 miles to the Interstate 605 north exit. Exit at the Santa Ana Freeway (Interstate 5) and continue south for 12 miles to the Disneyland Drive exit. Follow signs to the resort. From Downtown, follow Interstate 5 south 28 miles and exit at Disneyland Drive. **Disneyland Resort Express** (☎ *800/828–6699* ⊕ *dre.coachusa.com*) offers daily nonstop bus service between LAX, John Wayne Airport, and Anaheim. Reservations are not required. The cost is $30 one-way from LAX, and $20 from John Wayne Airport.

SAVING TIME AND MONEY

If you plan to visit for more than a day, you can save money by buying two- three-, four-, and five-day Park Hopper tickets that grant same-day "hopping" privileges between Disneyland and Disney's California Adventure. You get a discount on the multiple-day passes if you buy online through the Disneyland website.

Single-day admission prices vary by date. A one-day Park Hopper pass costs $147–$185 for anyone 10 or older, $141–$177 for kids ages three to nine depending on what day you go. Admission to either park (but not both) is $97–$135 or $91–$127 for kids three to nine; kids two and under are free.

In addition to tickets, parking is $20–$35 (unless your hotel has a shuttle or is within walking distance), and meals in the parks and at Downtown Disney range from $10 to $60 per person.

Disneyland

★ Disneyland

AMUSEMENT PARK/WATER PARK | FAMILY |
An imaginative original, Disneyland was an unproven concept when it opened in 1955. But Walt Disney himself could never have predicted the park's success and its beloved place in the hearts of Southern Californians. It is the only one of the parks to have been overseen by Walt himself, has a genuine historic feel, and occupies a unique place in the Disney legend. Expertly run, perfectly maintained, with polite and helpful staff ("cast members" in the Disney lexicon), the park has plenty that you won't find anywhere else—such as the Indiana Jones Adventure ride and Storybook Land, with its miniature replicas of animated Disney scenes from classics such as *Frozen* and *Alice in Wonderland*. Characters appear for autographs and photos throughout the day; times and places are posted at the entrances. Live shows, parades, strolling musicians, fireworks on weekends, and endless snack choices add to the carnival atmosphere. You can also meet some of the animated icons at one of the character meals served at the three Disney hotels (open to the public). Belongings can be stored in lockers just off Main Street; stroller rentals at the entrance gate are a convenient option for families with small tykes. The park's popularity means there are crowds year-round, even on the rare Southern California rainy days. ✉ *1313 S. Disneyland Dr., between Ball Rd. and Katella Ave., Anaheim* ☎ *714/781–4636 guest information* ⊕ *www.disneyland. com* ✉ *From $97; parking $20.*

PARK NEIGHBORHOODS

Neighborhoods for Disneyland are arranged in geographic order.

MAIN STREET, U.S.A.

Walt's hometown of Marceline, Missouri, was the inspiration behind this romanticized image of small-town America, circa 1900. The sidewalks are lined with a penny arcade and shops that sell everything from tradeable pins to Disney-themed clothing, an endless supply of sugar confections, and a photo shop that offers souvenirs created via Disney's PhotoPass (on-site photographers capture memorable moments digitally—you can access them in person or online via the Disneyland app). Main Street opens half an hour before the rest of the park, so it's a good place to explore if you're getting an early start to beat the crowds (it's also open an hour after the other attractions close, so you may want to save your shopping for the end of the day). **Main Street Cinema** offers a cool respite from the crowds and six classic Disney animated shorts, including *Steamboat Willie.* There's rarely a wait to enter. Grab a cappuccino and fresh-made pastry at the Jolly Holiday bakery to jump-start your visit. Board the **Disneyland Railroad** here to save on walking; it tours all the lands and offers unique views of Splash Mountain, the Grand Canyon, and Primeval World dioramas.

NEW ORLEANS SQUARE

This mini–French Quarter, with narrow streets, hidden courtyards, and live street performances, is home to two iconic attractions and the Cajun-inspired Blue Bayou restaurant. **Pirates of the Caribbean** now features Jack Sparrow and the cursed Captain Barbossa of the blockbuster series, plus enhanced special effects and battle scenes (complete with cannonball explosions). Nearby **Haunted Mansion** continues to spook guests with its stretching room and "doombuggy" rides (there's now an expanded storyline for the beating-heart bride). The *Nightmare Before Christmas* holiday overlay is an annual tradition. This is a good area to get a casual bite to eat; the clam chowder in sourdough bread bowls, sold at the French Market Restaurant and Royal Street Veranda, is a popular choice. Food carts offer everything from just-popped popcorn to churros and even fresh fruit.

Disneyland

MICKEY'S TOONTOWN

San Diego Freeway 5

Minnie's House
Mickey's House
Chip 'n Dale Treehouse
Gadget's Go Coaster
Goofy's Playhouse
Roger Rabbit's Car Toon Spin
Donald's Boat
Fantasyland Theatre

It's A Small World

FANTASYLAND
Dumbo the Flying Elephant
Casey Jr. Circus Train
Storybook Land Canal Boats

DISNEYLAND PARK

King Arthur Carousel
Peter Pan's Flight
Mad Tea Party
Mr. Toad's Wild Ride
Alice in Wonderland

FRONTIERLAND
Rivers of America
Big Thunder Mountain RR
Pinocchio's Daring Journey
Snow White's Scary Adventures
Matterhorn Bobsleds
Finding Nemo's Submarine Voyage
Autopia

The Many Adventures of Winnie the Pooh
Canoes
Tom Sawyer Island
Fantasy Faire
Fantasy Land
Plaza Garden Stage
Buzz Lightyear Astro Blasters
Star Wars Launch Bay

CRITTER COUNTRY
Sailing Ship Columbia
Mark Twain Riverboat
Shootin' Exposition
Central Plaza
Astro Orbiter
Star Tours- The Adventure Continues
Star Wars, Path of the Jedi

Splash Mountain
Golden Horseshoe Stage
Enchanted Tiki Room
Haunted Mansion
Rafts
TOMORROWLAND

Pirates of the Caribbean
Jungle Cruise
Tarzan's Treehouse
Parade Route
Space Mountain

NEW ORLEANS SQUARE
ADVENTURELAND

Indiana Jones Adventure
Main Street Cinema

MAIN STREET, U.S.A.

Disneyland Railroad

House of Blues Stage

DOWNTOWN DISNEY

AMC Theaters
LEGO Imagination Center

Red Car Trolley
Soarin' Around the World
Monsters Inc. Mike & Sulley to the Rescue

Disneyland Hotel
Grand Californian Hotel
Sunset Showcase Theatre
Hollywood Backlot Stage
HOLLYWOOD LAN[...]
Turtle Talk with Crush
Frozen
Disney Animation

SUNSHINE PLAZA
Disney Junior

Paradise Pier Hotel
Grizzly River Run
GRIZZLY PEAK
BUENA VISTA STREET
It's Tough To Be a Bug
Flik's Flyers
Guardians of the Galaxy- Mission:BREAKOUT!

Redwood Creek Challenge Trail
Wine Country Trattoria
"A BUG'S LAND"
Tuck and Roll's Drive 'Em Buggies

Little Mermaid- Ariel's Undersea Adventure
The Bakery Tour
DISNEY CALIFORNIA ADVENTURE

Goofy's Sky School
Jumpin' Jellyfish
PARADISE GARDENS PARK
PACIFIC WHARF
Luigi's Rollickin' Roadsters

Golden Zephyr
Silly Symphony Swings
Lamplight Lounge
Radiator Springs Racers
CARS LAND

PIXAR PIER
Pixar Pal-A-Round
Toy Story Midway Mania!
California Screamin'
Games of the Boardwalk
King Triton's Carousel
Incredicoaster

Disneyland Drive

Parking

Katella Avenue

KEY	
🚻	Restrooms
┼┼┼	Rail Line
⊂⊃⊂⊃	Monorail

FRONTIERLAND

Between Adventureland and Fantasyland, Frontierland transports you to the wild, wild West with its rustic buildings, shooting gallery, mountain range, and foot-stompin' dance hall. The marquee attraction, **Big Thunder Mountain Railroad,** is a relatively tame roller coaster ride (no steep descents) that takes the form of a runaway mine car as it rumbles past desert canyons and an old mining town. Tour the Rivers of America on the **Mark Twain Riverboat** in the company of a grizzled old river pilot or circumnavigate the globe on the **Sailing Ship Columbia,** though its operating hours are usually limited to weekends. From here, you can raft over to Pirate's Lair on **Tom Sawyer Island,** which now features pirate-themed caves, treasure hunts, and music, along with plenty of caves and hills to climb and explore. If you don't mind tight seating, have a snack at the Golden Horseshoe saloon, where Walt himself used to hang out.

CRITTER COUNTRY

Down-home country is the theme in this shaded corner of the park, where Winnie the Pooh and Davy Crockett make their homes. Here you can find **Splash Mountain,** a classic flume ride with music, and appearances by Brer Rabbit and other *Song of the South* characters. Don't forget to check out your photo (the camera snaps close-ups of each car just before it plunges into the water) on the way out. The patio of the popular Hungry Bear Restaurant has great views of Tom Sawyer's Island and Davy Crockett's Explorer Canoes, which ply the waters on weekends only.

ADVENTURELAND

Modeled after the lands of Africa, Polynesia, and Arabia, this tiny tropical paradise is worth braving the crowds that flock here for the ambience and better-than-average food. Sing along with the animatronic birds and tiki gods in the **Enchanted Tiki Room,** sail the rivers of the world with

Disney's Top Attractions

- **Indiana Jones:** You're at the wheel for this thrilling ride through a cursed temple.

- **Haunted Mansion:** A "doombuggy" takes you through a spooky old plantation mansion.

- **Matterhorn Bobsleds:** At the center of the Magic Kingdom, this roller coaster simulates bobsleds.

- **Pirates of the Caribbean:** Watch buccaneers wreak havoc as you float along in a rowboat.

- **Space Mountain:** This scary-but-thrilling roller coaster is indoors—and mostly in the dark.

joke-cracking skippers on **Jungle Cruise,** and climb the *Disneyodendron semperflorens* (the always-blooming Disney tree) to **Tarzan's Treehouse,** where you can walk through scenes, some interactive, from the 1999 animated film. Cap off the visit with a wild jeep ride at **Indiana Jones Adventure,** where the special effects and decipherable hieroglyphics distract you while you're waiting in line. There's a single-rider option for a quicker ride. The skewers (some vegetarian options available) at Bengal Barbecue and pineapple whip at Tiki Juice Bar are some of the best fast-food options in the park.

FANTASYLAND

Sleeping Beauty Castle marks the entrance to Fantasyland, a visual wonderland of princesses, spinning teacups, flying elephants, and other classic storybook characters. Rides, and shops such as the princess-themed Bibbidi Bobbidi Boutique, take precedence over restaurants in this area of the park, but outdoor carts sell everything from churros to turkey legs. Tots love the **King**

Best Tips for Disneyland

■TIP➜ **As of 2017, all visitors must pass through metal detectors, and bags are searched before entering the Disneyland Resort. Allot 10–15 extra minutes for passing through the security line.**

Download the Disneyland app. The app provides access to FASTPASS tickets via the digital MAXPASS, shows attraction wait times in real time, lists entertainment and parade times, and can guide you through the park.

Buy entry tickets in advance. Nearby hotels sell park admission tickets; you can also buy them through Disney's website and the Disneyland app. With package deals, like those offered through AAA, tickets are included.

Lines at ticket booths can take more than an hour on busy days. Save time by buying in advance.

Come midweek. Weekends, especially in summer, are a mob scene. Holidays are crowded, too. A rainy winter weekday is often the least crowded time to visit.

Plan your times to hit the most popular rides. Get to the park as early as possible, even before the gates open, and make a beeline for the top rides before the crowds reach a critical mass. Late evening is when the hordes thin out, and you can catch a special show or parade. Save the quieter attractions for mid-afternoon.

Use FASTPASS. These passes allow you to reserve your place in line at some of the most crowded attractions (only one at a time). Distribution machines are posted near the entrances of each attraction. Feed in your park admission ticket, and you'll receive a pass with a printed time frame (generally up to 1–1½ hours later) during which you can return to wait in a much shorter line.

Avoid peak mealtime crowds. Start the day with a big breakfast so you won't be too hungry at noon, when restaurants and vendors get slammed. Wait to have lunch until after 1 pm.

If you want to eat at the **Blue Bayou** in New Orleans Square, you can make a reservation up to six months in advance online. Another (cheaper) option is to bring your own snacks. It's always a good idea to bring water.

Check the daily events schedule online or at the park entrance. During parades, fireworks, and other special events, sections of the parks are filled with crowds. This can work in your favor or against you: an event could make it difficult to get around a park—but if you plan ahead, you can take advantage of the distraction to hit popular rides.

Send the teens next door. Disneyland's newer sister park, California Adventure, features more intense rides suitable for older kids (Park Hopper passes include admission to both parks).

Arthur Carousel, Casey Jr. Circus Train, and **Storybook Land Canal Boats.** This is also home to **Mr. Toad's Wild Ride, Peter Pan's Flight,** and **Pinocchio's Daring Journey,** all classic movie-theater-dark rides that immerse riders in Disney fairy tales. The Abominable Snowman pops up on the **Matterhorn Bobsleds,** a roller coaster that twists and turns up and around on a made-to-scale model of the real Swiss mountain. Anchoring the east end of Fantasyland is **It's a Small World,** a smorgasbord of dancing animatronic dolls, cuckoo clock–covered walls, and variations of the song everyone knows, or soon *will* know, by heart. Beloved Disney characters like Ariel from *The Little Mermaid* are also part of the mix. Fantasy Faire is a fairy tale–style village that collects all the Disney princesses together. Each has her own reception nook in the Royal Hall. Condensed retellings of *Tangled* and *Beauty and the Beast* take place at the Royal Theatre.

MICKEY'S TOONTOWN

Geared toward small fries, this lopsided cartoonlike downtown, complete with cars and trolleys that invite exploring, is where Mickey, Donald, Goofy, and other classic Disney characters hang their hats. One of the most popular attractions is **Roger Rabbit's Car Toon Spin,** a twisting, turning cab ride through the Toontown of *Who Framed Roger Rabbit?* You can also walk through **Mickey's House** to meet and be photographed with the famous mouse, take a low-key ride on **Gadget's Go Coaster,** or bounce around the fenced-in playground in front of **Goofy's Playhouse.**

TOMORROWLAND

This popular section of the park continues to tinker with its future, adding and enhancing rides regularly. *Star Wars*–themed attractions can't be missed, like the immersive, 3-D **Star Tours – The Adventures Continue,** where you can join the Rebellion in a galaxy far, far away. **Finding Nemo's Submarine Voyage** updates the old Submarine Voyage ride with the

exploits of Nemo, Dory, Marlin, and other characters from the Disney-Pixar film. Try to visit this popular ride early in the day if you can, and be prepared for a wait. The interactive **Buzz Lightyear Astro Blasters** lets you zap your neighbors with laser beams and compete for the highest score. Hurtle through the cosmos on **Space Mountain** or check out mainstays like the futuristic **Astro Orbiter** rockets, **Star Wars Launch Bay,** which showcases costumes, models, and props from the franchise, and **Star Wars, Path of the Jedi,** which catches viewers up on all the movies with a quick 12-minute film. Disneyland Monorail and Disneyland Railroad both have stations here. There's also a video arcade and dancing water fountain that makes a perfect playground for kids on hot summer days. The Jedi Training Academy spotlights future Luke Skywalkers in the crowd.

Besides the eight lands, the daily live-action shows and parades are always crowd pleasers. Among these is **Fantasmic!,** a musical, fireworks, and laser show in which Mickey and friends wage a spellbinding battle against Disneyland's darker characters. ■TIP➔ **Arrive early to secure a good view; if there are two shows scheduled for the day, the second one tends to be less crowded. A fireworks display lights up weekends and most summer evenings.** Brochures with maps, available at the entrance, list show and parade times.

Disney California Adventure

⭐ **Disney California Adventure**
AMUSEMENT PARK/WATER PARK | FAMILY | The sprawling Disney California Adventure, adjacent to Disneyland (their entrances face each other), pays tribute to the Golden State with seven theme areas that re-create vintage architectural styles and embrace several hit Pixar films via engaging attractions. Visitors enter through the art deco–style Buena Vista Street, past shops and a

Did You Know?

The plain purple teacup in Disneyland's Mad Tea Party ride spins the fastest—though no one knows why.

helpful information booth that advises wait times on attractions. The 12-acre Cars Land features Radiator Springs Racers, a speedy trip in six-passenger speedsters through scenes featured in the blockbuster hit. (FASTPASS tickets for the ride run out early most days.) Other popular attractions include the free-falling Guardians of the Galaxy–Mission: BREAKOUT!; World of Color, a nighttime water-effects show; and Toy Story Midway Mania!, an interactive adventure ride hosted by Woody and Buzz Lightyear. At night the park takes on neon hues as glowing signs light up Route 66 in Cars Land and Pixar Pal-A-Round, a giant Ferris wheel on the Pixar Pier. Cocktails, beer, and wine are available; craft beers and premium wines from California are poured. Live nightly entertainment also features a 1930s jazz troupe that arrives in a vintage jalopy. Some rides have a minimum height limit of 40 inches. ⊠ *1313 S. Disneyland Dr., between Ball Rd. and Katella Ave., Anaheim* ☏ *714/781–4636* ⊕ *www.disneyland.com* ⊠ *From $97; parking $20.*

PARK NEIGHBORHOODS
BUENA VISTA STREET
California Adventure's grand entryway re-creates the lost 1920s Los Angeles that Walt Disney encountered when he moved to the Golden State. There's a **Red Car trolley** (modeled after Los Angeles's bygone streetcar line); hop on for the brief ride to Hollywood Land. Buena Vista Street is also home to a Starbucks outlet—within the Fiddler, Fifer and Practical Café—and the upscale Carthay Circle Restaurant and Lounge, which serves modern craft cocktails and beer. The comfy booths of the Carthay Circle restaurant on the second floor feel like a relaxing world away from the theme park outside.

GRIZZLY PEAK
This woodsy land celebrates the great outdoors. Test your skills on the **Redwood Creek Challenge Trail,** a challenging

trek across net ladders and suspension bridges. **Grizzly River Run** mimics the river rapids of the Sierra Nevadas; be prepared to get soaked.

Soarin' Around the World is a spectacular simulated hang-gliding ride over internationally known landmarks like Switzerland's Matterhorn and India's Taj Mahal.

HOLLYWOOD LAND
With a main street modeled after Hollywood Boulevard, a fake sky backdrop, and real sound stages, this area celebrates California's film industry. **Disney Animation** gives you an insider's look at how animators create characters. **Turtle Talk with Crush** lets kids have an unscripted chat with a computer-animated Crush, the sea turtle from *Finding Nemo*. The Hyperion Theater hosts **Frozen,** a 45-minute live performance from a Broadway-size cast with terrific visual effects. ■TIP→ **Plan on getting in line about half an hour in advance; the show is worth the wait.** On the film-inspired ride **Monsters, Inc. Mike & Sulley to the Rescue,** visitors climb into taxis and travel the streets of Monstropolis on a mission to safely return Boo to her bedroom. **Guardians of the Galaxy – Mission: BREAKOUT!,** which opened in summer 2017, replaced the now-closed Twilight Zone Tower of Terror.

CARS LAND
Amble down Route 66, the main thoroughfare of Cars Land, and discover a pitch-perfect re-creation of the vintage highway. Quick eats are found at the Cozy Cone Motel (in a teepee-shape motor court) while Flo's V8 café serves hearty comfort food. Start your day at Radiator Springs Racers, the park's most popular attraction, where waits can be two hours or longer. Strap into a nifty sports car and meet the characters of Pixar's *Cars*; the ride ends in a speedy auto race through the red rocks and desert of Radiator Springs. ■TIP→ **To bypass the line, there's a single-rider option for Radiator Springs Racers.**

PACIFIC WHARF

In the midst of the California Adventure you'll find 10 different dining options, from light snacks to full-service restaurants. The Wine Country Trattoria is a great place for Italian specialties; relax outside on the restaurant's terrace for a casual bite while sipping a California-made craft beer or wine. Mexican cuisine and potent margaritas are available at the Cocina Cucamonga Mexican Grill and Rita's Baja Blenders, and Lucky Fortune Cookery serves Chinese stir-fry dishes.

PARADISE GARDENS PARK

The far corner of California Adventure is a mix of floating, zigzagging, and flying rides: soar via the **Silly Symphony Swings**; **Goofy's Sky School** rollicks and rolls through a cartoon-inspired landscape; and the sleek retro-styled gondolas of the **Golden Zephyr** mimic 1920s movies and their sci-fi adventures. Journey through Ariel's colorful world on **The Little Mermaid—Ariel's Undersea Adventure.** The best views of the nighttime music, water, and light show, **World of Color,** are from the paths along Paradise Bay. FASTPASS tickets are available. Or for a guaranteed spot, book dinner at the Wine Country Trattoria that includes a ticket to a viewing area to catch all the show's stunning visuals.

PIXAR PIER

This section re-creates the glory days of California's seaside piers, themed with Pixar film characters. If you're looking for thrills, join The Incredibles family on the **Incredicoaster** as the fast moving roller coaster takes its riders from 0 to 55 mph in about four seconds and proceeds through scream tunnels, steeply angled drops, and a 360-degree loop. **Pixar Pal-A-Round,** a giant Ferris wheel, provides a good view of the grounds, though some cars spin and sway for more kicks. There are also carnival games, an aquatic-themed carousel, and **Toy Story Midway Mania!,** an interactive ride where you can take aim at a series of cartoon targets. Soft-serve ice cream, turkey legs, hot dogs, and churros are readily available for quick snacking. At the **Lamplight Lounge** adults can chill out and overlook the action while sipping on craft cocktails.

OTHER ATTRACTIONS
Downtown Disney District

AMUSEMENT PARK/WATER PARK | FAMILY | The Downtown Disney District is a 20-acre promenade of dining, shopping, and entertainment that connects the resort's hotels and theme parks. **The Void** provides an immersive virtual reality experience with special effects and more; the current game, **Star Wars: Secrets of the Empire,** transforms visitors into participants in an intergalactic battle. Refresh afterward at the bar or dining room at Splitsville, a mid-century modern–style bowling alley serving American comfort food. At **Ralph Brennan's Jazz Kitchen** you can dig into New Orleans–style food and music. Save room for sweets: **Salt and Straw** has gourmet ice cream while **Sprinkles** offers ultrarich cupcakes. Disney merchandise and artwork is showcased at the brightly lit **World of Disney** store. At the megasize **Lego Store** there are hands-on demonstrations and space to play with the latest Lego creations. **Anna and Elsa's Boutique** speedily makes over kids into their favorite character from the hit film *Frozen*. All visitors must pass through a security checkpoint and metal detectors before entering. With a minimum purchase of $20, parking is free for the first three hours. ✉ *1580 Disneyland Dr., Anaheim* ☎ *714/300–7800* ⊕ *disneyland.disney.go.com/downtown-disney* 🎫 *Free.*

🍴 Restaurants

Anaheim White House

$$$ | ITALIAN | Although a massive fire gutted the Anaheim White House in 2017, owner Bruno Serato rebuilt and expanded the local landmark known for its specialty pastas. The 1909-built original mansion

was the inspiration for the complete renovation. ⑤ *Average main: $38 ✉ 887 S. Anaheim Blvd., Anaheim* ☎ *714/772–1381* ⊕ *www.anaheimwhitehouse.com* ⊘ *No lunch.*

Catal Restaurant and Uva Bar

$$$ | **MEDITERRANEAN** | Famed chef Joachim Splichal guides his staff to take a relaxed approach at this bi-level Mediterranean spot, where more than 30 wines by the glass, craft beers, and craft cocktails pair well with his Spanish-influenced dishes. Upstairs, Catal's menu has tapas, a variety of flavorful paellas, and charcuterie. **Known for:** people-watching; gourmet burgers; happy hour. ⑤ *Average main: $30 ✉ Downtown Disney District, 1580 S. Disneyland Dr., Suite 103, Anaheim* ☎ *714/781–3463* ⊕ *www.patinagroup.com.*

Napa Rose

$$$$ | **AMERICAN** | Done up in a handsome Craftsman style, Napa Rose's rich seasonal cuisine is matched with an extensive wine list, with 1,500 labels and 80 available by the glass. For a look into the open kitchen, sit at the counter and watch the chefs as they whip up such signature dishes as grilled diver scallops and chanterelles, and lamb pot roast topped with a pomegranate mint glaze. **Known for:** excellent wine list; kid-friendly options; gorgeous dining room. ⑤ *Average main: $48 ✉ Disney's Grand Californian Hotel, 1600 S. Disneyland Dr., Anaheim* ☎ *714/300–7170, 714/781–3463 reservations* ⊕ *disneyland.disney.go.com/grand-californian-hotel/napa-rose.*

Hotels

Candy Cane Inn

$ | **HOTEL** | **FAMILY** | One of the Disneyland area's first hotels, the Candy Cane is one of Anaheim's most relaxing properties, with spacious and understated rooms and an inviting palm-fringed pool. **Pros:** proximity to everything Disney; friendly service; free breakfast. **Cons:** dated

decor; all rooms face parking lot; no elevator. ⑤ *Rooms from: $179 ✉ 1747 S. Harbor Blvd., Anaheim* ☎ *714/774–5284, 800/345–7057* ⊕ *www.candycaneinn.net* ⇆ *171 rooms* ⦿ *Breakfast.*

★ Disney's Grand Californian Hotel and Spa

$$$$ | **RESORT** | **FAMILY** | The most opulent of Disneyland's three hotels, the Craftsman-style Grand Californian offers views of Disney California Adventure and Downtown Disney. **Pros:** gorgeous lobby; family friendly; direct access to California Adventure. **Cons:** the $20 self-parking lot is across the street; standard rooms are on the small side; $30 valet parking. ⑤ *Rooms from: $625 ✉ 1600 S. Disneyland Dr., Anaheim* ☎ *714/635–2300* ⊕ *disneyland.disney.go.com/grand-californian-hotel* ⇆ *1019 rooms* ⦿ *No meals.*

Doubletree Suites by Hilton Hotel Anaheim Resort-Convention Center

$ | **HOTEL** | This busy hotel near the Anaheim Convention Center and a 20-minute walk from Disneyland caters to business travelers and vacationers alike. **Pros:** huge suites; walking distance to a variety of restaurants; chocolate chip cookies at check-in. **Cons:** a bit far from Disneyland; pool area is small; $21 daily parking fee. ⑤ *Rooms from: $153 ✉ 2085 S. Harbor Blvd., Anaheim* ☎ *714/750–3000, 800/215–7316* ⊕ *doubletreeanaheim.com* ⇆ *252 rooms* ⦿ *No meals.*

Hilton Anaheim

$ | **HOTEL** | **FAMILY** | Next to the Anaheim Convention Center, this busy Hilton is the third-largest hotel in Southern California, with a restaurant and food court, hopping lobby lounge with communal tables, a full-service gym, and its own Starbucks. **Pros:** efficient service; fast-casual dining options; some rooms have views of the park fireworks. **Cons:** huge size can be daunting; fee to use health club; megasize parking lot. ⑤ *Rooms from: $159 ✉ 777 Convention Way, Anaheim* ☎ *714/750–4321, 800/445–8667* ⊕ *www.hiltonanaheimhotel.com* ⇆ *1572 rooms* ⦿ *No meals.*

Park Vue Inn

$ | HOTEL | FAMILY | Watch the frequent fireworks from the rooftop sundeck at this bougainvillea-covered Spanish-style inn, one of the closest lodgings to the Disneyland Resort main gate. **Pros:** easy walk to Disneyland, Downtown Disney, and Disney California Adventure; free parking until midnight on checkout day; some rooms have bunk beds. **Cons:** all rooms face the parking lot; rooms near the breakfast room can be noisy; inefficient room air conditioners. ⑤ *Rooms from: $159* ⊠ *1570 S. Harbor Blvd., Anaheim* ☎ *714/772–3691, 800/334–7021* ⊕ *www.parkvueinn.com* ⌁ *86 rooms* ⑩ *Breakfast.*

Knott's Berry Farm

25 miles south of Los Angeles, via I–5, in Buena Park.

Knott's Berry Farm

AMUSEMENT PARK/WATER PARK | FAMILY | The land where the boysenberry was invented (by crossing raspberry, blackberry, and loganberry bushes) is now occupied by Knott's Berry Farm. In 1934 Cordelia Knott began serving chicken dinners on her wedding china to supplement her family's income. The dinners and her boysenberry pies proved more profitable than husband Walter's farm, so the two moved first into the restaurant business and then into the entertainment business. The park is now a 160-acre complex with close to 40 rides, dozens of restaurants and shops, arcade games, live shows, a brick-by-brick replica of Philadelphia's Independence Hall, and loads of Americana. Although it has plenty to keep small children occupied, the park is best known for its awesome thrill rides. The boardwalk area is home to several coasters, including the zooming HangTime that pauses dramatically then drops nearly 15 stories, plus water features to cool things off on hot days, and a lighted promenade. And, yes, you

can still get that boysenberry pie (and jam, juice—you name it). Buy adult tickets online for a major discount; FastLane wristbands—for quicker access to the most popular rides—cost $70 online. ⊠ *8039 Beach Blvd., Buena Park* ✛ *Between La Palma Ave. and Crescent St., 2 blocks south of Hwy. 91* ☎ *714/220–5200* ⊕ *www.knotts.com* ⌁ *$82.*

Park Neighborhoods

THE BOARDWALK

Not-for-the-squeamish thrill rides and skill-based games dominate the scene at the **boardwalk.** Roller coasters—Coast Rider, Surfside Glider, and Pacific Scrambler—surround a pond that keeps things cooler on hot days. **HangTime** towers 150 feet above the boardwalk as coaster cars hang, invert and drop the equivalent of 15 stories. The boardwalk is also home to a string of test-your-skill games that are fun to watch whether you're playing or not, and Johnny Rockets, the park's all-American diner.

CAMP SNOOPY

It can be gridlock on weekends, but kids love this miniature High Sierra wonderland where the *Peanuts* gang hangs out. Tykes can push and pump their own mini-mining cars on **Huff and Puff,** soar around via **Charlie Brown's Kite Flyer,** and hop aboard **Woodstock's Airmail,** a kids' version of the park's Supreme Scream ride. Most of the rides here are geared toward kids only, leaving parents to cheer them on from the sidelines. **Sierra Sidewinder,** a roller coaster near the entrance of Camp Snoopy, is aimed at older children, with spinning saucer-type vehicles that go a maximum speed of 37 mph.

FIESTA VILLAGE

Over in **Fiesta Village** are two more musts for adrenaline junkies: **Montezooma's Revenge,** a roller coaster that goes from 0 to 55 mph in less than five seconds, and **Jaguar!,** which simulates the motions of a cat stalking its prey, twisting, spiraling, and speeding up and slowing down as it takes you on its stomach-dropping course. There's also **Hat Dance,** a version of the spinning teacups but with sombreros, and a 100-year-old **Dentzel carousel,** complete with an antique organ and menagerie of hand-carved animals. In a nod to history, there are restored scale models of the California Missions at Fiesta Village's southern entrance.

GHOST TOWN
Clusters of authentic old buildings relocated from their original mining-town sites mark this section of the park. You can stroll down the street, stop and chat with a blacksmith, pan for gold (for a fee), crack open a geode, check out the chalk-board of a circa-1875 schoolhouse, and ride an original Butterfield stagecoach. Looming over it all is **GhostRider,** Orange County's first wooden roller coaster. Traveling up to 56 mph and reaching 118 feet at its highest point, the park's biggest attraction is riddled with sudden dips and curves, subjecting riders to forces up to three times that of gravity. On the Western-theme **Silver Bullet,** riders are sent to a height of 146 feet and then back down 109 feet. Riders spiral, corkscrew, fly into a cobra roll, and experience overbanked curves. The **Calico Mine** ride descends into a replica of a working gold mine complete with 50 animatronic figures. The **Timber Mountain Log Ride** is a visitor favorite: the flume ride tours through pioneer scenes before splashing down. Also found here is the **Pony Express,** a roller coaster that lets riders saddle up on packs of "horses" tethered to platforms that take off on a series of hairpin turns and travel up to 38 mph. Take a step inside the **Western Trails Museum,** a dusty old gem full of Old West memorabilia and rural Americana, plus menus from the original chicken restaurant and an impressive antique button collection. **Calico Railroad** departs regularly from Ghost

Town station for a round-trip tour of the park (bandit holdups notwithstanding).

This section is also home to **Big Foot Rapids,** a splash-fest of white-water river rafting over towering cliffs, cascading waterfalls, and wild rapids. Don't miss the visually stunning show at **Mystery Lodge,** which tells the story of Native Americans in the Pacific Northwest with lights, music, and special effects.

INDIAN TRAILS
Celebrate Native American traditions through interactive exhibits like tepees and daily dance and storytelling performances.

Knott's Soak City Waterpark is directly across from the main park on 13 acres next to Independence Hall. It has a dozen major water rides; **Pacific Spin** is an oversize waterslide that drops riders 75 feet into a catch pool. There's also a children's pool, a 750,000-gallon wave pool, and a fun house. Soak City's season runs mid-May to mid-September. It's open daily after Memorial Day, weekends only after Labor Day, and then closes for the season.

🍴 Restaurants

Mrs. Knott's Chicken Dinner Restaurant
$$ | AMERICAN | FAMILY | Cordelia Knott's fried chicken and boysenberry pies drew crowds so big that Knott's Berry Farm was built to keep the hungry customers occupied while they waited. The restaurant's current incarnation (outside the park's entrance) still serves crispy fried chicken, along with fluffy handmade biscuits, mashed potatoes, and Mrs. Knott's signature chilled cherry-rhubarb compote. **Known for:** fried chicken; family friendliness; outdoor dining. ⑤ *Average main: $22* ✉ *Knott's Berry Farm Marketplace, 8039 Beach Blvd., Buena Park* ☎ *714/220–5200* ⊕ *www.knotts.com/california-marketplace/mrs-knott-s-chicken-dinner-restaurant.*

A mural at Huntington Beach

Hotels

Knott's Berry Farm Hotel

$ | RESORT | FAMILY | This convenient high-rise hotel is run by the park and sits right on park grounds surrounded by graceful palm trees. **Pros:** easy access to Knott's Berry Farm; plenty of family activities; extra-large swimming pool. **Cons:** lobby and hallways can be noisy; public areas show significant wear and tear; dated room decor. $ *Rooms from: $129* ✉ *7675 Crescent Ave., Buena Park* ☎ *714/995–1111, 866/752–2444* ⊕ *www.knottshotel. com* ⇩ *320 rooms* ❍ *No meals.*

The Coast

Running along the Orange County coastline is scenic Pacific Coast Highway (Highway 1, known locally as the PCH). Older beachfront settlements, with their modest bungalow-style homes, are joined by posh gated communities. The pricey land between Newport Beach and Laguna Beach is where ex-Laker Kobe Bryant, novelist Dean Koontz, those infamous Real Housewives of Bravo, and a slew of finance moguls live.

Though the coastline is rapidly being filled in, there are still a few stretches of beautiful, protected open land. And at many places along the way you can catch an idealized glimpse of the Southern California lifestyle: surfers hitting the beach, boards under their arms.

Long Beach

About 25 miles southeast of Los Angeles, via I–110 south.

Sights

★ Aquarium of the Pacific

ZOO | FAMILY | Sea lions, zebra sharks, and penguins, oh my!—this aquarium focuses on creatures of the Pacific Ocean and is home to more than 11,000 animals. The main exhibits include large tanks of sharks, stingrays, and ethereal sea dragons, which the aquarium has successfully bred in captivity. The Ocean Theater features the multimedia attraction *Penguins 4D,* a panoramic film that captures the world of this endangered species. Be sure to say hello to Betty, a rescue at the engaging sea otter exhibit. For a non-aquatic experience, head to Lorikeet Forest, a walk-in aviary full of the friendliest parrots from Australia. Buy a cup of nectar and smile as you become a human bird perch. If you're a true animal lover, book an up-close-and-personal Animal Encounters Tour ($109) to learn about and assist in the care and feeding of sharks, penguins, and other aquarium residents; or find out how the aquarium functions with the extensive Behind the Scenes Tour ($19 for adults, not including admission). Certified divers can book a supervised dive in the aquarium's Tropical Reef Habitat ($299). Twice daily whale-watching trips on Harbor Breeze Cruises depart from the dock adjacent to the aquarium; summer sightings of blue whales are an unforgettable thrill. ⊠ *100 Aquarium Way, Long Beach* ☎ *562/590–3100* ⊕ *www.aquariumofpacific.org* ✉ *$30.*

Queen Mary

LIGHTHOUSE | FAMILY | The *Queen Mary,* though berthed, is an impressive example of 20th-century cruise ship opulence and sadly the last of its kind. The beautifully preserved art deco–style ocean liner was launched in 1936 and made 1,001 transatlantic crossings before finally berthing in Long Beach in 1967. Today there are multiple diversions on board from ongoing theatrical performances by illusionist Aiden Sinclair, *Illusions of the Passed: Legends of the Queen Mary*, a wine tasting room, and a daily British-style high tea.

Also on board you can take one of three daily or five weekend tours, such as the informative Glory Days Historical walk or the downright spooky Haunted Encounters tour. (Spirits have reportedly been

spotted in the pool and engine room.) You could stay for dinner at one of the ship's restaurants, listen to live jazz in the original first-class lounge, or even spend the night in one of the 347 wood-panel cabins. The ship's neighbor, a geodesic dome originally built to house Howard Hughes's *Spruce Goose* aircraft, now serves as a terminal for Carnival Cruise Lines, making the *Queen Mary* the perfect pit stop before or after a cruise. Anchored next to the *Queen* is the *Scorpion,* a Russian submarine you can tour for a look at Cold War history. ⊠ *1126 Queens Hwy., Long Beach* ☎ *877/342–0738* ⊕ *www.queenmary.com* ✉ *Tours from $16.*

Hotels

Queen Mary Hotel

$ | HOTEL | FAMILY | Experience the golden age of transatlantic travel without the seasickness: a 1936 art deco–style reigns on the *Queen Mary,* from the ship's mahogany paneling to its nickel-plated doors to the majestic Grand Salon. **Pros:** a walkable historic Promenade deck; views from Long Beach out to the Pacific; art deco details. **Cons:** spotty service; vintage soundproofing makes for a challenging night's sleep; mandatory facility fee. ⑤ *Rooms from: $129* ⊠ *1126 Queens Hwy., Long Beach* ☎ *562/435–3511, 877/342–0742* ⊕ *www.queenmary.com* ⇨ *347 staterooms* ⎟⊙⎟ *No meals.*

The Varden

$ | B&B/INN | Constructed in 1929 to house Bixby Knolls Sr.'s mistress, Dolly Varden, this small, historic, European-style hotel, on the metro line in downtown Long Beach, now caters to worldly budget travelers. Compact rooms are mostly white and blend modern touches like flat-screen TVs and geometric silver fixtures with period details like exposed beams, Dakota Jackson periwinkle chairs, and round penny-tile baths. **Pros:** great value for downtown location; discount passes to Gold's Gym across the street; complimentary continental

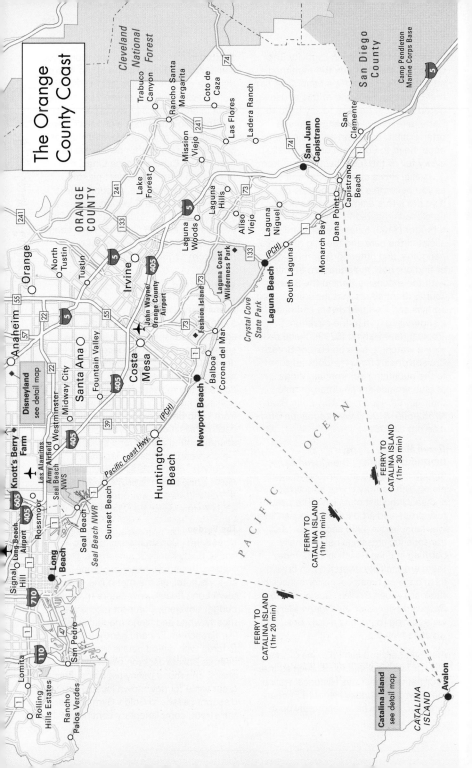

breakfast. **Cons:** no resort services; small rooms; no elevator. $ *Rooms from: $129* ⊠ *335 Pacific Ave., Long Beach* ☎ *562/432–8950* ⊕ *www.thevardenhotel. com* ⌁ *35 rooms* ⏐○⏐ *Free Breakfast.*

Newport Beach

6 miles south of Huntington Beach via the Pacific Coast Hwy.

Newport Beach has evolved from a simple seaside village to an icon of chic coastal living. Its ritzy reputation comes from mega-yachts bobbing in the harbor, boutiques that rival those in Beverly Hills, and spectacular homes overlooking the ocean.

The city boasts some of the cleanest beaches in Southern California; inland Newport Beach's concentration of high-rise office buildings, shopping centers, and luxury hotels drives the economy. But on the city's Balboa Peninsula, you can still catch a glimpse of a more humble, down-to-earth town scattered with taco spots, tackle shops, and sailor bars.

ESSENTIALS
VISITOR AND TOUR INFORMATION
Visit Newport Beach Concierge. ⊠ *Atrium Court at Fashion Island, 401 Newport Center Dr.* ☎ *855/563–9767* ⊕ *www. visitnewportbeach.com.*

Sights

Balboa Island
COMMERCIAL CENTER | FAMILY | This sliver of terra firma in Newport Harbor boasts quaint streets tightly packed with impossibly charming multimillion-dollar cottages. The island's main drag, Marine Avenue, is lined with equally picturesque cafés and shops. A car-free bike path and boardwalk encircles much of the island for an easy and scenic ramble.

Balboa Peninsula
BEACH—SIGHT | FAMILY | Newport's best beaches are on Balboa Peninsula, where many jetties pave the way to ideal swimming areas. The most intense spot for bodysurfing in Orange County, and arguably on the West Coast, known as the **Wedge,** is at the south end of the peninsula. It was created by accident in the 1930s when the Federal Works Progress Administration built a jetty to protect Newport Harbor. ■TIP➜ **Rip currents and punishing waves mean it's strictly for the pros—but it sure is fun to watch an experienced local ride it.** ⊠ *2172 E. Ocean Front* ⊕ *www.visitnewportbeach.com/ beaches-and-parks/the-wedge.*

Discovery Cube's Ocean Quest
MUSEUM | FAMILY | This family-friendly destination has exhibits on the history of the harbor, ocean explorers, and scientific aspects of the Pacific Ocean. Other fun features include a touch tank holding local sea creatures and a lab for kids that encourages innovation. ⊠ *600 E. Bay Ave.* ☎ *949/675–8915* ⊕ *www.oceanquestoc.org* ⌁ *$5* ☉ *Closed weekdays.*

Newport Harbor
BODY OF WATER | FAMILY | Sheltering nearly 16,000 small boats, Newport Harbor may seduce even those who don't own a yacht. Spend an afternoon exploring the charming avenues and surrounding alleys; take California's longest-running auto ferry across to Balboa Island. The fare is $2 for car and driver for the scenic crossing. Several grassy areas on the primarily residential Lido Isle have views of the water. To truly experience the harbor, rent an electric boat for a pleasant day cruise or try stand-up paddleboarding in the sheltered waters. ⊠ *Pacific Coast Hwy.* ⊕ *www.balboaislandferry.com.*

Newport Pier
MARINA | FAMILY | Jutting out into the ocean near 20th Street, Newport Pier is a popular fishing spot. Street parking is difficult, so grab the first space you find and be prepared to walk. Early on

Wednesday–Sunday mornings you're likely to encounter dory fishermen hawking their predawn catches, as they've done for generations. On weekends the area is alive with kids of all ages on in-line skates, skateboards, and bikes dodging pedestrians and whizzing past fast-food joints and classic dive bars. ☒ 72 McFadden Pl.

Restaurants

Basilic

$$$ | **BRASSERIE** | This intimate French-Swiss bistro adds a touch of old-world elegance to the island with its white linen and flower-topped tables. Chef Bernard Althaus grows the herbs used in his classic French dishes. **Known for:** French classics; fine wine; old-school ambience. ⑤ Average main: $32 ☒ 217 Marine Ave., Balboa Island ☎ 949/673–0570 ⊕ www. basilicrestaurant.com ☺ Closed Sun.

Bear Flag Fish Co.

$ | **SEAFOOD** | **FAMILY** | Expect long lines in summer at this indoor/outdoor dining spot serving up the freshest local fish (swordfish, sea bass, halibut, and tuna) and a wide range of creative seafood dishes (the Hawaiian-style *poke* salad with ahi tuna is a local favorite). Order at the counter, which doubles as a seafood market, and sit inside the airy dining room or outside on a grand patio. **Known for:** freshest seafood; fish tacos; craft beers. ⑤ Average main: $12 ☒ Newport Peninsula, 3421 Via Lido ☎ 949/673–3474 ⊕ www.bearflagfishco.com.

The Cannery

$$$ | **SEAFOOD** | This 1920s cannery building still teems with fish, but now they go into dishes on the eclectic Pacific Rim menu rather than being packed into crates. Settle in at the sushi bar, in the dining room, or on the patio before choosing between sashimi, freshly shucked oysters, or cilantro-marinated fish tacos. **Known for:** waterfront views; seafood specialties; craft cocktails.

⑤ Average main: $35 ☒ 3010 Lafayette Rd. ☎ 949/566–0060 ⊕ www.canerynewport.com ☺ No lunch Mon.

Gulfstream

$$$ | **SEAFOOD** | **FAMILY** | This on-trend restaurant has an open kitchen, comfortable booths, and outdoor seating. The patio is a fantastic place to hang out. **Known for:** oysters on the half shell; local hangout; outdoor patio. ⑤ Average main: $33 ☒ 850 Avocado Ave. ☎ 949/718–0188 ⊕ www.gulfstreamrestaurant.com.

3-Thirty-3

$$ | **AMERICAN** | This stylish eatery attracts a convivial crowd—both young and old—for midday, sunset, and late-night dining. A long list of small, shareable plates heightens the camaraderie. **Known for:** happy hour; brunch burritos; generous portions. ⑤ Average main: $26 ☒ 333 Bayside Dr. ☎ 949/673–8464 ⊕ www.3thirty3nb.com.

Hotels

Balboa Bay Resort

$$$ | **RESORT** | **FAMILY** | Sharing the same frontage as the private Balboa Bay Club that long ago hosted Humphrey Bogart, Lauren Bacall, and the Reagans, this waterfront resort has one of the best bay views around. **Pros:** exquisite bayfront views; comfortable beds; a raked beach for guests. **Cons:** not much within walking distance; $34 nightly hospitality fee; some rooms have courtyard-only views. ⑤ Rooms from: $339 ☒ 1221 W. Coast Hwy. ☎ 949/645–5000 ⊕ www. balboabayresort.com ☞ 159 rooms ⑩ No meals.

Fashion Island Hotel

$$ | **HOTEL** | **FAMILY** | Across a palm tree–lined boulevard from stylish Fashion Island, this 20-story tower caters to business types during the week and luxury seekers on weekends. **Pros:** lively lounge scene; large heated pool; great location. **Cons:** steep valet parking prices; some rooms have views of

Riding the waves at Newport Beach

mall parking; destination fee add-on.
$ *Rooms from: $295* ✉ *690 Newport Center Dr.* ☎ *949/759–0808, 877/591–9145* ⊕ *www.fashionislandhotel.com* ⮑ *295 rooms* ○| *No meals.*

★ Lido House, Autograph Collection

$$ | **RESORT** | **FAMILY** | Close to the Balboa Peninsula, the Lido House is modeled after a New England–style beach cottage, one grand enough to welcome you and all your family and friends. **Pros:** large hot tub and pool deck; lively hotel bar; free bikes to cruise the nearby beach boardwalk. **Cons:** pricey restaurant; $33 resort fee add-on; $40 valet parking.
$ *Rooms from: $300* ✉ *3300 Newport Blvd., Balboa Island* ☎ *949/524–8500* ⮑ *130 rooms* ○| *No meals.*

Newport Beach Marriott Hotel and Spa

$$ | **RESORT** | Here you'll be smack in the busy part of town: across from Fashion Island, next to a country club, and with a view toward Newport Harbor. **Pros:** four concierge floors offer enhanced amenities; large spa; across from Fashion Island. **Cons:** sprawling floor plan; small

bathrooms; car is essential for exploring beyond Fashion Island. $ *Rooms from: $229* ✉ *900 Newport Center Dr.* ☎ *949/640–4000* ⊕ *www.marriott.com* ⮑ *532 rooms.*

Activities

BOAT RENTALS
Balboa Boat Rentals

BOATING | **FAMILY** | You can tour the waterways surrounding Lido and Balboa isles with kayaks ($18 an hour), stand-up paddleboards ($25 for two hours), small motorboats ($75 an hour), and electric boats ($80 to $105 an hour) at Balboa Boat Rentals. ✉ *510 E. Edgewater Ave., Balboa Island* ☎ *855/690–0794* ⊕ *www.boats4rent.com.*

BOAT TOURS
Catalina Flyer

TOUR—SPORTS | **FAMILY** | At Balboa Pavilion, the *Catalina Flyer* operates a 90-minute daily round-trip passage to Catalina Island for $70 in season. Reservations are required; check the schedule,

A whimbrel hunts for mussels at Crystal Cove State Park.

as crossings may be canceled due to annual maintenance. ✉ *400 Main St., Balboa Island* ☎ *949/673–5245* ⊕ *www. catalinainfo.com.*

Hornblower Cruises and Events

TOUR—SPORTS | This operator books three-hour weekend dinner cruises with dancing for $95. The two-hour Sunday brunch cruise starts at $75. Cruises traverse the mostly placid and scenic waters of Newport Harbor. ✉ *2431 W. Coast Hwy.* ☎ *888/467–6256* ⊕ *www. hornblower.com.*

FISHING
Davey's Locker

FISHING | **FAMILY** | In addition to a complete tackle shop, Davey's Locker offers half-day sportfishing trips starting at $41.50. Whale-watching excursions begin at $26 for weekdays. ✉ *Balboa Pavilion, 400 Main St., Balboa Island* ☎ *949/673– 1434* ⊕ *www.daveyslocker.com.*

👜 Shopping

★ Fashion Island

STORE/MALL | Shake the sand out of your shoes to head inland to the ritzy Fashion Island outdoor mall, a cluster of arcades and courtyards complete with koi pond, fountains, and a family-friendly trolley—plus some awesome ocean views. It has the luxe department stores Neiman Marcus and Bloomingdale's, plus expensive spots like Jonathan Adler, Kate Spade, and Michael Stars. ✉ *401 Newport Center Dr., between Jamboree and MacArthur Blvds., off PCH* ☎ *949/721–2000, 855/658–8527* ⊕ *www. shopfashionisland.com.*

Laguna Beach

10 miles south of Newport Beach on PCH, 60 miles south of Los Angeles, I–5 south to Hwy. 133, which turns into Laguna Canyon Rd.

Driving in along Laguna Canyon Road from the Interstate 405 freeway gives you the chance to cruise through a gorgeous coastal canyon, large stretches of which remain undeveloped, before arriving at a glistening wedge of ocean. There are 30 coves and beaches to visit, all with some of the cleanest water in Southern California. There's a convenient and free trolley service through town; service is extended on weekends and holidays.

Laguna's welcome mat is legendary. On the corner of Forest and Park avenues is a gate proclaiming, "This gate hangs well and hinders none, refresh and rest, then travel on." A gay community has long been established here; art galleries dot the village streets, and there's usually someone daubing up in Heisler Park. Along the Pacific Coast Highway you'll find dozens of clothing boutiques, jewelry stores, and cafés.

ESSENTIALS
VISITOR AND TOUR INFORMATION
Visit Laguna Beach Visitors Center. ✉ *381 Forest Ave.* ☎ *949/497–9229, 800/877–1115* ⊕ *www.visitlagunabeach.com.*

 Sights

Laguna Art Museum
MUSEUM | This museum displays American art, with an emphasis on California artists from all periods. Special exhibits change quarterly. ✉ *307 Cliff Dr.* ☎ *949/494–8971* ⊕ *www.lagunaartmuseum.org* 🖼 *$7* 🕙 *Closed Wed.*

Laguna Coast Wilderness Park
HIKING/WALKING | **FAMILY** | The Laguna Coast Wilderness Park is spread over 7,000 acres of fragile coastal territory, including the canyon. The 40 miles of trails are great for hiking and mountain biking, and are open daily, weather permitting. Docent-led hikes are given most weekends. No dogs are allowed in the park. ✉ *18751 Laguna Canyon Rd.* ☎ *949/923–2235* ⊕ *www.ocparks.com/parks/lagunac* 🖼 *$3 parking.*

 Beaches

⭐ Main Beach Park
BEACH—SIGHT | **FAMILY** | A stocky 1920s lifeguard tower marks Main Beach Park, where a wooden boardwalk separates the sand from a strip of lawn. Walk along this soft-sand beach, or grab a bench and watch people bodysurfing, playing volleyball, or scrambling around two half-basketball courts. The beach also has children's play equipment. Most of Laguna's hotels are within a short (but hilly) walk. **Amenities:** lifeguards; toilets; showers. **Best for:** sunset; swimming; walking. ✉ *Broadway at S. Coast Hwy.* ⊕ *www.visitlagunabeach.com.*

1,000 Steps Beach
BEACH—SIGHT | **FAMILY** | Off South Coast Highway at 9th Street, 1,000 Steps Beach is a hard-to-find spot tucked away in a neighborhood with great waves and hard-packed, white sand. There aren't really 1,000 steps down (but when you hike back up, it'll certainly feel like it). Sea caves and tide pools enhance this already beautiful natural spot. The beach is a rare dog-friendly spot. **Amenities:** showers. **Best for:** snorkeling; surfing; swimming. ✉ *S. Coast Hwy., at 9th St.*

Wood's Cove
BEACH—SIGHT | **FAMILY** | Off South Coast Highway, Wood's Cove is especially quiet during the week. Big rock formations hide lurking crabs. This is a prime scuba-diving spot, and at high tide much of the beach is underwater. Climbing the steps to leave, you can see a Tudor-style mansion that was once home to Bette Davis. Street parking is limited. **Amenities:** none. **Best for:** snorkeling; scuba diving; sunset. ✉ *Diamond St. and Ocean Way* ⊕ *www.visitlagunabeach.com.*

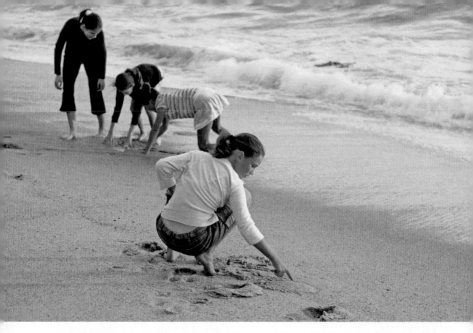

Looking for shells on Laguna Beach, one of the nicest stretches of sand in Southern California

Restaurants

Ocean at Main

$$$ | AMERICAN | Set in a handsomely renovated former bank from the 1940s, Ocean at Main's dishes are artfully presented and feature the best of California produce. Owned by the O.C.'s favorite chef, Craig Strong (who guided Studio at Montage for almost a decade), there's an expected emphasis on service but without pretension. **Known for:** handsome dining room; local ingredients; California-focused wine list. ⑤ *Average main: $38* ✉ *222 Ocean Ave.* ☎ *949/715–3870* ⊕ *www.oceanatmain.com.*

Sapphire Laguna

$$ | INTERNATIONAL | FAMILY | This Laguna Beach establishment set in a historic Craftsman is part gourmet pantry (a must-stop for your every picnic need) and part global dining adventure. Iranian-born chef Azmin Ghahreman takes you on a journey through Europe and Asia with dishes ranging from coconut macaroon pancakes to Malaysian black pepper shrimp. **Known for:** fried chicken sandwich; weekend brunch; pet-friendly patio. ⑤ *Average main: $27* ✉ *The Old Pottery Place, 1200 S. Coast Hwy.* ☎ *949/715–9888* ⊕ *www.sapphirelaguna.com.*

★ Studio

$$$$ | MODERN AMERICAN | In a nod to Laguna's art history, Studio has housemade specialties that entice the eye as well as the palate. The restaurant occupies its own Craftsman-style bungalow, atop a 50-foot bluff overlooking the Pacific. **Known for:** attentive service; chef's tasting menu; being great for special occasions. ⑤ *Average main: $60* ✉ *Montage Laguna Beach, 30801 S. Coast Hwy.* ☎ *949/715–6420* ⊕ *www. studiolagunabeach.com* ⊙ *Closed Mon. No lunch.*

Taco Loco

$ | MEXICAN | FAMILY | This may look like a fast-food taco stand, and the hemp brownies on the menu may make you think the kitchen's *really* laid-back, but the quality of the food here equals that in many higher-price restaurants. Some

Mexican standards get a Louisiana twist, like Cajun-spiced seafood tacos. **Known for:** vegetarian tacos; sidewalk seating; surfer clientele. ⑤ *Average main: $12* ✉ *640 S. Coast Hwy.* ☎ *949/497–1635* ⊕ *www.tacoloco.net.*

Zinc Café and Market

$ | **VEGETARIAN** | **FAMILY** | Families flock to this small Laguna Beach institution for reasonably priced breakfast and lunch options. Try the signature quiches or poached egg dishes in the morning, or swing by later in the day for healthy salads, house-made soups, quesadillas, or pizzettes. **Known for:** gourmet goodies; avocado toast; busy outdoor patio. ⑤ *Average main: $15* ✉ *350 Ocean Ave.* ☎ *949/494–6302* ⊕ *www.zinccafe.com* ◷ *No dinner Nov.–Apr.*

 ## Hotels

Inn at Laguna Beach

$$$ | **HOTEL** | **FAMILY** | This bright yellow local landmark is stacked neatly at the north end of Laguna's Main Beach and it's one of the few hotels in SoCal set almost on the sand. **Pros:** rooftop bar; beach essentials provided; beachfront location. **Cons:** ocean-view rooms are pricey; small hot tub; limited breakfast menu. ⑤ *Rooms from: $379* ✉ *211 N. Coast Hwy.* ☎ *949/497–9722, 800/544–4479* ⊕ *www.innatlagunabeach.com* ⇆ *70 rooms.*

La Casa del Camino

$$ | **HOTEL** | The look is Old California at the 1929-built La Casa del Camino, with dark woods, arched doors, and wrought iron in the lobby. **Pros:** breathtaking views from rooftop lounge; personable service; close to beach. **Cons:** some rooms face the highway; frequent events can make hotel noisy; some rooms are very small. ⑤ *Rooms from: $229* ✉ *1289 S. Coast Hwy.* ☎ *949/497–2446, 855/634–5736* ⊕ *www.lacasadelcamino.com* ⇆ *36 rooms* ⑩ *No meals.*

★ Montage Laguna Beach

$$$$ | **RESORT** | **FAMILY** | Laguna's connection to the Californian plein-air artists is mined for inspiration at this head-turning, lavish hotel. **Pros:** top-notch, enthusiastic service; idyllic coastal location; numerous sporty pursuits available offshore. **Cons:** rates can be more than $1,100 per night for holidays or summer weekends; $50 valet parking; $42 daily resort fee. ⑤ *Rooms from: $695* ✉ *30801 S. Coast Hwy.* ☎ *949/715–6000, 866/271–6953* ⊕ *www.montagehotels.com/lagunabeach* ⇆ *250 rooms* ⑩ *No meals.*

Surf and Sand Resort

$$$$ | **RESORT** | **FAMILY** | One mile south of downtown, on an exquisite stretch of beach with thundering waves and gorgeous rocks, this is a getaway for those who want a boutique hotel experience without all the formalities. **Pros:** easy beach access; intimate property; slightly removed from Main Street crowds. **Cons:** pricey valet parking; surf can be quite loud; no air conditioning. ⑤ *Rooms from: $575* ✉ *1555 S. Coast Hwy.* ☎ *949/497–4477, 877/741–5908* ⊕ *www.surfandsandresort.com* ⇆ *167 rooms* ⑩ *No meals.*

 ## Shopping

Coast Highway, Forest and Ocean avenues, and Glenneyre Street are full of art galleries, fine jewelry stores, souvenir shops, and clothing boutiques.

Adam Neeley Fine Art Jewelry

JEWELRY/ACCESSORIES | Be prepared to be dazzled at Adam Neeley Fine Art Jewelry, where artisan proprietor Adam Neeley creates one-of-a-kind modern pieces. ✉ *352 N. Coast Hwy.* ☎ *949/715–0953* ⊕ *www.adamneeley.com* ◷ *Closed Sun. and Mon.*

Art for the Soul

CRAFTS | A riot of color, Art for the Soul has hand-painted furniture, crafts, and unusual gifts. ✉ *272 Forest Ave.* ☎ *949/675–1791* ⊕ *www.art4thesoul.com.*

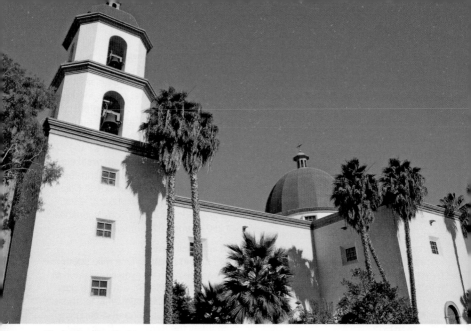

Mission San Juan Capistrano

Candy Baron

FOOD/CANDY | FAMILY | Get your sugar fix at the time-warped Candy Baron, filled with old-fashioned goodies like gumdrops, bull's-eyes, and more than 50 flavors of saltwater taffy. ⊠ *231 Forest Ave.* ☎ *949/497–7508* ⊕ *www.thecandy-baron.com.*

Fetneh Blake

CLOTHING | Hit Fetneh Blake for pricey, Euro-chic clothes. The emerging designers found here lure Angelenos to make the trek south. ⊠ *427 N. Coast Hwy.* ☎ *949/494–3787* ⊕ *www.fetnehblake.com.*

La Rue du Chocolat

FOOD/CANDY | This shop dispenses chocolate-covered strawberries and handcrafted chocolates in seasonal flavors. ⊠ *Peppertree La., 448 S. Coast Hwy., Suite B* ☎ *949/494–2372* ⊕ *www. larueduchocolat.com.*

San Juan Capistrano

5 miles north of Dana Point, Hwy. 74, 60 miles north of San Diego, I–5.

San Juan Capistrano is best known for its historic mission, where the swallows traditionally return each year, migrating from their winter haven in Argentina, but these days they are more likely to choose other local sites for nesting. St. Joseph's Day, March 19, launches a week of fowl festivities. Charming antiques stores, which range from pricey to cheap, line Camino Capistrano.

GETTING HERE AND AROUND

If you arrive by train, which is far more romantic and restful than battling freeway traffic, you'll be dropped off across from the mission at the San Juan Capistrano depot. With its appealing brick café and preserved Santa Fe cars, the depot retains much of the magic of early American railroads. If driving, park near Ortega and Camino Capistrano, the city's main streets.

Sights

★ Mission San Juan Capistrano

ARCHAEOLOGICAL SITE | FAMILY | Founded in 1776 by Father Junípero Serra (consecrated as St. Serra), Mission San Juan Capistrano was one of two Roman Catholic outposts between Los Angeles and San Diego. The Great Stone Church, begun in 1797, is the largest structure created by the Spanish in California. After extensive retrofitting, the golden-hued interiors are open to visitors who may feel they are touring among ruins in Italy rather than the O.C. Many of the mission's adobe buildings have been restored to illustrate mission life, with exhibits of an olive millstone, tallow ovens, tanning vats, metalworking furnaces, and the padres' living quarters. The gardens, with their fountains and koi pond, are a lovely spot in which to wander. The bougainvillea-covered Serra Chapel is believed to be the oldest church still standing in California and is the only building remaining in which St. Serra actually led Mass. Mass takes place weekdays at 7 am in the chapel. Enter via a small gift shop in the gatehouse. ⊠ *26801 Ortega Hwy.* ☎ *949/234–1300* ⊕ *www.missionsjc.com* 🎫 *$10.*

San Juan Capistrano Library

LIBRARY | FAMILY | Near Mission San Juan Capistrano is the San Juan Capistrano Library, a postmodern structure built in 1983. Architect Michael Graves combined classical and Mission styles to striking effect. Its courtyard has secluded places for reading. ⊠ *31495 El Camino Real* ☎ *949/493–1752* ⊕ *ocpl.org/libloc/sjc* ⊙ *Closed Fri.*

Restaurants

Cedar Creek Inn

$$$ | AMERICAN | FAMILY | Just across the street from Mission San Juan Capistrano, this restaurant has a patio that's perfect for a late lunch or a romantic dinner. The menu is fairly straightforward, dishes are tasty, and portions are substantial—try the Cobb salad or a burger at lunch, or splurge on the prime rib for dinner. **Known for:** brunch; rich desserts; comfortable seating. ⑤ *Average main: $30* ⊠ *26860 Ortega Hwy.* ☎ *949/240–2229* ⊕ *www.cedarcreekinn.com.*

L'Hirondelle

$$$ | FRENCH | Locals have romanced at cozy tables for decades at this delightful restaurant. Such classic dishes as beef bourguignonne and a New York strip in a black-peppercorn-and-brandy sauce are the hallmark of this French and Belgian restaurant, whose name means "the little swallow." The extensive wine list is matched by an impressive selection of Belgian beers. **Known for:** Sunday brunch; traditional French cuisine; composed salads. ⑤ *Average main: $35* ⊠ *31631 Camino Capistrano* ☎ *949/661–0425* ⊕ *www.lhirondellesjc.com* ⊙ *Closed Mon.*

The Ramos House Cafe

$$ | AMERICAN | It may be worth hopping the Amtrak to San Juan Capistrano just for the chance to have breakfast or lunch at one of Orange County's most beloved restaurants, located in a historic board-and-batten home dating back to 1881. This café sits practically on the railroad tracks across from the depot—nab a table on the patio and dig into a hearty breakfast featuring seasonal items, such as the smoked bacon scramble with wilted rocket. **Known for:** southern specialties; weekend brunch; historic setting. ⑤ *Average main: $20* ⊠ *31752 Los Rios St.* ☎ *949/443–1342* ⊕ *www.ramoshouse.com* ⊙ *Closed Mon. No dinner.*

Nightlife

Swallow's Inn

BARS/PUBS | Across the way from Mission San Juan Capistrano you may spot a line of Harleys in front of the down-home and downright funky Swallow's Inn. Despite a somewhat tough look, it attracts all kinds—bikers, surfers, modern-day cowboys, grandparents—for a drink, a casual bite, karaoke nights, and some rowdy live country music. ✉ *31786 Camino Capistrano* ☎ *949/493–3188* ⊕ *www.swallowsinn.com.*

Catalina Island

Just 22 miles out from the L.A. coastline, across from Newport Beach and Long Beach, Catalina has virtually unspoiled mountains, canyons, coves, and beaches; best of all, it gives you a glimpse of what undeveloped Southern California once looked like.

Water sports are a big draw, as divers and snorkelers come for the exceptionally clear water surrounding the island. Kayakers are attracted to the calm cove waters and thrill seekers book the eco-themed zipline that traverses a wooded canyon. The main town, Avalon, is a charming, old-fashioned beach community, where yachts and pleasure boats bob in the crescent bay. Wander beyond the main drag and find brightly painted little bungalows fronting the sidewalks; golf carts are the preferred mode of transport.

In 1919, William Wrigley Jr., the chewing-gum magnate, purchased a controlling interest in the company developing Catalina Island, whose most famous landmark, the Casino, was built in 1929 under his orders. Because he owned the Chicago Cubs baseball team, Wrigley made Catalina the team's spring training site, an arrangement that lasted until 1951.

In 1975, the Catalina Island Conservancy, a nonprofit foundation, acquired about 88% of the island to help preserve the area's natural flora and fauna, including the bald eagle and the Catalina Island fox. These days the conservancy is restoring the rugged interior country with plantings of native grasses and trees. The organization helps oversee the interior's 50 miles of bike trails and 165 miles of

hiking trails and helps protect the island's 60 endemic species. Along the coast you might spot oddities like electric perch, saltwater goldfish, and flying fish.

GETTING HERE AND AROUND
FERRY TRAVEL

Two companies offer ferry service to Catalina Island. The boats have both indoor and outdoor seating and snack bars. Excessive baggage is not allowed, and there are extra fees for bicycles and surfboards. The waters around Catalina can get rough, so if you're prone to seasickness, come prepared. Winter, holiday, and weekend schedules vary, so reservations are strongly recommended.

Catalina Express makes an hour-long run from Long Beach or San Pedro to Avalon and a 90-minute run from Dana Point to Avalon with some stops at Two Harbors. Round-trip fares begin at $73.50, with discounts for seniors and kids. On busy days, a $15 upgrade to the Commodore Lounge, when available, is worth it. Service from Newport Beach to Avalon is available through the *Catalina Flyer.* The boat leaves from Balboa Pavilion at 9 am (in season), takes 75 minutes to reach the island, and costs $70 round-trip. The return boat leaves Catalina at 4:30 pm. Reservations are required for the *Catalina Flyer* and recommended for all weekend and summer trips. ■ **TIP→ Keep an eye out for dolphins, which sometimes swim alongside the ferries.**

FERRY CONTACTS Catalina Flyer.
☎ *949/673–5245* ⊕ *www.catalinainfo.com.*

GOLF CARTS

Golf carts constitute the island's main form of transportation for sightseeing in the area; however, some parts of town are off-limits, as is the island's interior. Drivers 21 and over with valid driver's license can rent them along Avalon's Crescent Avenue and Pebbly Beach Road for about $45 per hour with a $45 deposit, payable via cash only.

GOLF CART RENTALS **Island Rentals.**
✉ *125 Pebbly Beach Rd., Avalon*
☎ *310/510–1456* ⊕ *www.catalinagolfcart-rentals.com.*

HELICOPTER TRAVEL
Island Express helicopters depart from San Pedro (Friday, Saturday, and Sunday only), John Wayne Airport, Burbank Airport, and Long Beach next to the *Queen Mary* (8 am–dusk). The trip from Long Beach takes about 15 minutes and costs $135 one way, $270 round-trip. Reservations a week in advance are recommended; some flights require a minimum passenger load.

TIMING
Although Catalina can be seen in one very hectic day, several inviting hotels make it worth extending your stay for one or more nights. A short itinerary might include breakfast on the pier, a tour of the interior, a snorkeling excursion at Casino Point, or beach day at the Descanso Beach Club and a romantic waterfront dinner in Avalon.

After late October, rooms are much easier to find on short notice, rates drop dramatically, and many hotels offer packages that include transportation from the mainland and/or sightseeing tours. January to March you have a good chance of spotting migrating gray whales on the ferry crossing.

TOURS
Santa Catalina Island Company runs nine land tours and six ocean tours, including the *Flying Fish* boat trip (summer evenings only); a comprehensive inland motor tour; a tour of Skyline Drive; several Casino tours; a scenic tour of Avalon; a glass-bottom-boat tour; an undersea tour on a semisubmersible vessel; an eco-themed zipline tour that traverses a scenic canyon; a speedy Ocean Runner expedition that searches for all manner of sea creatures and a fast Cyclone boat tour that takes you to the less populated center of the island, Two Harbors. Reservations are highly recommended for

the inland tours. Tours cost $14 to $129. There are ticket booths on the Green Pleasure Pier, at the Casino, in the plaza, and at the boat landing. Catalina Adventure Tours, which has booths at the boat landing and on the pier, also arranges excursions at comparable prices.

The Catalina Island Conservancy organizes custom ecotours and hikes of the interior. Naturalist guides drive open jeeps through some gorgeously untrammeled parts of the island. Tours start at $70 per person for a two-hour trip (two-person minimum). The tours run year-round.

ESSENTIALS
VISITOR AND TOUR INFORMATION
Catalina Adventure Tours. ☎ 877/510–2888 ⊕ *www.catalinaadventuretours.com.* **Catalina Island Chamber of Commerce and Visitors Bureau.** ✉ *1 Green Pleasure Pier, Avalon* ☎ *310/510–1520* ⊕ *www.catalinachamber.com.* **Catalina Island Conservancy.** ✉ *125 Claressa Ave., Avalon* ☎ *310/510–2595* ⊕ *www.catalinaconservancy.org.* **Santa Catalina Island Company.** ☎ *877/778–8322* ⊕ *www.visitcatalinaisland.com.*

Avalon

A 1- to 2-hour ferry ride from Long Beach, Newport Beach, or San Pedro; a 15-minute helicopter ride from Long Beach or San Pedro, slightly longer from Santa Ana.

Avalon, Catalina's only real town, extends from the shore of its natural harbor to the surrounding hillsides. Its resident population is about 3,800, but it swells with tourists on summer weekends. Most of the city's activity, however, is centered on the pedestrian mall on Crescent Avenue, and most sights are easily reached on foot. Private cars are restricted and rental cars aren't allowed, but taxis, trams, and shuttles can take you anywhere you need to go. Bicycles, electric bikes, and golf carts can be rented from shops along Crescent Avenue.

◉ Sights

★ Casino

BUILDING | This circular white structure is one of the finest examples of art deco architecture anywhere. Its Spanish-inspired floors and murals gleam with brilliant blue and green Catalina tiles. In this case, *casino,* the Italian word for "gathering place," has nothing to do with gambling. First-run movies are screened nightly at the Avalon Theatre, noteworthy for its classic 1929 theater pipe organ and art deco wall murals. The circular ballroom once famously hosted 1940s big bands and is still used for gala events.

The Santa Catalina Island Company leads three tours of the Casino— the 30-minute basic tour ($14), the 90-minute behind-the-scenes tour ($28), which leads visitors through the green room and into the Wrigleys' private lounge, and a weekend nights evening tour ($45), where guests enjoy wine on the scenic terrace after touring the historic building. ⊠ *1 Casino Way* ☎ *310/510–0179 theater* ⊕ *www.visit-catalinaisland.com.*

Casino Point Dive Park

BEACH—SIGHT | **FAMILY** | In front of the Casino are the crystal-clear waters of the Casino Point Dive Park, a protected marine preserve where moray eels, bat rays, spiny lobsters, harbor seals, and other sea creatures cruise around kelp forests and along the sandy bottom. No need to don a wet suit: the brilliantly orange garibaldi, California's state marine fish, can sometimes be viewed from the seawall. It's a terrific site for scuba diving, with some shallow areas suitable for snorkeling. Equipment can be rented on and near the pier. The shallow waters of Lover's Cove, east of the boat landing, are also good for snorkeling. ⊠ *Avalon.*

Where the Buffalo Roam

Zane Grey, the writer who put the Western novel on the map, spent a lot of time on Catalina, and his influence is still evident in a peculiar way. As the story goes, when the movie version of Grey's book *The Vanishing American* was filmed here in 1924, American bison were ferried across from the mainland to give the land that Western plains look. After the crew packed up and left, the buffalo stayed, and a small herd of about 150 still remains, grazing the interior and reinforcing the island's image as the last refuge from SoCal's urban sprawl.

Catalina Island Museum

LOCAL INTEREST | **FAMILY** | The exterior of the Catalina Island Museum is a nod to Catalina Island's developer William Wrigley Jr.—it's modeled after Wrigley Field in Chicago. Inside, the museum traces the island's history from it's precontact days and native Chumash to its role in Hollywood history and beyond. Two galleries host traveling exhibitions. The view from the outside terrace takes in lovely Avalon and its picturesque harbor. A small gift shop offers reproductions of the island's signature colorful Catalina pottery tiles. ⊠ *217 Metropole Ave.* ☎ *310/510–2414* ⊕ *www.catalinamuseum.org* 🎟 *$17.*

Green Pleasure Pier

LOCAL INTEREST | **FAMILY** | Head to the Green Pleasure Pier for a good vantage point of Avalon. On the pier you can find the visitor information, snack stands, and scads of squawking sea gulls. It's also the landing where visiting cruise-ship passengers catch tenders back out to their ship. ⊠ *End of Catalina Ave.*

Wrigley Memorial and Botanic Garden

GARDEN | Two miles south of the bay is Wrigley Memorial and Botanic Garden, home to plants native to Southern California. Several grow only on Catalina Island—Catalina ironwood, wild tomato, and rare Catalina mahogany. The Wrigley family commissioned the garden as well as the monument, which has a grand staircase and a Spanish-style mausoleum inlaid with colorful Catalina tile. Wrigley Jr. was once buried here but his remains were moved to Pasadena during World War II. ⊠ *Avalon Canyon Rd.* ☎ *310/510–2897* ⊕ *www.catalina-conservancy.org* ⊅ *$8.*

Restaurants

Bluewater Grill

$$ | SEAFOOD | FAMILY | Overlooking the ferry landing and the entire harbor, the open-to-the-salt-air Bluewater Grill offers freshly caught fish, savory chowders, and all manner of shellfish. If they're on the menu, don't miss the swordfish steak or the sand dabs. **Known for:** fresh local fish; happy hour (October–May); harbor views. ⑤ *Average main: $27* ⊠ *306 Crescent Ave.* ☎ *310/510–3474* ⊕ *www.bluewatergrill.com.*

Descanso Beach Club

$ | AMERICAN | FAMILY | Set on an expansive deck overlooking the water, Descanso Beach Club serves a wide range of favorites: buffalo wings, hamburgers, salads, nachos, and tacos are all part of the selection. Watch the harbor seals frolic just offshore while sipping the island's super-sweet signature cocktail, the Buffalo Milk, a mix of fruit liqueurs, vodka, and whipped cream. **Known for:** tropical beach vibe; scenic views; chic cabana rentals. ⑤ *Average main: $15* ⊠ *Descanso Beach, 1 Descanso Ave.* ☎ *310/510–7410.*

The Lobster Trap

$$ | SEAFOOD | Seafood rules at the Lobster Trap—the restaurant's owner has his own boat and fishes for the catch of the day and, in season, spiny lobster. Ceviche is a great starter, always fresh and brightly flavored. **Known for:** locally caught seafood; convivial atmosphere; locals' hangout. ⑤ *Average main: $26* ⊠ *128 Catalina St.* ☎ *310/510–8585* ⊕ *catalinalobstertrap.com.*

Hotels

Aurora Hotel

$$ | HOTEL | In a town dominated by historic properties, the Aurora is refreshingly contemporary, with a hip attitude and sleek furnishings. **Pros:** trendy design; quiet location off main drag; close to restaurants. **Cons:** standard rooms are small, even by Catalina standards; no elevator; small bathrooms. ⑤ *Rooms from: $270* ⊠ *137 Marilla Ave.* ☎ *310/510–0454* ⊕ *www.auroracatalina.com* ⊅ *18 rooms* ⑩| *Breakfast.*

Hotel Vista del Mar

$$ | HOTEL | FAMILY | On the bay-facing Crescent Avenue, this third-floor property is steps from the beach, where complimentary towels, chairs, and umbrellas await guests. **Pros:** comfortable beds; central location; in-room fireplace. **Cons:** no restaurant or spa facilities; few rooms with ocean views; no elevator. ⑤ *Rooms from: $235* ⊠ *417 Crescent Ave.* ☎ *310/510–1452, 800/601–3836* ⊕ *www.hotel-vistadelmar.com* ⊅ *14 rooms* ⑩| *Breakfast.*

Mt. Ada

$$$$ | B&B/INN | If you stay in the mansion where Wrigley Jr. once lived, you can enjoy all the comforts of a millionaire's home—at a millionaire's prices. **Pros:** timeless charm; shuttle from heliport and dock; incredible views. **Cons:** smallish rooms and bathrooms; expensive; queen-size beds only. ⑤ *Rooms from: $480* ⊠ *398 Wrigley Rd.* ☎ *310/510–2030, 877/778–8322* ⊘ *Closed mid-Jan.–early Feb.* ⊅ *6 rooms* ⑩| *Some meals.*

Pavilion Hotel

$$ | **HOTEL** | **FAMILY** | This mid-century modern–style hotel is Avalon's most citified spot, though just a few steps from the sand. **Pros:** centrally located, steps from the beach and harbor; friendly staff; plush bedding. **Cons:** no pool; rooms near stairs can be noisy; some rooms fully shaded. ⑤ *Rooms from: $265* ✉ *513 Crescent Ave.* ☎ *310/510–1788, 877/778–8322* ⊕ *www.visitcatalinaisland.com* ⇨ *71 rooms* ❖ *Breakfast.*

Portofino Hotel

$$ | **HOTEL** | **FAMILY** | Steps from the Green Pleasure Pier, this European-style hotel creates an intimate feel with brick courtyards and walkways and suites named after Italian cities. **Pros:** romantic; close to beach; incredible sundeck. **Cons:** ground-floor rooms can be noisy; some rooms are on small side; no elevator. ⑤ *Rooms from: $209* ✉ *111 Crescent Ave.* ☎ *310/510–0555, 888/510–0555* ⊕ *www.hotelvillaportofino.com* ⇨ *35 rooms* ❖ *Breakfast.*

 # Activities

BICYCLING
Brown's Bikes

BICYCLING | **FAMILY** | Look for rentals on Crescent Avenue and Pebbly Beach Road, where Brown's Bikes is located. Beach cruisers start at $25 per day, mountain bikes are $30 per day, and electric bikes are $50 for a day rental and a good choice for Catalina's hills. ✉ *107 Pebbly Beach Rd.* ☎ *310/510–0986* ⊕ *www.catalinabiking.com.*

DIVING AND SNORKELING

The Casino Point Underwater Park, with its handful of wrecks and ample sea life, is best suited for diving. Lover's Cove is better for snorkeling (but you'll share the area with glass-bottom boats). Both are protected marine preserves.

Catalina Divers Supply

SCUBA DIVING | Head to Catalina Divers Supply to rent equipment, sign up for guided scuba and snorkel tours, and attend certification classes. It also has an outpost at the Dive Park at Casino Point that offers gear rental and tank air fills. ✉ *7 Green Pleasure Pier* ☎ *310/510–0330* ⊕ *www.catalinadiverssupply.com.*

Chapter 7

LOS ANGELES

Updated by
Paul Feinstein,
Michelle Rae Uy,
and Candice Yacono

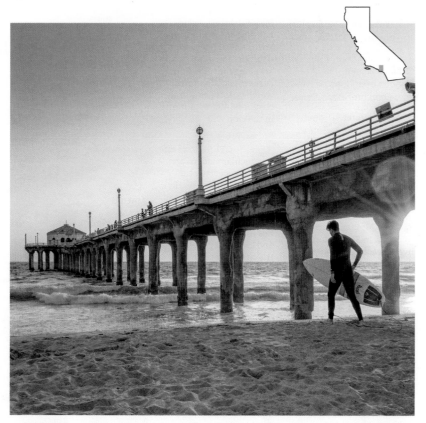

◉ Sights	🍴 Restaurants	🛏 Hotels	🛍 Shopping	🍸 Nightlife
★★★★★	★★★★★	★★★★★	★★★★★	★★★★☆

WELCOME TO LOS ANGELES

TOP REASONS TO GO

★ **Stargazing:** Both through the telescope atop Griffith Park and among the residents of Beverly Hills.

★ **Eating:** From food trucks to fine dining, an unparalleled meal awaits your palate.

★ **Beaches and Boardwalks:** The dream of '80s Venice is alive in California.

★ **Shopping:** Peruse eclectic boutiques or window-shop on Rodeo Drive.

★ **Architecture:** Art-deco wonders to Frank Gehry masterpieces abound.

★ **Scenic Drives:** You haven't seen the sunset until you've seen it from a winding L.A. road.

1 Santa Monica and the Beaches. In Santa Monica, a lively beach scene plays out daily. Venice is a more raffish mix of artists, beach punks, and yuppies. Drive up the Pacific Coast Highway to Malibu, where the rich and famous reside.

2 Beverly Hills, West Hollywood, and the Westside. Rodeo Drive is particularly good for a look at wretched or ravishing excess. West Hollywood is an area for urban indulgences—shopping, restaurants, nightlife— rather than sightseeing.

3 Hollywood and the Studios. Glitzy and tarnished, good and bad— Hollywood is just like the entertainment business itself. The Walk of Fame, Chinese Theatre, and the Hollywood Bowl keep the romantic past alive. Universal Studios Hollywood is in the Valley.

4 Mid-Wilshire and Koreatown. In Mid-Wilshire is a glorious hodgepodge of manicured lawns and art-deco high-rises. Here you can peruse art along Museum Row. Just east is Koreatown, which boasts some of the best bars and restaurants in the city.

5 Downtown Los Angeles. DTLA shows off spectacular modern architecture, especially the Walt Disney Concert Hall. The MOCA and the Broad anchor a world-class art scene, while El Pueblo de Los Angeles, Chinatown, and Little Tokyo reflect the city's diversity.

6 Pasadena. It's a quiet, genteel area, with outstanding Arts and Crafts homes and a pair of exceptional museums: the Norton Simon Museum and the Huntington Library.

7 Los Feliz and the Eastside. This is a land of good eats and better booze. Dine in Los Feliz and Silver Lake and go drinking in Echo Park and Highland Park.

SOUTH-OF-THE-BORDER FLAVOR

From Cal-Mex burritos to Mexico City–style tacos, Southern California is a top stateside destination for experiencing Mexico's myriad culinary styles.

Many Americans are surprised to learn that the Mexican menu goes far beyond Tex-Mex (or Cal-Mex) favorites like burritos, chimichangas, enchiladas, fajitas, and nachos—many of which were created or popularized stateside. Indeed, Mexico has rich, regional food styles, like the complex *mole* sauces of Puebla and Oaxaca and the fresh *ceviches* of Veracruz, as well as the trademark snack of Mexico City: tacos.

In Southern California tacos are an obsession, with numerous blogs and websites dedicated to the quest for the perfect taco. They're everywhere—in ramshackle taco stands, roving trucks, and strip-mall taquerias. Whether you're looking for a cheap snack or a lunch on-the-go, SoCal's taco selection can't be beat. But be forewarned: there may not be an English menu. Here we've noted unfamiliar taco terms, along with other potentially new-to-you items from the Mexican menu.

THIRST QUENCHERS

Spanish for "fresh water," *agua fresca* is made from fruit, rice, or seeds that are blended with sugar and water. Lemon, lime, and watermelon are common flavors. Other varieties include *agua de Jamaica*, flavored with red hibiscus petals; *agua de horchata*, a cinnamon-scented rice milk; and *agua de tamarindo*, a bittersweet variety flavored with tamarind. For a little more kick, try a *Michelada*, a beer spiked with lime juice and chili sauce, served in a salt-rimmed glass with ice.

Decoding the Menu

Ceviche—Citrus-marinated raw seafood appetizer from the Gulf shores of Veracruz. Often eaten with tortilla chips.

Chile relleno—Roasted poblano pepper stuffed with ground meat or cheese, then dipped in egg batter, fried, and served in tomato sauce.

Fish taco—A specialty in Southern California, the fish taco is a soft corn tortilla stuffed with grilled or fried white fish (mahimahi, tilapia, or wahoo), pico de gallo, *crema*, and shredded cabbage.

Gordita—"Little fat one" in Spanish, this dish is like a taco, but the cornmeal shell is thicker, similar to pita bread.

Mole—A complex sauce with Aztec roots made from more than 20 ingredients, including chilies, cinnamon, cumin, anise, sesame seeds, and Mexican chocolate. There are many variations, but the most common is *mole poblano* from the Puebla region.

Quesadilla—A snack made from a fresh tortilla that is folded over and stuffed with simple fillings, then toasted on a griddle. Elevated versions of the quesadilla may be stuffed with sautéed *flor de calabaza* (squash blossoms) or *huitlacoche* (corn mushrooms).

Tacos

Tamales

Salsa—A cooked or raw sauce. Popular salsas include *pico de gallo,* a fresh sauce made from chopped tomatoes, onions, chilies, cilantro, and lime; *salsa verde,* made with tomatillos; and *salsa roja,* a cooked sauce made with chilies, tomatoes, onion, garlic, and cilantro.

Sope—A small, fried corn cake topped with ingredients like refried beans, shredded chicken, and salsa.

Taco—Tacos are made from soft, palm-sized corn tortillas folded over and filled with meat, chopped onion, cilantro, and salsa with meats like *al pastor* (spiced pork), *barbacoa* (braised beef), *carnitas* (roasted pork), *cecina* (chili-coated pork), *carne asada* (roasted, chopped beef), *chorizo* (spicy sausage), *lengua* (beef tongue), *sesos* (cow brain), and *tasajo* (spiced, grilled beef).

Tamales—Sweet or savory corn cakes that are steamed, and may be filled with cheese, roasted chilies, shredded meat, or other fillings.

Torta—A Mexican sandwich served on a crusty sandwich roll. Fillings often include meat, refried beans, and cheese.

Los Angeles is a polarizing place, but those who hate it just haven't found their niche—there's truly a corner of the city for everyone. Drive for miles between towering palm trees, bodega-lined streets, and Downtown's skyscrapers, and you'll still never discover all of L.A.'s hidden gems.

Yes, you'll encounter traffic-clogged freeways, but there are also walkable pockets like Venice's Abbot Kinney. You'll drive past Beverly Hills mansions and spy palaces perched atop hills, but you'll also see the roots of mid-century modern architecture in Silver Lake. You'll soak up the sun in Santa Monica and then find yourself barhopping in the city's revitalized Downtown while enjoying scrumptious fish tacos along the way.

You might think that you'll have to spend most of your visit in a car, but that's not the case. In fact, exploring by foot is the only way to really get to know the various fringe neighborhoods and mini-cities that make up the vast L.A. area. But no single locale—whether it's Malibu, Downtown, Beverly Hills, or Burbank—fully embodies Los Angeles. It's in the mix that you'll discover the city's character.

Planning

When to Go

Almost any time of the year is the right time to go to Los Angeles; the climate is mild and pleasant year-round. Winter brings crisp, sunny, unusually smogless days from about November to May (expect brief rains from December to April). Los Angeles summers, which are virtually rainless, can lead to air-quality alerts. Prices skyrocket and reservations are a must when tourism peaks from July through early October.

Getting Here and Around

AIR TRAVEL

It's generally easier to navigate the secondary airports than to get through sprawling LAX, the city's major gateway. Bob Hope Airport in Burbank is closest to Downtown, and domestic flights to it can be cheaper than those to LAX—it's definitely worth checking out. From Long Beach Airport it's equally convenient to go north to central Los Angeles or south to Orange County. Flights to Orange County's John Wayne Airport are often more expensive than those to the other secondary airports. Parking at the smaller airports is cheaper than at LAX.

At LAX, SuperShuttle allows walk-on shuttle passengers without prior reservations. FlyAway buses travel between LAX and Van Nuys, Westwood, La Brea, and Union Station in Downtown.

AIRPORTS Hollywood Burbank Airport
(*BUR*). ✉ *2627 N. Hollywood Way, near I–5 and U.S. 101, Burbank* ☎ *818/840–8840* ⊕ *www.hollywoodburbankairport. com.* **John Wayne Airport** (*SNA*). ✉ *18601 Airport Way, Santa Ana* ☎ *949/252–5200* ⊕ *www.ocair.com.* **L.A./Ontario International Airport** (*ONT*). ✉ *E. Airport Dr., off I–10, Ontario* ☎ *909/544–5300* ⊕ *www. flyontario.com.* **Long Beach Airport** (*LGB*). ✉ *4100 Donald Douglas Dr., Long Beach* ☎ *562/570–2600* ⊕ *www.lgb.org.* **Los Angeles International Airport** (*LAX*). ✉ *1 World Way, off Hwy. 1* ☎ *855/463–5252* ⊕ *www.flylax.com.*

SHUTTLES FlyAway. ☎ *866/435–9529* ⊕ *www.flylax.com/en/flyaway-bus.* **Super-Shuttle.** ☎ *323/775–6600, 800/258–3826* ⊕ *www.supershuttle.com.*

BUS TRAVEL

Inadequate public transportation has plagued L.A. for decades. That said, many local trips can be made, with time and patience, by buses run by the Los Angeles County Metropolitan Transit Authority. In certain cases—visiting the Getty Center, for instance, or Universal Studios—buses may be your best option. There's a special Dodger Stadium Express that shuttles passengers between Union Station and the world-famous ballpark for home games. It's free if you have a ticket in hand and saves you parking-related stress.

Metro buses cost $1.75, plus 50¢ for each transfer to another bus or to the subway. A one-day pass costs $7, and a weekly pass is $25 for unlimited travel on all buses and trains. Passes are valid from Sunday through Saturday. For the fastest service, look for the red-and-white Metro Rapid buses; these stop less frequently. There are 25 Metro Rapid routes, including along Wilshire and Vermont boulevards.

Other bus services make it possible to explore the entire metropolitan area. DASH minibuses cover six different circular routes in Hollywood, Mid-Wilshire, and Downtown. You pay 50¢ every time you get on. The Santa Monica Municipal Bus Line, also known as the Big Blue Bus, is a pleasant and inexpensive way to move around the Westside. Trips cost $1.25. An express bus to and from Downtown L.A., run by Culver CityBus, costs $2.50. Transfers to Metro or Metro Rail are 50¢.

You can pay your fare in cash on MTA, Santa Monica, and Culver City buses, but you must have exact change. You can buy MTA TAP cards at Metro Rail stations, customer centers throughout the city, and some convenience and grocery stores.

BUS INFORMATION Culver CityBus.
☎ *310/253–6510* ⊕ *www.culvercity.org.* **DASH.** ☎ *310/808–2273* ⊕ *www.ladottransit.com.* **Los Angeles County Metropolitan Transit Authority.** ☎ *323/466–3876* ⊕ *www. metro.net.* **Santa Monica Municipal Bus Line.** ☎ *310/451–5444* ⊕ *www.bigbluebus.com.*

CAR TRAVEL

If you're used to urban driving, you shouldn't have too much trouble navigating the streets of Los Angeles. If not, L.A. can be unnerving. However, the city has evolved with drivers in mind. Streets are wide and parking garages abound, so it's more car friendly than many older big cities.

Remember that most freeways are known by a name and a number; for example, the San Diego Freeway is Interstate 405 (or just The 405), the Hollywood Freeway is U.S. 101, the Ventura Freeway is a different stretch of U.S. 101, the Santa Monica Freeway is Interstate 10, and the Harbor Freeway is Interstate 110. It helps, too, to know which direction you're traveling; say, west toward Santa Monica or east toward Downtown Los Angeles. Distance in miles doesn't mean much, depending on the time of day you're traveling: the short 10-mile drive between the San Fernando Valley and Downtown Los Angeles might take an hour to travel during rush hour but only 20 minutes at other times.

There are plenty of identical or similarly named streets in L.A. (Beverly Boulevard and Beverly Drive, for example), so be as specific as you can when asking directions. Expect sudden changes in addresses as streets pass through neighborhoods, then incorporated cities, then back into neighborhoods. This can be most bewildering on Robertson Boulevard, an otherwise useful north–south artery that, by crossing through L.A., West Hollywood, and Beverly Hills, dips in and out of several such numbering shifts in a matter of miles.

INFORMATION Caltrans Current Highway Conditions. ☎ *800/427–7623 for road conditions* ⊕ *www.dot.ca.gov.*

EMERGENCY SERVICES Metro Freeway Service Patrol. ☎ *511 for breakdowns* ⊕ *www.go511.com.*

METRO RAIL TRAVEL

Metro Rail covers only a small part of L.A.'s vast expanse, but it's convenient, frequent, and inexpensive. Most popular with visitors is the underground Red Line, which runs from Downtown's Union Station through Mid-Wilshire, Hollywood, and Universal City on its way to North Hollywood, stopping at the most popular tourist destinations along the way.

The light-rail Green Line stretches from Redondo Beach to Norwalk, while the partially underground Blue Line travels from Downtown to the South Bay. The monorail-like Gold Line extends from Union Station to Pasadena and out to the deep San Gabriel Valley and Azusa. The Orange Line, a 14-mile bus corridor, connects the North Hollywood subway station with the western San Fernando Valley.

Most recently extended was the Expo Line, which connects Downtown to the Westside, and terminates in Santa Monica, two blocks from the Pacific Ocean.

Daily service is offered from about 4:30 am to 12:30 am, with departures every 5 to 15 minutes. On weekends trains run until 2 am. Buy tickets from station vending machines; fares are $1.75, or $7 for an all-day pass. Bicycles are allowed on Metro Rail trains at all times.

METRO RAIL INFORMATION Los Angeles County Metropolitan Transit Authority. ☎ *213/922–6235* ⊕ *www.metro.net.*

RIDE-SHARING AND TAXI TRAVEL

Request a ride using apps like Lyft, and a driver will usually arrive within minutes. Fares increase during busy times, but it's often the most affordable option, especially for the convenience.

Instead of trying to hail a taxi on the street, phone one of the many taxi companies. The Curb Taxi app allows for online hailing of L.A. taxis. The metered rate is $2.70 per mile, plus a $2.85 perfare charge. Taxi rides from LAX have an additional $4 surcharge. Be aware that distances are greater than they might appear on the map so fares add up quickly.

TAXI COMPANIES Beverly Hills Cab Co. ☎ *800/273–6611* ⊕ *www.beverlyhillscabco.com.* **Independent Cab Co.** ☎ *800/521–8294* ⊕ *www.taxi4u.com.* **LA Checker Cab.** ☎ *800/300–5007* ⊕ *www.ineedtaxi.com.* **United Independent Taxi.** ☎ *800/822–8294, 323/207–8294 text to order taxi* ⊕ *www.unitedtaxi.com.* **Yellow Cab Los Angeles.** ☎ *424/222–2222* ⊕ *www.layellowcab.com.*

TRAIN TRAVEL

Downtown's Union Station is one of the great American railroad terminals. The interior includes comfortable seating, a restaurant, and several snack bars. As the city's rail hub, it's the place to catch an Amtrak, Metrolink commuter train, or the Red, Gold, or Purple lines. Among

Amtrak's Southern California routes are 11 daily trips to San Diego and 6 to Santa Barbara. Amtrak's luxury *Coast Starlight* travels along the spectacular coastline from Seattle to Los Angeles in just a day and a half (though it's often a little late). The *Sunset Limited* arrives from New Orleans, and the *Southwest Chief* comes from Chicago.

INFORMATION Amtrak. ☎ *800/872–7245* ⊕ *www.amtrak.com.* **Metrolink.** ☎ *800/371–5465* ⊕ *www.metrolinktrains. com.* **Union Station.** ✉ *800 N. Alameda St.* ☎ *213/683–6979* ⊕ *www.unionstationla. com.*

Restaurants

Los Angeles may be known for its beach living and celebrity-infused backdrop, but it was once a farm town. The hillsides were covered in citrus orchards and dairy farms, and agriculture was a major industry. Today, even as L.A. is urbanized, the city's culinary landscape has reembraced a local, sustainable, and seasonal philosophy at many levels—from fine dining to street snacks.

With a growing interest in farm-to-fork, the city's farmers' market scene has exploded, becoming popular at big-name restaurants and small eateries alike. In Hollywood and Santa Monica you can often find high-profile chefs scouring farm stands for fresh produce.

The status of the celebrity chef carries weight around this town. People follow the culinary zeitgeist with the same fervor as celebrity gossip. You can queue up with the hungry hordes at Nancy Silverton's **Mozza,** or try and snag a reservation to Ludo Lefebvre's ever-popular **Trois Mec** or David Chang's L.A. outpost, **Majordomo.**

Global eats continue to be a backbone of the L.A. dining scene. People head to Koreatown for epic Korean cooking and late-night coffeehouses and to West L.A. for phenomenal sushi. Latin food is

well represented in the city, making it tough to choose between Guatemalan eateries, Peruvian restaurants, nouveau Mexican bistros, and Tijuana-style taco trucks. With so many dining options, sometimes the best strategy is simply to drive and explore.

What It Costs			
$	$$	$$$	$$$$
RESTAURANTS			
under $14	$14–$22	$23–$31	over $31

Hotels

When it comes to finding a place to stay, travelers have never been more spoiled for choice than in today's Los Angeles. From luxurious digs in Beverly Hills and along the coast to budget boutiques in Hollywood, hotels are stepping up service, upgrading amenities, and trying all-new concepts, like upscale hostels and retro-chic motels. Hotels in Los Angeles today are more than just a place to rest your head; they're a key part of the experience.

What It Costs			
$	$$	$$$	$$$$
HOTELS			
under $200	$200–$300	$301–$400	over $400

Nightlife

Los Angeles is not the city that never sleeps—instead it parties until 2 am (save for the secret after-hours parties at private clubs or warehouses) and wakes up to imbibe green juices and breakfast burritos as hangover cures or to sweat it out in a yoga class. Whether you plan to test your limit at historic establishments

Downtown or take advantage of a cheap happy hour at a Hollywood dive, this city's nightlife has something for you.

A night out in Los Angeles can simultaneously surprise and impress. Seeing an unscheduled set by an A-list comedian at the stand-up comedy club, being talked into singing karaoke at the diviest place you've ever seen, dancing at a bar with no dance floor because, well, the DJ is just too good at his job—going out isn't always what you expect, but it certainly is never boring.

The focus of nightlife once centered on the Sunset Strip, with its multitude of bars, rock clubs, and dance spots, but more neighborhoods are competing with each other and forcing the nightlife scene to evolve. Although the Strip can be a worthwhile trip, other areas of the city are catching people's attention. Downtown Los Angeles, for instance, is a destination in its own right. Other areas foster more of a neighborhood vibe. Silver Lake and Los Feliz have both cultivated a relaxed environment.

So if you find yourself disappointed with a rude bouncer, or drinks that are too watery, or a cover charge that just isn't worth it, try again. Eventually you'll find that perfect place where each time is the best time. If not, at least you'll walk away with a good story.

Performing Arts

The art scene in Los Angeles extends beyond the screen and onto the stage. A place of artistic innovation and history, one can discover new and challenging theatrical works across L.A. stages, while the city still maintains a respect for tradition with its restored theaters and classic plays. See live music at impeccably designed amphitheaters like the Hollywood Bowl or listen in on captivating lectures by authors and directors at various intimate spaces. In homage to the city's

roots as a filmmaking mecca, there are also retrospectives and rare screenings in movie theaters all over the city, often followed by Q&As with the cast.

Visitor Information

Discover Los Angeles, the official tourism site, has an annually updated general information packet that includes suggestions for entertainment, lodging, and dining and a list of special events. There are two visitor information centers, both accessible to Metro stops: the Hollywood & Highland Center and Union Station.

CONTACTS Discover Los Angeles.
☎ *213/624–7300, 800/228–2452*
⊕ *www.discoverlosangeles.com.*

Santa Monica and the Beaches

Hugging the Santa Monica Bay in an arch, the desirable communities of Malibu, Santa Monica, and Venice move from ultrarich and ultracasual Malibu to bohemian, borderline-seedy Venice. What they have in common is cleaner air, mild temperatures, heavy traffic, and an emphasis on beach culture.

Santa Monica

 Sights

Santa Monica Pier
AMUSEMENT PARK/WATER PARK | FAMILY |
Souvenir shops, carnival games, arcades, eateries, an outdoor trapeze school, a small amusement park, and an aquarium all contribute to the festive atmosphere of this truncated pier at the foot of Colorado Boulevard below Palisades Park. The pier's trademark 46-horse Looff Carousel, built in 1922, has appeared in several films, including *The Sting*. The

Santa Monica Pier's West Coaster and Pacific Wheel provide incredible ocean views.

Soda Jerks ice cream fountain (named for the motion the attendant makes when pulling the machine's arm) inside the carousel building is a pier staple. Free concerts are held on the pier in the summer. ⊠ *Colorado Ave. and the ocean, Santa Monica* ☎ *310/458–8901* ⊕ *www. santamonicapier.org.*

Santa Monica State Beach

BEACH—SIGHT | The first beach you'll hit after the Santa Monica Freeway (Interstate 10) runs into the Pacific Coast Highway, wide and sandy Santa Monica is *the* place for sunning and socializing. Be prepared for a mob scene on summer weekends, when parking becomes an expensive ordeal. Swimming is fine (with the usual post-storm-pollution caveat); for surfing, go elsewhere. For a memorable view, climb up the stairway over PCH to Palisades Park, at the top of the bluffs. Free summer concerts are held on the pier on Thursday evening. **Amenities:** parking; lifeguards; toilets; food and drink; showers; water sports. **Best for:** partiers; sunset; surfing; swimming; walking. ⊠ *1642 Promenade, PCH at California Incline, Santa Monica* ☎ *310/458–8573* ⊕ *www.smgov.net/ portals/beach* 🅿 *Parking from $6.*

Third Street Promenade and Santa Monica Place

COMMERCIAL CENTER | Stretch your legs along this pedestrian-only, three-block stretch of 3rd Street, close to the Pacific, lined with jacaranda trees, ivy-topiary dinosaur fountains, strings of lights, and branches of nearly every major U.S. retail chain. Outdoor cafés, street vendors, movie theaters, and a rich nightlife make this a main gathering spot for locals, visitors, street musicians, and performance artists. Plan a night just to take it all in or take an afternoon for a long people-watching stroll. There's plenty of parking in city structures on the streets flanking the promenade. **Santa Monica Place,** at the south end of the promenade, is a sleek outdoor mall and foodie haven. Its three stories are home to Nordstrom, Louis Vuitton, Coach, and other upscale retailers. Don't miss

Santa Monica, Venice, and Malibu

KEY

- ① Exploring Sights
- ① Restaurants
- ① Hotels

0 — 1/2 mi
0 — 1/2 km

Sights ▼
1 The Getty Center......... E1
2 Muscle Beach D6
3 Santa Monica Pier...... B3
4 Santa Monica State
  Beach.................... A3
5 3rd Street Promenade... B2
6 Venice Beach
  Boardwalk.............. D6

Restaurants ▼
1 Bay Cities Italian Deli... C2
2 Gjelina..................... E6
3 Melisse B1
4 Rose Cafe................ D5
5 Rustic Canyon Wine Bar
  & Seasonal Kitchen B1
6 Santa Monica
  Seafood.................. B2
7 Tar & Roses B2
8 Toscana.................... C1
9 The Venice Whaler...... E7

Hotels ▼
1 The Ambrose............. C1
2 Channel Road Inn....... A2
3 Fairmont Miramar Hotel &
  Bungalows A2
4 Hotel Erwin D6
5 Palihouse
  Santa Monica A2
6 Sea Shore Motel........ C4
7 Shore Hotel............. B3
8 Shutters on the
  Beach.................... B4

the ocean views from the rooftop food court. ✉ *3rd St., between Colorado and Wilshire Blvds., Santa Monica* ⊕ *www. downtownsm.com.*

🍴 Restaurants

Bay Cities Italian Deli

$ | **DELI** | Part deli, part market, Bay Cities has been home to incredible Italian subs since 1925. This renowned counter-service spot is always crowded (best to order ahead), but monster subs run the gamut from the mighty meatball to the signature Godmother, made with prosciutto, ham, capicola, mortadella, Genoa salami, and provolone. **Known for:** market with rare imports; excellent service. ⑤ *Average main: $10* ✉ *1517 Lincoln Blvd., Santa Monica* ☎ *310/395–8279* ⊕ *www.baycitiesitaliandeli.com* ⊘ *Closed Mon.*

★ Mélisse

$$$$ | **FRENCH** | Chef-owner Josiah Citrin enhances his modern French cooking with seasonal California produce at this Santa Monica institution. The tasting menu might feature egg caviar with smoked lemon crème fraiche, wild Scottish red partridge with chocolate persimmons, or Kagoshima Wagyu beef rib eye. **Known for:** domestic and European cheese cart; contemporary/elegant decor. ⑤ *Average main: $145* ✉ *1104 Wilshire Blvd., Santa Monica* ☎ *310/395–0881* ⊕ *www.melisse.com* ⊘ *Closed Sun. and Mon. No lunch.*

★ Rustic Canyon Wine Bar and Seasonal Kitchen

$$$ | **MODERN AMERICAN** | A Santa Monica mainstay, the seasonally changing menu at this farm-to-table restaurant consistently upends norms. The homey, minimalist space offers sweeping views of Wilshire Boulevard, and on any given night the menu of California cuisine may include Channel Island rockfish with shelling beans and Sun Gold tomatoes, or buttered ricotta dumplings with golden chanterelles and Coolea cheese. **Known for:** never-ending wine list; knowledgeable staff. ⑤ *Average main: $35* ✉ *1119 Wilshire Blvd., Santa Monica* ☎ *310/393–7050* ⊕ *www.rusticcanyon-winebar.com.*

Santa Monica Seafood

$$ | **SEAFOOD | FAMILY** | A Southern California favorite, this Italian seafood haven has been serving up fresh fish since 1939. This freshness comes from its pedigree as the largest seafood distributor in the Southwest. **Known for:** deliciously seasoned rainbow trout; oyster bar; kids' meals. ⑤ *Average main: $20* ✉ *1000 Wilshire Blvd., Santa Monica* ☎ *310/393–5244* ⊕ *www.santamonicaseafood.com.*

Tar and Roses

$$$ | **MODERN AMERICAN** | This small and dimly lit romantic spot in Santa Monica is full of adventurous options, like octopus skewers and venison loin. The new American cuisine also features standouts like braised lamb belly with minted apple chutney and drool-worthy strawberry ricotta crostata with honeycomb ice cream for dessert. **Known for:** phenomenal oxtail dumplings; delicious hanger steak. ⑤ *Average main: $30* ✉ *602 Santa Monica Blvd., Santa Monica* ☎ *310/587–0700* ⊕ *www.tarandroses.com.*

🛏 Hotels

The Ambrose

$$$ | **HOTEL** | Tranquility pervades the airy, California Craftsman–style, four-story Ambrose, which blends right into its mostly residential Santa Monica neighborhood. **Pros:** "green" practices like nontoxic cleaners and recycling bins; partial ocean view. **Cons:** quiet, residential area of Santa Monica; parking fee ($27); not walking distance to beach. ⑤ *Rooms from: $359* ✉ *1255 20th St., Santa Monica* ☎ *310/315–1555, 877/262–7673* ⊕ *www.ambrosehotel.com* ⟿ *77 rooms* ⦿| *Breakfast.*

★ Channel Road Inn

$$ | B&B/INN | A quaint surprise in Southern California, the Channel Road Inn is every bit the country retreat bed-and-breakfast lovers adore, with four-poster beds, fluffy duvets, and a cozy living room with a fireplace. **Pros:** free wine and hors d'oeuvres every evening; home-cooked breakfast included; meditative rose garden on-site. **Cons:** no pool; need a car to get around. $ *Rooms from: $225* ✉ *219 W. Channel Rd., Santa Monica* ☎ *310/459–1920* ⊕ *www.channelroadinn. com* ⌁ *15 rooms* ⚬ *Breakfast.*

Fairmont Miramar Hotel and Bungalows Santa Monica

$$$$ | HOTEL | A mammoth Moreton Bay fig tree dwarfs the main entrance of the 5-acre, beach-adjacent Santa Monica wellness retreat and lends its name to the inviting on-site Mediterranean-inspired restaurant, FIG, which focuses on local ingredients and frequently refreshes its menu. **Pros:** guests can play games on the heated patio; swanky open-air cocktail spot, the Bungalow, on-site; stay in retrofitted '20s and '40s bungalows. **Cons:** all this luxury comes at a big price. $ *Rooms from: $599* ✉ *101 Wilshire Blvd., Santa Monica* ☎ *310/576–7777, 866/540–4470* ⊕ *www. fairmont.com/santamonica* ⌁ *334 rooms* ⚬ *No meals.*

Palihouse Santa Monica

$$$ | HOTEL | Tucked in a posh residential area three blocks from the sea and lively Third Street Promenade, Palihouse Santa Monica caters to design-minded world travelers, with spacious rooms and suites decked out in whimsical antiques. **Pros:** Apple TV in rooms; walking distance to Santa Monica attractions; fully equipped kitchens. **Cons:** no pool; decor might not appeal to more traditional travelers; parking fee ($45). $ *Rooms from: $355* ✉ *1001 3rd St., Santa Monica* ☎ *310/394– 1279* ⊕ *www.palihousesantamonica.com* ⌁ *38 rooms* ⚬ *No meals.*

Sea Shore Motel

$ | HOTEL | On Santa Monica's busy Main Street, the Sea Shore is a charming throwback to Route 66 and to '60s-style, family-run roadside motels and is surrounded by an ultratrendy neighborhood. **Pros:** close to beach and restaurants; free Wi-Fi, parking, and use of beach equipment; popular rooftop deck and on-site restaurant, Amelia's. **Cons:** street noise; motel-style decor and beds. $ *Rooms from: $159* ✉ *2637 Main St., Santa Monica* ☎ *310/392–2787* ⊕ *www.seashoremotel.com* ⌁ *25 rooms* ⚬ *No meals.*

★ Shore Hotel

$$$$ | HOTEL | With views of the Santa Monica Pier, this hotel with a friendly staff offers eco-minded travelers stylish rooms with a modern design, just steps from the sand and sea. **Pros:** near beach and Third Street Promenade; rainfall showerheads; solar-heated pool and hot tub. **Cons:** expensive rooms and parking fees; fronting busy Ocean Avenue; some sharing a room may be wary of the see-through shower. $ *Rooms from: $432* ✉ *1515 Ocean Ave., Santa Monica* ☎ *310/458–1515* ⊕ *shorehotel.com* ⌁ *164 rooms* ⚬ *No meals.*

★ Shutters on the Beach

$$$$ | HOTEL | FAMILY | Set right on the sand, this inn has become synonymous with staycations. **Pros:** built-in cabinets filled with art books and curios; rooms designed by Michael Smith; rooms come with whirlpool tub. **Cons:** have to pay for extras like beach chairs; very expensive. $ *Rooms from: $675* ✉ *1 Pico Blvd., Santa Monica* ☎ *310/458–0030, 800/334– 9000* ⊕ *www.shuttersonthebeach.com* ⌁ *198 rooms* ⚬ *No meals.*

LOS ANGELES INTERNATIONAL AIRPORT

Custom Hotel

$ | HOTEL | Close enough to LAX to see the runways, the Custom Hotel is a playful and practical redo of a 12-story, mid-century modern tower by famed L.A. architect Welton Becket (of

Hollywood's Capitol Records building and the Dorothy Chandler Pavilion). **Pros:** shuttle to LAX; close to beach and airport; socializing at poolside restaurant/lounge, Deck 33. **Cons:** at the desolate end of Lincoln Boulevard; thin walls; in need of updating. $ *Rooms from: $183* ☒ *8639 Lincoln Blvd., Los Angeles International Airport* ☎ *310/645–0400, 877/287–8601* ⊕ *www.customhotel.com* ⇱ *250 rooms* ⏏ *No meals.*

Nightlife

★ Chez Jay
BARS/PUBS | Around since 1959, this dive bar continues to be a well-loved place in Santa Monica. Everyone from the young to the old (including families) frequents this historical landmark. It's a charming place, from the well-worn booths with their red checkered tablecloths to the ship's wheel near the door. Be on the lookout for ongoing *Goliath* filmings, and consider the patio for private parties. ☒ *1657 Ocean Ave., Santa Monica* ☎ *310/395–1741* ⊕ *www.chezjays.com.*

The Galley
BARS/PUBS | Santa Monica's oldest restaurant and bar, the Galley has a consistent nautical theme inside and out: the boatlike exterior features wavy blue neon lights and porthole windows; inside, fishing nets and anchors adorn the walls, and the whole place is aglow with colorful string lights. Most patrons tend to crowd the center bar, with the more dinner-oriented folks frequenting the booths. Prices are a good deal during "most hours" and a steal during "happy hours." ☒ *2442 Main St., Santa Monica* ☎ *310/452–1934.*

UnUrban Coffee House
CAFES—NIGHTLIFE | Looking for a real neighborhood experience, with mismatched furniture and undiscovered talent? This is the place to enjoy a laid-back evening of entertainment by local performers (and good espresso drinks and organic pastries). The music and poetry open-mic nights attract interesting and talented folks, and the musical showcase draws a random mix of musicians. There's no cover to get in, but it typically costs $5 to participate in the open mics. ☒ *3301 Pico Blvd., at Urban Ave., Santa Monica* ☎ *310/315–0056* ⊕ *www.unurban.com.*

Shopping

Lady Chocolatt
FOOD/CANDY | This is the shop where chocolate dreams are made. The purveyor of the finest Belgian chocolate in all of Los Angeles, Lady Chocolatt is the perfect answer to the age-old question "What should we buy for our loved one's birthday, anniversary, baby shower, celebration, etc.?" The ornate display case is filled with dark chocolate truffles, hazelnut pralines, Grand Marnier ganaches, and so much more. Post up for a late-afternoon espresso and let your chocolate dreams wander. ☒ *12008 Wilshire Blvd., Santa Monica* ☎ *310/442–2245* ⊕ *www.chocolatt.com.*

Planet Blue
CLOTHING | The beachy bohemian style is the focus at this small local chain, with an abundance of jeans, breezy dresses, turquoise jewelry, bikinis, and other SoCal staples. ☒ *800 14th St., Santa Monica* ☎ *310/394–0135* ⊕ *www.shopplanetblue.com.*

Third Street Promenade
SHOPPING CENTERS/MALLS | There is no shortage of spots to shop everything from sporting goods to trendy fashions on this pedestrian-friendly strip. Outposts here are mainly of the chain variety, and in between splurging on books, clothing, sneakers, and more, shoppers can pop into one of the many eateries to stay satiated or even catch a movie at one of the theaters. Additionally, the chef-approved Farmers Market takes over twice a week, and with the beach

just a few steps away, the destination is a quintessential California stop. ✉ *3rd St., between Broadway and Wilshire Blvd., Santa Monica.*

Wasteland

CLOTHING | This vintage emporium, a block from the Third Street Promenade, sells gently used items for both women and men. You'll find everything from wide-lapel polyester shirts to last year's Michael Kors bag. There is also a location on Ventura Boulevard. ✉ *1330 4th St., between Arizona Ave. and Santa Monica Blvd., Santa Monica* ☎ *310/395–2620* ⊕ *www.shopwasteland.com.*

Venice

◉ Sights

Muscle Beach

LOCAL INTEREST | Bronzed young men bench-pressing five girls at once, weight lifters doing tricks on the sand—the Muscle Beach facility fired up the country's imagination from the get-go. There are actually two spots known as Muscle Beach. The original Muscle Beach, just south of the Santa Monica Pier, is where bodybuilders Jack LaLanne and Vic and Armand Tanny used to work out in the 1950s. When it was closed in 1959, the bodybuilders moved south along the beach to Venice, to a city-run facility known as "the Pen," and the Venice Beach spot inherited the Muscle Beach moniker. The spot is probably best known now as a place where a young Arnold Schwarzenegger first came to flex his muscles in the late '60s and began his rise to fame. The area now hosts a variety of sports and gymnastics events and the occasional "beach babe" beauty contests that always draw a crowd. But stop by any time during daylight for an eye-popping array of beefcakes (and would-be beefcakes). ✉ *1800 Ocean Front Walk, Venice* ⊕ *www.musclebeach.net.*

Venice Beach Boardwalk

MARINA | The surf and sand of Venice are fine, but the main attraction here is the boardwalk scene, which is a cosmos all its own. Go on weekend afternoons for the best people-watching experience. You can also swim, fish, surf, and skateboard, or play racquetball, handball, shuffleboard, and basketball (the boardwalk is the site of hotly contested pickup games). You can rent a bike or in-line skates and hit the Strand bike path, then pull up a seat at a sidewalk café and watch the action unfold. ✉ *1800 Ocean Front Walk, west of Pacific Ave., Venice* ☎ *310/392–4687* ⊕ *www.venicebeach.com.*

Restaurants

Gjelina

$$ | **AMERICAN** | Gjelina comes alive the minute you walk through the rustic wooden door and into a softly lit dining room with long communal tables. The menu is seasonal, with outstanding small plates, charcuterie, pastas, and pizza. **Known for:** lively crowd on the patio; late-night menu; inventive pizzas and salads. ⑤ *Average main: $20* ✉ *1429 Abbot Kinney Blvd., Venice* ☎ *310/450–1429* ⊕ *www.gjelina.com.*

Rose Cafe

$$ | **MODERN AMERICAN** | **FAMILY** | This indoor-outdoor restaurant has served Venice for decades but constantly reinvents itself, serving mouthwatering California cuisines with multiple patios, a full bar, and a bakery. Creative types loiter for the Wi-Fi and sip espressos, while young families gather out back to nibble on yellowtail crudo and crispy brussels sprouts. **Known for:** sophisticated but unpretentious vibe; location in the heart of Venice; being L.A. in a nutshell. ⑤ *Average main: $25* ✉ *220 Rose Ave., Venice* ☎ *310/399–0711* ⊕ *www.rosecafevenice.com.*

Venice Whaler

$$ | **AMERICAN** | This beachfront bar that's been the local watering hole for musicians like the Doors and the Beach Boys since

1944 boasts an amazing view and serves tasty California pub food like fish tacos, pulled pork sliders, and avocado toast with a basic selection of beers. Be prepared for rowdy crowds of sports fans and beachgoers at happy hour and on weekends. **Known for:** rock-n-roll history; pub food; brunch. $ *Average main: $15 ☒ 10 W. Washington Blvd., Venice ☎ 310/821–8737 ⊕ www.venicewhaler.com.*

Hotels

Hotel Erwin

$$$ | HOTEL | A boutique hotel a block off the Venice Beach Boardwalk, the newly renovated Erwin will make you feel like a hipper version of yourself. **Pros:** dining emphasizes fresh ingredients; playful design in guest rooms; free Wi-Fi. **Cons:** some rooms face a noisy alley; no pool. $ *Rooms from: $369 ☒ 1697 Pacific Ave., Venice ☎ 310/452–1111, 800/786–7789 ⊕ www.hotelerwin.com ⤴ 119 rooms* ⦿| *No meals.*

★ The Kinney

$$ | HOTEL | Walking distance to Venice Beach and Abbot Kinney's artsy commercial strip, this playful new hotel announces itself boldly with wall murals by Melissa Scrivner before you even enter the lobby. **Pros:** affordable, artistic rooms; Ping-Pong area; Jacuzzi bar. **Cons:** valet parking is a must ($15). $ *Rooms from: $239 ☒ 737 Washington Blvd., Venice ☎ 310/821–4455 ⊕ www.thekinneyvenicebeach.com ⤴ 68 rooms* ⦿| *No meals.*

Nightlife

The Brig

BARS/PUBS | This charming bar has its pluses (interesting drinks, talented DJs) and minuses (ugh, parking) but is worth a look if you're in the area. There's always a food truck around, and the bar's fine with you bringing in outside food. ☒ *1515 Abbot Kinney Blvd., Venice ☎ 310/399–7537 ⊕ www.thebrig.com.*

Shopping

General Store

GIFTS/SOUVENIRS | Right at home in the beachy, bohemian neighborhood, this well-curated shop is a decidedly contemporary take on the concept of general stores. The very definition of "California cool," General Store offers beauty and bath products loaded with organic natural ingredients, handmade ceramics, linen tea towels, and a spot-on selection of art books. Featuring an impressive number of local makers and designers, the boutique also sells modern, minimal clothing and has a kids' section that will wow even the hippest moms and dads. ☒ *1801 Lincoln Blvd., Venice ☎ 310/751–6393 ⊕ www.shop-generalstore.com.*

Heist

CLOTHING | Owner Nilou Ghodsi has admitted that she stocks her Westside shop like an extension of her own closet, which in her case means keeping the focus on modern-yet-classic pieces as opposed to trendy ones. The airy boutique offers elegantly edgy separates from American designers like Nili Lotan and Ulla Johnson, as well as from hard-to-find French and Italian designers. ☒ *1100 Abbot Kinney Blvd., Venice ☎ 310/450–6531 ⊕ www.shopheist.com.*

Strange Invisible Perfumes

PERFUME/COSMETICS | Finding your signature fragrance at this sleek Abbot Kinney boutique won't come cheap, but perfumer Alexandra Balahoutis takes creating her scents as seriously as a seasoned winemaker—and they're just as nuanced as a well-balanced glass of vino. Essences for the perfumes are organic, wild crafted, biodynamic, and bottled locally. Highlights from SI's core collection include the cacao-spiked Dimanche and leathery Black Rosette. ☒ *1138 Abbot Kinney Blvd., Venice ☎ 310/314–1505 ⊕ www.siperfumes.com.*

Malibu

Sights

★ Getty Villa Malibu

HOUSE | Feeding off the cultures of ancient Rome, Greece, and Etruria, the villa exhibits astounding antiquities, though on a first visit even they take a backseat to their environment. This megamansion sits on some of the most valuable coastal property in the world. Modeled after the Villa dei Papiri in Herculaneum, a Roman estate owned by Julius Caesar's father-in-law that was covered in ash when Mt. Vesuvius erupted, the Getty Villa includes beautifully manicured gardens, reflecting pools, and statuary. The structures blend thoughtfully into the rolling terrain and significantly improve the public spaces, such as the new outdoor amphitheater, gift store, café, and entry arcade. Talks, concerts, and educational programs are offered at an indoor theater. ■ **TIP→ An advance timed entry ticket is required for admission. Tickets are free and may be ordered from the museum's website or by phone.** ✉ *17985 Pacific Coast Hwy., Pacific Palisades* ☎ *310/440–7300* ⊕ *www.getty. edu* ☞ *Free, tickets required; parking $15* ✲ *Closed Tues.*

Beaches

Malibu Lagoon State Beach

BEACH—SIGHT | Bird-watchers, take note: in this 5-acre marshy area near Malibu Beach Inn you can spot egrets, blue herons, avocets, and gulls. (You need to stay on the boardwalks so as not to disturb their habitats.) The path leads out to a rocky stretch of Surfrider Beach and makes for a pleasant stroll. The sand is soft, clean, and white, and you're also likely to spot a variety of marine life. Look for the signs to help identify these sometimes exotic-looking creatures. The lagoon is particularly enjoyable in the early morning and at sunset—and even

more so now, thanks to a restoration effort that improved the lagoon's scent. The parking lot has limited hours, but street-side parking is usually available at off-peak times. Close by are shops and a theater. **Amenities:** parking (fee); lifeguards; toilets; showers. **Best for:** sunset; walking. ✉ *23200 Pacific Coast Hwy., Malibu* ☎ *310/457–8143* ⊕ *www.parks. ca.gov* ☞ *Parking $12.*

Westward Beach–Point Dume

BEACH—SIGHT | Go tide pooling, fishing, snorkeling, or bird-watching (prime time is late winter to early spring). Hike to the top of the sandstone cliffs at Point Dume to whale-watch—their migrations can be seen between December and April—and take in dramatic coastal views. Westward is a favorite surfing beach, but the steep surf isn't for novices. The Sunset restaurant is between Westward and Point Dume (at 6800 Westward Beach Road). Bring your own food, since the nearest concession is a long hike away. **Amenities:** parking (fee); lifeguards; toilets; food and drink; showers. **Best for:** surfing; walking. ✉ *71030 Westward Beach Rd., Malibu* ☎ *310/305–9503* ☞ *Parking $14.*

Zuma Beach Park

BEACH—SIGHT | This 2-mile stretch of white sand, usually dotted with tanning teenagers, has it all, from fishing and kitesurfing to swings and volleyball courts. Beachgoers looking for quiet or privacy should head elsewhere. Stay alert in the water: the surf is rough and inconsistent. **Amenities:** parking; lifeguards; toilets; food and drink; showers. **Best for:** partiers; sunset; swimming; walking. ✉ *30000 Pacific Coast Hwy., Malibu* ☎ *310/305–9522* ⊕ *www.zuma-beach. com* ☞ *Parking $10.*

🍴 Restaurants

Nobu Malibu

$$$$ | **JAPANESE** | At famous chef-restaurateur Nobu Matsuhisa's coastal outpost, super-chic clientele sails in for morsels of the world's finest fish. It's hard not to be seduced by the oceanfront property, and stellar sushi and ingenious specialties match the upscale setting. **Known for:** exotic fish; toro with truffle teriyaki; bento box Valrhona chocolate soufflé. ⑤ *Average main: $35* ⊠ *22706 Pacific Coast Hwy., Malibu* ☎ *310/317–9140* ⊕ *www.noburestaurants.com.*

Reel Inn
$$ | SEAFOOD | FAMILY | Long wooden tables and booths are often filled with fish-loving families chowing down on mahimahi sandwiches and freshly caught swordfish. Get in line and choose your fish and sides, then nab a table. **Known for:** easy-to-miss spot on PCH; fresh catches. ⑤ *Average main: $17* ⊠ *18661 Pacific Coast Hwy., Malibu* ☎ *310/456–8221* ⊕ *www.reelinnmalibu.com.*

Hotels

Malibu Beach Inn
$$$$ | B&B/INN | Set right on exclusive Carbon Beach, Malibu's hideaway for the super-rich remains the room to nab along the coast, with an ultrachic new look thanks to designer Waldo Fernandez, and an upscale restaurant and wine bar perched over the Pacific. **Pros:** see the ocean from your private balcony; wine list curated by sommelier Laurie Sutton; world-class chocolate chip cookies at reception. **Cons:** billionaire's travel budget required; some in-room noise from PCH; no pool, gym, or hot tub. ⑤ *Rooms from: $749* ⊠ *22878 Pacific Coast Hwy., Malibu* ☎ *310/456–6444* ⊕ *www.malibubeachinn.com* ⇆ *47 rooms* ⦿ *No meals.*

Nightlife

Duke's Barefoot Bar
BARS/PUBS | FAMILY | With a clear view of the horizon from almost everywhere, a sunset drink at Duke's Barefoot Bar is how many beachgoers like to end their day. The entertainment is in keeping with the bar's theme, with Hawaiian dancers as well as live music on Friday night by Hawaiian artists. The menu features island favorites like *poke* tacos, macadamia-crusted fish, and kalua pork and a Sunday brunch buffet from 10 to 2. Just don't expect beach-bum prices, unless you stop by the happy hour weekday events like Taco Tuesday ($3 fish, kalua pork, or grilled chicken tacos, along with $3 beer). ⊠ *21150 Pacific Coast Hwy., Malibu* ☎ *310/317–0777* ⊕ *www.dukesmalibu.com.*

Moonshadows
BARS/PUBS | This newly renovated outdoor lounge attracts customers with its modern look and views of the ocean. Think dark woods, cabana-style draperies, and ambient lighting in the Blue Lounge. DJs are constantly spinning lounge music in the background, and there's never a cover charge. Try the new lobster roll and dessert lineup. This restaurant maintains some amount of notoriety as the establishment frequented by Mel Gibson just before his infamous 2006 arrest. ⊠ *20356 Pacific Coast Hwy., Malibu* ☎ *310/456–3010* ⊕ *www.moonshadowsmalibu.com.*

Shopping

Malibu Country Mart
SHOPPING CENTERS/MALLS | Have the quintessential beachside shopping experience complete with browsing designer clothing (Morgane le Fay, Ron Herman, or Madison) and eclectic California housewares and gifts (Burro), picking up body-boosting wellness goodies at Sunlife Organics, and finishing the day off with dinner at iconic eatery Mr. Chow. If you can squeeze in a workout, there's a Pure Barre and 5 Point Yoga to choose from, plus tarot readings at metaphysical outpost Malibu Shaman, and Eastern medicine treatments at Malibu Acupuncture. Then reward yourself for your good health habits by stopping at fan-favorite Italian gelateria Grom's Malibu outpost for out-of-this-world

fresh pistachio or *gianduia* (chocolate hazelnut) gelato. ⊠ *3835 Cross Creek Rd., Malibu* ☎ *310/456–7300* ⊕ *www. malibucountrymart.com.*

Malibu Lumber Yard

SHOPPING CENTERS/MALLS | Emblematic Malibu lifestyle stores in this shopping complex include James Perse, Maxfield, and too-chic Intermix. The playground and alfresco dining area make this an ideal weekend destination for families. ⊠ *3939 Cross Creek Rd., Malibu* ⊕ *www. themalibulumberyard.com.*

Brentwood

 Sights

★ The Getty Center

MUSEUM | FAMILY | With its curving walls and isolated hilltop perch, the Getty Center resembles a pristine fortified city of its own. You may have been lured there by the beautiful views of Los Angeles—on a clear day stretching all the way to the Pacific Ocean—but the amazing architecture, uncommon gardens, and fascinating art collections will be more than enough to capture and hold your attention. When the sun is out, the complex's rough-cut travertine marble skin seems to soak up the light.

Getting to the center involves a bit of anticipatory lead-up. At the base of the hill, a pavilion disguises the underground parking structure. From there you either walk or take a smooth, computer-driven tram up the steep slope, checking out the Bel Air estates across the humming 405 freeway. The five pavilions that house the museum surround a central courtyard and are bridged by walkways. From the courtyard, plazas, and walkways, you can survey the city from the San Gabriel Mountains to the ocean.

In a ravine separating the museum and the Getty Research Institute, conceptual artist Robert Irwin created the playful Central Garden in stark contrast to Richard Meier's mathematical architectural geometry. The garden's design is what Hollywood feuds are made of: Meier couldn't control Irwin's vision, and the two men sniped at each other during construction, with Irwin stirring the pot with every loose twist his garden path took. The result is a refreshing garden walk whose focal point is an azalea maze (some insist the Mickey Mouse shape is on purpose) in a reflecting pool.

Inside the pavilions are the galleries for the permanent collections of European paintings, drawings, sculpture, illuminated manuscripts, and decorative arts, as well as world-class temporary exhibitions and photographs gathered internationally. The Getty's collection of French furniture and decorative arts, especially from the early years of Louis XIV (1643–1715) to the end of the reign of Louis XVI (1774–92), is renowned for its quality and condition; you can even see a pair of completely reconstructed salons. In the paintings galleries, a computerized system of louvered skylights allows natural light to filter in, creating a closer approximation of the conditions in which the artists painted. Notable among the paintings are Rembrandt's *The Abduction of Europa*, Van Gogh's *Irises,* Monet's *Wheatstack, Snow Effects,* and *Morning,* and James Ensor's *Christ's Entry into Brussels.*

If you want to start with a quick overview, pick up the brochure in the entrance hall that guides you to collection highlights. There's also an instructive audio tour (free, but you have to leave your ID) with commentaries by art historians and other experts. Art information rooms with multimedia computer stations contain more details about the collections. The Getty also presents lectures, films, concerts, art workshops, and special programs for kids, families, and all-around culture lovers. The complex includes an upscale restaurant and downstairs cafeteria with panoramic window views. There are also outdoor coffee carts. ■ TIP→ **On-site parking is subject to availability and can fill up by midday on holidays and in the summer, so try to come early in the day or after lunch.** A tram takes you from the street-level entrance to the top of the hill. Public buses (Metro Rapid Line 734) also serve the center and link to the Expo Rail extension. ⊠ *1200 Getty Center Dr., Brentwood* ☎ *310/440–7300* ⊕ *www.getty.edu* ▢ *Free; parking $15* ⊘ *Closed Mon.*

Restaurants

Toscana

$$$$ | **ITALIAN** | This rustic trattoria along San Vicente is a favorite celebrity haunt. Expect elevated sensory offerings, from its cozy atmosphere to its mouthwatering Tuscan fare and excellent wine list. **Known for:** excellent wine list; white truffles; celeb-spotting. $ *Average main: $35* ⊠ *11633 San Vicente Blvd., Brentwood* ☎ *310/820–2448* ⊕ *www.toscana-brentwood.com.*

Beverly Hills, West Hollywood, and the Westside

The rumors are true: Beverly Hills delivers on a dramatic, cinematic scale of wealth and excess. A known celebrity haunt, come here to daydream or to live like the rich and famous for a day. Window-shop or splurge at tony stores, and keep an eye out for filming locales; just walking around here will make you feel like you're on a movie set.

West Hollywood is not a place to see things (like museums or movie studios) as much as it is a place to do things—like go to a nightclub, eat at a world-famous restaurant, or attend an art gallery opening. Since the end of Prohibition, the **Sunset Strip** has been Hollywood's nighttime playground, where stars headed to such glamorous nightclubs as the Trocadero, the Mocambo, and Ciro's. It's still going strong, with crowds still filing into well-established spots like Whisky A Go Go and paparazzi staking out the members-only Soho House. But hedonism isn't all that drives West Hollywood. Also thriving is an important interior design and art gallery trade exemplified by the Cesar Pelli–designed **Pacific Design Center.** The three-block stretch of Wilshire Boulevard known as Museum Row, east of Fairfax Avenue, features intriguing museums and a prehistoric tar pit. Wilshire Boulevard itself is something of a cultural monument—it begins its grand 16-mile sweep to the sea in Downtown L.A.

West Hollywood has emerged as one of the most progressive cities in Southern California. It's also one of the most gay-friendly cities anywhere, with a large LGBTQ community. Its annual Gay Pride Parade is one of the largest in the nation, drawing tens of thousands of participants each June.

The historic **Farmers Market** and **The Grove** shopping mall are both great places to people-watch over breakfast.

Beverly Hills

Sights

Museum of Tolerance

MUSEUM | **FAMILY** | This museum unflinchingly confronts bigotry and racism. One of the most affecting sections covers the Holocaust, with film footage of deportations and concentration camps. Upon entering, you are issued a "passport" bearing the name of a child whose life was dramatically changed by the Nazis; as you go through the exhibit, you learn the fate of that child. An exhibit called *Anne: The Life and Legacy of Anne Frank*

Sights ▼

1 Museum of
  Tolerance **C7**

2 Pierce Brothers
  Westwood Village
  Memorial Park and
  Mortuary **A7**

3 Rodeo Drive **B7**

4 Santa Monica
  Boulevard **F2**

5 Spadena House **A6**

6 Sunset Boulevard **E2**

7 West Hollywood
  Design District **E4**

Restaurants ▼

1 Angelini Osteria **J5**

2 Animal **H4**

3 A.O.C. **E5**

4 The Bazaar by
  José Andrés **F6**

5 Canter's **H4**

6 Craig's **E4**

7 Crustacean **B6**

8 Dan Tana's **D4**

9 El Coyote
  Mexican Food **J5**

10 Greenblatt's Deli **H1**

11 Maude **C7**

Beverly Hills, West Hollywood, and the West Side

KEY

1 Exploring Sights

1 Restaurants

1 Hotels

brings her story to life through immersive environments, multimedia presentations, and interesting artifacts. Simon Wiesenthal's Vienna office is set exactly as the famous "Nazi hunter" had it while conducting his research that brought more than 1,000 war criminals to justice.

Interactive exhibits include the Millennium Machine, which engages visitors in finding solutions to human rights abuses around the world; Globalhate.com, which examines hate on the Internet by exposing problematic sites via touch-screen computer terminals; and the Point of View Diner, a re-creation of a 1950s diner that "serves" a menu of controversial topics on video jukeboxes.

■ TIP➜ **Plan to spend at least three hours touring the museum; making a reservation is especially recommended for Friday, Sunday, and holiday visits.** ⊠ *9786 W. Pico Blvd., south of Beverly Hills* ☎ *310/772–2505 for reservations* ⊕ *www.museumoftolerance.com* ➥ *From $16* ⊘ *Closed Sat.*

Pierce Brothers Westwood Village Memorial Park and Mortuary

CEMETERY | The who's who of the dearly departed can all be found at this peaceful, though unremarkable, cemetery. Notable residents include Marilyn Monroe and Joe DiMaggio; authors Truman Capote, Ray Bradbury, and Jackie Collins; actors Natalie Wood, Rodney Dangerfield, Farrah Fawcett, Jack Lemmon, and Dean Martin; and directors Billy Wilder and John Cassavetes. ⊠ *1218 Glendon Ave., Westwood.*

Rodeo Drive

NEIGHBORHOOD | The ultimate shopping indulgence, Rodeo Drive is one of L.A.'s bona fide tourist attractions. The art of window-shopping (and reenacting your *Pretty Woman* fantasies) is prime among the retail elite: Tiffany & Co., Gucci, Jimmy Choo, Valentino, Harry Winston, Prada—you get the picture. Near the southern end of Rodeo Drive is Via Rodeo, a curvy cobblestone street designed to resemble a European shopping area and

the perfect backdrop to pose for your Instagram feed. To give your feet a rest, free trolley tours depart from the southeast corner of Rodeo Drive and Dayton Way from 11:30 to 4:30. They're a terrific way to get an overview of the neighborhood. ⊠ *Rodeo Dr., Beverly Hills* ⊕ *www.rodeodrive-bh.com.*

Spadena House

BUILDING | Otherwise known as the Witch's House in Beverly Hills, the Spadena House has an interesting history. First built on the Willat Studios lot in 1920, the house was physically moved to its current ritzy location in 1924. The house is not open for tourists, but the fairy-tale-like appearance is viewable from the street for onlookers to snap pics. Movie buffs will also recognize it from a background shot in the film *Clueless*. ⊠ *516 Walden Dr., Beverly Hills.*

🍴 Restaurants

The Bazaar by José Andrés

$$$$ | SPANISH | Spanish celebrity chef José Andrés has conquered L.A. with this colorful and opulent Beverly Hills spot, which features a bar stocked with liquid nitrogen and a super-flashy patisserie. Pore over a menu of items like Spanish tapas (with a twist) and "liquid" olives (created using a technique called spherification). **Known for:** molecular gastronomy; foie gras cotton candy. ⑤ *Average main: $65* ⊠ *SLS Hotel at Beverly Hills, 465 S. La Cienega Blvd., Beverly Hills* ☎ *310/246–5555* ⊕ *slshotels.com/beverlyhills/bazaar* ⊘ *No lunch.*

Crustacean

$$$$ | VIETNAMESE | Crustacean, the Euro-Vietnamese fusion gem in the heart of Beverly Hills, received a $10 million makeover in 2018. You can still walk on water above exotic fish, but now you can see the kitchen preparing your perfect garlic noodles through a glass window. **Known for:** sake-simmered dishes; colossal tiger prawns; no-grease garlic

noodles. $ *Average main: $36 ⊠ 468 N. Bedford Dr., Beverly Hills ☎ 310/205–8990 ⊕ crustaceanbh.com ⊗ Closed Mon. No lunch weekends.*

Maude

$$$$ | INTERNATIONAL | Maude is a much-needed addition to the Beverly Hills dining scene as it bucks a traditional tried-and-true menu for a tasting explosion that changes four times a year (we'd say seasonally, but it's L.A.). Helmed by celeb chef Curtis Stone, the cuisine ranges from Spanish and Italian influences to French and coastal Californian. **Known for:** titillating tasting menus; intimate dining. $ *Average main: $185 ⊠ 212 S. Beverly Dr., Beverly Hills ☎ 310/859–3418 ⊕ www.mauderestaurant.com ⊗ Closed Sun. and Mon.*

★ Spago Beverly Hills

$$$$ | MODERN AMERICAN | Wolfgang Puck's flagship restaurant is a modern L.A. classic. Spago centers on a buzzing redbrick outdoor courtyard (with retractable roof) shaded by 100-year-old olive trees, and a daily-changing menu that offers dishes like smoked salmon pizza or off-menu schnitzel. **Known for:** great people-watching; off-menu schnitzel; sizzling smoked salmon pizza. $ *Average main: $35 ⊠ 176 N. Canon Dr., Beverly Hills ☎ 310/385–0880 ⊕ www.wolfgang-puck.com ⊗ No lunch Sun. or Mon.*

Hotels

Beverly Wilshire, a Four Seasons Hotel

$$$$ | HOTEL | Built in 1928, this Rodeo Drive–adjacent hotel is part Italian Renaissance (with elegant details like crystal chandeliers) and part contemporary. **Pros:** complimentary car service; Wolfgang Puck restaurant on-site; first-rate spa. **Cons:** small lobby; valet parking is expensive. $ *Rooms from: $545 ⊠ 9500 Wilshire Blvd., Beverly Hills ☎ 310/275–5200, 800/427–4354 ⊕ www.fourseasons.com/beverlywilshire ⊋ 395 rooms* †○† *No meals.*

★ The Crescent Beverly Hills

$$ | HOTEL | Built in 1927 as a dorm for silent-film actors, the Crescent is now a fanciful boutique hotel with a great location—within the Beverly Hills shopping triangle—and with an even better price (for the area). **Pros:** indoor/outdoor fireplace; lively on-site restaurant, Crescent Bar and Terrace; economic room available for $148. **Cons:** resort fee is $30 and not optional; no elevator. $ *Rooms from: $245 ⊠ 403 N. Crescent Dr., Beverly Hills ☎ 310/247–0505 ⊕ www.crescentbh.com ⊋ 35 rooms* †○† *Free Breakfast.*

★ Montage Beverly Hills

$$$$ | HOTEL | FAMILY | The nine-story, Mediterranean-style palazzo is dedicated to welcoming those who relish luxury, providing classic style and exemplary service. **Pros:** secret whiskey bar tucked upstairs; Gornick and Drucker barbershop on-site; obliging, highly trained staff; lots of activities and amenities for kids. **Cons:** the hefty tab for all this finery. $ *Rooms from: $550 ⊠ 225 N. Canon Dr., Beverly Hills ☎ 310/860–7800, 855/691–1162 ⊕ www.montagebeverlyhills.com/beverlyhills ⊋ 201 rooms* †○† *No meals.*

★ Peninsula Beverly Hills

$$$$ | HOTEL | This French Riviera–style palace overflowing with antiques and art is a favorite of boldface names, but visitors consistently describe a stay here as near perfect. **Pros:** 24-hour check-in/check-out policy; sunny pool area with cabanas; complimentary Rolls-Royce takes you to nearby Beverly Hills. **Cons:** very expensive; room decor might feel too ornate for some. $ *Rooms from: $600 ⊠ 9882 S. Santa Monica Blvd., Beverly Hills ☎ 310/551–2888, 800/462–7899 ⊕ www.peninsula.com/en/beverly-hills/5-star-luxury-hotel-beverly-hills ⊋ 195 rooms* †○† *No meals.*

SLS Hotel Beverly Hills

$$$ | HOTEL | From the sleek, Philippe Starck–designed lobby and lounge with fireplaces, hidden nooks, and a communal table, to poolside cabanas with DVD players, this hotel offers a cushy, dream-like stay. **Pros:** on-property cuisine masterminded by José Andrés; free shuttle to nearby Beverly Hills; dreamy Ciel spa. **Cons:** standard rooms are compact; pricey dining and parking; on a busy intersection outside of Beverly Hills. ⑤ *Rooms from: $365* ✉ *465 S. La Cienega Blvd., Beverly Hills* ☎ *310/247–0400* ⊕ *slshotels.com/beverlyhills* ⇨ *297 rooms* ⍟ *No meals.*

★ Viceroy L'Ermitage Beverly Hills

$$$$ | **HOTEL** | This all-suite hotel is the picture of luxury: French doors open to a mini balcony with views of the Hollywood sign; inside rooms you'll find soaking tubs and oversize bath towels, and they even have fully curated packages for your pet. **Pros:** traditional French cuisine at Avec Nous on-site; free shuttle service with 2-mile radius; all suite rooms. **Cons:** small spa and pool; very expensive; a bit of a trek to the Beverly Hills shopping. ⑤ *Rooms from: $495* ✉ *9291 Burton Way, Beverly Hills* ☎ *310/278–3344* ⊕ *www.viceroyhotelsandresorts.com/en/beverlyhills* ⇨ *116 rooms* ⍟ *No meals.*

Shopping

Barneys New York

DEPARTMENT STORES | This is truly an impressive one-stop shop for high fashion. Deal hunters will appreciate the co-op section, which introduces indie designers before they make it big. Shop for beauty products, shoes, and accessories on the first floor, then wind your way up the staircase for couture. Keep your eyes peeled for fabulous and/or famous folks spearing salads at Fred's on the top floor. ✉ *9570 Wilshire Blvd., Beverly Hills* ☎ *310/276–4400* ⊕ *www.barneys.com.*

Cartier

JEWELRY/ACCESSORIES | Cartier has a bridal collection to sigh for in its chandeliered and respectfully hushed showroom, along with more playful pieces (chunky, diamond-encrusted panther cocktail rings, for example), watches, and accessories. The stop itself feels like the ultimate playground for A-list clientele, complete with a red-carpeted spiral staircase. ✉ *370 N. Rodeo Dr., Beverly Hills* ☎ *310/275–4272* ⊕ *www.cartier.com.*

Céline

CLOTHING | Under designer Hedi Slimane's creative direction, the Parisian brand has entered a new chapter. At the Beverly Hills brick-and-mortar, fashion lovers looking for French Cool Girl clothing will love the selection of the label's leather handbags, heels, and chic ready-to-wear clothing. ✉ *319 N. Rodeo Dr., Beverly Hills* ☎ *310/888–0120* ⊕ *www.celine.com.*

Gearys of Beverly Hills

GIFTS/SOUVENIRS | Since 1930, this has been the ultimate destination for those seeking the most exquisite fine china, crystal, silver, and jewelry, mostly from classic sources like Christofle, Baccarat, and Waterford. No wonder it's a favorite for registries of the rich and famous. ✉ *351 N. Beverly Dr., Beverly Hills* ☎ *310/273–4741* ⊕ *www.gearys.com.*

Neiman Marcus

DEPARTMENT STORES | Luxury shopping at its finest, this couture salon frequently trots out designer trunk shows, and most locals go right for the shoe department, which features high-end footwear favorites like Giuseppe Zanotti and Christian Louboutin. A café on the third floor keeps your blood sugar high during multiple wardrobe changes, while a bar on the fourth is for celebrating those perfect finds with a glass of champagne. ✉ *9700 Wilshire Blvd., Beverly Hills* ☎ *310/550–5900* ⊕ *www.neimanmarcus.com.*

Taschen

BOOKS/STATIONERY | Philippe Starck designed the Taschen space to evoke a cool 1920s Parisian salon—a perfect showcase for the publisher's design-forward coffee-table books about architecture, travel, culture, and photography. A suspended glass cube gallery in back hosts art exhibits and features

From celebrity mansions to rock 'n' roll lore, Sunset Boulevard is a drive through Hollywood history.

limited-edition books. *354 N. Beverly Dr., Beverly Hills* ☎ *310/274–4300* ⊕ *www.taschen.com.*

Tory Burch

CLOTHING | Preppy, stylish, and colorful clothes appropriate for a road trip to Palm Springs or a flight to Palm Beach fill this flagship boutique. ⊠ *142 S. Robertson Blvd., Beverly Hills* ☎ *310/248–2612* ⊕ *www.toryburch.com.*

West Hollywood

👁 Sights

Santa Monica Boulevard

NEIGHBORHOOD | From La Cienega Boulevard in the east to Doheny Drive in the west, Santa Monica Boulevard is the commercial core of West Hollywood's gay community, with restaurants and cafés, bars and clubs, bookstores and galleries, and other establishments catering largely to the LGBTQ scene. Twice a year—during June's L.A. Pride and on Halloween—the boulevard becomes an open-air festival. ⊠ *Santa Monica Blvd., between La Cienega Blvd. and Doheny Dr., West Hollywood* ⊕ *weho.org.*

Sunset Boulevard

NEIGHBORHOOD | One of the most fabled avenues in the world, Sunset Boulevard began humbly enough in the 18th century as a route from El Pueblo de Los Angeles to the Pacific Ocean. Today, as it passes through West Hollywood, it becomes the sexy and seductive Sunset Strip, where rock and roll had its heyday and cocktail bars charge a premium for the views. It slips quietly into the tony environs of Beverly Hills and Bel Air, twisting and winding past gated estates and undulating vistas. ⊠ *Sunset Blvd., West Hollywood* ⊕ *www.weho.org.*

West Hollywood Design District

STORE/MALL | More than 200 businesses—art galleries, antiques shops, fashion outlets (including Rag & Bone and Christian Louboutin), and interior design stores—are found in the design district. There are also about

30 restaurants, including the famous paparazzi magnet, the Ivy. All are clustered within walking distance of each other—rare for L.A. ✉ *Melrose Ave. and Robertson and Beverly Blvds., West Hollywood* ☎ *310/289–2534* ⊕ *westhollywooddesigndistrict.com.*

Restaurants

★ Angelini Osteria

$$$$ | ITALIAN | Despite its modest, rather congested dining room, this is one of L.A.'s most celebrated Italian restaurants. The keys are chef-owner Gino Angelini's consistently impressive dishes, like whole branzino, *tagliolini al limone,* veal chop *alla* Milanese, as well as lasagna oozing with *besciamella* (Italian béchamel sauce). **Known for:** large Italian wine selection; bold flavors; savory pastas. Ⓢ *Average main: $40* ✉ *7313 Beverly Blvd., West Hollywood* ☎ *323/297–0070* ⊕ *www.angeliniosteria. com* ⊗ *No lunch weekends.*

Animal

$$$ | AMERICAN | Owned by Jon Shook and Vinny Dotolo of *Iron Chef* fame, this oft-packed James Beard Award–winning restaurant offers shareable plates with a focus on meat. Highlights include barbecue pork belly sandwiches, poutine with oxtail gravy, and foie gras *loco moco* (a hamburger topped with foie gras, quail egg, and Spam). **Known for:** bacon-chocolate crunch bar; reputation as a must for foodies; being carnivore heaven. Ⓢ *Average main: $30* ✉ *435 N. Fairfax Ave., Fairfax District* ☎ *323/782–9225* ⊕ *www. animalrestaurant.com* ⊗ *No lunch.*

A.O.C.

$$$ | MEDITERRANEAN | An acronym for Appellation d'Origine Contrôlée, the regulatory system that ensures the quality of local wines and cheeses in France, A.O.C. upholds this standard of excellence from shared plates to perfect wine pairings in its stunning exposed-brick and vine-laden courtyard. Try the Spanish fried chicken; wood-oven brioche with prosciutto, Gruyère, and egg; or *arroz negro* (black rice) with squid. **Known for:** amazing cocktail hour; quaint outdoor courtyard; fireplaces indoors. Ⓢ *Average main: $25* ✉ *8700 W. 3rd St., West Hollywood* ☎ *310/859–9859* ⊕ *www. aocwinebar.com.*

Canter's

$ | DELI | FAMILY | This granddaddy of L.A. delicatessens (it opened in 1931) cures its own corned beef and pastrami and features delectable desserts from the in-house bakery. It's not the best (or friendliest) deli in town, but it's a classic. **Known for:** location adjacent to Kibitz Room bar; plenty of seating and short wait times. Ⓢ *Average main: $12* ✉ *419 N. Fairfax Ave., Fairfax District* ☎ *323/651–2030* ⊕ *www.cantersdeli.com.*

Craig's

$$$$ | AMERICAN | Behind the unremarkable facade is an uber-trendy—yet decidedly old-school—den of American cuisine that doubles as a safe haven for the movie industry's most important names and well-known faces. We're not going to lie: this joint is always busy so you might not even get a table and reservations are hard to come by. **Known for:** celebrities; chick Parm; strong drinks. Ⓢ *Average main: $32* ✉ *8826 Melrose Ave, West Hollywood* ☎ *310/276–1900* ⊕ *craigs.la.*

Dan Tana's

$$$$ | ITALIAN | If you're looking for an Italian vibe straight out of *Goodfellas,* your search ends here. Checkered tablecloths cover the tightly packed tables as Hollywood players dine on the city's best chicken and veal Parm, and down Scotches by the finger. **Known for:** elbow-room-only bar; lively atmosphere; celeb spotting. Ⓢ *Average main: $35* ✉ *9071 Santa Monica Blvd., West Hollywood* ☎ *310/275–9444* ⊕ *www.dantanasrestaurant.com.*

★ El Coyote Mexican Food

$$ | **MEXICAN** | **FAMILY** | Open since 1931, this landmark spot is perfect for those on a budget or anyone after an authentic Mexican meal. The traditional fare is decadent and delicious; the margaritas are sweetened to perfection. **Known for:** affordable, quality cuisine; festive atmosphere; being an L.A. staple. $ *Average main: $14* ✉ *7312 Beverly Blvd., Fairfax* ☎ *323/939–2255* ⊕ *www.elcoyotecafe.com.*

Greenblatt's Deli

$$ | **DELI** | In 1926, Herman Greenblatt opened his eponymous deli which serves Jewish deli food, wine, and spirits. The restaurant claims to have the rarest roast beef in town—and they're probably right. **Known for:** matzo ball soup; pastrami sandwiches; old-school vibe. $ *Average main: $18* ✉ *8017 Sunset Blvd., West Hollywood* ☎ *323/656–0606* ⊕ *www.greenblattsdeli.com.*

The Nice Guy

$$$ | **ITALIAN** | This dark and brooding Italian restaurant sits discretely on La Cienega Boulevard and hides one of the cooler scenes in L.A. A favorite among privacy-minded celebs (there's a no-photo policy), the Nice Guy is known for its cavatelli *alla* vodka and mouthwatering chicken Parm. **Known for:** mouthwatering pastas; see-and-be-seen crowd. $ *Average main: $25* ✉ *401 N. La Cienega Blvd., West Hollywood* ☎ *310/360–9500* ⊕ *www.theniceguyla.com.*

★ Republique

$$$$ | **FRENCH** | **FAMILY** | This stunning expansive space, originally built for Charlie Chaplin back in the 1920s, serves French delicacies for breakfast, lunch, and dinner every day of the week. The scent of homemade croissants wafts through the building in the morning; steak frites can be enjoyed at night. **Known for:** classics like escargot; unbeatable pastries. $ *Average main: $35* ✉ *624 S. La Brea Ave., West Hollywood* ☎ *310/362–6115* ⊕ *www.republiquela.com.*

Hotels

★ Farmer's Daughter Hotel

$$ | **HOTEL** | A favorite of *Price Is Right* and *Dancing with the Stars* hopefuls (both TV shows tape at the CBS studios nearby), this hotel has a tongue-in-cheek country style with a hopping Sunday brunch and a little pool accented by giant rubber duckies and a living wall. **Pros:** bikes for rent; daily yoga; book lending library. **Cons:** shaded pool; no bathtubs; restaurant is just okay. $ *Rooms from: $200* ✉ *115 S. Fairfax Ave., Fairfax District* ☎ *323/937–3930, 800/334–1658* ⊕ *www.farmersdaughterhotel.com* ⇄ *65 rooms* ⦿ *No meals.*

The London West Hollywood at Beverly Hills

$$$ | **HOTEL** | Cosmopolitan and chic, especially after the recent multimillion-dollar renovation, the London West Hollywood is known for its large suites, rooftop pool with citywide views, and luxury touches throughout. **Pros:** state-of-the-art fitness center; chef Anthony Keene oversees dining program; 110-seat screening room. **Cons:** too refined for kids to be comfortable; lower floors have mundane views. $ *Rooms from: $350* ✉ *1020 N. San Vicente Blvd., West Hollywood* ☎ *310/854–1111* ⊕ *www.thelondonwesthollywood.com* ⇄ *226 suites* ⦿ *No meals.*

Mondrian Los Angeles

$$ | **HOTEL** | The Mondrian has a city club feel; socializing begins in the lobby bar and lounge and extends from the Ivory on Sunset restaurant to the scenic patio and pool, where you can listen to music underwater, and the lively Skybar. **Pros:** acclaimed Skybar on property; Benjamin Noriega-Ortiz guest room design; double-paned windows keep out noise. **Cons:** pricy valet parking only ($44); late-night party scene; no free Wi-Fi. $ *Rooms from: $300* ✉ *8440 Sunset Blvd., West Hollywood* ☎ *323/650–8999, 800/606–6090* ⊕ *www.mondrianhotel.com* ⇄ *237 rooms* ⦿ *No meals.*

Palihouse West Hollywood

$$ | HOTEL | Inside an unassuming condo complex just off West Hollywood's main drag, you'll find DJs spinning tunes on the ground floor and a gorgeous collection of assorted suites with fully equipped kitchens upstairs. **Pros:** fun scene at lobby bar; eclectic design; kitchens in all rooms. **Cons:** lobby can be loud in the evenings; no pool. $ *Rooms from: $280* ✉ *8465 Holloway Dr., West Hollywood* ☎ *323/656–4100* ⊕ *www.palihousewesthollywood.com* ⌕ *36 suites* ⦿❘ *No meals.*

The Standard

$$ | HOTEL | Hotelier André Balazs created this kitschy Sunset Strip hotel out of a former retirement home, and a '70s aesthetic abounds with pop art, shag carpets, and suede sectionals in the lobby, and beanbag chairs, surfboard tables, and Warhol poppy-print curtains in the rooms. **Pros:** late-night dining on-site; choose-your-own checkout time; secret nightclub, mmhmmm. **Cons:** for partying more than for resting; staff can be aloof. $ *Rooms from: $250* ✉ *8300 Sunset Blvd., West Hollywood* ☎ *323/650–9090* ⊕ *www.standardhotels.com* ⌕ *139 rooms* ⦿❘ *No meals.*

★ Sunset Marquis Hotel and Villas

$$$ | HOTEL | If you're in town to cut your new hit single, you'll appreciate this near-the-Strip hidden retreat in the heart of WeHo, with two on-site recording studios. **Pros:** favorite among rock stars; 53 villas with lavish extras; exclusive Bar 1200. **Cons:** rooms can feel dark; small balconies. $ *Rooms from: $365* ✉ *1200 N. Alta Loma Rd., West Hollywood* ☎ *310/657–1333, 800/858–9758* ⊕ *www.sunsetmarquis.com* ⌕ *154 rooms* ⦿❘ *No meals.*

Nightlife

The Abbey

BARS/PUBS | The Abbey in West Hollywood is one of the most famous gay bars in the world. And rightfully so. Seven days a week, a mixed and very good-looking crowd comes to eat, drink, dance, and flirt. Creative cocktails are whipped up by buff bartenders with a bevy of themed nights and parties each day. A generous happy hour runs 4–7 pm on weekdays and until 9 on Friday with $8 apps and $6 cocktails. ✉ *692 N. Robertson Blvd., West Hollywood* ☎ *310/289–8410* ⊕ *www.theabbeyweho.com.*

Comedy Store

COMEDY CLUBS | Three stages give seasoned and unseasoned comedians a place to perform and try out new material, with big-name performers dropping by just for fun. The front bar along Sunset Boulevard is a popular hangout after or between shows, oftentimes with that night's comedians mingling with fans. ✉ *8433 Sunset Blvd., West Hollywood* ☎ *323/650–6268* ⊕ *www.thecomedystore.com.*

Delilah

THEMED ENTERTAINMENT | Reservations are definitely required for this swanky, New York–style space in West Hollywood. Waiters in white coats serve a mix of upscale American cuisine, but the true reason to come happens a little later when live jazz and burlesque dancers turn the night into a sultry singles scene that's visited by the who's who of Hollywood celebrity royalty. ✉ *7969 Santa Monica Blvd., West Hollywood* ☎ *323/745–0600* ⊕ *www.delilahla.com.*

Employees Only

BARS/PUBS | If you're looking for the best cocktail program in L.A., you'll find it at Employees Only. This very chic spot is a sister of the New York original and is consistently awarded worldwide for its delicious drinks. At this iteration, there are various themed nights with burlesque on Saturday and sporadic live music. In the back is a speakeasy called Harry's, which is a more intimate space where you can get up close and personal with the master barkeeps to tailor you the perfect drink. ✉ *7953 Santa Monica Blvd., West Hollywood* ☎ *323/536–9045* ⊕ *www.employeesonlyla.com.*

Jones

BARS/PUBS | Italian food and serious cocktails are the mainstays at Jones. Whiskey is a popular choice for the classic cocktails, but the bartenders also do up martinis properly (read: strong). The Beggar's Banquet is their version of happy hour (10 pm to 2 am, Sunday through Thursday), with specials on drinks and pizza. ⊠ *7205 Santa Monica Blvd., West Hollywood* ☎ *323/850–1726* ⊕ *www. joneshollywood.com.*

Laugh Factory

COMEDY CLUBS | Top stand-up comics appear at this Sunset Boulevard mainstay, often working out the kinks in new material in advance of national tours. Stars such as Whitney Cummings and Tim Allen sometimes drop by unannounced, and themed nights like Midnight Madness and Chocolate Sundaes are extremely popular, with comics performing more daring sets. ⊠ *8001 W. Sunset Blvd., West Hollywood* ☎ *323/656–1336* ⊕ *www.laughfactory. com* ⊠ *$17.*

Rage

DANCE CLUBS | The various events at this gay bar and dance club draw different crowds—show queens for Broadway musical sing-alongs on Mondays, drag queens (and more show queens) on themed nights, half-nude chiseled-bodied men most nights, as well as Latin Saturdays and Starboy Sundays. There's lots of eye candy, even more so on weekends. ⊠ *8911 Santa Monica Blvd., West Hollywood* ☎ *310/652–7055* ⊕ *www. ragenightclub.com.*

Rainbow Bar and Grill

BARS/PUBS | Its location next door to a long-running music venue, the Roxy, helped cement this bar and restaurant's status as a legendary watering hole for musicians (as well as their entourages and groupies). The Who, Guns N' Roses, Poison, Kiss, and many others have all passed through the doors. Expect a $5–$10 cover, but you'll get the money back in drink tickets or a food discount. ⊠ *9015 W. Sunset Blvd., West Hollywood* ☎ *310/278–4232* ⊕ *www.rainbowbarandgrill.com.*

The Troubadour

MUSIC CLUBS | The intimate vibe of the Troubadour helps make this club a favorite with music fans. Around since 1957, this venue has a storied past where legends like Elton John and James Taylor have graced the stage. These days, the eclectic lineup is still attracting crowds, with the focus mostly on rock, indie, and folk music. Those looking for drinks can imbibe to their heart's content at the adjacent bar. ⊠ *9081 Santa Monica Blvd., West Hollywood* ⊕ *www.troubadour.com.*

Whisky A Go Go

MUSIC CLUBS | The hard-core metal and rock scene is alive and well at the legendary Whisky A Go Go (the full name includes the prefix "World Famous"), where Janis Joplin, Led Zeppelin, Alice Cooper, Van Halen, the Doors (they were the house band for a short stint), and Frank Zappa have all played. On the Strip for more than five decades, the club books both underground acts and huge names in rock. ⊠ *8901 Sunset Blvd., West Hollywood* ☎ *310/652–4202* ⊕ *www.whiskyagogo.com.*

🛍 Shopping

⭐ American Rag Cie

CLOTHING | Half the store features new clothing from established and emerging labels, while the other side is stocked with well-preserved vintage clothing organized by color and style. You'll also find plenty of shoes and accessories being picked over by the hippest of Angelenos. ⊠ *150 S. La Brea Ave., West Hollywood* ☎ *323/935–3154* ⊕ *americanrag.com.*

Beverly Center

SHOPPING CENTERS/MALLS | Having gone through a massive renovation in 2018, this eight-level shopping center is home to luxury retailers like Bloomingdale's,

Henri Bendel, and Dolce & Gabbana but also offers plenty of outposts for more affordable brands including Aldo, H&M, and Uniqlo. The refurb also introduced a bevy of great dining options like Farmhouse, a seed-to-table spot with amazing pizzas; Eggslut, an extraordinarily popular breakfast joint; and Yardbird, a fried-chicken lovers' favorite, plus many, many more. ⊠ 8500 Beverly Blvd., West Hollywood ☎ 310/854–0070 ⊕ www. beverlycenter.com.

★ Fred Segal

CLOTHING | One of the most well-known boutiques in all of Los Angeles, Fred Segal is a fashion design mecca that has been clothing the rich, famous, and their acolytes since the 1960s. Since moving from its original location on Melrose, the new flagship store sits atop Sunset Boulevard with more than 21,000 square feet of space that showcases innovative brands and high-end threads. Inside is also Tesse Café and Bakery, which offers fashionistas some fast casual fare as they peruse the merchandise. ⊠ 8500 Sunset Blvd., West Hollywood ☎ 310/432-0560 ⊕ www. fredsegal.com.

The Grove

OUTDOOR/FLEA/GREEN MARKETS | Come to this popular outdoor mall for familiar names like Apple, Nike, and Nordstrom; stay for the central fountain with "dancing" water and light shows, people-watching from the trolley, and, during the holiday season, artificial snowfall and a winter wonderland. Feel-good pop blasting over the loudspeakers aims to boost your mood while you spend, and a giant cineplex gives shoppers a needed break with the latest box office blockbusters. The adjacent Farmers Market offers dozens of freshly farmed food stalls and tons of great restaurants. ⊠ 189 The Grove Dr., West Hollywood ☎ 323/900–8080 ⊕ www.thegrovela.com.

★ Maxfield

CLOTHING | This modern concrete structure is one of L.A.'s most desirable destinations for ultimate high fashion. The space is stocked with sleek offerings from Givenchy, Saint Laurent, Valentino, and Rick Owens, plus occasional pop-ups by fashion's labels-of-the-moment. For serious shoppers (or gawkers) only. ⊠ 8825 Melrose Ave., West Hollywood ☎ 310/274–8800 ⊕ www.maxfieldla.com.

Paul Smith

CLOTHING | You can't miss the massive, minimalist pink box that houses Paul Smith's fantastical collection of clothing, boots, hats, luggage, and objets d'art (seriously, there will be hordes of Instagrammers shooting selfies in front of the bright facade). Photos and art line the walls above shelves of books on pop culture, art, and Hollywood. As for the clothing here, expect the British brand's signature playfully preppy style, with vibrant colors and whimsical patterns mixed in with well-tailored closet staples. ⊠ 8221 Melrose Ave., West Hollywood ☎ 323/951–4800 ⊕ www. paulsmith.com/uk.

Reformation

CLOTHING | Local trendsetters flock here for the sexy, easy-to-wear silhouettes of Reformation's dresses (including a totally affordable bridal line), jumpsuits, and separates—it's a welcome bonus that the pieces here are sustainably manufactured using recycled materials. ⊠ 8000 Melrose Ave., West Hollywood ☎ 323/852–0005 ⊕ www.thereformation.com.

The Way We Wore

CLOTHING | Beyond the over-the-top vintage store furnishings, you'll find one of the city's best selections of well-cared-for and one-of-a-kind items, with a focus on sequins and beads. Upstairs, couture from Halston, Dior, and Chanel can cost up to $20,000. ⊠ 334 S. La Brea Ave., West Hollywood ☎ 323/937–0878 ⊕ www.thewaywewore.com.

Hollywood and the Studios

The Tinseltown mythology of Los Angeles was born in Hollywood, still one of the city's largest and most vibrant neighborhoods. In the Hollywood Hills to the north of Franklin Avenue sit some of the most marvelous mansions the moguls ever built; in the flats below Sunset and Santa Monica boulevards are the classic Hollywood bungalows where studio workers once resided. Reputation aside, though, it's mostly a workaday neighborhood without the glitz and glamour of places like Beverly Hills. The only major studio still located in Hollywood is Paramount; Warner Bros., Disney, and Universal Studios Hollywood are to the north in Burbank and Universal City.

Of course, the notion of Hollywood as a center of the entertainment industry can be expanded to include more than one neighborhood: to the north is Studio City, a thriving strip at the base of the Hollywood Hills, which is home to many smaller film companies; Universal City, where you'll find Universal Studios Hollywood; and Burbank, home to several major studios. North Hollywood, a suburban enclave that's actually in the San Fernando Valley, has its own thriving arts district.

Hollywood

Sights

Dolby Theatre

ARTS VENUE | More than just a prominent fixture on Hollywood Boulevard, the Dolby Theatre has a few accolades under its belt as well, most notably as home to the Academy Awards. The theater is the blend of the traditional and the modern, where an exquisite classical design inspired by the grand opera houses of Europe meets a state-of-the-art sound and technical system for an immersive,

theatrical experience. Watch a concert or a show here to experience it fully, but before you do, take a tour for an informative, behind-the-scenes look and to step into the VIP lounge where celebrities rub elbows on the big night. ✉ *6801 Hollywood Blvd., Hollywood* ☎ *323/308–6300* ⊕ *www.dolbytheatre.com* 🎟 *Tour $22.*

★ Hollywood Museum

MUSEUM | Don't let its kitschy facade turn you off. The Hollywood Museum, nestled at the busy intersection of Hollywood and Highland, is worth it, especially for film aficionados. A museum deserving of its name, it boasts an impressive collection of exhibits from the moviemaking world, spanning several film genres and eras. Start in its pink, art-deco lobby where the Max Factor exhibit pays tribute to the cosmetics company's pivotal role in Hollywood, make your way to the dark basement, where the industry's penchant for the macabre is on full display, and wrap up your visit by admiring Hollywood's most famous costumes and set props on the top floor. ✉ *1660 N. Highland Ave., at Hollywood Blvd., Hollywood* ☎ *323/464–7776* ⊕ *www.thehollywoodmuseum.com* 🎟 *$15* ⊘ *Closed Mon. and Tues.*

Hollywood Sign

MEMORIAL | With letters 50 feet tall, Hollywood's trademark sign can be spotted from miles away. The icon, which originally read "Hollywoodland," was erected in the Hollywood Hills in 1923 to advertise a segregated housing development and was outfitted with 4,000 light bulbs. In 1949 the "land" portion of the sign was taken down. By 1973 the sign had earned landmark status, but because the letters were made of wood, its longevity came into question. A makeover project was launched and the letters were auctioned off (rocker Alice Cooper bought an "O" and singing cowboy Gene Autry sponsored an "L") to make way for a new sign made of sheet metal. Inevitably, the sign has drawn pranksters who have altered it over the years, albeit temporarily, to spell

out "Hollyweed" (in the 1970s, to push for more lenient marijuana laws), "Go Navy" (before a Rose Bowl game), and "Perotwood" (during businessman Ross Perot's 1992 presidential bid). A fence and surveillance equipment have since been installed to deter intruders, but another vandal managed to pull the "Hollyweed" prank once again in 2017 after Californians voted to make recreational use of marijuana legal statewide. ⚠ **Use caution if driving up to the sign on residential streets; many cars speed around the blind corners.** ⊠ *Griffith Park, Mt. Lee Dr., Hollywood* ⊕ *www.hollywoodsign.org.*

Hollywood Walk of Fame

ARTS VENUE | Along Hollywood Boulevard (and part of Vine Street) runs a trail of affirmations for entertainment-industry overachievers. On this mile-long stretch of sidewalk, inspired by the concrete handprints in front of TCL Chinese Theatre, names are embossed in brass, each at the center of a pink star embedded in dark gray terrazzo. They're not all screen deities; many stars commemorate people who worked in a technical field, such as sound or lighting. The first eight stars were unveiled in 1960 at the northwest corner of Highland Avenue and Hollywood Boulevard: Olive Borden, Ronald Colman, Louise Fazenda, Preston Foster, Burt Lancaster, Edward Sedgwick, Ernest Torrence, and Joanne Woodward (some of these names have stood the test of time better than others). Since then, more than 2,000 others have been immortalized, though that honor doesn't come cheap—upon selection by a special committee, the personality in question (or more likely his or her movie studio or record company) pays about $30,000 for the privilege. To aid you in spotting celebrities you're looking for, stars are identified by one of five icons: a motion-picture camera, a radio microphone, a television set, a record, or a theatrical mask. ⊠ *Hollywood Blvd. and Vine St., Hollywood* ☎ *323/469–8311* ⊕ *www.walkoffame.com.*

★ Paramount Pictures

FILM STUDIO | With a history dating to the early 1920s, the Paramount lot was home to some of Hollywood's most luminous stars, including Mary Pickford, Rudolph Valentino, Mae West, Marlene Dietrich, and Bing Crosby. Director Cecil B. DeMille's base of operations for decades, Paramount offers probably the most authentic studio tour, giving you a real sense of the film industry's history. This is the only major studio from film's golden age left in Hollywood—all the others are in Burbank, Universal City, or Culver City.

Memorable movies and TV shows with scenes shot here include *Sunset Boulevard, Forrest Gump,* and *Titanic.* Many of the *Star Trek* movies and TV series were shot entirely or in part here, and several seasons of *I Love Lucy* were shot on the portion of the lot Paramount acquired in 1967 from Lucille Ball. You can take a 2-hour studio tour or a 4½-hour VIP tour, led by guides who walk and trolley you around the back lots. As well as gleaning some gossipy history, you'll spot the sets of TV and film shoots in progress. Reserve ahead for tours, which are for those ages 10 and up. ◼**TIP**→ **You can be part of the audience for live TV tapings (tickets are free), but you must book ahead.** ⊠ *5515 Melrose Ave., Hollywood* ☎ *323/956–1777* ⊕ *www.paramountstudiotour.com* ⊡ *From $58.*

TCL Chinese Theatre

ARTS VENUE | The stylized Chinese pagodas and temples of the former Grauman's Chinese Theatre have become a shrine both to stardom and the combination of glamour and flamboyance that inspire the phrase "only in Hollywood." Although you have to buy a movie ticket to appreciate the interior trappings, the courtyard is open to the public. The main theater itself is worth visiting, if only to see a film in the same setting as hundreds of celebrities who have attended big premieres here.

A concert at the Hollywood Bowl is a summertime tradition for Angelenos.

And then, of course, outside in front are the oh-so-famous cement hand- and footprints. This tradition is said to have begun at the theater's opening in 1927, with the premiere of Cecil B. DeMille's *King of Kings,* when actress Norma Talmadge just happened to step in wet cement. Now more than 160 celebrities have contributed imprints for posterity, including some oddball specimens, such as casts of Whoopi Goldberg's dreadlocks. ⊠ *6925 Hollywood Blvd., Hollywood* ☎ *323/461–3331* ⊕ *www.tclchinesetheatres.com* 🎟 *Tour $18.*

Restaurants

Café Gratitude

$$ | **VEGETARIAN** | **FAMILY** | Of L.A.'s long list of vegan restaurants, this is among the best, with luscious dishes that are also social media worthy. But it's more than just gourmet, plant-based dining—Café Gratitude is also about leading a sustainable lifestyle full of positivity and (obviously) gratitude. **Known for:** vegan fare; the Mucho Mexican Bowl; pressed juices.

$ *Average main: $16* ⊠ *639 N. Larchmont Blvd., Hollywood* ☎ *323/580–6383* ⊕ *www.cafegratitude.com.*

★ Gwen

$$$$ | **STEAKHOUSE** | Upscale carnivores: this is your heaven. A fine-dining restaurant that serves impossibly exquisite dishes in a copper-and-marble setting. **Known for:** steak; duck fat potatoes; house-cured meats. $ *Average main: $50* ⊠ *6600 Sunset Blvd., Hollywood* ☎ *323/946–7513* ⊕ *www.gwenla.com/butcher-shop-about.html.*

★ Osteria Mozza

$$$ | **ITALIAN** | How close do you think you can get to divinity? At chef Nancy Silverton's passion project–slash–culinary masterpiece, you'll come pretty damn close after sampling a few of its celestial dishes. **Known for:** ricotta-and-egg ravioli; all-Italian wine; artisanal spirits. $ *Average main: $30* ⊠ *6602 Melrose Ave., Hollywood* ☎ *323/297–0100* ⊕ *osteriamozza.com.*

★ Pink's Hot Dogs

$ | HOT DOG | FAMILY | Since 1939, Angelenos and tourists alike have been lining up at this roadside hot dog stand. But Pink's is more than just an institution, it's a beloved family-run joint that serves a damn good hot dog. **Known for:** the Brando Dog; late-night dining; chili fries. *Average main: $6* ⊠ *709 N. La Brea Ave., Hollywood* ☎ *323/931–4223* ⊕ *www.pinkshollywood.com.*

Pizzeria Mozza

$$ | ITALIAN | Chef Nancy Silverton, of Osteria Mozza, owns this upscale pizza and antipasto eatery. The pies—thin-crusted delights with golden, blistered edges—are more Campania than California and are served piping hot daily. **Known for:** late-night eats; goat cheese, leek, scallion, garlic, and bacon pizza; family friendliness. *Average main: $20* ⊠ *641 N. Highland Ave., Hollywood* ☎ *323/297–0101* ⊕ *www.pizzeriamozza.com.*

★ Providence

$$$$ | SEAFOOD | This is widely considered one of the best seafood restaurants in the country, and chef-owner Michael Cimarusti elevates sustainably driven fine dining to an art form. The elegant space is the perfect spot to sample exquisite seafood with the chef's signature application of French technique, traditional American themes, and Asian accents. **Known for:** seafood; immaculate presentation; excellent wine list. *Average main: $120* ⊠ *5955 Melrose Ave., Hollywood* ☎ *323/460–4170* ⊕ *www.providencela.com* ☺ *No lunch Mon.–Thurs. and weekends.*

Roscoe's House of Chicken and Waffles

$$ | SOUTHERN | FAMILY | Roscoe's is *the* place for down-home Southern cooking in Southern California. Just ask the patrons who drive from all over L.A. for bargain-priced fried chicken and waffles. The name of this casual eatery honors a late-night combo popularized in Harlem jazz clubs. **Known for:** chicken and waffles; soul food; eggs with cheese and onions. *Average main: $15* ⊠ *1514 N. Gower St., Hollywood* ☎ *323/466–7453* ⊕ *www.roscoeschickenandwaffles.com.*

Sqirl

$ | CAFÉ | Sitting on the fringe of East Hollywood where L.A.'s most touristy neighborhood transitions into the city's hippest zip code, it's hardly a surprise that Sqirl is every bit as trendy as Silver Lake—from the beautiful twenty- and thirtysomethings that frequent it to the vegan and gluten-free options the café has on hand. But don't let that tidbit turn you off—its worldly breakfast menu is just the ticket to sustain you for a busy day ahead. **Known for:** crispy rice salad; breakfast all day; sorrel-pesto rice. *Average main: $12* ⊠ *720 N. Virgil Ave. Suite 4, Hollywood* ☎ *323/284–8147* ⊕ *www.sqirlla.com.*

Hotels

★ Hollywood Roosevelt Hotel

$$$$ | HOTEL | Poolside cabana rooms are adorned with cow-skin rugs and marble bathrooms, while rooms in the main building accentuate the property's history at this party-centric hotel in the heart of Hollywood. **Pros:** Spare Room bowling alley on-site; pool is a popular weekend hangout; great burgers at the on-site 25 Degrees restaurant. **Cons:** reports of noise and staff attitude; stiff parking fees ($42). *Rooms from: $419* ⊠ *7000 Hollywood Blvd., Hollywood* ☎ *323/466–7000, 800/950–7667* ⊕ *www.hollywoodroosevelt.com* ⇲ *353 rooms* ✿ *No meals.*

★ Magic Castle Hotel

$ | HOTEL | FAMILY | Guests at the hotel can secure advance dinner reservations and attend magic shows at the Magic Castle, a private club in a 1908 mansion next door for magicians and their admirers. **Pros:** heated pool; near Hollywood & Highland; lush patio. **Cons:** strict dress code; no elevator; highly trafficked street. *Rooms from: $199* ⊠ *7025 Franklin*

Ave., Hollywood ☎ 323/851–0800, 800/741–4915 ⊕ magiccastlehotel.com ⇱ 43 rooms ⏇ Breakfast.

★ Mama Shelter

$ | HOTEL | Even locals are just catching on to Hollywood's sexiest new property, complete with a rooftop bar populated with beautiful people lounging on love seats, simple affordable rooms with quirky amenities like Bert and Ernie masks, and a down-home lobby restaurant that serves a mean Korean-style burrito. **Pros:** delicious food and cocktails on the property; affordable rooms don't skimp on style; foosball in lobby. **Cons:** spare and small rooms; creaky elevators. ⑤ *Rooms from: $159* ✉ *6500 Selma Ave., Hollywood* ☎ *323/785–6666* ⊕ *www. mamashelter.com/en/los-angeles* ⇱ *70 rooms* ⏇ *No meals.*

★ Palihotel

$ | HOTEL | Catering to young and hip budget travelers who crave style over space, this design-centric boutique property on Melrose Avenue is in the heart of Hollywood's best shopping and dining, including hot spot Hart and the Hunter. **Pros:** funky aesthetic; sweet-corn hush puppies at the Hart and the Hunter restaurant are delish; fantastic location in a walkable neighborhood. **Cons:** small rooms; congested lobby; decor might not appeal to everyone. ⑤ *Rooms from: $190* ✉ *7950 Melrose Ave., Hollywood* ☎ *323/272–4588* ⊕ *www.pali-hotel.com* ⇱ *33 rooms* ⏇ *No meals.*

W Hollywood

$$$$ | HOTEL | This centrally located, ultra-modernly lit location is outfitted for the wired traveler and features a rooftop pool deck and popular on-site bars, like the Station Hollywood and the mod Living Room lobby bar. **Pros:** Metro stop outside the front door; comes with in-room party necessities, from ice to cocktail glasses; comfy beds with petal-soft duvets. **Cons:** small pool; pricey dining and valet parking; in noisy part of Hollywood. ⑤ *Rooms from: $659* ✉ *6250 Hollywood Blvd.,*

Hollywood ☎ 323/798–1300, 888/625–4955 ⊕ www.whotels.com/hollywood ⇱ 305 rooms ⏇ No meals.

Activities

Bronson Canyon

HIKING/WALKING | Bronson Canyon—or more popularly, Bronson Caves—is one of L.A.'s most famous filming locations, especially for western and sci-fi flicks. This section of Griffith Park, easily accessible through a trail that's less than half a mile, is a great place to visit whether you're a film buff or an exercise junkie. ✉ *3200 Canyon Dr., Hollywood.*

Runyon Canyon Trail and Park

HIKING/WALKING | Is Runyon Canyon the city's most famous trail? To the world, it just might be, what with so many A-listers frequenting it. Many folks visiting L.A. take the trail specifically for celebrity spotting. But, if that's not something you're into, this accessible trail right in the middle of Hollywood is also a good place to hike, run, see the Hollywood sign, photograph the city skyline, or simply get a bit of fresh air. If you just happen to run into a famous face, well that's just the cherry on the cake. ✉ *2000 N. Fuller Ave., Hollywood* ☎ *805/370–2301* ⊕ *www.nps.gov/samo/planyourvisit/runyoncanyon.htm.*

Nightlife

Birds

BARS/PUBS | They call it your neighborhood bar, because even if you don't live in the neighborhood you'll feel at home at this Alfred Hitchcock–themed eatery. Located in Franklin Village, a block-long stretch of bars, cafés, and bookstores, come here for pub food or a cheap poultry-centric dinner. Weekend nights mean cheap beer and well drinks, crowds spilling onto the streets, and a few rounds of oversized Jenga. Right next to the UCB Theatre, you're likely to see a few comedians grabbing a drink here after their shows. ⊠ *5925 Franklin Ave., Hollywood* ☎ *323/465–0175* ⊕ *www.birdshollywood.com.*

Burgundy Room

BARS/PUBS | Around since 1919, Burgundy Room attracts a fiercely loyal crowd of locals, as well as the occasional wandering tourists. The bar is supposedly haunted (check out the Ouija boards toward the back), but that just adds to its charm. Its rock-and-roll vibe, strong drinks, and people-watching opportunities make this a worthy detour on any night out on the town. ⊠ *1621 N. Cahuenga Blvd., Hollywood* ☎ *323/465–7530.*

★ Dirty Laundry

BARS/PUBS | Tucked away in a basement on the quiet Hudson Avenue, Dirty Laundry is a former speakeasy turned proper cocktail bar with live music and DJs spinning both fresh and throwback music, not to mention jazz-inspired details. There's beer on hand, but here, cocktails are king. ⊠ *1725 Hudson Ave., Hollywood* ☎ *323/462–6531.*

★ Good Times at Davey Wayne's

BARS/PUBS | It's a fridge; it's a door; it's the entrance to Davey Wayne's, a bar and lounge that pulls out all the stops to transport you back in time to the '70s. The interior is your living room; the outside is an ongoing backyard barbecue with all of your friends. Except, wait, I don't recognize anyone … who invited all these drunk people to my house?! Come early to beat the crowds or be prepared to get up close and personal with your neighbors. ⊠ *1611 N. El Centro Ave., Hollywood* ☎ *323/962–3804* ⊕ *www.goodtimesatdaveywaynes.com.*

Hotel Cafe

MUSIC CLUBS | This intimate venue caters to fans of folk, indie rock, and music on the softer side. With red velvet backdrops, hardwood furnishings, and the occasional celebrity surprise performance—notably John Mayer—musicophiles will not only be very happy but will receive a respite from the ordinary Hollywood experience. ⊠ *1623½ N. Cahuenga Blvd., Hollywood* ☎ *323/461–2040* ⊕ *www.hotelcafe.com.*

★ Musso and Frank Grill

BARS/PUBS | **FAMILY** | The prim and proper vibe of this old-school steak house won't appeal to those looking for a raucous night out; instead, its appeal lies in its history and sturdy drinks. Established a century ago, its dark wood decor, red tuxedo–clad waiters, and highly skilled bartenders can easily shuttle you back to its Hollywood heyday when Marilyn Monroe, F. Scott Fitzgerald, and Greta Garbo once hung around and sipped martinis. ⊠ *6667 Hollywood Blvd., Hollywood* ☎ *323/467–7788* ⊕ *www.mussoandfrank.com.*

No Vacancy

BARS/PUBS | Though at first glance, No Vacancy might boast an air of exclusivity and pretentiousness, its relaxed interiors and welcoming staff will almost instantly make you feel like you're at a house party. You know, the kind with burlesque shows, tightrope performances, a speakeasy secret entrance, and mixologists who can pretty much whip up any drink your heart desires. ⊠ *1727 N. Hudson Ave., Hollywood* ☎ *323/465–1902* ⊕ *www.novacancyla.com.*

Sassafras Saloon

BARS/PUBS | Put on your dancing shoes (or your cowboy boots) and step back in time. The Sassafras boasts not only an oddly cozy, Western atmosphere but plenty of opportunities to strut your moves on the dance floor. Indulge in exquisite craft mezcal, whiskey, and tequila cocktails for some liquid courage before you salsa the night away. ⊠ *1233 N. Vine St., Hollywood* ☎ *323/467–2800* ⊕ *www.sassafrassaloon.com.*

Three Clubs

BARS/PUBS | Cocktail bars are a dime a dozen in Hollywood, but there's something about this Vine Street joint that makes patrons keep coming back for more. Maybe it's the down-to-earth attitude, delicious no-frills cocktails, and the fact that a taco stand serving greasy grub is right next door. Come to see one of the burlesque or comedy shows for a full experience. ⊠ *1123 Vine St., Hollywood* ☎ *323/462–6441* ⊕ *www. threeclubs.com.*

★ Upright Citizens Brigade

COMEDY CLUBS | The L.A. offshoot of New York's famous troupe continues its tradition of sketch comedy and improv with weekly shows like "Facebook," where the audience's online profiles are mined for material, and "ASSSSCAT," an improv show with rotating comedians including Zach Woods (*Silicon Valley*) and Matt Walsh (*Veep*). Arrive early as space is limited. A second theater on Sunset Boulevard opened in 2014. ⊠ *5919 Franklin Ave., Hollywood* ☎ *323/908–8702* ⊕ *ucbtheatre.com.*

🎭 Performing Arts

★ ArcLight

FILM | This big multiplex includes the historic Cinerama Dome, that impossible-to-miss golf ball–looking structure on Sunset Boulevard, which was built in 1963. Like many L.A. theaters, the ArcLight has assigned seating (you will be asked to select seats when purchasing tickets). The complex is a one-stop shop with a parking garage, shopping area, restaurant, and in-house bar. The events calendar is worth paying attention to, as directors and actors often drop by to chat with audiences. Amy Adams and Samuel L. Jackson, for example, have both made time for postscreening Q&As. Movies here can be pricey, but the theater shows just about every new release. ■TIP→ **Evening shows on the weekend feature "21+" shows, during which moviegoers can bring alcoholic beverages into the screening rooms.** ⊠ *6360 Sunset Blvd., Hollywood* ☎ *323/615–2550* ⊕ *www. arclightcinemas.com.*

★ Hollywood Bowl

CONCERTS | For those seeking a quintessential Los Angeles experience, a concert on a summer night at the Bowl, the city's iconic outdoor venue, is unsurpassed. The Bowl has presented world-class performers since it opened in 1920. The L.A. Philharmonic plays here from June to September; its performances and other events draw large crowds. Parking is limited near the venue, but there are additional remote parking locations serviced by shuttles. You can bring food and drink to any event, which Angelenos often do, though you can only bring alcohol when the L.A. Phil is performing. (Bars sell alcohol at all events, and there are dining options.) It's wise to bring a jacket even if daytime temperatures have been warm—the Bowl can get quite chilly at night. ■TIP→ **Visitors can sometimes watch the L.A. Phil practice for free, usually on a weekday; call ahead for times.** ⊠ *2301 Highland Ave., Hollywood* ☎ *323/850–2000* ⊕ *www.hollywoodbowl.com.*

Pantages Theatre

THEATER | For the grand-scale theatrics of a Broadway show, such as *Hamilton* and *The Book of Mormon,* the 2,703-seat Pantages Theatre (the last theater built by Greek American vaudeville producer Alexander Pantages) lights up Hollywood Boulevard on show nights, when lines of excited patrons extend down the block. ⊠ *6233 Hollywood Blvd., Hollywood* ☎ *323/468–1770* ⊕ *www. hollywoodpantages.com.*

🛍 Shopping

★ Amoeba Records

MUSIC STORES | Touted as the "World's Largest Independent Record Store," Amoeba is a playground for music lovers, with a knowledgeable staff and a focus on local artists. Catch free in-store appearances and signings by artists and bands that play sold-out shows at venues down the road. There's a massive and eclectic collection of vinyl records, CDs, and cassette tapes, not to mention VHS tapes, DVDs, and Blu-Ray discs. It's a paradise for both music and movie lovers. ⊠ *6400 W. Sunset Blvd., at Cahuenga Blvd., Hollywood* ☎ *323/245–6400* ⊕ *www.amoeba.com.*

Hollywood & Highland Center

SHOPPING CENTERS/MALLS | If you're on the hunt for unique boutiques, look elsewhere. However, if you prefer the biggest mall retail chains America has to offer, Hollywood & Highland is a great spot for a shopping spree. The design of the complex pays tribute to the city's film legacy, with a grand staircase leading up to a pair of three-story-tall stucco elephants, a nod to the 1916 movie *Intolerance*. Pause at the entrance arch, called Babylon Court, which frames a picture-perfect view of the Hollywood sign. This place is a huge tourist magnet, so don't expect to mingle with the locals. ⊠ *6801 Hollywood Blvd., at Highland Ave., Hollywood* ☎ *323/467–6412* ⊕ *www.hollywoodandhighland.com.*

Larry Edmunds Bookshop

BOOKS/STATIONERY | Cinephiles have long descended upon this iconic 70-plus-year-old shop that in addition to stocking tons of texts about motion picture history offers film fans the opportunity to pick up scripts, posters, and photographs from Hollywood's Golden Era to the present. ⊠ *6644 Hollywood Blvd., Hollywood* ☎ *323/463–3273* ⊕ *www.larryedmunds.com.*

The Record Parlour

MUSIC STORES | Vinyl records and music memorabilia abound in this hip yet modest record store–slash–music lover magnet that also touts vintage audio gear and retro jukeboxes. A visit here is usually a multihour affair, one that involves more than just browsing through display cases, digging through wooden carts of used vinyls, and playing your picks at the listening station. ⊠ *6408 Selma Ave., Hollywood* ☎ *323/464–7757* ⊕ *therecordparlour.com.*

Studio City

 Restaurants

Good Neighbor Restaurant

$ | **DINER** | Its walls may be heavy with framed photographs of film and TV stars, and folks from the biz might regularly grace its tables, but this Studio City diner is every bit as down-to-earth as your next-door neighbor, even after 40-some years. It gets pretty busy from the Universal City crowd, but a plateful of that home cooking is worth the wait; or if you're in a mad dash, grab a caffeine or fruit smoothie fix from the Neighbarista. **Known for:** omelet; cottage fries; breakfast food. ⑤ *Average main: $13* ⊠ *3701 Cahuenga Blvd., Studio City* ☎ *818/457–6050* ⊕ *goodneighborrestaurant.com.*

Hot Stone Slow Food from Korea

$ | **KOREAN FUSION** | **FAMILY** | Hot Stone Slow Food might sound more like the title of an indie band rather than a legitimate restaurant, but trust that this spot on Ventura is indeed the perfect place to partake in L.A.'s massive Korean gastronomy scene. There'll be no cooking your own meats over a hot grill here; but you may be creating your own bibimbap. **Known for:** Hot Stone bibimbap or dupbap; Hot Stone BBQ; dak kang jung. ⑤ *Average main: $8* ⊠ *12265 Ventura Blvd., Suite 102, Studio City* ☎ *818/358–4223* ⊕ *hotstone.net* ⊙ *Closed Mon.*

 Hotels

Sportsmen's Lodge

$$ | **HOTEL** | **FAMILY** | This sprawling five-story hotel, a San Fernando Valley landmark just a short jaunt over the Hollywood Hills, has an updated contemporary look highlighted by the Olympic-size pool and summer patio with an outdoor bar. **Pros:** close to Ventura Boulevard restaurants; free shuttle to Universal Hollywood; quiet garden-view rooms worth asking for. **Cons:** pricey daily self-parking fee ($18);

a distance from the city. $ *Rooms from: $249* ✉ *12825 Ventura Blvd., Studio City* ☎ *818/769–4700, 800/821–8511* ⊕ *www.sportsmenslodge.com* ⇄ *190 rooms* ⦿ *No meals.*

Nightlife

Baked Potato

MUSIC CLUBS | Baked Potato might be a strange name to give a world-famous jazz club that's been holding performances of well-known acts (Allan Holdsworth and Michael Landau) under its roof since the '70s, but it only takes a quick peek at the menu to understand. Twenty-four different types of baked potatoes dominate its otherwise short menu, each of which come with sour cream, butter, and salad to offset all that carb intake. ✉ *3787 Cahuenga Blvd., Studio City* ☎ *818/980–1615* ⊕ *www.thebakedpotato.com.*

Pinz Bowling Alley

BOWLING | "Bowl. Eat. Drink. Repeat" might be this bowling alley's motto, but thanks to its neon-slash-backlit lanes—each fully equipped with a touch-screen food and drink ordering system—and its very own arcade, Pinz is more than just your typical bowling experience. A few A-list names are among its loyal clientele, but you don't visit for celebrity sightings; all bells and whistles aside, it's a proper bowling alley and you come here to bowl. ✉ *12655 Ventura Blvd., Studio City* ☎ *818/769–7600* ⊕ *pinzla.com.*

Universal City

⊙ Sights

Universal Studios Hollywood

AMUSEMENT PARK/WATER PARK | **FAMILY** | A theme park with classic attractions like roller coasters and thrill rides, Universal Studios also provides a tour of some beloved television and movie sets. A favorite attraction is the tram tour, during which you can duck from King Kong; see the airplane wreckage of *War of the Worlds*; ride along with the cast of the *Fast and the Furious*; and get chills looking at the house from *Psycho.* ■ **TIP** → **The tram ride is usually the best place to begin your visit, because the lines become longer as the day goes on.**

Most attractions are designed to give you a thrill in one form or another, including the thrilling Revenge of the Mummy and immersive rides like the 4D Simpsons Ride, where you can actually smell Maggie Simpson's baby powder. The Wizarding World of Harry Potter, however, is the crown jewel of the park, featuring magical rides, pints of frozen butterbeer, and enough merchandise to drain you wallet faster than you can shout "Expecto Patronum." If you're in town in October, stop by for Halloween Horror Nights, featuring mazes full of monsters, murderers, and jump scares.

Geared more toward adults, CityWalk is a separate venue run by Universal Studios, where you'll find shops, restaurants, nightclubs, and movie theaters. ✉ *100 Universal City Plaza, Universal City* ☎ *800/864–8377* ⊕ *www.universalstudioshollywood.com* 🎟 *$99.*

Restaurants

Café Sierra

$$$ | **SEAFOOD** | **FAMILY** | Don't let the fact that this airy Californian and pan-Asian spot is located inside a Hilton Hotel scare you; Café Sierra has a drool-worthy seafood and prime rib buffet. Lunching here can be a splurge, but it's worth every penny. **Known for:** champagne brunch; Alaskan king crab; live jazz music. $ *Average main: $30* ✉ *555 Universal Hollywood Dr., Universal City* ☎ *818/824–4237* ⊕ *www.cafesierrahilton.com.*

Dongpo

$$ | **SICHUAN** | **FAMILY** | Upmarket regional Chinese cuisine chain Meizhou Dongpo tries its hand at bringing its modern take on authentic Sichuanese cuisine with

Dongpo Kitchen, and it's exactly what the CityWalk needed to up its dining game. This bright, contemporary-meets-traditional Chinese restaurant serves delightful, affordable fare right in the middle of a sea of tourists. **Known for:** Dongpo roast duck; Sichuan dumplings; kung pao chicken. $ *Average main: $19* ⊠ *1000 Universal Studios Blvd. V103, Universal City* ☎ *818/358–3272* ⊕ *www.citywalk-hollywood.com.*

 Hotels

Sheraton Universal

$$ | **HOTEL** | **FAMILY** | With large meeting spaces and a knowledgeable staff, this Sheraton buzzes year-round with business travelers and families, providing easy access to the free shuttle that takes guests to adjacent Universal Studios and CityWalk. **Pros:** pool area with cabanas and bar; oversize desks and office chairs in room. **Cons:** average in-house restaurant; touristy. $ *Rooms from: $299* ⊠ *333 Universal Hollywood Dr., Universal City* ☎ *818/980–1212, 888/627–7184* ⊕ *www.sheratonuniversal.com* ☞ *457 rooms* ❌ *No meals.*

Burbank

 Sights

Warner Bros. Studios

FILM STUDIO | You don't need to be a big film nerd to appreciate a visit to the Warner Bros. Studios, where you can pretend to be your favorite TV or movie characters, whether at a working replica of Central Perk from *Friends* or at a sorting ceremony from Harry Potter. You'll also visit backlots and sound stages to see how the magic is made.

If you're looking for an authentic behind-the-scenes look at how films and TV shows are made, head to this major studio center, one of the world's busiest. After a short film on the studio's movies

and TV shows, hop aboard a tram for a ride through the sets and sound stages of such favorites as *Casablanca* and *Rebel Without a Cause.* You'll see the bungalows where Marlon Brando, Bette Davis, and other icons relaxed between shots, and the current production offices for Clint Eastwood and George Clooney. You might even spot a celeb or see a shoot in action—tours change from day to day depending on the productions taking place on the lot. ⊠ *3400 W. Riverside Dr., Burbank* ☎ *818/977–8687* ⊕ *www.wbstudiotour.com* ☞ *From $65.*

 Restaurants

Bea Bea's

$ | **DINER** | Just because Bea Bea's is a no-nonsense kind of place, it doesn't mean the food isn't special. This diner serves breakfast food that is about as close to extraordinary as the most important meal of the day can be. **Known for:** large selection of pancakes and French toast; Happy Mornings; friendly staff. $ *Average main: $12* ⊠ *353 N. Pass Ave., Burbank* ☎ *818/846–2327* ⊕ *www.beabeas.com.*

Centanni Trattoria

$$ | **ITALIAN** | In a city full of adventurous restaurants touting new takes on traditional dishes and swanking about with bells and whistles and stunning interiors, a run-of-the-mill-looking place like Centanni Tratorria might never make it onto the radar. But what this authentic Italian spot lacks in swagger, it more than makes up for in delicious home cooking. **Known for:** homemade pasta; panini; seafood. $ *Average main: $20* ⊠ *117 N. Victory Blvd., Burbank* ☎ *818/561–4643* ⊕ *www.centannivenice.com.*

Los Amigos

$$ | **MEXICAN** | **FAMILY** | If you're in the mood for good old-fashioned fun coupled with hearty Mexican fare and delicious margaritas, then you'll want to consider Los Amigos, whose legendary fruity

margaritas alone are worth the drive. Pair those with something from the Platillos Mexicanos menu on karaoke night, and you're guaranteed a good time until the wee hours of the night. **Known for:** molcajete; guacamole; signature cocktails. ⑤ *Average main: $18* ⊠ *2825 W. Olive Ave., Burbank* ☎ *818/842–3700* ⊕ *www. losamigosbarandgrill.com.*

Porto's Bakery
$ | **CUBAN** | **FAMILY** | Waiting in line at Porto's is as much a part of the experience as is indulging in a roasted pork sandwich or a chocolate-dipped croissant. This Cuban bakery and café has been an L.A. staple for more than 50 years, often bustling during lunch. **Known for:** counter service; potato balls; roasted pork sandwiches. ⑤ *Average main: $8* ⊠ *3614 W. Magnolia Blvd., Burbank* ☎ *818/846–9100* ⊕ *www.portosbakery.com.*

 ## Hotels

Hotel Amarano Burbank
$$ | **HOTEL** | Close to Burbank's TV and movie studios, the smartly designed Amarano feels like a Beverly Hills boutique hotel, complete with 24-hour room service, a homey on-site restaurant and lounge, and spiffy rooms. **Pros:** fireplace, cocktails, and tapas in lobby; penthouse with private gym; saltwater pool. **Cons:** street noise. ⑤ *Rooms from: $269* ⊠ *322 N. Pass Ave., Burbank* ☎ *818/842–8887, 888/956–1900* ⊕ *www.hotelamarano. com* ⊋ *98 rooms, 34 suites* �ⓄⒾ *No meals.*

 ## Nightlife

Flappers Comedy Club
COMEDY CLUBS | Even though this live comedy club doesn't exactly have as long a history as others in town (it opened in 2010), it's attracted an impressive list of big names like Jerry Seinfeld, Maria Bamford, and Adam Sandler thanks to its Celebrity Drop-In Tuesdays. The food and drinks are good though not great, but you're here for the laughs not the grub. ⊠ *102 E. Magnolia Blvd., Burbank* ☎ *818/845–9721* ⊕ *www. flapperscomedy.com.*

The Snug
BARS/PUBS | If you think that Magnolia Boulevard's the Snug is your typical Irish pub, think again. This neighborhood watering hole, which has a wide selection of whiskey, 28 draft and bottled beers, and cocktails, plays host to a number of events throughout the year, from holiday parties to chili cook-offs and trivia nights, not to mention a $3 happy hour on weekdays. ⊠ *4108 W. Magnolia Blvd., Burbank* ☎ *818/557–0018* ⊕ *www. thesnugburbank.com.*

 ## Shopping

Magnolia Park Vintage
SHOPPING NEIGHBORHOODS | Melrose Avenue might be Los Angeles's most well-known vintage shopping destination, but to many locals, especially those on the Eastside, Burbank's Magnolia Park is, in many ways, better. Spanning several blocks around Magnolia Avenue, this revitalized section blends convenience, plenty of vintage, thrift, and antiques shopping opportunities and has that laid-back small-town vibe that Melrose lacks. Great dining spots and excellent coffee shops abound, as well as foot and nail spas for a bit of pampering. ⊠ *W. Magnolia Blvd., between N. Niagara and N. Avon St., Burbank* ⊕ *www.visitmagnoliapark.com.*

North Hollywood

 ## Sights

NoHo Arts District
NEIGHBORHOOD | In only a few years, North Hollywood's performance arts hub has grown from the residential home of aspiring actors who frequent a few small theaters and several chain restaurants to a completely revitalized district that boasts its own, albeit small, collection of

new coffee shops and restaurants, bars serving up craft beer, and colorful street art. ✉ *Lankershim and Magnolia Blvds., North Hollywood* ⊕ *www.nohoartsdistrict.com.*

 Restaurants

Mofongo's

$$ | **PUERTO RICAN** | Mofongo's small storefront represents one of the best and only venues to get authentic Puerto Rican food in L.A. Stop by and try the namesake dish (a delectable mash of fried plantains), but stay for the *pasteles* (cakes) and *rellenos de papa* (stuffed potatoes). **Known for:** mofongo de lechon (fried plantains with pork); Puerto Rican food; flan de queso (cream cheese flan). ⑤ *Average main: $20* ✉ *5757 Lankershim Blvd., North Hollywood* ☎ *818/754–1051* ⊕ *www.mofongosrestaurant.com.*

Rodini Park

$ | **MEDITERRANEAN** | Nestled in the heart of the NoHo Arts District amid newly minted high-rises, Rodini Park's "build your own" concept and highly rated house-made pastries make it the place to go for a quick, fresh, and delicious take on Greek cuisine. Between the multiple protein, topping, and sauce offerings, it offers something for all palates. **Known for:** chicken shawarma; baklava cheesecake; Mount Olympus sauce. ⑤ *Average main: $10* ✉ *11049 Magnolia Blvd., North Hollywood* ☎ *818/358–4802* ⊕ *www.rodinipark.com.*

TeaPop

$ | **CAFÉ** | At first glance, TeaPop may seem to be doing too many things at once, but this tea-centric café, with its art gallery–slash–industrial modern interior and picturesque patio, is a perfect spot to not only study or take a breather, but also to catch pop-up events like comedy nights and workshops. Don't let the hipster vibes turn you off—the service is fantastic and the drinks delicious. **Known for:** vintage milk tea; bubble tea; loose-leaf

tea. ⑤ *Average main: $4* ✉ *5050 Vineland Ave., North Hollywood* ☎ *323/927–0330* ⊕ *teapopla.com.*

 Nightlife

California Institute of Abnormal Arts

MUSIC CLUBS | What do a mummified clown, an alley full of Chinese red lanterns, and a collection of sideshow memorabilia have in common? They can all be found in the California Institute of Abnormal Arts, or CIA for short. This is a bar that proudly showcases the freak side of L.A., from the wonderfully bonkers decor to the utterly bizarre performances that often frequent its stage. ✉ *11334 Burbank Ave., North Hollywood* ☎ *818/221–8065.*

Catcher in the Rye

PIANO BARS/LOUNGES | Catcher in the Rye's theme is not specific to Holden Caulfield but rather to literature. Other odes to fictional greats can be found name-checked on the menu, including Huck Finn and Jay Gatsby. Should you have forgotten your book at home, check one out from the bar's bookshelf, or if reading's not your thing (you're in the wrong bar, pal), you can grab a board game instead. ✉ *10550 Riverside Dr., North Hollywood* ☎ *818/853–7835* ⊕ *www.catcherbar.com.*

The Other Door

BARS/PUBS | The Other Door occupies a strange space, somewhere between a steampunk-themed bar, a dive bar, and a music venue with a varied calendar featuring live music, karaoke, and silent disco. It also has a pool table and a vintage photo booth on hand, in case all these diversions aren't enough to distract you. ✉ *10437 Burbank Blvd., North Hollywood* ☎ *818/508–7008* ⊕ *theotherdoorbar.com.*

 Shopping

Blastoff Comics

BOOKS/STATIONERY | Blastoff rises above L.A.'s collection of fantastic comic book stores. This is a wonderland for the serious collector, especially those looking to dive deep into vintage and rare comics. New comics are also on offer and a friendly, knowledgeable staff makes this a must-visit for any comic fan. ✉ *5118 Lankershim Blvd., North Hollywood* ☎ *323/980–2665* ⊕ *www. blastoffcomics.com.*

The Iliad Book Shop

BOOKS/STATIONERY | For 30 years, Iliad not only has been selling used books but has been a set piece on a number of TV shows and movies, including *Lethal Weapon 3*. But with a collection of 125,000 books of all genres, including a solid selection of graphic novels, it's worth a visit just to peruse the aisles and find that next favorite novel. ✉ *5400 Cahuenga Blvd., North Hollywood* ☎ *818/509–2665* ⊕ *www.iliadbooks.com.*

Mid-Wilshire and Koreatown

While they're two distinctly different neighborhoods, Mid-Wilshire and Koreatown sit side by side and offer Angelenos some of the most interesting sights, sounds, and bites in the city. Mid-Wilshire is broadly known for its wide variety of museums, but there's also a strip called Little Ethiopia, where you can find incredible cuisine. Koreatown, meanwhile, is a haven for Seoul food (pun intended) but also an area with multiethnic dining nuggets that hit the top of many restaurant lists. Once your stomach is sated, check out a Korean spa, where scrubbing and pampering can close out a perfectly long day.

Sandwiched between some of L.A.'s coolest neighborhoods, Culver City has spent the past few years forming its own identity. A place for adventurous eaters, here you can find cuisines spanning the globe.

Mid-Wilshire

⊙ Sights

★ Los Angeles County Museum of Art (LACMA)

MUSEUM | Los Angeles has a truly fabulous museum culture and everything that it stands for can be epitomized by the massive, eclectic, and ever-changing Los Angeles County Museum of Art. Opened at its current location in 1965, today the museum boasts the largest collection of art in the western United States with more than 135,000 pieces from 6,000 years of history across multiple buildings atop over 20 acres. Highlights include the *Urban Light* sculpture by Chris Burden (an Instagram favorite), *Levitated Mass* by Michael Heizer, and prominent works by Frida Kahlo, Wassily Kandinsky, Henri Matisse, and Claude Monet. With an illustrative permanent collection to go along with an ever-rotating array of temporary exhibits, film screenings, educational programs, and more, the museum is a beacon of culture that stands alone in the middle of the city.

◼ **TIP** → **Temporary exhibitions sometimes require tickets purchased in advance.** ✉ *5905 Wilshire Blvd., Miracle Mile* ☎ *323/857–6000* ⊕ *www.lacma.org* 🎟 *$20* ⊙ *Closed Wed.*

Petersen Automotive Museum

MUSEUM | **FAMILY** | L.A. is a mecca for car lovers, which explains the popularity of this museum with a collection of more than 300 automobiles and other motorized vehicles. But you don't have to be a gearhead to appreciate the Petersen; there's plenty of fascinating history here for all to enjoy. Learn how Los Angeles grew up around its freeways, how cars evolve from the design phase to the production line, and how automobiles have influenced film and television. To see how the vehicles, many of them quite rare, are preserved and maintained, take the 90-minute tour of the basement-level

Vault (young kids aren't permitted in the Vault, but they'll find plenty to keep them occupied throughout the museum). ✉ *6060 Wilshire Blvd., Mid-Wilshire* ☎ *323/964–6331* ⊕ *www.petersen.org* 🎟 *From $16.*

⍟ Restaurants

★ Meals by Genet

$$ | ETHIOPIAN | In a tucked-away stretch along Fairfax Avenue is Little Ethiopia, where Angelenos of all stripes flock for the African country's signatures like *tibs*, *wat*, and *kitfo*. And while there is a plethora of Ethiopian options, no one does the cuisine justice quite like Meals by Genet. **Known for:** authentic Ethiopian cuisine; jovial atmosphere; unreal tibs. ⑤ *Average main: $20* ✉ *1053 S. Fairfax Ave., Mid-Wilshire* ☎ *323/938–9304* ⊕ *www.mealsbygenetla.com* ⊙ *Closed Mon.–Wed.*

Sky's Gourmet Tacos

$ | MEXICAN | If you're searching for some of the spiciest and most succulent tacos in L.A., look no further than Sky's. This quaint taco joint offers up beef, chicken, turkey, seafood, and vegan options that will leave your mouth on fire and your belly full in all the best ways possible. **Known for:** tacos; spices; jovial atmosphere. ⑤ *Average main: $10* ✉ *5303 Pico Blvd., Mid-Wilshire* ☎ *323/932–6253* ⊕ *www.skysgourmettacos.com.*

Koreatown

⍟ Restaurants

The Boiling Crab

$$ | SEAFOOD | FAMILY | Put on your bib and prepare to get messy, because this crab shack is not for stodgy eaters. Choices of blue, Dungeness, snow, king, and southern king, are brought out in plastic bags where you can rip, tear, twist, and yank the meaty goodness out of their shells. **Known for:** giant crab legs; unfussy environment; long lines. ⑤ *Average main:*

$20 ✉ *3377 Wilshire Blvd., Suite 115, Koreatown* ☎ *213/389–2722* ⊕ *www.theboilingcrab.com* ⊙ *Lunch on weekends only* Ⓜ *Wilshire/Normandie Station.*

Guelaguetza

$$ | MEXICAN | FAMILY | A classic L.A. Mexican eatery, Guelaguetza serves the complex but not overpoweringly spicy cooking of Oaxaca, one of Mexico's most renowned culinary capitals. Inside, you'll find a largely Spanish-speaking clientele bobbing their heads to nightly jazz and marimba while wolfing down the restaurant's specialty: the moles. **Known for:** salsa-covered chorizo; chili-marinated pork; family-owned restaurant. ⑤ *Average main: $15* ✉ *3014 W. Olympic Blvd., Koreatown* ☎ *213/427–0608* ⊕ *www.ilovemole.com.*

★ Here's Looking At You

$$$ | ECLECTIC | Hawaiian and Asian-inspired dishes can be found on this menu featuring veggie, meat, poultry, and seafood. The environment is eclectic, as is the food, with signature dishes like blood cake with duck egg and pork belly with *nam jim.* **Known for:** pie; exceptional cocktails; inventive dishes. ⑤ *Average main: $25* ✉ *3901 W. 6th St., Koreatown* ☎ *213/568–3573* ⊕ *www.hereslookingatyoula.com.*

Kobawoo House

$$ | KOREAN | FAMILY | Nestled into a dingy strip mall, this Korean powerhouse is given away by the lines of locals waiting outside. Once inside, scents of grilled meats and kimchi immediately fill your nostrils. **Known for:** kalbi beef; long lines; cheap eats. ⑤ *Average main: $17* ✉ *698 S. Vermont Ave., Koreatown* ☎ *213/389–7300* ⊕ *www.kobawoola.com* Ⓜ *Wilshire/Vermont.*

Hotels

Hotel Normandie

$ | HOTEL | Originally built in 1926, this Renaissance Revival gem has been renovated to today's standards and is now a hip and not-so-pricey spot to post up in the ever-booming center of Koreatown.

Pros: free wine happy hour; complimentary breakfast; cheap prices. **Cons:** feels dated; tiny bathrooms. $ *Rooms from: $190* ⊠ *605 Normandie Ave., Koreatown* ☎ *213/388–8138* ⊕ *www.hotelnormandiela.com* ⮑ *92 rooms.*

The Line

$$ | **HOTEL** | This boutique hotel pays homage to its Koreatown address with dynamic dining concepts and a hidden karaoke speakeasy. **Pros:** on-site bikes to explore the area; cheery staff; houses the Houston Brothers' '80s-themed bar. **Cons:** expensive parking; lobby club crowds public spaces; far from parts of the city you may want to explore. $ *Rooms from: $250* ⊠ *3515 Wilshire Blvd., Koreatown* ☎ *213/381–7411* ⊕ *www.thelinehotel.com* ⮑ *384 rooms* ⊗ *No meals* Ⓜ *Wilshire/Normandie Station.*

Nightlife

Dan Sung Sa

BARS/PUBS | Step through the curtained entrance and back in time to 1970s Korea at Dan Sung Sa, which gained wider popularity after Anthony Bourdain paid a visit. At this quirky time-capsule bar, wood-block menus feature roughly 100 small eats. You'll see much that looks familiar, but fortune favors the bold. Take a chance on corn cheese, or try the *makgeolli*: a boozy Korean rice drink you sip from a bowl. It pairs perfectly with good conversation and snacking all night long. ⊠ *3317 W. 6th St., Koreatown* ☎ *213/487–9100* Ⓜ *Wilshire/Vermont Station.*

★ HMS Bounty

BARS/PUBS | This super-kitschy nautical-themed bar in the heart of Koreatown offers drink specials and food at prices that will make you swoon. Make sure you speak to the grandmotherly Korean bartender—introduce yourself once and she'll never forget your name and order. ⊠ *3357 Wilshire Blvd., Koreatown* ☎ *213/385–7275* ⊕ *www.thehmsbounty.com* Ⓜ *Wilshire/Normandy Station.*

The Prince

BARS/PUBS | *Mad Men* and *New Girl* both had multiple scenes filmed in this Old Hollywood relic, which dates back to the early 1900s. The Prince is trimmed with vintage fabric wallpaper and bedecked with a stately mahogany bar; the grand piano waits in the wings. Squire lamps punctuate red leather booths where you can enjoy Korean fare and standard cocktails, wine, and beer. Whatever you do, get the deep-fried chicken. ⊠ *3198 W. 7th St., Koreatown* ☎ *213/389–1586* Ⓜ *Wilshire/Vermont Station.*

Shopping

Aroma Spa

SPA/BEAUTY | It's not difficult to find amazing spa experiences throughout Koreatown. Most places will offer up standard scrubs, hot and cold baths, dry and wet saunas, and more. Aroma takes things to another level as the spa is just the centerpiece of an entire entertainment complex. Spa services include all the traditional treatments, but when you're done getting pampered, the rest of the facility includes a gym, a swimming pool, restaurants, and a state-of-the-art golf driving range. ⊠ *3680 Wilshire Blvd., Koreatown* ☎ *213/387–2111* ⊕ *www.aromaresort.com.*

Wi Spa

SPA/BEAUTY | Koreatown is filled with endless spa experiences, but there are a few that rise above the rest. Wi Spa is a 24/7 wonderland of treatments that includes hot and cold baths, unique sauna rooms, and floors for men, women, or co-ed family spa fun. Signature sauna rooms vary from intense 231-degree thermotherapy to salt-enriched stations and specialty clay imported from Korea. Just remember, Korean spas are not for the shy at heart—you will be nude, you will get scrubbed, and you will feel like a million bucks after. ⊠ *2700 Wilshire Blvd., Koreatown* ☎ *213/487–2700* ⊕ *www.wispausa.com.*

Culver City

Restaurants

★ n/naka

$$$$ | JAPANESE | Chef's Table star Niki Nakayama helms this *omakase* (chef-selected) fine-dining establishment. Small and intimate, any given night will feature sashimi with *kanpachi*, sea bass with *uni* butter, or Myazaki Wagyu beef. **Known for:** three-hour meals; excellent sake pairings. ⑤ *Average main: $185* ✉ *3455 Overland Ave., Culver City* ☎ *310/836–6252* ⊕ *www.n-naka.com* ⊙ *Closed Sun. and Mon.*

Vespertine

$$$$ | AMERICAN | Vespertine isn't a restaurant. It's a multisensory event. **Known for:** elaborate tasting menu; modern design; unique everything. ⑤ *Average main: $250* ✉ *3599 Hayden Ave., Culver City* ☎ *323/320–4023* ⊕ *vespertine.la* ⊙ *Closed Sun. and Mon.*

Downtown

If there's one thing Angelenos love, it's a makeover, and city planners have put the wheels in motion for a dramatic revitalization. Downtown is both glamorous and gritty and is an example of Los Angeles's complexity as a whole. There's a dizzying variety of experiences not to be missed here if you're curious about the artistic, historic, ethnic, or sports-loving sides of L.A.

Downtown Los Angeles isn't just one neighborhood: it's a cluster of pedestrian-friendly enclaves where you can sample an eclectic mix of flavors, wander through world-class museums, and enjoy great live performances or sports events.

Sights

★ Angels Flight Railway

HISTORIC SITE | The turn-of-the-20th-century funicular, dubbed "the shortest railway in the world," operated between 1901 and 1969, when it was dismantled to make room for an urban renewal project. Almost 30 years later, Angels Flight returned with its original orange-and-black wooden cable cars hauling travelers up a 298-foot incline from Hill Street to the fountain-filled Watercourt at California Plaza. Your reward is a stellar view of the neighborhood. Tickets are $1 each way, but you can buy a souvenir round-trip ticket for $2 if you want something to take home with you. ✉ *351 S. Hill St., between 3rd and 4th Sts., Downtown* ☎ *213/626–1901* ⊕ *www.angelsflight.org.*

Bradbury Building

BUILDING | Stunning wrought-iron railings, ornate plaster moldings, pink marble staircases, a birdcage elevator, and a skylighted atrium that rises almost 50 feet—it's easy to see why the Bradbury Building leaves visitors awestruck. Designed in 1893 by a novice architect who drew his inspiration from a science-fiction story and a conversation with his dead brother via Ouija board, the office building was originally the site of turn-of-the-20th-century sweatshops, but now it houses a variety of businesses. Scenes from *Blade Runner* and *Chinatown* were filmed here, which means there's often a barrage of tourists snapping photos. Visits are limited to the lobby and the first-floor landing. ■TIP→ **Historic Downtown walking tours hosted by the L.A. Conservancy cost $15 and include the Bradbury Building.** ✉ *304 S. Broadway, Downtown* ☎ *213/626–1893* ⊕ *www.laconservancy.org/locations/bradbury-building* Ⓜ *Pershing Square Station.*

★ The Broad Museum

MUSEUM | The talk of Los Angeles's art world when it opened in 2015, this museum in an intriguing, honeycomb-looking building was created by philanthropists Eli and Edythe Broad (rhymes with "road") to showcase their stunning private collection of contemporary art, amassed over five decades and still growing. With upward of 2,000 pieces by more than 200 artists, the collection has in-depth representations of the work of such prominent names as Jean Michel Basquiat, Jeff Koons, Ed Ruscha, Cindy Sherman, Cy Twombly, Kara Walker, and Christopher Wool. The "veil and vault" design of the main building integrates gallery space and storage space (visitors can glimpse the latter through a window in the stairwell): the veil refers to the fiberglass, concrete, and steel exterior; the vault is the concrete base. Temporary exhibits and works from the permanent collection are arranged in the small first-floor rooms and in the more expansive third floor of the museum, so you can explore everything in a few hours. Next door to the Broad is a small plaza with olive trees and seating, as well as the museum restaurant, Otium. Admission to the museum is free, but book timed tickets in advance to guarantee entry. ⊠ 221 S. Grand Ave., Downtown ☎ 213/232–6200 ⊕ www.thebroad.org ☑ Free ⊘ Closed Mon.

California African American Museum
MUSEUM | With more than 4,500 historical artifacts, this museum showcases contemporary art of the African diaspora. Artists represented here include Betye Saar, Charles Haywood, and June Edmonds. The museum has a research library with more than 6,000 books available for public use. ■ TIP→ If possible, visit on a Sunday, when there's almost always a diverse lineup of speakers and performances. ⊠ 600 State Dr., Exposition Park ☎ 213/744–2084 ⊕ www.caamuseum. org ☑ Free; parking $12 ⊘ Closed Mon. Ⓜ Expo/Vermont Station.

California Science Center
MUSEUM | FAMILY | You're bound to see excited kids running up to the dozens of interactive exhibits here that illustrate the prevalence of science in everyday life.

Clustered in different "worlds," the center keeps young guests busy for hours. They can design their own buildings and learn how to make them earthquake-proof; watch Tess, the dramatic 50-foot animatronic star of the exhibit Body Works, demonstrate how the body's organs work together; and ride a bike across a trapeze wire three stories high in the air. One of the exhibits in the Air and Space section shows how astronauts Pete Conrad and Dick Gordon made it to outer space in the Gemini 11 capsule in 1966; also here is NASA's massive space shuttle Endeavor, located in the Samuel Oschin Pavilion, for which a timed ticket is needed to visit. The IMAX theater screens science-related large-format films. ⊠ 700 Exposition Park Dr., Exposition Park ☎ 323/724–3623 ⊕ www.californiasciencecenter.org ☑ Permanent exhibits free; fees for some attractions, special exhibits, and IMAX screenings vary.

Cathedral of Our Lady of the Angels
RELIGIOUS SITE | A half block from Frank Gehry's curvaceous Walt Disney Concert Hall sits the austere Cathedral of Our Lady of the Angels—a spiritual draw as well as an architectural attraction. Controversy surrounded Spanish architect José Rafael Moneo's unconventional design for the seat of the Archdiocese of Los Angeles. But judging from the swarms of visitors and the standing-room-only holiday masses, the church has carved out a niche for itself in Downtown L.A.

The plaza in front is glaringly bright on sunny days, though a children's play garden with bronze animals mitigates the starkness somewhat. Head underground to wander the mausoleum's mazelike white-marble corridors. Free guided tours start at the entrance fountain at 1 pm on weekdays. ■ TIP→ There's plenty of underground visitors parking; the vehicle entrance is on Hill Street. ⊠ 555 W. Temple St., Downtown ☎ 213/680–5200 ⊕ www.olacathedral.org ☑ Free Ⓜ Civic Center/Grand Park.

Sights ▼

Restaurants ▼

Hotels ▼

Chinatown

NEIGHBORHOOD | Smaller than San Francisco's Chinatown, this neighborhood near Union Station still represents a slice of East Asian life. Sidewalks are usually jammed with tourists, locals, and residents hustling from shop to shop picking up goods, spices, and trinkets from small shops and miniplazas that line the street. Although some longtime establishments have closed in recent years, the area still pulses with its founding culture. During Chinese New Year, giant dragons snake down the street. And, of course, there are the many restaurants and quick-bite cafés specializing in Chinese feasts. In recent years, a slew of hip eateries like Howlin' Ray's and Majordomo have injected the area with vibrancy.

An influx of local artists has added a spark to the neighborhood by taking up empty spaces and opening galleries along Chung King Road, a faded pedestrian passage behind the West Plaza shopping center between Hill and Yale. Also look for galleries along a little side street called Gin Ling Way on the east side of Broadway. Chinatown has its main action on North Broadway. There are several garages available for parking here that range from $5 to $10 per day. ⊠ *Bordered by the 110, 101, and 5 freeways, Downtown* ⊕ *chinatownla.com* Ⓜ *Union Station.*

El Pueblo de Los Angeles

NEIGHBORHOOD | The oldest section of the city, known as El Pueblo de Los Angeles, represents the rich Mexican heritage of L.A. It had a close shave with disintegration in the early 20th century, but key buildings were preserved, and eventually **Olvera Street,** the district's heart, was transformed into a Mexican American marketplace. Today vendors still sell puppets, leather goods, sandals, and woolen shawls from stalls lining the narrow street. You can find everything from salt and pepper shakers shaped like donkeys to gorgeous glassware and pottery.

At the beginning of Olvera Street is the Plaza, a Mexican-style park with plenty of benches and walkways shaded by a huge Moreton Bay fig tree. On weekends, mariachi bands and folkloric dance groups perform. Nearby places worth investigating include the historic Avila Adobe, the Chinese American Museum, the Plaza Firehouse Museum, and the America Tropical Interpretive Center. Exhibits at the Italian American Museum of Los Angeles chronicle the area's formerly heavy Italian presence. ⊠ *Avila Adobe/Olvera Street Visitors Center, 125 Paseo De La Plaza, Downtown* ☎ *213/628–1274* ⊕ *www.elpueblo.lacity. org* ☞ *Free for Olvera St. and guided tours; fees at some museums.*

Geffen Contemporary at MOCA

MUSEUM | The Geffen Contemporary is one of architect Frank Gehry's boldest creations. The largest of the three MOCA branches, with 40,000 square feet of exhibition space, it was once used as a police car warehouse. Works from the museum's permanent collection on display here include the artists Willem de Kooning, Franz Kline, Jackson Pollock, Mark Rothko, and Cindy Sherman. ∎**TIP→ Present your TAP metro card to get two-for-one admission.** ⊠ *152 N. Central Ave., Downtown* ☎ *213/626–6222* ⊕ *www.moca.org/exhibitions* ☞ *$12; free Thurs. 5–8 and weekends through Mar. 25* ☾ *Closed Tues.*

GRAMMY Museum

MUSEUM | The GRAMMY Museum brings the music industry to life. Throughout four floors and 30,000 square feet of space, the museum showcases rare footage of GRAMMY performances, plus rotating and interactive exhibits on award-winning musicians and the history of music. A 200-seat theater is great for live events that include screenings, lectures, interviews, and intimate music performances. ⊠ *800 W. Olympic Blvd., Downtown* ☎ *213/765–6800* ⊕ *www.grammymuseum.org* ☞ *$15* ☾ *Closed Tues.*

★ Grand Central Market

MARKET | Handmade white-corn tamales, warm olive bread, dried figs, Mexican fruit drinks. Hungry yet? This mouthwatering gathering place is the city's largest and most active food market. Treated to a makeover in 2013, Grand Central Market is now the home to various artisanal food vendors. The spot bustles nonstop with locals and visitors surveying the butcher shop's display of everything from lambs' heads to pigs' tails. Produce stalls are piled high with locally grown avocados and heirloom tomatoes. Stop by **Chiles Secos** at stall C-12 for a remarkable selection of rare chilies and spices; **Ramen Hood** at C-2, for sumptuous vegan noodles and broth; or **Sticky Rice** at stall C-5, for fantastic Thai-style chicken. Even if you don't plan on buying anything, it's a great place to browse and people-watch. ⊠ 317 S. Broadway, Downtown ☎ 213/624–2378 ⊕ www.grandcentral-market.com 🎫 Free.

L.A. Live

ARTS VENUE | The mammoth L.A. Live entertainment complex was opened in 2007 when there was little to do or see in this section of Downtown. Since its inception, this once creepy ghost town has become a major hub for sports, concerts, award shows, and more. The first things you'll notice as you emerge from the parking lot are the giant LED screens and sparkling lights, and the buzz of crowds as they head out to dinner before or after a Lakers game, movie, or live show at the Microsoft Theater. There are dozens of restaurants and eateries here, including Los Angeles favorite Katsuya, the spot for sizzling Kobe beef platters and excellent sushi (the crab rolls are not to be missed). ■ TIP→ **Park for free on weekdays from 11 am to 2 pm if you eat at one of the dozen or so restaurants here.** ⊠ 800 W. Olympic Blvd., Downtown ☎ 213/763–5483 ⊕ www.lalive.com.

Little Tokyo

NEIGHBORHOOD | One of three official Japantowns in the country—all of which are in California—Little Tokyo is blossoming again thanks to the next generation of Japanese Americans setting up small businesses. Besides dozens of sushi bars, tempura restaurants, and karaoke bars, there's a lovely garden at the Japanese American Cultural and Community Center and a renovated 1925 Buddhist temple with an ornate entrance at the Japanese American National Museum.

On 1st Street you'll find a strip of buildings from the early 1900s. Look down when you get near San Pedro Street to see the art installation called Omoide no Shotokyo ("Remembering Old Little Tokyo"). Embedded in the sidewalk are brass inscriptions naming the original businesses, quoted reminiscences from residents, and steel time lines of Japanese American history up to World War II. Nisei Week (a nisei is a second-generation Japanese American) is celebrated every August with traditional drums, dancing, a carnival, and a huge parade. ■ TIP→ **Docent-led walking tours are available the last Saturday of every month starting at 10:15 am. The cost is $15 and includes entry to the Japanese American National Museum.** ⊠ Bounded by 1st and 3rd Sts., the 101 and 110 freeways, and LA River, Downtown ⊕ www.visitlittletokyo.com Ⓜ Civic Center/Grand Park Station.

MOCA Grand Avenue

MUSEUM | The main branch of the Museum of Contemporary Art, designed by Arata Isozaki, contains underground galleries and presents elegant exhibitions. A huge Nancy Rubins sculpture fashioned from used airplane parts graces the museum's front plaza. The museum gift shop offers apothecary items, modernist ceramics, and even toys and games for children to appease any art lover. ■ TIP→ **Take advantage of the free audio tour.** ⊠ 250 S. Grand Ave.,

Downtown ☎ 213/626–6222 ⊕ www.
moca.org ✉ $15; free Thurs. 5–8
🕗 Closed Tues.

Natural History Museum of Los Angeles County

MUSEUM | FAMILY | The hot ticket at this
Beaux Arts–style museum completed in
1913 is the Dinosaur Hall, whose more
than 300 fossils include adult, juvenile,
and baby skeletons of the fearsome
Tyrannosaurus rex. The Discovery Center
lets kids and curious grown-ups touch
real animal pelts, and the Insect Zoo
gets everyone up close and personal
with the white-eyed assassin bug and
other creepy crawlers. A massive hall
displays dioramas of animals in their
natural habitats. Also look for pre-Columbian artifacts and crafts from the South
Pacific, or priceless stones in the Gem
and Mineral Hall. Outdoors, the 3½-acre
Nature Gardens shelter native plant and
insect species and contain an expansive
edible garden. ■ TIP➔ Don't miss out on
the Dino lab, where you can watch pale-
ontologists unearth and clean real fossils.
✉ 900 W. Exposition Blvd., Exposition
Park ☎ 213/763–3466 ⊕ www.nhm.org
✉ $15.

Orpheum Theatre

ARTS VENUE | Opened in 1926, the opu-
lent Orpheum Theatre played host to live
attractions including classic comedians,
burlesque dancers, jazz greats like
Lena Horne, Ella Fitzgerald, and Duke
Ellington, and later on rock-and-roll
performers such as Little Richard. After
extensive restorations, the Orpheum
once again revealed a stunning
white-marble lobby, majestic auditorium
with fleur-de-lis panels, and two dazzling
chandeliers. A thick red velvet and gold-
trimmed curtain opens at showtime, and
a white Wurlitzer pipe organ (one of the
last remaining organs of its kind from
the silent movie era) is at the ready. The
original 1926 rooftop neon sign again
shines brightly, signaling a new era for
this theater. Today the theater plays host
to live concerts, comedy shows, and
movie screenings. ✉ 842 S. Broadway,
Downtown ☎ 877/677–4386 ⊕ www.
laorpheum.com.

Richard J. Riordan Central Library

LIBRARY | The nation's third-largest public
library, the handsome Richard J. Riordan
Central Library was designed in 1926
by Bertram Goodhue. Restored to their
pristine condition, a pyramid tower and a
torch symbolizing the "light of learning"
crown the building. The Cook rotunda
on the second floor features murals by
Dean Cornwell depicting the history of
California, and the Tom Bradley Wing,
named for another mayor, has a soaring
eight-story atrium.

The library offers frequent special exhibits, plus a small café where you can refuel. Don't ignore the gift shop, which is
loaded with unique items for readers and
writers. Free docent walking tours are
offered Monday through Friday at 12:30,
Saturday at 11 and 2, and Sunday at 2. An
Art-in-the-Garden tour is on Saturdays at
12:30 pm. A self-guided tour map is also
available on the library's website. ✉ 630
W. 5th St., Downtown ☎ 213/228–7000
⊕ www.lapl.org ✉ Free.

★ Walt Disney Concert Hall

CONCERTS | One of the architectural won-
ders of Los Angeles, the 2,265-seat hall
is a sculptural monument of gleaming,
curved steel designed by Frank Gehry.
It's part of a complex that includes a public park, gardens, shops, and two outdoor
amphitheaters, one of them atop the
concert hall. The acoustically superlative
venue is the home of the city's premier
orchestra, the Los Angeles Philharmonic,
whose music director, Gustavo Dudamel,
is an international celebrity in his own
right. The orchestra's season runs from
late September to early June, before it
heads to the Hollywood Bowl for the
summer. Attached to the hall is Patina,
an exquisite fine-dining French restaurant
that's the perfect date-night spot for
predinner shows. ■ TIP➔ Free 60-minute

guided tours are offered on most days, and there are self-guided audio tours. ⌧ *111 S. Grand Ave., Downtown* ☎ *323/850–2000* ⊕ *www.laphil.org* ✉ *Tours free.*

Union Station

HISTORIC SITE | Even if you don't plan on traveling by train anywhere, head here to soak up the ambience of a great rail station. Envisioned by John and Donald Parkinson, the architects who also designed the grand City Hall, the 1939 masterpiece combines Spanish Colonial Revival and art-deco elements that have retained their classic warmth and quality. The waiting hall's commanding scale and enormous chandeliers have provided the backdrop for countless scenes in films, TV shows, and music videos. Recently added to the majesty are the Imperial Western Beer Company and the Streamliner, two bars that pay homage to the station's original architecture while serving homemade brews and inventive classic cocktails. ■**TIP→ Walking tours of Union Station are on Saturday at 10 and cost $15.** ⌧ *800 N. Alameda St., Downtown* ⊕ *www.unionstationla.com.*

Restaurants

★ Bavel

$$$$ | **MIDDLE EASTERN** | Fans of Bestia have been lining up for stellar Mediterranean cuisine at this Arts District hot spot, which is owned by the same restaurateurs. Rose gold stools give way to marble tabletops as the open kitchen bangs out hummus and baba ghanoush spreads, along with flatbreads and lamb neck shawarma. **Known for:** Mediterranean cuisine; sceney atmosphere; great vibe. ⑤ *Average main: $40* ⌧ *500 Mateo St., Downtown* ☎ *213/232–4966* ⊕ *baveldtla.com.*

Bottega Louie

$$$ | **ITALIAN** | A Downtown dining staple, this lively Italian restaurant and gourmet market features open spaces, stark white walls, and majestic floor-to-ceiling windows. If the wait is too long at this no-reservations eatery, you can sip on Prosecco and nibble on pastries at the bar. **Known for:** mouthwatering chicken Parm; one-of-a-kind portobello fries. ⑤ *Average main: $25* ⌧ *700 S. Grand Ave., Downtown* ☎ *213/802–1470* ⊕ *www.bottegalouie.com.*

★ Broken Spanish

$$$$ | **MEXICAN FUSION** | Prepare for a taste explosion at this modern Mexican restaurant. Every dish on the menu is packed with flavor in ways you wouldn't think are possible. **Known for:** modern Mexican; taste explosions; super-friendly staff. ⑤ *Average main: $35* ⌧ *1050 S. Flower St., Downtown* ☎ *213/749–1460* ⊕ *brokenspanish.com.*

★ Cole's French Dip

$ | **AMERICAN** | There's a fight in Los Angeles over who created the French dip sandwich. The first contender is Cole's, whose sign on the door says it's the originator of the salty, juicy, melt-in-your-mouth meats. ⑤ *Average main: $10* ⌧ *118 E. 6th St., Downtown* ☎ *213/622–4090* ⊕ *www.213hospitality.com/coles.*

Guerrilla Tacos

$ | **MEXICAN FUSION** | What started as a food truck serving gourmet tacos has turned into a brick-and-mortar that also has an excellent (and cheap) bar. East L.A. native chef Wes Avila fires up some of the most inventive tacos in the city—sweet potato with almond chili and feta or the Baja fried cod with chipotle crema. **Known for:** gourmet tacos; cheap drinks; long lines. ⑤ *Average main: $11* ⌧ *2000 E. 7th St., Downtown* ☎ *213/375–3300* ⊕ *www.guerrillatacos.com.*

★ Howlin' Ray's

$$ | **SOUTHERN** | **FAMILY** | Don't let the hour-long waits deter you—if you want the best Nashville fried chicken in L.A., Howlin' Ray's is worth the effort. Right in the middle of Chinatown, this tiny chicken joint consists of a few bar seats, a few side tables, and a kitchen that sizzles as staff yell out "yes, chef" with each incoming order. **Known for:** spicy fried chicken; classic Southern sides. $ *Average main: $15* ✉ *727 N. Broadway, Suite 128, Downtown* ☎ *213/935–8399* ⊕ *www.howlinrays.com* ◷ *Closed Mon.*

★ Majordomo

$$$$ | ECLECTIC | You would never just stumble upon this out-of-the-way spot in Chinatown, but world-famous celeb chef David Chang likes it that way. This is a dining destination, and it's worth the trip. **Known for:** minimal design; chuck short rib with raclette; rice-based drinks. $ *Average main: $40* ✉ *1725 Naud St., Downtown* ☎ *323/545–4880* ⊕ *www. majordomo.la.*

★ Philippe the Original

$ | AMERICAN | FAMILY | First opened in 1908, Philippe's is one of L.A.'s oldest restaurants and claims to be the originator of the French dip sandwich. While the debate continues around the city, one thing is certain: the dips made with beef, pork, ham, lamb, or turkey on a freshly baked roll stand the test of time. **Known for:** 50¢ coffee; communal tables; post–Dodgers game eats. $ *Average main: $8* ✉ *1001 N. Alameda St., Downtown* ☎ *213/628–3781* ⊕ *www.philippes.com.*

71Above

$$$$ | ECLECTIC | As its name suggests, this sky-high dining den sits on the 71st floor, 950 feet above ground level. With that elevation come the most stunning views of any restaurant in L.A., and the food comes close to matching it. **Known for:** sky-high views; fine dining. $ *Average main: $39* ✉ *633 W. 5th St., 71st fl., Downtown* ☎ *213/712–2683* ⊕ *www.71above.com* Ⓜ *Pershing Square Station.*

Sushi Gen

$$ | JAPANESE | Consistently rated one of the top sushi spots in L.A., Sushi Gen continues to dole out the freshest and tastiest fish in town. Sit at the elongated bar and get to know the sushi

masters while they prepare your lunch. **Known for:** chef recommendations; limited seating; great lunch specials. $ *Average main: $20* ✉ *422 E. 2nd St., Downtown* ☎ *213/617–0552* ⊕ *www. sushigen-dtla.com* ◷ *Closed Sun. and Mon. No lunch Sat.*

Hotels

Ace Hotel Downtown Los Angeles

$$ | HOTEL | The L.A. edition of this bohemian-chic hipster haven is at once a hotel, theater, bar, and poolside lounge, housed in the gorgeous Spanish Gothic–style United Artists building in the heart of Downtown. **Pros:** lively rooftop lounge/pool area, aptly named Upstairs; gorgeous building and views; heart of Downtown. **Cons:** expensive parking rates compared to nightly rates ($36); some kinks in the service; compact rooms. $ *Rooms from: $239* ✉ *929 S. Broadway, Downtown* ☎ *213/623–3233* ⊕ *www. acehotel.com/losangeles* ⇆ *183 rooms* ⦿❚ *No meals.*

★ Freehand Los Angeles

$ | HOTEL | Part hotel, part hostel, the Freehand is one of the newest hotels in Downtown Los Angeles and also one of the coolest. **Pros:** range of rooms from lofts to bunk beds; active social scene; great rooftop pool and bar. **Cons:** sketchy area at night around the hotel; free lobby Wi-Fi attracts dubious crowds at times. $ *Rooms from: $100* ✉ *416 W. 8th St., Downtown* ☎ *213/612–0021* ⊕ *freehand-hotels.com/los-angeles* ⇆ *59 shared rooms, 167 private rooms* ⦿❚ *No meals* Ⓜ *Pershing Square.*

Hotel Figueroa

$$ | HOTEL | After years of renovation, the Hotel Figueroa has finally made its return to the Downtown hospitality scene, and it was well worth the wait. **Pros:** a short walk to Nokia Theatre, L.A. Live, and the convention center; great poolside bar; in-room iPads and complimentary minibar snacks. **Cons:** the area can be sketchy

at night; expensive parking ($45/night). [$] *Rooms from: $200* ✉ *939 S. Figueroa St., Downtown* ☎ *866/734–6018* ⊕ *www. hotelfigueroa.com* ↻ *268 rooms* ⧈ *No meals* Ⓜ *Olympic/Figueroa.*

InterContinental Los Angeles Downtown

$$ | **HOTEL** | This five-star addition to the Downtown L.A. scene impresses with views, an enormous gym, dining, and an outdoor pool. **Pros:** best views; incredible F&B outlets; top-rate service. **Cons:** too big and impersonal; busy and tricky intersection. [$] *Rooms from: $300* ✉ *900 Wilshire Blvd., Downtown* ☎ *213/688–7777* ⊕ *dtla.intercontinental. com* ↻ *889 rooms* ⧈ *No meals* Ⓜ *7th Street/Metro Center.*

Millennium Biltmore Hotel

$$ | **HOTEL** | As the local headquarters of John F. Kennedy's 1960 presidential campaign and the location of some of the earliest Academy Awards ceremonies, this Downtown treasure, with its gilded 1923 Beaux Arts design, exudes ambience and history. **Pros:** 24-hour business center; tiled indoor pool and steam room; multimillion-dollar refurbishment in 2017. **Cons:** pricey valet parking ($45); standard rooms are compact. [$] *Rooms from: $200* ✉ *506 S. Grand Ave., Downtown* ☎ *213/624–1011, 866/866–8086* ⊕ *www. millenniumhotels.com* ↻ *683 rooms* ⧈ *No meals* Ⓜ *Pershing Square.*

The NoMad Hotel

$$ | **HOTEL** | This stunningly refurbished property used to house the Bank of Italy and touches of the old bank can still be seen throughout—most notably in the lobby bathrooms that are cut out of the original vault. **Pros:** freestanding tubs; smart TVs in rooms; 24-hour gym. **Cons:** sketchy area at night; expensive parking ($48/night). [$] *Rooms from: $250* ✉ *649 S. Olive St., Downtown* ☎ *213/358–0000* ⊕ *www.thenomadhotel.com/los-angeles* ↻ *241 rooms* ⧈ *No meals* Ⓜ *7th Street/ Metro Center.*

Westin Bonaventure Hotel and Suites

$$ | **HOTEL** | **FAMILY** | Step inside the futuristic lobby of L.A.'s largest hotel to be greeted by fountains, an indoor lake and track, and 12 glass elevators leading up to the historic rooms of this 35-story property. Color-coded hotel floors help newcomers navigate the hotel, which takes up an entire city block. **Pros:** spa with shiatsu massage; revolving rooftop lounge; many on-site restaurants. **Cons:** massive hotel might feel too corporate; mazelike lobby and public areas. [$] *Rooms from: $250* ✉ *404 S. Figueroa St., Downtown* ☎ *213/624–1000* ⊕ *westin.marriott. com* ↻ *1493 rooms* ⧈ *No meals.*

Nightlife

Blue Whale

MUSIC CLUBS | This unassuming jazz club in Little Tokyo caters to a serious crowd, bringing progressive and modern jazz to the stage. Although the venue is focused on the music (yes, you may get shushed for talking—that's how small it is), there is a kitchen and bar for snacks and drinks. The club is on the third floor of Weller Court, and the cover runs around $10 to $20. ✉ *Weller Court Plaza, 123 Astronaut E. S. Onizuka St., Suite 301, Downtown* ☎ *213/620–0908* ⊕ *www. bluewhalemusic.com.*

Broadway Bar

BARS/PUBS | This watering-hole-meets-dive sits in a flourishing section of Broadway (neighbors include the swank Ace Hotel). Bartenders mix creative cocktails while DJs spin tunes nightly. The two-story space includes a smoking balcony overlooking the street. The crowd is often dressed to impress. ✉ *830 S. Broadway, Downtown* ☎ *213/614–9909* ⊕ *213hospitality.com/broadwaybar.*

★ Golden Gopher

BARS/PUBS | Craft cocktails, beers on tap, an outdoor smoking patio, and retro video games—this bar in the heart of Downtown is not to be missed. With one of the oldest liquor licenses in Los Angeles (issued in 1905), the Golden Gopher is the only bar in Los Angeles with an on-site liquor store for to-go orders—just in case you want to buy another bottle before you head home. ✉ *417 W. 8th St., Downtown* ☎ *213/614–8001* ⊕ *213hospitality.com/project/goldengopher.*

La Cita

DANCE CLUBS | This dive bar may not look like much, but it more than makes up for it with an interesting mix of barflies, urban hipsters, and reasonable drink prices. Friday and Saturday nights, DJs mix Top 40 hits and a tiny dance floor packs in the crowd. For those more interested in drinking and socializing, head to the back patio where a TV plays local sports. Every day has a differently themed happy hour—hip-hop happy hour on Wednesday or rockabilly happy hour on Thursday. Specials vary from $3 Tecates to free pizza. ✉ *336 S. Hill St., Downtown* ☎ *213/687–7111* ⊕ *www.lacitabar.com* Ⓜ *Pershing Square Station.*

Love Song Bar

BARS/PUBS | Lovers of T. S. Eliot and vinyl will find themselves instantly at home inside this cozy establishment named after Eliot's "The Love Song of J. Alfred Prufrock." When not pouring drinks, bartenders often act as DJs, playing records (the best of the '60s through the '80s) in their entirety. As it's housed inside the Regent Theater, the cozy nature of the place can be disrupted when there's a concert scheduled. For those with an appetite, fantastic food can be ordered from the pizza parlor next door—naturally, it's called Prufrock's. ✉ *446 S. Main St., Downtown* ☎ *323/284–5661.*

Redwood Bar & Grill

BARS/PUBS | If you're looking for a place with potent drinks and a good burger, this kitschy bar fits the bill perfectly. Known today as the "pirate bar" because of its nautical decor, the place dates back to the 1940s, when it was rumored to attract mobsters, politicians, and journalists due to its proximity to City Hall, the Hall of Justice, and the original location of the *Los Angeles Times*. There's nightly music from local rock bands, though it comes with a cover charge. ✉ *316 W. 2nd St., Downtown* ☎ *213/680–2600* ⊕ *www.theredwoodbar.com.*

★ Resident

MUSIC CLUBS | Catch a lineup of indie tastemakers inside this converted industrial space, or hang outdoors in the beer garden while trying bites from on-site food truck KTCHN (on cooler evenings you can congregate around the fire pits). A wide variety of draft beers and a specially curated cocktail program are available inside at the bar or at the trailer bar outside. ✉ *428 S. Hewitt St., Downtown* ☎ *213/628–7503* ⊕ *www.residentdtla.com.*

Seven Grand

BARS/PUBS | The hunting lodge vibe makes you feel like you need a whiskey in hand—luckily, this Downtown establishment stocks more than 700 of them. Attracting whiskey novices and connoisseurs, the bartenders here are more than willing to help you make a selection. Live jazz and blues bands play every night, so even if you're not a big drinker there's still some appeal (although you're definitely missing out). For a more intimate setting, try the on-site **Bar Jackalope,** a bar within a bar, which has a "whiskey tasting library" specializing in Japanese varieties and seats only 18. ✉ *515 W. 7th St., 2nd fl., Downtown* ☎ *213/614–0737* ⊕ *www.sevengrandbars.com* Ⓜ *7th Street/Metro Center.*

★ The Varnish

BARS/PUBS | Beeline through the dining room of Cole's to find an unassuming door that leads to this small, dimly lit bar within a bar. Wooden booths line the walls, candles flicker, and live jazz is performed Sunday through Wednesday. The bartenders take their calling to heart and shake and stir some of the finest cocktails in the city. Those who don't have a drink of choice can list their wants ("gin-based and sweet," "strong whiskey and herbaceous") and be served a custom cocktail. Be warned: patrons requiring quick drinks will want to go elsewhere—perfection takes time. ⊠ *118 E. 6th St., Downtown* ☎ *213/265–7089* ⊕ *213hospitality.com/the-varnish.*

Performing Arts

Ahmanson Theatre

THEATER | The largest of L.A.'s Center Group's three theaters, the 2,100-seat Ahmanson Theatre presents larger-scale classic revivals, dramas, musicals, and comedies like *Into the Woods,* which are either going to or coming from Broadway and the West End. The ambience is a theater lover's delight. ⊠ *135 N. Grand Ave., Downtown* ☎ *213/628–2772* ⊕ *www.centertheatregroup.org* Ⓜ *Civic Center/Grand Park Station.*

★ Dorothy Chandler Pavilion

CONCERTS | Though half a century old, this theater maintains the glamour of its early years, richly decorated with crystal chandeliers, classical theatrical drapes, and a 24-karat gold dome. Part of the Los Angeles Music Center, this pavilion is home to the L.A. Opera though a large portion of programming is made up of dance and ballet performances as well. Ticket holders can attend free talks that take place an hour before opera performances. ■ **TIP→ Reservations for the talks aren't required, but it's wise to arrive early as space is limited.** ⊠ *135 N. Grand Ave., Downtown* ☎ *213/972–0711* ⊕ *www. musiccenter.org or www.dorothychandlerpavilion.net.*

Microsoft Theater

CONCERTS | The Microsoft Theater is host to a variety of concerts and big-name awards shows—the Emmys, American Music Awards, BET Awards, and the ESPYs. This theater and the surrounding L.A. Live complex are a draw for those looking for a fun night out. The building's emphasis on acoustics and versatile seating arrangements means that all 7,100 seats are good, whether you're at an intimate Neil Young concert or the People's Choice Awards. Outside, the L.A. Live complex hosts restaurants and attractions, including the GRAMMY Museum, to keep patrons entertained before and after shows (though it's open whether or not there's a performance). ⊠ *777 Chick Hearn Ct., Downtown* ☎ *213/763–6030* ⊕ *www.microsofttheater.com.*

The REDCAT (Roy and Edna Disney/Cal Arts Theater)

DANCE | Located inside the Walt Disney Concert Hall, this 288-seat theater serves as a space for innovative performance and visual art in addition to film screenings and literary events. The gallery features changing art installations. Tickets are reasonably priced at $25 and under for most events. ⊠ *631 W. 2nd St., Downtown* ☎ *213/237–2800* ⊕ *www. redcat.org.*

Shrine Auditorium

CONCERTS | Since opening in 1926, the auditorium has hosted nearly every major awards show at one point or another, including the Emmys and the GRAMMYs. Today, the venue and adjacent Expo Hall hosts concerts, film premieres, award shows, pageants, and special events. The Shrine's Moorish Revival–style architecture is a spectacle all its own. ⊠ *665 W. Jefferson Blvd., Downtown* ☎ *213/748–5116* ⊕ *www.shrineauditorium.com.*

Shopping

Alchemy Works

CLOTHING | This beautifully curated shop specializes in goods by local brands including hats by Janessa Leone, jewelry by Gabriela Artigas, and bags by Clare V., much of which is decidedly contemporary and minimal. There's also an in-store Warby Parker Glass House, where shoppers can try on different styles by the affordable eyewear brand. Besides wearables, Alchemy Works also offers housewares, apothecary items, books and magazines, and more must-haves for modern design lovers. ⊠ *826 E. 3rd St., Downtown* ☎ *323/487–1497* ⊕ *www. alchemyworks.us.*

★ The Last Bookstore

BOOKS/STATIONERY | California's largest used and new book and record shop is a favorite for both book lovers and fans of a good photo op, thanks to elements like an archway created from curving towers of books, a peephole carved into the stacks, and an in-store vault devoted to horror texts. Aside from the awesome aesthetics, shoppers will love to get lost in the store's collection of affordable books, art, and music. ⊠ *453 S. Spring St., ground fl., Downtown* ☎ *213/488–0599* ⊕ *www.lastbookstorela. com* Ⓜ *Pershing Square Station.*

Pasadena Area

Although seemingly absorbed into the general Los Angeles sprawl, Pasadena is a separate and distinct city. It's best known for the Tournament of Roses, or more commonly, the Rose Bowl, seen around the world every New Year's Day. But the city has sites worth seeing year-round—from gorgeous Craftsman homes to exceptional museums, particularly the Norton Simon and the Huntington Library, Art Collections, and Botanical Gardens. Note that the Huntington and the Old Mill reside in San Marino, a wealthy, 4-square-mile residential area just over the Pasadena line.

Sights

The Gamble House

HOUSE | Built by Charles and Henry Greene in 1908, this American Arts and Crafts bungalow illustrates the incredible craftsmanship that went into early L.A. architecture. The term "bungalow" can be misleading, since the Gamble House is a huge three-story home. To wealthy Easterners such as the Gambles (as in Procter & Gamble), this type of vacation home seemed informal compared with their mansions back home. Admirers swoon over the teak staircase and cabinetry, the Greene and Greene–designed furniture, and an Emil Lange glass door. The dark exterior has broad eaves, with sleeping porches on the second floor. An hour-long, docent-led tour of the Gamble's interior will draw your eye to the exquisite details. For those who want to see more of the Greene and Greene homes, there are guided walks around the historic Arroyo Terrace neighborhood. Advance tickets are highly recommended. ◼ TIP➡ **Film buffs might recognize this as Doc Brown's house from Back to the Future.** ⊠ *4 Westmoreland Pl., Pasadena* ☎ *626/793–3334* ⊕ *www.gamblehouse. org* ▣ *$15* ◷ *Closed Mon.*

★ Huntington Library, Art Collections, and Botanical Gardens

GARDEN | If you have time for just one stop in the Pasadena area, be sure to see this sprawling estate built for railroad tycoon Henry E. Huntington in the early 1900s. Henry and his wife, Arabella (who was also his aunt by marriage), voraciously collected rare books and manuscripts, botanical specimens, and 18th-century British art. The institution they established became one of the most extraordinary cultural complexes in the world.

The library contains more than 700,000 books and 4 million manuscripts, including one of the world's biggest history of science collections.

Don't resist being lured outside into the Botanical Gardens, which extend out from the main building. The 10-acre Desert Garden has one of the world's largest groups of mature cacti and other succulents (visit on a cool morning or late afternoon). The Shakespeare Garden, meanwhile, blooms with plants mentioned in Shakespeare's works. The

Japanese Garden features an authentic ceremonial teahouse built in Kyoto in the 1960s. A waterfall flows from the teahouse to the ponds below. In the Rose Garden Tea Room, afternoon tea is served (reserve in advance). The Chinese Garden, which is among the largest outside of China, sinews around waveless pools.

The Bing Children's Garden lets tiny tots explore the ancient elements of water, fire, air, and earth. A 1¼-hour guided tour of the Botanical Gardens is led by docents at posted times, and a free brochure with a map and property highlights is available in the entrance pavilion. ✉ *1151 Oxford Rd., San Marino* ☎ *626/405–2100* ⊕ *www.huntington.org* 💲 *From $25; free admission 1st Thurs. of every month* ⊙ *Closed Tues.*

★ Norton Simon Museum

MUSEUM | As seen in the New Year's Day Tournament of Roses Parade, this low-profile brown building is one of the finest midsize museums anywhere, with a collection that spans more than 2,000 years of Western and Asian art. It all began in the 1950s when Norton Simon (Hunt-Wesson Foods, McCalls Corporation, and Canada Dry) started collecting works by Degas, Renoir, Gauguin, and Cézanne. His collection grew to include works by Old Masters and impressionists, modern works from Europe, and Indian and Southeast Asian art.

Today the Norton Simon Museum is richest in works by Rembrandt, Picasso, and, most of all, Degas.

Head down to the bottom floor to see temporary exhibits and phenomenal Southeast Asian and Indian sculptures and artifacts, where pieces like a Ban Chiang black ware vessel date back to well before 1000 BC. Don't miss a living-artwork outdoors: the garden, conceived by noted Southern California landscape designer Nancy Goslee Power. The tranquil pond was inspired by Monet's

gardens at Giverny. ✉ *411 W. Colorado Blvd., Pasadena* ☎ *626/449–6840* ⊕ *www.nortonsimon.org* 💲 *$15; free 1st Fri. of month 5–8* ⊙ *Closed Tues.*

The Old Mill (El Molino Viejo)

BUILDING | Built in 1816 as a gristmill for the San Gabriel Mission, the mill is one of the last remaining examples in Southern California of Spanish Mission architecture. The thick adobe walls and textured ceiling rafters give the interior a sense of quiet strength. Be sure to step into the back room, now a gallery with rotating quarterly exhibits. Outside, a chipped section of the mill's exterior reveals the layers of brick, ground seashell paste, and ox blood used to hold the structure together. The surrounding gardens are reason enough to visit, with a flower-decked arbor and old sycamores and oaks. In summer the Capitol Ensemble performs in the garden. ✉ *1120 Old Mill Rd., San Marino* ☎ *626/449–5458* ⊕ *www.old-mill.org* 💲 *Free* ⊙ *Closed Mon.*

Old Town Pasadena

NEIGHBORHOOD | This 22-block historic district contains a vibrant mix of restored 19th-century brick buildings interspersed with contemporary architecture. Chain stores have muscled in, but there are still some homegrown shops, plenty of tempting cafés and restaurants, and a bustling beer scene. In recent years, a vibrant Asian food scene has popped up in the vicinity as well. In the evening and on weekends, the streets are packed with people. Old Town's main action takes place on Colorado Boulevard between Pasadena Avenue and Arroyo Parkway. ✉ *Pasadena* ☎ *626/356–9725* ⊕ *www.oldpasadena.org.*

🍴 Restaurants

Lincoln

$$ | CAFÉ | This adorable little café should be a go-to for any and all light breakfast and lunch needs. Healthy breakfast bowls get your body moving, while pesto

Pasadena and Environs

PASADENA

SAN MARINO

SOUTH PASADENA

Sights ▼
1 The Gamble House **A3**
2 Huntington Library, Art Collections, and Botanical Gardens....... **E5**
3 Norton Simon Museum **A3**
4 The Old Mill (El Molino Viejo)......... **D6**
5 Old Town Pasadena **B4**

Restaurants ▼
1 Lincoln **A1**
2 Pie'n Burger............. **D4**
3 The Raymond 1886...... **B6**

KEY
① Exploring Sights
① Restaurants

0 ——————— 1/2 mi
0 ——————— 1/2 km

turkey sandwiches fill you up just right. **Known for:** light bites; great patio; strong coffee. $ *Average main: $15 ☒ 1992 Lincoln Ave., Pasadena ☎ 626/765–6746 ⊕ lincolnpasadena.com.*

Pie 'n Burger
$ | **DINER** | Since 1963, this small and charming diner has done two things really well—pie and burgers. Most seats are counter-style, with a griddle searing up patties. **Known for:** simple burgers; enormous pie slices; retro style. $ *Average main: $13 ☒ 913 E. California Blvd., Pasadena ☎ 626/795–1123 ⊕ pienburger.com.*

The Raymond 1886
$$$ | **MODERN AMERICAN** | The Raymond 1886 is the coolest kid on the Pasadena block. Carved out of an old cottage, the bar and restaurant has an expansive patio with long wooden tables and hanging lights. **Known for:** solid happy hour; great bar food; expansive patio. $ *Average main: $30 ☒ 1250 S. Fair Oaks Ave., Pasadena ☎ 626/441–3136 ⊕ theraymond. com ⊗ Closed Mon.*

Shopping

★ Rose Bowl Flea Market
OUTDOOR/FLEA/GREEN MARKETS | This massively popular flea market, which happens the second Sunday of each month (rain or shine), deservedly draws crowds that come for deals on goods including mid-century furniture, vintage clothing, pop culture collectibles, books, and music. Food and drink options are on hand to keep shoppers satiated, and general admission is just $9, but VIP/ early-bird options are available for a little extra dough. Bring cash to avoid an inevitable line at the ATM, and feel free to try your hand at haggling. ☒ *1001 Rose Bowl Dr., Pasadena ☎ 323/560–7469 ⊕ www. rgcshows.com.*

Vroman's Bookstore
BOOKS/STATIONERY | Southern California's oldest and largest independent bookseller is justly famous for its great service.

A newsstand, café, and stationery store add to the appeal. A regular rotation of events including trivia night, kids' story time, author meet-and-greets, crafting sessions, discussions, and more get the community actively involved. ☒ *695 E. Colorado Blvd., Pasadena ☎ 626/449– 5320 ⊕ www.vromansbookstore.com.*

Los Feliz and the Eastside

The neighborhoods in L.A.'s Eastside are talked about with the same oh-my-god-it's-so-cool reverence by Angelenos as Brooklyn is by New Yorkers. These streets are dripping with trendiness— which will delight some and enrage others. Almost 20 years ago, Los Feliz was the first of these reinvented neighborhoods, then came Silver Lake, then Echo Park. As each one became more expensive, the cool kids relocated, leaving behind their style and influence. Now Highland Park is the center of the oh-so-hip universe. But, the epicenter is constantly shifting. No doubt, by the next edition of this guide, it'll be someplace else.

Los Feliz

Sights

Barnsdall Art Park
HOUSE | **FAMILY** | The panoramic view of Hollywood alone is worth a trip to this hilltop cultural center. On the grounds you'll find the 1921 **Hollyhock House,** a masterpiece of modern design by architect Frank Lloyd Wright. It was commissioned by philanthropist Aline Barnsdall to be the centerpiece of an arts community. While Barnsdall's project didn't turn out the way she planned, the park now hosts the L.A. Municipal Art Gallery and Theatre, which provides exhibition space for visual and performance artists.

Wright dubbed this style "California Romanza" (*romanza* is a musical term meaning "to make one's own form"). Stylized depictions of Barnsdall's favorite flower, the hollyhock, appear throughout the house in its cement columns, roof line, and furnishings. The leaded-glass windows are expertly placed to make the most of both the surrounding gardens and the city views. On summer weekends, there are wildly popular wine tastings and outdoor movie screenings. Self-guided tours are available Thursday through Sunday from 11 to 4. ⊠ *4800 Hollywood Blvd., Los Feliz* ☎ *323/644–6296* ⊕ *www.barnsdall. org* ✑ *Free; house tours $7* ⊙ *House closed Mon.*

★ Griffith Observatory

OBSERVATORY | Most visitors barely skim the surface of this gorgeous spot in the Santa Monica Mountains, but those in the know will tell you there's more to the Griffith Observatory than its sweeping views and stunning Greek Revival architecture. To start, this free-to-the-public mountaintop observatory is home to the Samuel Oschin Planetarium, a state-of-the-art theater with an aluminum dome and a Zeiss star projector that plays a number of ticketed shows. Those spectacular shows are complemented by a couple of space-related exhibits, and several telescopes (naturally), as well as theater programs and events at the Leonard Nimoy Event Horizon Theater. For visitors who are looking to get up close and personal with the cosmos, monthly star-viewing parties with local amateur astronomers are also on hand. ■**TIP**➜ **For a fantastic view, come at sunset to watch the sky turn fiery shades of red with the city's skyline silhouetted.** ⊠ *2800 E. Observatory Ave., Los Feliz* ☎ *213/473–0800* ⊕ *www. griffithobservatory.org* ⊙ *Closed Mon.* ☞ *Observatory grounds and parking are open daily.*

Griffith Park

CITY PARK | **FAMILY** | The country's largest municipal park, the 4,310-acre Griffith Park is a must for nature lovers, the perfect spot for respite from the hustle and bustle of the surrounding urban areas. Plants and animals native to Southern California can be found within the park's borders, including deer, coyotes, and even a reclusive mountain lion. Bronson Canyon (where the Batcave from the 1960s *Batman* TV series is located) and Crystal Springs are favorite picnic spots.

The park is named after Colonel Griffith J. Griffith, a mining tycoon who donated 3,000 acres to the city in 1896. As you might expect, the park has been used as a film and television location for at least a century. Here you'll find the Griffith Observatory, the Los Angeles Zoo, the Greek Theater, two golf courses, hiking and bridle trails, a swimming pool, a merry-go-round, and an outdoor train museum. ⊠ *4730 Crystal Springs Dr., Los Feliz* ☎ *323/913–4688* ⊕ *www.laparks.org/dos/ parks/griffithpk* ✑ *Free; attractions inside park have separate admission fees.*

🍴 Restaurants

The Best Fish Taco in Ensenada

$ | **MEXICAN** | **FAMILY** | In mirroring the taco stands of Ensenada, Mexico—simple, cheap, unceremonious, with a selection of spicy house-made salsas—this little local treasure has achieved what many restaurants serving Baja tacos haven't: an authentic (and delicious) experience. **Known for:** fish-and-shrimp tacos; mango salsa; horchata. ⑤ *Average main: $6* ⊠ *1650 Hillhurst Ave., Los Feliz* ☎ *323/466–5552* ⊕ *www.bestfishtacoin-ensenada.com.*

Kismet

$$ | **MEDITERRANEAN** | You may feel like you're about to walk into a sauna rather than a restaurant because of its minimalist light-color wood on white paint interior, but Kismet's colorful gorgeous Middle

Eastern dishes tell a different story. This James Beard nominee perfectly blends comforting Middle Eastern and Israeli cuisine with Californian flavors and plant-based flair, all served in a modern space. **Known for:** freekeh fritters; jeweled crispy rice with egg yolk; dessert. ⑤ *Average main: $18 ⊠ 4648 Hollywood Blvd., Los Feliz ☎ 323/409–0404 ⊕ www.kismet-losangeles.com.*

Little Dom's
$$ | ITALIAN | With a vintage bar and dapper barkeep who mixes up season-ally inspired retro cocktails, an attached Italian deli where you can pick up a pork-cheek sub, and an $18 Monday-night supper, it's not surprising that Little Dom's is a neighborhood gem. Cozy and inviting, with big leather booths you can sink into for the night, the restaurant puts a modern spin on classic Italian dishes such as *burrata* agnolotti and meatballs. **Known for:** ricotta cheese and fresh blueberry pancakes; pizza with sunny-side up egg; breakfast. ⑤ *Average main: $20 ⊠ 2128 Hillhurst Ave., Los Feliz ☎ 323/661–0055 ⊕ www.littledoms.com.*

Nightlife

Covell
WINE BARS—NIGHTLIFE | Covell is the embodiment of what every unpretentious wine drinker wishes a wine bar should be—laid back. It's thankfully lacking in servers who might turn up their noses should you—for shame!—forget to swirl the glass. But what else would you expect from a spot with shabby furnishings and a vintage motorcycle mounted to the wall? ⊠ *4628 Hollywood Blvd., Los Feliz ☎ 323/660–4400 ⊕ www.barcovell.com.*

Dresden Room
PIANO BARS/LOUNGES | This bar's 1940s lounge decor makes it a favorite with folks in Los Angeles. The long-running house band, Marty and Elayne, has entertained patrons for more than three decades. (They found a new generation of fans, thanks to the film *Swingers*.) Other than the entertainment, perhaps the best reason to wander in is to sip on a Blood and Sand cocktail, self-proclaimed to be "the world's most tantalizing drink." ⊠ *1760 N. Vermont Ave., Los Feliz ☎ 323/665–4294 ⊕ www.thedresden.com.*

Performing Arts

Greek Theatre
CONCERTS | With a robust lineup from May through November, acts such as Bruce Springsteen, John Legend, and Aretha Franklin (RIP) have all graced the stage at this scenic outdoor venue. The 5,900-capacity amphitheater is at the base of Griffith Park, and you may want to make a day of it by hiking or stargazing beforehand. There is usually slow, preshow traffic on concert nights, but it'll give you a chance to take in the beautiful park foliage and homes in the Hollywood Hills. Paid lots are available for parking, but wear comfortable shoes and expect to walk, as some lots are fairly far from the theater. Or, park and enjoy cocktails in the trendy and chic Los Feliz neighborhood below before a show, then walk up to the venue. ⊠ *2700 N. Vermont Ave., Los Feliz ☎ 844/524–7335 ⊕ www.greektheatrela.com.*

Rockwell Table and Stage
THEATER | Great comfort food, decent cocktails, and a boisterous night of fun await at one of L.A.'s most idiosyncratic nighttime diversions. At the Rockwell Table and Stage performance venue, it's the shows and their hilarious cast that are the main attractions, whether they're doing an unofficial parody of a famous TV show or movie or putting on a political cabaret. ⊠ *1714 N. Vermont Ave., Los Feliz ☎ 323/669–1550 ⊕ rockwell-la.com.*

🛍 Shopping

Skylight Books

BOOKS/STATIONERY | A neighborhood bookstore through and through, Skylight has excellent sections devoted to kids, fiction, travel, food, and it even has a live-in cat. Be sure to browse the Staff Picks section, as the well-informed employees have the inside scoop on new or under-the-radar must-reads. The space also hosts book discussion groups, panels, and author readings with hip literati. Art lovers can peruse texts on design and photography, graphic novels, and indie magazines at Skylight's annex a few doors down. ✉ *1818 N. Vermont Ave., Los Feliz* ☎ *323/660–1175* ⊕ *www. skylightbooks.com.*

Soap Plant/Wacko

GIFTS/SOUVENIRS | This pop-culture supermarket offers a wide range of items, including rows of books on art and design. But it's the novelty stock that makes the biggest impression, with ant farms, X-ray specs, and anime figurines. An adjacent gallery space, La Luz de Jesus, focuses on underground art. ✉ *4633 Hollywood Blvd., Los Feliz* ☎ *323/663–0122* ⊕ *www.soapplant.com.*

Vamp Shoes

CLOTHING | From well-known designers to up-and-comers and handcrafters who make their shoes in small batches, boutique store Vamp Shoes has a solid collection of footwear for women who appreciate and are not afraid to invest in gorgeous, excellent-quality soles. Inventory here also includes cool bags, hosiery, jewelry, and handcrafted ceramics. ✉ *1951 Hillhurst Ave., Los Feliz* ☎ *323/662–1150* ⊕ *www.vamp-shoeshop.com.*

Silver Lake

🍴 Restaurants

★ Alimento

$$$ | **ITALIAN** | There's little surprise that Chef Zach Pollack's soulful Italian masterpiece in Silver Lake features a lot of influences and inspirations; the true Angelenos, after all, grew up in a melting pot. Alimento's dishes are modern takes on traditional Italian cuisine, using locally sourced ingredients and varying in influences—from your classic American to Chinese and Mexican. **Known for:** yellowtail-collar affumicato; chicken liver crostone; dinner only. ⑤ *Average main: $25* ✉ *1710 Silver Lake Blvd., Silver Lake* ☎ *323/928–2888* ⊕ *www.alimentola.com* ☾ *Closed Mon. No lunch.*

Cafe Stella

$$$$ | **FRENCH** | This strange den of eclectic decor and peeling paint feels undoubtedly French. Come for the aperitifs (Kir Royal, perhaps?), but stick around for the food for an exquisite blend of French and American bistro cuisine, prepared for lunch and dinner using traditional French techniques. **Known for:** brunch; Moroccan eggs; eggs Benedict. ⑤ *Average main: $34* ✉ *3932 Sunset Blvd., Silver Lake* ☎ *323/666–0265* ⊕ *www.cafestella.com* ☾ *No brunch Mon.*

Daw Yee Myanmar Corner

$ | **BURMESE** | Burmese food is hard to find in Los Angeles so it's a good thing that tucked away in a Silver Lake strip mall sits the unassuming Daw Yee Myanmar Corner, a restaurant that's as good as it is rare. The food is an explosion of flavors and textures (there's a lot of roasted peanuts and toasted sesame). **Known for:** tea leaf salad; Burmese cuisine; mohinga. ⑤ *Average main: $12* ✉ *2837 Sunset Blvd., Silver Lake* ☎ *213/413–0568* ⊕ *www.dawyeesilverlake.com* ☾ *Closed Tues.*

LaMill Coffee

$$ | CAFÉ | These folks take their coffee seriously, sourcing estate-grown beans that are prepared in a variety of ways (French press or Clover, to name but two) and offering an inventive list of espresso-based drinks. To go along with the requisite coffee fix is a menu put together by renowned chef Michael Cimarusti of Providence fame, as well as a serious tea list. **Known for:** blanco y negro; orange-infused cappucino; extensive tea list. $ *Average main: $14* ⊠ *1636 Silver Lake Blvd., Silver Lake* ☎ *323/663–4441* ⊕ *www.lamillcoffee.com.*

Pine and Crane

$ | TAIWANESE | FAMILY | This is not the typical Chinese restaurant one might expect; it's a fast casual, often locally sourced Taiwanese restaurant housed in a modern setting. The menu changes based on season, the wine and beer list updates constantly, and the tea menu is carefully curated. **Known for:** dan dan noodles; beef rolls; Taiwanese food. $ *Average main: $12* ⊠ *1521 Griffith Park Blvd., Silver Lake* ☎ *323/668–1128* ⊕ *www.pineandcrane. com* ⊗ *Closed Tues.*

Sawyer

$$$ | SEAFOOD | Simply put, Sawyer is a stunner with its restored brick wall, beautiful hardwood floor, and tiled patio, flourished with mid-century modern furniture; it's exactly the kind of bright and airy place you'd want to start off your day in. Yet most patrons come here less for the ambience and more for the food, with a menu that might lean on the healthy side but isn't afraid to indulge in the hearty stuff, touting an assortment of traditional and modern American fare. **Known for:** seafood boil; oysters; fries. $ *Average main: $23* ⊠ *3709 Sunset Blvd., Silver Lake* ☎ *323/641–3709* ⊕ *www.sawyerlosangeles.com* ⊗ *No brunch weekdays.*

Nightlife

Akbar

BARS/PUBS | This bar's welcoming feel is one of the reasons many people consider it their neighborhood bar, even if they don't live in the neighborhood. The crowd is friendly and inviting, and theme nights attract all sorts of folks, gay or straight. The comedy nights are favorites, as are weekends, when DJs get everyone on the dance floor. ⊠ *4356 W. Sunset Blvd., Silver Lake* ☎ *323/665–6810* ⊕ *www. akbarsilverlake.com.*

Cha Cha Lounge

BARS/PUBS | If chaos and the assortment of ill-matched furnishings and decor is something you can forgive—or revel in— then this import from Seattle is a Silver Lake staple you should be partaking in, as there's never a dull moment. Grab your (cheap) poison then meander through the Mexican fiesta-themed bar. Foosball tables, a photo booth, and a vending machine will give you plenty to occupy your time … that is, if you're not already having a swell time. ⊠ *2375 Glendale Blvd., Silver Lake* ☎ *323/660–7595* ⊕ *www.chachalounge.com.*

★ 4100

BARS/PUBS | With swaths of fabric draped from the ceiling, this low-lit bar with a bohemian vibe makes it perfect for dates. Groups of locals also come through for the night, making the crowd a plentiful mix of people. The bartenders know how to pour drinks that are both tasty and potent. There's plenty of seating at the tables and stools along the central bar, which gets crowded on the weekends. ⊠ *1087 Manzanita St., Silver Lake* ☎ *323/666–4460* ⊕ *213hospitality.com/ project/4100bar.*

★ The Satellite

MUSIC CLUBS | Once known as Spaceland, the Satellite holds nightly shows filled with underground musicians, both touring and local, all trying to make a dent. Many of them play indie rock, punk, or something else outside the mainstream, so it's a must-stop for music fans who abhor the Billboard Top 100. If you're around, make sure to take advantage of the free residencies where bands get to take center stage every Monday for an entire month. ✉ *1717 Silver Lake Blvd., Silver Lake* ☎ *323/661–4380* ⊕ *www.thesatellitela.com.*

Silverlake Lounge

MUSIC CLUBS | Rock bands, burlesque, comedy, and even open-mic nights all have a home at the cross section of Sunset and Silver Lake at a little dive bar called the Silverlake Lounge. This small club with the yellow awning is a neighborhood spot—cash only, by the way—in the best way possible, with cheap drinks and local talent deserving of their time in the limelight. ✉ *2906 W. Sunset Blvd., Silver Lake* ☎ *323/663–9636* ⊕ *www.thesilverlakelounge.com.*

Thirsty Crow

BARS/PUBS | This whiskey bar serves up seasonal cocktails in a fun, rustic environment. Though small, it manages to find space for live musicians and an open-mic night on Saturday. Part of the same hospitality group as Bigfoot Lodge and Highland Park Bowl, this watering hole has a locals-only feel. As local L.A. musician Father John Misty once said, "nothing good ever happens at the goddamn Thirsty Crow," but we think you should go and see for yourself. ✉ *2939 W. Sunset Blvd., Silver Lake* ☎ *323/661–6007* ⊕ *www.thirstycrowbar.com.*

🛍 Shopping

Mohawk General Store

CLOTHING | Filled with a brilliant marriage of indie and established designers, this upscale boutique is a mainstay for the modern minimalist. Pick up the wares of local favorites Black Crane and Jesse Kamm, as well as internationally loved labels like Commes des Garcons, Issey Miyake, and Levi's Vintage Clothing. The Sunset Boulevard store stocks goods for men and women, as well as children, plus accessories and some home goods. ✉ *4011 W. Sunset Blvd., Silver Lake* ☎ *323/522–6459* ⊕ *www.mohawkgeneralstore.com.*

Secret Headquarters

BOOKS/STATIONERY | This could be the coolest comic-book store on the planet, with a selection to satisfy both the geekiest of collectors and those more interested in artistic and literary finds. Rich wood floors and a leather chair near the front window of this intimate space mark the sophisticated setting, which features wall displays neatly organized with new comics and filing cabinets marked DC and Marvel. ✉ *3817 W. Sunset Blvd., Silver Lake* ☎ *323/666–2228* ⊕ *www.thesecretheadquarters.com.*

Silver Lake Wine

WINE/SPIRITS | Boutique wineries from around the world provide this shop with the vintages that fill the floor-to-ceiling racks. Looking unassuming in jeans and T-shirts, the knowledgeable staff can steer you to the right wine or spirits for any occasion. You can wet your whistle at tastings on Monday and Thursday. ✉ *2395 Glendale Blvd., Silver Lake* ☎ *323/662–9024* ⊕ *www.silverlakewine.com.*

Echo Park

👁 Sights

Dodger Stadium

SPORTS VENUE | **FAMILY** | Home of the Dodgers since 1962, it's the third-oldest baseball stadium still in use and has had quite the history in baseball, including Sandy Koufax's perfect game in 1965 and Kirk Gibson's 1988 World Series home run. Not only has it played host to the Dodgers' ups and downs and World Series runs, it's also has been the venue for some of the biggest performers in the world, including the Beatles, Madonna, and Beyonce. The stadium can be tough to get into on game day so consider getting dropped off in the park and walking up. Alternately, arrive early as locals tend not to roll up until the third inning. If you have the opportunity to take in a Friday night game, make sure to stick around for the fireworks show that follows—if you're patient, you can even wait in line and watch it from the field. ⊠ *1000 Vin Scully Ave., Echo Park* ☎ *866/363–4377* ⊕ *dodgers.mlb.com/la/ballpark* ۞ *Check schedule.*

Echo Park Lake
BODY OF WATER | FAMILY | If this charming little park and its lake of swan boats looks a little familiar to you, it's most likely because you've seen it in one L.A.-shot movie or another (*Chinatown*, for instance). After a major overhaul, the park has blossomed into a beautiful urban landscape, set against the backdrop of the Downtown skyline. Weekends are always bustling, as are mornings when joggers and early risers take laps around the lake. There's a tiny breakfast-slash-lunch spot that serves healthy nosh and good coffee. ⊠ *751 Echo Park Ave., Echo Park* ⊕ *www.laparks.org/aquatic/lake/echo-park-lake.*

🍽 Restaurants

Dinette
$ | CAFÉ | Coffee shops may be a dime a dozen, but Dinette stands out. First of all, this is a walk-up-window-only establishment, which gives it a nice vintage-diner feel. **Known for:** coffee; avocado toast; waffle with bacon and poached egg. ⑤ *Average main: $11* ⊠ *1608½ Sunset Blvd., Echo Park* ☎ *213/278–0301* ⊕ *dinettela.com* ۞ *Closed Mon.*

Masa of Echo Park
$$ | PIZZA | FAMILY | While Masa of Echo Park does do excellent "bistro pizzas," as the restaurant calls them, it's mostly known for their delectable deep-dish pies that may just be the best you'll find this side of Chicago. Be prepared though—it can take a while to get seated and up to 45 minutes to get that deep dish you ordered, so it might be best to call ahead. **Known for:** vegan menu; family-style dining; Italian classics. ⑤ *Average main: $20* ⊠ *1800 W. Sunset Blvd., Echo Park* ☎ *213/989–1558* ⊕ *www.masaofechopark.com.*

Taix
$$ | FRENCH | FAMILY | Serving French cuisine since 1927—and at its current location since 1962—Taix is the opportunity to peek at a time in L.A. that's mostly disappeared. Dark, wooden tables, intimate booths, low lighting, and portrait-adorned walls all help to set the scene. **Known for:** steak frites; being a local institution; French onion soup. ⑤ *Average main: $21* ⊠ *1911 W. Sunset Blvd., Echo Park* ☎ *213/484–1265* ⊕ *taixfrench.com.*

🍸 Nightlife

Button Mash
BARS/PUBS | FAMILY | Button Mash hits all the right buttons (sorry), with a wide selection of rotating arcade games, most of which are from the golden age, not to mention a fantastically curated wine and beer list, and a menu put together by the old Starry Kitchen pop-up team that specializes in Asian fusion bar food. Before 9, this bar-cade is all ages, so everyone can be the next pinball wizard between bites of double-fried chicken wings. ⊠ *1391 Sunset Blvd., Echo Park* ☎ *213/250–9903* ⊕ *www.buttonmashla.com.*

★ The Echo and Echoplex
MUSIC CLUBS | These two venues, one sitting on top of the other, are the heart of live music in Echo Park. Both offer a full bar and the ability to order pizza from Two Boots next door as well as recurring themed nights like Part-Time Punks. While they both host cutting-edge music, the Echo usually has up-and-coming local and touring acts whereas more well-known bands play downstairs. ⊠ *1822 Sunset Blvd., Echoplex entrance at 1154 Glendale Blvd, Echo Park* ☎ *213/413–8200* ⊕ *www.theecho.com.*

⭐ Mohawk Bend

BARS/PUBS | There are so many reasons to stop by Mohawk Bend: 72 craft beers on tap, a wide range of California-only liquor, a vegetarian and vegan-friendly menu that includes tailored-to-your-wants pizza, and a buffalo cauliflower that—rumor has it—started the whole trend. There might be a long line to get into this 100-year-old former restaurant in the evenings, but it's worth it. ✉ *2141 Sunset Blvd., Echo Park* ☎ *213/483–2337* ⊕ *mohawk.la.*

⭐ 1642 Beer and Wine

BARS/PUBS | This romantically lit hole-in-the-wall is easy to miss. Perfect for first dates, come here to experiment with craft beers or to warm up with wine. On the first Thursday of every month, get a free tamale with your drink, and hear some live old-time fiddle tunes. ✉ *1642 W. Temple St., Echo Park* ☎ *213/989–6836.*

 # Shopping

Esqueleto

JEWELRY/ACCESSORIES | There's a bit of the macabre on display at Esqueleto, but what do you expect from a jewelry boutique with a name meaning "skeleton" in Spanish? But that doesn't mean the light, airy, contemporary shop is stereotypically Goth in style; both its design and the inventory it stocks are perfectly polished and selected with a discerningly artistic eye. With a mix of excellent vintage finds and emerging designers (Melissa Joy Manning, Lauren Wolf, and Satomi Kawakita are favorites here), the shop has become a go-to destination for alternative brides' engagement rings and wedding bands. ✉ *1928 W. Sunset Blvd., Echo Park* ☎ *213/947–3508* ⊕ *www.shopesqueleto.com.*

Stories Books and Café

BOOKS/STATIONERY | With an off-the-beaten path collection of new and used literature, a café catering to freelancers and free thinkers, and a back patio that showcases singer-songwriters, Stories Books and Café is an authentic reflection of Echo Park. Readings, signings, and other events are a regular occurrence. ✉ *1716 Sunset Blvd., Echo Park* ☎ *213/413–3733* ⊕ *www.storiesla.com.*

Time Travel Mart

SPECIALTY STORES | **FAMILY** | You probably won't find anything useful in the Time Travel Mart and that's exactly the point. From dinosaur eggs to robot milk, this is a store that touts the ridiculous—all of which should bring back memories of your childhood and maybe a little bit of joy. But that's because the store holds a secret: it's really a fundraiser for the nonprofit 826LA, which tutors neighborhood kids in the back section. So, know when you're buying that totally unnecessary, but absolutely wonderful, samurai umbrella, the proceeds are going to a good cause. ✉ *1714 W. Sunset Blvd., Echo Park* ☎ *213/413–3388* ⊕ *826la.org/store.*

Atwater Village

⊕ Restaurants

Dune

$ | **MEDITERRANEAN** | **FAMILY** | Simple, small, and understated, it's easy to miss the best falafel spot in town. Hearty Middle Eastern falafel and chicken shawarma are piled on house-made flatbread. **Known for:** organic green-herb falafel sandwich; fried chicken shawarma sandwich; lunch and dinner. 💲 *Average main: $12* ✉ *3143 Glendale Blvd., Atwater Village* ☎ *323/486–7073* ⊕ *www.dune.kitchen.*

⭐ Good Measure

$$ | **CONTEMPORARY** | Good Measure's proprietors decided to mix their love of travel with their passion for wine and start their own space offering a by-the-glass selection that spans the globe. The result is this romantic restaurant with an eclectic and excellent wine menu, not to mention an incredible dining menu with a quarterly On Tour section, which explores the food and wines of various regions. **Known for:** crispy chicken confit; chickpea fries; desserts. ⓢ *Average main: $18* ✉ *3224 Glendale Blvd., Atwater Village* ☎ *323/426–9461* ⊕ *www.goodmeasurela.com.*

Link N Hops

$ | HOT DOG | Link N Hops is your typical sports bar, almost. There are a couple things that elevate it: excellent hot dog sandwiches and 24 craft beers on tap. **Known for:** Atwater knackwurst; smoked Portuguese Hawaiian; happy hour specials. ⓢ *Average main: $10* ✉ *3111 Glendale Blvd., Atwater Village* ☎ *323/426–9049* ⊕ *linknhops.com.*

Sepan Chicken

$ | MIDDLE EASTERN | Don't knock it until you've tried it. Despite appearances (it looks like a fast-food chicken shack), Sepan Chicken serves one of the best rotisserie chickens in town, or at least this side of Hollywood. **Known for:** Middle Eastern dishes; chicken kebabs; hummus. ⓢ *Average main: $10* ✉ *3324 Glendale Blvd., Atwater Village* ☎ *323/669–0616* ⊕ *sepan-chicken.com.*

Tacos Villa Corona

$ | MEXICAN | You likely won't notice this cramped little spot on Glendale Boulevard unless there's a line or you're a fan of the late, great Anthony Bourdain, who was a big fan. About that line—it's almost always there, especially weekend mornings, when Tacos Villa Corona caters to the hangover crowd. **Known for:** chorizo and potato burrito; tacos. ⓢ *Average main: $4* ✉ *3185 Glendale Blvd., Atwater Village* ☎ *323/661–3458.*

Tam O'Shanter

$$$$ | IRISH | It's a bit of a specific recognition, but Tam O'Shanter is the oldest restaurant run by the same family in the same location in Los Angeles, operating for more than 90 years in its Tudor-style spot—that alone makes this place a worthy addition to any Atwater Village visit. Then there's their delicious food whose $30 prices are completely worth it, not to mention the fact that, once upon a time, it was Walt Disney's favorite restaurant. **Known for:** steak; toad-in-the-hole; Scottish decor. ⓢ *Average main: $32* ✉ *2980 Los Feliz Blvd., Atwater Village* ☎ *323/664–0228* ⊕ *www.lawrysonline.com/tam-oshanter.*

Nightlife

★ Bigfoot Lodge

BARS/PUBS | Don't be turned off by the glaring log cabin theme (which is intensified by signature cocktails called Scout's Honor and Roasted Marshmallow). Bigfoot Lodge is beloved by Eastside denizens, and despite appearances, it's every bit a low-key, unpretentious neighborhood bar that specializes in shots and beer and welcomes the occasional tourist that happens to stumble inside. ✉ *3172 Los Feliz Blvd., Atwater Village* ☎ *323/662–9227* ⊕ *www.bigfootlodge.com.*

Moonlight Rollerway Skating Rink

SPORTS VENUE | It seems like every night there's a hubbub at Moonlight Rollerway, whether it's skating to *Purple Rain* for a Prince tribute night, a tricky mannequin challenge, or a Harry Potter–themed skate night. If you're looking for a quick throwback to your childhood or a simple break from life, this is just the ticket. This vintage roller rink also offers affordable lessons, in case you're rusty and need a crash course. ✉ *5110 San Fernando Rd., Atwater Village* ☎ *818/241–3630* ⊕ *moonlightrollerway.com.*

Verdugo Bar

BARS/PUBS | It's hard to decide whether the best thing about this place is its selection of 22 craft beers on tap and menu of "to-go" beer or the large beer garden furnished with picnic tables. It's probably a tie. But be warned, this place can get crowded, but it's worth it, especially on a hot sunny day (so pretty much every day). ✉ *3408 Verdugo Rd., Atwater Village* ☎ *323/257–3408* ⊕ *www.verdugobar.com.*

Shopping

Potted

FLOWERS | There's something comforting about Potted, like you've just walked into your parents' sunroom or a woodland fairy's home. This is a garden full of colors, nooks and crannies to tuck yourself into, and treasures of the botanic kind waiting to be discovered. It's every plant lover's paradise, but even those who wouldn't consider themselves to be plant fiends will be tempted to spend a fortune here. ⊠ *3158 Los Feliz Blvd., Atwater Village* ☎ *323/665–3801* ⊕ *pottedstore.com*.

Treehaus

CLOTHING | The beauty of Treehaus isn't that it's an independent boutique—Los Angeles has plenty of those—but that it carries a great assortment of retail pieces, from women's and children's clothing to accessories and home goods, all in a cozy rectangular space. ⊠ *3153 Glendale Blvd., Atwater Village* ☎ *323/230–6776* ⊕ *www.treehaus.biz*.

Highland Park

Sights

Heritage Square Museum

MUSEUM | Looking like a prop street set up by a film studio, Heritage Square resembles a row of bright dollhouses in the modest Highland Park neighborhood. Five 19th-century residences, a train station, a church, a carriage barn, and a 1909 boxcar that was originally part of the Southern Pacific Railroad, all built between the Civil War and World War I, were moved to this small park from various locations in Southern California to save them from the wrecking ball. The latest addition, a re-creation of a World War I–era drugstore, has a vintage soda fountain and traditional products. Docents dressed in period costume lead visitors through the lavish homes, giving an informative picture of Los Angeles in the early 1900s. Don't miss the unique 1893 Octagon House, one of just a handful of its kind built in California. ⊠ *3800 Homer St., Highland Park* ☎ *323/225–2700* ⊕ *www.heritagesquare. org* ⊠ *$10* ☉ *Closed Tues.–Thurs. and federal holiday Mon.* ☞ *Tour included with admission price.*

Restaurants

Cafe Birdie

$$ | **MEDITERRANEAN** | Though it only opened in 2016, this spacious 1920s spot along this quickly revitalizing stretch of Figueroa has already established itself as a neighborhood bistro frequented by Highland Park residents, as well as folks from nearby neighborhoods. The eclectic menu skillfully blends elements of European, Southern, and Japanese cuisines, tying them together with a fresh California flair and a gorgeous interior inspired by a fictional meeting-of-two-souls narrative. **Known for:** Mediterranean dishes; cocktails; great ambience. ⑤ *Average main: $19* ⊠ *5631 N. Figueroa St., Highland Park* ☎ *323/739–6928* ⊕ *www. cafebirdiela.com*.

★ Dave's Chillin'-n-Grillin'

$ | **AMERICAN** | **FAMILY** | Dave's Chillin'-n-Grillin' has been making the kind of sandwiches people dream about for more than 10 years. On a couple of griddles, Dave himself often turns out no-nonsense wonders. **Known for:** Rosemary's Turkey; the Pilgrim; the Surf and Turf. ⑤ *Average main: $12* ⊠ *5715 N. Figueroa St., Highland Park* ☎ *323/490–0988* ☉ *Closed Sun.*

★ Donut Friend

$ | **BAKERY** | When this music-influenced donut shop first opened on York Boulevard in the early days of Highland Park's renaissance, there wasn't much there, and its arrival helped shape the now bustling strip and its vegan inclinations. Donut Friend had evolved into a destination in its own right, touting both a signature and limited menu of purely vegan donuts—which also happen to be inspired by the pop punk and emo music scene—that taste better than Dunkin'. **Known for:** Green Teagan and Sara; Jets to Basil; make-your-own donut. ⑤ *Average main: $4* ✉ *5107 York Blvd., Highland Park* ☎ *213/995–6191* ⊕ *www.donutfriend.com.*

El Huarache Azteca

$ | **MEXICAN** | **FAMILY** | While you definitely should try the flat shoe-shaped dish El Huarache Azteca is named after—think somewhere between a flatbread and a tostada—you cannot go wrong with any of the other options at this family restaurant that's been a fixture in the area for the last couple decades. Just be aware there's often a wait for the food to come out. **Known for:** huarache; agua fresca; barbacoa de barrego. ⑤ *Average main: $10* ✉ *5225 York Blvd., Highland Park* ☎ *323/478–9572* ⊕ *elhuaracheaztecalive.com* ▭ *No credit cards.*

★ Knowrealitypie

$ | **BAKERY** | The award-winning Knowrealitypie, hidden in a shop the size of a large walk-in closet, serves homemade pies every Friday through Saturday and only stays open until it sells out, which it often does. So hurry on down to partake in a rotating menu of seasonal savory and sweet pies, turnovers, and other pastries while supplies last. **Known for:** triple cherry Cabernet pie; caramel mango passion pie; minipies. ⑤ *Average main: $6* ✉ *5106 Townsend Ave., Highland Park* ☎ *323/610–2244* ⊕ *www.knowrealitypie.com* ⊘ *Closed Mon.–Thurs.*

Polka Polish Cuisine

$$ | **POLISH** | There's a coziness in Polka Polish Cuisine that can only be matched by a grandmother's living room. The food here, traditional Polish fare, also has that same comfort. **Known for:** royal platter; pierogi; stuffed cabbage. ⑤ *Average main: $20* ✉ *4112 Verdugo Rd., Highland Park* ☎ *323/255–7887* ⊕ *www.polkarestaurant.com* ⊘ *Closed Mon. and Tues.*

 ## Nightlife

The Hermosillo

BARS/PUBS | The Hermosillo is the kind of laid-back pub every neighborhood should have, with an excellent selection of locally focused draft beer on tap, rotating wine list, and mouthwatering food. To add to its allure, award-winning Highland Park Brewery got its start in the pub's back storage room and is still featured prominently on the menu. ✉ *5125 York Blvd., Highland Park* ☎ *323/739–6459* ⊕ *thehermosillo.com.*

The Hi Hat

MUSIC CLUBS | The only thing left from its previous life as a pool hall are the two tables that greet customers as they enter. Now, it's the epicenter of live music in Highland Park and part of the revitalization of York Boulevard. Its exposed brick walls and pop-up kitchen are the cherry on top of the real treat—the local, underground bands performing here. ✉ *5043 York Blvd., Highland Park* ⊕ *hihat.la.*

Highland Park Bowl

BARS/PUBS | **FAMILY** | Highland Park Bowl was an ambitious restoration project and is now a massive throwback to its Prohibition Era roots as an alcohol-prescribing doctor's office and drugstore with its own bowling alley. That bowling alley remains, complete with the original pin machine. The hooch-pushing doctor and druggist, however, are long gone. But now there's an Italian restaurant that serves excellent pizza made from scratch using a mother dough brought all the way from Italy. ✉ *5621 N. Figueroa St., Highland Park* ☎ *323/257–2695* ⊕ *www.highlandparkbowl.com.*

★ The Old Chalet

BARS/PUBS | This ski lodge–inspired neighborhood bar may have changed ownership and management, but that doesn't mean that it's gotten a major and pretentious overhaul. In fact, besides its beefed-up whiskey and agave spirit lists (which desperately needed to be updated), new seasonal cocktails, and a new wave of eclectic clientele, it's still pretty much the same neighborhood bar the local residents have come to know and love. Plus, it's got a karaoke night that can't be beat. ⊠ *1630 Colorado Blvd., Highland Park* ☎ *323/508–5058* ⊕ *www.theoldchalet.com.*

The York

BARS/PUBS | Since 2007, before Highland Park became trendy, the York has been holding its own as the neighborhood bar. It's not just that the aesthetic gives off that neighborhood vibe (think exposed brick and chalkboard menus), but the craft beers on tap are great, and the pub food is delicious—the cheddar burger and the fish-and-chips are favorites. ⊠ *5018 York Blvd., Highland Park* ☎ *323/255–9675* ⊕ *theyorkonyork.wordpress.com.*

Shopping

Galco's Soda Pop Stop

FOOD/CANDY | **FAMILY** | Galco's, a local fixture in Highland Park for decades, is in some ways a trip down memory lane, carrying more than 600 sodas—most of which harken back to the days when soda was a regional affair—and options from all over the world. They also have a collection of retro candies, a soda creation station with more than 100 syrups to choose from, and a selection of alcohol that would put most liquor stores to shame. ⊠ *5702 York Blvd., Highland Park* ☎ *323/255–7115* ⊕ *sodapopstop.com.*

Permanent Records

MUSIC STORES | Permanent Records has been a part of the vinyl resurgence since 2013, stocking new and used vinyl for every musical taste and doing it without any snobbery. The record store, which often has in-store performances, also runs its own label that focuses on local bands, limited-edition runs, and reissues. ⊠ *5116 York Blvd., Highland Park* ☎ *323/739–6141* ⊕ *www.permanentrecordsla.com.*

Chapter 8

JOSHUA TREE NATIONAL PARK

Updated by
Sarah Amandolare

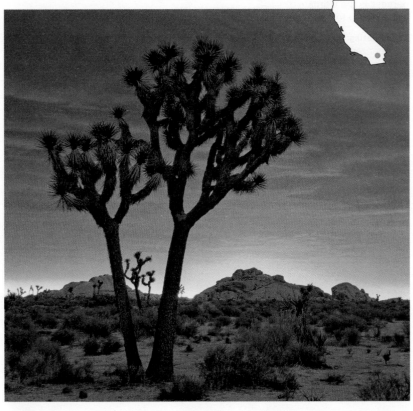

👁 Sights	🍴 Restaurants	🛏 Hotels	💼 Shopping	🍸 Nightlife
★★★★★	★★★★☆	★★★★★	★☆☆☆☆	★☆☆☆☆

WELCOME TO
JOSHUA TREE NATIONAL PARK

TOP REASONS TO GO

★ **Rock climbing:** Joshua Tree is a world-class site with challenges for climbers of just about every skill level.

★ **Peace and quiet:** Roughly two hours from Los Angeles, this great wilderness is the ultimate escape from technology.

★ **Stargazing:** You'll be mesmerized by the Milky Way flowing across the summer sky. For spectacular natural fireworks, visit in mid-August during the Perseid meteor shower and watch shooting stars streak overhead.

★ **Wildflowers:** In spring, the hillsides explode in a patchwork of yellow, blue, pink, and white.

★ **Sunsets:** Twilight is a magical time here, especially during the winter, when the setting sun casts a golden glow on the mountains.

1 **Keys View.** This is the most dramatic overlook in the park—on clear days you can see Signal Mountain in Mexico.

2 **Hidden Valley.** Crawl between the big rocks and you'll understand why this boulder-strewn area was once a cattle rustlers' hideout.

3 **Cholla Cactus Garden.** Come here in the late afternoon, when the spiky stalks of the bigelow (jumping) cholla cactus are backlit against an intense blue sky.

4 **Oasis of Mara.** Walk the nature trail around this desert oasis, which the first settlers, the Serrano, dubbed "the place of little springs and much grass."

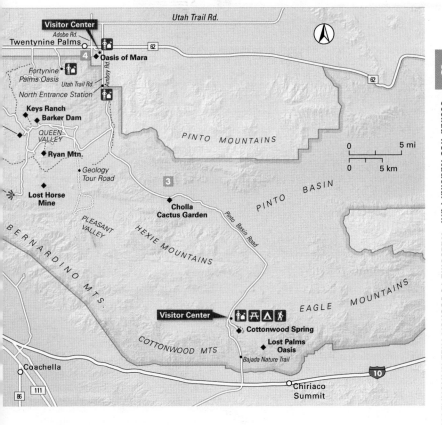

Joshua Tree National Park teems with fascinating landscapes and life-forms. It attracts around 1.5 million visitors each year, yet is mysteriously quiet at dawn and dusk. The landscape shifts abruptly from the arid stubble of the low Sonoran Desert to vast stands of the park's namesake Joshua trees in the higher, wetter Mojave Desert.

Planning

When to Go

October through May, when the desert is cooler, is when most visitors arrive. Daytime temperatures range from the mid-70s in December and January to mid-90s in October and May. Lows can dip to near freezing in midwinter, and you may even encounter snow at the higher elevations. Summers can be torrid, with daytime temperatures reaching 110°F.

Festivals and Events

Pioneer Days
FESTIVAL | FAMILY | Outhouse races, live music, and arm wrestling mark this celebration held annually, during the third full October weekend, in Twentynine Palms. The event also features a parade, carnival, chili dinner, and an old timers' gathering. ⊠ *Twentynine Palms* ☎ *760/367-3445* ⊕ *www.visit29.org.*

Riverside County Fair & National Date Festival
FESTIVAL | FAMILY | Head to Indio for camel and ostrich races. ⊠ *Riverside County Fairgrounds, 82-503 Hwy. 111, Indio* ☎ *800/811-3247* ⊕ *www.datefest.org.*

Planning Your Time

JOSHUA TREE IN ONE DAY
After stocking up on water, snacks, and lunch in Yucca Valley or Joshua Tree (you won't find any supplies inside the park), begin your visit at the **Joshua Tree Visitor Center,** where you can pick up maps and peruse exhibits to get acquainted with what awaits you. Enter the park itself at the nearby **West Entrance Station** and continue driving along the highly scenic and well-maintained **Park Boulevard.** Stop first at **Hidden Valley,** where you can relax at the picnic area or hike the easy 1-mile loop trail. After a few more miles turn left onto the spur road that takes you to the trailhead for the **Barker Dam Nature Trail.** Walk the easy 1.1-mile loop to view a water tank ranchers built to quench their cattle's thirst; along the way you'll spot birds and a handful of cactus

AVERAGE HIGH/LOW TEMPERATURES					
JAN.	**FEB.**	**MAR.**	**APR.**	**MAY**	**JUNE**
62/32	65/37	72/40	80/50	90/55	100/65
JULY	**AUG.**	**SEPT.**	**OCT.**	**NOV.**	**DEC.**
105/70	101/78	96/62	85/55	72/40	62/31

varieties. Return to Park Boulevard and head south; you'll soon leave the main road again for the drive to **Keys View.** The easy loop trail here is only 0.25 mile, but the views extend for miles in every direction—look for the San Andreas Fault, the Salton Sea, and nearby mountains. Return to Park Boulevard, where you'll find **Cap Rock,** another short loop trail winding amid rock formations and Joshua trees.

Continuing along Park Boulevard, the start of the 18-mile self-guided **Geology Tour Road** will soon appear on your right. A brochure outlining its 16 stops is available at visitor centers; note that the round-trip will take about two hours, and high-clearance, four-wheel-drive vehicles are recommended after stop 9. ■TIP→ **Do not attempt if it has recently rained.** Back on Park Boulevard, you'll soon arrive at the aptly named **Skull Rock.** This downright spooky formation is next to the parking lot; a nearby trailhead marks the beginning of a 1.7-mile nature trail. End your day with a stop at the **isitor Center** in Twentynine Palms, where you can stroll through the historic **Oasis of Mara,** popular with area settlers.

Getting Here and Around

AIR TRAVEL
Palm Springs International Airport is the closest major airport to Joshua Tree National Park. It's about 45 miles from the park. The drive from Los Angeles International Airport to Joshua Tree takes about two to three hours.

CAR TRAVEL
An isolated island of pristine wilderness—a rarity these days—Joshua Tree National Park is within a short drive of 11 million Southern California residents. Most visitors, in fact, make the two- to three-hour drive from the Los Angeles area to enjoy a weekend of solitude in 792,726 acres of untouched desert. The urban sprawl of Palm Springs (home to the nearest airport) is 45 miles away, but gateway towns Joshua Tree, Yucca Valley, and Twentynine Palms are just north of the park. If you're staying in the Palm Springs area, you can enjoy the highlights of the park in one day, including a stop for a picnic at a scenic spot.

■TIP→ **If you'd prefer not to drive, most Palm Springs area hotels can arrange a half- or full-day tour that hits the highlights of Joshua Tree National Park.** But you'll need to spend two or three days camping here to truly experience the quiet beauty of the desert.

Park Essentials

ACCESSIBILITY
Black Rock Canyon and Jumbo Rocks campgrounds have one accessible campsite each. Nature trails at Oasis of Mara, Bajada, Keys View, and Cap Rock are accessible. Some trails at roadside viewpoints can be negotiated by those with limited mobility.

PARK FEES AND PERMITS
Park admission is $30 per car, $15 per person on foot, bicycle, or horse, and $25 per person by motorcycle. The Joshua Tree Pass, good for one year, is $55.

PARK HOURS

The park is open every day, around the clock, but visitor centers are staffed from approximately 8 am to 5 pm. The park is in the Pacific time zone.

CELL PHONE RECEPTION

Cell phones don't work in most areas of the park. There are no telephones in the interior of the park.

Educational Offerings

LECTURES

The Desert Institute at Joshua Tree National Park

COLLEGE | The nonprofit educational partner of the park offers a full schedule of lectures, classes, and hikes. Class topics include basket making, painting, and photography, while field trips include workshops on cultural history, natural science, and how to survive in the desert. ⊠ *74485 National Park Dr., Twentynine Palms* ☎ *760/367–5525* ⊕ *www.joshuatree.org.*

Stargazing

COLLEGE | At Joshua Tree National Park you can tour the Milky Way on summer evenings using binoculars. Rangers also offer programs on some evenings when the moon isn't visible. Browse the schedule online. ⊠ *Cottonwood Campground Amphitheater and Oasis Visitor Center* ⊕ *www.nps.gov/jotr/planyourvisit/calendar.htm.*

RANGER PROGRAMS

Evening Programs

TOUR—SIGHT | Rangers present 45-minute-long programs, often on Friday or Saturday evening, at Cottonwood Amphitheater, Indian Cove Amphitheater, and Jumbo Rocks Campground. Topics range from natural history to local lore. The schedule is posted online. ⊠ *Joshua Tree National Park* 🎫 *Free.*

★ **Keys Ranch Tour**

HOUSE | A guide takes you through the former home of a family that homesteaded here for 60 years. In addition to the ranch, a workshop, store, and schoolhouse are still standing, and the grounds are strewn with vehicles and mining equipment. The 90-minute tour, which begins at the Keys Ranch gate, tells the history of the family that built the ranch. Tickets are $10, and reservations are required. ⊠ *Keys Ranch gate* ☎ *760/367–5522* ⊕ *www.nps.gov/jotr.*

Restaurants

Dining options in the gateway towns around Joshua Tree National Park are extremely limited—you'll mostly find fast-food outlets and a few casual cafés in Yucca Valley and Twentynine Palms. The exception is the restaurant at 29 Palms Inn, which has an interesting California-cuisine menu that features lots of veggies. Still, you'll have to travel to the Palm Springs desert resort area for a fine-dining experience.

Hotels

Lodging choices in the Joshua Tree National Park area are limited to a few motels, chain hotels, and a luxury bed-and-breakfast establishment in the gateway towns. In general, most offer few amenities and are modestly priced. Book ahead for the spring wildflower season—reservations may be difficult to obtain then.

For a more extensive range of lodging options, you'll need to head to Palm Springs and the surrounding desert resort communities. *Hotel reviews have been shortened. For full information, visit Fodors.com.*

What It Costs			
$	$$	$$$	$$$$
RESTAURANTS			
under $12	$12–$20	$21–$30	over $30
HOTELS			
under $100	$100–$150	$151–$200	over $200

Tours

Big Wheel Tours

TOUR—SIGHT | Based in Palm Desert, Big Wheel Tours offers van excursions, jeep tours, and hiking trips through the park. Bicycle tours (road and mountain bike) are available outside the park boundary. Pickups are available at Palm Springs area hotels. ✉ 42160 State St., Palm Desert ☎ 760/779–1837 ⊕ www.bwbtours.com 🚲 From $119.

Trail Discovery

TOUR—SIGHT | You can get a full day of exploring Joshua Tree with Trail Discovery, along with information on the park's plants, animals, geography, and history. Sunrise treks are offered in hot, summer months. Park admission, bottled water, hip packs, snacks, and fruit are included. Transportation is not provided. ☎ 760/413–1575 ⊕ www.palmspringshiking.com 🚲 From $125.

Visitor Information

PARK CONTACT INFORMATION Joshua Tree National Park. ✉ 74485 National Park Dr., Twentynine Palms ☎ 760/367–5522 ⊕ www.nps.gov/jotr.

VISITOR CENTERS

Cottonwood Visitor Center

INFO CENTER | The south entrance is the closest to Interstate 10, the east–west highway from Los Angeles to Phoenix. Exhibits in this small center, staffed by rangers and volunteers, illustrate the region's natural history. The center also has restrooms with flush toilets. ✉ Cottonwood Spring, Pinto Basin Rd. ⊕ www.nps.gov/jotr.

Joshua Tree Visitor Center

INFO CENTER | This visitor center has maps and interesting exhibits illustrating park geology, cultural and historic sites, and hiking and rock-climbing activities. There's also a small bookstore and café. Restrooms with flush toilets are on the premises. ✉ 6554 Park Blvd., Joshua Tree ☎ 760/366–1855 ⊕ www.nps.gov/jotr.

Oasis Visitor Center

INFO CENTER | Exhibits here illustrate how Joshua Tree was formed, reveal the differences between the park's two types of desert, and demonstrate how plants and animals eke out an existence in this arid climate. Take the ½-mile nature walk through the nearby Oasis of Mara, which is alive with cottonwood trees, palm trees, and mesquite shrubs. Facilities include picnic tables, restrooms, and a bookstore. ✉ 74485 National Park Dr., Twentynine Palms ☎ 760/367–5500 ⊕ www.nps.gov/jotr.

Plants and Wildlife in Joshua Tree

Joshua Tree will shatter your notions of the desert as a wasteland. Life flourishes here, as flora and fauna have adapted to heat and drought. In most areas you'll be walking among native Joshua trees, ocotillos, and yuccas. One of the best spring desert wildflower displays in Southern California blooms here. You'll see plenty of animals—reptiles such as nocturnal sidewinders, birds like golden eagles or burrowing owls, and occasionally mammals like coyotes and bobcats.

Sights

You can experience Joshua Tree National Park on several levels. Even on a short excursion along Park Boulevard between the Joshua Tree entrance station and Oasis of Mara, you'll see the essence of North American desert scenery—including a staggering abundance of flora visible along a dozen self-guided nature trails. You'll also see remnants of homesteads from a century ago, now mostly abandoned and wind-worn. If rock climbing is your passion, this is the place for you; boulder-strewn mountaintops and slopes beckon. But in the end, Joshua Tree National Park is a pristine wilderness where you can enjoy a solitary stroll along an animal trail and commune with nature. Be sure to take some time to explore on your own and enjoy the peace and quiet.

SCENIC DRIVES

Geology Tour Road

SCENIC DRIVE | Some of the park's most fascinating landscapes can be observed from this 18-mile dirt road. Parts of the journey are rough; a 4X4 vehicle is required after mile marker 9. Sights to see include a 100-year-old stone dam called Squaw Tank, defunct mines, and a large plain with an abundance of Joshua trees. There are 16 stops along the way, so give yourself about two hours to complete the round-trip trek. ⊠ *South of Park Blvd., west of Jumbo Rocks.*

Park Boulevard

SCENIC DRIVE | If you have time only for a short visit, driving Park Boulevard is your best choice. Traversing the most scenic portions of Joshua Tree, this well-paved road connects the north and west entrances in the park's high desert section. Along with some sweeping desert views, you'll see jumbles of splendid boulder formations, stands of Joshua trees, and Hidden Valley and Barker Dam, remnants of the area's wild and woolly past. From the Oasis Visitor Center, drive south. After about 5 miles, the road forks; turn right and head west toward Jumbo Rocks (clearly marked with a road sign). ⊠ *Joshua Tree National Park.*

Pinto Basin Road

SCENIC DRIVE | This paved road takes you from high Mojave desert to low Colorado desert. A long, slow drive, the route runs from the main part of the park to Interstate 10; it can add as much as an hour to and from Palm Springs (round-trip), but the views and roadside exhibits make it worth the extra time. From the Oasis Visitor Center, drive south. After about 5 miles, the road forks; take a left and continue another 9 miles to the Cholla Cactus Garden, where the sun fills the cactus needles with light. Past that is the Ocotillo Patch, filled with spindly plants bearing razor-sharp thorns and, after a rain, bright green leaves and brilliant red flowers. Side trips from this route require a 4X4. ⊠ *Joshua Tree National Park.*

HISTORIC SITES

Hidden Valley

NATURE SITE | **FAMILY** | This legendary cattle-rustlers' hideout is set among big boulders along a 1-mile loop trail. Kids love to scramble on and around the rocks. There are shaded picnic tables here. ⊠ *Park Blvd.* ✛ *14 miles south of west entrance.*

★ Keys Ranch

TOUR—SIGHT | This 150-acre ranch, which once belonged to William and Frances Keys and is now on the National Historic Register, illustrates one of the area's most successful attempts at home-steading. The couple raised five children under extreme desert conditions. Most of the original buildings, including the house, school, store, and workshop, have been restored to the way they were when William died in 1969. The only way to see the ranch is on one of the 90-minute walking tours usually offered Friday–Sunday, October–May, and weekends in summer; advance reservations required. ⊠ *Joshua Tree National Park* ✛ *2 miles north of Barker Dam Rd.* ☎ *760/367–5522* ⊕ *www.nps. gov/jotr/planyourvisit/ranchtour.htm* ⊠ *$10, available at Oasis Visitor Center or reserve by phone.*

Lost Horse Mine

MINE | This historic mine, which produced 10,000 ounces of gold and 16,000 ounces of silver between 1894 and 1931, was among Southern California's most productive mines. The 10-stamp mill is considered one of the best preserved of its type in the park system. The site is accessed via a fairly strenuous 4-mile round-trip hike. Mind the park warnings and don't enter any mine in Joshua Tree. ⊠ *Keys View Rd.* ✛ *About 15 miles south of west entrance.*

SCENIC STOPS

Barker Dam

DAM | Built around 1900 by ranchers and miners to hold water for cattle and mining operations, the dam now collects rainwater and is a good place to spot wildlife such as the elusive bighorn sheep. ⊠ *Barker Dam Rd.* ✛ *Off Park Blvd., 10 miles south of west entrance.*

Cholla Cactus Garden

GARDEN | This stand of bigelow cholla (sometimes called jumping cholla, because its hooked spines seem to jump at you) is best seen and photographed in late afternoon, when the backlit spiky stalks stand out against a colorful sky. ⊠ *Pinto Basin Rd.* ✛ *20 miles north of Cottonwood Visitor Center.*

Cottonwood Spring

NATIVE SITE | Home to the native Cahuilla people for centuries, this spring provided water for travelers and early prospectors. The area, which supports a large stand of fan palms and cottonwood trees, is one of the best stops for bird-watching, as migrating birds (and bighorn sheep) rely on the water as well. A number of gold mines were located here, and the area still has some remains, including concrete pillars. ⊠ *Cottonwood Visitor Center.*

Fortynine Palms Oasis

NATIVE SITE | A short drive off Highway 62, this site is a bit of a preview of what the park's interior has to offer: stands of fan palms, interesting petroglyphs, and evidence of fires built by early Native Americans. Because animals frequent this area, you may spot a coyote, bobcat, or roadrunner. ⊠ *End of Canyon Rd.* ✛ *4 miles west of Twentynine Palms.*

★ Keys View

VIEWPOINT | At 5,185 feet, this point affords a sweeping view of the Santa Rosa Mountains and Coachella Valley, the San Andreas Fault, the peak of 11,500-foot Mt. San Gorgonio, the shimmering surface of Salton Sea, and—on a rare clear day—Signal Mountain in Mexico. Sunrise and sunset are magical times, when the light throws rocks and trees into high relief before bathing the hills in brilliant shades of red, orange, and gold. ⊠ *Keys View Rd.* ✛ *16 miles south of park's west entrance.*

Lost Palms Oasis

TRAIL | More than 100 fan palms comprise the largest group of the exotic plants in the park. A spring bubbles from between the rocks, but disappears into the sandy, boulder-strewn canyon. The 7.5-mile round-trip hike is not for everyone, and not recommended during summer months. Bring plenty of water! ⊠ *Cottonwood Visitor Center.*

Ocotillo Patch

GARDEN | Stop here for a roadside exhibit on the dramatic display made by the red-tipped succulent after even the shortest rain shower. ⊠ *Pinto Basin Rd.* ✛ *About 3 miles east of Cholla Cactus Gardens.*

8

Joshua Tree National Park

Activities

BICYCLING

Mountain biking is a great way to see Joshua Tree. Bikers are restricted to roads that are used by motorized vehicles, including the main park roads and a few four-wheel-drive trails. Bicycling on dirt roads is not recommended during the summer. Most scenic stops and picnic areas, and the Wall Street Mill trailhead, have bike racks.

Black Eagle Mine Road

BICYCLING | This 9-mile dead-end road is peppered with defunct mines, the entrances of which should be avoided. It runs along the edge of a former lake bed, then crosses a number of dry washes before navigating several of Eagle Mountain's canyons. ⊠ *Joshua Tree National Park* ✛ *Trailhead: off Pinto Basin Rd., 6½ miles north of Cottonwood Visitor Center.*

Covington Flats

BICYCLING | This 4-mile route takes you past impressive Joshua trees as well as pinyon pines, junipers, and areas of lush desert vegetation. It's tough going toward the end, but once you reach 5,518-foot Eureka Peak you'll have great views of Palm Springs, the Morongo Basin, and the surrounding mountains. ⊠ *Joshua Tree National Park* ✛ *Trailhead: at Covington Flats picnic area, La Contenta Rd., 10 miles south of Rte. 62.*

Pinkham Canyon and Thermal Canyon Roads

BICYCLING | This challenging 20-mile route begins at the Cottonwood Visitor Center and loops through the Cottonwood Mountains. The unpaved trail follows Smoke Tree Wash through Pinkham Canyon, rounds Thermal Canyon, and loops back to the beginning. Rough and narrow in places, the road travels through soft sand and rocky floodplains. ⊠ *Joshua Tree National Park* ✛ *Trailhead: at Cottonwood Visitor Center.*

Queen Valley

BICYCLING | This 13.4-mile network of mostly level roads winds through one of the park's most impressive groves of Joshua trees. You can also leave your bike at one of the racks placed in the area and explore on foot. ⊠ *Joshua Tree National Park* ✛ *Trailhead: at Hidden Valley Campground, and accessible opposite Geology Tour Rd. at Big Horn Pass.*

BIRD-WATCHING

Joshua Tree, located on the inland portion of the Pacific Flyway, hosts about 240 species of birds, and the park is a popular seasonal location for bird-watching. During the fall migration, which runs mid-September through mid-October, there are several reliable sighting areas. At Barker Dam you might spot white-throated swifts, several types of swallows, or red-tailed hawks. Lucy's warbler, flycatchers, and Anna's hummingbirds cruise around Cottonwood Spring, a serene palm-shaded setting; occasional ducks, herons, and egrets, as well as migrating rufous and calliope hummingbirds, wintering prairie falcons, and a resident barn owl could show up. Black Rock Canyon sees pinyon jays, while Covington Flats reliably gets mountain quail, and you may see La Conte's thrashers, ruby-crowned kinglets, and warbling vireos at either locale. Rufous hummingbirds, Pacific slope flycatchers, and various warblers are frequent visitors to Indian Cove. Lists of birds found in the park, as well as information on recent sightings, are available at visitor centers.

HIKING

There are more than 190 miles of hiking trails in Joshua Tree, ranging from quarter-mile nature trails to 35-mile treks. Some connect with each other, so you can design your own desert maze. Remember that drinking water is hard to come by—you won't find water in the park except at the entrances. Bring along at least a gallon per person for all but the shortest hikes, more if the weather is hot.

Did You Know?

Found only in Arizona, California, Nevada, and Utah, the Joshua tree (*Yucca brevifolia*) is actually a member of the agave family. Native Americans used the Joshua tree's hearty foliage like leather, forming it into everyday items like baskets and shoes. Later, early settlers used its core and limbs for building fences to contain their livestock.

Bajada All Access

HIKING/WALKING | Learn all about what plants do to survive in the desert on this wheelchair-accessible ¼-mile loop. *Easy.* ⊠ *Joshua Tree National Park* ⊹ *Trailhead: south of Cottonwood Visitor Center, ½ mile from park entrance.*

Boy Scout Trail

HIKING/WALKING | The moderately strenuous 8-mile trail, suitable for backpackers, extends from Indian Cove to Park Boulevard. It runs through the westernmost edge of the Wonderland of Rocks (where you're likely to see climbers on the outcroppings), passing through a forest of Joshua trees, past granite towers, and around willow-lined pools. Completing the round-trip journey may require camping along the way, so you may want to hike only part of the trail or have a car waiting at the other end. *Difficult.* ⊠ *Joshua Tree National Park* ⊹ *Trailhead: between Quail Springs Picnic Area and Indian Cove Campground.*

California Riding and Hiking Trail

HIKING/WALKING | You'll need a backcountry camping pass to traverse this 35-mile route between the Black Rock Canyon entrance and the north entrance. You can access the trail for a short or long hike at several points. The visitor centers have trail maps. *Difficult.* ⊠ *Joshua Tree National Park* ⊹ *Trailheads: at Upper Covington Flats, Ryan Campground, Twin Tanks, south of north park entrance, and Black Rock Campground.*

Cap Rock

HIKING/WALKING | This ½-mile wheelchair-accessible loop—named after a boulder that sits atop a huge rock formation like a cap—winds through fascinating rock formations and has signs that explain the geology of the Mojave Desert. *Easy.* ⊠ *Joshua Tree National Park* ⊹ *Trailhead: Keys View Rd. near junction with Park Blvd.*

Fortynine Palms Oasis Trail

HIKING/WALKING | Allow three hours for this moderately strenuous 3-mile trek. There's no shade, and the trail makes a steep climb in both directions, eventually dropping down into a canyon where you'll find an oasis lined with fan palms, which can be viewed from boulders above, but not accessed. If you look carefully, you'll find evidence of Native Americans in this area, from traces of cooking fires to rocks carved with petroglyphs. *Difficult.* ⊠ *Joshua Tree National Park* ⊹ *Trailhead: at end of Canyon Rd., 4 miles west of Twentynine Palms.*

Hidden Valley

HIKING/WALKING | FAMILY | Crawl through the rocks surrounding Hidden Valley to see where cattle rustlers supposedly hung out on this 1-mile loop. *Easy.* ⊠ *Joshua Tree National Park* ⊹ *Trailhead: at Hidden Valley Picnic Area.*

Hi-View Nature Trail

HIKING/WALKING | This 1.3-mile loop climbs nearly to the top of 4,500-foot Summit Peak. The views of nearby Mt. San Gorgonio (snowcapped in winter) make the moderately steep journey worth the effort. You can pick up a pamphlet describing the vegetation you'll see along the way at any visitor center. *Moderate.* ⊠ *Joshua Tree National Park* ⊹ *Trailhead: ½ mile west of Black Rock Canyon Campground.*

Indian Cove Trail

HIKING/WALKING | Look for lizards and roadrunners along this ½-mile loop that follows a desert wash. A walk along this well-signed trail reveals signs of Indian habitation, animals, and flora such as desert willow and yucca. *Easy.* ⊠ *Joshua Tree National Park* ⊹ *Trailhead: at west end of Indian Cove Campground.*

Lost Horse Mine Trail

HIKING/WALKING | This fairly strenuous 4-mile round-trip hike follows a former mining road to a well-preserved mill that was used in the 1890s to crush gold-encrusted rock mined from the nearby mountain. The operation was one of the area's most successful, and the mine's cyanide settling tanks and stone buildings are the area's best-preserved structures. From the mill area, a short but steep 10-minute side trip takes you to the top of a 5,278-foot peak with great views of the valley. *Difficult.* ⊠ *Joshua Tree National Park* ⊹ *Trailhead: 1¼ miles east of Keys View Rd.*

Lost Palms Oasis Trail

HIKING/WALKING | Allow four to six hours for the moderately strenuous, 7¼-mile round-trip, which leads to the most impressive oasis in the park. It's uphill on the way back to the trailhead. You'll find more than 100 fan palms and an abundance of wildflowers here. *Difficult.* ⊠ *Joshua Tree National Park* ⊹ *Trailhead: at Cottonwood Spring Oasis.*

Mastodon Peak Trail

HIKING/WALKING | Some boulder scrambling is optional on this 3-mile hike that loops up to the 3,371-foot Mastodon Peak, and the journey rewards you with stunning views of the Salton Sea. The trail passes through a region where gold was mined from 1919 to 1932, so be on the lookout for open mines. The peak draws its name from a large rock formation that early miners believed looked like the head of a prehistoric behemoth. *Moderate.* ⊠ *Joshua Tree National Park* ⊹ *Trailhead: at Cottonwood Spring Oasis.*

Oasis of Mara

HIKING/WALKING | A stroll along this short, wheelchair-accessible trail, located just outside the visitor center, reveals how early settlers took advantage of this oasis, which was first settled by the Serrano tribe. *Mara* means "place of little springs and much grass" in their language. The Serrano, who farmed the oasis until the mid-1850s, planted one palm tree for each male baby born during the first year of the settlement. *Easy.* ⊠ *Joshua Tree National Park* ⊹ *Trailhead: at Oasis Visitor Center.*

★ **Ryan Mountain Trail**

HIKING/WALKING | The payoff for hiking to the top of 5,461-foot Ryan Mountain is one of the best panoramic views of Joshua Tree. From here you can see Mt. San Jacinto, Mt. San Gorgonio, Lost Horse Valley, and the Pinto Basin. You'll need two to three hours to complete the 3-mile round-trip with 1,000-plus feet of elevation gain. *Moderate.* ⊠ *Joshua Tree National Park* ⊹ *Trailhead: at Ryan Mountain parking area, 13 miles southeast of park's west entrance, or Sheep Pass, 16 miles southwest of Oasis Visitor Center.*

Skull Rock Trail

HIKING/WALKING | The 1.7-mile loop guides hikers through boulder piles, desert washes, and a rocky alley. It's named for what is perhaps the park's most famous rock formation, which resembles the eye sockets and nasal cavity of a human skull. Access the trail from within Jumbo Rocks Campground or from a small parking area on the highway just east of the campground. *Easy.* ⊠ *Joshua Tree National Park* ⊹ *Trailhead: at Jumbo Rocks Campground.*

ROCK CLIMBING

With an abundance of weathered igneous boulder outcroppings, Joshua Tree is one of the nation's top winter-climbing destinations. There are more than 4,500 established routes offering a full menu of climbing experiences—from bouldering for beginners in the Wonderland of Rocks to multiple-pitch climbs at Echo Rock and Saddle Rock. The best-known climb in the park is Hidden Valley's Sports Challenge Rock. A map inside the *Joshua Tree Guide* shows locations of selected wilderness and nonwilderness climbs.

Joshua Tree Rock Climbing School

CLIMBING/MOUNTAINEERING | The school offers several programs, from one-day introductory classes to multiday programs for experienced climbers, and provides all needed equipment. Beginning classes, offered year-round on most weekends, are limited to six people age eight or older. ✉ *Joshua Tree National Park* ☎ *760/366–4745* ⊕ *www.joshuatreerockclimbing.com* 🖃 *From $195.*

Vertical Adventures Rock Climbing School
CLIMBING/MOUNTAINEERING | About 1,000 climbers each year learn the sport in Joshua Tree National Park through this school. Classes, offered September–May, meet at a designated location in the park, and all equipment is provided. ✉ *Joshua Tree National Park* ☎ *800/514–8785* ⊕ *www.verticaladventures.com* 🖃 *From $155.*

Nearby Towns

About 9 miles north of Palm Springs and closer to the park is **Desert Hot Springs,** which has more than 1,000 natural hot mineral pools and 40 health spas ranging from low-key to luxurious. **Yucca Valley** is the largest and fastest growing of the communities straddling the park's northern border. The town boasts a handful of motels, supermarkets, and a Walmart. Tiny **Joshua Tree,** the closest community to the park's west entrance, is where the serious rock climbers make their headquarters. **Twentynine Palms,** known as "two-nine" by locals, is sandwiched between the Marine Corps Air Ground Task Force Center to the north and Joshua Tree National Park to the south. Here you'll find a smattering of coffeehouses, antiques shops, and cafés.

VISITOR INFORMATION California Welcome Center Yucca Valley. ✉ *56711 Twentynine Palms Hwy., Yucca Valley* ☎ *760/365–5464* ⊕ *www.californiawelcomecenter.com.* **Joshua Tree Chamber of Commerce.** ✉ *6448 Hallee Rd., Joshua Tree* ☎ *760/366–3723* ⊕ *www.joshuatreechamber.org.* **Palm Springs Visitor Center.** ✉ *2109 N. Palm Canyon Dr., Palm Springs* ☎ *760/778–8415, 800/348–7746* ⊕ *www.visitpalmsprings.com.* **Twentynine Palms Chamber of Commerce.** ✉ *73484 Twentynine Palms Hwy., Twentynine Palms*

☎ *760/367–3445* ⊕ *www.29chamber.org.* **Yucca Valley Chamber of Commerce.** ✉ *56711 Twentynine Palms Hwy., Yucca Valley* ☎ *760/365–6323* ⊕ *www.yuccavalley.org.*

 Sights

Hi-Desert Nature Museum
MUSEUM | FAMILY | Natural and cultural history of the Morongo Basis and High Desert are the focus here. A small live-animal display includes scorpions, snakes, lizards, and small mammals. You'll also find gems and minerals, fossils from the Paleozoic era, taxidermy, and Native American artifacts. There's also a children's area and art exhibits. ✉ *Yucca Valley Community Center, 57090 Twentynine Palms Hwy., Yucca Valley* ☎ *760/369–7212* ⊕ *hidesertnaturemuseum.org* 🖃 *Free* ⊙ *Closed Sun.–Tues.*

Oasis of Murals
PUBLIC ART | Twenty-six murals painted on the sides of buildings depict the history, wildlife, and landscape of Twentynine Palms. If you drive around town you can't miss the murals, but you can also pick up a free map from the visitor center. ✉ *Twentynine Palms* ⊕ *www.action-29palmsmurals.com.*

Pioneertown
TOWN | In 1946 Roy Rogers, Gene Autry, the Sons of the Pioneers (the music group for whom the town is named), and Russ Hayden built Pioneertown, an 1880s-style Wild West movie set complete with hitching posts, saloon, and an OK Corral. You can stroll past wooden and adobe storefronts and feel like you're back in the Old West. Pappy & Harriet's Pioneertown Palace, now the town's top draw, has evolved into a hip venue for indie and mainstream performers such as Dengue Fever, Neko Case, and Robert Plant. ✉ *53688 Pioneertown Rd., Pioneertown* ✚ *4 miles north of Yucca Valley* ⊕ *pappyandharriets.com.*

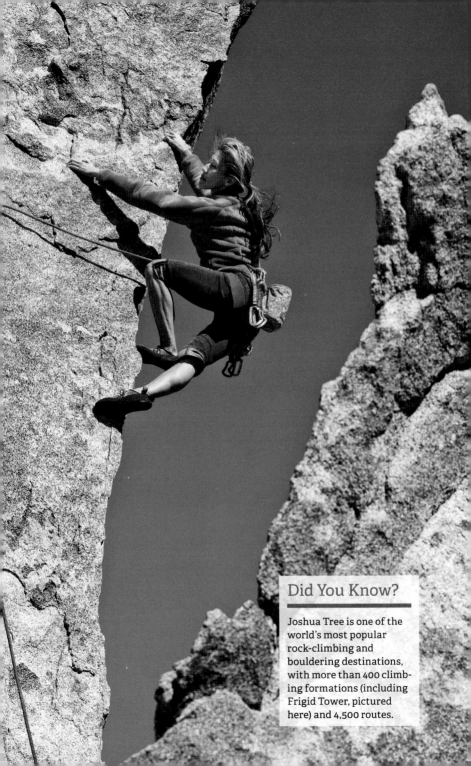

Did You Know?

Joshua Tree is one of the world's most popular rock-climbing and bouldering destinations, with more than 400 climbing formations (including Frigid Tower, pictured here) and 4,500 routes.

Learn about the park's flora and fauna by attending the ranger programs.

🍴 Restaurants

IN THE PARK
PICNIC AREAS
Black Rock Canyon

CANYON | Set among Joshua trees, pinyon pines, and junipers, this popular picnic area has barbecue grills and drinking water. It's one of the few with flush toilets. ⊠ *Joshua Tree National Park ✛ End of Joshua La. at Black Rock Canyon Campground.*

Covington Flats

RESTAURANT—SIGHT | This is a great place to get away from crowds. There's just one table, and it's surrounded by flat, open desert dotted here and there by Joshua trees. ⊠ *La Contenta Rd. ✛ 10 miles from Rte. 62.*

Hidden Valley

RESTAURANT—SIGHT | Set among huge rock formations, with picnic tables shaded by dense trees, this is one of the most pleasant places in the park to stop for lunch. ⊠ *Park Blvd. ✛ 14 miles south of the west entrance.*

OUTSIDE THE PARK
C&S Coffee Shop

$ | AMERICAN | If you're yearning for pork chops and gravy for breakfast or eggs over easy for dinner, head to this tidy diner, which has been a local hangout since 1946. The typical diner menu also features soups, salads, and sandwiches, all cooked to order and presented in heaping portions. **Known for:** perfectly cooked fries; prompt service. ⑤ *Average main: $8* ⊠ *55795 Twentynine Palms Hwy., Yucca Valley* ☎ *760/365–9946.*

Edchada's

$$ | MEXICAN | Rock climbers who spend their days in Joshua Tree swear by the margaritas at this Mexican eatery. Specialties include prodigious portions of fajitas, carnitas, seafood enchiladas, and fish tacos. **Known for:** margaritas; large portions. ⑤ *Average main: $12* ⊠ *73502 Twentynine Palms Hwy., Twentynine Palms* ☎ *760/367–2131.*

Best Campgrounds in Joshua Tree

Camping is the best way to experience the stark, exquisite beauty of Joshua Tree. You'll also have a rare opportunity to sleep outside in a semi-wilderness setting. The campgrounds, set at elevations from 3,000 to 4,500 feet, have only primitive facilities; few have drinking water. Black Rock, Indian Cove, Jumbo Rocks, and Cottonwood campgrounds accept reservations up to six months in advance, and only for October through Memorial Day. Campsites elsewhere are on a first-come, first-served basis. Belle and White Tank campgrounds, and parts of Black Rock Canyon, Cottonwood, and Indian Cove campgrounds, are closed from the day after Memorial Day to September.

Belle Campground. This small campground is popular with families, as there are a number of boulders kids can scramble over and around. ⊠ *9 miles south of Oasis of Mara* ☎ *760/367–5500* ⊕ *www.nps.gov/jotr.*

Black Rock Canyon Campground. Set among juniper bushes, cholla cacti, and other desert shrubs, Black Rock Canyon is one of the prettiest campgrounds in Joshua Tree. ⊠ *Joshua La., south of Hwy. 62 and Hwy. 247* ☎ *877/444–6777* ⊕ *www. recreation.gov.*

Cottonwood Campground. In spring this campground, the southernmost one in the park (and therefore often

the last to fill up), is surrounded by some of the desert's finest wildflowers and is a great spot to watch the night sky. ⊠ *Pinto Basin Rd., 32 miles south of North Entrance Station* ☎ *877/444–6777* ⊕ *www.nps.gov/jotr.*

Hidden Valley Campground. This campground is a favorite with rock climbers, who make their way up valley formations that have names like the Blob, Old Woman, and Chimney Rock. ⊠ *Off Park Blvd., 20 miles southwest of Oasis of Mara* ☎ *760/367–5500* ⊕ *www.nps.gov/jotr.*

Indian Cove Campground. This is a sought-after spot for rock climbers, primarily because it lies among the 50 square miles of rugged terrain at the Wonderland of Rocks. ⊠ *Indian Cove Rd., south of Hwy. 62* ☎ *877/444–6777* ⊕ *www.nps.gov/jotr.*

Jumbo Rocks. Each campsite at this well-regarded campground tucked among giant boulders has a bit of privacy. It's a good home base for visiting many of Joshua Tree's attractions. ⊠ *Park Blvd., 11 miles from Oasis of Mara* ☎ *877/444–6777* ⊕ *www. nps.gov/jotr.*

White Tank. This small, quiet campground is popular with families because a nearby trail leads to a natural arch. ⊠ *Pinto Basin Rd., 11 miles south of Oasis of Mara* ☎ *760/367–5500* ⊕ *www.nps.gov/jotr.*

Park Rock Café

$ | CAFÉ | If you're on your way to the national park on Highway 62, stop in the town of Joshua Tree to grab a hearty breakfast bagel sandwich and order a box lunch to take with you. The café creates some tasty sandwiches, including a healthy option with avocado and

pesto mayo. **Known for:** takeout; outdoor dining; lentil barley soup. ⑤ *Average main: $9* ⊠ *6554 Park Blvd., Joshua Tree* ☎ *760/366–8200* ⊕ *jtparkrockcafe.com* ⌚ *No dinner.*

Hotels

OUTSIDE THE PARK

★ 29 Palms Inn

$$$ | B&B/INN | FAMILY | The closest lodging to the entrance to Joshua Tree National Park, the funky 29 Palms Inn scatters a collection of adobe and wood-frame cottages, some dating back to the 1920s and 1930s, over 70 acres of grounds that include the ancient Oasis of Mara, a popular destination for birds and bird-watchers year-round. **Pros:** gracious hospitality; exceptional bird-watching; art gallery, pool, and on-site restaurant. **Cons:** rustic accommodations; limited amenities. ⓢ *Rooms from: $165* ✉ *73950 Inn Ave., Twentynine Palms* ☎ *760/367–3505* ⊕ *www.29palmsinn.com* ⤳ *20 rooms, 4 guesthouses* ⫤ *Breakfast.*

MOJAVE DESERT

Updated by
Cheryl Crabtree

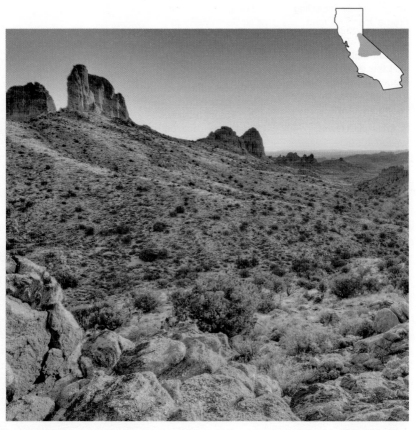

👁 **Sights** | 🍴 **Restaurants** | 🛏 **Hotels** | 🛍 **Shopping** | 🍸 **Nightlife**
★★★★★ | ★★★★☆ | ★★★★★ | ★☆☆☆☆ | ★☆☆☆☆

WELCOME TO MOJAVE DESERT

TOP REASONS TO GO

★ **Nostalgia:** Old neon signs, historic motels, and restored (or neglected but still striking) rail stations abound across this desert landscape. Don't miss the classic eateries along the way, including Emma Jean's Holland Burger Cafe in Victorville.

★ **Death Valley wonders:** Visit this distinctive landscape to tour some of the most varied desert terrain in the world.

★ **Great ghost towns:** California's gold rush brought miners to the Mojave, and the towns they left behind have their own unique charms.

★ **Desert flora and fauna:** Explore the Mojave National Preserve to view Joshua trees, volcanic cinder cones, huge sand dunes, desert tortoises, and other natural wonders.

★ **Explore ancient history:** The Mojave Desert is replete with rare petroglyphs, some dating back almost 16,000 years.

The Mojave Desert, once part of an ancient inland sea, is one of the largest swaths of open land in Southern California. Its boundaries include the San Gabriel and San Bernardino mountain ranges to the south; Palmdale and Ridgecrest to the west; Death Valley to the north; and Needles and Lake Havasu in Arizona to the east. The area is distinguishable by its wide-open sandy spaces, peppered with creosote bushes, Joshua trees, cacti, and abandoned homesteads. Access the Mojave via Interstates 40 and 15, Highways 14 and 95, and U.S. 395.

1 **Lancaster.**

2 **Red Rock Canyon State Park.**

3 **Ridgecrest.**

4 **Randsburg.**

5 **Victorville.**

6 **Barstow.**

7 **Mojave National Preserve.**

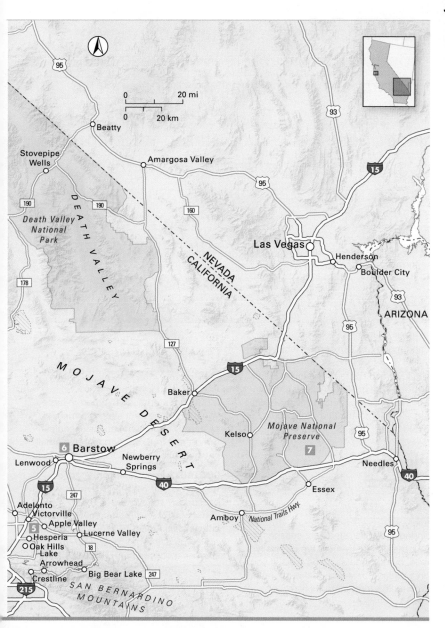

Dust and desolation, tumbleweeds and rattlesnakes, barren landscapes and failed dreams—these are the bleak images that come to mind when most people hear the word desert. Yet the remote regions east of the Sierra Nevada possess a singular beauty, the vast open spaces populated with spiky Joshua trees, undulating sand dunes, faulted mountains, and dramatic rock formations. With a few exceptions the area is not heavily peopled, providing expanses in which visitors can both lose and find themselves.

The topography is extreme; while Death Valley drops to almost 300 feet below sea level and contains the lowest (and hottest) spot in North America, the Mojave Desert, which lies to the south, has elevations ranging from 3,000 to 5,000 feet.

Planning

When to Go

Spring and fall are the best seasons to tour the desert. Winters are generally mild, but summers can be cruel. If you're on a budget, be aware that room rates drop as the temperatures rise.

Getting Here and Around

AIR TRAVEL
McCarran International Airport in Las Vegas is the nearest airport to many eastern Mojave destinations. Needles Airport and Inyokern Airport serve small, private planes.

CONTACTS Inyokern Airport. ✉ 1669 Airport Rd., off Hwy. 178, 9 miles west of Ridgecrest, Inyokern ☎ 760/377–5844 ⊕ www.inyokernairport.com. **McCarran International Airport.** ✉ 5757 Wayne Newton Blvd., Las Vegas ☎ 702/261–5211 ⊕ www.mccarran.com. **Needles Airport.** ✉ 711 Airport Rd., Needles ☎ 760/247–2371 ⊕ cms.sbcounty.gov/airports.

9

BUS TRAVEL

Greyhound provides bus service to Barstow, Victorville, and Palmdale; check with the chambers of commerce about local bus service, which is generally more useful to residents than to tourists.

CONTACTS Greyhound. ☎ 800/231–2222, 214/849–8100 international ⊕ www. greyhound.com.

CAR TRAVEL

The major north–south route through the western Mojave is U.S. 395, which intersects with Interstate 15 between Cajon Pass and Victorville. Farther west, Highway 14 runs north–south between Inyokern (near Ridgecrest) and Palmdale. Two major east–west routes travel through the Mojave: to the north, Interstate 15 to Las Vegas, Nevada; to the south, Interstate 40 to Needles. At the intersection of the two interstates, in Barstow, Interstate 15 veers south toward Victorville and Los Angeles, and Interstate 40 gives way to Highway 58 west toward Bakersfield.

■**TIP→ For the latest Mojave traffic and weather, tune in to the Highway Stations (98.1 FM near Barstow, 98.9 FM near Essex, and 99.7 FM near Baker).** Traffic can be especially troublesome Friday through Sunday, when thousands of Angelenos head to Las Vegas for a bit of R&R.

CONTACTS Caltrans Current Highway Conditions. ☎ 800/427–7623 ⊕ www.dot. ca.gov.

TRAIN TRAVEL

Amtrak trains traveling east and west stop in Victorville, Barstow, and Needles, but the stations aren't staffed, so you'll have to purchase tickets in advance and handle your own baggage. The Barstow station is served daily by Amtrak California motor coaches that stop in Los Angeles, Bakersfield, Las Vegas, and elsewhere. Metrolink's Antelope Valley line travels from Los Angeles Union Station north to Burbank Airport, Palmdale, and Lancaster.

CONTACTS Amtrak. ☎ 800/872–7245, 215/856–7924 international ⊕ www. amtrak.com. **Metrolink.** ☎ 800/371–5465 ⊕ metrolinktrains.com.

Health and Safety

Let someone know your trip route, destination, and estimated time of return. Before setting out, make sure your vehicle is in good condition. Carry water, a jack, tools, and towrope or chain. Keep an eye on your gas gauge and try to keep the needle above half. Stay on main roads, and watch out for wildlife, horses, and cattle.

Drink at least a gallon of water a day (more if you're hiking or otherwise exerting yourself). Dress in layered clothing and wear comfortable, sturdy shoes and a hat. Keep snacks, sunscreen, and a first-aid kit on hand. If you have a headache or feel dizzy or nauseous, you could be suffering from dehydration. Get out of the sun immediately and drink plenty of water. Dampen your clothing to lower your body temperature. Do not enter abandoned mine tunnels or shafts of which there are hundreds in the Mojave Desert. The structures may be unstable, and there may be hidden dangers such as pockets of bad air. Avoid canyons during rainstorms. Floodwaters can quickly fill up dry riverbeds and cover or wash away roads. Never place your hands or feet where you can't see them: rattlesnakes, scorpions, and black widow spiders may be hiding there.

CONTACTS Barstow Community Hospital. ✉ 820 E. Mountain View St., Barstow ☎ 760/256–1761 ⊕ www.barstowhospital.com. **BLM Rangers.** ☎ 916/978–4400 ⊕ www.blm.gov/california. **San Bernardino County Sheriff.** ☎ 760/256–4838 in Barstow, 760/326–9200 in Needles ⊕ wp. sbcounty.gov/sheriff/.

Hours of Operation

Early morning is the best time to visit sights and avoid crowds, but some museums and visitor centers don't open until 10. If you schedule your town arrivals for the late afternoon, you can drop by the visitor centers just before closing hours to line up an itinerary for the next day.

Restaurants

Throughout the desert, dining is a fairly simple affair. There are chain establishments in Ridgecrest, Victorville, and Barstow, as well as some ethnic eateries. *Restaurant reviews have been shortened. For full information, visit Fodors.com.*

Hotels

Chain hotel properties and roadside motels are the desert's primary lodging options. The tourist season runs from late May through September. Reservations are rarely a problem, but it's still wise to make them. *Hotel reviews have been shortened. For full information, please visit Fodors.com.*

What it Costs

	$	$$	$$$	$$$$
RESTAURANTS				
	under $16	$16–$22	$23–$30	over $30
HOTELS				
	under $120	$120–$175	$176–$250	over $250

Tours

Sierra Club

SPECIAL-INTEREST | The San Gorgonio Chapter of the Sierra Club and the chapter's Mojave Group conduct interesting field trips and desert excursions.

Activities are often volunteer-run and free, but participants are sometimes required to cover parking and other expenses. ☎ 951/684–6203 ⊕ sangorgonio2.sierraclub.org ✉ Some free; fee tour prices vary.

Visitor Information

CONTACTS Bureau of Land Management. ⊠ California Desert District Office, 22835 Calle San Juan De Los Lagos, Moreno Valley ☎ 951/697–5200 ⊕ www.blm.gov/office/california-desert-district-office. **California Welcome Center Barstow.** ⊠ 2796 Tanger Way, Barstow ☎ 760/253–4782 ⊕ www.visitcalifornia.com/attraction/california-welcome-center-barstow. **Death Valley Chamber of Commerce.** ☎ 888/600–1844 ⊕ www.deathvalleychamber.org.

Lancaster

8 miles north of Palmdale.

Points of interest around Lancaster include a state poppy reserve that bursts to life in the spring and Edwards Air Force Base, which offers a fascinating tour of historical military aircraft. Lancaster was founded in 1876, when the Southern Pacific Railroad arrived. Before that, several Native American tribes, some of whose descendants still live in the surrounding mountains, inhabited it.

GETTING HERE AND AROUND

From the Los Angeles basin, take Highway 14, which proceeds north to Mojave and Highway 58, a link between Bakersfield and Barstow. Regional Metrolink trains serve Lancaster from the Los Angeles area. Local transit exists, but a car is the best way to experience this area.

ESSENTIALS

VISITOR INFORMATION Destination Lancaster. ⊠ 554 W. Lancaster Blvd. ☎ 661/948–4518 ⊕ www.destinationlancasterca.org.

👁 Sights

Air Force Flight Test Museum at Edwards Air Force Base

MILITARY SITE | This museum, at what many consider to be the birthplace of supersonic flight, chronicles the rich history of flight testing. Numerous airplanes are on exhibit, from the first F-16B to the only remaining YF-22. While those with approved base entry have access to regular museum hours, a general-public tour takes place once a month. The 3½-hour tour includes indoor museum exhibits and driving tours of the base. The tour requires a reservation and you have to provide basic information for a background check at least two weeks in advance (a month for non-U.S. residents), but be aware that slots fill up fast. On the base's website, click Tours for details. ✉ Edwards Air Force Base Visitor Control Center, 405 S. Rosamond Blvd., Edwards ☎ 661/277–8050, 661/277–3510 ⊕ www.afftcmuseum.org ✉ Free.

Antelope Valley California Poppy Reserve

NATIONAL/STATE PARK | The California poppy, the state flower, can be spotted throughout the state, but this quiet park holds the densest concentration. Eight miles of trails wind through 1,745 acres of hills carpeted with poppies and other wildflowers, including a paved section that allows wheelchair access. Keep in mind that poppy flowers will curl up their petals if it's too windy or cold, so plan accordingly. ⚠ Heed the rules and stay on the official trails when taking photos. ■TIP→ **Blooming season is usually March through May.** On a clear day at any time of year, you'll be treated to sweeping views of Antelope Valley. Visit the website or call the wildflower hotline for the current bloom status. ✉ 15101 Lancaster Rd., west off Hwy. 14, Ave. I Exit ☎ 661/724–1180 wildflower hotline, 661/946–6092 administration ⊕ www.parks.ca.gov/poppyreserve ✉ $10 per vehicle ⊙ Visitor center closed mid-May–Feb.

Antelope Valley Indian Museum

MUSEUM | FAMILY | This museum got its start as a private collection of American Indian antiquities gathered in the 1920s by artist and amateur naturalist Howard Arden Edwards. Today, his Swiss chalet–style home is a state museum known for one-of-a-kind artifacts from California, Southwest, and Great Basin native cultures, including ancient tools, artwork, basketry, and rugs. To get here, exit north off Highway 138 at 165th Street East and follow the signs, or take the Avenue K exit off Highway 14. ✉ 15701 E. Ave. M ☎ 661/946–3055 ⊕ www.avim.parks.ca.gov ✉ $3 ⊙ Closed weekdays.

Antelope Valley Winery/Donato Family Vineyard

STORE/MALL | Cyndee and Frank Donato purchased the Los Angeles–based McLester Winery in 1990 and moved it to Lancaster, where the high-desert sun and nighttime chill work their magic on wine grapes such as Merlot, Zinfandel, and Sangiovese. In addition to tastings, the winery hosts a Saturday farmers' market (from May through November between 9 and noon) and sells grass-fed buffalo and other game and exotic meats such as venison, pheasant, and wild boar. ✉ 42041 20th St. W, at Ave. M ☎ 661/722–0145, 888/282–8332 ⊕ www.avwinery.com ✉ Winery free, tastings from $8 ⊙ Closed Mon. and Tues.

The BLVD

ARTS VENUE | Lancaster's downtown arts and culture district and social hub, The BLVD, stretches for nine blocks along West Lancaster Boulevard from 10th Street West to Sierra Highway. Boeing Plaza anchors the east end and marks the start of the Aerospace Walk of Honor—a series of murals and monuments lauding 100 legendary figures, including Neil Armstrong and Chuck Yeager. The district is also home to the Lancaster Performing Arts Center, the

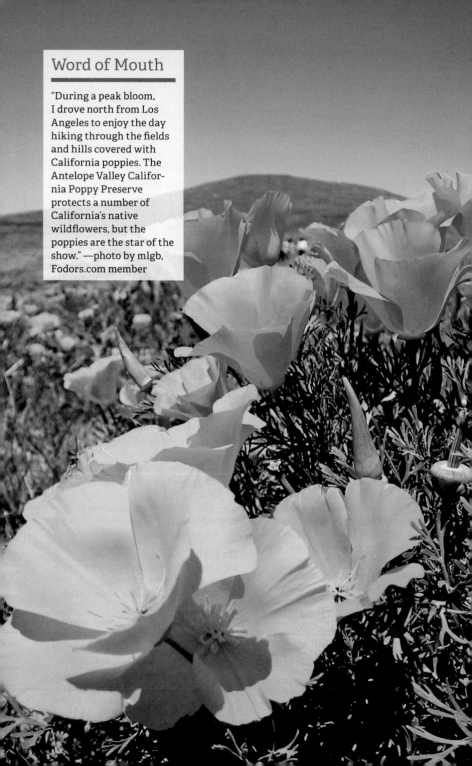

Word of Mouth

"During a peak bloom, I drove north from Los Angeles to enjoy the day hiking through the fields and hills covered with California poppies. The Antelope Valley California Poppy Preserve protects a number of California's native wildflowers, but the poppies are the star of the show." —photo by mlgb, Fodors.com member

Lancaster Museum of Art & History, galleries, restaurants, boutiques, coffee and tea shops, craft breweries, and entertainment venues. ⊠ *W. Lancaster Blvd.* ✛ *10th St. W to Sierra Hwy. and Jackman to Milling Sts.* ☎ *661/723–6074* ⊕ *www.theblvdlancaster.com.*

Devil's Punchbowl Natural Area

NATURE SITE | A mile from the San Andreas Fault, the namesake of this attraction is a natural bowl-shape depression in the earth, framed by 300-foot rock walls. At the bottom is a stream, which you can reach via a moderately strenuous 1-mile hike. You also can detour on a short nature trail; at the top an interpretive center has displays of native flora and fauna, including live animals such as snakes, lizards, and birds of prey. ⊠ *28000 Devil's Punchbowl Rd., south of Hwy. 138, Pearblossom* ☎ *661/944–2743* ⊕ *parks.lacounty.gov/devils-punchbowl-natural-area-and-nature-center/* 🖾 *Free.*

Exotic Feline Breeding Compound's Feline Conservation Center

ZOO | About two dozen species of wild cats, from the unusual, weasel-size jaguarundi to leopards, tigers, and jaguars, inhabit this small, orderly facility. You can see the cats up close (behind barrier fences) in the parklike public zoo and research center, and docents are available to answer questions. ⊠ *Rhyolite Ave. off Mojave-Tropico Rd., Rosamond* ☎ *661/256–3793* ⊕ *www.wildcatzoo.org* 🖾 *$10* 🕑 *Closed Wed.*

St. Andrew's Abbeys

RELIGIOUS SITE | Nestled in the foothills of the Antelope Valley, this peaceful enclave is both Benedictine monastery and restful retreat for those wanting to get away from the bustle of everyday life. Day visitors can walk the lush tree-lined grounds, including a large, shaded pond teeming with ducks and red-eared turtles, or browse the well-stocked gift shop for religious keepsakes. An extensive collection of ceramic tiles in the image of saints and angels by Father Maur van Doorslaer, a Belgian monk whose work U.S. and Canadian collectors favor, are among the items sold here to help sustain the monastery and its good works. ⊠ *31001 N. Valyermo Rd., south of Hwy. 138, Valyermo* ☎ *888/454–5411, 661/944–2178 ceramics studio* ⊕ *www.saintandrewsabbey.com* 🖾 *Free.*

Red Rock Canyon State Park

48 miles north of Lancaster.

On the stretch of Highway 14 that slices through Red Rock Canyon State Park, it's easy to become caught up in the momentum of rushing to your "real" destination. But it would be a shame not to stop for this deeply beautiful canyon, with its rich, layered colors and Native American heritage.

GETTING HERE AND AROUND
The only practical way to get here is by car, taking Highway 14 north from the Palmdale-Lancaster area or south from Ridgecrest.

Sights

Red Rock Canyon State Park

NATIONAL/STATE PARK | A geological feast for the eyes with its layers of pink, white, red, and brown rock, this remote canyon is also a region of fascinating biological diversity—the ecosystems of the Sierra Nevada, the Mojave Desert, and the Basin Range all converge here. Native Americans known as the Kawaiisu lived here some 20,000 years ago; later, Mojave Indians roamed the land for centuries. You can still see remains of gold mining operations in the park, and movies such as *Jurassic Park* have been shot here. For a quiet nature trail a little off the beaten path try

Mojave Desert

the 0.75-mile loop at Red Cliffs Natural Preserve on Highway 14, across from the entrance to the Ricardo Campground. ⊠ *Visitor Center, 37749 Abbott Dr., off Hwy. 14, Cantil* 🕾 *661/946–6092* ⊕ *www.parks.ca.gov* 🗺 *$6 per vehicle.*

Ridgecrest

28 miles northeast of Red Rock Canyon State Park, 77 miles south of Lone Pine.

A military town that serves the U.S. Naval Weapons Center to its north, Ridgecrest has scores of stores, restaurants, and hotels. With about 29,000 residents, it's the last city of any significant size you'll encounter as you head northeast toward Death Valley National Park. It's a good base for visiting regional attractions such as the Trona Pinnacles and Petroglyph Canyons.

GETTING HERE AND AROUND

Arrive here by car via U.S. 395 or, from the Los Angeles area, Highway 14. The local bus service is of limited use to tourists.

ESSENTIALS

TRANSPORTATION CONTACTS Ridgerunner Transit. 🕾 *760/499–5040* ⊕ *ridgecrest-ca.gov/transit/transit.*

VISITOR INFORMATION Ridgecrest Area Convention and Visitors Bureau. ⊠ *643 N. China Lake Blvd., Suite C* 🕾 *760/375–8202, 800/847–4830* ⊕ *www.racvb.com.*

 Sights

Indian Wells Brewing Company

WINERY/DISTILLERY | After driving through the hot desert, you'll surely appreciate a cold one at Indian Wells Brewing Company, where master brewer Rick Lovett lovingly crafts his Lobotomy Bock, Amnesia I.P.A., and Lunatic Lemonade, among others. If you have the kids along, grab a six-pack of his specialty root beer, black cherry, orange, or cream soda. ⊠ *2565 N. Hwy. 14, 2 miles west of U.S. 395, Inyokern* 🕾 *760/377–5989* ⊕ *www.mojavered.com.*

Maturango Museum

CANYON | FAMILY | The museum contains interesting exhibits that survey the Upper Mojave Desert area's art, history, and geology, and sponsors tours of the amazing rock drawings in Petroglyph Canyons. ⊠ *100 E. Las Flores Ave., at Hwy. 178* 🕾 *760/375–6900* ⊕ *www.maturango.org* 🗺 *$5.*

⭐ Petroglyph Canyons

CANYON | FAMILY | Thousands of well-preserved images of animals and humans are scratched or pecked into dark basaltic rocks at Big Petroglyph and Little Petroglyph canyons in the Coso Mountain range, the largest concentration of ancient rock art in the Northern Hemisphere. The canyons lie within the million-acre U.S. Naval Weapons Center at China Lake. Only the drawings of Little Petroglyph can be visited, and only on a guided tour arranged in advance through the Maturango Museum. Tour participants must be U.S. citizens over 10 years of age, and fill out an online application to obtain security clearance. Detailed information about the spring and fall tours, which fill up fast, is provided on the museum's website. ⊠ *100 E. Las Flores Ave.* 🕾 *760/375–6900* ⊕ *www.maturango.org* 🗺 *$60* ⊗ *Closed Dec.–Feb. and June–mid-Sept.*

Trona Pinnacles National Natural Landmark

ARCHAEOLOGICAL SITE | Fantastic-looking formations of calcium carbonate, known as tufa, were formed underwater along fault lines in the bed of what is now Searles Dry Lake. Some of the more than 500 spires stand as tall as 140 feet, creating a landscape so surreal that it doubled for outer-space terrain in the film *Star Trek V.*

An easy-to-walk ½-mile trail allows you to see the tufa up close, but wear sturdy shoes—tufa cuts like coral. The

best road to the area can be impassable after a rainstorm. ✉ *Pinnacle Rd.* ✛ *5 miles south of Hwy. 178, 18 miles east of Ridgecrest* ☎ *760/384–5400 Ridgecrest BLM office* ⊕ *www.blm.gov/visit/ trona-pinnacles.*

Hotels

Hampton Inn & Suites Ridgecrest
$$ | HOTEL | Clean and reliable, the Hampton has a well-equipped exercise room, pool, spotless Internet service, and complimentary breakfast. **Pros:** attentive, friendly service; good breakfast; big rooms. **Cons:** a rather strong chain vibe; thin walls; basic breakfast. ⑤ *Rooms from: $159* ✉ *104 E. Sydnor Ave.* ☎ *760/446–1968* ⊕ *hamptoninn3.hilton. com* ⌁ *93 rooms* ⦿*❙ Breakfast.*

SpringHill Suites Ridgecrest
$$ | HOTEL | The spacious rooms and contemporary feel of this all-suites Marriott brand hotel make this a welcome choice after a long drive in the desert. **Pros:** spacious rooms; good breakfast; helpful staff. **Cons:** small fitness room; basic bathrooms; property needs updating. ⑤ *Rooms from: $159* ✉ *113 E. Sydnor Ave.* ☎ *888/236–2427, 760/446–1630* ⊕ *www.marriott.com/hotels/travel/ iyksh-springhill-suites-ridgecrest* ⌁ *93 studio suites* ⦿*❙ Breakfast.*

Randsburg

21 miles south of Ridgecrest, 26 miles east of Red Rock Canyon State Park.

Randsburg and nearby Red Mountain and Johannesburg make up the Rand Mining District, which first boomed with the discovery of gold in the Rand Mountains in 1895. Rich tungsten ore, used in World War I to make steel alloy, was discovered in 1907, and silver was found in 1919. The boom has gone bust, but the area still has some residents, a few antiques shops, and plenty of

character. Butte Avenue is the main drag in Randsburg, whose tiny city jail, just off Butte, is among the original buildings still standing. An archetypal Old West cemetery perched on a hillside looms over Johannesburg.

GETTING HERE AND AROUND
Arriving by car is the best transportation option. From Red Rock Canyon, drive east on Redrock Randsburg Road. From Ridgecrest, drive south on South China Lake Road and U.S. 395.

Sights

Desert Tortoise Natural Area
NATURE PRESERVE | It may not always be easy to spot the elusive desert tortoise in this peaceful protected habitat but the approximately 40-square-mile area often blazes with wildflowers in the spring and early summer. It is also a great spot to see desert kit fox, red-tailed hawks, cactus wrens, and Mojave rattlesnakes; walking paths and a small interpretive center are part of the experience. ✉ *8 miles northeast of California City via Randsburg Mojave Rd.* ☎ *951/683–3872* ⊕ *www.tortoise-tracks.org* ⌸ *Free.*

General Store
RESTAURANT—SIGHT | Built as Randsburg's Drug Store in 1896, the General Store is one of the area's few surviving ghost-town buildings with an original tin ceiling, light fixtures, and 1904-era marble-and-stained-glass soda fountain. You can still enjoy a phosphate soda from that same fountain, or a lunch of burgers, hot dogs, and chili. ✉ *35 Butte Ave.* ☎ *760/374–2143* ⊕ *www.randsburggeneralstore.com* ⦿ *Closed Tues. and Wed.*

Rand Desert Museum
MUSEUM | The colorful history of the Rand Mining District during its heyday is celebrated in this small museum, including historical mining photographs, documents, and artifacts. ✉ *161 Butte Ave.* ☎ *760/371–0965* ⊕ *www.randdesertmuseum.com* ⌸ *Free* ⦿ *Closed weekdays.*

White House Saloon

BUILDING | This still-surviving saloon served miners and cowboys when it was first established way back in 1897; nowadays tourists and bikers sidle up to the bar for a burger, ice-cold brew, and a giant dose of Old West nostalgia. ⊠ *168 Butte Ave.* ☎ *760/374–2464* ⊘ *Closed Mon.–Thurs.*

Victorville

87 miles south of Ridgecrest.

At the southwest corner of the Mojave is the sprawling town of Victorville, a town with a rich Route 66 heritage and a museum dedicated to the Mother Road. Victorville was named for Santa Fe Railroad pioneer Jacob Nash Victor, who drove the first locomotive through the Cajon Pass here in 1885. Once home to Native Americans, the town later became a rest stop for Mormons and missionaries. In 1941 George Air Force Base, now an airport and storage area, brought scores of military families to the area, many of which have stayed on to raise families of their own.

GETTING HERE AND AROUND

Drive here on Interstate 15 from Los Angeles or Las Vegas, or from the north via U.S. 395. Amtrak and Greyhound also serve the town. There are local buses, but touring by car is more practical.

ESSENTIALS

TRANSPORTATION INFORMATION
Victor Valley Transit Authority. ☎ *760/948–3030* ⊕ *www.vvta.org.*

VISITOR INFORMATION Victor Valley Chamber of Commerce. ⊠ *14174 Green Tree Blvd., at St. Andrews Dr.* ☎ *760/245–6506* ⊕ *www.vvchamber.com.*

Sights

California Route 66 Museum

MUSEUM | Visitors from around the world still think of Historic Route 66 as one of the best ways to see the real America and this 4,500-square-foot museum is chock-full of memorabilia such as maps and postcards, photographs, paintings, and nostalgic displays that bring the iconic highway's history to life. Friendly museum volunteers are more than happy to answer questions and take your picture inside the flower-painted VW Love Bus. ⊠ *16825 S. D St., between 5th and 6th Sts.* ☎ *760/951–0436* ⊕ *califrt66museum.org* ⊠ *Free* ⊘ *Closed Tues. and Wed.*

Mojave Narrows Regional Park

CITY PARK | FAMILY | This 840-acre park is one of the few spots where the Mojave River flows aboveground and the result is open pastures, wetlands, and two lakes surrounded by cottonwoods and cattails. Amenities include camping, fishing, equestrian/walking trails, and a large playground with water park. ⊠ *18000 Yates Rd., north on Ridgecrest Rd. off Bear Valley Rd.* ☎ *760/245–2226* ⊕ *cms.sbcounty.gov/parks* ⊠ *From $8* ⊘ *Closed Tues. and Wed.*

Silverwood Lake State Recreation Area

NATIONAL/STATE PARK | One of the desert's most popular boating and fishing areas, 1,000-acre Silverwood Lake also has campgrounds and a beach with a lifeguard. You can rent boats; fish for trout, largemouth bass, crappie, and catfish; and hike and bike the trails. In winter, bald eagles nest in the tall Jeffrey pines by the shore. ⊠ *14651 Cedar Cir., at Cleghorn Rd., off Hwy. 138, Hesperia* ☎ *760/389–2281* ⊕ *www.parks.ca.gov* ⊠ *$10 per car, $10 per boat.*

Restaurants

Emma Jean's Holland Burger Cafe

$ | DINER | The short-order cook and his grill are literally center stage in this tiny, family-owned restaurant along Historic Route 66, which has changed little since it first opened in 1947. It's the peach cobbler, Brian burger, and fried chicken that keep locals lining up at the door, but anyone wanting a glimpse of 20th-century Americana can get their kicks here, too. **Known for:** Route 66 memorabilia; historical diner; hearty breakfasts. $ *Average main: $9* ⊠ *17143 N. D St., at Water Power Housing Dr.* ☎ *760/243-9938* ⊕ *www.hollandburger.com* ▭ *No credit cards* ☉ *Closed Sun. No dinner.*

Molly Brown's Country Cafe

$ | AMERICAN | FAMILY | There's no mystery why this place is a locals' favorite—the cozy eatery offers a mouthwatering breakfast menu that includes everything from chicken fried steak to a sizzling garden skillet brimming with fresh vegetables. Lunch includes sandwiches, salads, and hot plates such as meat loaf with potatoes, veggies, and corn bread. **Known for:** hearty breakfasts; locals' favorite; homemade breads. $ *Average main: $10* ⊠ *15775 Mojave Dr.* ☎ *760/241-4900* ⊕ *www.mollybrownscountrycafe.com.*

Hotels

Courtyard Marriott Victorville Hesperia

$$ | HOTEL | FAMILY | Rooms are spacious and contemporary, and there is both an indoor pool and large outdoor patio and pool area ideal for large groups. **Pros:** convenient location off Interstate 15; some rooms with desert views; two pools. **Cons:** breakfast only with certain room rates; bistro menu options limited; some rooms close to freeway noise. $ *Rooms from: $136* ⊠ *9619 Mariposa Rd., Hesperia* ☎ *760/956-3876* ⊕ *www.marriott.com* ⇗ *131 rooms.*

La Quinta Inn and Suites Victorville

$ | HOTEL | FAMILY | This small hotel offers a touch more than your typical chain, with contemporary decor in cozy earth tones and spacious rooms. **Pros:** near shopping mall; helpful staff; outdoor pool and Jacuzzi. **Cons:** some freeway noise; aging building; fronts a busy street. $ *Rooms from: $109* ⊠ *12000 Mariposa Rd., Hesperia* ☎ *760/949-9900* ⊕ *www.lq.com* ⇗ *75 rooms* �� *Breakfast.*

Barstow

32 miles northeast of Victorville.

Barstow was born in 1886, when a subsidiary of the Atchison, Topeka, and Santa Fe Railway began construction of a Harvey House depot and hotel here. The depot has been restored and includes two free museums, the family-friendly Calico Ghost Town is just north of town, and there are well-known chain motels and restaurants right off Interstate 15 if you need a rest and refuel before the next stop.

GETTING HERE AND AROUND

Driving here on Interstate 15 from Los Angeles or Las Vegas is the best option, although you can reach Barstow via Amtrak or Greyhound. The local bus service is helpful for sights downtown.

ESSENTIALS

**TRANSPORTATION INFORMATION
Barstow Area Transit/Victor Valley Transit.** ☎ *760/948-3030* ⊕ *vvta.org.*

VISITOR INFORMATION Barstow Area Chamber of Commerce and Visitors Bureau. ⊠ *229 E. Main St.* ☎ *760/256-8617* ⊕ *www.barstowchamber.com.* **California Welcome Center.** ⊠ *2796 Tanger Way, Suite 100, off Lenwood Rd.* ☎ *760/253-4782* ⊕ *www.visitcalifornia.com/attraction/california-welcome-center-barstow.* **Mojave National Preserve Headquarters.** ⊠ *2701 Barstow Rd.* ☎ *760/252-6100* ⊕ *www.nps.gov/moja/planyourvisit/visitorcenters.htm.*

Many of the buildings in the popular Calico Ghost Town are authentic.

 Sights

Afton Canyon

CANYON | Because of its colorful, steep walls, Afton Canyon is often called the Grand Canyon of the Mojave. It was carved over thousands of years by the rushing waters of the Mojave River, which makes one of its few aboveground appearances here. The dirt road that leads to the canyon is ungraded in spots, so it is best to explore it in an all-terrain vehicle. ⊠ *Off Afton Rd., 36 miles northeast of Barstow via I–15* ⊕ *www.recreation.gov.*

Bagdad Café

RESTAURANT—SIGHT | Tourists from all over the world flock to this Route 66 eatery where the 1987 film of the same name was shot. Built in the 1940s, the divey Bagdad Café's walls are crammed with memorabilia donated by visitors famous and otherwise. The very limited bill of fare includes the Bagdad omelet and a buffalo burger with fries, but this place is really about soaking up the Route

66-Americana vibe. ⊠ *46548 National Trails Hwy., at Nopal La., Newberry Springs* ☎ *760/257–3101.*

★ Calico Ghost Town

GHOST TOWN | FAMILY | This former silver-mining boom town was started in 1881 and within a few years boasted 500 mines and 22 saloons. Its reconstruction by Walter Knott of Knott's Berry Farm makes it more about G-rated family entertainment than the town's gritty past, but that doesn't seem to take away from the fun of panning for (fool's) gold, touring the original tunnels of Maggie Mine, or taking a leisurely ride on the Calico Odessa Railroad. Five of the original buildings are still standing, such as the impressive Lane's General Store, and its setting among the stark beauty of the Calico Hills can make a stroll along this once-bustling Main Street downright peaceful. ■ TIP→ **Calico also has ghost tours and regular events such as the yearly bluegrass festival on Mother's Day weekend.** ⊠ *36600 Ghost Town Rd., off I–15,*

Yermo ☎ 760/254–2122 ⊕ cms.sbcounty.gov/parks/Parks/CalicoGhostTown.aspx 🖅 $8.

Casa Del Desierto Harvey House

HISTORIC SITE | This historic train depot was built around 1911 (the original 1885 structure was destroyed by fire) and was one of the original Harvey Houses, providing dining and lodging for weary travelers along the rail lines. Waitresses at the depots were popularized in movies such as *The Harvey Girls* with Judy Garland. It now houses offices and two museums: the Western American Railroad and Route 66 Mother Road, but you can still walk along the porticos of the impressive Spanish Renaissance Classical building, or stroll into the restored lobby where you'll find the original staircase, terrazzo floor, and copper chandeliers. ⊠ 681 N. 1st Ave., near Riverside Dr. ☎ 760/818–4400 ⊕ www.barstowharveyhouse.com 🖅 Free ⊙ Closed Sun.

Desert Discovery Center

MUSEUM | FAMILY | The center's main attraction is Old Woman Meteorite, the second-largest such celestial object ever found in the United States. It was discovered in 1976 about 50 miles from Barstow. The center also has exhibits of fossils, plants, and local animals. Environmental education, history, and the arts are among the topics of workshops and presentations the center hosts. Follow the outdoor desert nature trail with interpretive signs on desert plants and early man's relationship with native plants for shelter, medicine, clothing, food, and weaponry. ■TIP➔ **Reserve a spot in advance for the Stone Age to Space Age tour, offered the first Saturday of the month at 10 am (about 1½ hours, donations appreciated). It begins with a Route 66 history presentation at the Desert Discovery Center, followed by visits to the Main Street Murals and the NASA Goldstone Visitor Center.** ⊠ 831 Barstow Rd. ☎ 760/252–6060 ⊕ www.desertdiscoverycenter.com 🖅 Free ⊙ Closed Sun. and Mon.

★ Goldstone Deep Space Communications Complex

MUSEUM | FAMILY | Friendly and enthusiastic staffers conduct guided tours of this 53-square-mile complex at Fort Irwin Military Base, 35 miles north of Barstow. Tours start at the Goldstone Museum, where exhibits detail past and present space missions and Deep Space Network history. From there, you'll drive out to see the massive concave antennas, starting with those used for early manned space flights and culminating with the 24-story-tall "listening" device. This is one of only three complexes in the world that make up the Deep Space Network, tracking and communicating with spacecraft throughout our solar system. Appointments are required; contact the complex to reserve a slot. ■TIP➔ **No time to tour? Stop by the NASA Goldstone Visitor Center in the Casa del Desierto Harvey House in Barstow to view exhibits and learn about the Deep Space Network and space missions.** ⊠ NASA Goldstone Visitor Center, 681 N. 1st Ave. ☎ 760/255–8688 ⊕ www.gdscc.nasa.gov 🖅 Free ⊙ Closed Sun.

Inscription Canyon

CANYON | Located 42 miles northwest of Barstow in the remote Black Mountains, Inscription has one of the world's largest collections of Native American petroglyphs and pictographs, but it is not an easy trek. Visitors need four-wheel-drive, high-clearance vehicles that are meant to go off road; portions of the journey include pockets of deep sand. It's also best to avoid in the hot summer months, but no matter the season, fill the gas tank and bring plenty of water. ⊠ Barstow ☎ 760/252–6000 ⊕ www.recreation.gov.

Main Street Murals

PUBLIC ART | FAMILY | A series of hand-painted murals (a total of 30 when all are completed) in downtown Barstow depicts the town's history, from prehistoric times and early explorers to pioneer caravans, mining eras, and Route 66. Walking tour guides are available at the Barstow Chamber of Commerce and the public library. Contact the Desert Discovery Center for more details on the murals and monthly guided tours. ⊠ *E. Main St.* ✛ *Between 1st and 7th Sts.* ☎ *760/252–6060* ⊕ *www. mainstreetmurals.com.*

Mojave River Valley Museum

MUSEUM | FAMILY | The floor-to-ceiling collection of local history, both quirky and conventional, includes Ice Age fossils such as a giant mammoth tusk dug up in 2006, Native American artifacts, 19th-century handmade quilts, and displays on early settlers. Entrance is free and there's a little gift shop with a nice collection of books about the area. ■**TIP**➔ **The story about Possum Trot and its population of folk-art dolls is not to be missed.** ⊠ *270 E. Virginia Way, at Barstow Rd.* ☎ *760/256–5452* ⊕ *www. mojaverivervalleymuseum.org* ⊠ *Free.*

Rainbow Basin National Natural Landmark

NATIONAL/STATE PARK | Many science-fiction movies set on Mars have been filmed at this landmark 8 miles north of Barstow. Huge slabs of red, orange, white, and green stone tilt at crazy angles like ships about to capsize and traces of ancient beasts such as mastodons and bear-dogs, which roamed the basin up to 16 million years ago have been discovered in its fossil beds. The dirt road around the basin is narrow and bumpy so vehicles with higher clearance are recommended and rain can quickly turn the road to mud; at times, only four-wheel-drive vehicles are permitted. ⊠ *Fossil Bed Rd., 3 miles west of Fort Irwin Rd. (head north from I–15)* ☎ *760/252–6000* ⊕ *www.recreation.gov.*

Skyline Drive-In Theatre

ARTS VENUE | Check out a bit of surviving Americana at this dusty drive-in, where you can watch the latest Hollywood flicks among the Joshua trees and starry night sky. Keep in mind the old-time

speakers are no more; sound is tuned in via car radio. ⊠ *31175 Old Hwy. 58* ☎ *760/256–3333* ⊠ *$9 per person* ☾ *Closed early Dec.–early Mar.*

Western America Railroad Museum

MUSEUM | FAMILY | You can almost hear the murmur of passengers and rhythmic, metal-on-metal clatter as you stroll past the old cabooses, railcars and engines, such as Sante Fe number 95, that are on display outside the historic Barstow station where this museum is located. The next stop is the indoor portion of the collection, including a train simulator, rail equipment, model railroad display, and other memorabilia. A handful of artifacts from the depot's Harvey House days are on display, as well as period dining-car china from railways around the country. ⊠ *Casa Del Desierto, 685 N. 1st Ave., near Riverside Dr.* ☎ *760/256–9276* ⊕ *www.barstowrailmuseum.org* ⊠ *Free* ☾ *Closed Mon.–Thurs.*

Restaurants

Idle Spurs Steakhouse

$$$ | STEAKHOUSE | This spacious steak-and-seafood restaurant, with its Western-style memorabilia and cheerful white fairy lights, has been a favorite among locals for decades. The menu is very basic no-frills steak-house fare, but the service is friendly and it's a bit of cozy, mid-century charm in the middle of the Mojave. **Known for:** locals' favorite; family run; dated but cozy. ⑤ *Average main: $28* ⊠ *690 Old Hwy. 58, at Camarillo Ave.* ☎ *760/256–8888* ⊕ *www.theidlespurs. com* ☾ *Closed Mon. No lunch.*

Peggy Sue's 50s Diner

$ | AMERICAN | FAMILY | Checkerboard floors and life-size versions of Elvis and Marilyn Monroe greet you at this funky '50s coffee shop and pizza parlor in the middle of the Mojave. The fare is basic American—fries, onion rings, burgers, pork chops—with some fun surprises such as pineapple pie and deep-fried dill pickles. **Known for:** movie, TV memorabilia; over-the-top '50s vibe; gift shop, jukebox, soda fountain, duck pond. ⑤ *Average main: $11* ✉ *35654 W. Yermo Rd., at Daggett-Yermo Rd., Yermo* ☎ *760/254–3370* ⊕ *www.peggysuesdiner.com.*

Hotels

Ayres Hotel Barstow

$$ | HOTEL | FAMILY | In a sea of chain hotels this one has a few homespun touches up its sleeves, such as fresh-baked cookies in the cozy lobby lounge every evening. **Pros:** clean rooms; engaged management; entirely non-smoking; Tesla charging stations. **Cons:** pricey for Barstow; near freeway; shared parking lot with other businesses. ⑤ *Rooms from: $139* ✉ *2812 Lenwood Rd.* ☎ *760/307–3121* ⊕ *www.ayreshotels.com/ayres-hotel-barstow* ⮌ *92 rooms* ⦿ *Breakfast.*

Mojave National Preserve

Visitor center 118 miles east of Barstow, 58 miles west of Needles.

The 1.6 million acres of the Mojave National Preserve hold a surprising abundance of plant and animal life—especially considering their elevation (nearly 8,000 feet in some areas). There are traces of human history here as well, including abandoned army posts and vestiges of mining and ranching towns. The Cinder Cone Lava Beds area holds 75 inactive volcanoes; the youngest is 11,500 years old. North Cima Road passes the world's largest Joshua tree forest. Mojave National Preserve rangers also oversee the adjacent 20,920-acre Castle Mountains National Monument, created in 2016.

GETTING HERE AND AROUND

A car is the best way to access the preserve, which lies between Interstates 15 and 40. Kelbaker Road bisects the park from north to south; northbound from Interstate 40, Essex Road gets you to Hole-in-the-Wall on pavement but is graveled beyond there.

Sights

Hole-in-the-Wall

NATURE SITE | Created millions of years ago by volcanic activity, Hole-in-the-Wall formed when gases were trapped between layers of deposited ash, rock, and lava; the gas bubbles left holes in the solidified material. You will encounter one of California's most distinctive hiking experiences here. Proceeding clockwise from a small visitor center, you walk gently down and around a craggy hill, past cacti and fading petroglyphs to Banshee Canyon, whose pockmarked walls resemble Swiss cheese. From there you head back out of the canyon, supporting yourself with widely spaced iron rings (some of which wiggle precariously from their rock moorings) as you ascend a 50-foot incline that deposits you back near the visitor center. The one-hour adventure can be challenging but wholly entertaining. ■ TIP➔ **There are no services (gas or food) nearby; be sure to fill your tank and pack some snacks before heading out here.** ✉ *Mojave National Preserve* ☎ *760/252–6104* ⊕ *www.nps.gov/moja* ⛺ *Free.*

★ Kelso Dunes

NATURE SITE | As you enter the preserve from the south, you'll pass miles of open scrub brush, Joshua trees, and beautiful red-black cinder cones before encountering the Kelso Dunes. These golden, fine-sand slopes cover 70 square miles, reaching heights of 600 feet. You can reach them via a short walk from the main parking area, but be prepared for a serious workout. When you reach the top of a dune, kick a little bit of sand down the lee side and listen to the sand "sing." North of the dunes, in the town of Kelso, is the Mission revival–style **Kelso Depot Visitor Center.** The striking building, which dates to 1923, contains several rooms of desert- and train-theme exhibits. ⊠ *For Kelso Depot Visitor Center, take Kelbaker Rd. exit from I–15 (head south 34 miles) or I–40 (head north 22 miles)* ☎ *760/252–6100, 760/252–6108* ⊕ *www.nps.gov/moja* ⊠ *Free* ⊘ *Kelso Depot visitor center closed Tues. and Wed.*

Chapter 10

SEQUOIA AND KINGS CANYON NATIONAL PARKS

10

Updated by
Cheryl Crabtree

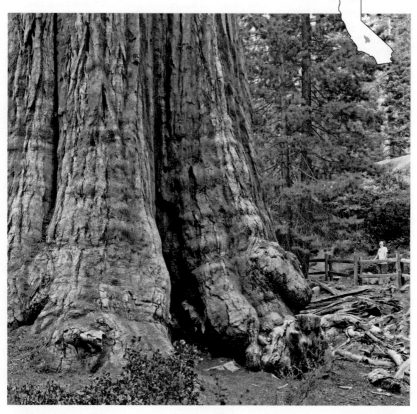

👁 **Sights**
★★★★★

🍴 **Restaurants**
★★★★☆

🛏 **Hotels**
★★★★★

🛍 **Shopping**
★☆☆☆☆

🍸 **Nightlife**
★☆☆☆☆

WELCOME TO SEQUOIA AND KINGS CANYON NATIONAL PARKS

TOP REASONS TO GO

★ **Gentle giants:** You'll feel small—in a good way—walking among some of the world's largest living things in Sequoia's Giant Forest and Kings Canyon's Grant Grove.

★ **Because it's there:** You can't even glimpse it from the main part of Sequoia, but the sight of majestic Mt. Whitney is worth the trip to the eastern face of the High Sierra.

★ **Underground exploration:** Far older even than the giant sequoias, the gleaming limestone formations in Crystal Cave will draw you along dark, marble passages.

★ **A grander-than-Grand Canyon:** Drive the twisting Kings Canyon Scenic Byway down into the jagged, granite Kings River canyon, deeper in parts than the Grand Canyon.

★ **Regal solitude:** To spend a day or two hiking in a subalpine world of your own, pick one of the many trailheads at Mineral King.

The two parks comprise 865,964 acres (1,353 square miles), mostly on the western flank of the Sierra. A map of the adjacent parks looks vaguely like a mitten, with the palm of Sequoia National Park south of the north-pointing, skinny thumb and long fingers of Kings Canyon National Park. Between the western thumb and eastern fingers, north of Sequoia, lies part of Sequoia National Forest, which includes Giant Sequoia National Monument.

1 **Giant Forest–Lodgepole Village.** One of the most heavily visited areas of Sequoia contains major sights such as Giant Forest, General Sherman Tree, Crystal Cave, and Moro Rock.

2 **Grant Grove Village–Redwood Canyon.** The "thumb" of Kings Canyon National Park is its busiest section, where Grant Grove, General Grant Tree, Panoramic Point, and Big Stump are the main attractions.

3 **Cedar Grove.** The drive through the high-country portion of Kings Canyon National Park to Cedar Grove Village, on the canyon floor, reveals magnificent granite formations of varied hues.

Rock meets river in breathtaking fashion at Zumwalt Meadow.

4 **Mineral King.** In the southeast section of Sequoia, the highest road-accessible part of the park is a good place to hike, camp, and soak up the unspoiled grandeur of the Sierra Nevada.

5 **Mount Whitney.** The highest peak in the Lower 48 stands on the eastern edge of Sequoia; to get there from Giant Forest you must either backpack eight days through the mountains or drive nearly 400 miles around the park to its other side.

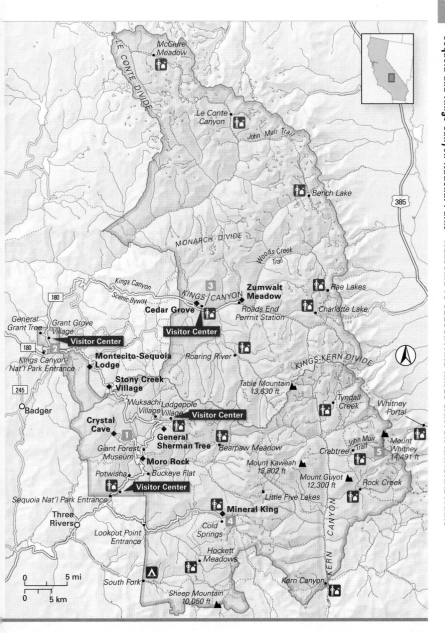

The monstrously thick trunks and branches, remarkably shallow root systems, and neck-craning heights of the sequoias are almost impossible to believe, as is the fact they can live for more than 2,500 years. Many of these towering marvels are in the Giant Forest stretch of Generals Highway, which connects Sequoia and Kings Canyon national parks.

Next to or a few miles off the 46-mile Generals Highway are most of Sequoia National Park's main attractions and Grant Grove Village, the orientation hub for Kings Canyon National Park. The two parks share a boundary that runs from the Central Valley in the west, where the Sierra Nevada foothills begin, to the range's dramatic eastern ridges. Kings Canyon has two portions: the smaller is shaped like a bent finger and encompasses Grant Grove Village and Redwood Mountain Grove (two of the parks' largest concentration of sequoias), and the larger is home to stunning Kings River Canyon, whose vast, unspoiled peaks and valleys are a backpacker's dream. Sequoia is in one piece and includes Mt. Whitney, the highest point in the lower 48 states (although it is impossible to see from the western part of the park and is a chore to ascend from either side).

Planning

When to Go

The best times to visit are spring and fall, when temperatures are moderate and crowds thin. Summertime can draw hordes of tourists to see the giant sequoias, and the few, narrow roads mean congestion at peak holiday times. If you must visit in summer, go during the week. By contrast, in wintertime you may feel as though you have the parks all to yourself. But because of heavy snows, sections of the main park roads can be closed without warning, and low-hanging clouds can move in and obscure mountains and valleys for days. From early October to late April, check road and weather conditions before venturing out.

■ TIP→ **Even in summer, you can escape hordes of people just walking ¼ to ½ mile off the beaten path on a less-used trail.**

Festivals and Events

Annual Trek to the Tree

FESTIVAL | On the second Sunday of December, thousands of carolers gather at the base of General Grant Tree, the nation's official Christmas tree. ☏ 559/565–3341.

Big Fresno Fair

FESTIVAL | Over 12 days in October, agricultural, home-arts, and other competitions, plus horse racing and a carnival make for a lively county fair. ✉ Fresno ☏ 559/650–3247 ⊕ www.fresnofair.com.

Blossom Days Festival

FESTIVAL | On the first Saturday of March, communities along Fresno County's Blossom Trail celebrate the flowering of the area's orchards, citrus groves, and vineyards. ☏ 559/981–5500 ⊕ www. goblossomtrail.com.

Jazzaffair

FESTIVAL | On the second weekend of April, a festival of mostly traditional jazz takes place at several venues just south of the parks. ⊕ sierratraditionaljazzclub.com.

Woodlake Rodeo

FESTIVAL | The local Lions Club sponsors this rousing rodeo that draws large crowds to Woodlake on Mother's Day weekend. ☏ 559/564–8555 ⊕ www. woodlakelionsclub.com.

Planning Your Time

SEQUOIA NATIONAL PARK IN ONE DAY

After spending the night in Visalia or Three Rivers—and provided your vehicle's length does not exceed 22 feet—take off early on Route 198 to the **Sequoia National Park entrance.** Pull over at the **Hospital Rock** picnic area to gaze up at the imposing granite formation of Moro Rock, which you later will climb. Heed signs that advise "10 mph" around tight turns as you climb

3,500 feet on **Generals Highway** to the **Giant Forest Museum.** Spend a half hour here, then examine trees firsthand by circling the lovely **Round Meadow** on the **Big Trees Trail,** to which you must walk from the museum or from its parking lot across the road.

Get back in your car and continue a few miles north on Generals Highway to see the jaw-dropping **General Sherman Tree.** Then set off on the **Congress Trail** so that you can be further awed by the Senate and House big-tree clusters. Buy lunch at the **Lodgepole** complex, 2 miles to the north, and eat at the nearby **Pinewood** picnic area. Now you're ready for the day's big exercise, climbing **Moro Rock.**

You can drive there or, if it is summer, park at the museum lot and take the free shuttle. Count on spending at least an hour for the 350-step ascent and descent, with a pause on top to appreciate the 360-degree view. Get back in the car, or on the shuttle, and proceed past the **Tunnel Log** to **Crescent Meadow.** Spend a relaxing hour or two strolling on the trails that pass by, among other things, **Tharp's Log.** By now you've probably renewed your appetite; head to **Lodgepole Grill & Market** or the restaurant at **Wuksachi Lodge.**

KINGS CANYON NATIONAL PARK IN ONE DAY

Enter the park via the **Kings Canyon Scenic Byway** (Route 180), having spent the night in Fresno or Visalia. Better yet, wake up already in **Grant Grove Village,** perhaps in the **John Muir Lodge.** Stock up for a picnic with takeout food from the **Grant Grove Restaurant,** or purchase prepackaged food from the nearby market. Drive east a mile to see the **General Grant Tree** and compact **Grant Grove's** other sequoias. If it's no later than mid-morning, walk up the short trail at **Panoramic Point,** for a great view of Hume Lake and the High Sierra. Either way, return to Route 180 and continue east. Stop at Junction View to

AVERAGE HIGH/LOW TEMPERATURES

JAN.	FEB.	MAR.	APR.	MAY	JUNE
42/24	44/25	46/26	51/30	58/36	68/44
JULY	AUG.	SEPT.	OCT.	NOV.	DEC.
76/51	76/50	71/45	61/38	50/31	44/27

take in several noteworthy peaks that tower over Kings Canyon. From here, visit **Boyden Cavern** or continue to **Cedar Grove Village,** pausing along the way for a gander at **Grizzly Falls.** Eat at a table by the **South Fork of the Kings River,** or on the deck off the Cedar Grove Snack Bar. Now you are ready for the day's highlight, strolling **Zumwalt Meadow,** which lies a few miles past the village.

After you have enjoyed that short trail and the views it offers of **Grand Sentinel** and **North Dome,** you might as well go the extra mile to **Roads End,** where backpackers embark for the High Sierra wilderness. Make the return trip—with a quick stop at **Roaring River Falls**—past Grant Grove and briefly onto southbound **Generals Highway.** Pull over at the **Redwood Mountain Overlook** and use binoculars to look down upon the world's largest sequoia grove, then drive another couple of miles to the **Kings Canyon Overlook,** where you can survey some of what you have done today. Make reservations for a late dinner at **Wuksachi Lodge.**

Getting Here and Around

AIR TRAVEL

The closest airport to Sequoia and Kings Canyon national parks is Fresno Yosemite International Airport (FAT).

AIRPORT CONTACTS Fresno Yosemite International Airport (*FAT*). ✉ *5175 E. Clinton Way, Fresno* ☎ *800/244–2359 automated info, 559/454–2052 terminal info desk* ⊕ *www.flyfresno.com.*

CAR TRAVEL

Sequoia is 36 miles east of Visalia on Route 198; Grant Grove Village in Kings Canyon is 56 miles east of Fresno on Route 180. There is no automobile entrance on the eastern side of the Sierra. Routes 180 and 198 are connected by Generals Highway, a paved two-lane road that sometimes sees delays at peak times due to ongoing improvements. The road is extremely narrow and steep from Route 198 to Giant Forest, so keep an eye on your engine temperature gauge, as the incline and congestion can cause vehicles to overheat; to avoid overheated brakes, use low gears on downgrades.

If you are traveling in an RV or with a trailer, study the restrictions on these vehicles. Do not travel beyond Potwisha Campground on Route 198 with an RV longer than 22 feet; take straighter, easier Route 180 instead. Maximum vehicle length on Generals Highway is 40 feet, or 50 feet combined length for vehicles with trailers.

Generals Highway between Lodgepole and Grant Grove is sometimes closed by snow. The Mineral King Road from Route 198 into southern Sequoia National Park is closed 2 miles below Atwell Mill either on November 1 or after the first heavy snow. The Buckeye Flat–Middle Fork Trailhead road is closed from mid-October to mid-April when the Buckeye Flat Campground closes. The lower Crystal Cave Road is closed when the cave closes (typically in November). Its upper 2 miles, as well as the Panoramic Point and Moro Rock–Crescent Meadow roads, close with the first heavy snow.

Because of the danger of rockfall, the portion of Kings Canyon Scenic Byway east of Grant Grove closes in winter. For current road and weather conditions, call ☎ 559/565–3341 or visit the park website: ⊕ www.nps.gov/seki.

■TIP➜ **Snowstorms are common from late October through April. Unless you have a four-wheel-drive vehicle with snow tires, you should carry chains and know how to install them.**

Park Essentials

ACCESSIBILITY

All the visitor centers, the Giant Forest Museum, and Big Trees Trail are wheelchair accessible, as are some short ranger-led walks and talks. General Sherman Tree can be reached via a paved, level trail near a parking area. None of the caves is accessible, and wilderness areas must be reached by horseback or on foot. Some picnic tables are extended to accommodate wheelchairs. Many of the major sites are in the 6,000-foot range and thin air at high elevations can cause respiratory distress for people with breathing difficulties. Carry oxygen if necessary. Contact the park's main number for more information.

PARK FEES AND PERMITS

The admission fee is $35 per vehicle, $30 per motorcycle, and $20 per person for those who enter by bus, on foot, bicycle, horse, or any other mode of transportation; it is valid for seven days in both parks. U.S. residents over the age of 62 pay $80 for a lifetime pass, and permanently disabled U.S. residents are admitted free.

If you plan to camp in the backcountry, you need a permit, which costs $15 for hikers or $30 for stock users (e.g., horseback riders). One permit covers the group. Availability of permits depends upon trailhead quotas. Reservations are accepted by mail or email for a $15

processing fee, beginning March 1, and must be made at least 14 days in advance (☎ 559/565–3766). Without a reservation, you may still get a permit on a first-come, first-served basis starting at 1 pm the day before you plan to hike. For more information on backcountry camping or travel with pack animals (horses, mules, burros, or llamas), contact the Wilderness Permit Office (☎ 530/565–3766).

PARK HOURS

The parks are open 24/7 year-round. They are in the Pacific time zone.

CELL PHONE RECEPTION

Cell phone reception is poor to nonexistent in the higher elevations and spotty even on portions of Generals Highway, where you can (on rare clear days) see the Central Valley. Public telephones may be found at the visitor centers, ranger stations, some trailheads, and at all restaurants and lodging facilities in the park.

Educational Offerings

Educational programs at the parks include museum-style exhibits, ranger- and naturalist-led talks and walks, film and other programs, and sightseeing tours, most of them conducted by either the park service or the nonprofit Sequoia Parks Conservancy. Exhibits at the visitor centers and the Giant Forest Museum focus on different aspects of the park: its history, wildlife, geology, climate, and vegetation—most notably the giant sequoias. Weekly notices about programs are posted at the visitor centers and elsewhere.

Grant Grove Visitor Center at Kings Canyon National Park has maps of self-guided park tours. Ranger-led walks and programs take place throughout the year in Grant Grove. Cedar Grove and Forest Service campgrounds have activities from Memorial Day to Labor Day. Check bulletin boards or visitor centers for schedules.

EXHIBITS
Giant Forest Museum
MUSEUM | Well-imagined and interactive displays at this worthwhile stop provide the basics about sequoias, of which there are 2,161 with diameters exceeding 10 feet in the approximately 2,000-acre Giant Forest. ⊠ *Sequoia National Park ⊕ Generals Hwy., 4 miles south of Lodgepole Visitor Center* ☎ *559/565–4436* ⊠ *Free* ☞ *Shuttle: Giant Forest or Moro Rock–Crescent Meadow.*

PROGRAMS AND SEMINARS
Evening Programs
TOUR—SIGHT | The Sequoia Parks Conservancy presents films, hikes, and evening lectures during the summer and winter. From May through October the popular Wonders of the Night Sky programs celebrate the often stunning views of the heavens experienced at both parks. ⊠ *Sequoia National Park* ☎ *559/565–4251* ⊕ *www.sequoiaparks-conservancy.org.*

Free Nature Programs
TOUR—SIGHT | Almost any summer day, ½-hour to 1½-hour ranger talks and walks explore subjects such as the life of the sequoia, the geology of the park, and the habits of bears. Giant Forest, Lodgepole Visitor Center, and Wuksachi Village are frequent starting points. Look for less frequent tours in the winter from Grant Grove. Check bulletin boards throughout the park for the week's offerings. ⊕ *www.sequoiaparksconservancy.org.*

Junior Ranger Program
TOUR—SIGHT | FAMILY | Children over age five can earn a patch upon completion of a fun set of age-appropriate tasks outlined in the Junior Ranger booklet. Pick one up at any visitor center. ☎ *559/565–3341.*

Seminars
TOUR—SIGHT | Expert naturalists lead seminars on a range of topics, including birds, wildflowers, geology, botany, photography, park history, backpacking, and pathfinding. Reservations are required. Information about times and prices is available at the visitor centers or through the Sequoia Parks Conservancy. ⊠ *Sequoia National Park* ☎ *559/565–4251* ⊕ *www.sequoiaparks-conservancy.org.*

TOURS
★ Sequoia Parks Conservancy Field Institute
TOUR—SIGHT | The Sequoia Parks Conservancy's highly regarded educational division conducts half-day, single-day, and multiday tours that include backpacking hikes, natural-history walks, cross-country skiing, kayaking excursions, and motor-coach tours. ⊠ *47050 Generals Hwy., Unit 10, Three Rivers* ☎ *559/565–4251* ⊕ *www.sequoiaparks-conservancy.org* ⊠ *From $40 for ½-day guided tour.*

Sequoia Sightseeing Tours
TOUR—SIGHT | This locally owned operator's friendly, knowledgeable guides conduct daily interpretive sightseeing tours in Sequoia and Kings Canyon. Reservations are essential. The company also offers private tours. ⊠ *Three Rivers* ☎ *559/561–4189* ⊕ *www.sequoiatours.com* ⊠ *From $79 tour of Sequoia; from $139 tour of Kings Canyon.*

Restaurants

In Sequoia and Kings Canyon national parks, you can treat yourself (and the family) to a high-quality meal in a wonderful setting in the Peaks restaurant at Wuksachi Lodge, but otherwise you should keep your expectations modest. You can grab bread, spreads, drinks, and fresh produce at one of several small grocery stores for a picnic, or get takeout food from the Grant Grove Restaurant, the Cedar Grove snack bar, or one of the two small Lodgepole eateries. Between the parks and just off Generals Highway, the Montecito Sequoia Lodge has a year-round buffet. *Restaurant reviews have been shortened. For full information, visit Fodors.com.*

Hotels

Hotel accommodations in Sequoia and Kings Canyon are limited, and—although they are clean and comfortable—tend to lack much in-room character. Keep in mind, however, that the extra money you spend on lodging here is offset by the time you'll save by being inside the parks. You won't be faced with a 60- to 90-minute commute from the less-expensive motels in Three Rivers (by far the most charming option), Visalia, and Fresno. Reserve as far in advance as you can, especially for summertime stays. *Hotel reviews have been shortened. For full information, visit Fodors.com.*

What It Costs			
$	$$	$$$	$$$$
RESTAURANTS			
under $12	$12–$20	$21–$30	over $30
HOTELS			
under $100	$100–$150	$151–$200	over $200

Visitor Information

NATIONAL PARK SERVICE Sequoia and Kings Canyon National Parks. ⊠ *47050 Generals Hwy. (Rte. 198), Three Rivers* ☎ *559/565–3341* ⊕ *nps.gov/seki.*

SEQUOIA VISITOR CENTERS
Foothills Visitor Center
INFO CENTER | Exhibits here focus on the foothills and resource issues facing the parks. You can pick up books, maps, and a list of ranger-led walks, and get wilderness permits. ⊠ *47050 Generals Hwy., Rte. 198, 1 mile north of Ash Mountain entrance, Sequoia National Park* ☎ *559/565–3341.*

Lodgepole Visitor Center
INFO CENTER | Along with exhibits on the area's history, geology, and wildlife, the center screens an outstanding 22-minute film about bears. You can buy books, maps, and tickets to cave tours here. ⊠ *Sequoia National Park ✛ Generals Hwy. (Rte. 198), 21 miles north of Ash Mountain entrance* ☎ *559/565–3341* ⊙ *Closed Oct.–Apr.* ☞ *Shuttle: Giant Forest or Wuksachi-Lodgepole-Dorst.*

KINGS CANYON VISITOR CENTERS
Cedar Grove Visitor Center
INFO CENTER | Off the main road and behind the Sentinel Campground, this small ranger station has books and maps, plus information about hikes and other activities. ⊠ *Kings Canyon National Park ✛ Kings Canyon Scenic Byway, 30 miles east of Rte. 180/198 junction* ☎ *559/565–3341* ⊙ *Closed mid-Sept.–mid-May.*

Kings Canyon Park Visitor Center
INFO CENTER | The center's 15-minute film and various exhibits provide an overview of the park's canyon, sequoias, and human history. Books, maps, and weather advice are dispensed here, as are (if available) free wilderness permits. ⊠ *Kings Canyon National Park ✛ Grant Grove Village, Generals Hwy. (Rte. 198), 3 miles northeast of Rte. 180, Big Stump entrance* ☎ *559/565–3341.*

Sequoia National Park

Sights

SCENIC DRIVES
★ Generals Highway
SCENIC DRIVE | One of California's most scenic drives, this 46-mile road is the main asphalt artery between Sequoia and Kings Canyon national parks. Some portions are also signed as Route 180, others as Route 198. Named after the landmark Grant and Sherman trees that leave so many visitors awestruck,

Western Sequoia and Kings Canyon National Parks

Yucca Point

180

Boyden Cavern

Kings Canyon Scenic Byway

South Fork Kings River

Grizzly Falls

Lewis Creek Trail

CONVERSE BASIN GROVE

Hume Lake

Sheep Creek

Cedar Grove Visitor Center

General Grant Tree

Crystal Springs

KINGS CANYON NATIONAL PARK

Azalea Sunset

Kings Canyon Park Visitor Center

Kings Canyon Overlook

245

180

Redwood Mountain Overlook

Redwood Mountain Sequoia Grove

Kings Canyon National Park Entrance

TO CAT HAVEN

Generals Highway

Eshom

Montecito Sequoia Lodge

Stony Creek

REDWOOD CANYON

SILLIMAN CREST

Stony Creek Village

Dorst Creek

Wuksachi Village

Lodgepole Visitor Center and Village

Twin Lakes Trail

Wolverton

Crystal Cave

Pinewood

General Sherman Tree

Kaweah River

Yucca Creek

Giant Forest Museum

Tharps Log

High Sierra Trail

Crescent Meadow

Auto Log

Tunnel Log

Moro Rock

Colony Mill Trail

North Fork

ASH PEAKS

Hospital Rock

Potwisha

Buckeye Flat

SEQUOIA NATIONAL PARK

Foothills Visitor Center

Generals Highway

TO MINERAL KING AREA

Sequoia National Park Entrance

Atwell Mill

0   3 mi

0   3 km

198

Kaweah River

Mineral King Rd

Lake Kaweah

Three Rivers

Lookout Point Entrance

Kaweah River

Generals Highway runs from Sequoia's Foothills Visitor Center north to Kings Canyon's Grant Grove Village. Along the way, it passes the turnoff to Crystal Cave, the Giant Forest Museum, Lodgepole Village, and other popular attractions. The lower portion, from Hospital Rock to the Giant Forest, is especially steep and winding. If your vehicle is 22 feet or longer, avoid that stretch by entering the parks via Route 180 (from Fresno) rather than Route 198 (from Visalia or Three Rivers). Take your time on this road—there's a lot to see, and wildlife can scamper across at any time. ⊠ *Sequoia National Park.*

Mineral King Road

SCENIC DRIVE | Vehicles longer than 22 feet are prohibited on this side road into southern Sequoia National Park, and for good reason: it contains 589 twists and turns. Anticipating an average speed of 20 mph is optimistic. The scenery is splendid as you climb nearly 6,000 feet from Three Rivers to the Mineral King Area. In addition to maneuvering the blind curves and narrow stretches, you might find yourself sharing the pavement with bears, rattlesnakes, and even softball-size spiders. Allow 90 minutes each way. ⊠ *Sequoia National Forest* ⊹ *East off Sierra Dr. (Rte. 198), 3.5 miles northeast of Three Rivers* ⊙ *Road typically closed Nov.–late May.*

SCENIC STOPS

Sequoia National Park is all about the trees, and to understand the scale of these giants you must walk among them. If you do nothing else, get out of the car for a short stroll through one of the groves. But there is much more to the park than the trees. Try to access one of the vista points that provide a panoramic view over the forested mountains. Generals Highway (on Routes 198 and 180) will be your route to most of the park's sights. A few short spur roads lead from the highway to some sights, and Mineral King Road branches off

Route 198 to enter the park at Lookout Point, winding east from there to the park's southernmost section.

Auto Log

FOREST | Before its wood showed signs of severe rot, cars drove right on top of this giant fallen sequoia. Now it's a great place to pose for pictures or shoot a video. ⊠ *Sequoia National Park* ⊹ *Moro Rock–Crescent Meadow Rd., 1 mile south of Giant Forest.*

Crescent Meadow

TRAIL | A sea of ferns signals your arrival at what John Muir called the "gem of the Sierra." Walk around for an hour or two and you might decide that the Scotland-born naturalist was exaggerating a bit, but the verdant meadow is quite pleasant and you just might see a bear. Wildflowers bloom here throughout the summer. ⊠ *Sequoia National Park* ⊹ *End of Moro Rock–Crescent Meadow Rd., 2.6 miles east off Generals Hwy.* ☞ *Shuttle: Moro Rock–Crescent Meadow.*

★ Crystal Cave

CAVE | One of more than 200 caves in Sequoia and Kings Canyon, Crystal Cave is composed largely of marble, the result of limestone being hardened under heat and pressure. It contains several eye-popping formations. There used to be more, but some were damaged or obliterated by early-20th-century dynamite blasting. You can only see the cave on a tour. The Daily Tour ($16), a great overview, takes about 50 minutes. To immerse yourself in the cave experience—at times you'll be crawling on your belly—book the exhilarating Wild Cave Tour ($135). Availability is limited—reserve tickets at least 48 hours in advance at ⊕ *www.recreation.gov* or stop by either the Foothills or Lodgepole visitor center first thing in the morning to try to nab a same-day ticket; they're not sold at the cave itself. ⊠ *Crystal Cave Rd., off Generals Hwy.* ☏ *877/444–6777* ⊕ *www.sequoiaparksconservancy.org/ crystalcave.html* ⊟ *$16* ⊙ *Closed Oct.– late May.*

★ General Sherman Tree

LOCAL INTEREST | The 274.9-foot-tall General Sherman is one of the world's tallest and oldest sequoias, and it ranks No. 1 in volume, adding the equivalent of a 60-foot-tall tree every year to its approximately 52,500 cubic feet of mass. The tree doesn't grow taller, though—it's dead at the top. A short, wheelchair-accessible trail leads to the tree from Generals Highway, but the main trail (½ mile) winds down from a parking lot off Wolverton Road. The walk back up the main trail is steep, but benches along the way provide rest for the short of breath. ⊠ *Sequoia National Park* ⊹ *Main trail Wolverton Rd. off Generals Hwy. (Rte. 198)* ⌁ *Shuttle: Giant Forest or Wolverton–Sherman Tree.*

Mineral King Area

NATURE PRESERVE | A subalpine valley of fir, pine, and sequoia trees, Mineral King sits at 7,500 feet at the end of a steep, winding road. This is the highest point to which you can drive in the park. It is open only from Memorial Day through late October. ⊠ *Sequoia National Park* ⊹ *Mineral King Rd., 25 miles east of Generals Hwy. (Rte. 198)* ⊗ *Closed late Oct.–May.*

★ Moro Rock

NATURE SITE | This sight offers panoramic views to those fit and determined enough to mount its 350 or so steps. In a case where the journey rivals the destination, Moro's stone stairway is so impressive in its twisty inventiveness that it's on the National Register of Historic Places. The rock's 6,725-foot summit overlooks the Middle Fork Canyon, sculpted by the Kaweah River and approaching the depth of Arizona's Grand Canyon, although smoggy, hazy air often compromises the view. ⊠ *Sequoia National Park* ⊹ *Moro Rock–Crescent Meadow Rd., 2 miles east off Generals Hwy. (Rte. 198) to parking area* ⌁ *Shuttle: Moro Rock–Crescent Meadow.*

Tunnel Log

LOCAL INTEREST | This 275-foot tree fell in 1937, and soon a 17-foot-wide, 8-foot-high hole was cut through it for vehicular passage (not to mention the irresistible photograph) that continues today. Large vehicles take the nearby bypass. ⊠ *Sequoia National Park* ⊹ *Moro Rock–Crescent Meadow Rd., 2 miles east of Generals Hwy. (Rte. 198)* ⌁ *Shuttle: Moro Rock–Crescent Meadow.*

🏃 Activities

The best way to see Sequoia is to take a hike. Unless you do so, you'll miss out on the up-close grandeur of mist wafting between deeply scored, red-orange tree trunks bigger than you've ever seen. If it's winter, put on some snowshoes or cross-country skis and plunge into the snow-swaddled woodland. There are not too many other outdoor options: no off-road driving is allowed in the parks, and no special provisions have been made for bicycles. Boating, rafting, and snowmobiling are also prohibited.

BICYCLING

Steep, winding roads and shoulders that are either narrow or nonexistent make bicycling here more of a danger than a pleasure. Outside of campgrounds, you are not allowed to pedal on unpaved roads.

BIRD-WATCHING

More than 200 species of birds inhabit Sequoia and Kings Canyon national parks. Not seen in most parts of the United States, the white-headed woodpecker and the pileated woodpecker are common in most mid-elevation areas here. There are also many hawks and owls, including the renowned spotted owl. Species are diverse in both parks due to the changes in elevation, and range from warblers, kingbirds, thrushes, and sparrows in the foothills to goshawk, blue grouse, red-breasted nuthatch, and brown creeper at the highest elevations. The Sequoia Parks Conservancy (☎ 559/565–4251 ⊕ www. sequoiaparksconservancy.org) has information about bird-watching in the southern Sierra.

CROSS-COUNTRY SKIING

For a one-of-a-kind experience, cut through the groves of mammoth sequoias in Giant Forest. Some of the Crescent Meadow trails are suitable for skiing as well; none of the trails is groomed. You can park at Giant Forest. Note that roads can be precarious in bad weather. Some advanced trails begin at Wolverton.

Alta Market and Ski Shop

SKIING/SNOWBOARDING | Rent cross-country skis and snowshoes here. Depending on snowfall amounts, instruction may also be available. Reservations are recommended. Marked trails cut through Giant Forest, about 5 miles south of Wuksachi Lodge. ⊠ Sequoia National Park ⚓ At Lodgepole, off Generals Hwy. (Rte. 198) ☎ 559/565–3301 ⓢ Shuttle: Wuksachi-Lodgepole-Dorst.

FISHING

There's limited trout fishing in the creeks and rivers from late April to mid-November. The Kaweah River is a popular spot; check at visitor centers for open and closed waters. Some of the park's secluded backcountry lakes have good fishing. A California fishing license, required for persons 16 and older, costs about $16 for one day, $24 for two days, and $48 for 10 days (discounts are available for state residents and others). For park regulations, closures, and restrictions, call the parks at ☎ 559/565–3341 or stop at a visitor center. Licenses and fishing tackle are usually available at Hume Lake.

California Department of Fish and Game

FISHING | The department supplies fishing licenses and provides a full listing of regulations. ☎ 916/928–5805 ⊕ www. wildlife.ca.gov.

HIKING

The best way to see the park is to hike it. The grandeur and majesty of the Sierra is best seen up close. Carry a hiking map and plenty of water. Visitor center gift shops sell maps and trail books and pamphlets. Check with rangers for current trail conditions, and be aware of rapidly changing weather. As a rule of thumb, plan on covering about a mile per hour.

★ Big Trees Trail

HIKING/WALKING | This hike is a must, as it does not take long and the setting is spectacular: beautiful Round Meadow surrounded by many mature sequoias, with well-thought-out interpretive signs along the path that explain the ecology on display. The 0.7-mile Big Trees Trail is wheelchair accessible. Parking at the trailhead lot off Generals Highway is for cars with handicap placards only. The round-trip loop from the Giant Forest Museum is about a mile long. Easy. ⊠ Sequoia National Park ⚓ Trailhead: off Generals Hwy. (Rte. 198), near the Giant Forest Museum ⓢ Shuttle: Giant Forest.

★ Congress Trail

HIKING/WALKING | This 2-mile trail, arguably the best hike in the parks in terms of natural beauty, is a paved loop that begins near General Sherman Tree. You'll get close-up views of more big trees here than on any other Sequoia hike. Watch for the clusters known as the House and Senate. The President Tree, also on the trail, supplanted the General Grant Tree in 2012 as the world's second largest in volume (behind the General Sherman). An offshoot of the Congress Trail leads to Crescent Meadow, where in summer you can catch a free shuttle back to the Sherman parking lot. Easy. ⊠ Sequoia National Park ⚓ Trailhead: off Generals Hwy. (Rte. 198), 2 miles north of Giant Forest ⓢ Shuttle: Giant Forest.

Crescent Meadow Trails

HIKING/WALKING | A 1-mile trail loops around lush Crescent Meadow to Tharp's Log, a cabin built from a fire-hollowed sequoia. From there you can embark on a 60-mile trek to Mt. Whitney, if you're prepared and have the time. Brilliant wild-flowers bloom here in midsummer. *Easy.* ⊠ *Sequoia National Park* ⊹ *Trailhead: the end of Moro Rock–Crescent Meadow Rd., 2.6 miles east off Generals Hwy. (Rte. 198)* ☞ *Shuttle: Moro Rock–Crescent Meadow.*

Little Baldy Trail

HIKING/WALKING | Climbing 700 vertical feet in 1.75 miles of switchbacking, this trail ends at a granite dome with a great view of the peaks of the Mineral King area and the Great Western Divide. The walk to the summit and back takes about four hours. *Moderate.* ⊠ *Sequoia National Park* ⊹ *Trailhead: Little Baldy Saddle, Generals Hwy. (Rte. 198), 9 miles north of General Sherman Tree* ☞ *Shuttle: Lodgepole-Wuksachi-Dorst.*

Marble Falls Trail

HIKING/WALKING | The 3.7-mile trail to Marble Falls crosses through the rugged foothills before reaching the cascading water. Plan on three to four hours one-way. *Moderate.* ⊠ *Sequoia National Park* ⊹ *Trailhead: off dirt road across from concrete ditch near site 17 at Potwisha Campground, off Generals Hwy. (Rte. 198).*

Mineral King Trails

HIKING/WALKING | Many trails to the high country begin at Mineral King. Two pop-ular day hikes are Eagle Lake (6.8 miles round-trip) and Timber Gap (4.4 miles round-trip). At the Mineral King Ranger Station (☎ *559/565–3768*) you can pick up maps and check about conditions from late May to late September. *Difficult.* ⊠ *Sequoia National Park* ⊹ *Trailheads: at end of Mineral King Rd., 25 miles east of Generals Hwy. (Rte. 198).*

Muir Grove Trail

HIKING/WALKING | You will attain solitude and possibly see a bear or two on this unheralded gem of a hike, a 4-mile round-trip from the Dorst Creek Campground. The remote grove is small but lovely, its sound track provided solely by nature. The trailhead is subtly marked. In sum-mer, park in the amphitheater lot and walk down toward the group campsite area. *Easy.* ⊠ *Sequoia National Park* ⊹ *Trailhead: Dorst Creek Campground, Generals Hwy. (Rte. 198), 8 miles north of Lodgepole Visitor Center* ☞ *Shuttle: Lodgepole-Wuksachi-Dorst.*

Tokopah Falls Trail

HIKING/WALKING | This trail with a 500-foot elevation gain follows the Marble Fork of the Kaweah River for 1.75 miles one-way and dead-ends below the impressive granite cliffs and cascading waterfall of Tokopah Canyon. The trail passes through a mixed-conifer forest. It takes 2½ to 4 hours to make the round-trip journey. *Moderate.* ⊠ *Sequoia National Park* ⊹ *Trailhead: off Generals Hwy. (Rte. 198), ¼ mile north of Lodgepole Campground* ☞ *Shuttle: Lodgepole-Wuksachi-Dorst.*

HORSEBACK RIDING

Trips take you through forests and flower-ing meadows and up mountain slopes.

Grant Grove Stables

HORSEBACK RIDING | Grant Grove Stables isn't too far from parts of Sequoia Nation-al Park, and is perfect for short rides from June to September. Reservations are recommended. ☎ *559/335–9292 sum-mer* ⊕ *www.nps.gov/seki/planyourvisit/horseride.htm* ⊠ *From $40.*

Horse Corral Packers

HORSEBACK RIDING | One- and two-hour trips through Sequoia are available for beginning and advanced riders. ⊠ *Big Meadow Rd., 12 miles east of Generals Hwy. (Rte. 198) between Sequoia and Kings Canyon national parks* ☎ *559/565–3404 summer, 559/565–6429 off-season,* ⊕ *hcpacker.com* ⊠ *From $45.*

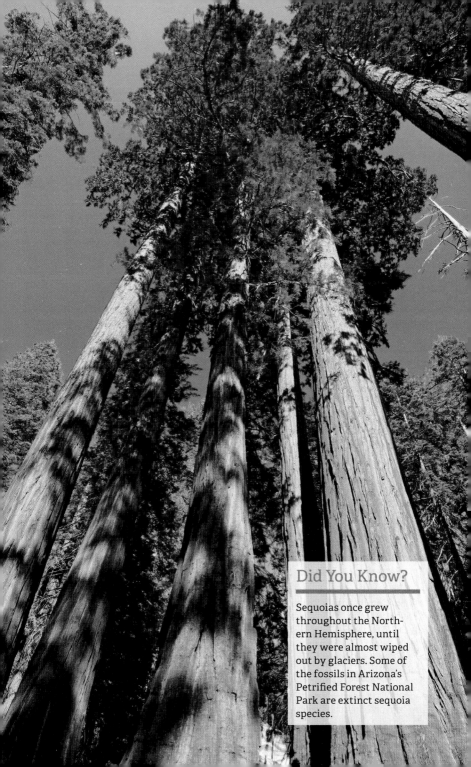

Did You Know?

Sequoias once grew throughout the Northern Hemisphere, until they were almost wiped out by glaciers. Some of the fossils in Arizona's Petrified Forest National Park are extinct sequoia species.

SLEDDING AND SNOWSHOEING

The Wolverton area, on Route 198 near Giant Forest, is a popular sledding spot, where sleds, inner tubes, and platters are allowed. You can buy sleds and saucers, with prices starting at $15, at the Alta Market and Ski Shop (☎ 559/565–3301), at the Lodgepole Visitor Center.

You can rent snowshoes for $18–$24 at the Alta Market and Ski Shop, at the Lodgepole Visitor Center. Naturalists lead snowshoe walks around Giant Forest and Wuksachi Lodge, conditions permitting, on Saturday and holidays. Make reservations and check schedules at Giant Forest Museum (☎ 559/565–3341) or Wuksachi Lodge.

SWIMMING

Drowning is the number-one cause of death in both Sequoia and Kings Canyon parks. Though it is sometimes safe to swim in the parks' rivers in the late summer and early fall, it is extremely dangerous to do so in the spring and early summer, when the snowmelt from the high country causes swift currents and icy temperatures. Stand clear of the water when the rivers are running, and stay off wet rocks to avoid falling in. Check with rangers for safety information.

Kings Canyon National Park

 Sights

SCENIC DRIVES

★ **Kings Canyon Scenic Byway**

SCENIC DRIVE | The 30-mile stretch of Route 180 between Grant Grove Village and Zumwalt Meadow delivers eye-popping scenery—granite cliffs, a roaring river, waterfalls, and Kings River canyon itself—much of which you can experience at vista points or on easy walks. The canyon comes into view about 10 miles east of the village at **Junction View.** Five miles beyond, at **Yucca Point,** the canyon is thousands of feet deeper than the more famous Grand Canyon. **Canyon View,** a special spot 1 mile east of the Cedar Grove Village turnoff, showcases evidence of the area's glacial history. Here, perhaps more than anywhere else, you'll understand why John Muir compared Kings Canyon vistas with those in Yosemite. Driving the byway takes about an hour each way without stops. ⊠ *Kings Canyon National Park* ⊕ *Rte. 180 north and east of Grant Grove village.*

HISTORIC SITES

Fallen Monarch

TOUR—SIGHT | This toppled sequoia's hollow base was used in the second half of the 19th century as a home for settlers, a saloon, and even to stable U.S. Cavalry horses. As you walk through it (assuming entry is permitted, which is not always possible), notice how little the wood has decayed, and imagine yourself tucked safely inside, sheltered from a storm or protected from the searing heat. ⊠ *Kings Canyon National Park* ⊕ *Grant Grove Trail, 1 mile north of Kings Canyon Park Visitor Center.*

Gamlin Cabin

BUILDING | Despite being listed on the National Register of Historic Places, this replica of a modest 1872 pioneer cabin is only borderline historical. The structure, which was moved and rebuilt several times over the years, once served as U.S. Cavalry storage space and, in the early 20th century, a ranger station. ⊠ *Grant Grove Trail.*

SCENIC STOPS

Kings Canyon National Park consists of two sections that adjoin the northern boundary of Sequoia National Park. The western portion, covered with sequoia and pine forest, contains the park's most visited sights, such as Grant Grove. The vast eastern portion is remote high country, slashed across half its southern

Kings Canyon's
Cedar Grove Area

breadth by the deep, rugged Kings River canyon. Separating the two is Sequoia National Forest, which encompasses Giant Sequoia National Monument. The Kings Canyon Scenic Byway (Route 180) links the major sights within and between the park's two sections.

General Grant Tree

LOCAL INTEREST | President Coolidge proclaimed this to be the "nation's Christmas tree," and 30 years later President Eisenhower designated it as a living shrine to all Americans who have died in wars. Bigger at its base than the General Sherman Tree, it tapers more quickly. It's estimated to be the world's third-largest sequoia by volume. A spur trail winds behind the tree, where scars from a long-ago fire remain visible. ⊠ *Kings Canyon National Park* ⊕ *Trailhead: 1 mile north of Grant Grove Visitor Center.*

Redwood Mountain Sequoia Grove

FOREST | One of the world's largest sequoia groves, Redwood contains within its 2,078 acres nearly 2,200 sequoias whose diameters exceed 10 feet. You can view the grove from afar at an overlook or hike 6 to 10 miles down into the richest regions, which include 2 of the world's 25 heaviest trees. ⊠ *Kings Canyon National Park* ⊕ *Drive 6 miles south of Grant Grove on Generals Hwy. (Rte. 198), then turn right at Quail Flat; follow it 2 miles to the Redwood Canyon trailhead.*

🏃 Activities

The siren song of beauty, challenge, and relative solitude (by national parks standards) draws hard-core outdoors enthusiasts to the Kings River canyon and the backcountry of the

Plants and Wildlife in Sequoia and Kings Canyon

The parks can be divided into three distinct zones. In the west (1,500–4,500 feet) are the rolling, lower-elevation foothills, covered with shrubby chaparral vegetation or golden grasslands dotted with oaks. Chamise, red-barked manzanita, and the occasional yucca plant grow here. Fields of white popcorn flower cover the hillsides in spring, and the yellow fiddleneck flourishes. In summer, intense heat and absence of rain cause the hills to turn golden brown. Wildlife includes the California ground squirrel, noisy blue-and-gray scrub jay, black bears, coyotes, skunks, and gray fox.

At middle elevation (5,000–9,000 feet), where the giant sequoia belt resides, rock formations mix with meadows and huge stands of evergreens—red and white fir, incense cedar, and ponderosa pines, to name a few. Wildflowers like yellow blazing star and red Indian paintbrush bloom in spring and summer. Mule deer, golden-mantled ground squirrels, Steller's jays, and black bears (most active in fall) inhabit the area, as does the chickaree.

The high alpine section of the parks is extremely rugged, with a string of rocky peaks reaching above 13,000 feet to Mt. Whitney's 14,494 feet. Fierce weather and scarcity of soil make vegetation and wildlife sparse. Foxtail and whitebark pines have gnarled and twisted trunks, the result of high wind, heavy snowfall, and freezing temperatures. In summer you can see yellow-bellied marmots, pikas, weasels, mountain chickadees, and Clark's nutcrackers.

park's eastern section. Backpacking, rock-climbing, and extreme-kayaking opportunities abound, but the park also has day hikes for all ability levels. Winter brings sledding, skiing, and snowshoeing fun. No off-road driving or bicycling is allowed in the park, and snowmobiling is also prohibited.

BICYCLING
Bicycles are allowed only on the paved roads in Kings Canyon. Cyclists should be extremely cautious along the steep highways and narrow shoulders.

CROSS-COUNTRY SKIING
Roads to Grant Grove are accessible even during heavy snowfall, making the trails here a good choice over Sequoia's Giant Forest when harsh weather hits.

FISHING
There is limited trout fishing in the park from late April to mid-November, and catches are minor. Still, Kings River is a popular spot. Some of the park's secluded backcountry lakes have good fishing. Licenses are available, along with fishing tackle, in Grant Grove and Cedar Grove. *See Activities, in Sequoia National Park, above, for more information about licenses.*

HIKING
You can enjoy many of Kings Canyon's sights from your car, but the giant gorge of the Kings River canyon and the sweeping vistas of some of the highest mountains in the United States are best seen on foot. Carry a hiking map—available at any visitor center—and plenty of water. Check with rangers for current

trail conditions, and be aware of rapidly changing weather. Except for one trail to Mt. Whitney, permits are not required for day hikes.

Big Baldy

HIKING/WALKING | This hike climbs 600 feet and 2 miles up to the 8,209-foot summit of Big Baldy. Your reward is the view of Redwood Canyon. Round-trip the hike is 4 miles. *Moderate.* ⊠ *Kings Canyon National Park* ✛ *Trailhead: 8 miles south of Grant Grove on Generals Hwy. (Rte. 198).*

Big Stump Trail

HIKING/WALKING | From 1883 until 1890, logging was done here, complete with a mill. The 1-mile loop trail, whose unmarked beginning is a few yards west of the Big Stump entrance, passes by many enormous stumps. *Easy.* ⊠ *Kings Canyon National Park* ✛ *Trailhead: near Big Stump Entrance, Generals Hwy. (Rte. 180).*

Buena Vista Peak

HIKING/WALKING | For a 360-degree view of Redwood Canyon and the High Sierra, make the 2-mile ascent to Buena Vista. *Difficult.* ⊠ *Kings Canyon National Park* ✛ *Trailhead: off Generals Hwy. (Rte. 198), south of Kings Canyon Overlook, 7 miles southeast of Grant Grove.*

★ Grant Grove Trail

HIKING/WALKING | Grant Grove is only 128 acres, but it's a big deal. More than 120 sequoias here have a base diameter that exceeds 10 feet, and the **General Grant Tree** is the world's third-largest sequoia by volume. Nearby, the Confederacy is represented by the **Robert E. Lee Tree,** recognized as the world's 11th-largest sequoia. Also along the easy-to-walk trail are the **Fallen Monarch** and the **Gamlin Cabin,** built by 19th-century pioneers. *Easy.* ⊠ *Kings Canyon National Park* ✛ *Trailhead: off Generals Hwy. (Rte. 180), 1 mile north of Kings Canyon Park Visitor Center.*

Hotel Creek Trail

HIKING/WALKING | For gorgeous canyon views, take this trail from Cedar Grove up a series of switchbacks until it splits. Follow the route left through chaparral to the forested ridge and rocky outcrop known as Cedar Grove Overlook, where you can see the Kings River canyon stretching below. This strenuous 5-mile round-trip hike gains 1,200 feet and takes three to four hours to complete. *Difficult.* ⊠ *Kings Canyon National Park* ✛ *Trailhead: at Cedar Grove Pack Station, 1 mile east of Cedar Grove Village.*

Mist Falls Trail

TRAIL | This sandy trail follows the glaciated South Fork Canyon through forest and chaparral, past several rapids and cascades, to one of the largest waterfalls in the two parks. Nine miles round-trip, the hike is relatively flat, but climbs 600 feet in the last 2 miles. It takes from four to five hours to complete. *Moderate.* ⊠ *Kings Canyon National Park* ✛ *Trailhead: at end of Kings Canyon Scenic Byway, 5½ miles east of Cedar Grove Village.*

Panoramic Point Trail

HIKING/WALKING | You'll get a nice view of whale-shape Hume Lake from the top of this Grant Grove path, which is paved and only 300 feet long. It's fairly steep—strollers might work here, but not wheelchairs. Trailers and RVs are not permitted on the steep and narrow road that leads to the trailhead parking lot. *Moderate.* ⊠ *Kings Canyon National Park* ✛ *Trailhead: at end of Panoramic Point Rd., 2.3 miles from Grant Grove Village.*

Redwood Canyon Trails

HIKING/WALKING | Two main trails lead into Redwood Canyon grove, the world's largest sequoia grove. The 6.5-mile **Hart Tree and Fallen Goliath Loop** passes by a 19th-century logging site, pristine Hart Meadow, and the hollowed-out Tunnel Tree before accessing a side trail to the grove's largest sequoia, the 277.9-foot-tall Hart Tree.

Mount Whitney

At 14,494 feet, Mt. Whitney is the highest point in the contiguous United States and the crown jewel of Sequoia National Park's wild eastern side. The peak looms high above the tiny, high-mountain desert community of Lone Pine, where numerous Hollywood Westerns have been filmed. The high mountain ranges, arid landscape, and scrubby brush of the eastern Sierra are beautiful in their vastness and austerity.

Despite the mountain's scale, you can't see it from the more traveled west side of the park because it is hidden behind the Great Western Divide. The only way to access Mt. Whitney from the main part of the park is to circumnavigate the Sierra Nevada via a 10-hour, nearly 400-mile drive outside the park. No road ascends the peak; the best vantage point from which to catch a glimpse of the mountain is at the end of Whitney Portal Road. The 13 miles of winding road leads from U.S. 395 at Lone Pine to the trailhead for the hiking route to the top of the mountain. Whitney Portal Road is closed in winter.

Mt. Whitney Trail. The most popular route to the summit, the Mt. Whitney Trail can be conquered by very fit and experienced hikers. If there's snow on the mountain, this is a challenge for expert mountaineers only. All overnighters must have a permit, as must day hikers on the trail beyond Lone Pine Lake, about 2½ miles from the trailhead. From May through October, permits are distributed via a lottery run each February by ⊕ *recreation.gov*. The Eastern Sierra Interagency Visitor Center (☎ 760/876–6200), on Route 136 at U.S. 395 about a mile south of Lone Pine, is a good resource for information about permits and hiking. ⊠ *Kings Canyon National Park* ☎ *760/873–2483 trail reservations* ⊕ *www.fs.usda.gov/inyo.*

The 6.4-mile **Sugar Bowl Loop** provides views of Redwood Mountain and Big Baldy before winding down into its namesake, a thick grove of mature and young sequoias. *Moderate.* ⊠ *Kings Canyon National Park* ⊹ *Trailhead: off Quail Flat. Drive 5 miles south of Grant Grove on Generals Hwy. (Rte. 198), turn right at Quail Flat and proceed 1½ miles to trailhead.*

Roads End Permit Station

HIKING/WALKING | You can obtain wilderness permits, maps, and information about the backcountry at this station, where bear canisters, a must for campers, can be rented or purchased. When the station is closed (typically October–mid-May), complete a self-service permit form. ⊠ *Kings Canyon National Park* ⊹ *Eastern end of Kings Canyon Scenic Byway, 6 miles east of Cedar Grove Visitor Center.*

Roaring River Falls Walk

HIKING/WALKING | Take a shady five-minute walk to this forceful waterfall that rushes through a narrow granite chute. The trail is paved and mostly accessible. *Easy.* ⊠ *Kings Canyon National Park* ⊹ *Trailhead: 3 miles east of Cedar Grove Village turnoff from Kings Canyon Scenic Byway.*

★ Zumwalt Meadow Trail

HIKING/WALKING | Rangers say this is the best (and most popular) day hike in the Cedar Grove area. Just 1.5 miles long, it offers three visual treats: the South Fork of the Kings River, the lush meadow, and the high granite walls above, including those of Grand Sentinel and North Dome. *Easy.* ⊠ *Kings Canyon National Park* ⚓ *Trailhead: 4½ miles east of Cedar Grove Village turnoff from Kings Canyon Scenic Byway.*

HORSEBACK RIDING

One-day destinations by horseback out of Cedar Grove include Mist Falls and Upper Bubb's Creek. In the backcountry, many equestrians head for Volcanic Lakes or Granite Basin, ascending trails that reach elevations of 10,000 feet. Costs per person range from $40 for a one-hour guided ride to around $300 per day for fully guided trips for which the packers do all the cooking and camp chores.

Cedar Grove Pack Station

HORSEBACK RIDING | Take a day ride or plan a multiday adventure along the Kings River canyon with Cedar Grove Pack Station. Popular routes include the Rae Lakes Loop and Monarch Divide. Closed early September–late May. ⊠ *Kings Canyon National Park* ⚓ *Kings Canyon Scenic Byway, 1 mile east of Cedar Grove Village* 📞 *559/565–3464 summer, 559/337–2413 off-season* ⊕ *www.nps.gov/seki/plan-yourvisit/horseride.htm* 💲 *From $40 per hr or $100 per day.*

Grant Grove Stables

HORSEBACK RIDING | A one- or two-hour trip through Grant Grove leaving from the stables provides a taste of horseback riding in Kings Canyon. Closed October–early June. ⊠ *Kings Canyon National Park* ⚓ *Rte. 180, ½ mile north of Grant Grove Visitor Center* 📞 *559/335–9292* ⊕ *www.nps.gov/seki/planyourvisit/horseride.htm* 💲 *From $40.*

SLEDDING AND SNOWSHOEING

In winter, Kings Canyon has a few great places to play in the snow. Sleds, inner tubes, and platters are allowed at both the Azalea Campground area on Grant Tree Road, ¼ mile north of Grant Grove Visitor Center, and at the Big Stump picnic area, 2 miles north of the lower Route 180 entrance to the park.

Snowshoeing is good around Grant Grove, where you can take occasional naturalist-guided snowshoe walks from mid-December through mid-March as conditions permit. Grant Grove Market rents sleds and snowshoes.

Nearby Towns

Numerous towns and cities tout themselves as "gateways" to the parks, with some more deserving of the title than others. One that certainly merits the name is frisky **Three Rivers,** a Sierra foothills hamlet (population 2,200) along the Kaweah River. Close to Sequoia's Ash Mountain and Lookout Point entrances, Three Rivers is a good spot to find a room when park lodgings are full. Either because Three Rivers residents appreciate their idyllic setting or because they know that tourists are their bread and butter, you'll find them almost uniformly pleasant and eager to share tips about the best spots for "Sierra surfing" the Kaweah's smooth, moss-covered rocks or where to find the best cell phone reception.

Visalia, a Central Valley city of about 128,000 people, lies 58 miles southwest of Sequoia's Wuksachi Village and 56 miles southwest of the Kings Canyon Park Visitor Center. Its vibrant downtown contains several good restaurants. If you're into Victorian and other old houses, drop by the visitor center and pick up a free map of them. A clear day's view of the Sierra from Main Street is spectacular, and even Sunday night can find the streets bustling with pedestrians. Visalia provides easy access to grand Sequoia National Park and the serene Kaweah Oaks Preserve.

Closest to Kings Canyon's Big Stump entrance, **Fresno,** the main gateway to the southern Sierra region, is about 55 miles west of Kings Canyon and about 85 miles northwest of Wuksachi

Village. This Central Valley city of nearly a half-million people is sprawling and unglamorous, but it has all the cultural and other amenities you'd expect of a major crossroads.

GETTING HERE AND AROUND
Sequoia Shuttle
In summer the Sequoia Shuttle connects Three Rivers to Visalia and Sequoia National Park. ☎ 877/287–4453 ⊕ www. sequoiashuttle.com ✉ $15 round-trip.

VISITOR INFORMATION
Fresno/Clovis Convention & Visitors Bureau. ✉ 1550 E. Shaw Ave., Suite 101, Fresno ☎ 559/981–5500, 800/788–0836 ⊕ www. playfresno.org. **Sequoia Foothills Chamber of Commerce.** ✉ 42268 Sierra Dr., Three Rivers ☎ 559/561–3300. **Visalia Convention & Visitors Bureau.** ✉ Kiosk, 303 E. Acequia Ave., at S. Bridge St., Visalia ☎ 559/334–0141, 800/524–0303 ⊕ www. visitvisalia.org.

 Sights

★ Colonel Allensworth State Historic Park
HISTORIC SITE | It's worth the slight detour off Highway 99 to learn about and pay homage to the dream of Allen Allensworth and other black pioneers who in 1908 founded Allensworth, the only California town settled, governed, and financed by African Americans. At its height, the town prospered as a key railroad transfer point, but after cars and trucks reduced railroad traffic and water was diverted for Central Valley agriculture, the town declined and was eventually deserted. Today the restored and rebuilt schoolhouse, library, and other structures commemorate Allensworth's heyday, as do festivities that take place each October. ✉ 4129 Palmer Ave., off Hwy. 43; from Hwy. 99 at Delano, take Garces Hwy. west to Hwy. 43 north; from Earlimart, take County Rd. J22 west to Hwy. 43 south, Allensworth ☎ 661/849–3433 ⊕ www.parks.ca.gov ✉ $6 per car.

Exeter Murals
PUBLIC ART | More than two dozen murals in the Central Valley city of Exeter's cute-as-a-button downtown make it worth a quick detour if you're traveling on Route 198. Several of the murals, which depict the area's agricultural and social history, are quite good. All adorn buildings within a few blocks of the intersection of Pine and E streets. If you're hungry, the **Wildflower Cafe,** at 121 South E Street, serves inventive salads and sandwiches. Shortly after entering Exeter head west on Pine Street (it's just before the water tower) to reach downtown. ✉ Exeter ✛ Rte. 65, 2 miles south of Rte. 198, about 11 miles east of Visalia ⊕ cityofexeter.com/galleries/exeter-murals.

★ Forestiere Underground Gardens
GARDEN | FAMILY | Sicilian immigrant Baldassare Forestiere spent four decades (1906–46) carving out an odd, subterranean realm of rooms, tunnels, grottoes, alcoves, and arched passageways that once extended for more than 10 acres between Highway 99 and busy, mall-pocked Shaw Avenue. Though not an engineer, Forestiere called on his memories of the ancient Roman structures he saw as a youth and on techniques he learned digging subways in New York and Boston. Only a fraction of his prodigious output is on view, but you can tour his underground living quarters, including bedrooms (one with a fireplace), the kitchen, living room, and bath, as well as a fishpond and auto tunnel. Skylights allow exotic full-grown fruit trees to flourish more than 20 feet belowground. ✉ 5021 W. Shaw Ave., 2 blocks east of Hwy. 99, Fresno ☎ 559/271–0734 ⊕ www.undergroundgardens.com ✉ $17 ⊗ Closed Dec.–Mar.

Kaweah Oaks Preserve
NATURE PRESERVE | Trails at this 344-acre wildlife sanctuary off the main road to Sequoia National Park lead past majestic valley oak, sycamore, cottonwood,

and willow trees. Among the 134 bird species you might spot are hawks, hummingbirds, and great blue herons. Bobcats, lizards, coyotes, and cottontails also live here. The Sycamore Trail has digital signage with QR codes you can scan with your smartphone to access plant and animal information. ⊠ *Follow Hwy. 198 for 7 miles east of Visalia, turn north on Rd. 182, and proceed ½ mile to gate on left side, Visalia* ☎ *559/738–0211* ⊕ *www.sequoiariverlands.org* ⊿ *Free.*

Project Survival's Cat Haven

ZOO | Take the rare opportunity to glimpse a Siberian lynx, a clouded leopard, a Bengal tiger, and other endangered wild cats at this conservation facility that shelters more than 30 big cats. A guided hour-long tour along a quarter mile of walkway leads to fenced habitat areas shaded by trees and overlooking the Central Valley. ⊠ *38257 E. Kings Canyon Rd. (Rte. 180), 15 miles west of Kings Canyon National Park, Dunlap* ☎ *559/338–3216* ⊕ *www.cathaven.com* ⊿ *$15.*

Sequoia National Forest and Giant Sequoia National Monument

FOREST | Delicate spring wildflowers, cool summer campgrounds, and varied winter-sports opportunities—not to mention more than half of the world's giant sequoia groves—draw outdoorsy types year-round to this sprawling district surrounding the national parks. Together, the forest and monument cover nearly 1,700 square miles, south from the Kings River and east from the foothills along the San Joaquin Valley. The monument's groves are both north and south of Sequoia National Park. One of the most popular is the **Converse Basin Grove,** home of the Boole Tree, the forest's largest sequoia. The grove is accessible by car on an unpaved road.

The Hume Lake Forest Service District Office, at 35860 Kings Canyon Scenic Byway (Route 180), has information about the groves, along with details about recreational activities. In springtime, diversions include hiking among the wildflowers that brighten the foothills. The floral display rises with the heat as the mountain elevations warm up in summer, when hikers, campers, and picnickers become more plentiful. The abundant trout supply attracts anglers to area waters, including 87-acre **Hume Lake,** which is also ideal for swimming and nonmotorized boating. By fall the turning leaves provide the visual delights, particularly in the Western Divide, Indian Basin, and the Kern Plateau. Winter activities include downhill and cross-country skiing, snowshoeing, and snowmobiling. ⊠ *Sequoia National Park ✢ Northern Entrances: Generals Hwy. (Rte. 198), 7 miles southeast of Grant Grove; Hume Lake Rd. between Generals Hwy. (Rte. 198) and Kings Canyon Scenic Byway (Rte. 180); Kings Canyon Scenic Byway (Rte. 180) between Grant Grove and Cedar Grove. Southern Entrances: Rte. 190 east of Springville; Rte. 178 east of Bakersfield* ☎ *559/784–1500 forest and monument, 559/338–2251 Hume Lake* ⊕ *www.fs.usda.gov/sequoia.*

 Activities

BOATING AND RAFTING

Hume Lake

BODY OF WATER | This reservoir, built by loggers in the early 1900s, is now the site of several church-affiliated camps, a gas station, and a public campground. Outside Kings Canyon's borders, Hume Lake offers intimate views of the mountains. Summer lodge room rentals start at $160. ⊠ *Hume Lake Rd., off Kings Canyon Hwy., 8 miles northeast of Grant Grove, 64144 Hume Lake Rd., Hume* ☎ *559/305–7770* ⊕ *www.humelake.org, visitsequoia.com.*

Kaweah White Water Adventures

BOATING | Kaweah's trips include a two-hour excursion (good for families) through Class III rapids, a longer paddle through Class IV rapids, and an extended trip (typically Class IV and V rapids). ✉ *40443 Sierra Dr., Three Rivers* ☎ *559/740–8251* ⊕ *www.kaweah-whitewater.com* 🖘 *From $50 per person.*

Kings River Expeditions

TOUR—SPORTS | This outfit arranges one- and two-day white-water rafting trips on the Kings River. The office is in Clovis, but all trips depart from Twin Pines Camp, 60 miles east of Fresno. ✉ *Twin Pines Camp, Clovis* ☎ *559/233–4881, 800/846–3674* ⊕ *www.kingsriver.com* 🖘 *From $145.*

HORSEBACK RIDING

Wood 'n' Horse Training Stables

HORSEBACK RIDING | For hourly horseback rides, riding lessons, or trail rides in the foothills, contact this outfit. From $45 for lessons; from $65 for trail rides. ✉ *42846 N. Fork Dr., Three Rivers* ☎ *559/561–4268* ⊕ *www.wdnhorse.com.*

Performing Arts

Fresno Philharmonic Orchestra

CONCERTS | The orchestra performs classical concerts from September through June. ✉ *Saroyan Theatre, 730 M St., near Inyo St., Fresno* ☎ *559/261–0600* ⊕ *fresnophil.org.*

Roger Rocka's Dinner Theater

THEATER | This Tower District venue stages Broadway-style musicals. ✉ *1226 N. Wishon Ave., at E. Olive Ave., Fresno* ☎ *559/266–9494* ⊕ *www.rogerrockas. com.*

Shopping

Cedar Grove Gift Shop and Market

GIFTS/SOUVENIRS | This place is small, but it's stocked with the essentials for RV and auto travelers. ✉ *Cedar Grove Village, Kings Canyon National Park* ☎ *559/565–3096* ☽ *Closed late Oct.–mid-May.*

Grant Grove Gift Shop

GIFTS/SOUVENIRS | This shop sells park-related gifts and souvenirs. ✉ *Grant Grove Village, Kings Canyon National Park* ☎ *559/335–5500.*

Lodgepole Market Center

GIFTS/SOUVENIRS | You'll find gifts, toys, books, souvenirs, and outdoor equipment in Sequoia National Park's largest store. Its grocery department has a fairly wide selection of items, some of them organic, including grab-and-go items for hikes and picnics. Across the hall is a café with various dishes for breakfast, lunch, and dinner. ✉ *63204 Lodgepole Rd., next to Lodgepole Visitor Center, Sequoia National Park* ☎ *559/565–3301.* ⊕ *www.visitsequoia.com.*

Wuksachi Gift Shop

GIFTS/SOUVENIRS | Souvenir clothing, Native American crafts, postcards, and snacks are for sale at this tasteful shop off the Wuksachi Lodge lobby. ✉ *Wuksachi Village* ☎ *559/625–7700.*

Restaurants

IN THE PARKS

SEQUOIA

Lodgepole Market and Grill

$$ | **CAFÉ** | The choices here run the gamut from simple to very simple, with several counters only a few strides apart in a central eating complex. The café also sells fresh and prepackaged salads, sandwiches, and wraps. **Known for:** quick and convenient dining; many healthful options; grab-and-go items for picnics. ⑤ *Average main: $12* ✉ *Next to Lodgepole Visitor Center, Sequoia National Park* ☎ *559/565–3301.*

The Peaks

$$$ | **MODERN AMERICAN** | Huge windows run the length of the Wuksachi Lodge's high-ceilinged dining room, and a large fireplace on the far wall warms both body and soul. The diverse dinner menu—by far the best at both parks—reflects a commitment to locally sourced and sustainable products. **Known for:** seasonal menus with fresh local ingredients; great views of sequoia grove; box lunches. $ *Average main: $28* ✉ *Wuksachi Lodge, 64740 Wuksachi Way, Wuksachi Village* ☎ *559/625–7700* ⊕ *www.visitsequoia.com/dine/the-peaks-restaurant.*

PICNIC AREAS

Take care to dispose of your food scraps properly (the bears might not appreciate this short-term, but the practice helps ensure their long-term survival).

Crescent Meadow

RESTAURANT—SIGHT | A mile or so past Moro Rock, this comparatively remote picnic area has meadow views and is close to a lovely hiking trail. Tables are under the giant sequoias, off the parking area. There are restrooms and drinking water. Fires are not allowed. ✉ *Sequoia National Park* ⊹ *End of Moro Rock–Crescent Rd., 2.6 miles east off Generals Hwy. (Rte. 198).*

Foothills Picnic Area

RESTAURANT—SIGHT | Near the parking lot at the southern entrance of the park, this area has tables, drinking water, and restrooms. ✉ *Sequoia National Park* ⊹ *Across Generals Hwy. from Foothills Visitor Center.*

Hospital Rock

RESTAURANT—SIGHT | Native Americans once ground acorns into meal at this site; outdoor exhibits tell the story. The picnic area's name, however, stems from a hunter/trapper who was treated for a leg wound here in 1873. Look up, and you'll see Moro Rock. Grills, drinking water, and restrooms are available. ✉ *Sequoia National Park* ⊹ *Generals Hwy. (Rte. 198), 6 miles north of Ash Mountain entrance.*

Pinewood Picnic Area

RESTAURANT—SIGHT | Picnic in Giant Forest, in the vicinity of sequoias if not actually under them. Drinking water, restrooms, grills, and wheelchair-accessible spots are provided in this expansive setting near Sequoia National Park's most popular attractions. ✉ *Sequoia National Park* ⊹ *Generals Hwy. (Rte. 198), 2 miles north of Giant Forest Museum, halfway between Giant Forest Museum and General Sherman Tree.*

Wolverton Meadow

RESTAURANT—SIGHT | At a major trailhead to the backcountry, this is a great place to stop for lunch before a hike. The area sits in a mixed-conifer forest adjacent to parking. Drinking water, grills, and restrooms are available. ✉ *Sequoia National Park* ⊹ *Wolverton Rd., 1½ miles northeast off Generals Hwy. (Rte. 198).*

KINGS CANYON

Cedar Grove Snack Bar

$$ | AMERICAN | The menu here is surprisingly extensive, with dinner entrées such as pasta, pork chops, trout, and steak. For breakfast, try the egg burrito, French toast, or pancakes; sandwiches, wraps, burgers (including vegetarian patties) and hot dogs dominate the lunch and dinner choices. **Known for:** scenic river views; extensive options; alfresco dining on balcony overlooking the Kings River. $ *Average main: $16* ✉ *Cedar Grove Village, Kings Canyon National Park* ☎ *559/565–3096* ⊕ *www.visitsequoia.com/dine/cedar-grove-snack-bar* ☉ *Closed Oct.–May.*

Grant Grove Restaurant

$$ | AMERICAN | Gaze at giant sequoias and a verdant meadow while dining in this eco-friendly restaurant's spacious dining room with fireplace, or outdoors on the expansive deck. The menu centers around locally sourced natural and organic ingredients and offers standard American fare. **Known for:** takeout service year-round; walk-up window for pizza, sandwiches, coffee, ice cream; picnic tables on outdoor deck. $ *Average main: $16* ✉ *Grant Grove Village, Kings Canyon National Park* ☎ *559/335–5500.*

PICNIC AREAS
Big Stump
RESTAURANT—SIGHT | Some trees still stand at this site at the edge of a logged sequoia grove. Near the park's entrance, the area is paved and next to the road. It's the only picnic area in either park that is plowed in the wintertime. Restrooms (portable toilets), grills, and drinking water are available, and the area is entirely accessible. ⊠ *Kings Canyon National Park* ✛ *Generals Hwy. (Rte. 180), just inside Big Stump entrance.*

Grizzly Falls
RESTAURANT—SIGHT | This little gem is worth a pull-over, if not a picnic at the roadside tables. A less-than-a-minute trek from the parking lot delivers you to the base of the delightful, 100-foot-plus falls. On a hot day, nothing feels better than dipping your feet in the cool water. An outhouse is on-site, but grills are not, and water is not available. ⊠ *Kings Canyon National Park* ✛ *Off Rte. 180, 2½ miles west of Cedar Grove entrance.*

OUTSIDE THE PARKS
Antoinette's Coffee and Goodies
$ | **CAFÉ** | For smoothies, well-crafted espresso drinks, breakfast bowls, and pumpkin chocolate-chip muffins and other homemade baked goods, stop for a spell at this convivial coffee shop. Antoinette's is known as the town's hub for vegan and gluten-free items. **Known for:** plentiful vegan and gluten-free items; Wi-Fi on-site; all organic, locally roasted coffee. ⑤ *Average main: $7* ⊠ *41727 Sierra Dr., Three Rivers* ☎ *559/561–2253* ⊕ *www.antoinettescoffeeandgoodies. com* ⊗ *Closed Tues. No dinner.*

Buckaroo Diner
$$ | **AMERICAN** | Set on a bluff overlooking the Kaweah River, the boho-chic Buckaroo serves fresh, house-made dishes made with seasonal organic ingredients. The restaurant's main dining room occupies a building that housed the original restaurant ('Ol Buckaroo) for decades; you can also sit in the cozy sun room or outdoor terrace overlooking the river. **Known for:** weekend beer garden; smoked foods; daily specials. ⑤ *Average main: $18* ⊠ *41695 Sierra Dr., Three Rivers* ☎ *559/465–5088* ⊕ *theolbuckaroo.com* ⊗ *Closed Tues. and Wed. No lunch weekdays.*

Café 225
$$$ | **MODERN AMERICAN** | High ceilings and contemporary decor contribute to the relaxed and sophisticated atmosphere at this popular downtown restaurant. Meats and fish grilled on a wood-fired rotisserie figure prominently on the menu, which also includes pastas and unusual treats such as artichoke fritters and goat cheese and roast lamb pizza. **Known for:** wood-fired rotisserie menu items; fresh local ingredients; sophisticated vibe. ⑤ *Average main: $22* ⊠ *225 W. Main St., Visalia* ☎ *559/733–2967* ⊕ *www.cafe225.com* ⊗ *Closed Sun.*

Gateway Restaurant and Lodge
$$$ | **AMERICAN** | The view's the draw at this roadhouse that overlooks the Kaweah River as it plunges out of the high country. The Gateway serves everything from osso buco and steaks to shrimp in Thai chili sauce; dinner reservations are essential on summer weekends. **Known for:** scenic riverside setting; fine dining in otherwise casual town; popular bar. ⑤ *Average main: $30* ⊠ *45978 Sierra Dr., Three Rivers* ☎ *559/561–4133* ⊕ *www.gateway-sequoia.com.*

School House Restaurant & Tavern
$$$ | **MODERN AMERICAN** | A Wine Country–style establishment that sources ingredients from the on-site gardens and surrounding farms and orchards, this popular restaurant occupies a redbrick 1921 schoolhouse in the town of Sanger. Chef Ryan Jackson, who grew up on local fruit farms, creates seasonal menus from the bounty of familiar backyards, mostly filled with classic American dishes with a contemporary twist. **Known for:** fresh ingredients

from neighboring farms and orchards; historic country setting; convenient stop between Kings Canyon and Fresno. ⑤ *Average main: $29 ⊠ 1018 S. Frankwood Ave., at Hwy. 180 (King's Canyon Rd.), 20 miles east of Fresno, Sanger ☎ 559/787–3271 ⊕ schoolhousesanger. com ⊘ Closed Mon. and Tues.*

Sierra Subs and Salads

$ | **AMERICAN** | This well-run sandwich joint satisfies carnivores and vegetarians alike with crispy-fresh ingredients prepared with panache. Depending on your preference, the centerpiece of the Bull's Eye sandwich, for instance, will be roast beef or a portobello mushroom, but whichever you choose, the accompanying flavors—of ciabatta bread, horseradish-and-garlic mayonnaise, roasted red peppers, Havarti cheese, and spinach—will delight your palate. **Known for:** many vegetarian, vegan, and gluten-free options; weekly specials; Wi-Fi. ⑤ *Average main: $9 ⊠ 41717 Sierra Dr., Three Rivers ☎ 559/561–4810 ⊕ www.sierrasubsandsalads.com ⊘ Closed Mon. No dinner.*

★ The Vintage Press

$$$$ | **EUROPEAN** | Built in 1966, this is one of the best restaurants in the Central Valley. The California–Continental cuisine includes dishes such as crispy veal sweetbreads with a port-wine sauce and filet mignon with a cognac-mustard sauce. **Known for:** wine list with more than 900 selections; chocolate Grand Marnier cake and other homemade desserts; sophisticated vibe. ⑤ *Average main: $32 ⊠ 216 N. Willis St., Visalia ☎ 559/733–3033 ⊕ www.thevintagepress.com.*

 Hotels

IN THE PARKS

SEQUOIA
Silver City Mountain Resort

$$$ | **RESORT** | High on Mineral King Road, this privately owned resort has rustic

cabins and deluxe chalets—all with a stove, refrigerator, and sink—plus three hotel rooms with private baths. **Pros:** rustic setting; friendly staff; great location for hikers. **Cons:** long, winding road is not for everybody; not much entertainment except hiking; some units have shared baths. ⑤ *Rooms from: $165 ⊠ Sequoia National Park ✛ Mineral King Rd., 21 miles southeast of Rte. 198 ☎ 559/561–3223 ⊕ www.silvercityresort.com ⊘ Closed Nov.–late May ➹ 13 cabins, 3 hotel rooms ⑩ No meals.*

★ Wuksachi Lodge

$$$$ | **HOTEL** | The striking cedar-and-stone main building is a fine example of how a structure can blend effectively with lovely mountain scenery. **Pros:** best place to stay in the parks; lots of wildlife; easy access to hiking and snowshoe/ski trails. **Cons:** rooms can be small; main lodge is a few-minutes' walk from guest rooms; slow Wi-Fi. ⑤ *Rooms from: $229 ⊠ 64740 Wuksachi Way, Wuksachi Village ☎ 559/625–7700, 888/252–5757 reservations ⊕ www.visitsequoia.com/lodging/wuksachi-lodge ➹ 102 rooms ⑩ No meals.*

KINGS CANYON
Cedar Grove Lodge

$$ | **HOTEL** | Backpackers like to stay here on the eve of long treks into the High Sierra wilderness, so bedtimes tend to be early. **Pros:** a definite step up from camping in terms of comfort; great base camp for outdoor adventures; on-site snack bar. **Cons:** impersonal; not everybody agrees it's clean enough; remote location. ⑤ *Rooms from: $147 ⊠ Kings Canyon Scenic Byway, Kings Canyon National Park ☎ 866/807–3598 ⊕ www.visitsequoia.com/lodging/cedar-grove-lodge ⊘ Closed mid-Oct.–mid-May ➹ 21 rooms ⑩ No meals.*

Grant Grove Cabins

$$ | **HOTEL** | Some of the wood-panel cabins here have heaters, electric lights, and private baths, but most have woodstoves, battery lamps, and shared baths.

Pros: warm, woodsy feel; clean; walk to Grant Grove Restaurant. **Cons:** can be difficult to walk up to if you're not in decent physical shape; costly for what you get; only basic amenities. ⑤ *Rooms from: $135* ✉ *Kings Canyon Scenic Byway in Grant Grove Village, Kings Canyon National Park* ☎ *866/807–3598* ⊕ *www.visitsequoia.com/Grant-Grove-Cabins.aspx* ⟳ *33 cabins, 9 with bath; 17 tent cabins* ⭕ *No meals.*

John Muir Lodge

$$$$ | **HOTEL** | In a wooded area in the hills above Grant Grove Village, this modern, timber-sided lodge has rooms and suites with queen- or king-size beds and private baths. **Pros:** open year-round; common room stays warm; quiet. **Cons:** check-in is down in the village; spotty Wi-Fi; remote location. ⑤ *Rooms from: $210* ✉ *Kings Canyon Scenic Byway, ¼ mile north of Grant Grove Village, 86728 Hwy. 180, Kings Canyon National Park* ☎ *866/807–3598* ⊕ *www.visitsequoia. com/john-muir-lodge.aspx* ⟳ *36 rooms* ⭕ *No meals.*

OUTSIDE THE PARKS

The only lodging immediately outside the parks is in Three Rivers. Options include inns, chain and mom-and-pop motels, and riverside cabins. Numerous chain properties operate in Visalia or Fresno (your favorite is likely represented in one or both cities), about an hour from the south and north entrances, respectively.

Montecito-Sequoia Lodge

$$$$ | **HOTEL** | **FAMILY** | Outdoor activities are what this year-round family resort is all about, including many that are geared toward teenagers and small children. **Pros:** friendly staff; great for kids; lots of fresh air and planned activities. **Cons:** can be noisy with all the activity; no TVs or phones in rooms; not within national park. ⑤ *Rooms from: $229* ✉ *63410 Generals Hwy., 11 miles south of Grant Grove, Sequoia National Forest* ☎ *559/565–3388, 800/227–9900* ⊕ *www.mslodge.com* ⊙ *Closed 1st 2 wks of Dec.* ⟳ *52 rooms* ⭕ *All meals.*

★ Rio Sierra Riverhouse

$$$ | **B&B/INN** | Guests at Rio Sierra come for the river views, the sandy beach, and the proximity to Sequoia National Park (6 miles away), but invariably end up raving equally about the warm, laid-back hospitality of proprietress Mars Roberts. **Pros:** seductive beach; add-on breakfast option; river views from all rooms; contemporary ambience. **Cons:** books up quickly in summer; some road noise audible in rooms; long walk or drive to restaurants. ⑤ *Rooms from: $200* ✉ *41997 Sierra Dr., Hwy. 198, Three Rivers* ☎ *559/561–4720* ⊕ *www.rio-sierra. com* ⟳ *5 rooms* ⭕ *No meals* ⟋ *2-night min stay on summer weekends. Closed Jan.–mid-Feb.*

Chapter 11

THE CENTRAL COAST

11

Updated by
Cheryl Crabtree

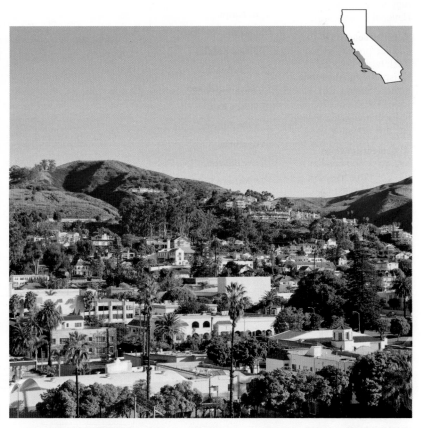

👁 Sights	🍴 Restaurants	🛏 Hotels	🛍 Shopping	🍸 Nightlife
★★★★★	★★★★☆	★★★★★	★☆☆☆☆	★☆☆☆☆

WELCOME TO THE CENTRAL COAST

TOP REASONS TO GO

★ **Incredible nature:**
The wild and wonderful Central Coast is home to Channel Islands National Park, two national marine sanctuaries, state parks and beaches, and the rugged Los Padres National Forest.

★ **Edible bounty:** Land and sea provide enough fresh regional foods to satisfy the most sophisticated foodies. Get your fill at countless farmers' markets, wineries, and restaurants.

★ **Outdoor activities:**
Kick back and revel in the California lifestyle. Surf, golf, kayak, hike, play tennis—or just hang out and enjoy the gorgeous scenery.

★ **Small-town charm, big-city culture:** With all the amazing cultural opportunities—museums, theater, music, and festivals—you might start thinking you're in L.A. or San Francisco.

★ **Wine tasting:** Central Coast wines earn high critical praise. Sample them in urban tasting rooms, dusty crossroads towns, and at high- and low-tech rural wineries.

1 **Ventura.**

2 **Channel Islands National Park.**

3 **Ojai.**

4 **Santa Barbara.**

5 **Santa Ynez.**

6 **Los Olivos.**

7 **Solvang.**

8 **Buellton.**

9 **Lompoc.**

10 **Pismo Beach.**

11 **Avila Beach.**

12 **San Luis Obispo.**

13 **Morro Bay.**

14 **Paso Robles.**

15 **Cambria.**

16 **San Simeon.**

17 **Southern Big Sur.**

18 **Central Big Sur.**

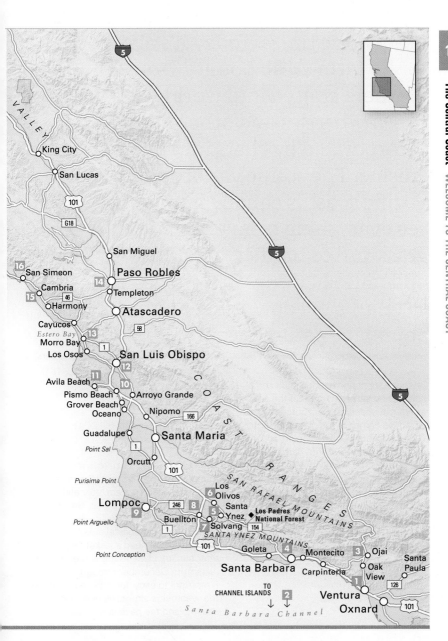

Balmy weather, glorious beaches, crystal-clear air, and serene landscapes have lured people to the Central Coast since prehistoric times. Today it's also known for its farm-fresh bounty, from grapes vintners crafted into world-class wines, to strawberries and other produce incorporated by chefs into distinctive cuisine. The scenic variety along the Pacific coast is equally impressive—you'll see everything from dramatic cliffs and grass-tufted bluffs to wildlife estuaries and miles of dunes. It's an ideal place to relax, slow down, and appreciate the abundant natural beauty.

Offshore, a pristine national park and a vast marine sanctuary protect the wild, wonderful underwater resources of this incredible corner of the planet. But not all of the Central Coast's top attractions are natural: Ventura, Santa Barbara, and San Luis Obispo are filled with sparkling examples of Spanish-Mediterranean architecture, bustling shopping districts, and first-rate restaurants showcasing regional foods and wines.

Planning

When to Go

The Central Coast climate is mild year-round. If you like to swim in warmer (if still nippy) ocean waters, July and August are the best months to visit. Be aware that this is also high season. Fog often rolls in along the coastal areas in early summer; you'll need a jacket, especially after sunset, close to the shore. It usually rains from December through March. From April to early June and early fall the weather is almost as fine as in high season, and the pace is less hectic.

Getting Here and Around

AIR TRAVEL

Alaska Air, American, Contour, Delta, Frontier, and United fly to Santa Barbara Airport (SBA), 9 miles from downtown. United, Alaska, and American provide service to San Luis Obispo County Regional Airport (SBP), 3 miles from downtown San Luis Obispo.

Santa Barbara Airbus shuttles travelers between Santa Barbara and Los Angeles for $55 one-way and $100 round-trip. The Santa Barbara Metropolitan Transit District Bus 11 ($1.75) runs every 30 minutes from the airport to the downtown transit center. A taxi between the airport and the hotel districts costs between $22 and $40.

AIRPORT CONTACTS San Luis Obispo County Regional Airport. ✉ 901 Airport Dr., off Hwy. 227, San Luis Obispo ☎ 805/781–5205 ⊕ sloairport.com. **Santa Barbara Airbus.** ☎ 805/964–7759, 800/423–1618 ⊕ www.sbairbus.com. **Santa Barbara Airport.** ✉ 500 Fowler Rd., off U.S. 101 Exit 104B, Santa Barbara ☎ 805/683–4011 ⊕ flysba.com. **Santa Barbara Metropolitan Transit District.** ☎ 805/963–3366 ⊕ sbmtd.gov.

BUS TRAVEL

Greyhound provides service from Los Angeles and San Francisco to San Luis Obispo, Ventura, and Santa Barbara. Local transit companies serve these three cities and several smaller towns. Buses can be useful for visiting some urban sights, particularly in Santa Barbara; they're less so for rural ones.

BUS CONTACTS Greyhound. ☎ 800/231–2222 ⊕ www.greyhound.com.

CAR TRAVEL

Driving is the easiest way to experience the Central Coast. U.S. 101 and Highway 1, which run north–south, are the main routes to and through the Central Coast from Los Angeles and

San Francisco. Highly scenic Highway 1 hugs the coast, and U.S. 101 runs inland. Between Ventura County and northern Santa Barbara County, the two highways are the same road. Highway 1 again separates from U.S. 101 north of Gaviota, then rejoins the highway at Pismo Beach. Along any stretch where these two highways are separate, U.S. 101 is the quicker route.

The most dramatic section of the Central Coast is the 70 miles between San Simeon and Big Sur. The road is narrow and twisting, with a single lane in each direction. In fog or rain the drive can be downright nerve-racking; in wet seasons mudslides can close portions of the road.

Other routes into the Central Coast include Highway 46 and Highway 33, which head, respectively, west and south from Interstate 5 near Bakersfield.

ROAD CONDITIONS Caltrans. ☎ 800/427–7623, 888/836–0866 Hwy. 1 visitor hotline (Cambria north to Carmel) ⊕ www.dot.ca.gov.

TRAIN TRAVEL

The Amtrak *Coast Starlight,* which runs between Los Angeles and Seattle via Oakland, stops in Paso Robles, San Luis Obispo, Santa Barbara, and Oxnard. Amtrak runs several *Pacific Surfliner* trains and buses daily between San Luis Obispo, Santa Barbara, Los Angeles, and San Diego. Metrolink Regional Rail Service trains connect Ventura and Oxnard with Los Angeles and points between.

TRAIN CONTACTS Amtrak. ☎ 800/872–7245 ⊕ www.amtrak.com. **Metrolink.** ☎ 800/371–5465 ⊕ metrolinktrains.com.

Restaurants

The cuisine in Ventura and Santa Barbara is every bit as eclectic as it is in California's bigger cities; fresh seafood is a standout. A foodie renaissance has overtaken the entire region from Ventura to Paso Robles, spawning dozens of restaurants touting locavore cuisine made with fresh organic produce and meats. Dining attire on the Central Coast is generally casual, though slightly dressy casual wear is the custom at pricier restaurants. *Restaurant reviews have been shortened. For full information, visit Fodors.com.*

Hotels

Expect to pay top dollar for rooms along the shore, especially in summer. Moderately priced hotels and motels do exist—most just a short drive inland from their higher-price counterparts. Make your reservations as early as possible, and take advantage of midweek specials to get the best rates. It's common for lodgings to require two-day minimum stays on holidays and some weekends, especially in summer, and to double rates during festivals and other events. *Hotel reviews have been shortened. For full information, visit Fodors.com.*

WHAT IT COSTS

	$	$$	$$$	$$$$
RESTAURANTS				
	under $16	$16–$22	$23–$30	over $30
HOTELS				
	under $120	$120–$175	$176–$250	over $250

Tours

Many tour companies will pick you up at your hotel or central locations; ask about this when booking.

Central Coast Food Tours

SPECIAL-INTEREST | Food and wine destinations are the focus of this outfit's walking tours of shops, restaurants, wineries, and other spots in San Luis Obispo, Paso Robles, and elsewhere. Some tours combine wine tasting with an ocean sail or a zip-line adventure. ☎ 844/337–1686 ⊕ centralcoastfoodtours.com ⧉ From $78.

Cloud Climbers Jeep and Wine Tours

SPECIAL-INTEREST | This outfit conducts trips in open-air, six-passenger jeeps to the Santa Barbara/Santa Ynez mountains and Wine Country. Tour options include wine tasting, mountain, sunset, and a discovery adventure for families. The company also offers a four-hour All Around Ojai Tour and arranges horseback riding and trap-shooting tours. ☎ 805/646–3200 ⊕ ccjeeps.com ⧉ From $89.

Grapeline Wine Tours

SPECIAL-INTEREST | Wine and vineyard picnic tours in Paso Robles and the Santa Ynez Valley are Grapeline's specialty. ☎ 951/693–5755 ⊕ gogrape.com ⧉ From $129.

Santa Barbara Wine Country Cycling Tours

BICYCLE TOURS | The company leads half- and full-day tours of the Santa Ynez wine region, conducts hiking and cycling tours, and rents out bicycles. ☎ 888/557–8687, 805/686–9490 ⊕ winecountrycycling.com ⧉ From $110.

Stagecoach Co. Wine Tours

SPECIAL-INTEREST | Locally owned and operated, Stagecoach runs daily wine-tasting excursions through the Santa Ynez Valley in vans, minicoaches, and SUVs. ✉ Solvang ☎ 805/686–8347 ⊕ winetourssantaynez.com ⧉ From $171.

Sustainable Vine Wine Tours

SPECIAL-INTEREST | This green-minded company specializes in eco-friendly Santa Ynez Valley wine tours in luxury vans and Tesla SUVs. Trips include tastings at limited-production wineries committed to sustainable practices. An organic picnic lunch is served. ☎ 805/698–3911 ⊕ sustainablevine.com ⧉ $150.

TOAST Tours

SPECIAL-INTEREST | Owned and operated by a sommelier couple with extensive guiding experience in Europe, Napa and Sonoma before relocating to Paso Robles, TOAST leads small-group tours to Central Coast wineries tasting rooms, and Hearst Castle. They also offer three-day tours from either Los Angeles or San Francisco to Central Coast wineries and Hearst Castle, and private tours, charters, and transportation. ☎ 805/400–3141 ⊕ *www.toasttours.com* ✉ *From $119.*

Wine Edventures

SPECIAL-INTEREST | This learning-oriented company conducts Santa Ynez Valley wine and craft beer tours in vans, minicoaches, and other vehicles. ⊠ *Santa Barbara* ☎ 805/965–9463 ⊕ *welovewines. com* ✉ *From $135.*

Visitor Information

CONTACTS Central Coast Tourism Council.
⊕ *centralcoast-tourism.com.*

Ventura

60 miles north of Los Angeles.

Like Los Angeles, the city of Ventura enjoys gorgeous weather and sun-kissed beaches—but without the smog and congestion. The miles of beautiful beaches attract athletes—body-surfers and boogie boarders, runners and bikers—and those who'd rather doze beneath an umbrella all day. Ventura Harbor is home to myriad fishing boats, restaurants, and water-activity centers where you can rent boats and take harbor cruises. Foodies can get their fix all over Ventura—dozens of upscale cafés and wine and tapas bars have opened in recent years. Arts and antiques buffs have long trekked downtown to browse the galleries and shops here. One of the greatest perks of Ventura is its walkability. If you drive here, park your car in one of the free 24-hour parking lots sprinkled around the city and hoof it on foot, or board a free trolley that cruises from downtown along the waterfront (Thursday–Sunday noon–9 pm).

GETTING HERE AND AROUND

Amtrak and Metrolink trains serve the area from Los Angeles. Greyhound buses stop in Ventura; Gold Coast Transit serves the city and the rest of Ventura County.

U.S. 101 is the north–south main route into town, but for a scenic drive, take Highway 1 north from Santa Monica. The highway merges with U.S. 101 just south of Ventura. ■ TIP➔ **Traveling north to Ventura from Los Angeles on weekdays, it's best to depart before 6 am, between 10 and 2, or after 7 pm, or you'll get caught in the extended rush-hour traffic. Coming south from Santa Barbara, depart before 1 or after 6 pm.** On weekends, traffic is generally fine except southbound on U.S. 101 between Santa Barbara and Ventura on Sunday late afternoon and early evening.

ESSENTIALS

BUS CONTACT Gold Coast Transit.
☎ 805/487–4222 ⊕ *www.goldcoasttransit.org.*

VISITOR INFORMATION Ventura Visitors and Convention Bureau. ⊠ *Downtown Visitor Center, 101 S. California St.* ☎ 805/648–2075 ⊕ *visitventuraca.com.*

Sights

Albinger Archaeological Museum

MUSEUM | More than three millennia of human history in the Ventura region is charted in the archaeological exhibits at the small Albinger Archaeological Museum. Some of the relics on display date back to 1600 BC. ⊠ *113 E. Main St.* ☎ 805/658–4728 ⊕ *www.cityofventura. ca.gov/639/Albinger-Archaeological-Museum* ✉ *Free* ☉ *Closed early Sept.–mid-June. Closed weekdays.*

Lake Casitas Recreation Area

AMUSEMENT PARK/WATER PARK | FAMILY | Lunker largemouth bass, rainbow trout, crappie, redears, and channel catfish live in the waters at this park, one of the country's best bass-fishing areas. Nestled below the Santa Ynez Mountains' Laguna Ridge, Lake Casitas is also a beautiful spot for pitching a tent or having a picnic. The Casitas Water Adventure, which has two water playgrounds and a lazy river for tubing and floating, provides kids with endless diversions in summer. ✉ *11311 Santa Ana Rd., off Hwy. 33, 13 miles northwest of Ventura* ☎ *805/649–2233, 805/649–1122 campground and water park reservations* ⊕ *www.lakecasitas.info* ⬥ *From $10 per vehicle, $13 per boat; Water Adventure $12 ($6, 5–7 pm).*

Mission San Buenaventura

HISTORIC SITE | The ninth of the 21 California missions, Mission San Buenaventura was established in 1782 and the current church was rebuilt and rededicated in 1809. A self-guided tour takes you through a small museum, a quiet courtyard, and a chapel with 250-year-old paintings. ✉ *211 E. Main St., at Figueroa St.* ☎ *805/648–4496 gift shop* ⊕ *www.sanbuenaventuramission.org* ⬥ *$5.*

Museum of Ventura County

MUSEUM | Exhibits in a contemporary complex of galleries and a sunny courtyard plaza tell the story of Ventura County from prehistoric times to the present. A highlight is the gallery that contains Ojai artist George Stuart's historical figures, dressed in exceptionally detailed, custom-made clothing reflecting their particular eras. In the courtyard, eight panels made with 45,000 pieces of cut glass form a history time line. ✉ *100 E. Main St., at S. Ventura Ave.* ☎ *805/653–0323* ⊕ *www.venturamuseum.org* ⬥ *$5, free 1st Sun. of month* ⊘ *Closed Mon.*

★ Ventura Oceanfront

PROMENADE | Four miles of gorgeous coastline stretch from the county fairgrounds at the northern border of the city of San Buenaventura, through San Buenaventura State Beach, down to Ventura Harbor in the south. The main attraction here is the San Buenaventura City Pier, a landmark built in 1872 and restored in 1993. Surfers rip the waves just north of the pier, and sunbathers relax on white-sand beaches on either side. The mile-long promenade and the Omer Rains Bike Trail north of the pier attract scores of joggers, surrey cyclers, and bikers throughout the year. ✉ *California St., at ocean's edge.*

🍴 Restaurants

Brophy Bros.

$$$ | SEAFOOD | The Ventura outpost of the wildly popular Santa Barbara restaurant provides the same fresh seafood-oriented meals in a spacious second-story setting overlooking the harbor. Feast on everything from fish-and-chips and crab cakes to chowder and delectable fish—often straight from the boats moored below. **Known for:** lively atmosphere; harbor views; killer clam bar. ⑤ *Average main: $26* ✉ *1559 Spinnaker Dr., in Ventura Harbor Village* ☎ *805/639–0865* ⊕ *brophybros.com.*

★ Café Zack

$$$ | AMERICAN | A local favorite for anniversaries and other celebrations, Zack's serves classic European dishes in an intimate, two-room 1930s cottage adorned with local art. Entrées of note include seafood specials (depending on the local catch), slow-roasted boar shank and filet mignon, the latter typically crusted in peppercorns or topped with porcini mushrooms. **Known for:** personal service; house-made desserts; excellent California wines. ⑤ *Average main: $30* ✉ *1095 E. Thompson Blvd., at S. Ann St.* ☎ *805/643–9445* ⊕ *cafezack.com* ⊘ *Closed Sun. No lunch Sat.*

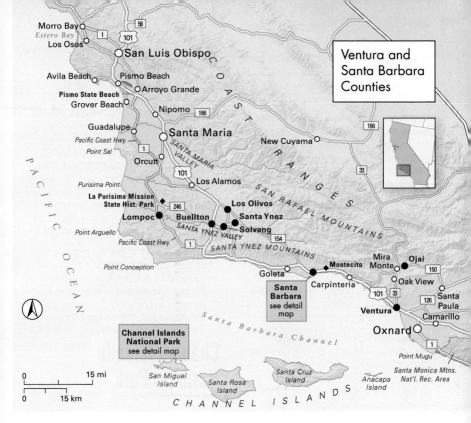

Ventura and Santa Barbara Counties

Lure Fish House

$$$ | SEAFOOD | Fresh, sustainably caught seafood charbroiled over a mesquite grill, a well-stocked oyster bar, specialty cocktails, and a wine list heavy on local vintages lure diners into this slick, nautical-theme space downtown. The menu centers on the mostly local catch and organic vegetables, and includes tacos, sandwiches, and salads. **Known for:** shrimp-and-chips; cioppino; citrus crab-cake salad. $ *Average main: $24* ✉ *60 S. California St.* ☎ *805/567–4400* ⊕ *lurefishhouse.com.*

Rumfish y Vino

$$$ | CARIBBEAN | The sibling of a popular namesake restaurant in Placencia, Belize, Rumfish y Vino serves up zesty Caribbean fare with a California Wine Country twist in a courtyard venue just off Main Street near the mission. Dine in the beach-chic dining room or in the heated patio with a roaring fireplace, where live music plays several nights a week, The seafood-heavy menu changes depending on the local catch. **Known for:** delectable fish tacos and flatbreads; happy hour and creative cocktails; Caribbean fish stew. $ *Average main: $26* ✉ *434 N. Palm St.* ☎ *805/667–9288* ⊕ *www.rumfishyvinoventura.com.*

 Hotels

Crowne Plaza Ventura Beach

$$$ | HOTEL | A 12-story hotel with an enviable location on the beach and next to a historic pier, the Crowne Plaza is within walking distance of downtown restaurants and nightlife. **Pros:** on the beach; near downtown; steps from waterfront. **Cons:** early-morning train noise; waterfront crowded in summer; self parking is in an adjacent public lot. $ *Rooms from: $200* ⊠ *450 E. Harbor Blvd.* ☎ *800/842–0800, 805/648–2100* ⊕ *cpventura.com* ⇆ *235 rooms* �|○| *No meals.*

Four Points by Sheraton Ventura Harbor Resort

$$$ | **RESORT** | An on-site restaurant, spacious rooms, and a slew of amenities make this 17-acre property—which includes sister hotel Holiday Inn Express—a popular and practical choice for Channel Islands visitors. **Pros:** close to island transportation; quiet location; short drive to historic downtown. **Cons:** not in the heart of downtown; noisy seagulls sometimes congregate nearby; service can be spotty. $ *Rooms from: $199* ⊠ *1050 Schooner Dr.* ☎ *805/658–1212, 800/368–7764* ⊕ *fourpoints.com/ventura* ⇆ *106 rooms* �|○| *No meals.*

Holiday Inn Express Ventura Harbor

$$$ | **HOTEL** | A favorite among Channel Islands visitors, this quiet, comfortable, lodge-inspired property sits right at the Ventura Harbor entrance. **Pros:** quiet at night; easy access to harbor restaurants and activities; five-minute drive to downtown. **Cons:** busy area on weekends; complaints of erratic service; fee for parking. $ *Rooms from: $189* ⊠ *1080 Navigator Dr.* ☎ *805/856–9533, 888/233–9450* ⊕ *hiexpress.com* ⇆ *69 rooms* �|○| *Breakfast.*

Ventura Beach Marriott

$$$ | **HOTEL** | Spacious, contemporary rooms, a peaceful location just steps from San Buenaventura State Beach, and easy access to downtown arts and culture make the Marriott a popular choice. **Pros:** walk to beach and biking/jogging trails; a block from historic pier; great value for location. **Cons:** close to highway; near busy intersection; special event noise some evenings. $ *Rooms from: $239* ⊠ *2055 E. Harbor Blvd.* ☎ *805/643–6000, 888/236–2427* ⊕ *marriottventurabeach.com* ⇆ *285 rooms* �|○| *No meals.*

Activities

The most popular outdoor activities in Ventura are beach-going and whale-watching. California gray whales migrate offshore through the Santa Barbara Channel from late December through March; giant blue and humpback whales feed here from mid-June through September. The channel teems with marine life year-round, so tours, which depart from Ventura Harbor, include more than just whale sightings.

Island Packers Cruises

TOUR—SPORTS | A cruise through the Santa Barbara Channel with Island Packers will give you the chance to spot dolphins, seals, and sometimes even whales. ⊠ *Ventura Harbor, 1691 Spinnaker Dr.* ☎ *805/642–1393* ⊕ *islandpackers.com.*

Channel Islands National Park

11 miles southwest of Ventura Harbor via boat.

On crystal-clear days the craggy peaks of the Channel Islands are easy to see from the mainland, jutting from the Pacific in such sharp detail it seems you could reach out and touch them. The islands are not too far away—a high-speed boat will whisk you to the closest ones in less than an hour—yet very few people ever visit them. Those who do venture out to the islands will experience one of the most splendid land-and-sea wilderness areas on the planet. Camping is your only lodging choice on the islands, but it's a fantastic way to experience the natural beauty and isolation of the park. Campsites are primitive, with no water (except on Santa Rosa and Santa Cruz) or electricity. Campsites are $15 per night; you must arrange your transportation before you reserve your site (☎ *877/444–6777*) or online (⊕ *www.recreation.gov*) up to five months in advance.

Channel Islands National Park includes five of the eight Channel Islands and the one nautical mile of ocean that surrounds them. Six nautical miles of surrounding channel waters are designated a National Marine Sanctuary, and are teeming with life, including giant kelp forests, 345 fish species, dolphins, whales, seals, sea lions, and seabirds. To maintain the integrity of their habitats, pets are not allowed in the park.

GETTING HERE AND AROUND

Most visitors access the Channel Islands via an Island Packers boat from Ventura Harbor. To reach the harbor by car, exit U.S. 101 in Ventura at Seaward Boulevard or Victoria Avenue and follow the signs to Ventura Harbor/Spinnaker Drive. An Island Packers boat heads to Anacapa Island from Oxnard's Channel Islands Harbor, which you can reach from Ventura Harbor by following Harbor Boulevard south about 6 miles and continuing south on Victoria Avenue. Private vehicles are not permitted on the islands.

BOAT TOURS
Island Packers

Sailing on high-speed catamarans from Ventura or a mono-hull vessel from Oxnard, Island Packers goes to Santa Cruz Island daily most of the year, weather permitting. The boats also go to Anacapa several days a week, and to the outer islands from April through November. They also cruise along Anacapa's north shore on three-hour wildlife tours (no disembarking) several times a week. ✉ *3550 Harbor Blvd., Oxnard* ☎ *805/642–1393* ⊕ *islandpackers.com* 💲 *$38.*

 Sights

Anacapa Island

ISLAND | Most people think of Anacapa as an island, but it's actually comprised of three narrow islets. Although the tips of these volcanic formations nearly touch, the islets are inaccessible from one another except by boat. All three

have towering cliffs, isolated sea caves, and natural bridges; Arch Rock, on East Anacapa, is one of the best-known symbols of Channel Islands National Park.

Wildlife viewing is the main activity on East Anacapa, particularly in summer when seagull chicks are newly hatched and sea lions and seals lounge on the beaches. Exhibits at East Anacapa's compact **museum** include the original lead-crystal Fresnel lens from the 1932 lighthouse.

On West Anacapa, depending on the season and the number of desirable species lurking about here, boats travel to **Frenchy's Cove.** On a voyage here you might see anemones, limpets, barnacles, mussel beds, and colorful marine algae in the pristine tide pools. The rest of West Anacapa is closed to protect nesting brown pelicans. ✉ *Channel Islands National Park.*

Channel Islands National Park Visitor Center

INFO CENTER | The park's Robert J. Lagomarsino Visitor Center has a museum, a bookstore, and a three-story observation tower with telescopes. The museum's exhibits and a 24-minute film, *Treasure in the Sea,* provide an engaging overview of the islands. In the marine life exhibit, sea stars cling to rocks, and a brilliant orange Garibaldi darts around. Also on display are full-size reproductions of a male northern elephant seal and the pygmy mammoth skeleton unearthed on Santa Rosa Island in 1994.

On weekends and holidays at 11 am and 3 pm, rangers lead various free public programs describing park resources, and from Wednesday through Saturday in summer the center screens live ranger broadcasts of hikes and dives on Anacapa Island. Webcam images of bald eagles and other land and sea creatures are shown at the center and on the park's website. ✉ *1901 Spinnaker Dr., Ventura* ☎ *805/658–5730* ⊕ *www.nps.gov/chis.*

Channel Islands

SANTA YNEZ MOUNTAINS

El Rio
Ventura
Oxnard
Channel Islands Harbor
Point Mugu

Visitor Center
Ventura Harbor

Santa Barbara
Montecito
Carpinteria
Santa Barbara Harbor
Goleta
Goleta Point

Santa Barbara Channel

Santa Barbara Island is approximately 52 miles southeast of Santa Cruz Island

Santa Barbara Island Light Beacon

Santa Barbara Island

Light Station & Museum
Summit Peak 936 ft
Anacapa Island
Anacapa Passage
Smugglers Cove

Scorpion Ranch
Visitor Center
CINP East Santa Cruz
Prisoners Harbor
Main Ranch
Central Valley
West Santa Cruz: The Nature - Conservancy
Santa Cruz Island
Painted Cave
Mount Diablo 2,450 ft
Morse Point
West Point
Santa Cruz Channel

Torrey Pines
East Point
Johnsons Lee
Bechers Bay
Carrington Point
Vail & Vickers Ranch
Santa Rosa Island
Soledad Peak 1,574 ft
South Point
San Miguel Passage
Sandy Point

Harris Point
Cuyler Harbor
Cabrillo Monument Lester Ranch site
San Miguel Island
Point Bennett
Tyler Bight

PACIFIC OCEAN

10 mi
0
10 km
0

San Miguel Island

ISLAND | The westernmost of the Channel Islands, San Miguel Island is frequently battered by storms sweeping across the North Pacific. The 15-square-mile island's wild windswept landscape is lush with vegetation. Point Bennett, at the western tip, offers one of the world's most spectacular wildlife displays when more than 30,000 pinnipeds hit its beach. Explorer Juan Rodríguez Cabrillo was the first European to visit this island; he claimed it for Spain in 1542. Legend holds that Cabrillo died on one of the Channel Islands—no one knows where he's buried, but there's a memorial to him on a bluff above Cuyler Harbor. ⊠ *Channel Islands National Park.*

Santa Barbara Island

ISLAND | At about 1 square mile, Santa Barbara Island is the smallest of the Channel Islands and nearly 35 miles south of the others. Triangular in shape, Santa Barbara's steep cliffs—which offer a perfect nesting spot for the Scripps's murrelet, a rare seabird—are topped by twin peaks. In spring you can enjoy a brilliant display of yellow coreopsis. Learn about the wildlife on and around the islands at the island's small museum. ⊠ *Channel Islands National Park.*

★ Santa Cruz Island

ISLAND | Five miles west of Anacapa, 96-square-mile Santa Cruz Island is the largest of the Channel Islands. The National Park Service manages the easternmost 24% of the island; the rest is owned by the Nature Conservancy, which requires a permit to land. When your boat drops you off on a portion of the 70 miles of craggy coastline, you see two rugged mountain ranges with peaks soaring to 2,500 feet and deep canyons traversed by streams. This landscape is the habitat of a remarkable variety of flora and fauna—more than 600 types of plants, 140 kinds of land birds, 11 mammal species, five varieties of reptiles, and three amphibian species live here. Bird-watchers may want to look for the endemic island scrub jay, which is found nowhere else in the world.

One of the largest and deepest sea caves in the world, **Painted Cave** lies along the northwest coast of Santa Cruz. Named for the colorful lichen and algae that cover its walls, Painted Cave is nearly ¼ mile long and 100 feet wide. In spring a waterfall cascades over the entrance. Kayakers may encounter seals or sea lions cruising alongside their boats inside the cave. The Channel Islands hold some of the richest archaeological resources in North America; all artifacts are protected within the park. Remnants of a dozen Chumash villages can be seen on the island. The largest of these villages, at the eastern end, occupied the area now called **Scorpion Ranch.** The Chumash mined extensive chert deposits on the island for tools to produce shell-bead money, which they traded with people on the mainland. You can learn about Chumash history and view artifacts, tools, and exhibits on native plant and wildlife at the interpretive visitor center near the landing dock. Visitors can also explore remnants of the early-1900s ranching era in the restored historic adobe and outbuildings. ⊠ *Channel Islands National Park.*

Santa Rosa Island

ISLAND | Between Santa Cruz and San Miguel, Santa Rosa is the second largest of the Channel Islands. The terrain along the coast varies from broad, sandy beaches to sheer cliffs—a central mountain range, rising to 1,589 feet, breaks the island's relatively low profile. Santa Rosa is home to about 500 species of plants, including the rare Torrey pine, and three unusual mammals, the island fox, the spotted skunk, and the deer mouse. They hardly compare, though, to their predecessors: a nearly complete skeleton of a 6-foot-tall pygmy mammoth was unearthed in 1994.

From 1901 to 1998, cattle were raised at the island's **Vail & Vickers Ranch.** The route from Santa Rosa's landing dock to the campground passes by the historic ranch buildings, barns, equipment, and the wooden pier where cattle were brought onto the island. ✉ *Channel Islands National Park.*

 ## Activities

Channel Islands Adventure Company (owned and operated by Santa Barbara Adventure Company) arranges paddling, kayaking, and other Channel Islands excursions out of Ventura, and various concessionaires at Ventura Harbor Village (☎ *805/477–0470* ⊕ *www.venturaharborvillage.com*) arrange diving, kayaking, and other rentals and tours. Island Packers conducts whale-watching cruises.

DIVING

Some of the best snorkeling and diving in the world can be found in the cool waters surrounding the Channel Islands. In the relatively warm water around Anacapa and eastern Santa Cruz, photographers can get great shots of rarely seen giant black bass swimming among the kelp forests. Here you also find a reef covered with red brittle starfish. If you're an experienced diver, you might swim among five species of seals and sea lions, or try your hand at spearing rockfish or halibut near San Miguel and Santa Rosa. The best time to scuba dive is in summer and fall, when the water is often clear up to a 100-foot depth.

KAYAKING

The most remote parts of the Channel Islands are accessible only by a sea kayak. Some of the best kayaking in the park can be found on Anacapa, Santa Barbara, and the eastern tip of Santa Cruz. It's too far to kayak from the mainland out to the islands, but outfitters have tours that take you to the islands. Tours are offered year-round, but high seas may cause trip cancellations between December and March. ⚠ **Channel waters can be unpredictable and challenging. Guided trips are highly recommended.**

WHALE-WATCHING

About a third of the world's cetacean species (27 to be exact) can be seen in the Santa Barbara Channel. In July and August, humpback and blue whales feed off the north shore of Santa Rosa. From late December through March, up to 10,000 gray whales pass through the Santa Barbara Channel on their way from Alaska to Mexico and back again; if you go on a whale-watching trip during this time frame you're likely to spot one or more of them. Other types of whales, but fewer in number, swim the channel from June through August.

Ojai

15 miles north of Ventura.

The Ojai Valley, which director Frank Capra used as a backdrop for his 1936 film *Lost Horizon,* sizzles in the summer when temperatures routinely reach 90°F. The acres of orange and avocado groves here evoke postcard images of long-ago agricultural Southern California. Many artists and celebrities have sought refuge from life in the fast lane in lush Ojai.

GETTING HERE AND AROUND

From northern Ventura, Highway 33 veers east from U.S. 101 and climbs inland to Ojai. From Santa Barbara, exit U.S. 101 at Highway 150 in Carpinteria, then travel east 20 miles on a twisting, two-lane road that is not recommended at night or during poor weather. You can also access Ojai by heading west from Interstate 5 on Highway 126. Exit at Santa Paula and follow Highway 150 north for 16 miles to Ojai. Gold Coast Transit provides service to Ojai from Ventura.

Ojai can be easily explored on foot; you can also hop on the Ojai Trolley ($1.50, or $2 day pass), which until about 5 pm follows two routes around Ojai and neighboring Miramonte on weekdays and one route on weekends. Tell the driver you're visiting and you'll get an informal guided tour.

ESSENTIALS

BUS CONTACTS Gold Coast Transit.
☎ 805/487–4222 ⊕ goldcoasttransit.org.
Ojai Trolley. ☎ 805/646–5581 ⊕ ojaitrolley.com.

VISITOR INFORMATION Ojai Visitors Bureau. ⊕ ojaivisitors.com.

 # Sights

Ojai Art Center

ARTS VENUE | California's oldest nonprofit, multipurpose arts center exhibits visual art from various disciplines and presents theater, dance, and other performances. ✉ 113 S. Montgomery St., near E. Ojai Ave. ☎ 805/646–0117 ⊕ www.ojaiartcenter.org ⊗ Closed Mon.

Ojai Avenue

NEIGHBORHOOD | The work of local artists is displayed in the Spanish-style shopping arcade along the avenue downtown. On Sunday between 9 and 1, organic and specialty growers sell their produce at the outdoor market behind the arcade.

Ojai Valley Museum

MUSEUM | FAMILY | The museum collects, preserves, and presents exhibits about the art, history, and culture of Ojai and Ojai Valley. Walking tours of Ojai depart from here. ✉ 130 W. Ojai Ave. ☎ 805/640–1390 ⊕ ojaivalleymuseum.org ☚ Museum $5, walking tours from $7 ⊗ Closed Mon.

Ojai Valley Trail

TRAIL | The 18-mile trail is open to pedestrians, joggers, equestrians, bikers, and others on nonmotorized vehicles. You can access it anywhere along its route. ✉ Parallel to Hwy. 33 from Soule Park in Ojai to ocean in Ventura ☎ 888/652–4669 ⊕ ojaivisitors.com.

🍴 Restaurants

Azu

$$$ | **MEDITERRANEAN** | Slick furnishings, piped-in jazz, craft cocktails, and local beers and wines draw diners to this artsy Mediterranean bistro known for tapas made from organic ingredients. You can also order soups, salads, and bistro fare such as steak frites and paella. **Known for:** many vegan and gluten-free options; amazing homemade gelato; more than 30 wines by the glass. ⑤ Average main: $25 ✉ 457 E. Ojai Ave. ☎ 805/640–7987 ⊕ azuojai.com.

Boccali's

$ | **ITALIAN** | Edging a ranch, citrus groves, and a seasonal garden that provides produce for menu items, the modest but cheery Boccali's attracts many loyal fans. When it's warm, you can dine alfresco in the oak-shaded patio and lawn area and sometimes listen to live music. **Known for:** family-run operation; hand-rolled pizzas and home-style pastas; seasonal strawberry shortcake. ⑤ Average main: $15 ✉ 3277 Ojai Ave., about 2 miles east of downtown ☎ 805/646–6116 ⊕ boccalis.com ⊗ No lunch Mon. and Tues.

Farmer and the Cook

$ | **AMERICAN** | An organic farmer and his chef-wife run this funky café/bakery/market in Meiners Oaks, just a few miles west of downtown Ojai. Fill up at the soup and salad bar, order a wood-fired pizza, bento box, sandwich, or a daily special, then grab a table indoors or out on the patio. **Known for:** many veggie, vegan, and gluten-free options; grab-and-go meals; Mexican-focused menu. ⑤ Average main: $14 ✉ 339 W. El Roblar ☎ 805/640–9608 ⊕ www.farmerandcook.com.

★ Nocciola

$$$ | **ITALIAN** | Authentic northern Italian dishes with a California twist, a cozy fireplace dining room in a century-old Craftsman-style house, and a covered

patio amid the oaks draw locals and visitors alike to this popular eatery, owned by an Italian chef and his American wife (the family lives upstairs). The menu changes seasonally, but regular stars include seared sea scallops with Parmesan fondue and truffle shavings, homemade pastas made with organic egg yolks, and *pappardelle* with slow-roasted wild boar. **Known for:** great wild fish and game; Moment Pink signature cocktail; five-course tasting menu. ⑤ *Average main: $30* ✉ *314 El Paseo Rd.* ☎ *805/640–1648* ⊕ *nocciolaojai.com* ☾ *No lunch.*

 Hotels

The Iguana Inns of Ojai

$$ | **B&B/INN** | Artists own and operate these two bohemian-chic inns: The Blue Iguana, a cozy Southwestern-style hotel about 2 miles west of downtown, and the Emerald Iguana, which has art nouveau rooms, suites, and cottages in a secluded residential setting near downtown Ojai. **Pros:** colorful art everywhere; secluded; pet-friendly (Blue Iguana). **Cons:** 2 miles from downtown; on a highway; no pets or children under 14 at Emerald Iguana. ⑤ *Rooms from: $159* ✉ *11794 N. Ventura Ave.* ☎ *805/646–5277* ⊕ *iguanainnsofojai.com* ☞ *12 rooms, 8 cottages* ⑩ *Breakfast.*

Ojai Rancho Inn

$$ | **HOTEL** | A collection of one-story buildings and cottages tucked between Ojai Avenue and the bike trail, this ranch-style motel attracts hipsters and those who appreciate a rustic getaway with modern comforts and a laid-back vintage vibe. **Pros:** free loaner cruiser bikes; small on-site bar; nice pool area with lounge chairs. **Cons:** not fancy or luxurious; rooms could use soundproofing; some road noise in rooms close to the road. ⑤ *Rooms from: $159* ✉ *615 W. Ojai Ave.* ☎ *805/646–1434* ⊕ *ojairanchoinn.com* ☞ *17 rooms* ⑩ *No meals.*

★ Ojai Valley Inn & Spa

$$$$ | **RESORT** | This outdoorsy, golf-oriented resort and spa is set on beautifully landscaped grounds, with hillside views in nearly all directions. **Pros:** Spanish-colonial architecture; exceptional outdoor activities; seven on-site restaurants serving regional cuisine. **Cons:** expensive; areas near restaurants can be noisy. ⑤ *Rooms from: $349* ✉ *905 Country Club Rd.* ☎ *805/646–1111, 855/697–8780* ⊕ *ojairesort.com* ☞ *303 rooms* ⑩ *No meals.*

Su Nido Inn

$$$ | **B&B/INN** | A short walk from downtown Ojai sights and restaurants, this posh Mission Revival–style inn sits in a quiet neighborhood a few blocks from Libbey Park. **Pros:** walking distance from downtown; homey feel; soaking tubs and private patios or balconies in some rooms. **Cons:** no pool; can get hot during summer; too quiet for some. ⑤ *Rooms from: $199* ✉ *301 N. Montgomery St.* ☎ *805/646–7080, 866/646–7080* ⊕ *www.sunidoinn.com* ☞ *12 rooms* ⑩ *No meals* ☞ *2-night minimum stay on weekends.*

Santa Barbara

27 miles northwest of Ventura and 29 miles west of Ojai.

Santa Barbara has long been an oasis for Los Angelenos seeking respite from big-city life. The attractions begin at the ocean and end in the foothills of the Santa Ynez Mountains. A few miles up the coast east and west—but still very much a part of Santa Barbara—are the exclusive residential districts of Montecito and Hope Ranch. Santa Barbara is on a jog in the coastline, so the ocean is actually to the south, instead of the west. "Up" the coast toward San Francisco is west, "down" toward Los Angeles is east, and the mountains are north.

GETTING HERE AND AROUND

U.S. 101 is the main route into Santa Barbara. If you're staying in town, a car is handy but not essential; the beaches and downtown are easily explored by bicycle or on foot. Visit the Santa Barbara Car Free website for bike-route and walking-tour maps, suggestions for car-free vacations, and transportation discounts.

Santa Barbara Metropolitan Transit District's Line 22 bus serves major tourist sights. Several bus lines connect with the very convenient electric shuttles that cruise the downtown and waterfront every 10 to 15 minutes (50¢ each way, $1 day pass).

Santa Barbara Trolley Co. operates a motorized San Francisco–style cable car that loops past major hotels, shopping areas, and attractions from 10 am to 4 pm. Get off whenever you like, and pick up another trolley (they come every hour) when you're ready to move on. The fare is $25 for the day.

TOURS

Land and Sea Tours
SPECIAL-INTEREST | This outfit conducts 90-minute narrated tours in an amphibious 49-passenger vehicle nicknamed the Land Shark. The adventure begins with a drive through the city, followed by a plunge into the harbor for a cruise along the coast. ⊠ *10 E. Cabrillo Blvd., at Stearns Wharf* ☎ *805/683–7600* ⊕ *out-2seesb.com* ⌓ *From $30.*

Segway Tours of Santa Barbara
SPECIAL-INTEREST | After a brief training session, a guide leads you around town on electric-powered personal balancing transporters. Tour options include the waterfront (1¼ hours), Butterfly Beach and Montecito (2 hours), historic downtown Santa Barbara (2½ hours), and through town to the mission (3 hours). ⊠ *122 Gray Ave., at E. Mason St.* ☎ *805/963–7672* ⊕ *segwayofsb.com* ⌓ *$75–$115.*

ESSENTIALS

TRANSPORTATION CONTACTS Santa Barbara Car Free. ☎ *805/696–1100* ⊕ *santabarbaracarfree.org.* **Santa Barbara Metropolitan Transit District.** ☎ *805/963–3366* ⊕ *sbmtd.gov.* **Santa Barbara Trolley Co.** ☎ *805/965–0353* ⊕ *www.sbtrolley.com.*

VISITOR INFORMATION Santa Barbara Visitor Center. ⊠ *1 Garden St., at Cabrillo Blvd.* ☎ *805/965–3021* ⊕ *www.sbchamber.org.* **Visit Santa Barbara.** ⊠ *500 E. Montecito St.* ☎ *805/966–9222* ⊕ *santabarbaraca.com.*

 # Sights

Santa Barbara's waterfront is beautiful, with palm-studded promenades and plenty of sand. In the few miles between the beaches and the hills are downtown, Mission Santa Barbara, and the Santa Barbara Botanic Garden.

Andree Clark Bird Refuge
NATURE PRESERVE | This peaceful lagoon and its gardens sit north of East Beach. Bike trails and footpaths, punctuated by signs identifying native and migratory birds, skirt the lagoon. ⊠ *1400 E. Cabrillo Blvd., near the zoo* ⌓ *Free.*

Carriage and Western Art Museum
MUSEUM | **FAMILY** | The country's largest collection of old horse-drawn vehicles—painstakingly restored—is exhibited here, everything from polished hearses to police buggies to old stagecoaches and circus vehicles. In August the Old Spanish Days Fiesta borrows many of the vehicles for a jaunt around town. Docents lead free tours from 1 to 4 pm the third Sunday of the month. ⊠ *Pershing Park, 129 Castillo St.* ☎ *805/962–2353* ⊕ *carriagemuseum.org* ⌓ *Free* ⌚ *Closed weekends.*

El Presidio State Historic Park
MILITARY SITE | Founded in 1782, El Presidio was one of four military strongholds established by the Spanish along the coast of California. The park

Be sure to visit Santa Barbara's beautiful—and usually uncrowded—beaches.

encompasses much of the original site in the heart of downtown. El Cuartel, the adobe guardhouse, is the oldest building in Santa Barbara and the second oldest in California. ■TIP→ **Admission is free for children 16 and under.** ⊠ *123 E. Canon Perdido St., at Anacapa St.* ☎ *805/965–0093* ⊕ *www.sbthp.org* ⊠ *$5.*

Funk Zone

NEIGHBORHOOD | A formerly run-down industrial neighborhood near the waterfront and train station, the Funk Zone has evolved into a hip hangout filled with wine-tasting rooms, arts-and-crafts studios, murals, breweries, distilleries, restaurants, and small shops. It's fun to poke around the three-square-block district. ■TIP→ **Street parking is limited, so leave your car in a nearby city lot and cruise up and down the alleys on foot.** ⊠ *Between State and Garden Sts. and Cabrillo Blvd. and U.S. 101* ⊕ *funkzone.net.*

Karpeles Manuscript Library

LIBRARY | Ancient political tracts and old Disney cartoons are among the holdings at this facility, which also houses one of the world's largest privately owned collections of rare manuscripts. Fifty display cases contain a sampling of the archive's million-plus documents. ⊠ *21 W. Anapamu St., near Chapala St.* ☎ *805/962–5322* ⊕ *www.rain. org/~karpeles* ⊠ *Free* ⊙ *Closed Mon. and Tues.*

★ Lotusland

GARDEN | FAMILY | The 37-acre estate called Lotusland—often ranked among the world's 10 best gardens—once belonged to the Polish opera singer Ganna Walska, who purchased it in 1941 and lived here until her death in 1984. Many of the exotic trees and other subtropical flora were planted in 1882 by horticulturist R. Kinton Stevens. On the two-hour guided tour—the only option for visiting unless you're a member (reserve well ahead in summer)—you'll see an outdoor theater, a topiary garden, a lotus pond, and a huge collection of rare cycads, an unusual plant genus that has been around since the time of the dinosaurs. ■TIP→ **Child-friendly family tours are available for groups with children under the age of 10; contact Lotusland for scheduling.** ✉ *695 Ashley Rd., off Sycamore Canyon Rd. (Hwy. 192), Montecito* ⊕ *Visitor entrance gate is on Cold Spring Rd., at Sycamore Canyon Rd.* ☏ *805/969–9990* ⊕ *lotusland.org* ✇ *$50* ⊗ *Closed mid-Nov.–mid-Feb. No tours Sun.–Tues.*

Montecito

TOWN | Since the late 1800s the tree-studded hills and valleys of this town have attracted the rich and famous: Hollywood icons, business tycoons, tech moguls, and old-money families who installed themselves years ago. Shady roads wind through the community, which consists mostly of gated estates. Swank boutiques line **Coast Village Road,** where well-heeled residents such as Oprah Winfrey sometimes browse for truffle oil, picture frames, and designer jeans. Residents also hang out in the Upper Village, a chic shopping area with restaurants and cafés at the intersection of San Ysidro and East Valley roads.

★ Mission Santa Barbara

RELIGIOUS SITE | Widely referred to as the "Queen of Missions," this is one of the most beautiful and frequently photographed buildings in coastal California. Dating to 1786, the architecture evolved from adobe-brick buildings with thatch roofs to more permanent edifices as the mission's population burgeoned. An earthquake in 1812 destroyed the third church built on the site. Its replacement, the present structure, is still a functioning Catholic church. Mission Santa Barbara has a splendid Spanish/Mexican colonial art collection, as well as Chumash sculptures and the only Native American–made altar and tabernacle left in the California missions. Docents lead

Best Views

Drive along Alameda Padre Serra, a hillside road that begins near the mission and continues to Montecito, to feast your eyes on spectacular views of the city and the Santa Barbara Channel.

60-minute tours ($13 adult) weekdays at 11 am, Saturday at 10:30 am, and Sunday at 12:30 pm. ✉ *2201 Laguna St., at E. Los Olivos St.* ☏ *805/682–4149 gift shop, 805/682–4713 tours* ⊕ *www.santabarbaramission.org* ✇ *$9 self-guided tour.*

★ MOXI–The Wolf Museum of Exploration and Innovation

MUSEUM | **FAMILY** | It took more than two decades of unrelenting community advocacy to plan and build this exceptional science hub, which opened in early 2017 in a gorgeous three-story Spanish-Mediterranean building next to the train station and a block from Stearns Wharf and the beach. MOXI ignites learning through interactive activities in science and creativity for curious minds of all ages, from pre-K to gray. The 70-plus interactive exhibits—devoted to science, technology, engineering, arts, and mathematics (STEAM)—are integrated so visitors can explore seven themed areas (called tracks) in concert with one another and discover connections between them, for example, the relationship between music and electricity. In the Speed and Motion track you can build a model car and challenge two others to a race on a test track—then use the collected data to reconfigure your car for improved performance. In the Fantastic Forces space, build a contraption to send on a test flight in a wind column. Other sections include Light and Color, The

California's Missions

California history changed forever in the 18th century when Spanish explorers founded a series of missions along the Pacific coast. Believing they were following God's will, they wanted to spread the gospel and convert as many natives as possible. The process produced a collision between the Hispanic and California Indian cultures, resulting in one of the most striking legacies of Old California: the Spanish mission churches. Rising like mirages in the middle of desert plains and rolling hills, these historic sites transport you back to the days of the Spanish colonial period.

assumed control of the territory, and California became part of the United States. Today, all 21 of these missions stand as extraordinary monuments to their colorful past. Many are found on or near the "King's Road"—El Camino Real—which linked these mission outposts. At the height of the mission system the trail was approximately 600 miles long, eventually extending from San Diego to Sonoma. Today the road is commemorated on portions of Routes 101 and 82 in the form of roadside bell markers erected by CalTrans every 1 to 2 miles between San Diego and San Francisco.

Father of the Missions
Father Junípero Serra is an icon of the Spanish colonial period. At the behest of the Spanish government, the diminutive padre—then well into his fifties, and despite a chronic leg infection—started out on foot from Baja California to search for suitable mission sites, with a goal of reaching Monterey. In 1769 he helped establish Alta California's first mission in San Diego and continued his travels until his death in 1784, by which time he had founded eight more missions.

El Camino Real
The system ended about a decade after the Mexican government took control of Alta California in the early 1820s and began to secularize the missions. In 1848, the Americans

Mission Architecture
Mission architecture reflects a gorgeous blend of European and New World influences. While naves followed the simple forms of Franciscan Gothic, cloisters (with beautiful arcades) adopted aspects of the Romanesque style, and ornamental touches of the Spanish Renaissance—including red-tiled roofs and wrought-iron grilles—added even more elegance. In the 20th century, the Mission Revival Style had a huge impact on architecture and design in California, as seen in examples ranging from San Diego's Union Station to Stanford University's main quadrangle. For information on California's missions, see ⊕ *california-missionsfoundation.org*.

Tech Track, Innovation Workshop, Sound Track, and interactive media spaces. Up on the rooftop Sky Garden, which has some of the best panoramic views in downtown, you can listen to an orchestra of wind and solar-powered instruments and peer down through glass floor-windows to view the happy faces of explorers on the floors below. ✉ *125 State St.* ☎ *805/770–5000* ⊕ *moxi.org* 🎟 *$15.*

Santa Barbara Botanic Garden

GARDEN | Five miles of scenic trails meander through the garden's 78 acres of native plants. The Mission Dam, built in 1806, stands just beyond the redwood grove and above the restored aqueduct that once carried water to Mission Santa Barbara. More than a thousand plant species thrive in various themed sections, including mountains, deserts, meadows, redwoods, and Channel Islands. ■TIP→ **A conservation center dedicated to rare and endangered plant species opened in 2016 and presents rotating exhibitions.** ⊠ *1212 Mission Canyon Rd., north of Foothill Rd. (Hwy. 192)* ☎ *805/682–4726* ⊕ *www.sbbg.org* ⊠ *$14.*

★ Santa Barbara County Courthouse

GOVERNMENT BUILDING | Hand-painted tiles and a spiral staircase infuse the courthouse, a national historic landmark, with the grandeur of a Moorish palace. This magnificent building was completed in 1929. An elevator rises to an arched observation area in the tower that provides a panoramic view of the city. Before or after you take in the view, you can (if it's open) visit an engaging gallery devoted to the workings of the tower's original, still operational Seth Thomas clock. The murals in the ceremonial chambers on the courthouse's second floor were painted by an artist who did backdrops for some of Cecil B. DeMille's films. ■TIP→ **Join a free guided tour weekdays at 10:30, daily at 2.** ⊠ *1100 Anacapa St., at E. Anapamu St.* ☎ *805/962–6464* ⊕ *sbcourthouse.org.*

Santa Barbara Historical Museum

MUSEUM | The historical society's museum exhibits decorative and fine arts, furniture, costumes, and documents from the town's past. Adjacent to it is the Gledhill Library, a collection of books, photographs, maps, and manuscripts. Tours are by appointment only. Admission is free for anyone under 18. ⊠ *136 E. De La Guerra St., at Santa Barbara St.* ☎ *805/966–1601* ⊕ *www.sbhistorical.org* ⊠ *Museum $7; library from $2 per hr for research* ⊘ *Closed Mon.*

Santa Barbara Maritime Museum

MUSEUM | FAMILY | California's seafaring history is the focus here. High-tech, hands-on exhibits, such as a virtual sportfishing activity that lets participants haul in a "big one" and a local surfing history retrospective, make this a fun stop for families. In 2018, the museum introduced a fascinating History of Oil in the Santa Barbara Channel exhibit that traces the Chumash Indians' use of natural seeps to the infamous 1969 oil spill that spawned the modern environmental movement. The museum's shining star is a rare, 17-foot-tall Fresnel lens from the historic Point Conception Lighthouse. Ride the elevator to the fourth-floor observation area for great harbor views. ⊠ *113 Harbor Way, off Shoreline Dr.* ☎ *805/962–8404* ⊕ *sbmm.org* ⊠ *$8* ⊘ *Closed Wed.*

Santa Barbara Museum of Art

MUSEUM | The highlights of this museum's permanent collection include ancient sculpture, Asian art, impressionist paintings, contemporary art, photography, and American works in several mediums. ⊠ *1130 State St., at E. Anapamu St.* ☎ *805/963–4364* ⊕ *sbma.net* ⊠ *$10, free Thurs. 5–8* ⊘ *Closed Mon.*

Santa Barbara Museum of Natural History

MUSEUM | FAMILY | The gigantic blue whale skeleton greets you at the entrance to this 17-acre complex whose major draws include its planetarium, paleo and marine life, and gem and mineral display. Startlingly alive-looking stuffed specimens in Mammal and Bird Halls include a smiling grizzly bear and nesting California condors. A room of dioramas illustrates Chumash Indian history and culture while a Santa Barbara Gallery showcases the region's unique biodiversity. Outdoors, nature trails wind through the serene oak woodlands and a summer butterfly pavilion.

Santa Barbara

KEY

1 *Exploring Sights*
1 *Restaurants*
1 *Hotels*
ℹ *Tourist information*

✉ *2559 Puesta del Sol Rd., off Mission Canyon Rd.* ☎ *805/682–4711* ⊕ *sbnature. org* ✉ *$15; free one Sun. of month Sept.–Apr.*

Santa Barbara Zoo

ZOO | FAMILY | This compact zoo's gorgeous grounds shelter elephants, gorillas, exotic birds, and big cats, and has many exhibits that educate visitors on conservation efforts to save endangered species like the California condor and the red-legged frog. For small children, there's a scenic railroad and barnyard area where they can feed domestic sheep. Three high-tech dinosaurs and an 8-foot-tall grizzly bear puppet perform in live stage shows (free with admission), daily in summer and on weekends the rest of the year. Kids especially love feeding the giraffes from a view deck overlooking the beach. ■TIP→ **The palm-studded lawns on a hilltop overlooking the beach are perfect spots for family picnics.** ✉ *500 Niños Dr., off El Cabrillo Blvd.* ☎ *805/962–5339 main line* ⊕ *santabarbarazoo.org* ✉ *Zoo $18, parking $11.*

Sea Center

ZOO | FAMILY | A branch of the Santa Barbara Museum of Natural History, the center specializes in Santa Barbara Channel marine life and conservation. Though small compared to aquariums in Monterey and Long Beach, this is a fascinating, hands-on marine science laboratory that lets you participate in experiments, projects, and exhibits, including touch pools. The two-story glass walls here open to stunning ocean, mountain, and city views. ✉ *211 Stearns Wharf* ☎ *805/962–2526* ⊕ *sbnature.org* ✉ *$9.*

Stearns Wharf

MARINA | Built in 1872, Stearns Wharf is Santa Barbara's most visited landmark. Expansive views of the mountains, cityscape, and harbor unfold from every vantage point on the three-block-long pier. Although it's a nice walk from the Cabrillo Boulevard parking areas, you can also park on the pier and then

Santa Barbara Style

After a 1925 earthquake demolished many buildings, the city seized a golden opportunity to assume a Spanish-Mediterranean style. It established an architectural board of review, which, along with city commissions, created strict building codes for the downtown district: red-tile roofs, earth-tone facades, arches, wrought-iron embellishments, and height restrictions (about four stories).

wander through the shops or stop for a meal at one of the wharf's restaurants. ✉ *Cabrillo Blvd. and State St.* ⊕ *stearnswharf.org.*

Urban Wine Trail

WINERY/DISTILLERY | Nearly 30 winery tasting rooms form the Urban Wine Trail; most are within walking distance of the waterfront and the lower State Street shopping and restaurant district. **Santa Barbara Winery,** at 202 Anacapa Street, and **Au Bon Climat,** at 813 Anacapa Street, are good places to start your oenological trek. ✉ *Santa Barbara* ⊕ *urbanwinetrailsb.com.*

🏖 Beaches

Arroyo Burro Beach

BEACH—SIGHT | FAMILY | The beach's usually gentle surf makes it ideal for families with young children. It's a local favorite because you can walk for miles in both directions when tides are low. Leashed dogs are allowed on the main stretch of beach and westward; they are allowed to romp off-leash east of the slough at the beach entrance. The parking lots fill early on weekends and throughout the summer, but the park is relatively quiet at other times. Walk along the beach just a few hundreds yards away from the main steps at the entrance to escape crowds on warm-weather days. Surfers, swimmers, stand-up paddlers, and boogie boarders regularly ply the waves, and photographers come often to catch the vivid sunsets. **Amenities:** food and drink; lifeguard in summer; parking, showers, toilets. **Best for:** sunset; surfing; swimming; walking. ⊠ *Cliff Dr. and Las Positas Rd.* ⊕ *countyofsb. org/parks.*

★ East Beach

BEACH—SIGHT | FAMILY | The wide swath of sand at the east end of Cabrillo Boulevard is a great spot for people-watching. East Beach has sand volleyball courts, summertime lifeguard and sports competitions, and arts-and-crafts shows on Sundays and holidays. You can use showers, a weight room, and lockers (bring your own towel) and rent umbrellas and boogie boards at the Cabrillo Bathhouse. Next door, there's an elaborate jungle-gym play area for kids. Hotels line the boulevard across from the beach. **Amenities:** food and drink; lifeguards in summer; parking (fee); showers; toilets; water sports. **Best for:** walking; swimming; surfing. ⊠ *1118 Cabrillo Blvd., at Ninos Dr.* ☎ *805/897–2680.*

 Restaurants

Arigato Sushi

$$$ | JAPANESE | You might have to wait for a table at this two-story restaurant and sushi bar—locals line up early for the wildly creative combination rolls and other delectables (first come, first served). Fans of authentic Japanese food sometimes disagree about the quality of the seafood, but all dishes are fresh and artfully presented. **Known for:** innovative creations; lively atmosphere; patio and second-floor balcony seating. Ⓢ *Average main: $30* ⊠ *1225 State St., near W. Victoria St.* ☎ *805/965–6074* ⊕ *www. arigatosb.com* ☾ *No lunch.*

Barbareño

$$$ | **MODERN AMERICAN** | Determined to push the boundaries of farm-to-table, college friends who worked at the same Los Angeles eatery banded together in 2014 to launch Barbareño. They churn their own butter, bake their own breads, make condiments from scratch, and forage mushrooms, eucalyptus leaves, and other ingredients from the wild. **Known for:** youthful, sophisticated vibe; chef's sampler plate; monthly seasonal menu. Ⓢ *Average main: $24* ⊠ *205 W. Canon Perdido St., at De La Vina St.* ☎ *805/963–9591* ⊕ *barbareno.com* ☾ *Closed Tues. No lunch.*

Brophy Bros.

$$$ | SEAFOOD | The outdoor tables at this casual harborside restaurant have perfect views of the marina and mountains. Staffers serve enormous, exceptionally fresh fish dishes and provide guests with a pager so you can stroll along the waterfront until the beep lets you know your table is ready. **Known for:** seafood salad and chowder; stellar clam bar; long wait times. Ⓢ *Average main: $26* ⊠ *119 Harbor Way, off Shoreline Dr.* ☎ *805/966–4418* ⊕ *brophybros.com.*

Jeannine's

$ | AMERICAN | Take a break from State Street shopping at Jeannine's, revered locally for its wholesome sandwiches, salads, and baked goods, made from scratch with organic and natural ingredients. Dine in the expansive dining room or patio, or pick up a turkey cranberry or chicken pesto sandwich to go, and picnic in the courthouse gardens a block away. **Known for:** fantastic pastries; hearty, healthful breakfasts; turkey roasted or smoked in house. Ⓢ *Average main: $15* ⊠ *La Arcada, 15 E. Figueroa St., at State St.* ☎ *805/966–1717* ⊕ *jeannines.com/restaurants.*

La Super-Rica

$ | MEXICAN | This food stand on the east side of town serves some of the spiciest and most authentic Mexican dishes between Los Angeles and San Francisco. Fans (the late chef Julia Child was one) fill up on the soft tacos served with yummy spicy or mild sauces and legendary beans; portions are on the small side; order several dishes and share. **Known for:** house-made tortillas; daily specials such as chilaquiles; vegetarian and gluten-free dishes. $ *Average main: $14* ⌧ *622 N. Milpas St., at Alphonse St.* ☎ *805/963–4940* ⊟ *No credit cards* ⊘ *Closed Tues. and Wed.*

★ The Lark

$$$ | MODERN AMERICAN | Shared dining—small plates and larger—and a seasonal menu showcasing local ingredients are the focus at this urban-chic restaurant named for an overnight all-Pullman train that chugged into the nearby railroad station for six decades. Sit at the 24-seat communal table set atop vintage radiators, or at tables and booths crafted from antique Spanish church pews and other repurposed or recycled materials. **Known for:** social environment; wines curated by a master sommelier; handcrafted locavore cocktails. $ *Average main: $30* ⌧ *131 Anacapa St., at E. Yanonali St.* ☎ *805/284–0370* ⊕ *www.thelarksb.com* ⊘ *Closed Mon. No lunch.*

Loquita

$$$ | SPANISH | In a cozy space in a prime corner at the gateway to the Funk Zone near Stearns Wharf, Loquita honors Santa Barbara's Spanish heritage by serving up authentic Spanish dishes, wines, and cocktails made with fresh, sustainably sourced local ingredients. The menu covers all bases, from tapas, to wood-fired seafood, and grilled meats, to Spanish wines, vermouth, gin and tonics, and sangria. **Known for:** multiple types of paella; counter and takeaway items; great gin and tonic. $ *Average main: $29* ⌧ *202 State St.* ☎ *805/880–3380* ⊕ *www.loquitasb.com.*

Take the Kids

Two fun playgrounds provide welcome interludes for the young set. Children love tooling around **Kids' World** (⌧ *Garden and Micheltorena Sts.*), a public playground with a castle-shaped maze of climbing structures, slides, and tunnels. At **Shipwreck Playground** (⌧ *Chase Palm Park, E. Cabrillo Blvd., east of Garden St.*), parents take as much pleasure in the waterfront views as the kids do in the nautical-theme diversions.

Olio e Limone

$$$$ | ITALIAN | Sophisticated Italian cuisine with an emphasis on Sicily is served at this restaurant near the Arlington. The juicy veal chop is popular, but surprises abound here; be sure to try unusual dishes such as ribbon pasta with quail and sausage in a mushroom ragout, or the duck ravioli. **Known for:** grilled veal and lamb chops; cozy white-tablecloth dining room; adjacent raw bar and casual pizzeria. $ *Average main: $32* ⌧ *17 W. Victoria St., at State St.* ☎ *805/899–2699* ⊕ *www.olioelimone.com* ⊘ *No lunch Sun.*

Palace Grill

$$$ | SOUTHERN | Mardi Gras energy, team-style service, lively music, and great Cajun, creole, and Caribbean food have made the Palace a Santa Barbara icon. Be prepared to wait for a table on Friday and Saturday nights (when reservations are taken for a 5:30 seating only), though the live entertainment and free appetizers, sent out front when the line is long, will whet your appetite for the feast to come. **Known for:** blackened fish and meats; Louisiana bread pudding soufflé; Cajun martini served in a mason jar. $ *Average main: $30* ⌧ *8 E. Cota St., at State St.* ☎ *805/963–5000* ⊕ *palacegrill.com.*

★ The Stonehouse

$$$$ | **AMERICAN** | The elegant Stonehouse—consistently lauded as one of the nation's top restaurants—is inside a century-old granite former farmhouse at the San Ysidro Ranch resort. The menu changes constantly, but might include pan-seared abalone or classic steak Diane flambéed table-side. **Known for:** ingredients from on-site garden; heated ocean-view deck with fireplace; elegant dining room. $ *Average main: $49* ✉ *900 San Ysidro La., off San Ysidro Rd., Montecito* ☎ *805/565–1700* ⊕ *www. sanysidroranch.com.*

★ Toma

$$$ | **ITALIAN** | Seasonal, locally sourced ingredients and softly lit muted-yellow walls evoke the flavors and charms of Tuscany and the Mediterranean at this rustic-romantic restaurant across from the harbor and West Beach. Ahi sashimi tucked in a crisp sesame cone is a popular appetizer, after which you can proceed to a house-made pasta dish or rock shrimp gnocchi. **Known for:** house-made pastas and gnocchi; wines from Italy and California's Central Coast; romantic waterfront setting. $ *Average main: $30* ✉ *324 W. Cabrillo Blvd., near Castillo St.* ☎ *805/962–0777* ⊕ *www. tomarestaurant.com* ☽ *No lunch.*

Wine Cask

$$$$ | **AMERICAN** | The Wine Cask serves bistro-style meals in a comfortable and classy dining room with a huge fireplace and wood-beam ceiling decorated with gold leaf. The more casual bar-café, Intermezzo, across the courtyard, serves pizzas, salads, small plates, wines, and cocktails and is open late. **Known for:** extensive wine list and pairing suggestions; historic courtyard patio; late hours. $ *Average main: $31* ✉ *El Paseo, 813 Anacapa St., at E. De La Guerra St.* ☎ *805/966–9463* ⊕ *winecask.com* ☽ *Closed Sun. and Mon.*

Hotels

★ Belmond El Encanto

$$$$ | **HOTEL** | Built in 1915 and following more than a $100 million of extensive renovations a century later, this Santa Barbara icon lives on to thrill a new generation of guests with its relaxed-luxe bungalow rooms, lush gardens, and personalized service. **Pros:** dining terrace with panoramic city and ocean views; stellar spa facility; infinity pool with ocean views. **Cons:** long walk to downtown; pricey; guests staying for more than a few days may find the restaurant menus limited. $ *Rooms from: $404* ✉ *800 Alvarado Pl.* ☎ *805/845–5800, 800/393–5315* ⊕ *www.belmond.com/ elencanto* ⇌ *92 rooms* ❑ *No meals.*

Canary Hotel

$$$$ | **HOTEL** | A full-service hotel in the heart of downtown, this Kimpton property blends a casual, beach-getaway feel with contemporary California style. **Pros:** upscale local cuisine at on-site Finch & Fork restaurant; rooms come with candles, yoga mats, and binoculars (for touring); adjacent fitness center. **Cons:** across from transit center; a mile from the beach; some rooms on the small side. $ *Rooms from: $415* ✉ *31 W. Carrillo St.* ☎ *805/884– 0300, 866/999–5401* ⊕ *www.canarysant- abarbara.com* ⇌ *97 rooms* ❑ *No meals.*

★ Four Seasons Resort The Biltmore Santa Barbara

$$$$ | **RESORT** | Surrounded by lush, perfectly manicured gardens and across from the beach, Santa Barbara's grande dame has long been a favorite for quiet, California-style luxury. **Pros:** spa with 11 treatment rooms; access to members-only clubs and restaurant on-site; steps from the beach. **Cons:** back rooms are close to train tracks; expensive; several miles from downtown hub. $ *Rooms from: $795* ✉ *1260 Channel Dr.* ☎ *805/969–2261, 805/565–8299 for reservations only* ⊕ *www.fourseasons.com/santabarbara* ⇌ *206 rooms* ❑ *No meals.*

The Goodland

$$$$ | HOTEL | A vintage Woody car, a silver Airstream trailer, and a lobby record shop are among the elements that bring 1960s California surf culture to life at this Kimpton hotel in Goleta. **Pros:** cool and casual vibe; live music or DJs several evenings a week; complimentary wine-and-beer social hour and s'mores by the fireside. **Cons:** not close to downtown Santa Barbara; some rooms on the small side; thin walls allow for noise transfer from neighboring rooms. $ *Rooms from: $284* ✉ *5650 Calle Real, Goleta* ☎ *877/480–1465, 805/964–6241* ⊕ *www.thegoodland.com* ⇔ *158 rooms* ◎| *No meals.*

Hilton Santa Barbara Beachfront Resort

$$$$ | RESORT | A full-scale resort with seven buildings spread over 24 landscaped acres across from East Beach, the hotel was founded by the late TV actor Fess Parker, best known for playing Davy Crockett and Daniel Boone. **Pros:** numerous amenities; right across from the beach; free shuttle to train station and airport. **Cons:** train noise filters into some rooms; too spread out for some; pricey. $ *Rooms from: $475* ✉ *633 E. Cabrillo Blvd.* ☎ *800/879–2929, 805/564–4333* ⊕ *www.hiltonsantabarbarabeachfrontresort.com* ⇔ *360 rooms* ◎| *No meals.*

★ Hotel Californian

$$$$ | HOTEL | A sprawling collection of Spanish-Moorish buildings that opened in summer 2017 at the site of the historic 1925 Hotel Californian, this sophisticated hotel with a hip youthful vibe occupies nearly three full blocks on State Street just steps from Stearns Wharf, MOXI, the Funk Zone, beaches, and the harbor. **Pros:** steps from the waterfront, Funk Zone, and beaches; resort-style amenities; on-site parking. **Cons:** pricey; must walk or ride the shuttle to downtown attractions; train whistle noise in rooms close to station. $ *Rooms from: $550* ✉ *36 State St.* ☎ *805/882–0100* ⊕ *www.thehotelcalifornian.com* ⇔ *121 rooms.*

Hotel Indigo

$$$ | HOTEL | The closest hotel to the train station and across the street from the Funk Zone, artsy Hotel Indigo is a fine choice for travelers who appreciate contemporary art and want easy access to dining, nightlife, and the beach. **Pros:** multilingual staff; a block from Stearns Wharf; great value for location. **Cons:** showers only (no bathtubs); train whistles early morning; rooms on small side. $ *Rooms from: $249* ✉ *121 State St.* ☎ *805/966–6586* ⊕ *www.indigosantabarbara.com* ⇔ *41 rooms* ◎| *No meals.*

Hyatt Santa Barbara

$$$$ | HOTEL | A complex of four buildings on 3 landscaped acres, the Hyatt provides an appealing lodging option in a prime location right across from East Beach. **Pros:** steps from the beach; many room types and rates; walk to the zoo and waterfront shuttle. **Cons:** motel feel; busy area in summer. $ *Rooms from: $289* ✉ *1111 E. Cabrillo Blvd.* ☎ *805/882–1234, 800/643–1994* ⊕ *santabarbara.centric.hyatt.com* ⇔ *174 rooms* ◎| *No meals.*

★ The Ritz-Carlton Bacara, Santa Barbara

$$$$ | RESORT | A luxury resort with four restaurants and a 42,000-square-foot spa and fitness center with 36 treatment rooms, the Ritz-Carlton Bacara provides a gorgeous setting for relaxing retreats. **Pros:** many diversions including hiking and stargazing; three zero-edge pools; three golf courses nearby. **Cons:** pricey; not close to downtown; sand on beach not pristine enough for some. $ *Rooms from: $475* ✉ *8301 Hollister Ave., Goleta* ☎ *805/968–0100* ⊕ *www.ritzcarlton.com/santabarbara* ⇔ *358 rooms* ◎| *No meals.*

★ Rosewood Miramar Beach

$$$$ | RESORT | This luxury resort, opened in 2019, sprawls across 16 lush acres on one of the area's most scenic and exclusive beaches. **Pros:** two cabana-lined pools; six restaurants and bars; steps to the beach. **Cons:** too exclusive

for some. $ Rooms from: $680 ✉ 1759 S. Jameson La., Montecito ☎ 214/880–4292 ⊕ www.rosewoodhotels.com/en/miramar-beach-montecito ⇨ 161 rooms ⦿ No meals.

★ San Ysidro Ranch

$$$$ | RESORT | At this romantic hideaway on a historic property in the Montecito foothills—where John and Jackie Kennedy spent their honeymoon and Oprah sends her out-of-town visitors—guest cottages are scattered among groves of orange trees and flower beds. **Pros:** rooms come with private outdoor spas; 17 miles of hiking trails nearby; Plow & Angel Bistro and Stonehouse restaurants on-site are Santa Barbara institutions. **Cons:** very expensive; too remote for some. $ Rooms from: $845 ✉ 900 San Ysidro La., Montecito ☎ 805/565–1700, 800/368–6788 ⊕ www.sanysidroranch.com ⇨ 41 rooms and cottages ⦿ No meals ⌲ 2-day minimum stay on weekends, 3 days on holiday weekends.

★ Santa Barbara Inn

$$$$ | HOTEL | This full-service, Spanish-Mediterranean, family-owned hotel occupies a prime waterfront corner across from East Beach. **Pros:** more than half the rooms have ocean views; suites come with whirlpool tubs; delicious on-site restaurant Convivo. **Cons:** on a busy boulevard; limited street parking; not withing easy walking distance of downtown. $ Rooms from: $350 ✉ 901 E. Cabrillo Blvd. ⊹ At Milpas St. ☎ 805/966–3636 ⊕ www.santabarainn.com ⇨ 70 rooms ⦿ Breakfast.

★ Simpson House Inn

$$$$ | B&B/INN | If you're a fan of traditional bed-and-breakfast inns, this property, with its beautifully appointed Victorian main house and acre of lush gardens, is for you. **Pros:** elegant furnishings; impeccable landscaping; within walking distance of downtown. **Cons:** some rooms in main building are small; two-night minimum stay on weekends May–October; no pets allowed. $ Rooms from:

$339 ✉ 121 E. Arrellaga St. ☎ 805/963–7067 ⊕ www.simpsonhouseinn.com ⇨ 15 rooms ⦿ Breakfast.

Spanish Garden Inn

$$$$ | B&B/INN | A half block from the Presidio in the heart of downtown, this Spanish-Mediterranean retreat celebrates Santa Barbara style, from the tile floors, wrought-iron balconies, and exotic plants to the original art by local plein-air artists. **Pros:** walking distance from downtown; classic Spanish-Mediterranean style; free parking. **Cons:** no restaurant; tiny fitness room; no hot tub. $ Rooms from: $339 ✉ 915 Garden St. ☎ 805/564–4700 ⊕ www.spanishgardeninn.com ⇨ 24 rooms ⦿ Breakfast.

The Upham

$$$$ | B&B/INN | Built in 1871, this downtown Victorian in the arts and culture district has been restored as a full-service hotel. **Pros:** 1-acre garden; easy walk to theaters; excellent on-site restaurant. **Cons:** some rooms are small; not near beach or waterfront; no in-room safes. $ Rooms from: $285 ✉ 1404 De la Vina St. ☎ 805/962–0058 ⊕ www.uphamhotel.com ⇨ 50 rooms ⦿ Breakfast ⌲ 2-night minimum stay on weekends.

The Wayfarer

$$$ | HOTEL | The hip and stylish Wayfarer occupies a prime Funk Zone location, three blocks from Stearns Wharf and the beach, and across the street from the train station. **Pros:** outdoor heated pool; breakfast included; free parking. **Cons:** some rooms on the small side; freeway and train noise bothers some guests; pricey during high season. $ Rooms from: $239 ✉ 12 E. Montecito St. ☎ 805/845–1000 ⊕ wayfarersb.com ⇨ 31 rooms ⦿ Breakfast.

Nightlife

The bar, club, and live music scene centers on lower State Street, between the 300 and 800 blocks.

Dargan's

BARS/PUBS | Lively Dargan's pub has pool tables, great draft beers and Irish whiskies, and serves a full menu of traditional Irish dishes. ⊠ *18 E. Ortega St., at Anacapa St.* ☎ *805/568–0702* ⊕ *darganssb.com.*

The Good Lion

BARS/PUBS | The cocktail menu at this intimate neighborhood bar near The Granada Theatre changes weekly, depending on the fresh organic bounty available at the markets. All juices are organic and squeezed fresh daily, and all syrups are made in house with organic produce and sweeteners. ⊠ *1212 State St.* ☎ *805/845–8754* ⊕ *www.goodlion-cocktails.com.*

James Joyce

BARS/PUBS | A good place to have a few beers and while away an evening; the James Joyce hosts rock, blues, jazz, and other performers six nights a week. ⊠ *513 State St., at W. Haley St.* ☎ *805/962–2688* ⊕ *sbjamesjoyce.com.*

Joe's Cafe

BARS/PUBS | Steins of beer and stiff cocktails accompany hearty bar food at Joe's. It's a fun, if occasionally rowdy, collegiate scene. ⊠ *536 State St., at E. Cota St.* ☎ *805/966–4638* ⊕ *joescafesb.com.*

Les Marchands

WINE BARS—NIGHTLIFE | A world-class team of sommeliers operates this European-styled wine bar, store, and eatery in the Funk Zone. ⊠ *131 Anacapa St., at Yananoli St.* ☎ *805/284–0380* ⊕ *www.lesmarchandswine.com.*

Lucky's

BARS/PUBS | A slick sports bar attached to an upscale steak house owned by the maker of Lucky Brand dungarees, this place attracts hip patrons hoping to see and be seen. ⊠ *1279 Coast Village Rd., near Olive Mill Rd., Montecito* ☎ *805/565–7540* ⊕ *luckys-steakhouse.com.*

Milk & Honey

BARS/PUBS | Artfully prepared tapas, mango mojitos, and exotic cocktails lure trendy crowds to swank M&H, despite high prices and a reputation for inattentive service. ⊠ *30 W. Anapamu St., at State St.* ☎ *805/275–4232* ⊕ *www.milknhoneytapas.com.*

SOhO

MUSIC CLUBS | A lively restaurant, bar, and music venue, SOhO books all kinds of musical acts, from jazz to blues to rock. ⊠ *1221 State St., at W. Victoria St.* ☎ *805/962–7776* ⊕ *www.sohosb.com.*

Performing Arts

The arts district, with theaters, restaurants, and cafés, starts around the 900 block of State and continues north to the 1300 block. To see what's scheduled around town, pick up the free weekly *Santa Barbara Independent* newspaper or visit its website, ⊕ *www.independent.com.*

Arlington Theatre

ARTS CENTERS | This Moorish-style auditorium presents touring performers and films throughout the year. ⊠ *1317 State St., at Arlington Ave.* ☎ *805/963–4408* ⊕ *thearlingtontheatre.com.*

Center Stage Theatre

ARTS CENTERS | This venue hosts plays, music, dance, and readings. ⊠ *Paseo Nuevo Center, Chapala and De la Guerra Sts., 2nd fl.* ☎ *805/963–0408* ⊕ *www.centerstagetheater.org.*

Ensemble Theatre Company (ETC)

THEATER | The company stages classic and contemporary comedies, musicals, and dramas. ⊠ *33 W. Victoria St., at Chapala St.* ☎ *805/965–5400* ⊕ *www.etcsb.org.*

The Granada Theatre

THEATER | A restored, modernized landmark that dates from 1924, the Granada hosts Broadway touring shows and dance, music, and other cultural events. ⊠ 1214 State St., at E. Anapamu St. ☎ 805/899–2222 ⊕ granadasb.org.

I Madonnari

ARTS FESTIVALS | Artists of all ages create 150 large-scale pastel drawings on the pavement near the Old Mission steps during an Italian street painting festival held Memorial Day weekend. ⊠ Santa Barbara ⊕ imadonnarifestival.com.

Lobero Theatre

THEATER | A state landmark, the Lobero hosts community theater groups and touring professionals. ⊠ 33 E. Canon Perdido St., at Anacapa St. ☎ 805/963–0761 ⊕ www.lobero.com.

Music Academy of the West

MUSIC | The academy presents orchestral, chamber, and operatic works every summer. ⊠ 1070 Fairway Rd., off Channel Dr. ☎ 805/969–4726, 805/969–8787 box office ⊕ www.musicacademy.org.

★ Old Spanish Days Fiesta

CULTURAL FESTIVALS | The city celebrates its Spanish, Mexican, and Chumash heritage in early August with events that include music, dancing, an all-equestrian parade, a carnival, and a rodeo. ⊠ Santa Barbara ⊕ oldspanishdays-fiesta.org.

★ Santa Barbara International Film Festival

FESTIVALS | The 12-day festival in late January and early February attracts film enthusiasts and major stars to downtown venues for screenings, panels, and tributes. ⊠ Santa Barbara ⊕ www.sbiff.org.

Summer Solstice Celebration

ARTS FESTIVALS | More than 100,000 revelers celebrate the arts at this mid-June event whose highlight is a huge parade of costumed participants who dance, drum, and ride people-powered floats up State Street. ⊠ Santa Barbara ☎ 805/965–3396 ⊕ www.solsticeparade.com.

Earth Day

In 1969, 200,000 gallons of crude oil spilled into the Santa Barbara Channel, causing an immediate outcry from residents. The day after the spill, Get Oil Out (GOO) was established; the group helped lead the successful fight for legislation to limit and regulate offshore drilling in California. The Santa Barbara spill also spawned Earth Day, which is still celebrated across the nation today.

🏃 Activities

BIKING

Cabrillo Bike Lane

BICYCLING | The level, two-lane, 3-mile Cabrillo Bike Lane passes the Santa Barbara Zoo, the Andree Clark Bird Refuge, beaches, and the harbor. Stop for a meal at one of the restaurants along the way, or for a picnic along the palm-lined path looking out on the Pacific.

Wheel Fun Rentals

BICYCLING | You can rent bikes, quadricycles, and skates here. ⊠ 24 E. Mason St, ☎ 805/966–2282 ⊕ wheelfunrentalssb.com.

BOATS AND CHARTERS

★ Condor Express

BOATING | From SEA Landing, the Condor Express, a 75-foot high-speed catamaran, whisks up to 149 passengers toward the Channel Islands on whale-watching excursions and sunset and dinner cruises. ⊠ 301 W. Cabrillo Blvd. ☎ 805/882–0088, 888/779–4253 ⊕ condorexpress.com.

Paddle Sports Center

WATER SPORTS | A full-service paddle-sports center in the harbor, this outfit rents kayaks, stand-up paddleboards, surfboards, boogie boards, and watersports gear. ⊠ 117 B Harbor Way, off

Shoreline Dr. ☎ *805/617–3425 rentals* ⊕ *www.paddlesportsca.com.*

Santa Barbara Sailing Center

BOATING | The center offers sailing instruction, rents and charters sailboats, kayaks, and stand-up paddleboards, and organizes dinner and sunset champagne cruises, island excursions, and whale-watching trips. ✉ *Santa Barbara Harbor launching ramp* ☎ *805/962–2826* ⊕ *sbsail.com.*

Santa Barbara Water Taxi

BOATING | FAMILY | Children beg to ride *Lil' Toot,* a cheery yellow water taxi that cruises from the harbor to Stearns Wharf and back again. The fare for kids is $2 each way. ✉ *Santa Barbara Harbor and Stearns Wharf* ☎ *805/465–6676* ⊕ *www.celebrationsantabarbara.com/* 🎫 *$5 one-way.*

SEA Landing

BOATING | This outfit operates surface and deep-sea fishing charters year-round. ✉ *Cabrillo Blvd., at Bath St., and breakwater in Santa Barbara Harbor* ☎ *805/963–3564* ⊕ *sealanding.net.*

Truth Aquatics

SCUBA DIVING | Truth runs kayaking, paddleboarding, hiking, snorkeling, and scuba excursions to the National Marine Sanctuary and Channel Islands National Park. ✉ *Departures from SEA Landing, Santa Barbara Harbor* ☎ *805/962–1127* ⊕ *truthaquatics.com* 🎫 *From $130.*

 # Shopping

CLOTHING

Channel Islands Surfboards

CLOTHING | Come here for top-of-the-line surfboards and the latest in California beachwear, sandals, and accessories. ✉ *36 Anacapa St., at E. Mason St.* ☎ *805/966–7213* ⊕ *www.cisurfboards.com.*

DIANI

CLOTHING | This upscale, European-style women's boutique dresses clients in designer clothing from around the world. Sibling shoe and home-and-garden shops are nearby. ✉ *1324 State St., at Arlington Ave.* ☎ *805/966–3114, 805/966–7175 shoe shop* ⊕ *dianiboutique.com.*

Surf N Wear's Beach House

CLOTHING | This shop carries surf clothing, gear, and collectibles; it's also the home of Santa Barbara Surf Shop and the exclusive local dealer of Surfboards by Yater. ✉ *10 State St., at Cabrillo Blvd.* ☎ *805/963–1281* ⊕ *www.surfnwear.com.*

Wendy Foster

CLOTHING | This store sells casual-chic women's fashions. ✉ *833 State St., at W. Canon Perdido St.* ☎ *805/966–2276* ⊕ *wendyfoster.com.*

FOOD AND WINE

Santa Barbara Public Market

FOOD/CANDY | A dozen food and beverage vendors occupy this spacious arts district galleria. Stock up on olive oils, vinegars, and other gourmet goodies; sip on hand-crafted wines and beers while watching sports events; and nosh on noodle bowls, sushi and baked goods. ✉ *38 W. Victoria St., at Chapala St.* ☎ *805/770–7702* ⊕ *sbpublicmarket.com.*

SHOPPING AREAS

★ El Paseo

SHOPPING NEIGHBORHOODS | Wine-tasting rooms, shops, art galleries, and studios share the courtyard and gardens of this historic arcade. ✉ *Canon Perdido St., between State and Anacapa Sts.*

★ State Street

SHOPPING NEIGHBORHOODS | Between Cabrillo Boulevard and Sola Street, State Street is a shopper's paradise. Chic malls, quirky storefronts, antiques emporia, elegant boutiques, and funky thrift shops abound. You can shop on foot or ride a battery-powered trolley (50¢ or $1 day pass) that runs between the waterfront and the 1300 block. Nordstrom and Macy's anchor **Paseo Nuevo,** an open-air mall in the 700 block. Shops, restaurants, galleries, and fountains line the tiled walkways of **La Arcada,** a small complex of landscaped courtyards in the 1100 block designed by architect Myron Hunt in 1926.

Summerland
SHOPPING NEIGHBORHOODS | Serious antiques hunters head southeast of Santa Barbara to Summerland, which is full of shops and markets. Several good ones are along Lillie Avenue and Ortega Hill Road. ✉ *Summerland.*

Santa Ynez

31 miles north of Goleta.

Founded in 1882, the tiny town of Santa Ynez still has many of its original frontier buildings. You can walk through the three-block downtown area in a few minutes, shop for antiques, and hang around the old-time saloon. At some of the Santa Ynez Valley's best restaurants, you just might bump into one of the celebrities who own nearby ranches.

GETTING HERE AND AROUND
Take Highway 154 over San Marcos Pass or U.S. 101 north 43 miles to Buellton, then 7 miles east.

Sights

Chumash Casino Resort
CASINO—SIGHT | Just south of Santa Ynez on the Chumash Indian Reservation lies this Las Vegas–style casino with 2,300 slot machines, three restaurants and a food court, a spa, and a 12-story upscale hotel with a rooftop pool. ✉ *3400 E. Hwy. 246* ☎ *800/248–6274* ⊕ *www. chumashcasino.com* ⌁ *Free.*

Gainey Vineyard
WINERY/DISTILLERY | The 1,800-acre Gainey Ranch, straddling the banks of the Santa Ynez River, includes about 100 acres of organic vineyards: Sauvignon Blanc, Merlot, Cabernet Sauvignon, and Cabernet Franc. The winery also makes

wines from Chardonnay, Pinot Noir, and Syrah grapes from the Santa Rita Hills. You can taste the latest releases—the estate Pinot Noir is especially good—in a Spanish-style hacienda overlooking the ranch. Barrel tasting on weekdays and jeep tours and tasting in the historic barn on weekends are also available (except in winter). ✉ *3950 E. Hwy. 246* ☎ *805/688–0558* ⊕ *www.gaineyvine-yard.com* ⌁ *Tastings from $15, jeep tour and barn tasting $25.*

⑪ Restaurants

Santa Ynez Kitchen
$$$ | **ITALIAN** | The owners of Toscana, a popular eatery in L.A.'s Brentwood neighborhood, run this rustic-chic restaurant with an Italy–meets–California Wine Country vibe. Chef and co-owner Luca Crestanelli, a native of Verona, Italy, typically offers about 10 seasonal daily specials. **Known for:** wood-fired pizzas and oak-grilled entrées; creative craft cocktails; gelatos and "not-so-classic" tiramisu. ⑤ *Average main: $28* ✉ *1110 Faraday St., at Sagunto St.* ☎ *805/691–9794* ⊕ *www.sykitchen.com.*

Trattoria Grappolo
$$$ | **ITALIAN** | Authentic Italian fare, an open kitchen, and festive, family-style seating make this trattoria equally popular with celebrities from Hollywood and ranchers from the Santa Ynez Valley. The noise level tends to rise in the evening, so this isn't the best spot for a romantic getaway. **Known for:** thin-crust wood-fired pizzas; risottos and homemade pastas; carpaccio. ⑤ *Average main: $28* ✉ *3687–C Sagunto St.* ☎ *805/688–6899* ⊕ *trattoriagrappolo.com* ⊙ *No lunch Mon.*

Hotels

ForFriends Inn
$$$$ | **B&B/INN** | Close friends own and operate this luxury bed-and-breakfast, designed as a social place where friends gather to enjoy good wine, food, and

music in a casual backyard setting. **Pros:** three-course breakfast, evening wine and appetizers included; friendly innkeepers; "Friendship Pass" provides perks and savings at restaurants and wineries. **Cons:** not suitable for children; no pets allowed; must climb stairs to second-floor rooms. $ *Rooms from: $295* ⊠ *1121 Edison St.* ☎ *805/693–0303* ⊕ *www.forfriendsinn.com* ⇌ *5 rooms, 2 cottages* ⊺⊚⨿ *Breakfast.*

Santa Ynez Inn

$$$$ | **B&B/INN** | This posh two-story Victorian inn in downtown Santa Ynez was built from scratch in 2002, and the owners have furnished all the rooms with authentic historical pieces. **Pros:** near restaurants; unusual antiques; spacious rooms. **Cons:** high price for location; building not historic. $ *Rooms from: $349* ⊠ *3627 Sagunto St.* ☎ *805/688–5588* ⊕ *www.santaynezinn.com* ⇌ *20 rooms* ⊺⊚⨿ *Breakfast.*

 ## Activities

Cloud Nine Glider Rides

FLYING/SKYDIVING/SOARING | The outfit's scenic glider rides last from 10 to 50 minutes. Tour options include the Santa Ynez Valley, coastal mountains and the Channel Islands, and celebrity homes. ⊠ *Santa Ynez Airport, 900 Airport Rd.* ☎ *805/602–6620* ⊕ *cloud9gliderrides.com* ⊠ *From $185.*

Los Olivos

4 miles north of Santa Ynez.

This pretty village was once on Spanish-built El Camino Real (Royal Road) and later a stop on major stagecoach and rail routes. Tasting rooms, art galleries, antiques stores, and country markets line Grand Avenue and intersecting streets for several blocks.

GETTING HERE AND AROUND
From U.S. 101 north or south, exit at Highway 154 and drive east about 8 miles. From Santa Barbara, travel 30 miles northwest on Highway 154.

 ## Sights

Blair Fox Cellars

WINERY/DISTILLERY | Blair Fox, a Santa Barbara native, crafts small-lot Rhône-style wines made from organic grapes. The bar in his rustic Los Olivos tasting room, where you can sample exceptional vineyard-designated Syrahs and other wines, was hewn from Australian white oak reclaimed from an old Tasmanian schoolhouse. ⊠ *2902–B San Marcos Ave.* ☎ *805/691–1678* ⊕ *www.blairfoxcellars.com* ⊠ *Tastings $15* ⊙ *Closed Tues. and Wed.*

Coquelicot Estate Vineyard

WINERY/DISTILLERY | Named for the vivid red poppy flowers that blanket the French countryside and appear on all its labels, this limited-production winery focuses on handcrafted Bordeaux wines made from grapes at its certified organic 58-acre Santa Ynez Valley vineyard. Don't miss samples of the flagship wines: Sixer (a Syrah and Viogner blend), Mon Amour (a Bordeaux blend), and the estate Sauvignon Blanc and Rosé. ⊠ *2884 Grand Ave.* ☎ *805/688–1500* ⊕ *www.coquelicotwines.com* ⊠ *Tastings from $15.*

Firestone Vineyard

WINERY/DISTILLERY | Heirs to the Firestone tire fortune developed (but no longer own) this winery known for Chardonnay, Gewürztraminer, Cabernet Sauvignon, and Syrah—and for the fantastic valley views from its tasting room and picnic area. The walking tour here (daily at 11:15 and 1:15) is highly informative. ⊠ *5017 Zaca Station Rd., off U.S. 101* ☎ *805/688–3940* ⊕ *www.firestonewine.com* ⊠ *Tastings from $10, tour $25.*

🍴 Restaurants

Los Olivos Wine Merchant Cafe

$$$ | **AMERICAN** | Part wine store and part social hub, this café focuses on wine-friendly fish, pasta, and meat dishes, plus salads, pizzas, and burgers. Don't miss the homemade muffuletta and olive tapenade spreads, or the homemade focaccia bread. **Known for:** nearly everything made in-house; ingredients from own organic café farm; wines from own estate winery. ⑤ *Average main: $23* ✉ *2879 Grand Ave.* ☎ *805/688–7265* ⊕ *www.winemerchant-cafe.com* ⊗ *No breakfast.*

Sides Hardware & Shoes: A Brothers Restaurant

$$$ | **AMERICAN** | Inside a historic storefront they renovated, brothers Matt and Jeff Nichols serve comfort food prepared with panache. The Kobe-style burgers, especially the one with bacon and white cheddar, make a great lunch, and the dinner favorites include Scottish salmon and lamb sirloin. **Known for:** in-house cured and smoked bacon; juicy burgers; jalapeño margaritas. ⑤ *Average main: $30* ✉ *2375 Alamo Pintado Ave.* ☎ *805/688–4820* ⊕ *sides-restaurant.com.*

🛏 Hotels

★ Ballard Inn & The Gathering Table

$$$$ | **B&B/INN** | Set among orchards and vineyards in the tiny town of Ballard, 2 miles south of Los Olivos, this inn makes an elegant Wine Country escape. **Pros:** exceptional food; attentive staff; secluded setting. **Cons:** some baths could use updating; restaurant noise sometimes travels upstairs; no in-room phones or TVs. ⑤ *Rooms from: $299* ✉ *2436 Baseline Ave., Ballard* ☎ *805/688–7770, 800/638–2466* ⊕ *ballardinn.com* ⇨ *15 rooms* ⑩ *Breakfast.*

Fess Parker's Wine Country Inn

$$$$ | **B&B/INN** | This luxury inn includes an elegant, tree-shaded French country–style main building and an equally attractive annex across the street with a pool and day spa. **Pros:** convenient wine-touring base; walking distance from restaurants and galleries; rate includes full breakfast at The Bear and Star on-site. **Cons:** pricey; not pet-friendly; thin walls between some rooms. ⑤ *Rooms from: $395* ✉ *2860 Grand Ave.* ☎ *805/688–7788, 800/446–2455* ⊕ *www.fessparker-inn.com* ⇨ *19 rooms* ⑩ *Breakfast.*

Solvang

5 miles south of Los Olivos.

You'll know you've reached the town of Solvang when the architecture suddenly changes to half-timber buildings and windmills. Danish educators settled the town in 1911—the flatlands and rolling green hills reminded them of home. Solvang has attracted tourists for decades, but it's lately become more sophisticated, with smorgasbords giving way to galleries, upscale restaurants, and wine-tasting rooms by day and wine bars by night. The visitor center on Copenhagen Drive has walking-tour maps (also available online). The Sweet Treats tour covers the town's Danish bakeries, confectionary stores, and ice-cream parlors. The Olsen's and Solvang bakeries and Ingeborg's Danish Chocolates are worth investigating.

GETTING HERE AND AROUND

Highway 246 West (Mission Drive) traverses Solvang, connecting with U.S. 101 to the west and Highway 154 to the east. Alamo Pintado Road connects Solvang with Ballard and Los Olivos to the north. Park your car in one of the free public lots and stroll the town. Or take the bus: Santa Ynez Valley Transit shuttles run between Solvang and nearby towns.

ESSENTIALS
VISITOR INFORMATION Solvang Conference & Visitors Bureau. ☒ *1639 Copenhagen Dr., at 2nd St.* ☎ *805/688–6144* ⊕ *www.solvangusa.com.*

Sights

Mission Santa Inés

RELIGIOUS SITE | The mission holds an impressive collection of paintings, statuary, vestments, and Chumash and Spanish artifacts in a serene bluff-top setting. You can tour the museum, sanctuary, and gardens. ☒ *1760 Mission Dr., at Alisal Rd.* ☎ *805/688–4815* ⊕ *missionsantaines.org* ☒ *$5.*

Rideau Vineyard

WINERY/DISTILLERY | This winery celebrates its locale's rich history—the King of Spain himself once owned this land, and the tasting room occupies a former guest ranch inn—but fully embraces the area's wine-making present. Wines made from the Rhône varietals Mourvèdre, Roussanne, Syrah, and Viognier are the specialty here. Winery and vineyard tours (free with tasting) are offered twice daily on weekdays (1:30 and 3) and thrice on weekends (12:30, 2, and 3:30). ☒ *1562 Alamo Pintado Rd., 2 miles north of Hwy. 246* ☎ *805/688–0717* ⊕ *rideauvineyard.com* ☒ *Tastings from $15.*

Sevtap

WINERY/DISTILLERY | Winemaker Art Sevtap, an Istanbul native, is often on hand to pour samples of his limited-production wines—mostly from Bordeaux varietals—in this artsy wine bar that's decked out with Tibetan prayer flags and chalkboard walls and has a stage where guests can pick up a guitar and strum away. ☒ *1622 Copenhagen Dr., at 2nd St.* ☎ *805/693–9200* ⊕ *www.sevtapwinery.com* ☒ *Tastings $15.*

🍴 Restaurants

★ First & Oak

$$$$ | AMERICAN | Create your own custom tasting menu by choosing among five different groups of eclectic California-French dishes paired with local wines at this elegant farm-to-table restaurant inside the Mirabelle Inn. The seasonal menu changes constantly, but regulars include smoked sweet-and-spicy duck wings, truffle-roasted cauliflower, local spot prawns, short rib bourguignonne, and pears poached in red wine from the sommelier-owner's organic Coceliquot Estate Vineyard. **Known for:** intimate fine-dining setting; sommelier-owner selected wine list; complex dishes and presentation. ⑤ *Average main: $36* ☒ *409 1st St.* ⊕ *At Oak St.* ☎ *805/688–1703* ⊕ *www.firstandoak.com.*

★ Root 246

$$$$ | AMERICAN | This chic restaurant's chefs tap local purveyors and shop for organic ingredients at farmers' markets before deciding on the day's menu. Depending on the season, you might feast on organic chicken liver pâté, grilled shrimp with peanut mole, butter-basted local fish, pork osso bucco with preserved lemon, lamb or Wagyu beef burger in a potato roll, or braised ribs with a slab of house-made cornbread. **Known for:** gorgeous contemporary Native American–influenced design; responsibly sourced meats, seafood, fruits, and veggies; popular happy hour with craft cocktails. ⑤ *Average main: $34* ☒ *Hotel Corque, 420 Alisal Rd., at Molle Way* ☎ *805/686–8681* ⊕ *www.root-246.com* ⊗ *Closed Mon. No lunch. No brunch weekdays.*

Succulent Café

$$$ | AMERICAN | Locals flock to this cozy café for its comfort cuisine and regional wines and craft beers. Order at the counter, and staffers will deliver your meal to the interior dining areas or the sunny outdoor patio. **Known for:** artisanal charcuterie plates; pet-friendly patio; homemade biscuits and gravy, house-roasted turkey. $ *Average main: $26* ⊠ *1555 Mission Dr., at 4th Pl.* ☎ *805/691–9444* ⊕ *succulentcafe.com* ⊗ *Closed Tues.*

Hotels

★ Alisal Guest Ranch and Resort

$$$$ | RESORT | Since 1946 celebrities and plain folk alike have come to this 10,000-acre ranch to join in a slew of activities, including horseback riding, tennis, golf, and archery, boating, and fishing You can also just lounge by the pool or book a treatment at the day spa. **Pros:** Old West atmosphere; breakfast and dinner included in the rate; free Wi-Fi. **Cons:** no in-room phones or TVs; not close to downtown; jacket required for dinner. $ *Rooms from: $600* ⊠ *1054 Alisal Rd.* ☎ *805/688–6411, 800/425–4725* ⊕ *alisal.com* ⇄ *73 rooms* ¶◉¶ *Some meals.*

★ Hotel Corque

$$$ | HOTEL | Owned by the Santa Ynez Band of Chumash Indians, the stunning three-story "Corque" provides a full slate of upscale amenities. **Pros:** friendly, professional staff; short walk to shops, tasting rooms and restaurants; free Wi-Fi. **Cons:** no kitchenettes or laundry facilities; some rooms need updating; not pet-friendly. $ *Rooms from: $239* ⊠ *400 Alisal Rd.* ☎ *805/688–8000* ⊕ *hotelcorque.com* ⇄ *132 rooms* ¶◉¶ *No meals.*

The Landsby

$$$ | B&B/INN | New owners remodeled the former old-world-style Petersen Village Inn and transformed it into a cozy, contemporary Scandinavian retreat that feels like a residence in downtown Copenhagen. **Pros:** in the heart of Solvang; easy parking; courtyard with fire pits. **Cons:** on highway; unusual hallway configuration can be confusing; thin walls in some rooms. $ *Rooms from: $195* ⊠ *1576 Mission Dr.* ☎ *805/688–3121* ⊕ *thelandsby.com* ⇄ *50 rooms* ¶◉¶ *No meals.*

★ Mirabelle Inn

$$$ | B&B/INN | French, Danish, and American flags at the entrance and crystal chandeliers, soaring ceilings, and skylights in the lobby set the tone from the get-go in this elegant four-story inn a few blocks from the main tourist hub. **Pros:** excellent farm-to-table restaurant (dinner only); full cook-to-order breakfast included; away from noisy crowds. **Cons:** some rooms on the small side; not in the heart of town; restaurant noise travels to nearby rooms. $ *Rooms from: $250* ⊠ *409 1st St.* ✛ *At Oak St.* ☎ *805/688–1703, 800/786–7925* ⊕ *mirabelleinn.com* ⇄ *12 rooms* ¶◉¶ *Breakfast.*

Performing Arts

Solvang Festival Theater

THEATER | Pacific Conservatory of the Performing Arts presents crowd-pleasing musicals like *A Gentleman's Guide to Love and Murder* and *Million Dollar Quartet*, as well as Oscar Wilde's *The Importance of Being Earnest*, and contemporary plays at this 700-seat outdoor amphitheater. ⊠ *420 2nd St., at Molle Way* ☎ *805/922–8313* ⊕ *pcpa.org* ☞ *Performances June–Oct.*

Buellton

3 miles west of Solvang.

A crossroads town at the intersection of U.S. 101 and Highway 246, Buellton has evolved from a sleepy gas and coffee stop into an enclave of wine-tasting rooms, beer gardens, and restaurants. It's also a gateway to Lompoc and the Santa Rita Hills Wine Trail to the west, and to Solvang, Santa Ynez, and Los Olivos to the east.

Driving is the easiest way to get to Buellton. From Santa Barbara, follow U.S. 101 north to the Highway 246 exit. Santa Ynez Valley Transit serves Buellton with shuttle buses from Solvang and nearby towns.

ESSENTIALS

VISITOR INFORMATION Discover Buellton. ⊠ *597 Ave. of the Flags, No. 101* ☎ *805/688–7829* ⊕ *visitbuellton.com.*
Santa Rita Hills Wine Trail. ⊕ *santaritahills-winetrail.com.*

Sights

Alma Rosa Winery

WINERY/DISTILLERY | Winemaker Richard Sanford helped put Santa Barbara County on the international wine map with a 1989 Pinot Noir. For Alma Rosa, started in 2005, he crafts wines from grapes grown on 100-plus acres of certified organic vineyards in the Santa Rita Hills. The Pinot Noirs and Chardonnays are exceptional. Vineyard tours and tastings are available by appointment, ⊠ *181 C Industrial Way, off Hwy. 246, west of U.S. 101* ☎ *805/688–9090* ⊕ *almarosaw-inery.com* ⊠ *Tastings $20.*

Industrial Way

NEIGHBORHOOD | A half mile west of U.S. 101, head south from Highway 246 on Industrial Way to explore a hip and happening collection of food and drink destinations. Top stops include **Industrial Eats** (a craft butcher shop and restaurant), **Figueroa Mountain Brewing Co.,** the **Alma Rosa Winery** tasting room, **Margerum Wine Company, Tesora Sweets,** and the **Ascendant Spirits Distillery.** ⊠ *Industrial Way, off Hwy. 246* ⊕ *www.industrialwaysbc.com.*

Lafond Winery and Vineyards

WINERY/DISTILLERY | A rich, concentrated Pinot Noir is the main attention-getter at this winery that also produces noteworthy Chardonnays and Syrahs. Bottles with Lafond's SRH (Santa Rita Hills) label are an especially good value. The winery also has a tasting room at 111 East Yanonali Street in Santa Barbara's Funk Zone. ⊠ *6855 Santa Rosa Rd., west off U.S. 101 Exit 139* ☎ *805/688–7921* ⊕ *lafondwinery.com* ⊠ *Tastings $15 (includes logo glass).*

Restaurants

The Hitching Post II

$$$$ | **AMERICAN** | You'll find everything from grilled artichokes to quail at this casual eatery, but most people come for the smoky Santa Maria–style barbecue. Be sure to try a glass of owner-chef-winemaker Frank Ostini's signature Highliner Pinot Noir, a star in the film *Sideways.* **Known for:** entrées grilled over local red oak; chef-owner makes his own wines; classic cocktails. ⑤ *Average main: $32* ⊠ *406 E. Hwy. 246, off U.S. 101* ☎ *805/688–0676* ⊕ *www.hitchingpost2.com* ⊗ *No lunch.*

Lompoc

20 miles west of Solvang.

Known as the flower-seed capital of the world, Lompoc is blanketed with vast fields of brightly colored flowers that bloom from May through August. Also home to a starkly beautiful mission, Lompoc has emerged as a major Pinot Noir and Chardonnay grape-growing region. Overlapping the Santa Rita Hills Wine Trail in parts, the Lompoc Wine Trail includes wineries in the Wine Ghetto, a downtown industrial park, and along Highway 246 and (to the south) Santa Rosa Road, which form a loop between Lompoc and Buellton.

Driving is the easiest way to get to Lompoc. From Santa Barbara, follow U.S. 101 north to Highway 1 exit off Gaviota Pass, or Highway 246 west at Buellton.

ESSENTIALS
VISITOR INFORMATION Lompoc Valley Chamber of Commerce & Visitors Bureau. ✉ *111 S. I St., at Hwy. 246* ☎ *805/736–4567* ⊕ *lompoc.com.*

 Sights

La Purísima Mission State Historic Park
RELIGIOUS SITE | **FAMILY** | The state's most fully restored mission, founded in 1787, stands in a stark and still remote location that powerfully evokes the lives and isolation of California's Spanish settlers. Docents lead afternoon tours Wednesday–Sunday (daily June–August), and vivid displays illustrate the secular and religious activities that formed mission life. ✉ *2295 Purisima Rd., off Hwy. 246* ☎ *805/733–3713* ⊕ *www.lapurisimamission.org* ✉ *$6 per vehicle* ⊗ *No tour Mon. and Tues. afternoon June.*

Lompoc Valley Flower Festival
FESTIVAL | Around the last weekend of June, Lompoc celebrates its floral heritage with a parade, a carnival, and a crafts show. ⊕ *explorelompoc.com.*

Lompoc Wine Ghetto
WINERY/DISTILLERY | Laid-back tasting rooms can be found in a downtown industrial park. Taste of Sta. Rita Hills and Flying Goat are two rooms worth checking out here. ✉ *200 N. 9th St.* ⊕ *lompoctrail.com* ✉ *Tasting fees vary, some free* ⊗ *Many tasting rooms closed Mon.–Wed.*

Pismo Beach

40 miles north of Lompoc.

About 20 miles of sandy shoreline—nicknamed the Bakersfield Riviera for the throngs of vacationers who come here from the Central Valley—begins at the town of Pismo Beach. The southern end of town runs along sand dunes, some of which are open to cars and off-road vehicles. Sheltered by the dunes,

Volcanoes?

Those eye-catching sawed-off peaks along the drive from Pismo Beach to Morro Bay are called the Nine Sisters—a series of ancient volcanic plugs. Morro Rock, the northernmost sibling and a state historic monument, is the most famous and photographed of the clan.

a grove of eucalyptus trees attracts thousands of migrating monarch butterflies from November through February. A long, broad beach fronts the center of town, where a municipal pier extends into the sea at the foot of shop-lined Pomeroy Street. To the north, hotels and homes perch atop chalky oceanfront cliffs. Fewer than 10,000 people live in this quintessential surfer haven, but Pismo Beach has a slew of hotels and restaurants with great views of the Pacific Ocean.

GETTING HERE AND AROUND
Pismo Beach straddles both sides of U.S. 101. If you're coming from the south and have time for a scenic drive, exit U.S. 101 in Santa Maria and take Highway 166 west for 8 miles to Guadalupe and follow Highway 1 north 16 miles to Pismo Beach. South County Area Transit (SCAT; ⊕ *www.slorta.org*) buses run throughout San Luis Obispo and connect the city with nearby towns. On summer weekends, the free Avila Trolley extends service to Pismo Beach.

ESSENTIALS
VISITOR INFORMATION California Welcome Center. ✉ *333 5 Cities Dr.* ☎ *805/773–7924.* **Pismo Beach Visitor Information Center.** ✉ *Dolliver St./Hwy. 1, at Hinds Ave.* ☎ *800/443–7778, 805/556–7397* ⊕ *classiccalifornia.com.*

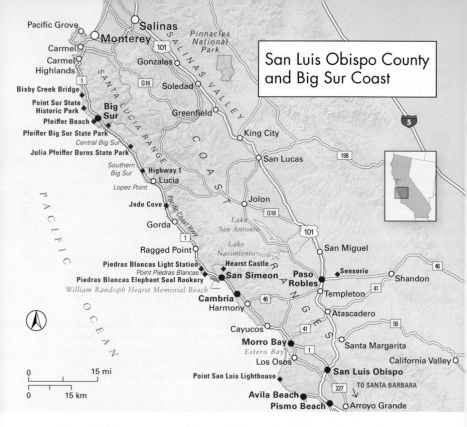

San Luis Obispo County and Big Sur Coast

Map labels include: Pacific Grove, Salinas, Monterey, Carmel, Carmel Highlands, Pinnacles National Park, Gonzales, 101, Soledad, G16, Bixby Creek Bridge, Point Sur State Historic Park, Big Sur, Pfeiffer Beach, Greenfield, Pfeiffer Big Sur State Park, Central Big Sur, Julia Pfeiffer Burns State Park, King City, SANTA LUCIA RANGE, SALINAS VALLEY, Southern Big Sur, Highway 1, Lucia, San Lucas, 198, Lopez Point, Jade Cove, Jolon, G18, Gorda, Lake San Antonio, 101, Ragged Point, Lake Nacimiento, San Miguel, Pacific Coast Hwy, Piedras Blancas Light Station, Point Piedras Blancas, Hearst Castle, San Simeon, Paso Robles, Sensorio, Shandon, 46, Piedras Blancas Elephant Seal Rookery, William Randolph Hearst Memorial Beach, Cambria, Templeton, 41, Harmony, 46, Atascadero, Cayucos, 41, 58, Morro Bay, Estero Bay, Santa Margarita, Los Osos, 1, California Valley, Point San Luis Lighthouse, San Luis Obispo, TO SANTA BARBARA, Avila Beach, 227, Pismo Beach, Arroyo Grande, PACIFIC OCEAN, COAST RANGES, 5, 0 15 mi, 0 15 km

🏛 Beaches

★ Oceano Dunes State Vehicular Recreation Area

BEACH—SIGHT | Part of the spectacular Guadalupe-Nipomo Dunes, this 3,600-acre coastal playground is one of the few places in California where you can drive or ride off-highway vehicles on the beach and sand dunes. Hike, ride horses, kiteboard, join a Hummer tour, or rent an ATV or a dune buggy and cruise up the white-sand peaks for spectacular views. At **Oso Flaco Lake Nature Area**—3 miles west of Highway 1 on Oso Flaco Road—a 1½-mile boardwalk over the lake leads to a platform with views up and down the coast. Leashed dogs are allowed in much of the park except Oso Flaco and Pismo Dunes Natural Reserve. **Amenities:** food and drink; lifeguards (seasonal); parking (fee); showers; toilets; water sports. **Best for:** sunset; surfing; swimming; walking. ⊠ *West end of Pier Ave., off Hwy. 1, Oceano* ☎ *805/473–7220* ⊕ *www.parks. ca.gov* 🖃 *$5 per vehicle.*

Pismo State Beach

BEACH—SIGHT | Hike, surf, ride horses, swim, fish in a lagoon or off the pier, and dig for Pismo clams at this busy state beach. One of the day-use parking areas is off Highway 1 near the **Monarch Butterfly Grove,** where from November through February monarch butterflies nest in eucalyptus and Monterey pines. The other parking area is about 1½ miles south at Pier Avenue. **Amenities:** food and drink; lifeguards (seasonal); parking (fee); showers; toilets; water sports. **Best for:** sunset; surfing; swimming; walking. ⊠ *555 Pier Ave., off Hwy. 1, 3 miles south of downtown Pismo Beach,*

Oceano ☎ *805/473–7220* ⊕ *www.parks.
ca.gov* ✉ *Day-use $10 per vehicle if
parking at beach.*

🍽 Restaurants

Cracked Crab

$$$ | SEAFOOD | This traditional New Eng-
land–style crab shack imports fresh sea-
food daily from Australia, Alaska, and the
East Coast. Fish is line-caught, much of
the produce is organic, and everything is
made from scratch. **Known for:** shellfish
meals in a bucket, dumped on the table;
casual setting; menu changes daily.
⑤ *Average main: $30* ✉ *751 Price St.,
near Main St.* ☎ *805/773–2722* ⊕ *www.
crackedcrab.com.*

Doc Burnstein's Ice Cream Lab

$ | AMERICAN | FAMILY | The delectable ice
creams are churned on-site at this belov-
ed old-fashioned parlor east of Pismo
Beach. Top-selling flavors include the
Elvis Special (banana and peanut butter)
and Motor Oil, a blend of dark chocolate
and Kahlua with a fudge swirl. **Known for:**
antique model train that chugs along a
circular ceiling track; different featured
flavors every month along with the clas-
sics; Wednesday afternoon creamery
tours. ⑤ *Average main: $7* ✉ *114 W.
Branch St., at Nevada St., east off U.S.
101, Arroyo Grande* ☎ *805/474–4688*
⊕ *docburnsteins.com.*

★ Ember

$$$ | MODERN AMERICAN | A barn-style
restaurant with high ceilings and an
open kitchen, Ember enjoys a red-hot
reputation for Italian-inflected dishes
prepared in an authentic Tuscan fireplace
or a wood-burning oven. Chef-owner
Brian Collins, a native of Arroyo Grande,
the town bordering Pismo Beach, honed
his culinary skills at Berkeley's legendary
Chez Panisse Restaurant. **Known for:** seasonal menu changes monthly; wood-fired
flatbread pizzas; long lines during prime
time (no reservations). ⑤ *Average main:
$26* ✉ *1200 E. Grand Ave., at Brisco Rd.,*

Arroyo Grande ☎ *805/474–7700* ⊕ *www.
emberwoodfire.com* ⊗ *Closed Mon. and
Tues. No lunch.*

Giuseppe's Cucina Italiana

$$$ | ITALIAN | The classic flavors of
southern Italy are highlighted at this
lively downtown spot. Most recipes
originate from Bari, a seaport on the
Adriatic; the menu includes breads
and pizzas baked in the wood-burning
oven, hearty dishes such as dry-aged
steak and rack of lamb, and homemade
pastas. **Known for:** lively family-style
atmosphere; daily specials; most fruits
and veggies come from owner's 12-acre
farm. ⑤ *Average main: $27* ✉ *891 Price
St., at Pismo Ave.* ☎ *805/773–2870*
⊕ *giuseppesrestaurant.com* ⊗ *No lunch
weekdays.*

Splash Café

$ | SEAFOOD | Folks stand in line down
the block for clam chowder served in
a sourdough bread bowl at this wildly
popular seafood stand. You can also
order beach food such as fresh steamed
clams, burgers, and fried calamari at
the counter (no table service) here and
at Splash's second location in San Luis
Obispo, which has an on-site bakery
and additional menu items. **Known for:**
famous clam chowder; sourdough bread
bowls baked in house; cheery hole-in-
the-wall. ⑤ *Average main: $10* ✉ *197
Pomeroy St., at Cypress St.* ☎ *805/773–
4653* ⊕ *splashcafe.com.*

The Spoon Trade

$$$ | AMERICAN | A silver spoon display
at the entrance reflects this casual
eatery's mission to "spoon food and
trade stories" with diners who indulge
in traditional American comfort food
with a modern twist. Perennial menu
faves include tri-tip tartare, deviled
eggs, meat loaf Stroganoff, and fried
chicken with sourdough waffles; save
room for a root beer float or brown sugar pot de creme for dessert. **Known for:**
pet-friendly patio; house-made pastas;
lively dining room with open kitchen.

$ Average main: $25 ⊠ 295 W Grand Ave. ☎ 805/904–6773 ⊕ www.thespoontrade.com ⊗ No lunch weekdays.

Ventana Grill

$$$ | FUSION | Perched on a bluff at the northern edge of Pismo Beach, Ventana Grill offers ocean views from nearly every table, unusual seafood-centered Latin American–California fusion dishes, and more than 50 tequilas plus craft cocktails at the bar. Reservations are essential—this place is almost always packed, especially during the weekday happy hour. **Known for:** happy hour with sunset views; salsas and sauces made from scratch; more than 50 tequila selections. *$ Average main: $27 ⊠ 2575 Price St. ☎ 805/773–0000 ⊕ ventana-grill.com.*

 Hotels

The Cliffs Hotel & Spa

$$$ | RESORT | Lawns and palm trees surround this full-service resort that perches dramatically on an oceanfront cliff. **Pros:** beach access via short downhill path; oceanfront restaurant and lounge; bluff-top walking trail. **Cons:** not close to downtown; rooms near service areas and elevator can be noisy; resort fee. *$ Rooms from: $209 ⊠ 2757 Shell Beach Rd. ☎ 805/773–5000, 800/826–7827 ⊕ www.cliffsresort.com ⊅ 160 rooms* †○† *No meals.*

Dolphin Bay Resort & Spa

$$$$ | RESORT | On grass-covered bluffs overlooking Shell Beach, this luxury resort looks and feels like an exclusive community of villas; choose among sprawling one- or two-bedroom suites, each with a gourmet kitchen, laundry room with washer and dryer, and contemporary furnishings. **Pros:** lavish apartment units; Lido farm-to-table restaurant; many suites have ocean views. **Cons:** hefty price tag; vibe too upper-crust for some; not close to downtown. *$ Rooms from: $489 ⊠ 2727 Shell Beach*

Rd. ☎ 805/773–4300, 800/516–0112 reservations, 805/773–8900 restaurant ⊕ www.thedolphinbay.com ⊅ 60 suites †○† No meals.

Hilton Garden Inn

$$$ | HOTEL | A slew of on-site amenities, easy access to the freeway and state beaches, and reasonable rates for the location make this chain hotel a good choice at the southern edge of Pismo Beach. **Pros:** newly renovated rooms with adjustable beds; on-site restaurant, bar and lounge; free parking and Wi-Fi. **Cons:** chain hotel; some rooms overlook freeway; not pet-friendly. *$ Rooms from: $199 ⊠ 601 James Way ☎ 805/773–6020 ⊕ www.sanluisobispopismobeach.hgi.com ⊅ 120 rooms* †○† *Breakfast.*

Inn at the Pier

$$$$ | HOTEL | The luxe Inn at the Pier opened in winter 2017, covering a prime city block just steps from the sand and across from the pier. **Pros:** walk to downtown restaurants, sights, shops; fitness center and cruiser bike rentals; new building. **Cons:** daily resort fee; valet parking only; bar noise travels to some rooms. *$ Rooms from: $269 ⊠ 601 Cypress St. ☎ 805/295–5565 ⊕ www.theinnatthepier.com ⊅ 104 rooms* †○† *No meals.*

Pismo Lighthouse Suites

$$$$ | HOTEL | Each of the well-appointed two-room, two-bath suites at this oceanfront resort has a private balcony or patio. **Pros:** sport court features life-size chess game; nautical-style furnishings; nice pool area. **Cons:** not easy to walk to main attractions; some units are next to busy road; first-floor units can hear footsteps from suites above. *$ Rooms from: $259 ⊠ 2411 Price St. ☎ 805/773–2411, 800/245–2411 ⊕ www.pismolighthousesuites.com ⊅ 70 suites* †○† *Breakfast.*

SeaVenture Beach Hotel & Restaurant

$$$ | **HOTEL** | The bright, homey rooms at this hotel all have fireplaces and featherbeds; most have balconies with private hot tubs, and some have beautiful ocean views. **Pros:** on the beach; excellent food; romantic rooms. **Cons:** touristy area; some rooms and facilities dated; dark hallways. $ *Rooms from: $249* ✉ *100 Ocean View Ave.* ☎ *805/773–4994* ⊕ *www.seaventure.com* 🛏 *50 rooms* ⦿ *No meals.*

Avila Beach

4 miles north of Pismo Beach.

Because the village of Avila Beach and the sandy, cove-front shoreline for which it's named face south into the Pacific Ocean, they get more sun and less fog than any other stretch of coast in the area. With its fortuitous climate and protected waters, Avila's public beach draws sunbathers and families; summer weekends are very busy. Downtown Avila Beach has a lively seaside promenade and some shops and hotels, but for real local color, head to the far end of the cove and watch the commercial fishers offload their catch on the old Port San Luis wharf. On Friday from mid-April through mid-September, a fish and farmers' market livens up the beach area with music, fresh local produce and seafood, and children's activities.

GETTING HERE AND AROUND

Exit U.S. 101 at Avila Beach Drive and head 3 miles west to reach the beach. The free Avila Trolley operates weekends year-round, plus Friday afternoon and evening from April to September. The minibuses connect Avila Beach and Port San Luis to Shell Beach, with multiple stops along the way. Service extends to Pismo Beach in summer.

ESSENTIALS

VISITOR INFORMATION Avila Beach Tourism Alliance. ⊕ *visitavilabeach.com.*

Sights

Avila Valley Barn

RESTAURANT—SIGHT | **FAMILY** | An old-fashioned, family-friendly country store jam-packed with local fruits and vegetables, prepared foods, and gifts, Avila Valley Barn also gives visitors a chance to experience rural American traditions. You can pet farm animals and savor homemade ice cream and pies daily, and on weekends ride a hay wagon out to the fields to pick your own produce. ✉ *560 Avila Beach Dr., San Luis Obispo* ☎ *805/595–2816* ⊕ *www.avilavalleybarn. com* ⊙ *Closed Tues. and Wed. Jan.–Mar.*

Central Coast Aquarium

MUSEUM | You'll learn all about local marine plants and animals from the hands-on exhibits at this science center next to the main beach. ✉ *50 San Juan St., at 1st St., off Avila Beach Dr.* ☎ *805/595–7280* ⊕ *www.central-coastaquarium.com* 🎟 *$8* ⊙ *Closed Mon.*

Point San Luis Lighthouse

LIGHTHOUSE | **FAMILY** | Docents lead hikes along scenic Pecho Coast Trail (3½ miles round-trip) to see the historic 1890 lighthouse and its rare Fresnel lens. **■ TIP➜ If you'd prefer a lift out to the lighthouse, join a trolley tour. Hikes and tours require reservations.** ✉ *Point San Luis, 1¾ miles west of Harford Pier, Port San Luis* ☎ *805/540–5771, 805/528–8758 hikes reservations* ⊕ *www.pointsanluislighthouse.org* 🎟 *Trolley tours $22; hikes free ($5 to enter lighthouse).*

Beaches

Avila City Beach

BEACH—SIGHT | **FAMILY** | At the edge of a sunny cove next to downtown shops and restaurants, Avila's ½-mile stretch of white sand is especially family-friendly, with a playground, barbecue and picnic tables, volleyball and basketball courts, and lifeguards on watch in summer and on many holiday weekends. The free beachfront parking fills up fast, but there's a nearby pay lot ($6 for the day, $2 after 4 pm). Dogs aren't allowed on the beach from 10 to 5. **Amenities:** food and drink; lifeguards (seasonal); parking; showers; toilets; water sports. **Best for:** sunset; surfing; swimming; walking. ⊠ *Avila Beach Dr., at 1st St.* ⊕ *www. visitavilabeach.com* ⮑ *Free.*

Restaurants

Mersea's

$ | SEAFOOD | Walk down the pier to this casual crab shack where you can order at the counter, grab a drink at the bar, and find a seat on the deck or in the casual indoor dining area to gaze at spectacular Avila Bay views while you dine. The menu includes chowder bowls, burgers, sandwiches, seafood, and salads, plus bowls of fish, shrimp, or chicken served over rice pilaf and veggies. **Known for:** clam chowder in sourdough bread bowls; fish tacos; fresh local ingredients. Ⓢ *Average main: $14* ⊠ *3985 Port San Luis Pier* ✛ *At Port San Luis* ☎ *805/548–2290* ⊕ *www. merseas.com.*

Ocean Grill

$$$ | SEAFOOD | Across from the promenade, beach, and pier, Ocean Grill serves up fresh seafood to diners who typically arrive before sunset to enjoy the views. Boats anchored in the bay provide much of the seafood, which pairs well with the mostly regional wines on the list. **Known for:** fantastic ocean views; wood-fired pizzas; gluten-free and vegetarian options. Ⓢ *Average main: $29* ⊠ *268 Front St.* ☎ *805/595–4050* ⊕ *www.oceangrillavila. com* ☽ *No lunch Mon.–Thurs.*

🛏 Hotels

Avila La Fonda

$$$$ | HOTEL | Modeled after a village in early California's Mexican period, Avila La Fonda surrounds guests with rich jewel tones, fountains, and upscale comfort; its facade replicates eight different casitas, including several famous historic homes in Mexico. **Pros:** one-of-a-kind theme and artwork; flexible room combinations; a block from the beach. **Cons:** pricey for the area; most rooms don't have an ocean view; spotty Wi-Fi. Ⓢ *Rooms from: $329* ⊠ *101 San Miguel St.* ☎ *805/595–1700* ⊕ *www.avilalafondahotel.com* ⮑ *28 rooms* ⦿ *No meals.*

Avila Lighthouse Suites

$$$$ | HOTEL | Families, honeymooners, and business travelers all find respite at this two-story, all-suites luxury hotel. **Pros:** directly across from beach; easy walk to restaurants and shops; free underground parking. **Cons:** noise from passersby can be heard in room; some ocean-view rooms have limited vistas; basic breakfast. Ⓢ *Rooms from: $359* ⊠ *550 Front St.* ☎ *805/627–1900, 800/372–8452* ⊕ *www.avilalighthousesuites.com* ⮑ *54 suites* ⦿ *Breakfast.*

Avila Village Inn

$$$ | HOTEL | This intimate hotel embraces Craftsman style in its wood-and-stone architecture and in custom furnishings such as faux-Tiffany lampshades. **Pros:** in a residential community; access to great fitness center with pool; gorgeous lobby. **Cons:** some rooms are small and dark; several miles from the beach; spotty Wi-Fi. Ⓢ *Rooms from: $200* ⊠ *6655 Bay Laurel Dr.* ☎ *800/454–0840, 805/627–1810* ⊕ *www.avilavillageinn. com* ⮑ *30 rooms* ⦿ *No meals.*

Sycamore Mineral Springs Resort & Spa

$$$ | RESORT | This wellness resort's hot mineral springs bubble up into private outdoor tubs on an oak-and-sycamore-forest hillside. **Pros:** great place to rejuvenate; nice hiking nearby; incredible spa with yoga classes, integrative healing arts, and many treatments. **Cons:** rooms vary in quality; 2½ miles from the beach; road noise can travel to certain areas of property. Ⓢ *Rooms from: $185* ⊠ *1215 Avila Beach Dr., San*

Luis Obispo ☎ 805/595–7302 ⊕ www.
sycamoresprings.com ⇆ 72 rooms
†⊙† No meals.

San Luis Obispo

8 miles north of Avila Beach.

About halfway between San Francisco and Los Angeles, San Luis Obispo spreads out below gentle hills and rocky extinct volcanoes. Its main appeal lies in its architecturally diverse, pedestrian-friendly downtown, which bustles with shoppers, restaurant goers, and students from California Polytechnic State University, known as Cal Poly. On Thursday evening from 6 to 9 the city's famed farmers' market fills Higuera Street with local produce, entertainment, and food stalls.

GETTING HERE AND AROUND
U.S. 101/Highway 1 traverses the city for several miles. From the north, Highway 1 merges with U.S. 101 when it reaches the city limits. The wineries of the Edna Valley and Arroyo Grande Valley wine regions lie south of town off Highway 227, the parallel (to the east) Orcutt Road, and connecting roads.

SLO City Transit buses operate daily; Regional Transit Authority (SLORTA) buses connect with north county towns. The Downtown Trolley provides evening service to the city's hub every Thursday, on Friday from June to early September, and Saturday from April through October.

ESSENTIALS
VISITOR INFORMATION San Luis Obispo Chamber of Commerce. ⊠ *895 Monterey St.* ☎ *805/781–2777* ⊕ *www.visitslo.com.* **San Luis Obispo City Visitor Information.** ☎ *877/756–8698* ⊕ *www.sanluisobispovacations.com.*

⊙ Sights

Biddle Ranch Vineyard
WINERY/DISTILLERY | Glass doors and walls in a converted dairy barn fill the Biddle Ranch Vineyard tasting room with light and sweeping valley, mountain, and vineyard views. The small-production winery focuses on estate Chardonnay (the adjacent 17-acre vineyard is planted exclusively to the grape), plus Pinot Noir and sparkling wines. The winery also crafts Sangiovese and Cabernet and Syrah blends. ⊠ *2050 Biddle Ranch Rd.* ⟱ *At Hwy. 227* ☎ *805/543–2399* ⊕ *www.biddleranch.com* ⊠ *Tastings $15.*

Claiborne & Churchill
WINERY/DISTILLERY | An eco-friendly winery built from straw bales, C&C makes small lots of aromatic Alsatian-style wines such as dry Riesling and Gewürztraminer, plus Pinot Noir blends, Syrah, and Chardonnay. ⊠ *2649 Carpenter Canyon Rd., at Price Canyon Rd.* ☎ *805/544–4066* ⊕ *www.claibornechurchill.com* ⊠ *Tastings $18.*

Edna Valley Vineyard
WINERY/DISTILLERY | For sweeping valley views and crisp Sauvignon Blancs and Chardonnays, head to the modern tasting bar here. ■TIP→ **The 18 Barrel Flight tasting ($35) that showcases five exclusive, limited production wines, is the best option.** ⊠ *2585 Biddle Ranch Rd., off Edna Rd.* ☎ *805/544–5855* ⊕ *www.ednavalleyvineyard.com* ⊠ *Tastings from $20.*

History Center of San Luis Obispo County
MUSEUM | **FAMILY** | Across the street from the old Spanish mission, the center presents exhibits that explore topics such as Native American life in the county, the California ranchos, and the impact of railroads. On the center's website are links to free downloadable video-podcast walking tours of historic San Luis Obispo. ⊠ *696 Monterey St., at Broad St.* ☎ *805/543–0638* ⊕ *www.historycenterslo.org* ⊠ *Free* ⊙ *Closed Tues.*

Mission San Luis Obispo de Tolosa

RELIGIOUS SITE | Sun-dappled Mission Plaza fronts the fifth mission established in 1772 by Franciscan friars. A small museum exhibits artifacts of the Chumash Indians and early Spanish settlers. ⊠ *751 Palm St., at Chorro St.* ☎ *805/543–6850* ⊕ *www.missionsanluisobispo.org* ☐ *$3.*

Niven Family Wine Estates

WINERY/DISTILLERY | A refurbished 1909 schoolhouse serves as tasting room for four Niven Family wineries: Baileyana, Tangent, True Myth, and Zocker. The winemaker for all these labels is Christian Roguenant, whose Cadre Pinot Noirs are worth checking out. ⊠ *5828 Orcutt Rd., at Righetti Rd.* ☎ *805/269–8200* ⊕ *www.nivenfamilywines.com* ☐ *Tastings from $15.*

Old Edna

TOWN | This peaceful, 2-acre site once *was* the town of Edna. Nowadays you can peek at the vintage 1897 and 1908 farmhouse cottages, taste Sextant wines, pick up sandwiches at the gourmet deli, and stroll along Old Edna Lane. ⊠ *1655 Old Price Canyon Rd., at Hwy. 227* ☎ *805/710–3701 Old Edna Townsite, 805/542–0133 tasting room and deli* ⊕ *oldedna.com.*

Parks and Recreation Department

INFO CENTER | Hilly greenbelts with extensive hiking trails surround San Luis Obispo. For information about trailheads, call the parks department or download a trail map on its website. ☎ *877/756–8696* ⊕ *www.slocity.org/parksandrecreation.*

San Luis Obispo Children's Museum

MUSEUM | FAMILY | Activities at this facility geared to kids under age 10 include an "imagination-powered" elevator that transports visitors to a series of underground caverns. Elsewhere, simulated lava and steam sputter from an active volcano. Kids can pick rubber fruit at a farmers' market and race in a fire engine to fight a fire. ⊠ *1010 Nipomo St., at Monterey St.* ☎ *805/544–5437* ⊕ *www.*

slocm.org ☐ *$8* ⊘ *Closed nonholiday Mon. Sept.–Apr.*

San Luis Obispo Museum of Art

MUSEUM | The permanent collection here focuses on the artistic legacy of the Central Coast. Temporary exhibits include traditional and cutting-edge arts and crafts by Central Coast, national, and international artists. ⊠ *Mission Plaza, 1010 Broad St., at Monterey St.* ☎ *805/543–8562* ⊕ *www.sloma.org* ⊘ *Closed Tues. early July–early Sept.*

★ Talley Vineyards

WINERY/DISTILLERY | Acres of Chardonnay and Pinot Noir, plus smaller parcels of Sauvignon Blanc, Syrah, and other varietals blanket Talley's mountain-ringed dell in the Arroyo Grande Valley. The estate tour ($45), worth a splurge, includes wine and cheese, a visit to an 1860s adobe, and barrel-room tastings of upcoming releases. ⊠ *3031 Lopez Dr., off Orcutt Rd., Arroyo Grande* ☎ *805/489–0446* ⊕ *www.talleyvineyards.com* ☐ *Tastings from $15; tours from $25.*

Wolff Vineyards

WINERY/DISTILLERY | Syrah, Petite Sirah, and Riesling join the expected Pinot Noir and Chardonnay as the stars at this family-run winery 6 miles south of downtown. The pourers are friendly, and you'll often meet one of the owners or their children in the tasting room. With its hillside views, the outdoor patio is a great place to enjoy an afternoon picnic.

6238 Orcutt Rd., near Biddle Ranch Rd.
805/781–0448 ⊕ www.wolffvineyards.
com ☷ Tastings $12.

🍽 Restaurants

Big Sky Café

$$ | **ECLECTIC** | Family-friendly Big Sky turns local and organically grown ingredients into global dishes, starting with breakfast. Just pick your continent: braised Argentinian lamb shanks, Southeast Asian noodle bowls, Middle Eastern lamb burger, Maryland crab cakes. **Known for:** artsy, creative vibe; ample choices for vegetarians; locavore pioneer. ⑤ Average main: $21 ✉ 1121 Broad St., at Higuera St. 805/545–5401 ⊕ bigskycafe.com.

Buona Tavola

$$$ | **ITALIAN** | Northern Italian dishes are this casual spot's specialty. You might find homemade pumpkin-stuffed tortellini in a creamy mascarpone sauce on the menu, or porcini-mushroom risotto with river shrimp. **Known for:** daily fresh fish and salad specials; impressive wine list; gluten-free menus. ⑤ Average main: $25 ✉ 1037 Monterey St., near Osos St. 805/545–8000 ⊕ btslo.com ⊗ No lunch weekends.

Café Roma

$$$ | **NORTHERN ITALIAN** | At this Railroad Square restaurant you can dine on authentic northern Italian cuisine in the warmly lit dining room or out on the covered patio. Menu favorites include ricotta-filled squash blossoms, and beef tenderloin glistening with porcini butter and a Pinot Noir reduction. **Known for:** classic Italian dining room and bar; well-selected international wine list with more than 200 choices; attentive service. ⑤ Average main: $26 ✉ 1020 Railroad Ave., at Osos St. 805/541–6800 ⊕ www.caferomaslo.com ⊗ No lunch weekends.

★ Giuseppe's Cucina Rustica

$$$ | **ITALIAN** | The younger sibling of the hugely popular Guiseppe's restaurant in Pismo Beach, this lively downtown eatery serves up authentic southern Italian fare in the historic Sinsheimer Bros. building, originally constructed in 1884. Dine in the spacious main restaurant amid high ceilings, fireplaces, and bar, or in the creekside courtyard beneath strings of twinkling lights. **Known for:** bread, sauce, pasta, gelato and other desserts made in-house; organic ingredients from the owner's 12-acre farm or sourced from local purveyors; historic ambience. ⑤ Average main: $27 ✉ 849 Monterey St. 805/541–9922 ⊕ www.giuseppesrestaurant.com.

Luna Red

$$$ | **INTERNATIONAL** | A spacious, contemporary space with a festive outdoor patio, this restaurant near Mission Plaza serves creative tapas and cocktails. The small plates include birria braised beef tacos, avocado-tuna ceviche, and empanadas stuffed with squash and goat cheese. **Known for:** excellent traditional Valencian paellas; craft cocktails; lively music scene. ⑤ Average main: $27 ✉ 1023 Chorro St., at Monterey St. 805/540–5243 ⊕ www.lunaredslo.com.

Mo's Smokehouse BBQ

$ | **SOUTHERN** | Barbecue joints abound on the Central Coast, but this one excels. Various Southern-style sauces season tender hickory-smoked ribs and shredded-meat sandwiches, and sides such as baked beans, coleslaw, homemade potato chips, and garlic bread extend the pleasure. **Known for:** barbecue sampler with ribs, pork, and chicken; barbecue chicken and other fresh salads; house-made potato chips, garlic fries, and other sides. ⑤ Average main: $15 ✉ 1005 Monterey St., at Osos St. 805/544–6193 ⊕ smokinmosbbq.com.

Novo Restaurant & Lounge

$$$ | **ECLECTIC** | In the colorful dining room or on the large creek-side deck, this animated downtown eatery will take you on a culinary world tour. The salads, small plates, and entrées come from nearly every continent. **Known for:** value-laden happy hour from 3 to 6; savory curry and noodle dishes; local farmers' market ingredients. $ *Average main: $25* ✉ *726 Higuera St., at Broad St.* ☎ *805/543–3986* ⊕ *www.novorestaurant.com.*

SLO Provisions

$ | **AMERICAN** | Stop at this casual café/market in the Upper Monterey neighborhood for a sit-down or take-away meal all day. Apart from full meals, order specialty sandwiches, farm-fresh salads, and baked goods, or hang out and taste wine or beer at the casual tasting bar. **Known for:** house-roasted rotisserie meats; family-style dinners; daily specials. $ *Average main: $14* ✉ *1255 Monterey St.* ☎ *805/439–4298* ⊕ *www.sloprovisions.com* ⊗ *Closed Sun.*

Vegetable Butcher

$$ | **AMERICAN** | Vegans, vegetarians, pescatarians, and carnivores alike can indulge in their preferred dietary choices in this casual downtown eatery in a spacious industrial-chic building, where organic and sustainably sourced Central Coast ingredients take center stage. Most menu choices (shared plates or larger mains, salads and rice bowls) begin with a plant-sourced foundation—add your preferred protein, or not. **Known for:** locally sourced premium meats and seafood; global flavors; happy hour weekdays. $ *Average main: $21* ✉ *712 Marsh St.* ☎ *805/439–4801* ⊕ *www.vegetablebutcherslo.com* ⊗ *Closed Sun. No lunch Mon.*

 Hotels

Apple Farm

$$$ | **HOTEL** | Decorated to the hilt with floral bedspreads and watercolors by local artists, this Wine Country–theme hotel is highly popular. **Pros:** flowers everywhere; convenient to Cal Poly and U.S. 101; creek-side setting. **Cons:** hordes of tourists during the day; some rooms too floral for some people's tastes; spotty Wi-Fi in some rooms. $ *Rooms from: $219* ✉ *2015 Monterey St.* ☎ *800/255–2040, 805/544–2040* ⊕ *www.applefarm.com* ⇴ *106 rooms* ⊘ *No meals.*

Garden Street Inn

$$$ | **B&B/INN** | From this restored 1887 Italianate Queen Anne downtown, you can walk to many restaurants and attractions; uniquely decorated rooms, each with private bath, are filled with antiques, and some rooms have stained-glass windows, fireplaces, and decks. **Pros:** lavish homemade breakfast; convenient location; complementary wine-and-cheese reception. **Cons:** city noise filters into some rooms; not great for families; no elevator. $ *Rooms from: $199* ✉ *1212 Garden St.* ☎ *805/545–9802, 800/488–2045* ⊕ *www.gardenstreetinn.com* ⇴ *13 rooms* ⊘ *Breakfast.*

Granada Hotel & Bistro

$$$$ | **HOTEL** | Built in 1922 in the heart of downtown and sparkling again after renovations completed in 2012, the two-story Granada is a vintage-style retreat with hardwood floors, redbrick walls, and antique rugs. **Pros:** one of a few full-service hotels in the heart of downtown; easy walk to restaurants, shops, and sights; farm-to-table Granada Bistro, Nightcap cocktail bar, and Nourish restaurant on-site. **Cons:** some rooms are tiny; sometimes noisy near restaurant kitchen; late-night bar noise travels to some rooms. $ *Rooms from: $279* ✉ *1126 Morro St.* ☎ *805/544–9100* ⊕ *www.granadahotelandbistro.com* ⇴ *17 rooms* ⊘ *No meals.*

★ Hotel Cerro

$$$$ | **HOTEL** | San Luis Obispo's Chumash, mission, and 19th-century industrial eras blend with urban sophistication

in this eco-friendly, four-story complex, which opened in summer 2019. **Pros:** on-site restaurant, café, and lobby lounge; tree-lined outdoor terrace; designed and built to meet LEED Silver status. **Cons:** in the heart of the downtown bar scene. $ *Rooms from: $275* ✉ *1125 Garden St.* ☎ *805/548–1000* ⊕ *www.hotelcerro.com* ⇨ *65 rooms* ❍ *No meals.*

Hotel San Luis Obispo

$$$$ | HOTEL | Completed in 2019, the sleek, three-story Hotel San Luis Obispo offers a full range of services and upscale amenities, just a block from the mission and steps from restaurants, shops, and nightlife. **Pros:** in the heart of the downtown historic district; park the car and walk to most attractions; new building. **Cons:** valet parking only. $ *Rooms from: $375* ✉ *877 Palm St.* ☎ *805/235–0700* ⊕ *hotel-slo.com* ⇨ *78 rooms* ❍ *No meals.*

The Kinney San Luis Obispo

$$ | HOTEL | Redesigned and renamed in 2018, The Kinney celebrates nearby Cal Poly's culture and history in fun, hipster fashion, with local photos, college sports equipment displays, and hanging wicker swings and vintage games and books in the lobby lounge. **Pros:** close to Cal Poly campus; heated pool and sundeck; free parking and Wi-Fi. **Cons:** air-conditioning less than adequate in some rooms; tiny fitness center; motel vibe. $ *Rooms from: $168* ✉ *1800 Monterey St.* ☎ *805/544–8600* ⊕ *www.thekinneyslo.com* ⇨ *100 rooms* ❍ *Free Breakfast.*

★ Madonna Inn

$$$ | HOTEL | From its rococo bathrooms to its pink-on-pink froufrou steak house, the Madonna Inn is fabulous or tacky, depending on your taste. **Pros:** fun, one-of-a-kind experience; infinity pool, exercise room, and day spa; each room has its own distinct identity, for example, Safari Room. **Cons:** rooms vary widely; must appreciate kitsch; no elevator.

$ *Rooms from: $209* ✉ *100 Madonna Rd.* ☎ *805/543–3000, 800/543–9666* ⊕ *www.madonnainn.com* ⇨ *110 rooms* ❍ *No meals.*

Petit Soleil

$$$ | B&B/INN | A cobblestone courtyard, country-French custom furnishings, and Gallic music piped through the halls evoke a Provençal mood at this cheery inn. **Pros:** includes wine and appetizers at cocktail hour; includes scrumptious breakfasts; cozy rooms with luxury touches. **Cons:** sits on a busy avenue; cramped parking; some rooms are tiny. $ *Rooms from: $179* ✉ *1473 Monterey St.* ☎ *805/549–0321, 800/676–1588* ⊕ *www.psslo.com* ⇨ *16 rooms* ❍ *Breakfast.*

SLO Brew Lofts

$$$$ | HOTEL | If you want to be in the heart of the downtown nightlife action, you can't get much closer than this contemporary collection of apartment-stye rooms on the second floor of the historic brick SLO Brew building. **Pros:** in the heart of downtown; upscale amenities; residential vibe. **Cons:** live music plays on the first floor Thursday–Monday; no on-site desk staff after business hours; parking is in a city lot several blocks away. $ *Rooms from: $350* ✉ *738 Higuera St,* ☎ *805/543–1843* ⊕ *www.slobrew.com/the-lofts* ⇨ *5 suites* ❍ *No meals.*

Nightlife

SLO's club scene is centered on Higuera Street, off Monterey Street.

Koberl at Blue

BARS/PUBS | A trendy crowd hangs out at this upscale restaurant's slick bar to sip on exotic martinis and the many local and imported beers and wines. ✉ *998 Monterey St., at Osos St.* ☎ *805/783–1135* ⊕ *www.epkoberl.com.*

The Libertine Brewing Company

BREWPUBS/BEER GARDENS | Come to Libertine to savor 76 craft beers and wines on tap, house-made brews of kombucha and cold brew coffee, and pub food infused with the brewery's own wild ales. ⊠ *1234 Broad St.* ☎ *805/548–2337* ⊕ *www.libertinebrewing.com/san-luis-obispo.*

Linnaea's

BARS/PUBS | A mellow java joint, Linnaea's hosts poetry readings, as well as blues, jazz, and folk music performances. ⊠ *1110 Garden St., at Higuera St.* ☎ *805/541–5888* ⊕ *linnaeas.com* ⌗ *No events Mon.*

MoTav

BARS/PUBS | Chicago-style MoTav draws crowds with good pub food and live entertainment in a turn-of-the-20th-century setting, complete with antique U.S. flags and a wall-mounted moose head. ⊠ *725 Higuera St., at Broad St.* ☎ *805/541–8733* ⊕ *motherstavern.com.*

Nightcap

BARS/PUBS | Indulge in craft and vintage cocktails at the Granada Hotel's artsy cocktail lounge, decked out in pink- and rose-colored velvet, mirrored ceilings, and marble tables and countertops. ⊠ *1130 Morro St.* ☎ *805/544–9100.*

SLO Brew

BARS/PUBS | Handcrafted microbrews and live music most nights make for a winning combination at this downtown watering hole and restaurant in a restored historic brick building. In 2017 SLO Brew opened The Rock, a satellite brewing and tasting facility near the airport with a beer garden, restaurant, and regular live music performances. ⊠ *736 Higuera St.* ☎ *805/543–1843* ⊕ *www.slobrew.com.*

Performing Arts

Festival Mozaic

FESTIVALS | The festival celebrates five centuries of classical music during popular concert series held intermittently from mid-summer to early spring. ☎ *805/781–3009, 877/881–8899* ⊕ *www.festivalmozaic.com.*

Performing Arts Center, San Luis Obispo

ARTS CENTERS | A truly great performance space, the center hosts live theater, dance, and music. ⊠ *Cal Poly, 1 Grand Ave., off U.S. 101* ☎ *805/756–4849* ⊕ *www.calpolyarts.org.*

San Luis Obispo Repertory Theatre

THEATER | SLO County's only nonprofit, fully professional theater group presents dramas, musicals, readings, and other performances year-round. ⊠ *888 Morro St.* ☎ *805/786–2440 box office* ⊕ *www.slolittletheatre.org.*

Shopping

Higuera Street

SHOPPING NEIGHBORHOODS | Many of San Luis Obispo's locally owned and operated shops cluster around downtown's Higuera Street in the blocks east of the mission. Also head up Monterey Street just north of the mission to find additional one-of-a-kind treasures at junkgirls, Taste of SLO, and other small storefronts. ⊠ *San Luis Obispo.*

Morro Bay

14 miles north of San Luis Obispo.

Commercial fishermen slog around Morro Bay in galoshes, and beat-up fishing boats bob in the bay's protected waters. Nature-oriented activities take center stage here: kayaking, hiking, biking, fishing, and wildlife-watching around the bay and national marine estuary and along the state beach.

GETTING HERE AND AROUND
From U.S. 101 south or north, exit at Highway 1 in San Luis Obispo and head west. Scenic Highway 1 passes through the eastern edge of town. From Atascadero, two-lane Highway 41 West treks

over the mountains to Morro Bay. San Luis Obispo RTA Route 12 buses travel year-round between Morro Bay, San Luis Obispo, Cayucos, Cambria, San Simeon, and Hearst Castle. The Morro Bay Shuttle picks up riders throughout the town from Friday through Monday in summer ($1.25 one-way, $3 day pass).

ESSENTIALS
VISITOR INFORMATION Morro Bay Visitors Center. ⊠ *695 Harbor St., at Napa Ave.* ☎ *805/225–1633, 800/231–0592* ⊕ *www.morrobay.org.*

Sights

Embarcadero
NEIGHBORHOOD | The center of Morro Bay action on land is the Embarcadero, where vacationers pour in and out of souvenir shops and seafood restaurants and stroll or bike along the scenic half-mile Harborwalk to Morro Rock. From here, you can get out on the bay in a kayak or tour boat. ⊠ *On waterfront from Beach St. to Tidelands Park.*

Montaña de Oro State Park
NATIONAL/STATE PARK | West of San Luis Obispo, Los Osos Valley Road winds past farms and ranches to this state park whose miles of nature trails traverse rocky shoreline, wild beaches, and hills overlooking dramatic scenery. Check out the tide pools, watch the waves roll into the bluffs, and picnic in the eucalyptus groves. From Montaña de Oro you can reach Morro Bay by following the coastline along South Bay Boulevard 8 miles through the quaint residential villages of Los Osos and Baywood Park. ⊠ *West about 13 miles from downtown San Luis Obispo on Madonna Rd., to Los Osos Valley Rd., to Pecho Valley Rd.; to continue on to Morro Bay, backtrack east to Los Osos Valley Rd., then head north on S. Bay Blvd., and west on State Park Rd., San Luis Obispo* ☎ *805/528–0513, 805/772–7434* ⊕ *www.parks.ca.gov.*

Morro Bay Maritime Museum
MUSEUM | At this tiny but fascinating museum in a parking lot across from the harbor you can learn about Morro Bay's colorful maritime history, dating back thousands of years to the native tribes that fished along the coast. Displays include a tule boat constructed by Salinan tribal members, explorers and traders, commercial fishing, abalone diving, and recreational sailing and boating. If the museum is closed, you can still check out the outdoor exhibits, including a tugboat that rescued sailors from a sinking oil tanker torpedoed by the Japanese during World War II. ⊠ *1210 Embarcadero* ☎ *805/225–5044* ⊕ *morrobaymaritime.org* ⊠ *Free* ☉ *Closed Sun.–Fri.*

Morro Bay State Park Museum of Natural History
MUSEUM | FAMILY | The museum's entertaining interactive exhibits explain the natural environment and how to preserve it—in the bay and estuary and on the rest of the planet. ■**TIP**➔ **Kids age 16 and under are admitted free.** ⊠ *20 State Park Rd., south of downtown* ☎ *805/772–2694* ⊕ *centralcoastparks.org* ⊠ *$3.*

Morro Rock
NATURE PRESERVE | At the mouth of Morro Bay stands 576-foot-high Morro Rock, one of nine small volcanic peaks, or morros, in the area. A short walk leads to a breakwater, with the harbor on one side and crashing ocean waves on the other. You may not climb the rock, where endangered falcons and other birds nest. Sea lions and otters often play in the water below the rock. ⊠ *Northern end of Embarcadero.*

Restaurants

Dorn's Original Breakers Cafe
$$ | SEAFOOD | This restaurant overlooking the harbor has satisfied local appetites since 1942. In addition to straight-ahead dishes such as cod or shrimp

fish-and-chips or calamari tubes sautéed in butter and wine, Dorn's serves breakfast. **Known for:** sweeping views of Morro Rock and the bay; fresh local seafood; friendly, efficient service. $ *Average main: $22* ✉ *801 Market Ave., at Morro Bay Blvd.* ☎ *805/772–4415* ⊕ *www. dornscafe.com.*

Taco Temple

$ | **SOUTHWESTERN** | This family-run diner serves some of the freshest food around. The seafood-heavy menu includes salmon burritos, superb fish tacos with mango salsa, and other dishes hailing from somewhere between California and Mexico. **Known for:** fresh seafood and salsa bar; hefty portions; daily specials. $ *Average main: $15* ✉ *2680 Main St., at Elena St., just north of Hwy. 1/Hwy. 41 junction* ☎ *805/772–4965* ⊕ *tacotemple.com.*

★ Tognazzini's Dockside

$$ | **SEAFOOD** | Captain Mark Tognazzini catches seasonal seafood and delivers the bounty to his family's collection of down-home, no-frills enterprises in the harbor: a fish market with patio dining and up-close views of Morro Rock (Dockside Too), and the original Dockside restaurant. Local musicians play live music nearly every day at the outdoor patio at Dockside Too. **Known for:** fresh-as-it-gets local seafood; live music nearly every day year-round; front-row seats to Morro Rock views. $ *Average main: $20* ✉ *1245 Embarcadero* ☎ *805/772–8100 restaurant, 805/772–8120 fish market and patio dining.*

Windows on the Water

$$$$ | **SEAFOOD** | Diners at this second-floor restaurant view the sunset through giant picture windows. Meanwhile, fresh fish and other dishes based on local ingredients emerge from the wood-fired oven in the open kitchen, and oysters on the half shell beckon from the raw bar. **Known for:** sustainably sourced seafood; 20-plus wines by the glass; menu changes nightly. $ *Average*

main: $37 ✉ *699 Embarcadero, at Pacific St.* ☎ *805/772–0677* ⊕ *www. windowsmb.com* ◷ *No lunch.*

 # Hotels

★ Anderson Inn

$$$$ | **B&B/INN** | Friendly, personalized service and an oceanfront setting keep loyal patrons returning to this Embarcadero inn, which was built from scratch in 2008, and features well-appointed rooms with state-of-the-art tiled bathrooms and cozy comforters atop queen beds. **Pros:** walk to restaurants and sights; spacious rooms; oceanfront rooms have fireplaces and private balconies. **Cons:** not low-budget; waterfront area can get crowded; need to book well in advance—fills quickly. $ *Rooms from: $269* ✉ *897 Embarcadero* ☎ *805/772–3434, 866/950–3434 toll-free reservations* ⊕ *andersoninnmorrobay. com* ⇆ *8 rooms* ❍ *No meals.*

Cass House

$$$$ | **B&B/INN** | In tiny Cayucos, 4 miles north of Morro Bay, a shipping pioneer's 1867 home is now a luxurious bed-and-breakfast surrounded by rose and other gardens. **Pros:** historic property; some ocean views; delicious lobster roll at The Grill. **Cons:** away from nightlife and attractions; not good for families; no elevator. $ *Rooms from: $265* ✉ *222 N. Ocean Ave., Cayucos* ☎ *805/995–3669* ⊕ *casshousecayucos.com* ⇆ *5 rooms* ❍ *Breakfast.*

456 Embarcadero Inn & Suites

$$$ | **HOTEL** | The rooms at this waterfront hotel are cheery and welcoming, and many have fireplaces. **Pros:** across from waterfront; free parking; in-room refrigerators and microwaves. **Cons:** tiny lobby; no pool; basic breakfast. $ *Rooms from: $189* ✉ *456 Embarcadero* ☎ *805/772–2700, 800/292–7625* ⊕ *www.embarcaderoinn.com* ⇆ *33 rooms* ❍ *Breakfast.*

The Inn at Morro Bay

$$$ | **RESORT** | Surrounded by eucalyptus trees, this inn abuts a heron rookery and Morro Bay State Park. **Pros:** great for wildlife lovers; stellar views from restaurant and some rooms; nearby golf course, wellness center on-site. **Cons:** some rooms on the small side; birds and seals can wake you early; some rooms need updating. ⑤ *Rooms from: $189* ✉ *60 State Park Rd.* ☎ *805/772–5651* ⊕ *innatmorrobay.com* ⇌ *98 rooms* ❑| *No meals.*

Activities

Kayak Horizons

KAYAKING | This outfit rents kayaks and paddleboards and gives lessons and guided tours. ✉ *551 Embarcadero, near Marina St.* ☎ *805/772–6444* ⊕ *kayakhorizons.com.*

The Paddleboard Co

WATER SPORTS | Come to this waterfront shop to rent stand-up paddleboards and to take paddleboard lessons and yoga and fitness classes (for all ages and skill levels), and stock up on outdoor wear and paddling gear. You can sign up for classes online as well. ✉ *575 Embarcadero* ☎ *805/225–5555* ⊕ *www.thepaddleboardcompany.com* ⊠ *Board rentals from $25 per hr, lessons from $85.*

Sub-Sea Tours & Kayaks

BOATING | You can view sea life aboard this outfit's glass-bottom boat, watch whales from its catamaran, or rent a kayak, canoe, or stand-up paddleboard. ✉ *699 Embarcadero* ☎ *805/772–9463* ⊕ *subseatours.com.*

Virg's Landing

FISHING | Virg's conducts deep-sea-fishing and whale-watching trips. ✉ *1169 Market Ave.* ☎ *805/772–1222* ⊕ *virgslanding.com.*

Paso Robles

30 miles north of San Luis Obispo, 25 miles northwest of Morro Bay.

In the 1860s, tourists began flocking to this ranching outpost to "take the cure" in a bathhouse fed by underground mineral hot springs. An Old West town emerged, and grand Victorian homes went up, followed in the 20th century by Craftsman bungalows. These days, the wooded hills of Paso Robles west of U.S. 101 and the flatter, more open land to the freeway's east hold more than 250 wineries, many with tasting rooms. Hot summer days, cool nights, and varied soils and microclimates allow growers to cultivate an impressive array of Bordeaux, Rhône, and other grape types. Cabernet Sauvignon grows well in the Paso Robles AVA—40,000 of its 600,000-plus acres are planted to grapes—as do Petit Verdot, Grenache, Syrah, Viognier, and Zinfandel. In recognition of the diverse growing conditions, the AVA was divided into 11 subappellations in 2014. Pick up a wine-touring map at lodgings, wineries, and attractions around town. The fee at most tasting rooms is between $10 and $25; many lodgings pass out discount coupons.

Upmarket restaurants, bars, antiques stores, and little shops fill the streets around oak-shaded City Park, where special events of all kinds—custom car shows, an olive festival, Friday-night summer concerts—take place on many weekends. Despite its increasing sophistication, Paso (as the locals call it) retains a small-town vibe. The city celebrates its cowboy roots in late July and early August with the two-week California Mid-State Fair, complete with livestock auctions, carnival rides, and corn dogs.

GETTING HERE AND AROUND

U.S. 101 runs north–south through Paso Robles. Highway 46 West links Paso Robles to Highway 1 and Cambria on the coast. Highway 46 East connects Paso Robles with Interstate 5 and the San Joaquin Valley. Public transit is not convenient for wine touring and sightseeing.

VISITOR INFORMATION Paso Robles CAB Collective. ☏ 805/543–2288 ⊕ pasoroblescab.com. **Paso Robles Wine Country Alliance.** ☏ 805/239–8463 ⊕ pasowine.com. **Paso Robles Visitor Center.** ✉ 1225 Park St., near 12th St. ☏ 805/238–0506 ⊕ travelpaso.com. **Rhone Rangers/Paso Robles.** ⊕ www.rhonerangers.org.

Sights

★ Calcareous Vineyard

WINERY/DISTILLERY | Elegant wines, a stylish tasting room, and knockout hilltop views make for a winning experience at this winery along winding Peachy Canyon Road. Cabernet Sauvignon, Syrah, and Zinfandel grapes thrive in the summer heat and limestone soils of the two vineyards near the tasting room; and a third vineyard on cooler York Mountain produces Pinot Noir, Chardonnay, and a Cabernet with a completely different character from the Peachy Canyon edition. ■ TIP➔ **The picnic area's expansive eastward views invite lingering.** ✉ 3430 Peachy Canyon Rd. ☏ 805/239–0289 ⊕ calcareous.com ⌲ Tastings $15; tour and tasting (reservations required) from $35.

Carnegie Historic Library

LIBRARY | Philanthropist and steel magnate Andrew Carnegie funded this sturdy and splendid structure, erected in 1908. The jewel of City Park, it hosts thoughtful exhibits on local history, many of which include quirky products and advertisements from days gone by. ✉ 800 12th St., at Park St. ☏ 805/238–4996 ⊕ www.pasorobleshistoricalsociety.org ۞ Closed Mon., Wed., and holidays.

Eberle Winery

WINERY/DISTILLERY | Even if you don't drink wine, stop here for a tour of the huge wine caves beneath the vineyards (departs every half hour all day). Eberle produces wines from Bordeaux, Rhône, and Italian varietals and makes intriguing blends including Grenache Blanc–Viognier and Cabernet Sauvignon–Syrah. ✉ 3810 Hwy. 46 E, 3½ miles east of U.S. 101 ☏ 805/238–9607 ⊕ www.eberlewinery.com ⌲ Basic tasting and tour free, private tour and tasting $35 by appointment.

Estrella Warbirds Museum

MUSEUM | **FAMILY** | An entertaining homage to fighter planes, flyboys, and flygirls, this museum maintains indoor exhibits about wartime aviation and displays retired aircraft outdoors and in repair shops. Bonus attraction: a huge building with spruced-up autos, drag racers, and "funny cars." ✉ 4251 Dry Creek Rd., off Airport Rd., north off Hwy. 46E ☏ 805/238–9317 ⊕ ewarbirds.org ⌲ $10 ۞ Closed Mon.–Wed. except legal holidays.

Firestone Walker Brewing Company

WINERY/DISTILLERY | At this working craft brewery you can sample medal-winners such as the Double Barrel Ale and learn about the beer-making process on 30-minute guided tours of the brew house and cellar. ✉ 1400 Ramada Dr., east side of U.S. 101; exit at Hwy. 46 W/Cambria, but head east ☏ 805/225–5911 ⊕ www.firestonebeer.com ⌲ Tastings from $2 per sample, tour $10 (includes 4 samples).

Halter Ranch Vineyard

WINERY/DISTILLERY | A good place to learn about contemporary Paso Robles wine making, this ultramodern operation produces high-quality wines from estate-grown Bordeaux and Rhône grapes grown in sustainably farmed vineyards. The gravity-flow winery, which you can view on tours, is a marvel of efficiency. Ancestor, the flagship wine, a potent Bordeaux-style blend of Cabernet Sauvignon, Petit Verdot, and Malbec, is named for the ranch's huge centuries-old coast oak tree. ⊠ *8910 Adelaida Rd., at Vineyard Dr.* ☎ *888/367–9977* ⊕ *www.halterranch. com* ⊠ *Tastings $20.*

★ HammerSky Vineyards

WINERY/DISTILLERY | Owner Doug Hauck handcrafts Bordeaux-centric wines on a 50-acre estate on the far western slopes of Paso Robles. Set amid rolling hills of vineyards punctuated by a huge oak, HammerSky's bright-white contemporary structure houses both the tasting and barrel-aging rooms; an outdoor patio has views of the estate vines. ⊠ *7725 Vineyard Dr., at Jensen Rd.* ☎ *805/239–0930* ⊕ *www.hammersky.com* ⊠ *Tastings $15.*

★ Jada Vineyard & Winery

WINERY/DISTILLERY | Jada biodynamically farms 65 acres of estate vineyards in the Templeton Gap/Willow Creek district, and uses the flavorful fruit to craft its nuanced, highly structured wines. Two worth checking out are Jack of Hearts, starring Petit Verdot, and Passing By, a Cabernet-heavy blend. Galzignato also shines with Tannat and with Rhône-style wines, particularly Grenache. ⊠ *5620 Vineyard Dr., north of Hwy. 46 W* ☎ *805/226–4200* ⊕ *jadavineyard.com* ⊠ *Tastings $15.*

JUSTIN Vineyards & Winery

WINERY/DISTILLERY | This suave winery built its reputation on Isosceles, a hearty Bordeaux blend, usually of Cabernet Sauvignon, Cabernet Franc, and Merlot. JUSTIN's Cabernet Sauvignon is also well regarded, as is the Right Angle blend of Cab and three other varietals. Tastings here take place in an expansive room whose equally expansive windows provide views of the hillside vineyards. ⊠ *11680 Chimney Rock Rd., 15 miles west of U.S. 101's Hwy 46 E exit; take 24th St. west and follow road (name changes along the way) to Chimney Rock Rd.* ☎ *805/238–6932* ⊕ *justinwine. com* ⊠ *Tastings $25, tour and tasting $30* ☞ *Tours 10 and 2:30 (reservations recommended).*

Paso Robles Pioneer Museum

MUSEUM | The delightful museum's one-room schoolhouse and its displays of ranching paraphernalia, horse-drawn vehicles, hot-springs artifacts, and photos evoke Paso's rural heritage. ⊠ *2010 Riverside Ave., at 21st St.* ☎ *805/239–4556* ⊕ *www.pasoroblespioneermuseum.org* ⊠ *Free* ☉ *Closed Mon.–Wed.*

Paso Robles Wine Festival

FESTIVAL | Most local wineries pour at this mid-May outdoor festival that has live bands and diverse food vendors. Winery open houses and winemaker dinners round out the weekend. ⊠ *City Park, Spring St., between 10th and 12th Sts.* ☎ *805/239–8463* ⊕ *www.pasowine. com* ⊠ *$80 basic admission, designated driver $25.*

★ Pasolivo

WINERY/DISTILLERY | While touring the idyllic west side of Paso Robles, take a break from wine tasting by stopping at Pasolivo. Find out how the artisans here make their Tuscan-style olive oils on a high-tech Italian press, and test the acclaimed results. ⊠ *8530 Vineyard Dr., west off U.S. 101 (Exit 224) or Hwy. 46 W (Exit 228)* ☎ *805/227–0186* ⊕ *www. pasolivo.com* ⊠ *Tastings $5.*

Pomar Junction Vineyard & Winery

WINERY/DISTILLERY | **FAMILY** | A vintage railroad boxcar and a caboose provide a visual change of pace at Pomar Junction. Its flagship wine, Train Wreck, is a daring but usually winning blend of Cabernet Sauvignon, Zinfandel, Mourvèdre, Syrah, and Petite Sirah. With sparkling wine, a Grenache Blanc, Pinot Noir, a smooth Merlot, and several white and red blends, there's something for pretty much everyone here. ■**TIP→ Picnic areas shaded by elms, oaks, and other trees—not to mention old farm equipment and those train cars— make this a popular stop for wine tasters with kids.** ⊠ *5036 S. El Pomar Rd., at El Pomar Dr.* ☎ *805/238–9940* ⊕ *pomarjunction.com* ⊠ *Tastings from $10.*

Re:Find Handcrafted Spirits

WINERY/DISTILLERY | The owners of Villacana Winery in west Paso Robles launched the first local distillery in 2011, aiming to repurpose the saignee (free-run juice) that's typically tossed out during the wine-making process. They ferment and distill the leftover high-quality juices into premium spirits, thus reclaiming about 60 acres of premium wine grapes. Taste vodka, gin, whiskey, bourbon, limoncello, and kumquat liqueurs in the tiny tasting space in the barrel room. ⊠ *2725 Adelaida Rd.* ☎ *805/239–9456* ⊕ *refind-distillery.com.*

River Oaks Hot Springs & Spa

SPA—SIGHT | The lakeside spa, on 240 hilly acres near the intersection of U.S. 101 and Highway 46 East, is a great place to relax after wine tasting or festival-going. Soak in a private indoor or outdoor hot tub fed by natural mineral springs, or indulge in a massage or facial. ⊠ *800 Clubhouse Dr., off River Oaks Dr., just north of River Oaks Golf Course* ☎ *805/238–4600* ⊕ *riveroakshotsprings. com* ⌒ *From $15 per hr.*

Robert Hall Winery

WINERY/DISTILLERY | The late Robert Hall's winery made its reputation on a well-made, reasonably priced Cabernet Sauvignon from Paso Robles AVA grapes, but at the high-ceilinged tasting room you can sample less widely distributed wines. These include a reserve Cabernet, a Merlot, a Malbec, a Bordeaux-style Meritage blend, and a Port made from Portuguese grapes. Whites of note include Roussanne, Sauvignon Blanc, and Viognier. ■ **TIP➔ Ask for a 30-minute tour if you'd like to see the production facilities.** ⊠ *3443 Mill Rd., at Hwy. 46E, 3 miles east of U.S. 101* ☎ *805/239–1616* ⊕ *roberthallwinery.com* ⌒ *Tastings $15; tour free.*

Sensorio

This 386-acre interactive garden engages the senses, honors the natural topography, and offers a wide range of amusing,

SIP Certification

Many wineries in Paso Robles take pride in being SIP (Sustainability in Practice) Certified, for which they undergo a rigorous third-party audit of their entire operations. Water and energy conservation practices are reviewed, along with pest management and other aspects of farming. Also considered are the wages, benefits, and working conditions of the employees, and the steps taken to mitigate the impact of grape growing and wine production on area habitats.

mystical, and kinetic experiences. It launches with an interactive light installation by Bruce Munro. ⊠ *Paso Robles.*

Studios on the Park

MUSEUM | A 1951 Hudson Hornet (a nod to the building's automotive past) greets visitors at the entrance to this nonprofit open studios art center on the east side of the downtown City Park. Interact with professional artists as they work on their latest pieces, browse the four galleries and gift shop, and on the first Saturday evening of the month, sip wine and listen to music while viewing the center's latest art exhibit. ⊠ *1130 Pine St.* ☎ *805/238–9800* ⊕ *www.studio-sonthepark.org.*

SummerWood Winery

WINERY/DISTILLERY | Rhône varietals do well in the Paso Robles AVA, where many wineries, including this one, produce "GSM" (Grenache, Syrah, Mourvèdre) red blends, along with whites such as Viognier, Marsanne, and Grenache Blanc. Winemaker Mauricio Marchant displays a subtle touch with Rhône whites and reds, as well as Sentio, a Petit Verdot–heavy Bordeaux red blend. Tastings here are relaxed and informal, and there's a patio from which you can enjoy the vineyard views. ⊠ *2175 Arbor Rd., off Hwy. 46W* ☎ *805/227–1365* ⊕ *summerwoodwine. com* ☎ *Tastings $15.*

Tablas Creek Vineyard

WINERY/DISTILLERY | Tucked in the western hills of Paso Robles, Tablas Creek is known for its blends of certified biodynamically grown, hand-harvested Rhône varietals. Roussanne and Viognier are the standout whites; the Mourvèdre-heavy blend called Panoplie (it also includes Grenache and Syrah) has received high praise in recent years. ■TIP→ **There's a fine picnic area here.** ⊠ *9339 Adelaida Rd., west of Vineyard Dr.* ☎ *805/237– 1231* ⊕ *www.tablascreek.com* ☎ *Tastings from $15 (reserve $40 by appointment), tour free.*

★ Tin City

WINERY/DISTILLERY | This industrial park on the southern border of Paso Robles houses a collection of wineries, craft breweries, distilleries, and specialty shops where you can pick up sheep's milk ice cream, fresh pasta, and other local wares. Good places to start your explorations include Giornata Winery, Levo Winery, Barrel House Brewery, and TinCity Cider House. Dine casually at Tin Canteen restaurant or upscale (dinner only) at Six Test Kitchen. ⊠ *Limestone Way* ✛ *East of Ramada Dr. via Marquita Ave.* ⊕ *www.tincitypaso.com.*

Villa San-Juliette Vineyard & Winery

WINERY/DISTILLERY | Nigel Lithgoe (co-creator of *So You Think You Can Dance* is one of his many titles), and Ken Warwick (executive producer of *American Idol*, among other programs) established this winery northeast of Paso Robles. With a cast that includes Petit Verdot, a fine Grenache, and a perky Albariño (a Spanish white varietal), their stylish operation is no flash in the pan. From 11 to 4 you can order snacks, panini, pizzas, soup and salad, and cheese and charcuterie

plates to enjoy with your wine in the tasting room or on the view-filled outdoor terrace. ⊠ *6385 Cross Canyons Rd., at Ranchita Canyon Rd., San Miguel* ☎ *805/467–0014* ⊕ *www.villasanjuliette. com* ☎ *Tastings $15* ◷ *Closed Tues. and Wed. except by appointment.*

Vina Robles

WINERY/DISTILLERY | "European inspiration, California character" is the motto of this winery whose owners hail from Switzerland. The flagship Suendero wine is a lush blend of Cabernet Sauvignon and Petit Verdot. You can enjoy it along with some winery-only whites and reds at the large hospitality center. ■TIP→ **In good weather the patio out back, outfitted with a fountain and a fire pit and shaded by a large oak tree, is a nice relaxing space to hang out.** ⊠ *3700 Mill Rd., at Hwy. 46E, 3 miles east of U.S. 101* ☎ *805/227–4812* ⊕ *vinarobles.com* ☎ *Tastings $15, wine and cheese pairing $35, wine and food pairing $70 by appointment.*

🍴 Restaurants

BL Brasserie

$$$$ | **FRENCH** | Owner-chef Laurent Grangien's handsome, welcoming French bistro occupies an 1890s brick building across from City Park. He focuses on traditional dishes such as duck confit, rack of lamb, and onion soup, but always prepares a few au courant daily specials as well. **Known for:** classic French dishes made with local ingredients; good selection of local and international wines; four- or five-course tasting menus. ⑤ *Average main: $32* ⊠ *1202 Pine St., at 12th St.* ☎ *805/226–8191* ⊕ *www.bistrolaurent. com* ◷ *Closed Sun. and Mon.*

The Hatch

$$ | **AMERICAN** | A wood-fired rotisserie in an open kitchen, simple but tasty comfort foods and a lively bar scene attract locals and visitors alike to this cozy, casual space in an historic brick building a block north from the main square. Fuel up body and soul with menu favorites like meat loaf, shrimp and grits, bacon burgers, donuts, cakes, and sundaes. **Known for:** house-made sauces, house-pickled fruits and veggies, house-cured ham; craft cocktails and small-batch whiskies; daily rotisserie specials: chicken, ribs, lamb, tri-tip. $ *Average main: $22* ⊠ *835 13th St.* ☎ *805/221–5727* ⊕ *hatchpasorobles.com* ⊗ *No lunch.*

★ Il Cortile

$$$$ | **MODERN ITALIAN** | One of two Paso establishments owned by chef Santos MacDonal and his wife, Carole, this Italian restaurant entices diners with complex flavors and a contemporary space with art-deco overtones. Consistent crowd-pleasers often on the menu include beef carpaccio with white truffle cream sauce and shaved black truffles and pappardelle with wild boar ragu. **Known for:** house-made pastas; excellent wine pairings; ingredients from chef's garden. $ *Average main: $38* ⊠ *608 12th St., near Spring St.* ☎ *805/226–0300* ⊕ *www.ilcortileristorante.com* ⊗ *Closed Tues. No lunch.*

Jeffry's Wine Country BBQ

$ | **AMERICAN** | Award-winning local chef Jeff Wiesinger and his wife Kathleen opened this casual eatery, tucked in a hidden courtyard a block from downtown City Park. Feast indoors or out on made-to-order sandwiches, hearty mac-and-cheese bowls, house-made potato chips, fresh salads, craft beer, and local wines while listening to throwback sound tracks from the '60s and '70s. **Known for:** delectable mac-and-cheese dishes; smoked tri-tip and other meats; savory paella. $ *Average main: $15* ⊠ *819 12th St., Suite B* ⊕ *In alley between 12th and 13th Sts.* ☎ *805/369–2132* ⊕ *jeffryswinecountrybbq.com* ⊗ *Closed Wed.*

La Cosecha

$$$ | **SOUTH AMERICAN** | At barlike, tin-ceilinged La Cosecha (Spanish for "the harvest"), Honduran-born chef Santos MacDonal faithfully re-creates dishes from Spain and South America. Noteworthy starters include *pastelitos catracho,* Honduran-style empanadas in a light tomato sauce served with *queso fresco* (fresh cheese) and micro cilantro. **Known for:** fusion of Latin spices and fresh local fare; daily paella special; artisanal cocktails. $ *Average main: $29* ⊠ *835 12th St., near Pine St.* ☎ *805/237–0019* ⊕ *www.lacosechabr. com* ⊗ *Closed Mon. Closed Tues. Jan. and Feb.*

McPhee's Grill

$$$$ | **AMERICAN** | Just south of Paso Robles in tiny Templeton, this casual chophouse in an 1860s wood-frame storefront serves sophisticated, contemporary versions of traditional Western fare such as oak-grilled filet mignon and fresh seafood tostadas. The house-label wines, made especially for the restaurant, are quite good. **Known for:** meats grilled over red oak; local seasonal menu; excellent wine selections. $ *Average main: $34* ⊠ *416 S. Main St., at 5th St., Templeton* ☎ *805/434–3204* ⊕ *mcpheesgrill.com* ⊗ *No lunch Sun.*

Tin Canteen

$ | **AMERICAN** | Decorated in industrial-chic style befitting its Tin City location, this lively eatery with an open kitchen and wood-fired oven showcases local and regional ingredients. The menu changes frequently depending on what's in season, but usually includes faves like garlic fries, burgers, and farm-to-table appetizers and salads. **Known for:** fresh pastas from the neighboring shop; lively local vibe; close to tasting rooms, distilleries, breweries, and shops. $ *Average main: $15* ⊠ *3070 Limestone Way* ⊕ *in Tin City* ☎ *805/369–2787* ⊕ *www.tincanteenpaso. net* ⊗ *Closed Mon. and Tues. No dinner Wed. and Sun.*

Hotels

★ Allegretto

$$$$ | **RESORT** | This swank, 20-acre Tuscan-style resort amid estate vineyards is also a private museum where owner Douglas Ayres displays hundreds of artworks and artifacts collected on his world travels: ancient Indian river stones and statues; a massive cross section from a giant sequoia; Russian and California impressionist paintings; mandalas; and more (nonguests are welcome to walk around). **Pros:** yoga in medieval abbey; full-service restaurant Cello and spa; bocce ball, fire pit, and other diversions. **Cons:** not close to downtown square; pricey; some rooms close to courtyard music. ⑤ *Rooms from: $349* ✉ *2700 Buena Vista Dr.* ☎ *805/369–2500* ⊕ *www. allegrettoresort.com* ⤤ *171 rooms.*

★ Hotel Cheval

$$$$ | **HOTEL** | Equestrian themes surface throughout this intimate European-style boutique hotel a half block from the main square and near some of Paso's best restaurants. **Pros:** most rooms have fireplaces; sip wine and champagne at the on-site Pony Club and zinc bar; extremely personalized service. **Cons:** views aren't great; no pool or hot tub; no elevator. ⑤ *Rooms from: $380* ✉ *1021 Pine St.* ☎ *805/226–9995, 866/522–6999* ⊕ *www.hotelcheval.com* ⤤ *16 rooms* ⦿ *Breakfast.*

JUST Inn

$$$$ | **B&B/INN** | Fine wines, a destination restaurant, and a vineyard's-edge setting make a stay at Justin winery's on-site inn an exercise in sophisticated seclusion. **Pros:** amazing night skies; vineyard views; destination restaurant. **Cons:** half-hour drive to town; location may be too secluded for some; spotty cell service. ⑤ *Rooms from: $475* ✉ *11680 Chimney Rock Rd.* ☎ *805/238–6932, 800/726–0049* ⊕ *www.justinwine.com* ⤤ *4 suites* ⦿ *Breakfast.*

La Bellasera Hotel & Suites

$$$ | **HOTEL** | A full-service hotel just off Highway 101 at the Highway 46 exit, La Bellasera caters to those looking for high-tech amenities and easy access to major Central Coast roadways. **Pros:** oversize rooms; Romanesque architectural features; close to freeways. **Cons:** far from downtown; at a major intersection; freeway noise heard in some rooms. ⑤ *Rooms from: $199* ✉ *206 Alexa Ct.* ☎ *805/238–2834, 866/782–9669* ⊕ *labellasera.com* ⤤ *60 rooms* ⦿ *No meals.*

La Quinta Inn & Suites

$$$ | **HOTEL** | A good value for Paso Robles, this three-story chain property attracts heavy repeat business with its upbeat staff and slew of perks. **Pros:** apartment-style suites in separate building; free happy hour with local wines and appetizers; good for leisure or business travelers. **Cons:** conventional decor; not downtown; basic breakfast. ⑤ *Rooms from: $189* ✉ *2615 Buena Vista Dr.* ☎ *805/239–3004, 800/753–3757* ⊕ *www. laquintapasorobles.com* ⤤ *101 rooms* ⦿ *Breakfast.*

Paso Robles Inn

$$ | **HOTEL** | On the site of an old spa hotel of the same name, the various buildings at this historic inn cluster around a lush, shaded garden with a pool. **Pros:** private hot tubs in many rooms; special touches like unique photography in each room; across from town square. **Cons:** fronts a busy street; rooms vary in size and amenities. ⑤ *Rooms from: $149* ✉ *1103 Spring St.* ☎ *805/238–2660, 800/676–1713* ⊕ *www.pasoroblesinn.com* ⤤ *122 rooms* ⦿ *No meals.*

★ SummerWood Inn

$$$$ | **B&B/INN** | Easygoing hospitality, vineyard-view rooms, and elaborate breakfasts make this inn a mile west of U.S. 101 worth seeking out. **Pros:** convenient wine-touring base; elaborate breakfasts; complimentary tastings at associated winery. **Cons:** some noise from nearby highway during the day;

no elevator; not close to downtown restaurants. ⑤ *Rooms from: $300* ✉ *2130 Arbor Rd., 1 mile west of U.S. 101, at Hwy. 46W* ☎ *805/227–1111* ⊕ *www.summerwoodwine.com/inn* ⇌ *9 rooms* ❍ *Breakfast.*

Nightlife

1122 Speakeasy

BARS/PUBS | Press the doorbell and request permission to enter this elegant, 1930s-era cocktail lounge and speakeasy on the back patio of Pappy McGregor's Pub on the main square. It has just 28 seats, so be prepared to wait in line on weekend nights. ✉ *1122 Pine St.* ✛ *Entrance on Railroad St. or walk through pub* ☎ *805/805–8055* ⊕ *www.eleven-twentytwo.com* ☞ *Closed Mon.*

Performing Arts

Vina Robles Amphitheatre

CONCERTS | At this 3,300-seat, Mission-style venue with good food, wine, and sight lines, you can enjoy acclaimed musicians in concert. ✉ *Vina Robles winery, 3800 Mill Rd., off Hwy. 46* ☎ *805/286–3680* ⊕ *www.vinarobles-amphitheatre.com* ☞ *Performances Apr.–Nov.*

Cambria

28 miles west of Paso Robles, 20 miles north of Morro Bay.

Cambria, set on piney hills above the sea, was settled by Welsh miners in the 1890s. In the 1970s the isolated setting attracted artists and other independent types; the town now caters to tourists, but it still bears the imprint of its bohemian past. Both of Cambria's downtowns, the original East Village and the newer West Village, are packed with art and crafts galleries, antiques shops, cafés, restaurants, and bed-and-breakfasts.

Two diverting detours lie between Morro Bay and Cambria. In the laid-back beach town of **Cayucos,** 4 miles north of Morro Bay, you can stroll the long pier, feast on chowder (at Duckie's), and sample the namesake delicacies of the Brown Butter Cookie Co. Over in **Harmony,** a quaint former dairy town 7 miles south of Cambria (population 18), you can take in the glassworks, pottery, and other artsy enterprises.

GETTING HERE AND AROUND

Highway 1 leads to Cambria from the north and south. Highway 246 West curves from U.S. 101 through the mountains to Cambria. San Luis Obispo RTA Route 12 buses stop in Cambria (and Hearst Castle).

ESSENTIALS

VISITOR INFORMATION Cambria Chamber of Commerce. ✉ *767 Main St.* ☎ *805/927–3624* ⊕ *www.cambriachamber.org.*

Sights

Covells California Clydesdales

NATURE PRESERVE | Come to the vast 2,000-acre Covells Ranch to see one of the world's largest private stands of endangered Monterey pines and witness herds of gentle Clydesdales roaming the range. Much of the ranch is in a conservation easement that will never be developed. The two-hour guided tours include a 3-mile ride that takes you through an historic picnic grove amid the pines to the barn. The ranch also offers trail rides and Saturday-night barbecue dinners at the barn, where you can take a hayride on a custom-built "people mover" wagon. ✉ *5694 Bridge St.* ☎ *805/975–7332* ⊕ *www.covellscaliforniaclydesdales.com* 🎫 *Tours $100 per person, Sat.-night barbecues $100 per person* ⊙ *Tours, trail rides, and barbecues by appointment only.*

Fiscalini Ranch Preserve

NATURE PRESERVE | Walk down a mile-long coastal bluff trail to spot migrating whales, otters, and shorebirds at this

450-acre public space. Miles of additional scenic trails crisscross the protected habitats of rare and endangered species of flora and fauna, including a Monterey pine forest, western pond turtles, monarch butterflies, and burrowing owls. Dogs are permitted on-leash everywhere and off-leash on all trails except the bluff. ⊠ *Hwy. 1, between Cambria Rd. and Main St. to the north, and Burton Dr. and Warren Rd. to the south; access either end of bluff trail off Windsor Blvd.* ☎ *805/927–2856* ⊕ *www.ffrpcambria.org.*

Leffingwell Landing

CITY PARK | A state picnic ground, the landing is a good place for examining tidal pools and watching otters as they frolic in the surf. ⊠ *North end of Moonstone Beach Dr.* ☎ *805/927–2070.*

Moonstone Beach Drive

SCENIC DRIVE | The drive runs along a bluff above the ocean, paralleled by a 3-mile boardwalk that winds along the beach. On this photogenic walk you might glimpse sea lions and sea otters, and perhaps a gray whale during winter and spring. Year-round, birds fly about, and tiny creatures scurry amid the tidepools. ⊠ *Off Hwy. 1.*

Nit Wit Ridge

HOUSE | Arthur Beal (aka Captain Nit Wit, Der Tinkerpaw) spent 51 years building a home above Cambria's West Village out of collected junk: beer cans, rocks, abalone shells, car parts, TV antennas—you name it. The site, sometimes signed as Nitt Witt Ridge, is a state landmark. ■TIP➜ **You can drive by and peek in—from the 700 block of Main Street, head southeast on Cornwall Street and east on Hillcrest Drive. Or, schedule a guided tour.** ⊠ *881 Hillcrest Dr.* ☎ *805/927–2690* ⊕ *visitcambriaca.com* ⊠ *$10.*

★ Stolo Family Vineyards

WINERY/DISTILLERY | Just 3 miles from the ocean and a short drive from Cambria's East Village, the 52-acre Stolo estate produces about 5,000 cases of premium wine each year. The estate Syrahs consistently win top awards; sample these and other estate wines, including Pinot Noir, dry Gewurztraminer, Sauvignon Blanc, and Chardonnays, in the hilltop tasting room on the site of a former dairy farm. If the weather's nice, sit out on the sprawling lawn near a 1920s barn and 1895 farmhouse. ⊠ *3776 Santa Rosa Creek Rd.* ☎ *805/924–3131* ⊕ *stolofamilyvineyards.com.*

🍴 Restaurants

Centrally Grown at Off the Grid

$$ | MODERN AMERICAN | A collection of sustainably conscious spaces fashioned from repurposed materials, Centrally Grown encompasses a coffee shop, wine tasting, exotic gardens, and a second-floor restaurant with fantastic views of San Simeon Bay and the Big Sur Coast. The restaurant, decorated in a "planet-friendly chic" style that includes a driftwood archway, serves classic California cuisine with global influences. **Known for:** all-day dining; great place to stop before or after driving the Big Sur Coast; exotic gardens with meandering paths. ⑤ *Average main: $22* ⊠ *7432 Exotic Garden Dr., off Hwy. 1* ☎ *800/927–3563* ⊕ *www.centrallygrown.com.*

Linn's Restaurant

$$$ | AMERICAN | FAMILY | Homemade olallieberry pies, soups, potpies, and other farmhouse comfort foods share the menu at this spacious East Village restaurant with fancier farm-to-table dishes such as organic, free-range chicken topped with raspberry-orange-cranberry sauce. Also on-site are a bakery, a café serving more casual fare (take-out available), and a gift shop that sells gourmet foods. **Known for:** olallieberry pie; numerous gluten-free and vegan options; family-owned-and-operated for decades. ⑤ *Average main: $25* ⊠ *2277 Main St., at Wall St.* ☎ *805/927–0371* ⊕ *www.linnsfruitbin.com.*

★ Madeline's

$$$$ | **FRENCH FUSION** | Dine on stellar French-American delights at a romantic, candlit table in this tiny restaurant within a tasting room and wineshop in Cambria's West Village. The menu changes seasonally, but you might start with crab and lobster cakes or lamb empanadas, then move on to Louisiana seafood gumbo or Long Island duck breast, and bananas foster or crème brûlée for dessert. **Known for:** unusual entrées like venison chops and rabbit; excellent selection of local wines; five-course chef's tasting menu ($55). ⑤ *Average main: $33* ⊠ *788 Main St.* ☎ *805/927–4175* ☾ *No lunch.*

Robin's

$$$ | **ECLECTIC** | An international, vegetarian-friendly dining experience awaits you at this cozy East Village cottage. Dinner choices include wild prawn enchiladas, grilled Skuna Bay salmon, lamb curry, and short ribs. **Known for:** savory curries; top-notch salmon bisque; secluded (heated) garden patio. ⑤ *Average main: $28* ⊠ *4095 Burton Dr., at Center St.* ☎ *805/927–5007* ⊕ *robinsrestaurant.com.*

★ Sea Chest Oyster Bar and Restaurant

$$$$ | **SEAFOOD** | Cambria's best place for seafood fills up soon after it opens at 5:30 (no reservations taken). Those in the know grab seats at the oyster bar and take in spectacular sunsets while watching the chefs broil fresh halibut, steam garlicky clams, and fry crispy calamari steaks; if you arrive to a wait, play cribbage or checkers in the game room. **Known for:** New England chowder house vibe; savory cioppino; waiting areas in wine bar, game room, and patio with fire pit. ⑤ *Average main: $32* ⊠ *6216 Moonstone Beach Dr., near Weymouth St.* ☎ *805/927–4514* ⊕ *www.seachestrestaurant.com* ▭ *No credit cards* ☾ *Closed Tues. mid-Sept.–May. No lunch.*

Hotels

Bluebird Inn

$$ | **HOTEL** | This sweet motel in Cambria's East Village sits amid beautiful gardens along Santa Rosa Creek. **Pros:** excellent value; well-kept gardens; friendly staff. **Cons:** few frills; basic rooms; not on beach. ⑤ *Rooms from: $125* ⊠ *1880 Main St.* ☎ *805/927–4634, 800/552–5434* ⊕ *www.bluebirdinncambria.com/* ⇱ *37 rooms* ⑪ *No meals.*

Cambria Pines Lodge

$$ | **RESORT** | This 25-acre retreat up the hill from the East Village is a good choice for families; accommodations range from basic fireplace cabins to motel-style standard rooms to large fireplace suites and deluxe suites with spa tubs. **Pros:** short walk from downtown; live music nightly in the lounge; verdant gardens. **Cons:** service and housekeeping not always top-quality; some units need updating; thin walls in some units. ⑤ *Rooms from: $149* ⊠ *2905 Burton Dr.* ☎ *805/927–4200, 800/966–6490* ⊕ *www.cambriapineslodge.com* ⇱ *152 rooms* ⑪ *Breakfast.*

Fog Catcher Inn

$$$ | **B&B/INN** | The landscaped gardens and 10 faux-thatched and timbered buildings here evoke an English-country village. **Pros:** romantic rooms; across from Moonstone Beach; updated furnishings. **Cons:** breakfast quality varies; pricey rates. ⑤ *Rooms from: $209* ⊠ *6400 Moonstone Beach Dr.* ☎ *805/927–1400, 800/425–4121* ⊕ *www.fogcatcherinn.com* ⇱ *60 rooms* ⑪ *Breakfast.*

J. Patrick House

$$$ | **B&B/INN** | Monterey pines and flower gardens surround this Irish-theme inn, which sits on a hilltop above Cambria's East Village. **Pros:** fantastic breakfasts; friendly innkeepers; quiet neighborhood. **Cons:** few rooms; fills up quickly; not pet- or kid-friendly. ⑤ *Rooms from: $195* ⊠ *2990 Burton Dr.* ☎ *805/927–3812* ⊕ *jpatrickhouse.com* ⇱ *7 rooms* ⑪ *Breakfast.*

Moonstone Landing

$$$ | HOTEL | This up-to-date motel's amenities, reasonable rates, and accommodating staff make it a Moonstone Beach winner. **Pros:** sleek furnishings; across from the beach; cheery lounge. **Cons:** narrow property; some rooms overlook a parking lot. $ *Rooms from: $189* ⊠ *6240 Moonstone Beach Dr.* ☎ *805/927–0012, 800/830–4540* ⊕ *www.moonstonelanding.com* ⇄ *29 rooms* ⦿ *Breakfast.*

★ Olallieberry Inn

$$$ | B&B/INN | The second-oldest home in Cambria (built in 1875) and a national historic monument, this painstakingly restored bed-and-breakfast inn offers luxurious creature comforts in a pristine English garden setting on the banks of Santa Rosa Creek. **Pros:** gourmet three-course breakfast; wine hour with homemade appetizers; walk to East Village restaurants and shops. **Cons:** no elevator; no children under 12; some rooms front busy road. $ *Rooms from: $225* ⊠ *2476 Main St.* ☎ *805/927–3222* ⊕ *www.olallieberry.com* ⇄ *9 rooms* ⦿ *Free Breakfast.*

San Simeon

9 miles north of Cambria, 65 miles south of Big Sur.

Whalers founded San Simeon in the 1850s, but had virtually abandoned it by 1865, when Senator George Hearst began purchasing most of the surrounding ranch land. Hearst turned San Simeon into a bustling port, and his son, William Randolph Hearst, further developed the area while erecting Hearst Castle (one of the many remarkable stops you'll encounter when driving along Highway 1). Today San Simeon is basically a strip of unremarkable gift shops and so-so motels that straddle Highway 1 about 4 miles south of the castle's entrance, but **Old San Simeon,** right across from the entrance, is worth a peek. Julia Morgan, William Randolph Hearst's architect, designed some of the village's Mission Revival–style buildings.

GETTING HERE AND AROUND

Highway 1 is the only way to reach San Simeon. Connect with the highway off U.S. 101 directly or via rural routes such as Highway 41 West (Atascadero to Morro Bay) and Highway 46 West (Paso Robles to Cambria).

San Simeon Chamber of Commerce Visitor Center

⊠ *250 San Simeon Ave.* ☎ *805/927–3500* ⊕ *www.visitsansimeonca.com.*

Sights

★ Hearst Castle

CASTLE/PALACE | Officially known as "Hearst San Simeon State Historical Monument," Hearst Castle sits in solitary splendor atop La Cuesta Encantada (the Enchanted Hill). Its buildings and gardens spread over 127 acres that were the heart of newspaper magnate William Randolph Hearst's 250,000-acre ranch. Hearst commissioned renowned California architect Julia Morgan to design the estate, but he was very much involved with the final product, a blend of Italian, Spanish, and Moorish styles. The 115-room main structure and three huge "cottages" are connected by terraces and staircases and surrounded by pools, gardens, and statuary. In its heyday the castle, whose buildings hold about 22,000 works of fine and decorative art, was a playground for Hearst and his guests—Hollywood celebrities, political leaders, scientists, and other well-known figures. Construction began in 1919 and was never officially completed. Work was halted in 1947 when Hearst had to leave San Simeon because of failing health. The Hearst Corporation donated the property to the State of California in 1958, and it is now part of the state park system.

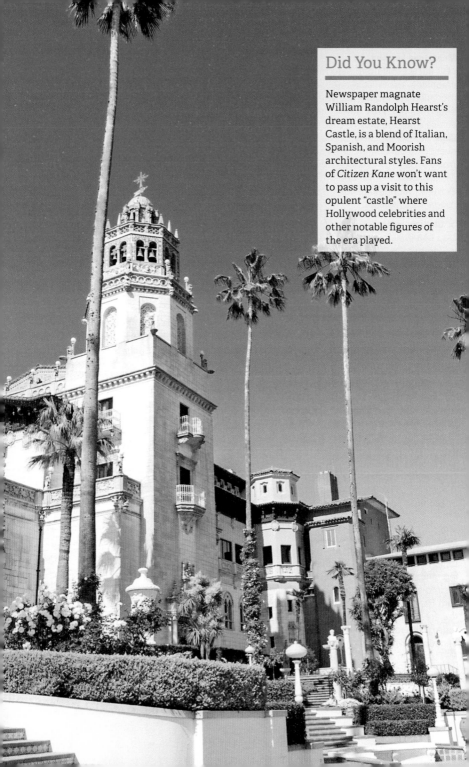

Access to the castle is through the visitor center at the foot of the hill, where you can view educational exhibits and a 40-minute film about Hearst's life and the castle's construction. Buses from the center zigzag up to the hilltop estate, where guides conduct four daytime tours, each with a different focus: Grand Rooms, Upstairs Suites, Designing the Dream, and Cottages and Kitchen. These tours take about three hours and include a movie screening, and time at the end to explore the castle's exterior and gardens. In spring and fall, docents in period costume portray Hearst's guests and staff for the Evening Tour, which begins around sunset. Reservations are recommended for all tours, which include a ½-mile walk and between 150 and 400 stairs. ⊠ *San Simeon State Park, 750 Hearst Castle Rd.* ☎ *800/444–4445, 518/218–5078 international reservations* ⊕ *www.hearstcastle.org* ✉ *Daytime tours from $25, evening tours $36.*

Hearst Ranch Winery

WINERY/DISTILLERY | Old whaling equipment and Hearst Ranch and Hearst Castle memorabilia decorate this winery's casual Old San Simeon outpost. The tasting room occupies part of Sebastian's, a former whaling store built in 1852 and moved by oxen to its present location in 1878. The flagship wines include a Bordeaux-style red blend with Petite Sirah added to round out the flavor, and Rhône-style white and red blends. Malbec and Tempranillo are two other strong suits. ■**TIP→ Templeton chef Ian McPhee serves burgers and other lunch items at the adjacent deli, whose outdoor patio is a delight in good weather.** ⊠ *442 SLO San Simeon Rd., off Hwy. 1* ☎ *805/927–4100* ⊕ *www.hearstranchwinery.com* ✉ *Tastings from $10.*

Piedras Blancas Elephant Seal Rookery

NATURE PRESERVE | FAMILY | A large colony of elephant seals (at last count 25,000) gathers every year at Piedras Blancas Elephant Seal Rookery, on the beaches near Piedras Blancas Lighthouse. The huge males with their pendulous, trunklike noses typically start appearing on shore in late November, and the females begin to arrive in December to give birth—most babies are born in the last two weeks of January. The newborn pups spend about four weeks nursing before their mothers head out to sea, leaving them on their own; the "weaners" leave the rookery when they are about 3½ months old. The seals return in the spring and summer months to molt or rest, but not en masse as in winter. You can watch them from a boardwalk along the bluffs just a few feet above the beach; do not attempt to approach them as they are wild animals. The nonprofit Friends of the Elephant Seal runs a small visitor center and gift shop (*250 San Simeon Ave.*) in San Simeon. ⊠ *Off Hwy. 1, 4½ miles north of Hearst Castle, just south of Piedras Blancas Lighthouse* ☎ *805/924–1628* ⊕ *www.elephantseal.org.*

Piedras Blancas Light Station

TOUR—SIGHT | If you think traversing craggy, twisting Highway 1 is tough, imagine trying to navigate a boat up the rocky coastline (*piedras blancas* means "white rocks" in Spanish) near San Simeon before lighthouses were built. Captains must have cheered wildly when the beam began to shine here in 1875. Try to time a visit to include a morning tour (reservations not required). Tours are at 9:45 am on Tuesday, Thursday, and Saturday year-round (except for on major holidays). ■**TIP→ Do not meet your guide at the gate to the lighthouse—you'll miss the tour. Meet instead at the former Piedras Blancas Motel, 1½ miles north of the light station.** ⊠ *San Simeon* ☎ *805/927–7361* ⊕ *www.piedrasblancas.org* ✉ *$10* ☞ *No pets allowed.*

Did You Know?

McWay Cove at Julia Pfeiffer Burns State Park is one of the most famous spots on the Big Sur Coast.

Beaches

William Randolph Hearst Memorial Beach
BEACH—SIGHT | This wide, sandy beach edges a protected cove on both sides of San Simeon Pier. Fish from the pier or from a charter boat, picnic and barbecue on the bluffs, or boogie board or bodysurf the relatively gentle waves. In summer you can rent a kayak and paddle out into the bay for close encounters with marine life and sea caves. The NOAA Coastal Discovery Center, next to the parking lot, has interactive exhibits and hosts educational activities and events. **Amenities:** food and drink; parking; toilets; water sports. **Best for:** sunset; swimming; walking. ⊠ *750 Hearst Castle Rd., off Hwy. 1, west of Hearst Castle entrance* ☎ *805/927–2020, 805/927–6575 Coastal Discovery Center* ⊕ *www.parks.ca.gov/?page_id=589* ☞ *Free.*

Hotels

Cavalier Oceanfront Resort
$$$ | HOTEL | Reasonable rates, an oceanfront location, evening bonfires, and well-equipped rooms—some with wood-burning fireplaces and private patios—make this motel a great choice. **Pros:** on the bluffs; fantastic views; close to Hearst Castle. **Cons:** room amenities and sizes vary; pools are small and sometimes crowded; some rooms need updating. ⑤ *Rooms from: $229* ⊠ *9415 Hearst Dr.* ☎ *805/927–4688, 800/826–8168* ⊕ *www.cavalierresort.com* ☞ *90 rooms* ⑩ *No meals.*

The Morgan San Simeon
$$ | HOTEL | On Highway 1's ocean side, the Morgan offers motel-style rooming options in two buildings designed to reflect the life and style of Hearst Castle architect, Julia Morgan. **Pros:** fascinating artwork; easy access to Hearst Castle; some ocean views. **Cons:** not right on beach; no fitness room or laundry facilities. ⑤ *Rooms from: $149* ⊠ *9135 Hearst*

Dr. ☎ *805/927–3878, 800/451–9900* ⊕ *www.hotel-morgan.com* ☞ *55 rooms* ⑩ *Breakfast.*

Southern Big Sur

Hwy. 1 from San Simeon to Julia Pfeiffer Burns State Park.

This especially rugged stretch of oceanfront is a rocky world of mountains, cliffs, and beaches.

GETTING HERE AND AROUND

Highway 1 is the only major access route from north or south. From the south, access Highway 1 from U.S. 101 in San Luis Obispo. From the north, take rural route Highway 46 West (Paso Robles to Cambria) or Highway 41 West (Atascadero to Morro Bay). Nacimiento-Fergusson Road snakes through mountains and forest from U.S. 101 at Jolon about 25 miles to Highway 1 at Kirk Creek, about 4 miles south of Lucia; this curving, at times precipitous road is a motorcyclist favorite, not recommended for the faint of heart or during inclement weather.

Sights

★ **Highway 1**
SCENIC DRIVE | One of California's most spectacular drives, Highway 1 snakes up the coast north of San Simeon. Numerous pullouts along the way offer tremendous views and photo ops. On some of the beaches huge elephant seals lounge nonchalantly, seemingly oblivious to the attention of rubberneckers. Heavy rain sometimes causes mudslides that block the highway north and south of Big Sur. ⚠ **Sections of Highway 1 are sometimes closed for general maintenance or to repair damage from natural incidents such as mudslides. It's wise to visit bigsurcalifornia.org and click on the Highway 1 Conditions and Information link for the latest news before you travel.** ⊕ *www.dot.ca.gov.*

Jade Cove

NATURE SITE | In Los Padres National Forest just north of the town of Gorda is Jade Cove, a well-known jade-hunting spot. Rock hunting is allowed on the beach, but you may not remove anything from the walls of the cliffs. ⊠ *Hwy. 1, 34 miles north of San Simeon.*

Julia Pfeiffer Burns State Park

NATIONAL/STATE PARK | The park provides fine hiking, from an easy ½-mile stroll with marvelous coastal views to a strenuous 6-mile trek through redwoods. The big draw here, an 80-foot waterfall that drops into the ocean, gets crowded in summer; still, it's an astounding place to contemplate nature. Migrating whales, harbor seals, and sea lions can sometimes be spotted just offshore. ⊠ *Hwy. 1, 15 miles north of Lucia* ☎ *831/667– 2315* ⊕ *www.parks.ca.gov* ⊠ *$10.*

 Hotels

Ragged Point Inn

$$$ | **HOTEL** | At this cliff-top resort— the only inn and restaurant for miles around—glass walls in most rooms open to awesome ocean views. **Pros:** on the cliffs; good burgers and locally made ice cream; idyllic views. **Cons:** busy road stop during the day; often booked for weekend weddings; spotty cell phone service. ⑤ *Rooms from: $219* ⊠ *19019 Hwy. 1, 20 miles north of San Simeon, Ragged Point* ☎ *805/927–4502, 805/927–5708 restaurant, 888/584–6374* ⊕ *www.raggedpointinn.com* ⊅ *39 rooms* ⑩ *No meals.*

Treebones Resort

$$$$ | **RESORT** | Perched on a hilltop surrounded by national forest and stunning, unobstructed ocean views, this yurt resort provides a stellar back-to-nature experience along with creature comforts. **Pros:** luxury yurts with cozy beds; lodge with fireplace and games; local food at Wild Coast Restaurant and decked sushi bar. **Cons:** steep paths; no private bathrooms; not good for families with young children. ⑤ *Rooms from: $370* ⊠ *71895 Hwy. 1, Willow Creek Rd., 32 miles north of San Simeon, 1 mile north of Gorda* ☎ *805/927–2390, 877/424–4787* ⊕ *www.treebonesresort. com* ⊅ *16 yurts, 1 autonomous tent, 5 campsites, 1 human nest w/campsite* ⑩ *Breakfast* ⊃ *2-night minimum.*

Central Big Sur

Hwy. 1, from Partington Cove to Bixby Bridge.

The countercultural spirit of Big Sur— which instead of a conventional town is a loose string of coast-hugging properties along Highway 1—is alive and well today. Its few residents include the very wealthy, the enthusiastically outdoorsy, and the thoroughly evolved: since the 1960s the Esalen Institute, a center for alternative education and East–West philosophical study, has attracted seekers of higher consciousness and devotees of the property's hot springs. Today posh and rustic resorts hidden among the redwoods cater to visitors drawn from near and far by the extraordinary scenery and serene isolation.

GETTING HERE AND AROUND

From the north, follow Highway 1 south from Carmel. From the south, continue the drive north from Julia Pfeiffer Burns State Park on Highway 1. Monterey-Salinas Transit operates the Line 22 Big Sur bus from Monterey and Carmel to Central Big Sur (the last stop is Nepenthe), daily from late May to early September and weekends only the rest of the year.

BUS CONTACT Monterey-Salinas Transit.
☎ *888/678–2871* ⊕ *www.mst.org.*

Sights

Bixby Creek Bridge

BRIDGE/TUNNEL | The graceful arc of Bixby Creek Bridge is a photographer's dream. Built in 1932, the bridge spans a deep canyon, more than 100 feet wide at the bottom. From the north-side parking area you can admire the view or walk the 550-foot structure. ☒ *Hwy. 1, 6 miles north of Point Sur State Historic Park, 13 miles south of Carmel, Big Sur.*

Pfeiffer Big Sur State Park

NATIONAL/STATE PARK | Among the many hiking trails at Pfeiffer Big Sur, a short route through a redwood-filled valley leads to a waterfall. You can double back or continue on the more difficult trail along the valley wall for views over miles of treetops to the sea. ☒ *47231 Hwy. 1, Big Sur* ☎ *831/667–2315* ⊕ *www.parks. ca.gov* ☒ *$10 per vehicle.*

★ Pfeiffer Canyon Bridge

BRIDGE/TUNNEL | In February 2017, heavy winter rains caused an old concrete bridge built in 1968 to crack and slip downhill at Pfeiffer Canyon, in the heart of Big Sur. Engineers deemed the old bridge irreparable, and auto and pedestrian access to Highway 1 south of the bridge was cut off indefinitely. CalTrans quickly made plans to construct a new, $24-million bridge to span the deep canyon. Normally, such a massive project would take at least seven years, but CalTrans accelerated the project and completed it in less than a year. The new bridge—a 21st-century engineering marvel—stretches 310 feet across the ravine without the need for column support. It's made of 15 steel girders, each weighing 62 tons and connected by steel plates holding 14,000 bolts. ☒ *Hwy. 1, Big Sur* ⊹ *0.7 mile south of Big Sur Station.*

Point Sur State Historic Park

NATIONAL/STATE PARK | An 1889 lighthouse at this state park still stands watch from atop a large volcanic rock. Four lighthouse keepers lived here with their families until 1974, when the light station became automated. Their homes and working spaces are open to the public only on 2½- to 3-hour ranger-led tours. Considerable walking, including up two stairways, is involved. Strollers are not allowed. ☒ *Hwy. 1, 7 miles north of Pfeiffer Big Sur State Park, Big Sur* ☎ *831/625–4419* ⊕ *www.pointsur.org* ☒ *$15* ☞ *Call or visit website for current tour schedule.*

Beaches

Pfeiffer Beach

BEACH—SIGHT | Through a hole in one of the gigantic boulders at secluded Pfeiffer Beach, you can watch the waves break first on the seaside and then on the beach side. Keep a sharp eye out for the unsigned, nongated road to the beach: it branches west of Highway 1 between the post office and Pfeiffer Big Sur State Park. The 2-mile, one-lane road descends sharply. **Amenities:** parking (fee); toilets. **Best for:** solitude; sunset. ☒ *Off Hwy. 1, 1 mile south of Pfeiffer Big Sur State Park, Big Sur* ☒ *$10 per vehicle.*

Restaurants

★ Deetjen's Big Sur Inn

$$$ | **AMERICAN** | The candle-lighted, creaky-floor restaurant in the main house at the historic inn of the same name is a Big Sur institution. It serves spicy seafood paella, grass-fed filet mignon, and rack of lamb for dinner and flavorful eggs Benedict for breakfast. **Known for:** rustic, romantic setting; ingredients from sustainable purveyors; stellar weekend breakfast. ⓢ *Average main: $30* ☒ *Hwy. 1, 3½ miles south of Pfeiffer Big Sur State Park, Big Sur* ☎ *831/667–2378* ⊕ *www.deetjens.com* ☾ *No lunch.*

★ Nepenthe

$$$$ | **AMERICAN** | It may be that no other restaurant between San Francisco and Los Angeles has a better coastal view than Nepenthe, named for an opiate mentioned in Greek literature that would induce a state of "no sorrow." For the real show, settle on the terraced deck in the late afternoon, order a glass from the extensive wine list, and watch the sun slip into the Pacific Ocean. **Known for:** ambrosia burger, fresh fish, hormone-free steaks; multiple view decks; brunch and lunch at casual outdoor Café Kevah. $ *Average main: $32 ⊠ 48510 Hwy. 1, 2½ miles south of Big Sur Station, Big Sur ☎ 831/667–2345 ⊕ nepenthebigsur.com.*

★ Sierra Mar

$$$$ | AMERICAN | At cliff's edge 1,200 feet above the Pacific at the ultrachic Post Ranch Inn, Sierra Mar serves cutting-edge American cuisine made from mostly organic, seasonal ingredients, some from the on-site chef's garden. The four-course prix-fixe option always shines, and the six-course tasting menu centers on ingredients grown or foraged on the property or sourced locally. **Known for:** stunning panoramic ocean views; one of the nation's most extensive wine lists; iconic Big Sur farm-to-table experience. $ *Average main: $125 ⊠ Hwy. 1, 1½ miles south of Pfeiffer Big Sur State Park, Big Sur ☎ 831/667–2800 ⊕ www.postranchinn.com/dining.*

★ The Sur House

$$$$ | AMERICAN | The Ventana Inn's restaurant sits high on a ridge, and magnificent terraces offer stunning ocean views and a full-service outdoor bar. Regional and international wines on a comprehensive list pair well with the California-inspired dishes, many of whose ingredients are sourced from local purveyors, and the bar serves seasonal specialty cocktails and California craft beers. **Known for:** stunning views; Pacific-sourced seafood and free-range meats and produce from local purveyors; excellent wine list. $ *Average main: $40 ⊠ 48123 Hwy. 1, 1½ miles south of Pfeiffer Big Sur State Park, Big Sur ☎ 831/667–2331 ⊕ www.ventanainn.com.*

Hotels

Big Sur Lodge

$$$$ | HOTEL | The lodge's modern, motel-style cottages with Mission-style furnishings and vaulted ceilings sit in a meadow surrounded by redwood trees and flowering shrubbery. **Pros:** secluded setting near trailheads; good camping alternative; rates include state parks pass. **Cons:** basic rooms; walk to main lodge; thin common walls in some units. $ *Rooms from: $279 ⊠ Pfeiffer Big Sur State Park, 47225 Hwy. 1, Big Sur ☎ 831/667–3100, 855/238–6950 reservations ⊕ www.bigsurlodge.com* ⌇ 62 rooms |○| No meals.

Big Sur River Inn

$$$$ | B&B/INN | During summer at this rustic property you can sip drinks beside— or in—the Big Sur River fronted by the inn's wooded grounds; if you're here on a Sunday afternoon between May and September you can enjoy live music on the restaurant's deck. **Pros:** riverside setting; next to a restaurant and small market, outdoor pool; recently renovated baths. **Cons:** standard motel rooms across the road; no phone in rooms; fronts busy road. $ *Rooms from: $275 ⊠ Hwy. 1, 2 miles north of Pfeiffer Big Sur State Park, Big Sur ☎ 831/667–2700, 831/667–2743, 800/548–3610 ⊕ www.bigsurriverinn.com* ⌇ 22 rooms |○| No meals.

Deetjen's Big Sur Inn

$$ | B&B/INN | This historic 1930s Norwegian-style property is endearingly rustic, with its village of cabins nestled in the redwoods; many of the very individual rooms have their own fireplaces. **Pros:** tons of character; wooded grounds; excellent food and wine in on-site restaurant. **Cons:** thin walls; some rooms don't have private baths; no TVs or Wi-Fi, limited cell service. $ *Rooms from: $170 ⊠ Hwy. 1, 3½ miles south of Pfeiffer Big Sur State Park, Big Sur ☎ 831/667–2377 ⊕ www.deetjens.com* ⌇ 20 rooms, 15 with bath |○| No meals ⌁ 2-night minimum stay on weekends.

Glen Oaks Big Sur

$$$$ | HOTEL | At this rustic-modern cluster of adobe-and-redwood buildings, you can choose between motel-style rooms, cabins, and cottages in the woods. **Pros:** in the heart of town; natural river-rock radiant-heated tiles; gas fireplaces in each room. **Cons:** near busy road and parking lot; no TVs; some cabins tiny. $ *Rooms from: $300* ⊠ *Hwy. 1, 1 mile north of Pfeiffer Big Sur State Park, Big Sur* ☎ *831/667–2105* ⊕ *www.glenoaksbigsur.com* ⌁ *16 rooms, 2 cottages, 10 cabins, 1 house* ❉❉ *No meals.*

★ Post Ranch Inn

$$$$ | RESORT | This luxurious retreat is perfect for getaways; the redwood guesthouses, all of which have views of the sea or the mountains, blend almost invisibly into a wooded cliff 1,200 feet above the ocean. **Pros:** units come with fireplaces and private decks; on-site activities like yoga and stargazing; gorgeous property with hiking trails and spectacular views. **Cons:** expensive; austere design; not a good choice if you're afraid of heights. $ *Rooms from: $995* ⊠ *Hwy. 1, 1½ miles south of Pfeiffer Big Sur State Park, Big Sur* ☎ *831/667–2200, 800/527–2200* ⊕ *www.postranchinn.com* ⌁ *39 rooms, 2 houses* ❉❉ *Breakfast.*

★ Ventana

$$$$ | HOTEL | Hundreds of celebrities, from Oprah Winfrey to Sir Anthony Hopkins, have escaped to Ventana, a romantic resort on 160 tranquil acres 1,200 feet above the Pacific. **Pros:** secluded; nature trails everywhere; rates include daily guided hike, yoga, wine and cheese hour. **Cons:** expensive; some rooms lack an ocean view; not family-friendly. $ *Rooms from: $750* ⊠ *Hwy. 1, almost 1 mile south of Pfeiffer Big Sur State Park, Big Sur* ☎ *831/667–2331, 800/628–6500* ⊕ *www.ventanainn.com* ⌁ *59 rooms, 15 tent cabins* ❉❉ *No meals.*

Chapter 12

DEATH VALLEY
NATIONAL PARK

Updated by
Deb Hopewell

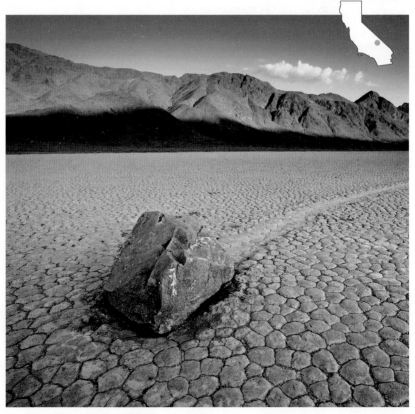

⊙ Sights   🍽 Restaurants   🛏 Hotels   🛍 Shopping   🍸 Nightlife

★★★★★   ★★★★☆   ★★★★★   ★☆☆☆☆   ★☆☆☆☆

WELCOME TO
DEATH VALLEY NATIONAL PARK

TOP REASONS TO GO

★ **Roving rocks:** Death Valley's Racetrack is home to moving boulders, an unexplained phenomenon that has scientists baffled.

★ **Lowest spot on the continent:** Stand on the lowest spot on the continent at Badwater, 282 feet below sea level.

★ **Wildflower explosion:** During the spring, this desert landscape is ablaze with greenery and colorful flowers, especially between Badwater and Ashford Mill.

★ **Ghost towns:** Death Valley is renowned for its Wild West heritage and is home to dozens of crumbling settlements including Ballarat, Cerro Gordo, Chloride City, Greenwater, Harrisburg, Keeler, Leadfield, Panamint City, Rhyolite, and Skidoo.

★ **Naturally amazing:** From canyons to sand dunes to salt flats and dry lake beds, Death Valley serves up plenty of geological treasures.

1 **Central Death Valley.** Furnace Creek sits in the heart of Death Valley—if you have only a short time in the park, head here. You can visit gorgeous Golden Canyon, Zabriskie Point, the Salt Creek Interpretive Trail, and Artist's Drive, among other popular points of interest.

2 **Northern Death Valley.** This region is uphill from Furnace Creek, which means marginally cooler temperatures. Be sure to stop by Rhyolite Ghost Town on Highway 374 before entering the park and exploring colorful Titus Canyon, and jaw-dropping Ubehebe Crater.

3 **Southern Death Valley.** This is a desolate area, but there are plenty of sights that help convey Death Valley's rich history. Don't miss the Dublin Gulch Caves.

4 **Western Death Valley.** Panamint Springs Resort is a nice place to grab a meal and get your bearings before moving on to quaint Darwin Falls, smooth rolling sand dunes, beehive-shaped Wildrose Charcoal Kilns, and historic Stovepipe Wells Village.

The natural riches of Death Valley—the largest national park outside Alaska—are overwhelming: rolling waves of sand dunes, black cinder cones thrusting up hundreds of feet from a blistered desert floor, riotous sheets of wildflowers, bizarrely shaped Joshua trees basking in the orange glow of a sunset, tiny pupfish, and a dramatic silence.

Planning

When to Go

Most of the park's one million annual visitors come between late fall and early spring, taking advantage of moderate temperatures and the lack of rainfall. During these cooler months you will need to book a room in advance, but don't worry: the park never feels crowded. If you visit in summer, believe everything you've ever heard about desert heat—it can be brutal, with temperatures often topping 120°F. The dry air wicks moisture from the body without causing a sweat, so drink plenty of water. Bring sunglasses, a hat, and sufficient clothing to block the sun's rays and the wind. Flash floods are fairly common; sections of roadway can be flooded or washed away, as they were after a major flood in 2015. The wettest month is February, when the park receives an average of 0.3 inches of rain.

Festivals and Events

Bishop Mule Days

FESTIVAL | Entertainment at this five-day festival over the Memorial Day weekend includes top country-music stars, an arts-and-crafts fair, barbecues, country dances, the longest-running nonmotorized parade in the United States, and more than 700 mules competing in 181 events. Admission is free. ✉ *1141 N. Main St., Bishop* ☎ *760/872–4263* ⊕ *www.muledays.org.*

Death Valley Chamber of Commerce Art Show

FESTIVAL | Admission is free for this arts-and-crafts show and sale weekend, held on the lawn of The Ranch at Death Valley (formerly Ranch at Furnace Creek). ✉ *The Ranch at Death Valley, Greenland Ranch Rd., Death Valley* ☎ *760/852–4420* ⊕ *www.deathvalleychamber.org.*

Death Valley 49er Encampment Days

FESTIVAL | FAMILY | Originally a centennial celebration held in 1949 to honor the area's first European visitors, this five-day event draws thousands of people from around the world to the Ranch at Death

AVERAGE HIGH/LOW TEMPERATURES					
JAN.	FEB.	MAR.	APR.	MAY	JUNE
65/39	72/46	80/53	90/62	99/71	109/80
JULY	AUG.	SEPT.	OCT.	NOV.	DEC.
115/88	113/85	106/75	92/62	76/48	65/39

Valley for art shows, a wagon train, live music, artisan booths, dancing, and even a poker tournament. ⊠ *Ranch at Death Valley, Greenland Ranch Rd., Death Valley* ⊕ *www.deathvalley49ers.org.*

Lone Pine Film Festival

FESTIVAL | Every Columbus Day weekend, this town pays tribute to its Hollywood history with three days of tours, films, lectures, and celebrity panels. ⊠ *701 S. Main St., Lone Pine* ☎ *760/876–9103* ⊕ *www.lonepinefilmfestival.org.*

Shoshone Old West Days

FESTIVAL | Just outside of Death Valley, this annual three-day festival celebrates Wild West heritage with live performances, arts-and-crafts, and deep-pit barbecue. ⊠ *Shoshone* ☎ *760/852–4335* ⊕ *www.shoshonevillage.com.*

Planning Your Time

DEATH VALLEY IN ONE DAY

If you begin the day in Furnace Creek, you can see several sights without doing much driving. Bring plenty of water with you, and some food, too. Get up early and drive the 20 miles on Badwater Road to **Badwater,** which looks out on the lowest point in the Western Hemisphere and is a dramatic place to watch the sunrise. Returning north, stop at **Natural Bridge,** a medium-size conglomerate rock formation that has been hollowed at its base to form a span across the canyon, and then at the **Devil's Golf Course,** so named because of the large pinnacles of salt present here. Detour to the right onto **Artist's Drive,** a 9-mile one-way, northbound route that passes **Artist's Palette.** The reds, yellows, oranges, and

greens come from minerals in the rocks and the earth. Four miles north of Artist's Drive you will come to the **Golden Canyon Interpretive Trail,** a 2-mile round-trip that winds through a canyon with colorful rock walls. Just before Furnace Creek, take Highway 190 3 miles east to **Zabriskie Point,** overlooking dramatic, furrowed red-brown hills and the **Twenty Mule Team Canyon.** Return to Furnace Creek, where you can grab a meal and visit the museum at the Furnace Creek Visitor Center. Heading north from Furnace Creek, pull off the highway and take a look at the **Harmony Borax Works.**

Getting Here and Around

AIR TRAVEL

The closest airport to the park with commercial service, Las Vegas McCarren International Airport, is 130 miles away, so you'll still need to drive a couple of hours to reach the park. Roughly 160 miles to the west, Burbank's Bob Hope Airport is the second-closest airport.

CAR TRAVEL

It can take more than three hours to cross from one side of the park to another, so it's important to choose an entrance point that makes sense for what you want to see. If you're driving from Los Angeles, enter through the western portion along Highway 395; if you're coming from Las Vegas, enter from the north at Beatty, Nevada, or via the central entrance at Death Valley Junction. Travelers from Orange County, San Diego, and the Inland Empire should access the park via Interstate 15 North at Baker.

Distances can be deceiving within the park: what seems close can be very far away. Much of the park can be viewed on regularly scheduled bus tours, but these often don't allow time for hikes to sites not seen from the road, such as Salt Creek, Golden Canyon, and Natural Bridge. The best option is to drive to a number of the sites, get out of the car, and walk.

When driving in Death Valley, reliable maps are important, as signage is often limited or, in a few places, nonexistent. Bring a phone but don't rely on cell coverage exclusively in every remote area, and pack plenty of food and water (3 gallons per person per day is recommended). Cars, especially in summer, should be prepared for the hot, dry weather, too. Some of the park's most spectacular canyons are only accessible via four-wheel-drive vehicles but if this is the way you want to travel, make sure the trip is well planned and use a backcountry map. Be aware of possible winter closures or driving restrictions because of snow. The National Park Service's website (⊕ nps.gov/deva) stays up-to-date on road closures during the wet (and popular) months. ⚠ **One of the park's signature landmarks, Scotty's Castle, and the 8-mile road connecting it to the park border may be closed until 2020 due to damage from a 2015 flood.**

DRIVING INFORMATION California Highway Patrol. ☎ *800/427–7623 recorded info from CalTrans, 760/872–5900 live dispatcher at Bishop Communications Center* ⊕ *www.chp.ca.gov*. **California State Department of Transportation Hotline.** ☎ *800/427–7623* ⊕ *www.dot.ca.gov*

Park Essentials

ACCESSIBILITY

All of Death Valley's visitor centers, contact stations, and museums are accessible to all visitors. The campgrounds at Furnace Creek, Sunset, and Stovepipe Wells have wheelchair-accessible sites. Highway 190, Badwater Road, and paved roads to Dante's View and Wildrose provide access to the major scenic viewpoints and historic points of interest.

PARK FEES AND PERMITS

The entrance fee is $30 per vehicle, $25 for motorcycles, and $15 for those entering on foot or bike. The payment, valid for seven consecutive days, is collected at the park's ranger stations, self-serve fee stations, and the visitor center at Furnace Creek. Annual park passes, valid only at Death Valley, are $55.

A permit is not required for groups of 14 or fewer, but if you're planning an overnight visit to the backcountry, complete a registration form at the Furnace Creek Visitor Center. Backcountry camping is allowed in areas that are at least 2 miles from maintained campgrounds and the main paved or unpaved roads and ¼ mile from water sources. Most abandoned mining areas are restricted to day use.

PARK HOURS

The park is open year-round, and can be visited day or night. Most facilities within the park remain open year-round, daily 8–6.

CELL PHONE RECEPTION

Results vary, but in general you should be able to get fairly good cell phone reception on the valley floor. In the surrounding mountains, however, don't count on it.

Educational Offerings

RANGER PROGRAMS

Junior Ranger Program
TOUR—SIGHT | FAMILY | Children can join this program at the Furnace Creek Visitor Center, where they can pick up a workbook and complete activities to earn a souvenir badge. ✉ *Death Valley National Park*.

Restaurants

Inside the park, if you're looking for a special evening out in Death Valley, head to the Inn at Death Valley Dining Room, where you'll be spoiled with fine wines and juicy steaks. It's also a great spot to start the day with a hearty gourmet breakfast. Most other eateries within the park are mom-and-pop-type places with basic American fare. Outside the park, dining choices are much the same, with little cafés and homey diners serving up coffee shop–style burgers, chicken, and steaks. If you're vegetarian or vegan, BYOB (bring your own beans). *Restaurant reviews have been shortened. For full information, visit Fodors.com.*

Hotels

It's difficult to find lodging anywhere in Death Valley that doesn't have breathtaking views of the park and surrounding mountains. Most accommodations, aside from the Inn at Death Valley, are homey and rustic. Rooms fill up quickly during the fall and spring seasons, and reservations are required about three months in advance for the prime weekends.

Outside the park, head to Beatty or Amargosa Valley in Nevada for a bit of nightlife and casino action. The western side of Death Valley, along the eastern Sierra Nevada, is a gorgeous setting, though it's quite a distance from Furnace Creek. Here, you can stay in the historic Dow Villa Motel, where John Wayne spent many a night, or head farther south to the ghost towns of Randsburg or Cerro Gordo for a true Wild West experience. *Hotel reviews have been shortened. For full information, visit Fodors.com.*

What It Costs

	$	$$	$$$	$$$$
RESTAURANTS				
	under $12	$12–$20	$21–$30	over $30
HOTELS				
	under $100	$100–$150	$151–$200	over $200

Tours

Death Valley Adventure Tour (*Adventure Motorcycle [AdMo] Tours*)

TOUR—SIGHT | Motorcycle enthusiasts can sign up for a guided Death Valley Adventure Tour that starts and ends in Las Vegas. The five-day tour through Death Valley covers 800 miles. The tours, which run October through May, include hotel accommodations, gasoline, breakfasts, two dinners, snacks, a support vehicle, and a professional guide. To join, you'll need a motorcycle driver's license and experience with off-road and all-terrain riding. ⊠ *Death Valley* ☎ *760/249–1105* ⊕ *www.admotours.com* 🖃 *From $3568.*

Furnace Creek Visitor Center programs

GUIDED TOURS | This center has many programs, including ranger-led hikes that explore natural wonders such as Golden Canyon, nighttime stargazing parties with telescopes, and evening ranger talks. Visit the website for a complete list. ⊠ *Furnace Creek Visitor Center, Rte. 190, 30 miles northwest of Death Valley Junction, Death Valley* ☎ *760/786–2331* ⊕ *www.nps.gov/deva/planyourvisit/tours. htm* 🖃 *Free.*

Pink Jeep Tours Las Vegas

GUIDED TOURS | A 10-passenger luxury vehicle with oversized viewing windows will pick you up at most Strip hotels for visits to landmarks such as Dante's View, Furnace Creek, Devil's Golf Course, Badwater Basin, and Artist's Palette. The tours run from about 7 am to 4 pm from September through May, are professionally narrated, and include lunch and bottled water. ✉ *3629 W. Hacienda Ave., Las Vegas* ☎ *888/900–4480* ⊕ *pinkjeeptourslasvegas.com* 🎫 *From $275.*

Visitor Information

MAPS AND INFO

The Death Valley Natural History Association sells a variety of books on the area and publishes a pamphlet outlining a self-guided tour of Golden Canyon, which is available from the association or the bookstore at the visitor center. The association also sells a waterproof, tear-proof topographical map of the entire park. Additional topo maps covering select areas are available at the visitor center or from the **Death Valley Natural History Association** (☎ *760/786–2146 or 800/478–8564* ⊕ *www.dvnha.org*).

PARK CONTACT INFORMATION Death Valley National Park. ☎ *760/786–3200* ⊕ *www.nps.gov/deva.*

VISITOR CENTERS

⚠ **The popular visitor center at Scotty's Castle is closed until at least 2020 as a result of a major flash flood in 2015 that damaged the structure and destroyed the access road.**

Furnace Creek Visitor Center and Museum
INFO CENTER | The exhibits and artifacts here provide a broad overview of how Death Valley formed; you can pick up maps at the bookstore run by the Death Valley Natural History Association. This is also the place to sign up for ranger-led walks (available November through April) or check out a live presentation about the valley's cultural and natural history. The helpful center offers regular showings of a 20-minute film about the park and children can get their free Junior Ranger booklet here, packed with games and information about the park and its critters. ✉ *Hwy. 190, Death Valley* ✛ *30 miles northwest of Death Valley Junction* ☎ *760/786–3200* ⊕ *www.nps.gov/deva.*

 Sights

SCENIC DRIVE
Artist's Drive
SCENIC DRIVE | This 9-mile, one-way route skirts the foothills of the Black Mountains and provides intimate views of the changing landscape. Once inside the palette, the huge expanses of the valley are replaced by the small-scale natural beauty of pigments created by volcanic deposits or sedimentary layers. It's a quiet, lonely drive, and shouldn't be rushed. Reach Artist's Palette by heading south on Badwater Road from its intersection with Route 190. ✉ *Death Valley National Park.*

HISTORIC SITES
Charcoal Kilns
MINE | Ten well-preserved stone kilns, each 25 feet high and 30 feet wide, stand as if on parade. The kilns, built by Chinese laborers for a mining company in 1877, were used to burn wood from pinyon pines to turn it into charcoal. The charcoal was then transported over the mountains into Death Valley, where it was used to extract lead and silver from the ore mined there. If you hike nearby Wildrose Peak, you will be rewarded with terrific views of the kilns. ✉ *Wildrose Canyon Rd., Death Valley* ✛ *37 miles south of Stovepipe Wells.*

Harmony Borax Works
HISTORIC SITE | Death Valley's mule teams hauled borax from here to the railroad town of Mojave, 165 miles away. The teams plied the route until 1889, when the railroad finally arrived in Zabriskie. Constructed in 1883, one of the oldest buildings in Death Valley houses the Borax Museum, 2 miles south of the borax works at the Ranch at Death Valley (between the restaurants and the post office). Originally a miners' bunkhouse, the building once stood in Twenty Mule Team Canyon. Now it displays mining machinery and historical exhibits. The adjacent structure is the original

Plants and Wildlife in Death Valley

There's a general misconception that Death Valley National Park consists of mile upon endless mile of flat desert sands, scattered cacti, and an occasional cow skull. Many people don't realize that across the valley floor from Badwater—the lowest point in the Western Hemisphere—Telescope Peak towers at 11,049 feet above sea level. The extreme topography of Death Valley is a lesson in geology. Two hundred million years ago seas covered the area, depositing layers of sediment and fossils. Between 3.5 million and 5 million years ago faults in the Earth's crust and volcanic activity pushed and folded the ground, causing mountain ranges to rise and the valley floor to drop. The valley was then filled periodically by lakes, which eroded the surrounding rocks into fantastic formations and deposited the salts that now cover the floor of the basin.

Most animal life in Death Valley (51 mammal, 36 reptile, 307 bird, and 3 amphibian species) is found near the limited sources of water. The bighorn sheep spend most of their time in the secluded upper reaches of the park's rugged canyons and ridges. Coyotes often can be seen lazing in the shade next to the golf course and have been known to run onto the fairways to steal a golf ball. The only native fish in the park is the pupfish, which grows to slightly longer than one inch. In winter, when the water is cold, the fish lie dormant in the bottom mud, becoming active again in spring. Because they are wary of large moving shapes, you must stand quietly over a pool at Salt Creek to see them.

Botanists say there are more than 1,000 species of plants here (21 exist nowhere else in the world), though many annual plants lie dormant as seeds for all but a few months in spring, when rains trigger a bloom. The rest congregate around the few water sources. Most of the low-elevation vegetation grows around the oases at Furnace Creek and Scotty's Castle, where oleanders, palms, and salt cedar grow. At higher elevations you will find pinyon, juniper, and bristlecone pine.

mule-team barn. ⊠ *Harmony Borax Works Rd., west of Hwy. 190 at Ranch at Death Valley* ⊕ *www.nps.gov/deva/historyculture/harmony.htm.*

SCENIC STOPS

Artist's Palette

NATURE SITE | So called for the contrasting colors of its volcanic deposits and sedimentary layers, this is one of the signature sights of Death Valley. Artist's Drive, the approach to the area, is one-way heading north off Badwater Road, so if you're visiting Badwater from Furnace Creek, come here on the way back. The drive winds through foothills of sedimentary and volcanic rocks. About 4 miles into the drive, a short side road veers right to a parking lot that's a few hundred feet before the "palette," whose natural colors include shades of green, gold, and pink. ⊠ *Off Badwater Rd., Death Valley* ⊹ *11 miles south of Furnace Creek.*

Badwater

SCENIC DRIVE | At 282 feet below sea level, Badwater is the lowest spot of land in North America—and also one of the hottest. Stairs and wheelchair ramps descend from the parking lot to a wooden platform that overlooks a sodium chloride pool, a small but remarkably persistent reminder that the valley floor used to contain a lake. You can continue past the platform on a broad, white path that peters out after a half mile or so. Badwater is one of the most popular and easily accessible sites within the park. From this lowest point, be sure to look across to Telescope Peak, which towers more than 2 miles above the valley floor. ⊠ *Badwater Rd., Death Valley* ⊕ *19 miles south of Furnace Creek.*

★ Dante's View

VIEWPOINT | This lookout is 5,450 feet above sea level in the Black Mountains. In the dry desert air you can see across most of 160-mile-long Death Valley. The view is astounding. Take a 10-minute, mildly strenuous walk from the parking lot toward a series of rocky overlooks, where with binoculars you can spot some of Death Valley's signature sites. A few interpretive signs point out the highlights below in the valley and across, in the Sierra. Getting here from Furnace Creek takes about an hour—time well invested. ⊠ *Dante's View Rd., Death Valley* ⊕ *Off Hwy. 190, 35 miles from Badwater, 20 miles south of Twenty Mule Team Canyon.*

Devil's Golf Course

NATURE SITE | Thousands of miniature salt pinnacles carved into surreal shapes by the desert wind dot this wildly varied landscape. The salt was pushed up to the earth's surface by pressure created as underground salt- and water-bearing gravel crystallized. Get out of your vehicle and take a closer look; you'll see perfectly round holes descending into the ground. ⊠ *Badwater Rd., Death Valley* ⊕ *13 miles south of Furnace Creek. Turn right onto dirt road and drive 1 mile.*

Golden Canyon

NATURE SITE | Just south of Furnace Creek, these glimmering mountains are perhaps best known for their role in the original *Star Wars*. The canyon is also a fine hiking spot, with gorgeous views

of the Panamint Mountains, ancient dry lake beds, and alluvial fans. ⊠ *Hwy. 178, Death Valley* ⊕ *From Furnace Creek Visitor Center, drive 2 miles south on Hwy. 190, then 2 miles south on Hwy. 178 to parking area; the lot has kiosk with trail guides.*

Racetrack

NATURE SITE | Getting here involves a 28-mile journey over a washboard dirt road, but the reward is well worth the trip. Where else in the world do rocks move on their own? This phenomenon has baffled scientists for years and is perhaps one of the last great natural mysteries. The best research on the rocks shows the movement requires a rare confluence of conditions: rain and then cold to create a layer of ice that becomes a sail for gusty winds that push the rocks along—sometimes for several hundred yards. When the mud dries, a telltale trail remains. The trek to the Racetrack can be made in a sedan, but beware—sharp rocks can slash tires; a truck or SUV with thick tires, high clearance, and a spare tire are suggested. ⊠ *Death Valley* ⊕ *27 miles west of Ubehebe Crater via rough dirt road.*

Sand Dunes at Mesquite Flat

NATURE SITE | These dunes, made up of minute pieces of quartz and other rock, are ever-changing products of the wind-rippled hills, with curving crests and a sun-bleached hue. The dunes are the most photographed destination in the park, and you can see them at their best at sunrise and sunset. Keep your eyes open for animal tracks—you may even spot a coyote or fox. Bring plenty of water, and note where you parked your car: It's easy to become disoriented in this ocean of sand. If you lose your bearings, climb to the top of a dune and scan the horizon for the parking lot. ⊠ *Death Valley* ⊕ *19 miles north of Hwy. 190, northeast of Stovepipe Wells Village.*

The Mesquite Flat Sand Dunes.

Stovepipe Wells Village

TOWN | This tiny 1926 town, the first resort in Death Valley, takes its name from the stovepipe that an early prospector left to indicate where he found water. The area contains a motel, restaurant, convenience store, gas station, RV hookups, swimming pool, and landing strip, though first-time park visitors are better off staying in Furnace Creek, which is more central. Off Highway 190, on a 3-mile gravel road immediately southwest, are the multicolor walls of Mosaic Canyon. ⊠ *Hwy. 190, Death Valley* ✛ *2 miles from Sand Dunes, 77 miles east of Lone Pine* ☎ *760/786–2387* ⊕ *www.deathvalleyhotels.com.*

Titus Canyon

SCENIC DRIVE | This popular one-way, 27-mile drive starts at Nevada Highway 374 (Daylight Pass Road), 2 miles from the park's boundary. Along the way you'll see Leadville Ghost Town and finally the spectacular limestone and dolomite narrows. Toward the end, a two-way section of gravel road leads you into the mouth of the canyon from Scotty's Castle Road. This drive is steep, bumpy, and narrow. High-clearance vehicles are strongly recommended. ⊠ *Death Valley National Park* ✛ *Access road off Nevada Hwy. 374, 6 miles west of Beatty, NV.*

Twenty Mule Team Canyon

CANYON | This canyon was named in honor of the 20-mule teams that, between 1883 and 1889, carried 10-ton loads of borax through the burning desert (though they didn't actually pass through this canyon). Along the 2.7-mile, one-way loop road off Highway 190, you'll find the soft rock walls reach high on both sides, making it seem like you're on an amusement-park ride. Remains of prospectors' tunnels are visible here, along with some brilliant rock formations. ⊠ *20 Mule Team Rd.* ✛ *Off Hwy. 190, 4 miles south of Furnace Creek, 20 miles west of Death Valley Junction.*

Ubehebe Crater

VOLCANO | At 500 feet deep and ½ mile across, this crater resulted from underground steam and gas explosions about

3,000 years ago. Volcanic ash spreads out over most of the area, and the cinders lie as deep as 150 feet, near the crater's rim. Trek down to the crater's floor or walk around it on a fairly level path. Either way, you need about an hour and will be treated to fantastic views. The hike from the floor can be strenuous. ⊠ *N. Death Valley Hwy., Death Valley* ✛ *8 miles northwest of Scotty's Castle.*

Zabriskie Point

VIEWPOINT | Although only about 710 feet in elevation, this is one of Death Valley National Park's most scenic spots, overlooking a striking panorama of wrinkled, multicolor hills. It's a great place to watch the sunrise, but it can be bustling any time of day. Pair it with a drive out to magnificent Dante's View. ⊠ *Hwy. 190, Death Valley* ✛ *5 miles south of Furnace Creek.*

 Activities

BICYCLING

Mountain biking is permitted on any of the back roads and roadways open to the public (bikes aren't permitted on hiking trails). Visit ⊕ *www.nps.gov/deva/ planyourvisit/bikingandmtbiking.htm* for a list of suggested routes for all levels of ability. Bicycle Path, a 4-mile round-trip trek from the visitor center to Mustard Canyon, is a good place to start. Bike rentals are available at the Oasis at Death Valley, by the hour or by the day.

Escape Adventures (*Escape Adventures*)
BICYCLING | Ride into the heart of Death Valley on the Death Valley & Red Rock Mountain Bike Tour, a five-day trip through the national park. The customizable two-day journey (on single-track trails and jeep roads) includes accommodations (both camping and inns). Bikes, tents, sleeping bags, helmets, and other gear may be rented for an additional price. Tours are available February–April and October only. ⊠ *Death Valley National Park* 🕿 *800/596–2953, 702/596–2953* ⊕ *www.escapeadventures.com* ⧓ *From $1720.*

BIRD-WATCHING

Approximately 350 bird species have been identified in Death Valley. The best place to see the park's birds is along the Salt Creek Interpretive Trail, where you can spot ravens, common snipes, killdeer, spotted sandpipers, and great blue herons. Along the fairways at Furnace Creek Golf Course, you can see kingfishers, peregrine falcons, hawks, Canada geese, yellow warblers, and the occasional golden eagle. Scotty's Castle, closed until at least 2020, draws wintering birds from around the globe that are attracted to its running water, shady trees, and shrubs. Other good spots to find birds are at Saratoga Springs, Mesquite Springs, Travertine Springs, and Grimshaw Lake near Tecopa.

You can download a complete park bird checklist, divided by season, at ⊕ *www. nps.gov/deva/learn/nature/upload/death-valley-bird-checklist.pdf.* Rangers at Furnace Creek Visitor Center often lead birding walks through various locations between November and March.

FOUR-WHEELING

Maps and SUV guidebooks for four-wheel-drive and other backcountry roads (including the popular Cottonwood/Marble canyons, Racetrack, Eureka Dunes, Saratoga Springs, and Warm Springs Canyon) are offered at the Furnace Creek Visitor Center. Remember: never travel alone and be sure to pack plenty of water and snacks. The park recommends checking ⊕ *www.nps.gov/deva/planyourvisit/backcountryroads.htm* for back-road conditions before setting out. Driving off established roads is strictly prohibited in the park.

Butte Valley

TOUR—SPORTS | This 21-mile road in the southwest part of the park climbs from 200 feet below sea level to an elevation of 4,700 feet. The geological formations along the drive reveal the development of Death Valley. High-clearance and four-wheel-drive required. If you have a

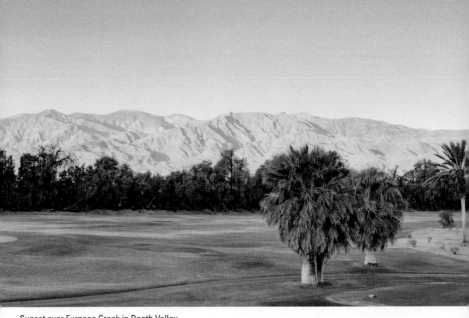

Sunset over Furnace Creek in Death Valley.

four-wheel-drive high-clearance vehicle and nerves of steel, this route takes you past Warm Springs talc mine and through Butte Valley to Geologist's Cabin, a charming and cheery little cabin where you can spend the night, if nobody else beats you to it. The park suggests checking their website or asking a ranger to check current conditions on all backcountry roads. The cabin, which sits under a cottonwood tree, has a fireplace, table and chairs, and a sink. Farther up the road, Stella's Cabin and Russell Camp are also open for public use. Keep the historic cabins clean and restock any items that you use. The road is even rougher if you continue over Mengel Pass. ⊠ *Trailhead on Warm Spring Canyon Rd., Death Valley ⊕ 50 miles south of Furnace Creek Visitor Center.*

GOLF

Furnace Creek Golf Course at the Oasis at Death Valley

GOLF | Golfers rave about how their drives carry at altitude, so what happens on the lowest golf course in the world (214 feet below sea level)? Its improbably green fairways are lined with date palms and tamarisk trees, and its level of difficulty is rated surprisingly high. You can rent clubs and carts, and there are golf packages available for The Oasis at Death Valley guests. In winter, reservations are essential. ⊠ *Hwy. 190, Furnace Creek* ☎ *760/786–2301* ⊕ *www.oasisatdeathvalley.com* ⊠ *From $35* ⅄. *18 holes, 6215 yards, par 70.*

HIKING

Plan to hike before or after midday in the spring, summer, or fall, unless you're in the mood for a masochistic baking. Carry plenty of water, wear protective clothing, and keep an eye out for black widows, scorpions, snakes, and other potentially dangerous creatures. Some of the best trails are unmarked; if the opportunity arises, ask for directions.

★ Darwin Falls

HIKING/WALKING | **FAMILY** | This lovely 2-mile round-trip hike rewards you with a refreshing year-round waterfall surrounded by thick vegetation and a rocky gorge.

No swimming or bathing is allowed, but it's a beautiful place for a picnic. Adventurous hikers can scramble higher toward more rewarding views of the falls. *Easy.* ⊠ *Death Valley National Park* ⊹ *Trailhead: access the 2-mile graded dirt road and parking area off Hwy. 190, 1 mile west of Panamint Springs Resort.*

Fall Canyon

HIKING/WALKING | This is a 3-mile, one-way hike from the Titus canyon parking area. First, walk ½ mile north along the base of the mountains to a large wash, then go 2½ miles up the canyon to a 35-foot dry fall. You can continue by climbing around to the falls on the south side. *Moderate.* ⊠ *Death Valley National Park* ⊹ *Trailhead: access road off Scotty's Castle Rd., 33 miles northwest of Furnace Creek.*

Keane Wonder Mine

HIKING/WALKING | This fascinating relic of Death Valley's gold-mining past, built in 1907, reopened in November 2017 after nine years of repair work. Its most unique feature is the mile-long tramway that descends 1,000 vertical feet, which once carried gold ore and still has the original cables attached. From here, a network of trails leads to other old mines. A climb to the uppermost tramway terminal is rewarded by expansive views of the valley. ⊠ *Access road off Beatty Cutoff Rd., 17½ miles north of Furnace Creek, Death Valley.*

Mosaic Canyon

HIKING/WALKING | **FAMILY** | A gradual uphill trail (4 miles round-trip) winds through the smoothly polished, marbleized limestone walls of this narrow canyon. There are dry falls to climb at the upper end. *Moderate.* ⊠ *Death Valley* ⊹ *Trailhead: access road off Hwy. 190, ½ mile west of Stovepipe Wells Village.*

Natural Bridge Canyon

HIKING/WALKING | A rough 2-mile access road from Badwater Road leads to a trailhead. From there, set off to see interesting geological features in addition to the bridge, which is a half mile away. The one-way trail continues for a few hundred yards, but scenic returns diminish quickly and eventually you're confronted with climbing boulders. *Easy.* ⊠ *Death Valley* ⊹ *Trailhead: access road off Badwater Rd., 15 miles south of Furnace Creek.*

Salt Creek Interpretive Trail

HIKING/WALKING | **FAMILY** | This trail, a ½-mile boardwalk circuit, loops through a spring-fed wash. The nearby hills are brown and gray, but the floor of the wash is alive with aquatic plants such as pickleweed and salt grass. The stream and ponds here are among the few places in the park to see the rare pupfish, the only native fish species in Death Valley. The pupfish are most easily observed during their spawning season in February and March. Animals such as bobcats, fox, coyotes, and snakes visit the spring, and you may also see ravens, common snipes, killdeer, and great blue herons. *Easy.* ⊠ *Death Valley* ⊹ *Trailhead: off Hwy. 190, 14 miles north of Furnace Creek.*

★ Telescope Peak Trail

HIKING/WALKING | The 14-mile round-trip (with 3,000 feet of elevation gain) begins at Mahogany Flat Campground, which is accessible by a rough dirt road. The steep and at some points treacherous trail winds through pinyon, juniper, and bristlecone pines, with excellent views of Death Valley and Panamint Valley. Ice axes and crampons may be necessary in winter—check at the Furnace Creek Visitor Center. It takes a minimum of six grueling hours to hike to the top of the 11,049-foot peak and then return. Getting to the peak is a strenuous endeavor; take plenty of water and only attempt it in fall unless you're an experienced hiker. *Difficult.* ⊠ *Death Valley* ⊹ *Trailhead: off Wildrose Rd., south of Charcoal Kilns.*

HORSEBACK AND CARRIAGE RIDES

Furnace Creek Stables

HORSEBACK RIDING | FAMILY | Set off on a one- or two-hour guided horseback, carriage, or hay wagon ride from Furnace Creek Stables. The rides traverse trails with views of the surrounding mountains, where multicolor volcanic rock and alluvial fans form a background for date palms and other vegetation. Evening carriage rides take passengers around the golf course and The Ranch at Death Valley. The stables are open October–May only. ⊠ *Hwy. 190, Furnace Creek* ☎ *760/614–1018* ⊕ *www.furnacecreekstables.net* 🎫 *From $55.*

Shopping

Experienced desert travelers carry a cooler stocked with food and beverages. You're best off replenishing your food stash in Ridgecrest, Barstow, or Pahrump, larger towns that have a better selection and nontourist prices.

Ranch General Store

CONVENIENCE/GENERAL STORES | This convenience store carries groceries, souvenirs, camping supplies, and other basics. ⊠ *Hwy. 190, Furnace Creek* ☎ *760/786–2345* ⊕ *www.oasisatdeathvalley.com.*

Restaurants

IN THE PARK

★ Inn at Death Valley Dining Room

$$$$ | AMERICAN | Fireplaces, beamed ceilings, and spectacular views provide a visual feast to match this fine-dining restaurant's ambitious menu. Dinner entrées include fare such as salmon, free-range chicken, and filet mignon, and there's a seasonal menu of vegetarian dishes. **Known for:** views of surrounding desert; old-school charm; can be pricey. ⑤ *Average main: $38* ⊠ *Inn at Death Valley, Hwy. 190, Furnace Creek* ☎ *760/786–3385* ⊕ *www.oasisatdeathvalley.com.*

19th Hole

$ | AMERICAN | Next to the clubhouse of the world's lowest golf course, this open-air spot serves hamburgers, hot dogs, chicken, and sandwiches. The full-service bar has a drive-through service for golfers in carts. **Known for:** kielbasa dog; breakfast burrito; golf cart drive-through. ⑤ *Average main: $8* ⊠ *Furnace Creek Golf Course, Hwy. 190, Furnace Creek* ☎ *760/786–2345* ⊕ *www.oasisatdeathvalley.com/dining/* 🕙 *Closed mid-May–mid-Oct. No dinner.*

Panamint Springs Resort Restaurant

$$ | AMERICAN | This is a great place for steak and a beer—choose from more than 150 different beers and ales—or pasta and a salad. In summer, evening meals are served outdoors on the porch, which has spectacular views of Panamint Valley. **Known for:** good burgers; extensive beer selection. ⑤ *Average main: $15* ⊠ *Hwy. 190, Death Valley* ✢ *31 miles west of Stovepipe Wells* ☎ *775/482–7680* ⊕ *www.panamintsprings.com/services/dining-bar.*

OUTSIDE THE PARK

Crowbar Café and Saloon

$$ | AMERICAN | FAMILY | In an old wooden building where antique photos adorn the walls and mining equipment stands in the corners, the Crowbar serves enormous helpings of regional dishes such as steak and taco salads. Home-baked fruit pies make fine desserts, and frosty beers are surefire thirst quenchers. **Known for:** home-baked fruit pies; rattlesnake chili; great breakfast spot. ⑤ *Average main: $15* ⊠ *Rte. 127, Shoshone* ☎ *760/852–4123* ⊕ *www.shoshonevillage.com/shoshone-crowbar-cafe-saloon.html.*

Mt. Whitney Restaurant

$ | AMERICAN | A boisterous family-friendly restaurant with four flat-screen televisions, this place serves the best burgers in town. In addition to the usual beef variety, you can choose from ostrich, elk, venison, and buffalo burgers. **Known**

Best Campgrounds in Death Valley

You'll need a high-clearance or 4X4 vehicle to reach these locations. To find out where you can camp in the backcountry, pick up a copy of the backcountry map at the visitor center, or check the website ⊕ *www.nps.gov/deva/planyourvisit/camping.htm.*

You can only build fires in the metal fire grates that are available at most campgrounds, though fires may be restricted in summer (check with rangers about current conditions). Wood gathering is prohibited at all campgrounds. A limited supply of firewood is available at general stores in Furnace Creek and Stovepipe Wells, but because prices are high and supplies limited, you're better off bringing your own if you intend to have a campfire. Camping is prohibited in the historic Inyo, Los Burro, and Ubehebe Crater areas, as well as all day-use spots, including Aguerberry Point Road, Cottonwood Canyon Road, Racetrack Road, Skidoo Road, Titus Canyon Road, Wildrose Road, and West Side Road.

Furnace Creek. This campground, 196 feet below sea level, has some shaded tent sites and is open all year. ⊠ *Hwy. 190, Furnace Creek* ☎ *760/786–2441.*

Mahogany Flat. If you have a four-wheel-drive vehicle and want to scale Telescope Peak, the park's highest mountain, you might want to sleep at one of the few shaded spots in Death Valley, at a cool 8,133 feet. ⊠ *Off Wildrose Rd., south of Charcoal Kilns* ☎ *No phone.*

Panamint Springs Resort. Part of a complex that includes a motel and cabin, this campground is surrounded by cottonwoods. The daily fee includes use of the showers and restrooms. ⊠ *Hwy. 190, 28 miles west of Stovepipe Wells* ☎ *775/482–7680.*

Sunset Campground. This first-come, first-served campground is a gravel-and-asphalt RV city. Closed mid-April to mid-October. ⊠ *Sunset Campground Rd., 1 mile north of Furnace Creek* ☎ *800/365–2267.*

Texas Spring. This campsite south of the Furnace Creek Visitor Center has good views and facilities and is a few dollars cheaper than Furnace Creek. Closed mid-May to mid-October. ⊠ *Off Badwater Rd., south of Furnace Creek Visitor Center* ☎ *800/365–2267.*

for: burgers; John Wayne memorabilia. ⑤ *Average main: $10* ⊠ *227 S. Main St., Lone Pine* ☎ *760/876–5751.*

Randsburg General Store

$ | **AMERICAN** | **FAMILY** | Built as Randsburg's Drug Store in 1896, this popular biker and family spot is one of the area's few surviving ghost-town buildings with original furnishings intact, such as a tin ceiling, light fixtures, and a 1904 marble-and-stained-glass soda fountain. You can still enjoy a phosphate soda from that same fountain, or lunch on slow-roasted barbecue sandwiches and blueberry milk shakes along with chili, hamburgers, and breakfast. **Known for:** friendly service; located in a ghost town. ⑤ *Average main: $10* ⊠ *35 Butte Ave., Randsburg* ☎ *760/374–2143* ⊕ *www.randsburggeneralstore.com* ⊗ *Closed Mon.–Thurs.; for extended opening during holiday wks, call ahead.*

Hotels

IN THE PARK

For the busy season (November–March) you should make reservations for lodgings within the park several months in advance.

★ The Inn at Death Valley

$$$$ | **HOTEL** | Built in 1927, this adobe-brick-and-stone lodge in one of the park's greenest oases reopened in 2018 after an extensive renovation, offering Death Valley's most luxurious accommodations, including 22 brand-new one- and two-bedroom casitas. **Pros:** refined; comfortable; great views. **Cons:** services reduced during low season (July and August); expensive; resort fee. $ *Rooms from: $499* ⊠ *Furnace Creek Village, near intersection of Hwy. 190 and Badwater Rd., Death Valley* 🕾 *760/786–2345* ⊕ *www.oasisatdeathvalley.com* ⤳ *88 rooms* ⦿ *No meals.*

Panamint Springs Resort

$ | **B&B/INN** | Ten miles inside the west entrance of the park, this low-key resort overlooks the sand dunes and peculiar geological formations of the Panamint Valley. **Pros:** slow-paced; friendly; peaceful and quiet after sundown. **Cons:** far from the park's main attractions; Internet very limited; most rooms don't have TV. $ *Rooms from: $94* ⊠ *Hwy. 190, Death Valley* ✛ *28 miles west of Stovepipe Wells* 🕾 *775/482–7680* ⊕ *www.panamintsprings.com* ⤳ *15 rooms, 8 cabins* ⦿ *No meals.*

The Ranch at Death Valley

$$$$ | **RESORT** | **FAMILY** | Originally the crew headquarters for the Pacific Coast Borax Company, the four buildings here have motel-style rooms that are a great option for families. **Pros:** good family atmosphere; central location. **Cons:** rooms can get hot despite air-conditioning; parking near your room can be problematic. $ *Rooms from: $279* ⊠ *Hwy. 190, Furnace Creek* 🕾 *760/786–2345, 800/236–7916* ⊕ *www.oasisatdeathvalley.com* ⤳ *224 rooms* ⦿ *No meals.*

Stovepipe Wells Village

$$ | **HOTEL** | If you prefer quiet nights and an unfettered view of the night sky and nearby Mesquite Flat Sand Dunes and Mosaic Canyon, this property is for you. **Pros:** intimate, relaxed; no big-time partying; authentic desert-community ambience. **Cons:** isolated; cheapest patio rooms very small; limited Wi-Fi access. $ *Rooms from: $140* ⊠ *Hwy. 190, Stovepipe Wells* 🕾 *760/786–2387* ⊕ *www.escapetodeathvalley.com* ⤳ *83 rooms* ⦿ *No meals.*

418

Index

Photo Credits

Front Cover: Jill Krueger [Description: Santa Monica, CA] **Back cover, from left to right:** Valhalla/Design & Conquer, Kimberly Beck Rubio/iStockphoto, Salvador Ceja/Dreamstime. Spine: Ken Wolter/Shutterstock. **Interior, from left to right:** Freesurf69/Dreamstime(1). Shaiith/Dreamstime (2). Mapics/Dreamstime (5). **Chapter 1: Experience Southern California:** Sean Xu/shutterstock (6-7). choness/istockphoto (8). Jill Krueger (9). Charlie Blacker/istockphoto (9). Brian Flaigmore/Dreamstime (10). Melanie Stocker/Courtesy sandiego.org (10). Chris Martin/Dreamstime.com (10). Hamilton Pytluk/Universal Studios Hollywood (10). rpac78/shutterstock (11). Sean Pavone/shutterstock (11). Visit California/Bongo (12). Jim Varley Photography/Alamy (12). Kelly vanDellen/istockphoto (12). Jose Angel Astor Rocha/Shutterstock (12). Lisa Field/Courtesy sandiego.org (13). Michele Kemper/Dreamstime.com (13). Visit California/thatgirlproductions.com/Jamie Williams (14). Visit California/Robert Holmes (14). Briana Edwards/Paramount studios (14). Visit California/Blaise (14). Blaise/Visit California (15). nisimo/shutterstock (20). Christian Heinz/shutterstock (21). joseph s giacalone/Alamy (22). Dancestrokes/Shutterstock (22). Sebastien Burel/Shutterstock (22). Marcel Fuentes/Shutterstock (23). Julia Hiebaum/Alamy (23). www.nicholasnicholas.com (24). Pinz Bowling Center (24). Courtesy of theHollywood Roosevelt (24). Courtesy of the Grove (24). ROB STARK (25). Henry Hargreaves (25). Catch Hospitality Group (25). Courtesy of Chateau Marmont (25). **Chapter 3: Southern California's Best Road Trips:** PauloZimmermann/istockphoto (41). **Chapter 4: San Diego:** Sierralara/shutterstock (55). alisafarov/Shutterstock (81). Dreyer Peter/agefotostock (81). Robert Holmes (82). Steve Snodgrass/Flickr, [CC BY 2.0] (83). Jim Epler/Flickr, [CC BY 2.0] (84). RENAULT Philippe/agefotostock (84). fPat (84). Chris Gotz/Shutterstock (84). fPat/Flickr, [CC BY 2.0] (84). Jose Angel Astor Rocha/Shutterstock (85). Howard Sandler/iStockphoto (100). **Chapter 5: Palm Springs:** Carol M. Highsmith/Visit California (111). sumikophoto/shutterstock (118). David Falk/iStockphoto (134). **Chapter 6: Orange County and Catalina Island:** Beach Media/shutterstock (151). www.ericcastro.biz/Flickr, [CC BY 2.0] (162). Robert Holmes (168). Scott Vickers/iStockphoto (173). www.rwongphoto.com/Alamy (174). Brett Shoaf/Artistic Visuals Photography (176). Lowe Llaguno/Shutterstock (178). Steve Heap/shutterstock.com (183). **Chapter 7: Los Angeles:** Jill Krueger (187). Jeff Morse/iStockphoto (190). wando studios inc/iStockphoto (191). Yelo34/Dreamstime (191). Paper Cat/shutterstock (197). Carl Yu (213). Adam Latham (223). **Chapter 8: Joshua Tree National Park:** Eric Foltz/iStockphoto (263). Dennis Silvas/shutterstock (273). Greg Epperson/shutterstock (277). miroslav_1/istockphoto (278). **Chapter 9: Mojave Desert:** Sierralara/shutterstock (281). Mlgb (288). DebsG/shutterstock (292). Maksershov/Dreamstime (296). **Chapter 10: Sequoia and Kings Canyon National Parks:** Robert Holmes (301). urosr/Shutterstock (315). **Chapter 11: The Central Coast:** jamesh1977/istockphoto (329). Davidmschrader/Dreamstime (346). Aimee M Lee/Shutterstock (392). lucky-photographer/istockphoto (394-395). **Chapter 12: Death Valley National Park:** Bryan Brazil/Shutterstock (401). kavram/shutterstock (411). LizzieMaher/istockphoto (413). **All photos are courtesy of the writers.**

*Every effort has been made to trace the copyright holders, and we apologize in advance for any accidental errors. We would be happy to apply the corrections in the following edition of this publication.

Notes

Notes

Notes

Notes

Notes

Fodor's SOUTHERN CALIFORNIA

Publisher: Stephen Horowitz, *General Manager*

Editorial: Douglas Stallings, *Editorial Director*; Jacinta O'Halloran, Amanda Sadlowski, *Senior Editors*; Kayla Becker, Alexis Kelly, Teddy Minford, Rachael Roth, *Editors*

Design: Tina Malaney, *Director of Design and Production*; Jessica Gonzalez, *Graphic Designer;* Mariana Tabares, *Design & Production Intern*

Production: Jennifer DePrima, *Editorial Production Manager*; Carrie Parker, *Senior Production Editor*; Elyse Rozelle, *Production Editor;* Jackson Pranica, *Editorial Production Assistant*

Maps: Rebecca Baer, *Senior Map Editor*; David Lindroth, Mark Stroud (Moon Street Cartography), *Cartographers*

Photography: Viviane Teles, *Senior Photo Editor;* Namrata Aggarwal, Ashok Kumar, Carl Yu, *Photo Editors;* Rebecca Rimmer, *Photo Intern*

Business & Operations: Chuck Hoover, *Chief Marketing Officer*; Robert Ames, *Group General Manager*; Tara McCrillis, *Director of Publishing Operations;* Victor Bernal, *Business Analyst*

Public Relations and Marketing: Joe Ewaskiw, *Senior Director Communications & Public Relations*; Esther Su, *Senior Marketing Manager*

Fodors.com: Jeremy Tarr, *Editorial Director;* Rachael Levitt, *Managing Editor*

Technology: Jon Atkinson, *Director of Technology;* Rudresh Teotia, *Lead Developer*; Jacob Ashpis, *Content Operations Manager*

Writers: Sarah Amandolare, Cheryl Crabtree, Paul Feinstein, Deb Hopewell, Marlise Kast-Myers, Daniel Mangin, Kathy A. McDonald, Kai Oliver-Kurtain, Jeff Terich, Michelle Rae Uy, Claire Deeks van der Lee, and Candice Yacono

Editor: Jeremy Tarr

Production Editor: Carrie Parker

Copyright © 2020 by Fodor's Travel, a division of MH Sub I, LLC, dba Internet Brands.

Fodor's is a registered trademark of Internet Brands, Inc. All rights reserved. Published in the United States by Fodor's Travel, a division of Internet Brands, Inc. No maps, illustrations, or other portions of this book may be reproduced in any form without written permission from the publisher.

16th Edition

ISBN 978-1-64097-190-5

ISSN 1543–1037

Library of Congress Control Number 2019903950

All details in this book are based on information supplied to us at press time. Always confirm information when it matters, especially if you're making a detour to visit a specific place. Fodor's expressly disclaims any liability, loss, or risk, personal or otherwise, that is incurred as a consequence of the use of any of the contents of this book.

SPECIAL SALES
This book is available at special discounts for bulk purchases for sales promotions or premiums. For more information, e-mail SpecialMarkets@fodors.com.

PRINTED IN THE UNITED STATES OF AMERICA

10 9 8 7 6 5 4 3 2 1

About Our Writers

Sarah Amandolare is a Los Angeles–based freelance journalist whose work has appeared in the Los Angeles Times, the New York Times online, BBC Travel, and Salon, among others. For this edition, she updated the Joshua Tree chapter.

Native Californian **Cheryl Crabtree** has worked as a freelance writer since 1987 and regularly travels up, down, and around California for work and fun. She has contributed to *Fodor's California* since 2003 and also contributes to the *Fodor's National Parks of the West* guide. Cheryl is editor of *Montecito Magazine* and co-authors *The California Directory of Fine Wineries* book series, Central Coast and Napa, Sonoma, Mendocino editions. Her articles have appeared in many regional and national magazines. Cheryl updated the Central Coast, Palm Springs, The Mojave Desert, and Sequoia & Kings Canyon National Park chapters this edition.

Deb Hopewell lives, surfs, and cycles in Santa Cruz, California. Before embracing the life of a freelance writer, she was the travel editor at Yahoo for six years, and a longtime editor and columnist at the San Jose Mercury News before that. Her writing has appeared in *Travel+Leisure, Outside, Architectural Digest, Sunset magazine, Yahoo,* and *Smarter Travel,* among others. She updated the Death Valley and Pinnacles chapters.

Finding the unexpected is Los Angeles freelance writer and frequent traveler **Kathy A. McDonald** 's favorite assignment. A writer with peripatetic beats, she covers the film business, design, and destinations, and is a frequent contributor to *Variety*, and other publications. Art galleries, historic architecture, and thrift stores entice her;

she rarely passes an open house or yard sale without stopping. She updated Orange County and Catalina Island.

Daniel Mangin returned to California, where he's maintained a home for three decades, after two stints at the Fodor's editorial offices in New York City, the second one as the editorial director of Fodors.com and the Compass American Guides. With several dozen wineries less than a half-hour's drive from home, he often finds himself transported as if by magic to a tasting room bar, communing with a sophisticated Cabernet or savoring the finish of a smooth Pinot Noir. For this edition, Daniel, the writer of *Fodor's Napa & Sonoma,* updated the Napa and Sonoma, North Coast, Redwood National Park, Far North, Sacramento & The Gold Country, Lake Tahoe, Best Road Trips, and Travel Smart chapters.

A veteran traveler, **Claire Deeks van der Lee** feels lucky to call San Diego home. Claire loves road-tripping around her adopted state of California, so it was a perfect fit for her to work on the Experience and Southern California's Best Road Trips chapters of this book. Claire has traveled to more than 40 countries, and has contributed to *Everywhere* magazine and several Fodor's guides.

Updating our Los Angeles chapter was a team of writers from *Fodor's Los Angeles*: **Paul Feinstein, Kathy A. McDonald,** and **Michelle Rae Uy**.

Updating our San Diego chapter was a team of writers from *Fodor's San Diego*: **Marlise Kast-Myers, Jeff Terich, Kai Oliver-Kurtain,** and **Claire Deeks van der Lee.**